CONTROVERSY

SAGE FOCUS EDITIONS

CONTROVERSY
POLITICS OF
TECHNICAL DECISIONS

Edited by
DOROTHY NELKIN

SAGE PUBLICATIONS   Beverly Hills   London

For information address:

SAGE PUBLICATIONS, INC. SAGE PUBLICATIONS LTD
275 South Beverly Drive   28 Banner Street
Beverly Hills, California 90212   London EC1Y 8QE

Printed in the United States of America

Library of Congress Cataloging in Publication Data

Main entry under title:

Controversy: politics of technical decisions

  (Sage focus editions; 8)
  Includes bibliographical references.
    1. Technology—Social aspects. 2. Science—Social
aspects. I. *Nelkin,* Dorothy. II. Series.
T14.5.C665   301.24'3   78-21339
ISBN 0-8039-1209-9

THIRD PRINTING, 1981

CONTENTS

PREFACE

The idea for this book originated in a Cornell University course which analyzed the political values and beliefs that underlie decisions about science and technology. In teaching, I have found that a useful way to convey the ideas in this and other courses was through the study of controversies. For in the course of disputes, the special interests, vital concerns, and hidden assumptions of various actors are clearly revealed.

The details of controversies can provide students with a sense of the kind of reasoning that motivates public agencies, government officials, scientists, and protest groups. They can provide a realistic understanding of science and technology policy, its social and political context, and its public impact. They can highlight social contradictions inherent in many decisions about science and technology, and the problems of developing public policies in the absence of definitive agreement about potential risks.

These studies of 12 controversies were written especially for this volume. I would like to thank the authors for their cooperation in organizing their studies around the appropriate themes and for tolerating a heavy editorial hand for the sake of the volume's coherence. In addition I would like to thank the Rockefeller Foundation for five weeks of splendid and productive isolation at the Villa Serbelloni in Bellagio, Italy. Work on some of these cases was done with support from the National Science Foundation and the National Endowment for the Humanities, EVIST Program. Finally I gratefully acknowledge the editorial assistance of Scott Montgomery and Scott Heyman, and the resources of the Cornell University Program on Science, Technology and Society.

SCIENCE, TECHNOLOGY, AND POLITICAL CONFLICT: ANALYZING THE ISSUES

Dorothy Nelkin

In the spring of 1977 at a forum on recombinant DNA research, protest groups invaded the austere quarters of the National Academy of Sciences singing: "We shall not be cloned." During that same spring, thousands of people camped at a reactor site in Seabrook, New Hampshire, to protest the construction of a nuclear power plant. Fundamentalists are increasingly open in their objections to the teaching of evolution in the public school system. Right-to-life groups bring lawsuits against scientists for fetal research. Citizens protest the decision to ban laetrile as a cancer therapy and question mandatory automobile safety devices as examples of government paternalism. Indeed controversy seems to erupt over nearly every aspect of science and technology as decisions once defined as technical (within the province of experts) have become intensely political.

The development of science and technology had remained largely unquestioned during the period of rapid economic growth that followed World War II. But belief in technological progress has since been tempered by awareness of its ironies. Technological "improvements" may cause disastrous environmental problems: drugs to stimulate the growth of beef cattle may cause cancer; "efficient" industrial processes may threaten worker health; biomedical research may be detrimental to human subjects; and a new airport may turn a neighborhood into a sonic garbage dump. Even efforts to control technology may impose inequities, as new standards and regulations pit quality of life against economic growth and the expectation of progress and prosperity.[1]

Thus the past decade has been remarkable for political action directed against science and technology. Issue-oriented organizations have formed to obstruct specific projects; scientists have called public attention to risks; and many groups demand greater accountability and public participation in technical policy decisions. Even scientific research has lost its exemption from political scrutiny. An issue of *Daedalus* on "The Limits of Scientific Inquiry" examines the proposition that some kinds of research should, in fact, not be done at all.[2] A conference on the "Social Assessment of Science" examines international efforts to impose regulations on research.[3] A political scientist writes about the "crisis" in science, "attacked from all sides through a significant coalition of reactionary and left wing thinking."[4]

Science has always faced ambivalent public attitudes. The acceptance of the authority of scientific judgment has coexisted with mistrust and fear, revealed, for example, in the response to innovations such as vaccination or research methods such as vivisection. The romantic view of the scientist as "a modern magician, a miracle man who can do incredible things" parallels negative images of:

> Dr. Faustus, Dr. Frankenstein, Dr. Moreau, Dr. Jekyll, Dr. Cyclops, Dr. Caligari, Dr. Strangelove. . . . In these images of our popular culture resides a legitimate public fear of the scientist's stripped down, depersonalized conception of knowledge—a fear that our scientists will go on being titans who create monsters.[5]

Even as attacks against science increase, public attitude surveys suggest that science and technology are favorably perceived as instrumental in achieving important social goals. About 70% of Americans believe that science and technology have changed life for the better.[6] Furthermore, the standing of scientists relative to other occupations has continually improved. In the United States scientists rank second only to physicians in occupational prestige (they were fifth in 1966). Similarly, in Europe a survey by the Commission on the European Communities finds widespread consensus that "science is one of the most important factors in the improvement of daily life."[7]

What then is the significance of the flare-up of disputes over science and technology? Are the recent controversies a manifestation of the "crisis of authority" associated with the 1960s, or are they simply local protests against decisions that affect particular and immediate interests? Do the disputes express widely shared ideological and political concerns, or do they simply reflect traditional antiscience sentiments and resistance to technological change?

From one viewpoint, the activities of protest groups resemble nineteenth-century Luddism—a wholesale rejection of technological change. Zbigniew Brzezinski calls such opposition "the death rattle of the historically obsolete."[8] But from another perspective, protest is a positive and necessary force in a society that, Theodore Roszak claims, "has surrendered responsibility for making morally demanding decisions, for generating ideals, for controlling public authority, for safeguarding the society against its despoilers."[9] Thus while most of us are "frozen in a position of befuddled docility," protest groups fight to preserve the values lost in the course of technological progress.

This book of controversies over science and technology describes and analyzes the struggles between different perspectives: between those who see technological development as a rational and objective process and those who see this process as primarily political. From a political perspective, the protests described may be less against science and technology than against the power relationships associated with them; less against specific technological decisions than against the declining capacity of citizens to shape policies that affect their interests; less against science than against the use of scientific rationality to mask political choices. This political challenge, this increasing politicization of science and technology, is common to all the cases in this book.

THE CASES

The case studies are selected to suggest the variety of political, economic, and ethical issues that provoke public debate. They include: siting of large scale technologies (nuclear power plants, airports, or industrial plants); implementation of safety technologies (automobile airbags); regulation of drugs or consumer goods (DES, laetrile); and even methods of scientific research. The cases are organized to emphasize the diversity in the concerns expressed by protests against science and technology—the questions of equity, the fears of risk, the constraints on freedom of choice, and the infringements of science on traditional values and cherished beliefs.

Many controversies arise when citizens in a community become aware that they must bear the costs of a project that will benefit a different or much broader constituency. Airports and power plants serve large regions, but near neighbors bear the environmental and social burden. Normally such projects are planned and sites selected on the basis of economic efficiency and technical criteria. But community protests raise basic questions of distributive justice: can any reduction in some citizens' welfare be justified by greater advantages to others? can the magnitude or intensity of costs borne by neighbors of a major project be reasonably incorporated into cost-benefit calculations? Three cases on such themes are presented in this section: an airport siting dispute, a nuclear power plant controversy, and, by way of contrast, some industrial siting disputes in the Soviet Union.

A second source of controversy over science and technology is the fear of potential health and environmental hazards. We are deluged with warnings about "invisible" hazards (PCBs, freon, radiation, cyclamates—the list is long and growing), so the fear of risk is inevitable. This fear is aggravated by the often poorly understood nature of risk.[10] How does one really know, for example, if a nuclear waste storage facility is adequately protected against long-term radiation leakage? Assessing risk is complicated. For often, while an accident could be catastrophic, the chances of one are small and difficult to calculate. In the case of nuclear waste disposal, it is the fear of an unlikely but potentially devastating catastrophe that sustains conflict. In other cases, risks are known but must be weighed against potential benefits; then dispute focuses on balancing competing priorities in decisions about regulation (for example, in setting worker safety standards).

New technology has increased our capability to detect potential risks, but technical uncertainties leave considerable leeway for conflicting interpretation.[11] The disputes among scientists that will be described in this book have caused public confusion and doubt. Moreover the possibility of risk poses the political question of how to regulate and control science and technology without imposing unreasonable constraints. These issues are developed in three cases: the controversies over nuclear waste disposal; over the regulation of the growth-promoting drug DES; and over the setting of worker safety standards for vinyl chloride production.

A third kind of controversy involves questions of freedom of choice when government regulates. Laetrile is banned, airbags are mandatory; both decisions infringe on freedom of choice—the freedom to choose one's own medication, the freedom to take one's own risks. If a water supply is fluoridated, airbags mandated, or universal vaccination required, everyone must partake of the decision and its consequences. And if the sale of laetrile or saccharin is prohibited, those who want these products are denied the right to buy them. Governments impose regulations on the assumption that individual choices have social costs or that individuals may fail to make rational and enlightened choices on their own behalf.

Such constraints, however, also may be viewed as protection of professional privilege, as unnecessary government paternalism, or as a violation of individual rights. These are the perceptions that have maintained the laetrile dispute. The three cases in this section describe the automobile airbag dispute, the laetrile controversy, and, in a historical parallel, several episodes in the development of smallpox immunization.

Finally, conflict occurs when science or technology is perceived to flaunt traditional values. Controversies over research procedures and over science education reflect a renewed concern with moral and religious values in American society. At a time when accomplishments of science have fostered in some a faith in rational explanations of nature, there are concerted efforts by others to reinvest educational systems with traditional faith. And even as biomedical research brings about dramatic improvements in medical care, there are always critics seeking to block research and to question areas of science that challenge traditional values.

For protest groups in such disputes, it is the moral implications of science and the potential for misuse of scientific findings that shape their dissent. They fear that science may change the normal state of nature, alter the genetic structure of mankind, or threaten deeply held beliefs about free will and self-determination. A major source of concern with respect to recombinant DNA research, for example, is the potential for removing the obstacles to genetic engineering by allowing scientists to transfer hereditary characteristics from one strain to another. This evokes images of eugenics and leads directly to questions about the wisdom of seeking certain kinds of knowledge at all. Thus the effort to defend moral values poses a threat to freedom of scientific inquiry, a deeply held value in itself. Part IV explores recent controversies over the teaching of evolution in public schools, over biomedical research using the human fetus, and over recombinant DNA research.

It is important to recognize that all the cases in this volume involve multiple issues. Conflicts over nuclear power plant or airport sitings, for example, may revolve around the equitable distribution of costs, but they also involve the fear of risks. The automobile airbag dispute focuses not only on freedom of individual choice but also on how to distribute the costs of this mandated technology. The nuclear debate raises questions about equity, but also about the values of a consumer society. To focus on the moral and value implications of recombinant DNA is not to ignore the fact that it involves tradeoffs of risk and benefit. Regulation of risks, especially in the workplace, necessarily raises questions about equity. And ideological concerns can pervade environmental disputes when moral values bump into pragmatic goals ("people versus penguins," "environment versus jobs").

The cases have been selected to illustrate the diverse concerns that underlie conflicts over science and technology. But each controversy has been analyzed to emphasize and clarify the political dimensions of "technical decisions." For while many of the debates are about technical questions, in the end they involve political choices from among competing social values. And while experts play a crucial role in all these controversies, the ultimate and ubiquitous question is "Who should control crucial policy choices?" Reflected in this question is a troubling feature of contemporary society—the impact of increased technical complexity and specialization on the decision-making process. Deference to technical knowledge enables those with specialized competence to exert a powerful influence on public agencies. These specialists are subject to only limited political constraints. The power afforded to those who control technical information can threaten democratic principles, reducing public control over many public policy choices.[12] This has been a driving force behind controversies over science and technology, expressed in the recurrent populist theme of participation. Indeed participation as an ideology in American society is increasing in importance even as technical complexity acts to limit effective political choice.

CONTROVERSY AS A POLITICAL CHALLENGE

Critics of science and technology perceive a vast distance between technology and human needs—indeed between the governing and the governed. They question the ability of representative institutions to serve their interests. They resent the concentration of authority over technology in private bureaucracies and public agencies responsible for technological change. And they challenge assumptions about the importance of technical competence as the basis for legitimate decision-making authority.

SOURCES OF OPPOSITION

Those who live in the vicinity of an airport, a nuclear waste disposal facility, or who work in a vinyl chloride plant, have practical reasons to protest. They are directly impacted by land appropriation, noise, immediate risks, local economic or social disruption, or by some encroachment on their individual rights. Others, including many environmentalists, creationists, and laetrile supporters, protest out of adherence to a "cause." And there are people not directly affected by a specific project or controversy who oppose science and technology because of global political concerns. Some nuclear critics, for example, see science as an instrument of military or economic domination and oppose technology for ideological reasons.

These conflicts over science and technology draw support from sharply contrasting social groups. Most active are middle-class, educated people with sufficient economic security and political skill to participate in decision-making. But conservative fundamentalists in California seeking to influence a science curriculum share concern about local control with citizens in a liberal university community seeking to influence the siting of a power plant.

Finally, an important source of criticism has been the scientific community itself. Many young scientists became politicized during the 1960s. At that time, they focused on antiwar activities, on university politics, and on the issue of military research in universities. More recently, their attention has turned to the environment, energy, biomedical research, and harmful industrial practices. These scientists often initiate controversies by raising questions about potential risks in areas obscured from public knowledge.

THE POLITICAL ROLE OF EXPERTS[13]

Technical expertise is a crucial political resource in conflicts over science and technology. For access to knowledge and the resulting ability to question the data used to legitimize decisions is an essential basis of power and influence. The cases will suggest the important role of the activist-scientist in formulating, legitimizing, and supporting the diverse concerns involved in the controversies. Scientists were the first to warn the public about the possible risks of recombinant DNA research. They were the first to call the public's attention to the problems of developing nuclear power before solving the problem of radiation disposal techniques. As various controversies develop, scientists are called upon to buttress political positions with the authority of their expertise. The willingness of scientists to expose technical uncertainties and to lend their expertise to citizen groups constitutes a formidable political challenge.

The authority of scientific expertise rests on assumptions about scientific rationality. Interpretations and predictions made by scientists are judged to be rational because they are based on data gathered through rational procedures. Their interpretations therefore serve as a basis for planning and as a means for defending the legitimacy of policy decisions.

The cases demonstrate how protest groups also exploit technical expertise to challenge policy decisions. Power plant opponents have their own scientists who legitimize their concerns about thermal pollution. Environmentalists hire their own experts to question the technical feasibility of questionable projects. Laetrile supporters have their own medical professionals. Even fundamentalists seeking to have the Biblical account of creation taught in the public schools present themselves as scientists and claim "creation theory" to be a scientific alternative to evolution theory.

Whatever political values motivate controversy, the debates usually focus on technical questions. The siting controversies develop out of concern with the quality of life in a community, but the debates revolve around technical questions—the physical requirements for the facility, the accuracy of the predictions establishing its need, or the precise extent of environmental risk. Concerns about the freedom to select a cancer therapy devolve into technical arguments about the efficacy of treatment. Moral opponents of fetal research engage in scientific debate about the precise point at which life begins.

This is tactically effective, for in all disputes broad areas of uncertainty are open to conflicting scientific interpretation. Decisions are often made in a context of limited knowledge about potential social or environmental impacts, and there is seldom conclusive evidence to reach definitive resolution. Thus power hinges on the ability to manipulate knowledge, to challenge the evidence presented to support particular policies, and technical expertise becomes a resource exploited by all parties to justify their political and economic views.[14] In the process, political values and scientific facts become difficult to distinguish.

The debates among scientists documented in these cases show how, in controversial situations, the value premises of the disputants color their findings. The boundaries of the problems to be studied, the alternatives weighed, and the issues regarded as appropriate—all tend to determine which data are selected as important, which facts emerge. The way project proponents or citizen groups use the work of "their" experts reflects their judgments about priorities or about acceptable levels of risk. Whenever such judgments conflict, this is reflected in the selective use of technical knowledge. Expertise is reduced to one more weapon in a political arsenal.

When expertise becomes available to both sides of a controversy, it further polarizes conflict by calling attention to areas of technical ambiguity and to the limited ability to predict and control risks. The very existence of conflicting technical interpretations generates political activity. And the fact that experts disagree, more than the substance of their disputes, fires controversy. After hearing 120 scientists argue over nuclear safety, for example, the California State Legislature concluded that the issues were not, in the end, resolvable by expertise. "The questions involved require value judgments and the voter is no less equipped to make such judgments than the most brilliant Nobel Laureate."[15] Thus the role of expertise in these disputes leads directly to demands for a greater public role in technical decision-making.

THE PARTICIPATORY IMPULSE

Most of the controversies described in this book were provoked by specific decisions: to expand an airport; to ban a drug; to site a power plant. Those who propose these projects define the decision and the issues involved primarily as technical—subject to objective criteria based on energy forecasts, studies of environmental impact, accident statistics, or predictions of future needs. Opposition groups, on the other hand, perceive such decisions in a political light. They use experts of their own, but mainly for tactical purposes—to prove that technical data are at best uncertain and subject to different interpretations. They try to show that important questions involve political choices and that these can be obscured by technical criteria. In the end, they seek a role in making social choices.

The cases suggest that the nature of public opposition depends on a number of circumstances. If a project in question (for example, an airport) directly affects a neighborhood, local activists are relatively easy to organize on the basis of immediate interests. Many issues (such as recombinant DNA research or the automobile airbag) have no such natural constituency. Risks may be diffuse. Affected interests may be hard to define, or so dispersed as to be difficult to organize. Or the significant affected interests may be more concerned with employment than with their environment and therefore willing to accept certain risks.[16] In such cases, participation is limited and the controversies involve mainly scientists or professional activists. Even in these conflicts, however, political protest can be maintained only if the leadership can count on support among a wider group of people who, though generally inactive, will lend support at public hearings, demonstrations, and other key events.

What channels do these groups exploit as they try to influence technology policy? First, they seek to capture technical resources. But those who oppose a project must also organize their activities to develop maximum public support. Expanding the scope of conflict is necessary to push decisions commonly defined as technical out into the political arena. Thus dramatic and highly publicized media events often are important. Tactics in the controversies described in this book range from routine political actions like lobbying or intervention in public hearings to litigation, referenda, and political demonstrations. These channels of participation depend on the institutional framework or political system in which opposition takes shape (note the tactics of environmental politics in the Soviet Union). In the United States litigation has become a major means for citizens to challenge technology. The role of the courts has expanded through the extension of the legal doctrine of standing—private citizens without alleged personal economic grievances may bring suit as advocates of the public interest.[17] The courts have been used by citizens not only in environmental cases, but in challenging research practices as well, as we see in the litigation over fetal research.

The participatory impulse has also forced elected representatives seeking to maintain their popular support to consider technical issues that are normally beyond their political jurisdiction. For example, the Cambridge City Council and local government bodies in a number of other university communities claim the authority to judge the adequacy of safety regulations in biology laboratories. Local townships forbid the transport and disposal of radioactive materials within their jurisdiction. And referenda on specific technologies such as nuclear power are increasingly common.

Such events evidence a changing relationship between science and the public. But it should not be assumed that demands for participation imply antiscience attitudes. More often they suggest a search for a more appropriate articulation between science and those affected by it. In its report on recombinant DNA research, the Cambridge Review Board thoughtfully expressed a prevailing view.

> Decisions regarding the appropriate course between the risks and benefits of potentially dangerous scientific inquiry must not be adjudicated within the inner circles of the scientific establishment. . . . We wish to express our sincere belief that a predominantly lay citizens' group can face a technical, scientific matter of general and deep public concern, educate itself appropriately to the task, and reach a fair decision.[18]

This view sees science and technology policy as no different from other policy areas, subject to political evaluation that includes intense public debate. This, indeed, is the political challenge posed by the current state of controversy over science and technology, and it has profound implications for their resolution.

THE RESOLUTION OF CONFLICT

How one perceives science and technology reflects special interests, personal values, attitudes toward risk, and general feelings about science and authority. The social and moral implications of science and technology, the threat to human values, may assume far greater importance than any details of scientific verification. Perceptions therefore differ dramatically.

• Is recombinant DNA research a potential boon to medical progress, or a risky procedure continued only because of vested interests among scientists?

• Is nuclear power a solution to the energy problem or a destructive force perpetuated because of existing industrial commitments?

• Is the air bag a solution to the problem of automobile safety, or a parternalistic mandate violating freedom of choice?

Resolution of a dispute depends on the nature of just such underlying perceptions. If the question at issue is merely one of specific interests, compensation measures could reduce conflict. But where more basic ideological principles or attitudes are at stake, no direct solutions will satisfy all protagonists—in the creationist controversy and in the debate over fetal research, all efforts to compromise have failed.

Nor is there much evidence that technical arguments change anyone's mind. In the disputes over fetal research and even in the various siting controversies no amount of data could resolve value differences. Each side used technical information mainly to legitimate a position based on existing priorities. Ultimately, dramatic events or significant political changes had more effect than expertise. For example, the growing base of technical information about the dangers of existing conditions in vinyl chloride plants did not lead to more stringent standards of occupational safety until the dramatic announcement of the death of several workers.

In some cases, increased knowledge may eventually depoliticize an issue by helping to separate facts from values or by clarifying the technical constraints that limit policy choices.[19] But even in the old conflict over compulsory vaccination, changing attitudes toward governmental regulation had more to do with reducing opposition than the obvious benefit of the vaccination program.

The outcome of many disputes depends on the relative political power of competing interests. In some cases industrial interests prevail; chemical firms were clearly influential in framing the principles that were to shape safety standards for the vinyl chloride industry. In other cases, powerful protest groups exercise sufficient economic leverage to determine the outcome; the ability of environmentalists to impose costly delays in the power plant siting controversy affected the ultimate decision not to build. In still other cases, external political factors are decisive. The election of minority governments in Ontario and Ottawa influenced the outcome of the Toronto airport controversy. Federal, state, and local government relationships affect decisions in the nuclear field. And because of the protracted nature of many controversies (for example, the air bag dispute), outcomes are influenced by changes in the political environment over time.

But ultimately the implementation of policies involving science and technology depend on public acceptance. Efforts to foster greater acceptance of science and technology are numerous.[20] United States legislation has provided greater public access to information, expanded public hearing procedures, and extended opportunities for intervention in rule-making and adjudicatory procedures. We shall see how these procedures operate in the controversies discussed in this book. Citizens are also appointed to advisory committees and institutional review boards, and public involvement is required in environmental impact statements. Standing advisory commissions (such as the National Commission for the Protection of Human Subjects of Biomedical Research) are established to interpret, clarify, and assure the quality of technical opinion and to gather information on public concerns as well. In the recombinant DNA case, we shall see the creation of a Citizens Review Board, formed to evaluate conflicting evidence about the adequacy of NIH guidelines for the research and advise on the wisdom of allowing a research facility in Cambridge, Massachusetts.

Whether such efforts will eventually help to resolve conflict remains to be seen, but many difficulties are apparent as we see these participatory mechanisms developed and used. Assessing science and technology may call for specialized knowledge, in turn creating problems for the layman. The vagueness of the boundaries between the technical and political dimensions of policies concerning science and technology—between questions of technical feasibility and political acceptability—itself enhances the difficulty of finding appropriate means to expand public choice. There are also problems in determining who should be involved in a decision—who is really representative of public interests. And finally the effect of a greater public role on the development of science and technology, on administrative efficiency, and on citizens' attitudes, is difficult to predict.

Controversies over science and technology develop over competing political, economic, or ethical values. But the dynamics of the disputes reflect a dialectic between the desire for efficiency and the demands of a democratic technology. The tendency to place a high value on efficiency leads to defining inherently political problems as technical. Yet technical planning limits public choice and threatens the widely held assumption that people should be able to influence decisions that affect their lives. And this assumption has considerable and increasing salience. Indeed of all the questions raised in the disputes over science and technology, the most pervasive have been: who should control? what is the relevant expertise? is responsibility for decisions to rest with those with technical knowledge or with those who bear the impact of technological choices? Does one rely on professionals to assess the impact of their research or on those who may be affected? Assumptions are changing about the importance of technical competence to assess science and technology. This challenging of authority is the most striking aspect of the many recent disputes.

The cases that follow explore such questions, providing concrete examples of actual decisions, of the tradeoffs among technical, ethical, and political considerations. Each case illustrates the interplay of the technical and political factors involved in choices about the siting of technology projects, the assessment of risks, and the setting of safety standards and regulations. The cases include material on the structure of decision-making authority, on the nature of the available technical alternatives, and on the social and ethical sources of conflict. They explore the groups engaged in the controversies, their diverse objectives, and the channels they exploit to influence policy. They analyze the role of experts in the disputes and how various groups employ technical information to further their political ends. And finally, they analyze the outcomes of disputes and their implications.

But even as these individual conflicts have been resolved, the same tensions recur in other contexts and in other places. Controversies erupt over the bans on saccharin and cyclamates, fluoridation, weather modification programs, research on the XYY chromosome, the swine flu vaccine, the use of pesticides, and genetic screening techniques. The persistence of controversy makes clear that the cases described in this book are not unique events, but are part of a significant movement to reassess the social values, the priorities, and the political relationships that are always present in technical decisions.

NOTES

1. For a review of the literature on science and technology policy emphasizing the increasing concern with the problems of technology, see Dorothy Nelkin, "Technology and Public Policy," Chapter 11, in I. Rosing and D. Price, *Science, Technology, and Society* (Beverly Hills, CA: Sage Publications, 1977), pp. 393-442.
2. *Daedalus,* March 1978.
3. This conference, organized by the International Council on Science Policy Studies, was held in Bielefeld, Germany, in May 1978.
4. Jean-Jacques Salomon, "Crisis of Science, Crisis of Society," *Science and*

Public Policy (October 1977), pp. 414-433.

5. Theodore Roszak, "The Monster and the Titan," *Daedalus* (Summer 1974), p. 31.

6. See annual Harris polls; also, A. Etzioni and C. Nunn, "The Public Appreciation of Science," in G. Holton and W. Blanpied, *Science and Its Public* (Holland: Reidel, 1976). Also, National Science Board, *Science Indicators 1976* (Government Printing Office, 1977).

7. Commission on the European Communities, *Science and European Public Opinion* (Brussels, 1977).

8. Zbigniew Brzezinski, "America and the Technetronic Age," in *Between Two Ages: America's Role in the Technetronic Era* (New York: Viking Press, 1970).

9. Theodore Roszak, *The Making of a Counter Culture* (New York: Doubleday, 1968), p. 22.

10. W. Lowrance, *Of Acceptable Risk* (Los Altos, CA: William Kaufman, 1976); W. D. Rowe, *An Anatomy of Risk* (New York: John Wiley, 1977).

11. See A. Mazur, "Disputes Between Experts," *Minerva* 11 (April 1973), pp. 213-262.

12. For an annotated bibliography of the impact of technology on the polity, see Harvard University, *Technology and the Polity,* Program on Technology and Society, Research Review 4, 1969.

13. For the changing role of experts see A. Teich (ed.), *Science and Public Affairs* (Cambridge, MA: MIT Press, 1974); J. Primack and F. Von Hippel, *Advice and Dissent: Scientists in the Political Arena* (New York: Basic Books, 1974).

14. G. Benveniste, *The Politics of Expertise* (Berkeley, CA: Glendessary Press, 1972).

15. Report on Hearings before the California State Committee on Resources, Land Use, and Energy, *New York Times,* June 2, 1976, 1: 1.

16. See R. Neuhaus, *In Defense of People* (New York: Macmillan, 1971).

17. For a review and bibliography on citizen litigation, see Joseph Dimento, "Citizen Environmental Litigation and Administrative Process," *Duke Law Journal* 22 (1977), pp. 409-452.

18. Cambridge City Council, Experimentation Review Board, "Guidelines for the Use of Recombinant DNA Molecule Technology," December 21, 1976.

19. This is the justification behind the idea for a Science Court. For a review of the literature on this proposal, see A. Mazur, "Science Courts," *Minerva* 15 (1977), pp. 1-14.

20. For examples of some of these efforts in a European context see: Dorothy Nelkin, *Technological Decisions and Democracy: European Experiments in Public Participation* (Beverly Hills, CA: Sage Publications, 1977).

PART I
EFFICIENCY VERSUS EQUITY

The siting of noxious facilities has generated a great number of protests over questions of equity—the way the costs and benefits of a disruptive technological facility are distributed. Nearly every decision to site an airport, a chemical plant, a power plant, or a hydroelectric dam generates opposition when neighboring communities realize they will bear the costs of a development that will benefit a much broader region. This section presents three such cases.

Jerome Milch examines the Toronto Airport controversy, one of many similar disputes throughout the world. The source of this dispute was the desire of airport neighbors to maintain an undisturbed life style. Despite the importance of this issue, much of the conflict revolved, for political reasons, around technical questions: the degree of harm involved, the actual need for the facility, and the facility's technical requirements.

Similarly, in Dorothy Nelkin's study of the Cayuga Lake nuclear power plant controversy, the central question was who should bear the cost of a facility designed to benefit a broad geographical region. Yet much of the dispute was played out in a scientific forum, as diverse groups for and against the facility used expertise to buttress their demands. This case, one of the earliest conflicts over nuclear power plant siting, also suggests the problems that participation in policy disputes pose for the scientific community.

23

By way of comparison, Thane Gustafson's study of environmental disputes in the Soviet Union reveals how scientists serve as surrogates for public opinion in the absence of other avenues for legitimate protest. In the USSR, the impact of scientific expertise is less important with respect to its public constituency than to existing attitudes at the top levels of political leadership. Experts can influence environmental policy, but only if their advice is consistent with government priorities.

In all these cases, decisions to develop a project proceed in similar fashion. Projects are planned and sites selected on the basis of economic efficiency and technical criteria. Planning and development are the responsibilities of public authorities or agencies whose autonomy is maintained by the complex and esoteric nature of the technology, and legitimized by the authority of the technical advice available to them. The degree of public consultation depends on legislative requirements such as those contained in the National Environmental Policy Act; but, characteristically, decisions are already made by the time approval-seeking consultation occurs. The cases illustrate the increased opposition to such procedures as people question the equity of the anticipated distribution of costs and benefits and seek to have their voices heard. Both planners and their critics exploit our inadequate knowledge about the environmental impacts of technology, and the uncertainties that permit diverse interpretation of data, by using experts to defend their priorities. In the process, however, the technical nature of the debates often tends to obscure their underlying political dimensions.

1

THE TORONTO AIRPORT CONTROVERSY

Jerome Milch

In December 1968, the Canadian government unveiled plans for the construction of a second international airport in metropolitan Toronto. The announcement followed a brief review of policy in the Ministry of Transport and reversed an earlier decision to expand the existing air facility in the region. From the outset, the project was steeped in controversy. A lengthy conflict with the provincial government over a suitable location for the airport was not resolved until March 1972. The selection of a site, however, simply motivated local citizen groups to organize an intensive campaign to prevent airport construction. Eventually the federal government concluded that the project was no longer worth the effort, and its demise was formally announced by Transport Minister Jean Marchand in September 1975.

The difficulties encountered by Canadian authorities in their efforts to construct the new Toronto airport have been experienced by developers throughout the industrial world. Construction of metropolitan air facilities has become increasingly controversial since the late 1960s.[1] Airport plans have been contested in virtually every Western country. In the United States and England, as well as Canada, bitter disputes forced authorities to terminate plans for construction. In Japan, opposition to the new Tokyo airport prevented the operation of a completed facility.

Conflict over airport development involves a number of policy issues, such as the adequacy of technical planning and the wisdom of devoting a scarce resource—undeveloped land on the urban periphery—to transportation purposes. Opponents are particularly critical of the narrow market criteria which dominate decision-making in nearly every instance.[2] But some aspects of airport development involve basic value questions for which there are no ready answers. Perhaps the most difficult issue is equity, for the construction and operation of air facilities creates costs and benefits which are distributed unevenly across the population. Airport developers trying to construct adequate facilities to meet the needs of the air traveler have tended to be oblivious to these inequities and their implications.

Distributional inequities underlie most airport controversies, but the issue does not always surface directly during a conflict. Developers are inclined to avoid the question altogether, since any effort to resolve inequities generates substantial costs. Airport opponents may be equally reluctant to formulate the issue in terms of equity; for they may be accused of promoting private concerns at the expense of the public interest. A safer strategy is to challenge the technical justification for decisions or the procedures employed in the decision-making process.[3] Thus, despite their importance in mobilizing opposition, equity issues are often downplayed.

To some extent, the conflict over the Toronto airport followed this pattern.[4] Citizens concerned with preserving the lifestyle which had drawn them to the suburbs objected to plans for airport construction on the grounds that the planning process was faulty. But the Toronto controversy was unique in one important respect: airport developers had by no means been oblivious to equity considerations in formulating plans for the facility. The bitter conflict over the proposed new airport had been foreshadowed by a brief but equally intense controversy over plans to expand the existing facility. During this earlier dispute, provincial politicians and airport neighbors had raised explicit demands for equity, and it was largely to accommodate them that the government agreed to consider an entire new airport system for the city.

Initially the policy was defended as a response to equity considerations, but transportation planners, requiring a technical argument to justify the scale of the proposed new airport, immediately commissioned additional forecasts. In the course of technical justification, the equity issue was forgotten. The federal government argued for the construction of a new airport on the basis of technical efficiency, even though its decision had been initially prompted by equity considerations. Meanwhile, airport critics opposed the new development on technical grounds, although their opposition actually stemmed from their concern about the inequitable distribution of costs and benefits.

INITIAL PLANNING

Airport development in Canada is the responsibility of the Ministry of Transport,[5] an agency of the federal government established in 1936 to rationalize transportation policy in the country. Federal control of the airways was established during aviation's early years. Airports, however, were excluded initially from the federal mandate. Government authorities regarded airports as service facilities, analogous to railroad terminals, and they presumed that the private sector or local municipalities would develop and operate them in response to market demand. This judgment proved unrealistic. As technological developments in aviation and intense competition with American airline interests raised costs beyond the means of these parties, the Ministry of Transport began to purchase and renovate existing airports and gradually assumed responsibility to develop new facilities. After World War II, all major construction projects were managed by Transport officials.[6]

Extensive experience with the construction and operation of airports did not shield the Ministry from criticism. Transport authorities had never developed a national airport plan; incrementalism was the rule, with air officials responding to demands for services as they arose. This approach had generated several major errors, such as the enormous investment poured into Gander Airport in Newfoundland during the 1950s, just before the introduction of jet aircraft made nonstop trans-Atlantic flights possible. But Transport also erred in not providing sufficient services for expanding air markets. A new passenger terminal constructed at Toronto International Airport during the early 1960s, for example, operated at near capacity levels from the day it was dedicated.

Senior air officials, conscious of such errors, attempted to rationalize the planning process. Consultants were employed in increasing numbers and with greater autonomy in order to broaden the perspective of in-house personnel. Systems analysis was accepted as the planning technique to elaborate the new air infrastructure. Project offices were established to strengthen coordination among the various sections of the Ministry.[7]

The first serious opportunity to incorporate the new, rational approach to planning came in 1966 during a review of plans for Toronto's air facilities. Toronto International Airport (known as Malton, after the nearby village of that name) was constructed in the late 1930s by the city government, with financial assistance from the Ministry of Transport. During the 1950s, the federal government purchased and renovated the airport, expropriated 3,000 acres of adjacent farmland, and invested more than $20 million in runway and terminal improvements. Transport's plans as of 1965 called for a gradual increase in terminal capacity at Malton but no additional runway development. Department officials assumed that annual increases in passenger traffic, though exceptionally high during the 1950s and early 1960s, would tail off in subsequent years. A 1965 forecast predicted that 6.5 million passengers would pass through the facility in 1980, a number which could be accommodated on existing runways.

Transport officials, however, were not comfortable with these plans. They had predicted declining growth at Malton by the mid-1960s; instead, traffic was increasing, and authorities were concerned that the airport's capacity might be reached sooner than anticipated. They were even more alarmed by the extraordinary population growth in the vicinity of Malton. Farms were disappearing as land near Metropolitan Toronto became too expensive for agricultural use. No effective zoning existed to control urban expansion near the airport, and Transport planners feared that Malton soon would be boxed in by such development.

The airport planning review was entrusted to Parkin and Associates, an architectural consulting firm. Parkin's study, completed in late 1967, recommended a major expansion of terminals, runways, and other ground facilities at Malton. According to Parkin, 19 million passengers would utilize Malton in 1985, nearly three times the original forecast. Malton would nevertheless be able to cope with this traffic if an additional 3,000 acres of land were expropriated.

Transport authorities endorsed the Parkin Plan but decided to postpone formal presentation to the Cabinet until a comprehensive program, which would include both Montreal and Toronto, could be formulated. A review of Montreal's air facilities, conducted by another consultant firm, was proceeding simultaneously. By the early summer of 1968, a package calling for a new airport in Montreal and an expanded facility in Toronto was submitted to the Cabinet. The Cabinet approved the plan in August and Minister of Transport Paul Hellyer released the details to the press with the remark that Malton's expansion would resolve Toronto's transport problems for at least a quarter of a century.

BEATING A HASTY RETREAT

The Cabinet decision was greeted with enthusiasm in Quebec, but the response to Malton's proposed expansion was entirely different in Ontario. Nearby residents, annoyed by the growth of air traffic and the introduction of noisy jet aircraft, were alarmed at the prospect of a major expansion program. The airport, situated on the northwestern fringe of the metropolitan area approximately 15 miles from the central business district, had been surrounded by farmland in the late 1950s. But no effort had been made to limit urbanization near the airport. In fact, both the provincial and federal governments had subsidized housing projects and encouraged development in the vicinity. By 1968, the character of the area had substantially altered and the new residents were determined to protect their financial investment and their quality of life.

The Society for Aircraft Noise Abatement (SANA) was established immediately after the announcement. Approximately 600 residents attended its first meeting in early September, during which a strategy of opposition was outlined and a formal protest drafted. Advertisements were placed in local newspapers to attract additional support, and 20,000 letters were sent to the Minister of Transport protesting the Cabinet decision.

Such organized protest startled Transport officials, but their primary concern was the opposition of key political leaders to the proposal. Ontario politicians, particularly the Members of Parliament representing the province, objected strenuously to the plan, for it implicitly relegated Toronto to the status of a second-class air center. The construction of a new international airport in Montreal would guarantee the future of that city as the "gateway to Canada." This, it was argued, was both unfair to Toronto and in conflict with market demand. Provincial authorities were also upset with the growing imbalance in federal investment policy. The proposed new airport in Montreal was the latest in a series of decisions committing substantial resources to Quebec. Ontario politicians argued that the federal government is obligated to spread its investments throughout the country.

Hellyer's determination to expand Malton began to waver under increasing pressure from these constituencies, and he agreed to authorize an in-house review of the plans. No objections to the continued operation of Malton emerged during a series of meetings with representatives of Malton-area communities and the Ontario Municipal Affairs Department, but local and provincial authorities were unanimously opposed to an expansion of the airport beyond its existing boundaries. This opposition was framed in terms of the welfare of the local residents; none of the participants challenged the technical basis of the Parkin Plan.[8]

One discordant note did emerge during the review. Air Canada warned Transport authorities, in a private letter in November 1968, that there was no economic justification for the construction of a new airport. The noise problem, airline officials insisted, was exaggerated and would be alleviated by the introduction of jumbo jets. They argued that air travel would not continue to expand at the same rate since passenger fares would be increasing. Malton, Air Canada suggested, needed a new passenger terminal, but was otherwise adequate for at least 10 or 15 years.[9]

The warning from Air Canada fell on deaf ears. The long-term costs which concerned airline officials were of little interest to the Minister. The economy was booming and the risk of overinvestment in aviation infrastructure was perceived by Transport officials as insignificant. In contrast, the political costs of adhering to the Parkin Plan appeared enormous. By mid-December, Hellyer had persuaded his Cabinet colleagues to authorize the construction of a new Toronto airport. The decision was justified to the public on the grounds that the consultant had used outdated maps of urban development, thereby underestimating the impact of expanding the facility at Malton. No mention was made of the pressure from provincial politicians or the concerns of Air Canada.

SITE SELECTION

This change in policy left Transport planners with the problem of locating a suitable site for a new air facility. No groundwork had been laid for a site selection process, and a special task force was quickly pulled together, directed by Ralph Gordon, that would conduct preliminary studies and recommend a site to the Minister. Although a number of civil servants from Transport were included on the team, the director relied heavily on private consultants.

The planning assumptions of the task force reflected the political origins of the project. Although the new airport was to supplement Malton rather than replace it, it would have to be as large as the proposed Montreal facility, that is 88,000 acres. Parkin's forecasts had provided no justification for an airport of this magnitude. Hence, the preparation of new forecasts became the first order of business for the team. Parkin had assumed an 8.8% average annual growth rate of passenger traffic through 1985; Gordon's team accepted that figure but projected growth at a 12%

rate after 1985, thereby arriving at an estimated 96 million passengers in the year 2000.

With these assumptions, the task force identified 60 potential sites for the airport within 50 miles of the central business district. Most were rapidly eliminated, and only four sites remained by the fall of 1969. Private consultants reviewed the problems of access, land use, and regional economic impact at each site and presented the results to the task force. The final recommendations, formulated in April 1970, identified a site to the northwest of the metropolitan area as the most promising location for the new airport.

Transport officials in Ottawa received these conclusions with little enthusiasm. An advisory committee established to oversee the activities of the project team questioned the technical justification for a new Toronto airport and the wisdom of Hellyer's change of policy. The committee also warned the Ministry that none of the four sites on the short list was technically acceptable for a major airport.

Transport department officials were equally concerned about a confrontation with the provincial government. They had instructed the task force to consult with provincial civil servants during the site selection process. The provincial Cabinet, in turn, established an interdepartmental committee to determine the provincial interest in airport development and to oversee site selection. These two groups could not reach an agreement on a site. The Transport task force believed that market considerations must determine airport location, and it advocated a westerly site along the principal axis of growth. The provincial committee was more concerned with the economic impact of an airport, and it sought a location east of the metropolitan area which would be consistent with Ontario's policy for regional development.

The critical factor which determined the response in Ottawa, however, was Canada's changing economic situation. The demand for air travel had not altered substantially, but the economy was no longer healthy. There was increasing indication from the Treasury Board that plans to develop a second major airport in eastern Canada might not be approved. As a result, Transport officials decided in May 1970 to reconsider the expansion of Malton as an alternative to the construction of a new airport.

The decision disappointed the task force, which was wedded to the concept of a new airport. Morale declined further when the Ministry hired Philip Beinhaker, the prime consultant for the Montreal airport, as a special adviser, for Beinhaker's support for Malton expansion was no secret to Transport planners. Irked by the Ministry's lack of confidence, Gordon resigned in July and his team disbanded. Beinhaker proceeded to prepare a report advocating the expansion of Malton as *the* solution to the problem, while the provincial committee conducted a similar study concluding that Malton expansion would not be harmful to Ontario's interests.

But Transport Minister Don Jamieson, who replaced Hellyer in April 1969, was not pleased with the recommendation. The federal government had pledged to build a new airport in Toronto, and Jamieson was committed to the eventual implementation of that policy. He was not opposed, however, to the expansion of Malton, and proposed a package deal: the immediate expansion of Malton and the future development of a major new airport at the western site identified by the project team. Ontario Prime Minister John Robarts, in turn, accepted the idea of expanding Malton but proposed that two smaller supplementary airports on either side of Toronto be developed instead of a single major facility. Jamieson was unwilling to accept the concept of a system of smaller airports, but he was equally unprepared to force the issue over the objections of the provincial government.

Following these difficulties, the Ministry of Transport reconstituted a planning team to reconsider the available options. Beinhaker, who remained a special consultant to the Ministry, and Gordon MacDowell, the new team manager, urged the Minister to scale down the size of the project, pointing out that additional sites were available if the required land package were smaller. By July 1971, Jamieson was persuaded that a system of smaller airports to supplement Malton was the only practical solution. The project team proposed a site southwest of Toronto for the first regional airport. Although little actual study had been made of the site's feasibility, Jamieson was prepared to announce this choice along with the concept of a regional airport system. But the problem was still not resolved, for the Ontario government remained committed to fostering growth *east* of the metropolitan area, and demanded that equal consideration be given to a site in Pickering Township. Jamieson reluctantly agreed to these demands and finally announced the selection of Pickering on March 2, 1972, more than three years after Ottawa had made its original decision to build a new airport.

OPPOSITION COALESCES

Pickering Township, situated northeast of Metropolitan Toronto, contains 32,000 people, 75,000 acres of land, three large towns, and a number of villages. The area is among the most productive agricultural land in

Canada, but active farming has declined steadily for the last century. The population also declined until the 1950s when an influx of exurbanites and "gentlemen farmers" helped reverse the trend. The site which Transport proposed to acquire contained, in 1972, 717 individual property owners and 126 working farms.[10] But by the late 1960s, land speculation and soaring property taxes had combined to discourage agriculture. According to Transport officials, only half the land on the site was occupied by owner-farmers, the remainder was owned by corporations and speculators.

The government's plans called for the expropriation of 18,000 acres for the operational zone of the airport. Ontario officials had succeeded in persuading Ottawa to situate the facility east of the metropolitan area, and now were prepared to cooperate by purchasing additional land for a proposed "airport city" and by zoning the remainder of the "noise lands" in conformity with federal plans. The agreement was formalized in an Annex of Understanding, signed by the two governments in March 1972.

Despite Ottawa's promise of an open-planning process for the new Toronto airport, virtually no one outside the federal and provincial governments was aware of the complex negotiations that had taken place during the three-year period. The March announcement, consequently, came as a surprise to the Toronto-area public.[11] Reaction was mixed: provincial politicians, including the opposition Liberal and New Democratic parties as well as the governing Conservatives, favored the project, but the opposition parties in Ottawa criticized the "costly duplication" implicit in the construction of a second major air facility. The *Globe and Mail,* a major Toronto newspaper, opposed the project on the grounds that the proposed facility would be too small to compete with the new Montreal airport.[12]

The reaction was also mixed in Pickering Township, particularly among farmers and long-time residents of the area. Some welcomed the prospect of selling their land; agricultural operations were becoming less lucrative and many farmers expected adequate compensation for their holdings. Others, however, were more attached to the land or were more skeptical of the price which the government would offer. There was little disagreement among the new residents, however: most had escaped the city in search of a tranquil lifestyle and were not inclined to accede quietly to the government's plans. The initial protest meetings attracted as many as 1000 people and generated considerable enthusiasm for keeping "the stench of the city out of Brougham's nostrils."[13]

Within a fortnight, opposition to the airport had coalesced, and a formal organization—People or Planes (POP)—was established. An executive committee was elected at the first meeting, chaired by Dr. Charles

Godfrey, a Toronto physician with a home in neighboring Uxbridge. The active core of POP consisted of 25 or 30 people, few of whom lived within the expropriated zone. Although not in jeopardy of losing their land, they feared that the pattern of development which often accompanies airport construction would eventually affect them. Consequently they were prepared to devote considerable time, energy, and money to oppose the airport plan.

The first major problem was to formulate an overall strategy. At first, support had been generated in the local area by appealing to residents to prevent the transformation of their peaceful countryside into a noisy concrete jungle. An array of arguments emphasizing equity issues could have been the basis for a powerful political campaign; after all, Malton-area residents had orchestrated a successful protest in 1968 on just such grounds. But POP leadership decided in early spring of 1972 to oppose the government's plans on the grounds that there was no *technical* justification for the construction of a new airport anywhere in the Toronto metropolitan area. The only logical choice to meet the airport demand, they argued, was to expand Malton; the construction of a new airport was a shortsighted solution to the problem of aircraft noise in the communities surrounding Malton.

The choice of strategy was influenced by several considerations. POP leaders were aware that many people in the local community in fact favored the airport plan. Moreover airport opponents were largely middle-class professionals while supporters came from lower socioeconomic groups. Many long-time residents relished the increased commerce and employment opportunities that they believed would accompany airport development. Several local town councils approved resolutions supporting construction, and a grass-roots organization, People over Welfare (POW) was formed as a counterweight to POP.[14] Under these circumstances, a campaign opposing airport construction which was based on equity considerations would be vulnerable to the criticism that opponents were in the minority even within the affected district. In fact, a subsequent survey conducted by the Pickering-area MP, Norman Cafik, found that the majority of respondents in the district supported the government decision.

Thus an attack on the technical justification for airport development seemed the most reasonable and feasible strategy for POP. The technical resources required to conduct a campaign of this nature were available within the organization, since a number of activists had extensive engineering experience. Moreover, by avoiding demands for a new site, POP was able to elicit support among those middle-class residents of Toronto who were becoming disenchanted with growth policies in general. Armed with the results of the 1970 Ministry of Transport study on the possibility of expanding Malton to meet the demand for air services, airport opponents knew that the need for a new facility would be difficult to demonstrate on technical grounds.

This strategic decision guided POP activists during a three and one-half year battle. Although their advocacy of expansion of the existing facilities created allies for the government within the Malton-area communities, the approach was judicious given its constituency, for POP would have gained little by raising questions of equity.

THE BATTLE FOR PICKERING

The stage was set for a long and protracted battle to determine the future of Pickering Township. The conflict evolved through four phases. Initially, airport opponents mobilized allies among citizen groups as well as local and provincial politicians to persuade the Ministry of Transport to reconsider its policy choice. The effort was unsuccessful and opponents then sought to generate public support by concentrating on the expropriations process. The third phase of the battle centered on the Airport Inquiry Commission, established by the federal government to review Transport's policy in response to electoral needs. In the final stages of the conflict, opponents physically obstructed the federal bulldozers.

ROUND ONE: SOLICITING ALLIES

In April 1972, POP launched a campaign for an official review of the airport decision and sought the support of organized citizen groups in the Toronto area. Disputes over proposed highway and urban renewal projects during the late 1960s and early 1970s had sensitized the urban middle class to environmental issues.[15] Thus the initial contacts were successful; both the Confederation of Residents and Ratepayers Associations (CORRA) and the Federation of Ontario Naturalists (FON) agreed to cooperate with POP. By late spring, sufficient support had been gathered to permit the creation of a new organization, the Metropolitan Toronto Airport Review Committee (MTARC), directed and financed through POP.

Airport opponents, however, encountered greater difficulty in eliciting support from local representatives and town councils. Norman Cafik, the Member of Parliament from Pickering and a member of the governing

Liberal Party, agreed to urge the Cabinet to conduct a formal review of the decision; he was unwilling, however, to challenge the selection of Pickering unless persuaded that the majority of his constituents opposed the project.[16] Several local councils had approved resolutions condemning the selection of Pickering, but others were enthusiastic about the choice.

The effort to elicit support from provincial officials for a formal policy review was particularly frustrating. The selection of Pickering had been influenced by the development plans of the Ontario government, and a portion of the land to be expropriated was to be taken by the province. Nevertheless the details of the decision process had not been made public, and provincial authorities denied any role in site selection. Since responsibility rested with the Ministry of Transport and the federal Cabinet, the Ontario government suggested that requests for review be directed to Ottawa.

The difficulties encountered by airport opponents in finding support for their campaign were exacerbated by the absence of technical information concerning the need for a new airport or the choice of site. The Ministry of Transport refused to release the task force studies and consultant reports prepared in connection with the site selection process. Transport officials were willing to make public the documents defending the need for a new airport, but the choice of Pickering had been a last-minute political compromise, and the site had not been subjected to detailed topographic, climatic, and environmental studies before the official announcement was made. Hence the Ministry required additional time to complete the required studies.

The inaccessibility of federal planning documents, however, was not entirely disadvantageous for opponents; indeed, the reluctance of Transport officials to offer technical support of its decision buttressed POP charges that the new airport was a political solution to the noise problem at Malton and that the Ministry of Transport was arrogant in refusing to provide information. But in late May, as soon as the technical studies were completed, Minister of Transport Don Jamieson agreed to meet with a POP delegation to discuss government policy. The meeting was well publicized and the Minister spent more than four hours with airport opponents, during which he patiently responded to all questions. Even the POP delegation was impressed by the effort. Jamieson further emphasized his good will by participating in a joint conference with POP leaders and releasing the planning documents to the public, along with additional information on the decision process. Jamieson nevertheless firmly denied the request for an open inquiry into the decision on the grounds that it would imply an abdication of government responsibility for policy choices. Similarly, the Minister offered to make Transport personnel available to respond to questions raised by opponents but refused to provide funds to conduct an "unfeasibility study," as demanded by POP. The critical demands of airport opponents were decisively rejected, and the meeting was a public relations coup for Jamieson, who appeared unruffled and conciliatory in the face of hostility.

This success was followed immediately by a series of public endorsements of government policy. On June 27, 1972, the Council of the Municipality of Metropolitan Toronto (the governing body of the Toronto region) gave its support to the airport in Pickering Township. The following day, the Toronto City Council approved a resolution to "endorse and support" the project. Airport opponents had anticipated the Metro Council vote, but the City Council resolution was unexpected. Opinion in the Council was divided and the decision was rescinded the following year, but the vote in 1972 constituted a crushing defeat for airport opponents, who had hoped to enlist city leaders in their battle with the Ministry of Transport.

ROUND TWO: THE EXPROPRIATIONS PROCESS

The second phase of the conflict began in September 1972, when the Ministry of Public Works informed property owners within the designated airport zone of its intention to expropriate their lands. The notification, required by the new Expropriations Act, was a break from previous procedures for land taking. Prior to the Act, the government took title to land by filing the proper papers in local land registry offices. Land owners were not specifically identified and no advance notice was required. The new law required the government to specify each parcel of land and to notify all property owners of its intention to expropriate. The detailed specification of properties had not been undertaken prior to the summer of 1972, so that the government could not proceed with the expropriation until September.

The new law allowed for additional delays by mandating a formal public hearing on the receipt of any written objections to a proposed expropriation. The hearing was not designed to review government policy. Moreover cross-examination of witnesses was not permitted; the Hearing Officer was simply to submit a summary of objections to the Minister of Public Works. The Ministry of Transport was not required to defend its policy or to participate in any way in the process. While this did not satisfy their demands for a formal inquiry, airport opponents saw the public hearing procedures as a means to delay further the development process.

Upon receipt of the Notice of Intent to Expropriate, they filed the requisite objections and the hearing was scheduled for late November. The Toronto airport project was the first major government expropriation subject to the new process, and both POP and the Ministry of Transport were determined to use the opportunity to further their own interests. Opposition leaders decided to challenge the need for a new facility in their testimony, even though the hearing was designed only to record objections to expropriations. Transport officials refused to participate but provided the media with information to refute the evidence presented at the hearing. Both parties understood that the critical audience was neither the Hearing Officer nor the Minister of Public Works, but public opinion.

During the eight days of hearings, the major objection raised by airport opponents was that the government's technical evidence was insufficient to support its policy position; neither the need for a new facility nor the selection of Pickering was substantiated in the documents made public by the Ministry of Transport. The real debate, however, took place outside the hearing room and before television cameras, where Transport officials complained of POP's "unjust allegations," while POP leaders compared the government planning studies to *Mein Kampf* because "they spell out what the government intends to do."[17]

After the hearings, attention shifted to Ottawa. The Minister of Public Works was allotted 30 days from the presentation of the Hearing Officer's report to confirm or deny the expropriation. Lobbying efforts intensified. Malton-area residents were particularly active in urging the Cabinet to proceed with the project; the media exposure enjoyed by POP during the hearings led Malton residents to believe that Transport's commitment to a second airport was weakening. The Society for Aircraft Noise Abatement (SANA), which had been essentially dormant since late 1968, publicly advocated confirmation, and the Mississauga town council offered to subsidize any ratepayer group that desired to participate in the campaign against Malton expansion. POP received some encouragement when the executive committee of the *new* Toronto City Council, elected in late 1972, resolved to oppose the new airport.

Many airport opponents believed that their presentation at the Expropriations Hearings had persuaded the Cabinet that it would be foolhardy to proceed with the project in the face of local resistance. Consequently the Minister of Public Works' decision to confirm the expropriation came as a disagreeable surprise. This time, however, the setback was not devastating, for just as the battle appeared to be over, opponents received a last-minute reprieve.

ROUND THREE: THE INQUIRY COMMISSION

On January 30, 1973, the new Minister of Transport, Jean Marchand, informed Parliament that although the government had decided to confirm the expropriation, it had agreed to postpone the project for one year pending completion of a review. This announcement marked the culmination of a gradual policy change within the Ministry of Transport. The determination to resist demands for review had begun to fade under the pressure of the approaching federal elections of October 1972. By late summer, the Minister of Transport indicated that the government might be willing to restudy the problem once the expropriation was confirmed; with the price of land frozen, an additional delay in the project would not increase the cost of assembling the required land for the airport. The elections left the Liberal Party in control but without an absolute majority. Thus a further delay in initiating the project was desirable for economic reasons and prudent for political purposes.

Despite Marchand's intention to complete the review within 12 months, the process of reassessment dragged on for two years. Organizational arrangements were not completed until the autumn of 1973, when the terms of reference and the membership of a Board of Inquiry were announced. The first public hearings were held in March 1974 and continued until June. The report was completed in December and the government's decision was formally announced in February 1975.

The initial delay in the review process resulted from the refusal of the provincial government to participate in the proceedings. Marchand's announcement had promised a joint federal-provincial study by a "board of examination," but Ontario Prime Minister William Davis was not persuaded of the utility of provincial participation. The Ontario government had consistently maintained that the airport decision was the responsibility of Ottawa, hence, any review should be conducted solely by the federal government. After several months of fruitless negotiations, federal officials decided to proceed under the terms of the Federal Inquiries Act and set up an independent Inquiry Commission.

Although airport opponents had eagerly sought a formal review of Transport's plans, they were far from pleased with the Inquiry Commission. The Order-in-Council which established the Commission instructed it "to receive and record new evidence" on the need for a new air facility and the choice of site. This vague wording was interpreted by the Commissioners to mean evidence developed after January 1973, thereby limiting the evidence which could be presented to the Commissioners. This, as well as the membership of the Commission, antagonized airport opponents. One of the members, Murray Jones, became the focus of controversy. Jones, an urban planner by profession, had been a representative of Mississauga during Hellyer's review of Malton expansion plans in the fall of 1968. In that capacity he had vigorously argued against Malton expansion. Convinced that Jones was biased, POP lodged a formal protest against his selection and eventually brought suit, but the protest was denied and the proceedings dismissed.[18]

Unable to broaden the terms of reference for the Inquiry Commission, airport opponents were faced with a dilemma. On the one hand, the Commission hearings offered an excellent opportunity to challenge the technical basis of government policy. But participation implied tacit approval of the process, and POP might encounter serious difficulties if it proved necessary to continue the battle once the Commission report was completed. After considerable debate, airport opponents opted to accept the risks involved in participation, but the vote on the issue was not unanimous and many activists were distressed by the outcome.

The decision to participate fully in the activities of the Commission, however, hinged on financial considerations. POP had amassed a substantial war chest, but much of the money had been spent on legal representation and media activities. Indeed the organization emerged from the Expropriations Hearings with a net deficit. The Inquiry Commission was prepared to cover the expenses involved to prepare evidence, but the cost of legal representation during the lengthy inquiry process was beyond the capacity of POP. It appeared, ironically, as if airport opponents would be unable to participate fully in the very mechanism for which they had fought.

Just as funds were running out, the Toronto City Council came to the rescue. The Council had expressed its opposition to the government project in January 1973, but had indicated to the Commission that it would take no formal stand at the hearings until its own technical studies were completed. Nonetheless city officials intended to participate, and appointed Donald Wright, the legal counsel for POP, as their representative. Wright formally severed his ties with POP, since the Toronto City Council was theoretically neutral, but his approach to the Inquiry process did not significantly change. In this manner, airport opponents continued to be represented without bearing the financial cost of participation.

Public hearings were conducted during the spring of 1974 at Malton, Pickering, and in downtown Toronto. They were dominated by the Ministry of Transport, which presented a bulky "Written Statement," scores of documents, and a series of witnesses in support of its plans for Pickering. More than 500 written statements were filed with the Commission and approximately 350 witnesses testified, each subject to extensive cross-examination by the Commission staff and the lawyers representing the concerned parties.

Discussion focused on three major issues: the noise problem at Malton, the impact of a new airport on Pickering, and the need for an additional air facility in the region. Transport officials presented technical data to support their position on each of these issues. During cross-examination, airport opponents raised questions about the accuracy of this evidence. They pointed out that Transport's emphasis on the noise at Malton and the absence of immediate technological remedies contrasted sharply with its assurances to the people of Vancouver that aircraft noise is a transient problem. The Commissioners heard a great deal of conflicting testimony; a spokesman for Air Canada questioned the reliability of the aviation forecasts developed by Transport planners; and a consultant for de Havilland Aircraft Corporation argued that the demand for air services could be accommodated through the use of STOL-craft, thereby eliminating the need for a new airport. But opponents encountered difficulty in presenting detailed technical data to support their position. A study prepared by consultants for the City of Toronto was pilloried during cross-examination, and one of its authors, Jack Ellis, was even forced to retract several statements.

Following the hearings, the Commissioners visited new air facilities in North America and Western Europe and spoke with airport developers. During the fall of 1974, they pieced together a final report and sent it to the Privy Council. The Commissioners accepted virtually all of the arguments presented by Transport, including forecasts of future demand, problems with Malton expansion, and the suitability of the Pickering site, and they recommended both immediate, full-scale development at Pickering and an additional runway at Malton.

The Inquiry Commission report touched off a furious battle in the Cabinet. Transport Minister Marchand welcomed the support for Pickering but opposed further development at Malton. A number of Ministers were concerned about the financial implications of the recommendations, while others were concerned about their potential political repercussions. The leading opponent was Barney Danson, Minister of State for Urban Affairs, whose constituency was adjacent to the proposed airport site. Danson and his allies succeeded in delaying the decision of the Cabinet for several weeks, until a compromise was reached; the Malton expansion project would be dropped, but Transport would proceed with a "minimum international airport," that is one runway and one terminal, at Pickering. The decision, announced on February 20, 1975, by Marchand, included a promise that any further work at the site would be preceded by another detailed reassessment.

ROUND FOUR: FACING THE BULLDOZERS

The revised plans stiffened the determination of airport opponents to continue the battle, but time was beginning to run out. In late February, the Department of Public Works, acting on behalf of Transport, mailed notices of possession to the 717 landowners in the expropriated zone. Only 70 parcels of land, approximately 1800 acres, were required during the first phase of construction, and Public Works offered three-year leases to the remaining residents. But the government could not actually take possession of the land, since the Expropriations Act allotted 90 days for residents to vacate the premises. Hence work could not commence at the site until the end of May.

Airport opponents frantically sought reinforcements to assist them. The defunct Metropolitan Toronto Airport Review Committee (MTARC) was resuscitated with the encouragement of the Toronto City Council. De Havilland Aircraft Corporation, whose opposition to the proposed airport was based on a marketing strategy for its STOL-craft, picked up some of MTARC's expenses.[19] Moral support was provided by Air Canada officials; as a Crown Corporation reporting to the Minister of Transport, Air Canada could not openly oppose the Cabinet decision, but corporate executives provided opponents with technical information to strengthen their case.

During the 90-day grace period, MTARC orchestrated an intensive campaign to persuade Ottawa to cancel the project. MTARC financed a public opinion survey and widely publicized the results. According to this survey, a majority of residents in Metropolitan Toronto disapproved of government plans for a new airport in Pickering Township; even more surprising, a slight majority in the Malton area were opposed to the project.[20] Glossy brochures were printed and copies sent to virtually every Minister in the federal government. Transport officials, however, were determined to proceed and the lobbying effort had little impact in Ottawa.

But the campaign was more successful in Ontario where provincial officials were beginning to doubt the wisdom of the project. The provincial Cabinet had insisted, as late as February 1975, that airport siting and development was a federal matter. But Prime Minister William Davis had never been persuaded that a new airport was necessary, and he had been careful to avoid public support for the project. As the construction date approached, he became increasingly concerned about the cost of the services which his government had agreed to provide, a sum which he estimated at $400 million. He was even more worried about the political consequences of proceeding with the project. The initial protest over Transport's plans had not dissipated and public opinion was turning against the airport. With provincial elections approaching in the fall, Davis was convinced that additional delay would be in the best interests of his party.

Airport opponents recognized that their most effective strategy would be to disrupt the alliance between the federal and provincial governments. MTARC quickly capitalized on Davis's growing uncertainty and arranged a meeting with the Prime Minister. The session was mutually beneficial; opponents were able to present their case against the airport while the Prime Minister could gauge the nature and extent of the opposition. Shortly thereafter, Davis officially requested clarification of Transport's long-range plans for the Pickering site. No mention was made of increasing provincial concern, but the inquiry alerted Transport officials that a reassessment was underway in Ontario.

On July 3, Marchand announced that preparatory work would begin before the end of the month. While airport opponents formulated strategies to obstruct the federal bulldozers, Davis dropped his bombshell. The provincial government, he announced, could not afford "at this time" to provide the infrastructure necessary for the functioning of the airport. The Cabinet, he explained, did not wish to see the project cancelled, but it desired an additional construction delay. Transport officials were dismayed but not entirely discouraged. Marchand interpreted Davis's actions as an effort to extract additional federal funds and he indicated that Ottawa was prepared to continue discussions of cost-sharing arrangements. He was not prepared, however, to tolerate prolonged delay in construction.

In mid-August, the bulldozers arrived on the airport site. Provincial elections were now less than one month away, and both opposition parties were strongly against the project. Davis feared that a confrontation between federal authorities and airport opponents could only help his political enemies, and he urged Marchand to postpone the work until after the election. Marchand agreed to an additional delay, but when the campaign was over Ottawa unleashed the bulldozers. POP activists occupied abandoned buildings on the site and committed small acts of sabotage. The media printed photos of people clinging to buildings which bulldozers were trying to level. One week later, Davis, who had lost his majority in the provincial parliament, had had enough; he announced on September 24 that his government was now firmly opposed to any further work on the site and would not cooperate in any way with federal authorities.

The withdrawal of provincial support was the final straw. The Ontario government had formally agreed to provide airport services and, technically, could be sued for breach of contract. But the federal Cabinet had no desire to pursue the matter further. If Ontario no longer desired the federal investment, the Cabinet had no intention of forcing it on them, and Marchand announced that work on the site would terminate immediately.

CONCLUSIONS

The decision to shelve the plans for airport development at Pickering concluded a seven-year battle over Toronto's air facilities. Few mourned the death of the project. Malton-area residents had perceived the new airport merely as a way to alleviate their own noise problem. The staff of the Ministry of Transport, the airport sponsor, had always been reluctant to build a second air facility. Neither was entirely unhappy with the Cabinet decision.

From the outset, the Pickering project had been influenced by efforts to find an equitable solution that would cater to diverse interests and concerns. The decision of the Minister of Transport in December 1968 to abandon plans for the expansion of Malton had reflected political sensitivity to these pressures. Despite warnings that a new airport was an unnecessary and inefficient use of resources, the Minister acceded to demands of Ontario politicians and Malton neighbors for the construction of another facility in a different part of the metropolitan area. Similarly, the protest in Pickering stemmed from the concern of local residents about bearing a disproportionate share of the costs of air services. But if the equity issue fueled the controversy, the battle itself centered on the technical justification for airport development. The terrain, which was consciously selected by opponents for strategic reasons, was appropriate in light of the political origins of the project. And in fact the outcome of the conflict reflected the priority of efficiency in public policy choices, rather than a newly discovered concern for equity.

Airport opponents were well organized to conduct a lengthy battle. Their choice of strategy was judicious, for it enabled them to assemble a coalition of interests. Technical resources were readily available from within the organization, and the financing was adequate to support a strong counter offensive through the local media. Influential allies within the Toronto City Council provided financial as well as moral support, and powerful political representatives in Parliament championed their cause. Organizational successes were facilitated by the nature of the local opposition, largely made up of highly educated, upper middle-class professionals.

But the political influence of airport opponents and the considerable resources employed in the conflict were not sufficient to persuade the federal government to abandon the project. To be sure, the perseverance of opposition provided a visible reminder of the political volatility of the issue. The airport question, however, was perceived as politically dangerous only because of chance political events such as the election of minority governments in Ottawa in the fall of 1972 and in Ontario in September 1975.

The airport battle, however, had a major impact on the two main combatants: Pickering-area residents and the Ministry of Transport. Airport opponents became increasingly cynical and distrustful of authority as the conflict proceeded. But the controversy created no revolutionaries among the middle-class participants. Instead it molded better citizens more conscious of government actions and ready to question them by active participation in the decision-making process.[21]

Ironically the impact of the conflict on the Ministry of Transport was broader and more disturbing. Oriented to the needs of the air traveler, Transport officials were prepared to ignore the concerns of the small core of activists in Pickering Township. Their inability to proceed with "business as usual" during the conflict persuaded them that public involvement in some form is inevitable in future airport development programs. Yet the essential orientation of these officials did not change in any significant respect as a result. Instead, Transport officials, like airport opponents, became increasingly cynical, concluding that the public's involvement must be carefully structured, indeed "managed," in order to assure the adoption and approval of technical plans. This combined effect of controversy on its participants has disturbing implications: increasing skepticism on the part of citizens may contribute to more active public involvement in policy decisions, but a heightened cynicism on the part of technocrats can seriously undermine the democratic process.

NOTES

1. For an overview of the problem in the American context, see Jerome Milch, "Feasible and Prudent Alternatives: Airport Development in the Age of Public Protest," *Public Policy* 1 (Winter 1976), 81-109; for comparative analyses, see Elliot J. Feldman, "Air Transportation Infrastructure as a Problem of Public Policy," *Policy Studies Journal* 1 (Autumn 1977), 20-28, and Elliot J. Feldman and Jerome Milch, "Options on the Metropolitan Fringe: Strategies of Airport Development," in Douglas Ashford (ed.), *Cities vs. Nations* (tentative title) (Chicago: Maaroufa Press, 1978).

2. Feldman, "Air Transportation" provides an excellent synopsis of this critique.

3. Much of the opposition to airport development projects in the United States, for example, has focused on the adequacy of environmental impact statements. Milch, "Feasible and Prudent Alternatives." Equity issues, however, remain directly on the agenda in some instances. See, for example, Dorothy Nelkin, *Jetport* (New Brunswick: Transaction Books, 1974).

4. The data base for this case study was collected by the author as part of a larger joint project with Elliot J. Feldman of Brandeis University. More than 50 interviews were conducted in Toronto and Ottawa in the course of this research, and numerous documents from government and private sources were collected. Specific citations to this material will be made only in reference to the more controversial arguments.

5. Prior to 1970, this bureaucracy was known as the Department of Transportation (DOT). The ministry concept and the new title are, consequently, recent developments, but in order to avoid confusion, the term—Ministry of Transport—will be used exclusively in this narrative.

6. For an account of the evolution of Canadian airport policies, see Jerome Milch, "One Step Ahead: The Impact of Economic Competition on the Development of Airport Policies in the United States and Canada," unpublished paper, February 1977.

7. They also reorganized the ministry. For a detailed account of these changes, see John W. Langford, *Transport in Transition* (Montreal: McGill-Queen's Press, 1976).

8. The Mississauga Homeowners Association, for example, presented a "Brief Opposing Expansion of Toronto International Airport" to Transport Minister Paul Hellyer on December 13, 1968, which argued that "expansion will seriously affect the health, safety, convenience, and welfare of the residents of Mississauga." Indeed, on those grounds alone the Association called for the construction of a second international airport in the Toronto region.

9. The contents of this letter were read to the author by Clayton Glenn, Vice President for Fleet Planning of Air Canada, during a personal interview on May 17, 1977.

10. The number of "working farms" in the airport zone proved to be a particularly controversial issue in the course of the Inquiry Commission Hearings. This figure was cited by Hector Massey and Charles Godfrey in *People or Planes* (Toronto: Copp Clark, 1972).

11. Budden and Ernst, *The Movable Airport* (Toronto: Hakkert, 1973), 99-100.

12. These responses are detailed in the *Toronto Globe and Mail* of March 3, 1972.

13. Massey and Godfrey, p. 46.

14. Airport opponents argued that People over Welfare (POW) was established and financed by the Ministry of Transport, but one leading activist admitted that the organization had considerable support in the area. However, it was unable to survive for very long, largely because its leadership lacked the technical and organizational skills available to People or Planes. Personal interview with Clark Muirhead, January 18, 1977.

15. Two prominent conflicts, both of which were eventually won by opponents, were the battle over the construction of the Spadina Expressway and the opposition to an urban renewal project in Trefann Court. The latter controversy is chronicled in Graham Fraser, *Fighting Back* (Toronto: Hakkert, 1972).

16. The results of Cafik's survey persuaded him to moderate his initial opposition to the airport. Instead he assumed the role of spokesman for the expropriated landowners and conducted a long and successful battle to extract additional compensation for them from the government.

17. *Toronto Globe and Mail,* November 30, 1972.

18. Irritated by the "frivolous and scandalous" nature of the suit, the Attorney General's office in Ottawa intervened in the court proceedings in opposition to People or Planes. The likelihood that the Court would assess costs to the organization, and particularly to its leader, Charles Godfrey, in the event that the suit was denied prompted POP to request termination of the proceedings. The government consented to the request, provided that Godfrey and his colleagues agree to take no other legal actions against the Commission (*Toronto Globe and Mail,* August 13, 1974). The incident is also noted in Airport Inquiry Commission, *Report* (Ottawa: Information Canada, 1974), 13ff.

19. Personal interview with Douglas Turner, Chairman of the Metropolitan Toronto Airport Review Committee, January 17, 1977.

20. The data from the survey, conducted by Elliott Research Corporation, have mysteriously disappeared. Neither aiport opponents nor the company have retained printouts of the data.

21. Angela Ferrante, "After the Protest Is Over," *Maclean's* (May 17, 1976).

2

NUCLEAR POWER AND ITS CRITICS:
A SITING DISPUTE

Dorothy Nelkin

In June 1967, the New York State Electric and Gas Corporation (NYSE&G) declared its intention to build a nuclear-fueled electric generating plant on the east shore of Cayuga Lake, in the heart of New York State. NYSE&G briefly described the details of the projected Bell Power Station to the press. The 830 megawatt plant, estimated to cost about $135 million, was scheduled for operation by mid-1973. Application for the required Atomic Energy Commission (AEC) construction permit to build "Bell Station #1" was made in March 1968 and site clearance began in April.

Five years later, plans for a nuclear plant were abandoned. What happened during this period is a story of controversy and opposition by scientists and citizens who perceived Bell Station (the first nuclear power station to be built on a deep, stratified lake) as a threat to the primary water and recreational resource of the upstate New York region.[1]

Many complex issues characteristic of nuclear power plant siting problems surfaced during this controversy. As new technical problems have been posed by nuclear power plants and the increased size of the generating units, the adequacy of the existing system of regulation has been challenged. The case brings into focus relationships among scientists, public agencies, citizens' groups, and policy makers. It illustrates the problem of developing policy in the absence of uniform standards and definitive scientific agreement on the character and dimensions of ecological damage. A major issue in the dispute was the character of scientific evidence itself and its interpretation for policy purposes. What are the obligations of scientists with respect to interpretation of their data? How can inconclusive scientific evidence be used as criteria for policy decisions? How does the behavior of opposition groups affect decisions concerning environmental issues? These are some of the questions raised when the siting of a nuclear power plant is under consideration.

CAYUGA'S WATERS

Cayuga Lake is the second largest of Central New York State's Finger Lakes. Formed as a result of the Pleistocene glacial advances, the lake is 38 miles long and 435 feet deep. Concern with the effects of the proposed power station rested on limited past experience with the ecological vulnerability of a slow-flushing inland lake. The immediate problem involved the impact of the heated effluent from the power plant on the thermal stratification pattern of deep lakes.[2]

Cayuga Lake has an annual thermal cycle consisting essentially of two stratification periods. From about the first week in May to the first week in December, the lake is stratified into three zones: the epilimnion or surface layer, the metalimnion or intermediate layer, and the hypolimnion or deepest and coldest layer. During the second period, from December to May, the lake is isothermal, reaching a uniform temperature of 35°-40°F. In the spring, heat is again absorbed by the surface and vertically diffused. Temperature changes decrease with water depth, however, and the hypolimnion is never warmed above about 45°F. Since the colder water in this layer is more dense than water of the upper layers, thermal stratification tends to be maintained until the cold winter months when temperature differences between levels decrease.

The stratification behavior of the lake affects the distribution of oxygen and nutrients. During the stratified period, the oxygen content of the hypolimnion decreases. Since there are no mechanisms other than molecular diffusion to provide transfer, the normal respiration of crustacea and other organisms, as well as decaying aerobic bacteria, reduce the existing supply of oxygen in this lower layer. Oxygen is annually replenished during the winter mixing period.

The hypolimnion also stores the concentrations of nutrients fed to the lake by runoff. Algae in the upper layers of the lake feed on and concentrate phosphorus. When they die and settle, the nutrient sinks out of the reach of plants. In this way, some nutrients are removed from the epilimnion, helping to reduce plant activity during the summer.

The proposed reactor, ordered by NYSE&G, would be cooled by water pumped in from the hypolimnion, a hundred feet below the surface (temperature of about 45°F). This would be discharged on the surface at about 65°F. The reactor, generating 830 megawatts, would circulate about 1,225 cubic feet of cooling water per second, and the maximum rate of heat discharged would be 5.55 billion BTUs per hour.

The NYSE&G decision to locate the Bell nuclear power station on Cayuga Lake was based on several considerations. Cayuga Lake was particularly desirable primarily because of its year-round cooling capacity. The lake was also navigable, allowing shipment of a large reactor vessel. The location was centrally placed in terms of the utility's transmission plans—in particular, in terms of its ties to other transmission systems. A plant on the lake could deliver power conveniently into the exchange system of the New York State Power Pool. Since the new plant would make available more capacity than needed by present NYSE&G customers, the plan was to sell about 70% of the new capacity during the first year.[3]

The utility's decision to build the power plant was greeted enthusiastically by the Tompkins County Board of Supervisors. There was no immediate public reaction, and several individuals who later actively opposed the utility's plans indicated that their initial response was a fleeting thought that "progress at last was coming to the area."

Many people welcomed the plans as an economic benefit. Bell Station would employ about 600 people during the construction phase, and about 60 on a permanent basis. It would also contribute significantly to the tax base of the small town of Lansing where it was to be located.

Early in June 1967, shortly after the first public announcement of the proposed plant, NYSE&G notified 25 property owners in the area that their property was condemned; for as a public utility NYSE&G has the right of eminent domain. Seven hundred and twenty-five acres were purchased adjacent to Milliken Station, the company's existing coal-fired installation, including 8,000 feet of lake frontage. NYSE&G bought the property for $700,000 even before applying for a construction permit to the AEC.

TECHNICAL DISPUTES

In February 1968, utility representatives spoke at an informal seminar sponsored by the Water Resources Center at Cornell University. The seminar, convened as a fact-finding session, was interpreted by some participants as indicating the group's tacit acceptance of the NYSE&G plans. This impression was buttressed by a research prospectus drafted at the Water Resources Center which implied that power plant construction was inevitable and that it would offer unique possibilities for studying thermal pollution. Seneca Lake, as yet unpolluted, was proposed as a control.[4] The Cornell Center submitted a proposal to NYSE&G for a study of the lake's ecology.

The subsequent reaction to the Bell Station plans must be considered in relation to the location of the site, 12 miles from Cornell University. Here was a high-powered cluster of scientists and engineers with concerns for the preservation of a major resource in their community. They were willing to use their expertise to enter the confrontation and to attempt an evaluation of potential damage to the ecology of the lake. Some of them (water resources engineers, ecologists, fishery biologists, conservationists, and limnologists) were professionally concerned with water resources; others, such as physical scientists, were concerned as citizens, but also had relevant professional expertise to contribute.

Evaluating the possibility of ecological damage to the lake required the cooperation of scientists from many disciplines. Professor Alfred Eipper, an ecologist specializing in fishery biology in the Department of Conservation at Cornell, organized the first of several interdisciplinary groups. From Eipper's point of view as an ecologist, scientists had to take a position on the utility's plans before irreversible damage to the lake occurred. His group agreed to develop a position paper summarizing the existing state of knowledge concerning the thermal properties of Cayuga lake.

Eipper wrote the initial draft, circulated it within the University and elsewhere, and received extensive comments and criticism. The report, considerably revised after circulation through four drafts, appeared on May 27, 1968. Seventeen contributors from several disciplines, including conservation, limnology, biology, botany, geology, and engineering, signed it. A preface noted that the paper, reflecting the knowledge of its authors, had "resulted from the conviction that . . . professionals should contribute to public decisions on the management of natural resources." The Eipper report summarized the known effects and raised several questions about possible consequences of a heat discharge on the thermal and nutrient constitution of the lake and, thus, its likely implications for the aquatic environment.[5]

The report predicted that as the normal stratification pattern is upset through the pumping of water from the hypolimnion, the natural eutrophication process would be augmented. Eutrophication is a process normally occurring when nutrients drain into lakes from the surrounding watershed and increase lake fertility. Biological production can eventually cause a lake to choke with algae and weed growth. Drawing the available nutrients from the hypolimnion and discharging them into the warmer waters of the epilimnion would increase biological productivity. Moreover, the continuous addition of heated water would extend the stratification period and consequently the biological growing season. At the same time, the oxygen available for animal life in the hypolimnion would be depleted, decreasing the food sources of fish. The Eipper report described the effects of eutrophication in other lakes, such as Lake Erie, pointing out the "pea soup" appearance caused by the proliferation of algae.

To minimize eutrophication, the report strongly recommended alternative methods of cooling the discharge water, either through the use of cooling towers or cooling ponds. The report concluded that although the increase in biological production, and therefore of eutrophication, was unpredictable, the practical impossibility of reversing cumulative damage imposed the need for cautious consideration of all alternatives.

When the report was distributed for revision, four of those initially involved in the early meetings of the Eipper Committee refused to sign. They considered it inappropriate for scientists to engage in a direct policy statement. In fact, the Eipper report, as it began to influence political activity, created increasing strains within the scientific community. This strain reflected not so much substantive disagreement as concern with the mode of presenting scientific data, the appropriate behavior of scientists with respect to public issues, and the effect of publicity on the scientific dimensions of the problem. At one extreme were those who felt that the "credibility" of science was threatened by scientists who took a position on a policy issue. At the other were those who felt that taking a firm policy stance was absolutely necessary. Disagreements were subtle and alliances shifting; strain persisted and was reinforced both by the inconclusiveness of the evidence available on the lake's ecology and by public pressure to take a stand.

Scientific uncertainty concerning the effects of the power station became increasingly apparent as new groups formed to study diverse technical aspects of the problem. In August 1968, Clarence A. Carlson, a fishery biologist from the Cornell Department of Conservation, brought together a group of 12 scientists representing the disciplines of medicine, limnology, ecology, conservation, physical biology, and physics, to study the radiological hazards of the proposed Bell Station. The group included five persons who had been on the Eipper Committee. The Carlson report, appearing in December 1968, aimed to "permit a better-informed decision as to whether the public benefits from the proposed station outweigh its liabilities."[6]

The report stated that nuclear accidents were unlikely, though not impossible. They were apprehensive, however, about the radiological wastes produced in the course of normal daily operation. Some low-radiation level wastes would be routinely released into the condenser cooling water and into the lake. While the company's estimates of radionuclide quantities to be released were well below AEC maxima, the report argued that "localized concentration of radionuclides by currents, eddies, or wave action, is a likely possibility." Moreover, the report argued, plants and animals may concentrate radionuclides which, through the food chain, could affect other aquatic organisms unpredictably. The report recommended that, in view of the difficulty of accurately predicting radionuclide concentrations and their possible effects on the lake ecology, the AEC tighten its requirements in this case. It advised that state agencies should consider radiological as well as thermal issues. It further urged a design modification which would virtually eliminate radionuclide discharge.

Cornell's Engineering College also undertook a study during the summer of 1968.[7] This report, appearing in February 1969, was a theoretical analysis of the physical consequences of the heat transfer underlying biological and ecological questions. It emphasized consideration of the lake's total parameters, taking issue with NYSE&G-supported research which focused only on the area near the site. Measurement programs, it claimed, should be undertaken not only near the plume created by the discharge, but over the entire lake. The report dealt with transport processes, or turbulence caused by winds, flushing, and discharge, estimating that the effect of forced mixing through pumping could cause a 10% increase in the vertical exchange of nutrients during the stratified period. The report also examined the heat balance of the lake, estimating that the plant's discharge would represent 7% of the direct solar heat received by the lake, "a neither overwhelming nor negligible perturbation." This contrasted with the claims of a NYSE&G engineer who calculated that the addition of the heat from the power plant would be from 1% to 4%, a much less significant perturbation.

The report further calculated that the increase in the yearly surface temperature would be $0.9°F$,[8] a temperature rise which, to some extent, would be shared by the hypolimnion, depending on unknown characteristics of the stratification process. In the absence of a theoretical basis on which to make predictions, the report urged a conservative thermal pollution standard and an increase in thermal efficiency.

While the earlier Eipper report focused on possible effects proximate to the proposed plant, several persons considered this approach too limited and demanded the development of a strategy which considered the lake as a whole. One of these, K. Bingham Cady, questioned the temperature and distance standards for heated water discharges which had been proposed, but not yet established, by the State Department of Health. On October 2, 1968, he and a group of colleagues drafted a letter to the Department of Health which proposed criteria for a lake standard based on the effects of heated water on the entire lake's ecology.[9] This clashed with the health department's intended temperature-distance standards. Cady believed his letter might be agreeable to NYSE&G, since it recognized that if heated water is floated onto the surface of the lake, a larger fraction of the heat is dissipated into the atmosphere. This would prevent complete mixing of the heat into the lake and at the same time would permit discharge of a heated plume on the surface. In terms of the ecological concerns of conservationists, it was a reasonable suggestion, one which NYSE&G could endorse since it would not require a change in their plans. In March 1969, at the Water Resources Commission hearings on the proposed standards, company engineers were in general agreement with Cady about the proposed standards. However, when a company engineer was asked to sign Cady's letter, he declined, and the compromise proposal was to have no effect whatsoever on health department regulations.

In October 1968, at the same time that Cady made his proposal, a physicist, James A. Krumhansl, advanced a broader research strategy with an approach to the technical problem which had been overlooked in other reports. Both Eipper's report and the NYSE&G-sponsored research restricted their concern to the damage that might result from the pumping and thermal effect of the power station. In contrast, the new analysis assumed the lake ecology was already damaged from a variety of continuing pollution sources and asked, "Is it possible to use a major energy source to beneficiate the lake, i.e., in some sense to combat these forces (chemical, biological, etc.) which are now driving it?"[10] It proposed to use the plant as an energy source to cool the epilimnion by circulating a volume of cold water from the hypolimnion. He calculated that a normal increase of 50% of the water pumped through condensers for cooling purposes would be sufficient to cool the epilimnion by about 10°F. Less costly than cooling towers, this process could have a positive effect on the lake by decreasing biological activity and reversing, in part, the existing state of eutrophication.

This proposal led to a new series of meetings from which other suggestions for dealing with overall lake problems developed, such as a pumped water scheme. NYSE&G rejected these on the basis of costs and the various suggestions were never seriously considered in the subsequent discussion of alternatives.

While these activities occurred, NYSE&G contracted its own research at a cost of about $500,000. Two major contracts were awarded. One was for about $320,000 to the Cornell Aeronautical Laboratory (CAL) in Buffalo, an independent research contract organization owned at the time by Cornell University. This contract was to study the physical effects of thermal discharge near the present fossil-fuel station. The other contract was for $135,000 to the Cornell Water Resources Center for studying the ecological effects of the proposed nuclear plant.

The CAL engineers concentrated on the area of the lake near the existing Milliken Station, studying the plume created by the discharge and its effect on the surface. Three types of data formed the basis of a new report which appeared in November 1969.[11] First, aerial measurements were taken of surface temperature profiles, using infra-red scanning devices. Second, the vertical structure of the lake was monitored from nine stations, all within three thousand feet of the site. These measured the diffusion and heat exchange caused by the existing power station. Finally, the engineers took measurements and used them to evaluate the effects of weather conditions on the rate at which the temperature of the plume decays. The conclusions were that the thermal impact of the proposed station would cause an overall increase in the surface temperature of $0.7°F$, or less than 10% of the normal fluctuation. The mechanical transfer of cooling water from the hypolimnion would increase the volume of the epilimnion during the stratification period, which would thus be lengthened, at most, by four to five days at each end. The increase in the maximum heat content of the lake would be about 2% of the annual heat budget.

Thus the CAL report suggested that the effects would be of the same order or less than normal fluctuations, though always unidirectional. It noted, however, that coming to firm conclusions required many more actual observations, as well as a greater understanding of the complexity of factors affecting turbulence.

Research supported by NYSE&G also was under way during the summer of 1968 at the Cornell Water Resources Center. Seven scientists, headed by a resource economist, David Allee, and an ecologist, Ray Oglesby, formed the research group. It was organized under strained circumstances. Several individuals, experts in relevant scientific fields, were logical choices, but their known concern with local environmental problems precluded their participation; for the utility insisted that no one who was likely to have already formed an opinion should work on the project. Thus a man from outside Cornell, Thomas D. Wright, was brought in as a research associate for the study and he was to author 14 of the 20 chapters in the final report. Bringing in an outsider unfamiliar with the research group posed problems of coordination in an interdisciplinary study. Moreover, Wright soon engendered controversy when he joined the Citizens Committee to Save Cayuga Lake (CSCL). Because Wright left Cornell after completing his research, the major editing and summarizing were done by Ray Oglesby, who had also joined the faculty well after the NYSE&G study was underway. Thus the constraints imposed by the utility's concern with objectivity in fact hampered the research.

The work of this group dealt basically with the same subject as the Eipper report, but its intention differed considerably. The work plan, formulated in May 1968, indicated that "the group would *not* attempt to comment upon the broader questions of public policy involved. Administrative, economic, political, or psychological questions would be put aside in order to objectively evaluate the physical, chemical, and biological impacts of heat addition to a water body."[12] The group members collected data in order to provide a base-line evaluation of the lake. In September 1969, they issued their report which contained 20 individually signed studies, as well as conclusions and recommendations.

The actual data collection for these studies was closely observed by NYSE&G engineers who met regularly with the group and participated in discussions. Their presence was described as being sometimes useful and sometimes irritating. It was emphasized, however, that this did not interfere with the results of the study. Sensitive to possible criticism concerning the source of support, the group insisted that the results be published without company editing.

The report began by interpreting historical data on the lake, indicating that it may just be entering a eutrophication stage. Samples were taken from seven stations at various times during the season to establish base-line information for biochemical and radionuclide studies. Members presented results with warnings as to the difficulty of drawing quantitative conclusions. It was estimated that at the time of greatest thermal effect, algae could increase by 5%. There could be a net seasonal decrease in the oxygen in the hypolimnion; but such changes were interpreted as insignificant. The effect of increased temperature and a longer stratification season were also predicted to be insignificant for the whole lake. They further stressed the uncertainty of knowledge in this area and suggested additional studies,

concluding that "Limnologists know so little about the ecological significance of some of these environmental parameters, that prediction of
biological effects would be highly conjectural even if exact descriptions of
the physical changes were available."[13] Despite problems, the study did
make publicly available a sizable body of empirical data about the lake.

During this period of research, NYSE&G proceeded with its plan by
applying for an AEC construction permit in March 1968, and beginning
site clearance next to Milliken Station in April. Excavation of 15 million
cubic feet of shale was completed and concrete forms installed before the
winter, at a cost of about $1 million in addition to the $700,000 purchase
price of the land. By September, however, it became evident to the utility
that it would have to contend not only with ambiguous standards of
thermal pollution and with conservationist criticism, but also with aroused
and organized community protest.

CITIZEN ACTIVITY AND NYSE&G RESPONSE

The Cayuga Lake Preservation Association (CLPA) was the most logical
of existing organizations to become involved in the issue. The CLPA
formed in 1956 to deal with sewage problems in the lake drainage area,
and by 1968 it included some 350 lakeshore property owners as members.
On July 15, 1968, in response to the Eipper report, the CLPA issued a
statement urging that, in the light of disagreement among scientists on the
effect of nuclear power plants, the company would delay construction
until definitive answers about potential damage to the lake environment
were obtained. It also urged the incorporation of an alternative cooling
system as recommended by the Eipper report. The CLPA was divided,
however, on whether to become directly involved in a political battle to
support its position, in part due to its recent heavy involvement in a
controversial campaign opposing fluoridation.

On August 15, Eipper called a community meeting in Ithaca for citizens
concerned about the lake. Thirty people attended. As a result of this
meeting, David D. Comey, director of a private research institute on Soviet
science, offered to form a citizens' organization, the Citizens' Committee
to Save Cayuga Lake (CSCL). In just a few weeks, officers were elected, a
press release issued, and a board of sponsors selected. The 33 members of
this board were respected and well-established members of the community, all active in other civic organizations. Professional men were dominant in the heterogeneous group: persons affiliated with universities in the

lake region, four local political figures, four attorneys, four physicians, a city planner, a newspaper publisher and former Commissioner of Construction of New York, a stock broker, and several insurance and real estate brokers. All the bank presidents in Ithaca were approached, but none would consider affiliation.

The organization's official purpose was "to inform citizens of the Cayuga Lake region about potential sources of bacterial, chemical, thermal, and radioactive pollution of the lake, and to coordinate the efforts of all concerned organizations and individuals to prevent and eradicate any pollution endangering the foremost natural resource of the region."[14] Its well-publicized position was not to oppose nuclear power but to question the design of the present plant and its adequacy to guarantee environmental protection. Attention was also directed to inadequacies in the system of regulation and the standards by which natural resources were protected.

Comey, the Executive Director of CSCL, was a skillful organizer and was highly successful in coordinating the efforts of those concerned with the issue. Sixty people attended the CSCL organizational meeting in September 1968, and within several months, the group boasted 300 core members as well as several thousand affiliated individuals who became associated with CSCL through their membership in various related organizations. These included local sportsmen's groups, the CLPA, the Seneca Lake Waterways Association, and the Lake Champlain Committee, a group which faced a similar threat and hoped to gain experience from the CSCL. By September 1969, the core paid membership had grown to 854 and $16,323 had been raised from dues and contributions.

The CSCL sought and received wide publicity. Newspaper coverage also helped to arouse citizen interest with headlines such as "Cayuga Lake Shouldn't Look Like Diluted 'Pea Soup'."

CSCL formed a science advisory committee composed of 20 scientists, including Eipper and Carlson, who worked closely with the Director and participated in all CSCL activities. All members volunteered their time. At a meeting in January 1969, the 200 members present were polled, and all but one supported a plan for the organization to appear as an intervening party, should there be an AEC hearing. This would be an expensive move, requiring legal counsel, and an attorney specializing in atomic energy was retained.

The autonomy of the Executive Director gave the CSCL a flexibility crucial to its aggressive strategy. He could transact most of the organization's business without consulting the membership, a fact which gave the

CSCL great tactical advantage in the controversy. Press releases were turned out in a matter of hours. Prompt and open responses were made to public inquiries. In contrast, NYSE&G was slow to release information, often inaccessible to the press, and cautious, if not defensive, regarding public controversy: at one point an officer claimed that "The company is not in the business of answering questions from the public."[15]

Although slow to respond, the utility did establish a Bell Station information program "to provide the public with an ongoing report of the Corporation's activities regarding the proposed nuclear plant." Public meetings and presentations were given to community leaders, planning and water management boards, and representatives from state and federal agencies.

The utility's strongest argument was the potential economic impact of Bell Station. At a meeting of 200 businessmen and government and labor representatives in February 1969, it gained substantial local support. The president of the Building Trades Council, impressed with the estimated construction payroll of $25 million, said, "We don't have the fears that some people have about this."[16]

But most of the company's presentations were defensive, seeking to reassure the public without refuting specific criticisms. NYSE&G never joined issue with its critics. There was little substantive response to the pollution charge. Defensiveness was rooted in the feeling that, as the accused party, they could not win the debate in direct confrontation with their critics; nothing they could say would persuade people they would not damage the lake. They saw their position as resting on their "credibility"; that is, on the good will accumulated through past customer relationships. From the company's point of view, their opponents, being accusers with a critical posture and emotional bias, could use indiscriminate evidence because they had little to lose.

Faced with attacks from scientists and citizens groups, NYSE&G management's main response was that the charges were "premature," based on conditions not yet definitively established. They repeatedly pointed to the extensive research under way as evidence of their intention to be "a good citizen operating in the public interest."[17] This argument, however, was not "good copy," and only about one-quarter of the extensive local press coverage on the controversy highlighted the NYSE&G position. And the media coverage of their views consisted largely of press releases and interviews. In contrast, David Comey, the CSCL Director, maintained close ties to the press; all CSCL meetings were covered, while few of the Bell Station information activities received any attention at all. Thus the

NYSE&G position was less clearly stated to the public than that of the CSCL, while the continual flow of publicity from the latter served to keep the company off balance and public concern alive.

The success of the CSCL helped it become a focus for local activity in various townships on the lake. Traditionally there is little cooperation and coordination between townships. Each municipality is empowered to manage its own waste water disposal and water supply program. On this issue, however, resolutions to halt power plant construction on the lake were passed by several town boards and mailed to the CSCL as evidence of their support.

The CSCL used other tactics: appearing at relevant hearings, establishing contacts and legal support, and generally working to delay construction. The group acted on the assumption that the delay in itself could deter NYSE&G, given rising costs of construction.[18] The Executive Director estimated, on the basis of experience in other controversies, that delays in the granting of an operating license could cost the utility $100,000 per day.

PUBLIC HEARINGS AND POLITICAL ACTIVITY

The Bell Station controversy was first brought up at a public hearing in April 1968. An exchange of letters between several citizens of Ithaca and NYSE&G engineers had been mailed to Edmund S. Muskie, chairman of the U.S. Senate Subcommittee on Air and Water Polution of the Committee on Public Works. The letters appeared as evidence in the subcommittee's hearing concerning the extent to which environmental factors should be considered in the selection of power plant sites.

Public hearings specifically related to the Cayuga Lake case were held in Ithaca on November 22, 1968, by the state joint Legislative Committee on Conservation, Natural Resources, and Scenic Beauty. In the climate of contention which prevailed by this time, several groups spoke for postponing the building of Bell Station until further evidence about possible damage could be accumulated. They also urged design changes to ensure minimal damage. These groups included the CLPA, the Tompkins County Chamber of Commerce, the New York State Conservation Council, the League of Women Voters, the Finger Lakes Chapter of the Sierra Club, and the Seneca Lake Waterways Association. Several others, however, indicated their support of the construction. Lansing Supervisor Harris Dates, thinking of tax benefits to Lansing Township, supported the utility.

Representatives of the Building Trades Council and the Builders' Exchange considered the benefits to the construction industry, and the Ithaca Taxpayers' Association said, "For once in our history let's try to get something on the local tax roll and not off it."[19]

The CSCL took the most active role at the hearings, but maintained a strategically moderate position. Its Director spoke about design alternatives aimed at minimizing thermal and radiological pollution, and stressed that the organization was not opposed to construction of the station, but merely sought to protect Cayuga Lake.

At the hearings, the CSCL also recommended that the State create definitive standards immediately relevant to the siting of power stations on thermally stratified lakes, and that it strengthen its control over the construction of nuclear units. Two petitions were presented which were later to go to the state legislature. One advised a more active role for the Department of Conservation in the licensing process; the other requested the establishment of basic criteria against which to evaluate thermal and radiological pollution.

Local political leaders were sympathetic to the CSCL. One U.S. Congressman, Samuel Stratton (Democrat), flew to Ithaca for the hearings to support the CSCL. However, another local Congressman, Howard Robison (Republican), resisted taking sides: "I do regret the aura of suspicion that has come to surround the NYSE&G effort to move forward with this project. . . . NYSE&G has for many years been a 'good neighbor' to those of us who have been its customers, and we are all indebted to it for its willingness to make the investment represented by the Cayuga Lake plant in an effort to meet our own future demands. . . . All of us want progress."[20]

Following further hearings, three bills on water quality standards of direct relevance to Cayuga Lake were introduced into the State legislature. Governor Nelson Rockefeller stifled these bills, declaring them "premature" in view of the fact that the State was, at that time, formulating an integrated package to safeguard the environment.

The turmoil at the state level concerning its environmental policy created a great deal of political uncertainty for utilities. Moreover, by early April 1969, it was clear that the company-sponsored scientific reports on Cayuga Lake would not be accepted as conclusive. In view of this state of affairs, William A. Lyons, the NYSE&G President, decided to postpone activity on the construction permit application to the AEC. On April 11, he formally recommended an indefinite postponement to the Board of Directors "to provide more time for additional research on cooling systems for thermal discharge from the plant and for consideration of the economic effects of such systems."[21] He projected a possible two- or three-year delay.

THE SECOND ROUND

In March 1973, NYSE&G again proposed a power station design similar to their earlier plan. This time, NYSE&G was determined to proceed on its plans without further delay. It anticipated that consumption of electric power in the service area would double by 1983, and that the load-generating capacity of its present facilities would be deficient by 1976. It was particularly anxious to build Bell Station on the Cayuga Lake site, since it had already expended nearly $9 million in planning and prepermit land development. When the March 1973 plan was proposed, it had also spent $1.5 million in environmental research and was armed with data supporting its claim that Bell Station, in essentially its original design, would not damage the lake. Yet the utility once more met organized public and scientific opposition.

A thousand citizens attended a public meeting organized by NYSE&G. Meanwhile, twenty-four Cornell scientists joined research groups formed to assess the environmental claims made by NYSE&G's consultants. They criticized the utility's data as "inadequate, misleading, and limited." As the utility's consultants responded, the battle resumed. Again each side operated from different premises that called for different sampling techniques; and these yielded different data. The utility claimed that their water quality studies focused on establishing base-line conditions that would help predict the changes caused by the power plant. Cornell's studies focused on limiting factors such as the impact of nutrients on lake growth. Finally, the dispute necessarily dealt with the genuine uncertainties that remained concerning the effects of drawing colder water from the lower level of a stratified lake and discharging it at the surface. Such uncertainties allowed NYSE&G and its opponents to offer different predictions from available data.

The Cornell experts soon found themselves involved in a widely publicized technical dispute that was, in itself, to be a decisive influence on the activities of local citizens and on the eventual decision. The citizen groups focused their campaign against the power plant not so much on the substantive details of the technical debate, but on the fact that there was disagreement among the technical experts, and emphasized that this was a key point in favor of abandoning the plan.

By the time of this second round of controversy over Bell Station, public attention was directed to a broader range of issues. State and federal regulations for environmental protection had been established for several years. And while the regulatory context remained controversial, it was no longer as ambiguous. Furthermore, by 1973 there had been years of discussion in the press and popular journals about the risks associated with the operation of nuclear reactors. Thus, the thermal pollution or waste heat issue which had dominated the 1968 controversy became, in 1973, only one of several problems of concern to NYSE&G's neighbors. The problems of transporting and disposing of nuclear wastes, the reliability of reactor safety mechanisms, reactor core defects that would allow the release of radioactive gases, and the danger of human error or sabotage were of greater importance to many people than the effect of waste heat on the lake.

The 1973 controversy also took place in a new organizational context. There was a residue of mistrust from the first round of controversy over Bell Station, and now a greater number of people were willing to become involved. CSCL once more mobilized its members, and several other groups also formed soon after the March 1973 announcement by NYSE&G. CSCL considered three alternative courses of action: (1) to oppose construction of any nuclear power plant on Cayuga Lake until the problems of reactor safety and disposal of radioactive wastes were resolved; (2) to adopt the Committee's 1969 position and oppose the current design of Bell Station; or (3) to support NYSE&G's plans. The first alternative, one of total opposition, won overwhelming support. The emphasis of the opposition was thereby shifted from thermal pollution to the risks associated with nuclear power.

A second citizens' group was formed by 16 people from Trumansburg, a small town on the west shore of Cayuga Lake across from the proposed power plant site. The group quickly grew to become the Coalition to Conserve Cayuga Lake (CCCL) and to include representatives from six regions in the lake area. The group's members disseminated technical information through mailings and regular radio and television interviews, and maintained contact with the AEC regulatory staff and congressional representatives in Washington and Albany. They also set up booths at supermarkets, shopping centers, and other public places to get signatures for a petition opposing the construction of Bell Station. Eventually they gathered more than 9,000 signatures. (The number of registered voters in Tompkins County is 32,410; Ithaca, the only city in the county, has 9,194 voters.)

The Finger Lakes division of the Sierra Club prepared and disseminated position papers emphasizing both the risks of nuclear fission technology and the problems caused by waste heat. Other participating groups included the League of Women Voters, the Cayuga Lake Preservation Association, and the Tompkins County Fish and Game Club. Each helped to mobilize opposition to the plant by distributing information to their members, communicating with public agencies, and providing services such as transportation to meetings. All agreed to cooperate in a legal intervention if NYSE&G filed formal application to the AEC, and tentative arrangements were made with an experienced attorney.

The groups opposed to Bell Station stressed two points. First, the risks involved.

As experience with the operation of fission reactors accumulates, more and more evidence of unreliability, malfunctioning, and unpredictability of the technology are appearing . . . e.g., the recent discovery of hundreds of bowed, cracked, and partially crushed fuel rods in the reactor core of the Rochester, N.Y., plant . . . expressed concern of AEC scientists about the AEC's recent deemphasizing of its entire safety research program. . . . Consolidated Edison's complaints about the poor operating record and high incidence of malfunction [CSCL, Newsletter, April 1973].

The second point emphasized by the citizen groups was the likelihood that their activities would be effective. Hopes were kindled by the growing number of signatures on petitions, but especially by the willingness of local scientists to question NYSE&G's evidence. This led to substantial expectation in the community that the effort involved in writing letters and going to meetings would not be wasted.

Community support for NYSE&G was less visible than the opposition, but many established organizations were involved. Five local building trades unions spoke at meetings of local political groups in favor of the power plant, and ran an ad in the newspaper indicating their support. The president of the chamber of commerce gave his unqualified vote of confidence to NYSE&G at the April 10 information meeting. Obstruction of such a facility, he observed, "would make earning a livelihood impossible." NYSE&G's decision was to be trusted as "the result of analysis by experts." The chamber of commerce polled their 550 members, writing a cover letter that indicated "deep concern about the energy crisis and a belief that provisions should be made today to provide for tomorrow's energy needs. . . . We cannot accept shutting off the lights and turning down the heat . . . as possible alternatives to Bell Station." Of the 221 responses received, 74% favored the plant.

Though not formally involved, county and city governments soon felt compelled to take action. The Tompkins County board of representatives asked various city and county organizations for their opinion. It was advised by the Environmental Management Council, a lay group appointed to advise the board on environmental matters. This council, which included representatives from county industries and localities, voted 13 to 7 against the Bell Station plan, with 13 abstentions. The county planning commission endorsed the station, claiming that "the issues are so complex that even if we have the so-called facts before us, it would still be a difficult question because so much depends on how we judge these facts." The county board of health thought that sophisticated technical questions should be left to the experts and to the government agencies established to protect the public. Similarly, the Cayuga Lake Basin Board, a nonpaid group appointed by the state water resources commission to develop a water management plan, maintained its 1968 position in favor of the plant. The Ithaca Common Council, however, voted 8 to 5 to oppose construction.

Although the intensity of public opinion, as expressed through letters and petitions, appeared to be strongly negative, most organizations were in favor of Bell Station. Despite this ambivalent situation, the county board endorsed the NYSE&G plan by a 10 to 6 vote, prompting NYSE&G opponents to assert that the body was irresponsible and unresponsive to voters.

When NYSE&G reopened the power plant issue by inviting written comments from all segments of the community, they had expected opposition but had not anticipated its extent and intensity. The letters to NYSE&G during the first few weeks after the April 10 public information meeting were largely favorable. On April 24, the company announced correspondence was 105 to 10 in favor of the power plant. At this time, NYSE&G made the letters available for public examination. Soon after, however, it refused to discuss the growing correspondence, claiming that it was "not playing a numbers game," that it was concerned with the quality not the quantity of the criticism. The company decided that arriving at a fair decision required "a sanitary period," and turned down requests to take part in public meetings. "We have adopted a posture of no public debate at this time." In thus isolating itself from the public the company undermined its credibility and stimulated further opposition.

In the face of disagreement among Cornell experts about numerous issues connected with construction of Bell Station, and in the face of the negative tone of the public correspondence which the company had requested, NYSE&G became convinced that it must abandon its plans in spite of its own unshaken conviction that nuclear generation was the most desirable source of energy. In discussing this decision, the company's president focused on the force of critical public sentiment.

Unfortunately, the critics of nuclear power have developed a national campaign to instill in the public's mind a psychology of fear through the dissemination of unsubstantiated claims and other controversial data relating to the safety of nuclear power plants. This propaganda campaign is having a very adverse impact on the major efforts . . . to provide clean, safe, and environmentally compatible sources of energy. . . . We must make our decisions recognizing that we have been threatened with like harassment.

Whereupon, claiming that there was no feasible alternative to immediate construction of a power plant in the area, NYSE&G's president recommended to his board of directors that an 850-megawatt coal-fired plant be constructed on the Cayuga Lake site.

Eventually, this plane also was abandoned in favor of a plant in a sparsely populated area on the shores of Lake Ontario—far from any major source of critical assessment.

NOTES

1. For a detailed analysis of this dispute, see Dorothy Nelkin, *Nuclear Power and Its Critics* (Ithaca, NY: Cornell University Press, 1971).

2. For technical information concerning this lake, see E. Henson et al., *The Physical Limnology of Cayuga Lake* (Cornell Agricultural Experiment Station, Memoir 378, August 1961).

3. *Nucleonics Week,* January 16, 1969.

4. Luther Carter, "Thermal Pollution: A Threat to Cayuga's Waters," *Science* 162 (November 8, 1967), 118-119.

5. Alfred W. Eipper et al., *Thermal Pollution of Cayuga Lake by a Proposed Power Plant* (Ithaca, NY, 1968).

6. Clarence A. Carlson et al., *Radioactivity and a Proposed Power Plant on Cayuga Lake* (Ithaca, NY, November 22, 1968).

7. F. K. Moore et al., *Engineering Aspects of Thermal Discharge to a Stratified Lake* (Cornell University College of Engineering, Ithaca, NY, 1969).

8. This assumed 100% utilization of the plant capacity. A realistic utilization of 80% would bring the temperature rise down to 0.7°F.

9. K. Bingham Cady et al. to Dwight Metzler, New York State Department of Health, October 2, 1968.

10. J. A. Krumhansl, *Ideas for Discussion of Thermal Pollution and Cayuga Lake, Protection or Beneficiation* (October 1, 1968), mimeo.

11. Cornell Aeronautical Laboratory, *Cayuga Lake and Bell Station Technical Reports,* VT 2616-0-3/VT 2161-0-2/VT 2616-0-1, November 1969.

12. Ray Oglesby and David Allee (eds.), *Ecology of Cayuga Lake and the Proposed Bell Station,* Publication 27, Water Resources and Marine Sciences Center, Ithaca, New York, September 1969, Introduction.

13. Ibid., 452.

14. David Comey (ed.), *Cayuga Lake Handbook* (Ithaca, NY, 1969), 102-105.

15. Quoted in a letter from Dean E. Arnold to the NYSE&G Ithaca Area Manager.

16. *Journal Courier,* February 20, 1969.

17. *Ithaca Journal,* September 11, 1969.

18. In 1967, the initial estimate of the total cost of construction was $135 million. In 1968, it was $170 million, and by April 1969 it was $245 million.

19. *Ithaca Journal,* November 23, 1968.

20. *Congressional Record,* March 10, 1969.

21. Statement to NYSE&G Board of Directors, April 11, 1969.

ENVIRONMENTAL CONFLICT
IN THE USSR

Thane Gustafson

For two generations, the Soviet Union has been engaged in the most single-minded drive to industrialize that the world has seen. So completely has this goal dominated all others that until recently even the provision of drinking water for the population often took second place behind industrial needs.[1] The Soviet Union more or less bypassed the successive reform movements that tempered the effects of industrialization in the West: sanitary engineering in the nineteenth century, conservation in the first half of the twentieth (despite the ritual references in Soviet books to conservation decrees adopted under Lenin). Until the mid-1960s, the Soviet Union looked as though it might skip the environmental movement as well. The bias toward industry appeared frozen into the very structure of the political system.

Then, in the mid-1960s, environmental issues abruptly burst into Soviet politics. Plans to build a viscose plant on the shores of Lake Baikal in Siberia touched off an aggressive protest campaign led by reporters and prominent scientists. Outraged local scientists took the fight to the doors of the top leadership in Moscow. Revelations that the pulp and paper industry had lied and bullied to get its way led to investigations by high-level commissions. The State Planning Committee (Gosplan), the Presidium of the USSR Academy of Sciences, the State Committee for Science and Technology, and finally the Party Politburo itself, all became involved. The protest had its effect. The plant was delayed for years while tens of millions of rubles were spent developing what is by now one of the most elaborate waste-treatment systems anywhere. Since then the government has begun regulating the use of the entire basin area through a series of high-level decrees.

At the same moment, another battle was starting, less well-known in the West. Scientists began studying and reporting the damage caused by large hydropower reservoirs. Until then hydropower construction had enjoyed top priority. But in the 1960s, a growing coalition of interests, including the scientists, found they could win battles against hydro builders, and forced a virtual halt to dam construction in European USSR.

Finally, in the early 1970s the cause of environmental quality gained official recognition with the launching of a multibillion ruble program, chiefly devoted to water quality. For the first time, environmentalists gained an established place in the official plan and growing powers of inspection and enforcement.

Clearly a very great change has taken place. Fifteen years ago, environmentalists had no official status, no institutional defenders, no base of scientific facts, and no funding. Now they have all of these. The environment has become an accepted (if far from dominant) part of debates over policy in the Soviet Union.

At first sight, we have here a remarkable case of the sort of politics one would least expect to find in Russia—an instance of grass-roots initiation of a major new policy, with scientists and the press bringing pressure and publicity to bear on politicians. But what emerges upon closer analysis is considerably different. In this chapter we shall examine the Baikal controversy, the antireservoir coalition, and the rise of the official environmental program. We shall see that specialists owed their apparent effectiveness to the presence of important ministerial allies and an initial receptiveness in the top leadership; this in turn was due to the changing economic circumstances of the country and the shifting priorities of the leaders. The appearance of grass-roots initiation is largely deceptive.

BAIKAL

The Baikal case was unique on several counts, and that is what made it possible for environmentalists to gain a hearing, using a combination of sentiment and economics. To begin with, the lake itself is unique. Several hundred miles long and in some places nearly a mile deep, Lake Baikal holds one-fifth of the world's fresh water in a state so pure that one can see far into its depths. Through literature and folklore, every Russian from childhood knows its beauty. Consequently, Lake Baikal was one of the few places in the Soviet Union where an argument based on environmental sentiment stood a chance against the normally overwhelming pressure for industrial growth. At the same time, the lake's pure water represented an invaluable resource for a region undergoing rapid growth, and so its preservation could be made to sound like sensible economic policy.

So scientists opposed to the viscose plant used a blend of appeals to both environmental sentiment and practicality. The President of the USSR Academy of Sciences, in a memorandum to the Council of Ministers, called for a multiple-purpose (*kompleksnyi*) approach to the development of the lake.[2] And two prominent Academicians described plans for a national "pazk-combine" (park-kombinat), which would be organized explicitly around the production of the nation's most valuable natural resource—fresh water of high purity.[3] But amidst these practical-minded arguments the appeal to sentiment was unmistakable.

> Science cannot oppose the exploitation of the natural wealth of Baikal, but it protests against arbitrary decisions about the pearl of the Soviet people, its national pride—Baikal.[4]

The second unique element in the Baikal case stems from the first: because of the lake's emotional value, the planners of the viscose plant were under pressure from the beginning to prove that they would not harm the lake. They were forbidden by a high-level order to start operating the plant until they had provided it with a waste-treatment facility in good working order.[5] But at that time industrial builders had had little experience with advanced waste-treatment facilities, and they soon ran into trouble. As early as 1962, the State Committee for Scientific Research (predecessor of the present State Committee on Science and Technology) warned that the plant's waste treatment plans were unsound.[6] Squeezed by tight deadlines, the builders resorted to lies and pressure tactics, giving their opponents a golden opportunity to discredit the project.

The first outcry came against the way the State Lumber Committee secured approval for its designs. The Committee had originally consulted a second-rank member of a fisheries institute for expert review, then used his statements to mislead other state agencies into giving their approval, even when the expert subsequently disavowed his earlier endorsement, and his institute disavowed *him*.[7] An angry open letter from the vice-president of the Academy of Sciences exclaimed, "The State Committee thought it possible to fool the government by justifying its choice of a building site in a seismic zone, and claiming that it was impossible to get clean water anywhere else. They submitted inflated estimates of the available stocks of raw materials in the Baikal area, and understated the expense of construction and operation."[8]

Reporters complained that they were being surrounded by a fog of ministerial optimism, which did not quite conceal that something unsavory was going on. For example, in 1965, the chief engineer of SibGIProBum offered assurances to a Pravda reporter that there would be no contamination of Baikal, thanks to the plant's elaborate treatment facilities.[9] Yet later in that same year, in an interview with a local newspaper, the same engineer stated, "The present design for the purification installations was developed not because of the danger of pollution to the lake, for that danger doesn't exist, but in order to quiet down the prolonged dispute between scientists and designers."[10] His designers, meanwhile, were careful to build the water intake three miles away from the wastepipe,[11] a more concrete indication of his true intentions.

The builders repeatedly violated their own agreements. When the plant itself was more than half completed, only one of three projected settling tanks had been dug, and no other work on the waste treatment complex had been done. In response to protests, the State Lumber Committee took measures in late 1964 to accelerate the work on the waste-treatment site, and they declared that their efforts had had a "positive effect."[12] Indeed, *Literaturnaia Gazeta* could report in early 1965 that the purification network was 40% complete, as opposed to 65% for the rest of the site.[13] But it came as a shock when it was realized just what part of the purification network this 40% represented. In a letter to *Literaturnaia Gazeta*, workers at the site reported that the builders were working round the clock to lead the main wastepipe directly to the lake, by-passing the site for the settling tanks altogether.[14] It was evident that the construction concern, if it could not make the water treatment process work, intended to begin without it.

A third unique feature of the Baikal case is that larger events then taking place in Soviet politics gradually weakened the backers of the viscose plant. When the project started in 1958, Khrushchev had just launched a radical decentralization program that abolished the central ministries and reorganized industrial production largely on a regional basis. This meant that the initial stages of the Baikal project probably by-passed Moscow, and when Moscow subsequently took a hand, it lacked effective leverage. In Eastern Siberia, the paper and logging industries were the heavyweights, with only embryonic scientific and regulatory agencies to oppose them. This explains why initial approval of the project by fisheries, public-health inspectors, and other local authorities was so easily obtained. The same lack of central authority and coordination during that period may also help to explain why the plant's designers were able to resist, until 1961, the Academy of Sciences' requests for an inspection of the designs.[15]

Starting in 1962, however, the decentralization movement was reversed, culminating after 1964 in a full restoration of the pre-1957 system of centralized ministries. In addition, in 1961 the State Scientific and Technical Committee was reorganized, renamed, and strengthened. Under its new name and powers (which increased still further in 1965) the State Committee played a prominent role in the subsequent debate over Baikal. The Soviet chemical industry began growing rapidly; viscose was soon replaced by more modern fibers; and this raised doubts about whether the Baikal site was needed at all. Finally, the steady growth of the Siberian Division of the Academy of Sciences gave a powerful voice for the scientists and direct access to Moscow. The Academy of Sciences was then at its height of independence and prestige. Thus by the mid-1960s the balance of forces around Baikal had changed substantially, much diminishing the power and latitude of the paper and pulp industry.

Since their victory of the 1960s, Baikal's defenders have managed to keep the attention of the political leadership. A series of top-level decrees provide for increasingly stiff protection and restoration: end-of-pipe treatment for surrounding industry, removal of sunken timber around the lake and the tributary streams, a ban on floating logs in the area and on cutting on steep slopes, and so on.[16] Yet it now appears that Baikal is still not safe. The surrounding region is developing rapidly; use of the lake for tourism and transportation is booming; and local Party officials, eager to get on with the development of the local economy, are growing impatient with the restrictions they operate under. What this shows is that the conflict of values contained in the Baikal affair has not yet really been addressed, but only postponed.

Likewise, victory for the environmentalists at Baikal set no automatic precedents for the rest of the country, precisely because of the unique circumstances of that case. Action at Baikal required no fundamental changes in the nationwide priority given to industrial development. Therefore its direct impact on subsequent policy was limited.

OPPOSITION TO BIG DAMS AND RESERVOIRS

The European region of the USSR, the most industrialized and populous area of the country, is chronically short of energy. Until recently, the Soviet answer to this was hydropower. By the 1960s, the map of European USSR was dotted with dams and reservoirs, and millions of acres of productive agricultural land lay under water. For thirty years the soundness of using land and water in this way was not publicly questioned. But in the 1960s for the first time, Soviet scientists began studying the resulting damage. Within a few years their findings, appearing in hundreds of specialized publications and papers, described cropland erosion, diminished water quality, declining commercial fishing, and many other severe effects.[17] During the second half of the 1960s, this work played a part in defeating several large reservoir projects and in bringing hydropower construction to a virtual end in the European USSR.

Here again we seem to have a striking case of effective intervention and influence by technical experts. But closer examination shows that what actually happened was more complicated: hydropower's position was already weakened by larger trends then occurring. The researchers' work, while it contributed to that weakening, was not the original cause of it. In fact, hydropower's troubles may have provided the stimulus for the reservoir research. The role of the scientists, in other words, was initially a symptom and then a contributing cause in a changing political environment.

The most prominent figures in this movement were geographers and hydrologists in the USSR Academy of Sciences (principally in the Institute of Geography and the Institute of Water Problems). Many of them came to the Academy from earlier careers in the water-resources field. The best-known and most interesting figure in this group is S. L. Vendrov, who came to the Academy of Sciences after an earlier career in river transportation. Vendrov launched a generation of graduate students into environmental studies. They traced in detail the effects of the Volga reservoirs on local climate, land, and hydrology,[18] and later did field studies of the proposed diversion of the Pechora River and many other projects. In the early 1970s, Vendrov and his students were filled with a crusading spirit. They saw themselves as the front line defense of the environment, and had detailed knowledge of the work done by similar groups in the West.[19] Vendrov himself enjoys a prominent position as an adviser; he sits on advisory panels (*ekspertnye komissii*) of Gosplan and of the State Committee on Science and Technology. In his books he ranges more widely and expresses himself more forcefully than any other specialist in this field. But he is not alone in the role he plays.

Researchers in the Academy were seconded by large numbers of hydrologists, icthyologists, soil scientists, and agronomists, all working for water-using agencies like the Ministry of the Fishing Industry. Many of these agencies competed with hydropower for the use of scarce water in the relatively arid southern half of the country, and bad news for hydropower was, in a sense, good news for them. Thus, for example, researchers in the fishing industry showed the devastating effect of reservoir construction on commercial catches in the lower reaches of rivers like the Volga, pointing out that fish yields from the reservoirs themselves were much lower than hydropower designers had claimed they would be.[20] Acting under a mixture of professional conviction and institutional interest, these specialists contributed a large volume of work. Thus in Soviet politics interagency rivalries can serve to some extent as a substitute for public opinion in dramatizing and documenting issues like safety and environmental quality.[21]

Perhaps the most important single contribution of their research was simply documenting the shocking damage done to agriculture by reservoir flooding: by the mid-1970s nearly 2.3 million hectares (roughly 5.7 million acres) of agricultural land had been flooded, about one-fifth of which consisted of highly productive plowland, mostly in the European USSR.[22] Much of this area was going under water even as the surveys were being done; the area submerged by reservoirs doubled during the 1960s.[23]

As the 1960s progressed, specialists and their agencies found official channels opening to them, through which they could present their findings and influence actual decisions. One example is the review procedure of Gosplan. Any project costing over 50 million rubles must go before a Review Division (*otdel ekspertizy*), which nominates an ad hoc advisory commission (*ekspertnaia komissiia*) to perform the review. Most of the members of such commissions are specialists from Academy and ministry institutes. But before this review even begins, the proposed project must run the gauntlet of review by other interested agencies.[24] Each of these stages provides the opportunity for technical specialists to express their views.

These are standard procedures in Soviet project planning. They can be an empty formality or the occasion for major changes in a project, depending on the relative clout of the participants and the type of arguments that have acknowledged standing at the time. In the case of hydropower, in the late 1950s Gosplan became more receptive to economic arguments than it had been before, and economists began appearing on Gosplan's *ekspertnye komissii*. This reflected larger changes taking place at the top. Starting in the late 1950s, Soviet leaders began attaching a higher value than before to capital, land, and water. This caused hydropower construction in European Russia to look economically unsound. Then, after 1965, the priority of agriculture began to rise, and with it the political influence of agricultural agencies, which began competing effectively with hydropower for land and water use. Until then, the objections of agencies affected by hydropower construction had had very little effect on the review process. Hydropower planners had been able to deal with the objections of agriculture and fisheries by incorporating vague provisions in their plans for dikes, levees, development of new land, and construction of artificial hatcheries to stock reservoirs. Since the cost of these measures was assigned to the affected ministries, it is not surprising that these provisions were usually not carried out. But by the late 1960s the situation was quite different. Hydropower planners found themselves so hampered by objections from other agencies that they were obliged to create "reservoir divisions" in their organization to improve their case before the reviewers. In sum, channels for review have long existed, but the rising clout of hydropower's competitors, and the growing responsiveness of Gosplan to them—both symptoms of shifting priorities at the top—turned them into effective vehicles for influence by technical specialists, to the exasperation of hydropower planners.[25]

Further channels of access to decision makers opened up during the 1960s. The Academy of Sciences created a Scientific Council on Water Resources Management (*nauchnyi soviet po vodnomu khoziaistvu*). In 1968 this Council became a full-fledged institute of the Academy. Similarly, the State Committee on Science and Technology organized a "Scientific Council for Multiple-Purpose Use and Protection of Water."[26] The Ministry of Power itself, upon instructions from the State Committee on Science and Technology, organized an interdisciplinary research program on the environmental problems of reservoirs, which ran from 1966 through the mid-1970s.[27] This program brought together thirty research design institutes representing all the affected agencies.

In the most serious cases, through channels like these, technical experts and their agencies could gain access to the highest authorities: arguments over agricultural compensation at the site of the Krasnoiarsk Dam in the 1960s were settled in the USSR Council of Ministers,[28] and disputes over the Cheboksar Dam on the Volga reached the Politburo itself.[29]

By the end of the decade, hydropower planners faced serious trouble. Projects proposed for the Middle Ob',[30] the lower Volga,[31] the Amur,[32] the Upper Kama,[33] the Middle Enisei,[34] and the Pechora[35] were cancelled or postponed after furious debate. Many more projects were redesigned, relocated, or seriously delayed by protests from technical experts and affected interests: the last three units of the Volga-Kama chain (at Saratov, Cheboksar, and the Lower-Kama[36]) were fought over at every stage. The Boguchansk reservoir on the lower Angara was moved upstream;[37] the use of Lake Sevan in Armenia as a source for hydropower was halted, and restoration of the severely depleted lake was begun.[38]

In interviews the geographers and hydrologists of the Academy institutes, and Vendrov in particular, observed that they would have had little success, but for the intervention of powerful industrial ministries whose missions were threatened by the plans of the dam builders. This sort of intervention is not new. Even in the 1940s, the heyday of hydropower construction, the site of the Volgograd project was changed because it would have flooded valuable mineral resources. In the 1950s the discovery of metal-ore deposits caused postponement of the Abalakovskoe dam on the middle Enisei. The same pattern continued in the following decade. In the 1960s, the coal-mining industry opposed the proposed diversion of the Pechora, and the petroleum industry fought the Middle Ob' project. But there was a new element in the 1960s; the priorities of political leaders had changed.

The lesson of this section appears to be that technical specialists defending the environment can gain a contingent, temporary sort of influence when shifting priorities among major policies and agencies create an opening. But they do not have much influence on their own. For example, opposition to hydropower has not been particularly effective in Siberia, where it faces little opposition from agriculture and can be justified as a sound use of capital. In the last few years, in fact, hydropower east of the Urals has gained a new lease on life, and in the current five-year plan it is scheduled to provide 20% of the country's net addition to electrical generating capacity.[39] Neither have environmentalists had much visible effect on nuclear power, which has replaced hydropower as the planners' main hope in European Russia, where energy remains as short as ever. Unlike hydropower, nuclear power does not compete with any agency of equal political weight, and so far has not faced any major public opposition.[40] The success of the scientists against hydropower in European Russia therefore appears in retrospect as the result of a temporary combination of forces directed against a program that was already on the way out.

Has nothing changed, then, in the Soviet scale of values? On the contrary. Largely because of the protesters' research and agitation, environmental issues now have standing as legitimate subjects for concern and public discussion. For example, recent debates over proposals to divert several of Russia's northward-flowing rivers to the south show clearly how accepted and prominent environmental concerns have become.[41] More important, an institutional base is gradually taking shape, giving environmental issues an established place in planning, policy formation, and implementation. This is the subject of the next section.

THE NEW ENVIRONMENTAL PROGRAM[42]

At the beginning of the 1970s, despite the cases we have just described, the Soviet Union did not yet have an environmental program worthy of the name. Except for Moscow, practically no money or equipment was allocated for treatment. Recycling of water or the development of waste-free industrial processes got little attention. There was no strong system of planning and enforcement for air and water quality. In 1972-1973, only one-quarter of the industrial wastes and process water discharged into the Volga, the most heavily industrialized artery in the USSR, were treated in even the most cursory way.[43] Municipal wastes were no better; throughout the country only 16% were treated by any method in 1970.[44] Meanwhile, the problem was growing rapidly worse, for the waste water discharged into the Volga was increasing by 4% a year,[45] and the rate of increase nationwide was much the same.[46] Yet despite growing evidence that the European USSR faced a serious problem, only in a handful of cases could one detect official concern.[47]

But since 1972 the Soviet Union has suddenly launched an environmental program with real teeth and real funding, mostly aimed at preserving clean water. In 1973, annual investment for water quality suddenly jumped fivefold, from 300 to 1,500 million rubles.[48] General Secretary Brezhnev, at the 25th Party Congress in the spring of 1976, announced a five-year, eleven-billion ruble program of capital expenditure for environmental protection, mostly for water. He added that in the future the size of the environmental program would grow still further.[49]

Simultaneously, the Soviet Union has set up legal and administrative machinery for reordering land-use and water-use policy. In 1970, a national water code appeared, followed over the next three years by detailed water legislation for each of the fifteen union-republics.[50] In 1972, a Party-State decree took a big step toward straightening chaotic agency jurisdictions by assigning the major responsibility for water-quality enforcement to the USSR Ministry of Water Management and Reclamation (Minvodkhoz), one of the fastest-growing agencies in the country.[51] For the first time this gave the responsibility for clean water to an institutional defender with potentially real clout and a real stake in the outcome. Then, in 1974, environmental protection was given a place of its own in the national economic plan, and a special division for the environment was created in the State Planning Committee (Gosplan), with subdivisions for air and water quality.[52]

Most of the pollution control program is directed toward the eleven river basins of the country's southern half, in which over 80% of the country's agricultural and industrial production is concentrated.[53] Within this group, top priority goes to the Volga and Ural basins. The Volga basin alone, which encompasses 25% of the country's population, industry, and agriculture, accounts for about one-third of the waste treatment capacity added during the ninth Five-Year Plan (1971-1975). The very selectivity of the program reflects the rapidly rising demand for clean water in the southern USSR, due in particular to the high priority of irrigation agriculture under Brezhnev.

Much of the sudden growth of the new program appears to be due to a crisis. By the early 1970s, the effects of water pollution in southern Russia were becoming alarming. Commercial yields of fresh-water fish had dropped sharply, including those of important earners of foreign exchange such as sturgeon, the source of caviar. Massive kills of valuable species were observed during the spring months, when factories discharged wastes they had stored over the winter. Then cholera, caused by untreated sewage, broke out in the southern river basins. Decisive action could not be delayed. The new program, in other words, differs fundamentally from the Baikal and reservoir controversies, and should not be seen as the final culmination of them. It did not follow a public campaign by scientists, nor was it directed at a single, temporarily vulnerable culprit. It is a centralized policy, precipitated by a crisis that was obvious to all, focused on a region for which the political leaders have big plans. In a sense, therefore, the new program marks the coming of age of environmental protection, as political leaders become increasingly aware of the larger implications of their own policies. This means, in turn, a new role for environmental specialists. Today they are no longer a handful of protesters taking advantage of chance political openings or occasional sympathy in high places to campaign for their odd ideas. Now specialists are being trained in recognized environmental professions; research institutes are being adapted to study pollution control; and state institutions are being built to administer official environmental programs. While it would be too much to claim that the environment has gained equal status with industry, it has become an established part of the system.

The contribution of technical specialists to this evolution was both vital and yet weak. To understand this, we must remember how different their situation is from that of their Western counterparts. In the USSR, scientists and other specialists cannot form independent groups to mobilize public opinion. They cannot use courts and parliaments to put pressure on political leaders. There are no elections to be influenced, and no independent political resources to turn to. There is little incentive to take one's case to the press; the well-timed leak of internal information is in any case prevented by detailed censorship rules. In the absence of countervailing political forces in society, petitioners and protesters have no leverage over political figures. Under these conditions the success of technical advice depends on the audience it finds within the state and the party. Technical experts may succeed in influencing policy-making, but only if their findings fit and amplify the views of political leaders or advance the interests of some state institution by adding to its power to win bureaucratic battles.

Yet, even so, technical specialists played a vital part in raising the awareness of decision makers and putting environmental issues on the list of "legitimate" issues for the government agenda. In this way, they serve, though in a very restricted sense, as surrogates for public opinion. They publicize and thrash out issues, call attention to implications, and stand in the way of ill-considered bureaucratic actions. And in this the technical specialists often have allies. In the Soviet Union, it is sometimes possible to fight one wing of city hall and win, provided some other wing of city hall overtly or covertly helps out.

NOTES

1. P.S. Neporozhnii, ed., *Gidroenergetika i kompleksnoe ispol zovanie vodnykh resursov SSSR* (Moscow, "Energiia," 1970), 101. For a more detailed discussion of the priority of industrial needs in a practice over requirements for drinking water, even as late as the 1960s, see *Kompleksnoe ispol'zovanie vodnykh resursov SSSR* (Report of the USSR Gosplan Soviet po izucheniiu proizvoditel'nykh sil, Otdel kompleksnogo ispol'zovaniia vodnykh resursov) Moscow, 1965. See also Marshall Goldman, *The Spoils of Progress: Environmental Pollution in the Soviet Union* (Cambridge, MIT Press, 1972), 104-108.

2. O. Volkov, "Tuman ne rasseialsia," *Literaturnaia Gazeta,* April 13, 1965.

3. A.A. Trofimuk and I.P. Gerasimov, "Sokhranit' chistotu vod ozera Baikala," *Priroda,* 11-1965, 59-60.

4. Ibid.

5. Marshall Goldman, *Spoils of Progress,* 189.

6. B.P. Konstantinov, "Baikal zhdet." *Komsomol'skaia Pravda,* May 11, 1966, 2.

7. O. Volkov, "Tuman ne rasseialsia."

8. B.P. Konstantinov, "Baikal zhdet."

9. A. Merkulov, "Alarm from Baikal," *Current Digest of the Soviet Press,* vol. XVII, No. 9 (1965).

10. S. Mokshin and N. Chernavin, "Gnev Baikala," *Sovetskaia Rossiia,* May 28, 1966, 3.

11. A.A. Trofimuk, "Tsena vedomstvennogo upriamstva," *Literaturnaia Gazeta,* April 15, 1965.

12. N. Chistiakov and E. Kuznetsov, "Neobkhodimye utochneniia," *Literaturnaia Gazeta,* April 10, 1965.

13. O. Volkov, "Tuman nad Baikalom," *Literaturnaia Gazeta,* February 6, 1965.

14. Volkov, "Tuman ne rasseialsia."

15. Ibid.

16. K. Prodai-Voda, "Chistye vody Baikala," *Trud,* September 7, 1976, 2; I. Borodavchenko, "Baikal: novaia stranitsa biografii," *Literaturnaia Gazeta,* no. 49, 4 December, 1974, 11; A. Golovanov, "Dar Baikala," *Sovetskaia Belorussiia,* 5 January

1975, 4; Iurii Khromov, "Zhemchuzhina Sibiri," *Sovetskaia Estoniia*, 10 December, 1974, 3; V. Khodii, "Baikalu–okhrannaia gramota," *Pravda*, 20 November, 1974, 6; Iurii Belichenko, "Chtoby sberech' Baikal," *Komsomol'skaia Pravda*, 23 November, 1974, 2; A. Larionov, "V listvianke na Baikale," *Sovetskaia Rossiia*, 18 March, 1975, 4. Also A. Veretennikov, "Preserve the Siberian Pearl" *Ekonomicheskaia Gazeta*, No. 4 (January, 1977), trans. in *Current Digest of the Soviet Press*, Vol. XXIX, No. 5 (1977), 15; A. Starukhin, "Ozero dlia vsekh," *Pravda* 15 May 1978; V. Riashin, "Zapret na pol'zu," *Literaturnaia Gazeta*, 21 December 1977, 13; O. Volkov, "Nad Baikalom veter peremen," *Pravda*, 3 December 1977.

17. These findings are summarized and discussed in S.L. Vendrov and K.N. D'iakonov, *Vodokhranilishcha i okruzhaiuschchaia prirodnaia sreda* (Moscow: "Navka," 1976) and S.L. Vendrov, *Problemy preobrazovaniia rechnykh sistem* (Leningrad, 1970).

18. S.L. Vendrov *et alii*, "O rabotakh IG AN SSSR v oblasti inzhenernogeograficheskikh problem proektirovaniia i ekspluatatsii krupynykh ravninnykh vodokhranilishch," *Trudy koordinatsionnykh soveshchanii po gidrotekhnike*, vyp. 53 (1969), 41-43.

19. Interviews conducted by the author during two six-week stays at the Institutes of Geography and Water Problems in late 1972 and early 1973.

20. P.L. Pirozhnikov, "Rybokhoziaistvennoe ispol'zovanie vodokhranilishch kompleksnogo naznacheniia," in *Koordinatsionnye soveshchaniia* (1969), 81-93. See also V.V. Delitsyn, "Razmnozhenie ryb na volgo-akhtubinskoi poime v usloviiakh zaregulirovannogo rechnogo stoka," in *Volga-1* (Abstracts from a Conference on the Reservoirs of the Volga Basin, sponsored by the Institute of Freshwater Biology of the USSR Academy of Sciences), Tol'iatti, 1968. These are just two examples from an enormous literature.

21. Robert Campbell, in a recent study on energy research in the Soviet Union, observes a similar phenomenon: safety issues have been brought out by the rivals of nuclear power. See Robert Campbell, *Soviet Energy R&D: Goals, Planning, and Organizations* R-2253-DOE (Santa Monica, CA: Rand Corporation, May, 1978).

22. Vendrov, 1976, 46.

23. A.I. Makarov and O.S. Ligun, "Nekotorye rezul'taty analiza svodnykh dannykh o vokokhranilishchakh SSSR," *Koordinatsionnye soveshchaniia po gidrotekhnike*, vyp. 70. Leningrad, "Energiia," 1972.

24. The project review process for the Krasnoiarsk Dam is described in detail in Iu.A. Kilinskii and V.S. Smetanich, *Kompensatsiia poter' sel'skogo khoziaistva pri sozdanii krupnykh vodokhranilishch: obzor literatury* (Moscow: VNII informatsii i tekhniko-ekonomicheskikh issledovanii po sel'skomu khoziaistvu, 1970), 40-41.

25. V.S. Matveev, "Sushchestvuiushchii poriadok soglasovaniia i utverzhdeniia proektov po organizatsii vodokhranilishch. Kriticheskie zamechaniia i predlozheniia po uluchsheniiu sushchestvuiushchego poriadka soglasovaniia i utverzhedeniia proektov," in *Tezisy dokladov seminara-soveshchaniia obobshcheniia opyta proektirovaniia vodokhranilishch* (Moscow, "Gidroproekt," 1969), 75-76.

26. A.A. Korobchenkov, "Osnovnye zadachi nauchno-issledovatel'-skikh rabot po obobshcheniiu opyta proektirovaniia, stroitel'stra i ekspluatatsii vodokhranilishch," *Trudy koordinatsionnykh soveshchanii po gidrotekhnike*, vyp. 53 (1969), 9.

27. The results were presented at periodic interagency conferences (*koordinatsionnye soveshchaniia*) hosted by the Vedeneev Research Institute for Hydro-Engineering in Leningrad. The proceedings of these conferences were published as *Trudy koordinatsionnykh soveshchanii po gidrotekhnike*, issues 53 (1969), 59 (1970), and 83 (1973).

28. Kilinskii and Smetanich.

29. Interview with A.B. Gokhshtein, formerly economist with the Central Scientific Research Institute for Inland Waterways (Moscow).

30. See *Kompleksnoe osvoenie vodnykh resursov obskogo basseina* (Novosibirsk, "Nauka," 1970), and A.B. Avakian et al., "Problemy sozdaniia vodokhranilishch v Sibiri," in *Prirodnye usloviia perspektivnykh raionov osvoeniia v Sibiri* (Novosibirsk, 1969).

31. Vendrov (1970), 115, 185, 188. See also P.S. Neporozhnii, "Gidroenergetika v vodokhoziaistvennom komplekse strany," *Vodnye Resursy*, No. 3, 1972, 11.

32. *Izuchenie i osvoenie rek Dal'nego Vostoka* (Moscow, "Nauka," 1969), esp. 25-29.

33. P.S. Neporozhnii, ed., *Gidroenergeticheskie resursy* (Moscow, "Nauka," 1967), 100.

34. P.M. Dmitrievskii, "Kompleksnyi metod issledovanii i proektirivaniia, ego primenenie pri razrabotke problemy Angary," In *Biulleten' po vodnomu khoziaistvu*, No. 3-1968, 99-106. See also A.I. Makarov, and G.V. Sergachev, "Perspektivy sozdaniia i ispol'zovaniia vodokhranilishch v basseine Eniseia i Angary," *Issledovaniia beregov vodokhranilishch* (Tezisy dokladov tret'ego soveshchaniia po izucheniiu beregov sibirskikh vokokhranilishch), Irkutsk, Siberian Division of the USSR Academy of Sciences, 1972), p. 15; and N.N. Iakovlev, "Ispol'zovanie unikal'nykh gidroenergoresursov v basseine Eniseia i Angary," *Trudy Gidroproekta* (Leningrad edition), No. 25 (13), Leningrad, 1971, 17-42.

35. See note 41.

36. A.D. Orlov, "Nekotorye itogi vypolneniia proektnykh i stroitel'nykh rabot sozdanii vodokhranilishcha saratovskoi GES," in *Tezisy dokladov*, 87.

37. Vendrov (1970), 135-136, 41-45.

38. O.A. Dzhougarian, "The Sevan Lake Problem: Economic and Ecological Aspects," U.S.-USSR Symposium on Economic Aspects of Environmental Protection, Erevan (October, 1977).

39. Robert Campbell, "Issues in Soviet R&D: the Energy Case," in U.S. Congress, Joint Economic Committee, *Soviet Economy in a New Perspective* (Washington, D.C.: USGPO, October, 1976), 97-112.

40. Soviet energy planning and forecasting contains little discussion of environmental issues. Campbell, 1978.

41. For a brief discussion of the proposed interbasin diversions, see Thane Gustafson, "Modernizing Soviet Agriculture: Brezhnev's Gamble on Reclamation," *Public Policy* (Summer, 1977). A more detailed review will be found in Gustafson, "Institutional and Regional Forces in Soviet Politics: The Debate over Re-routing Major Rivers to the South," (Unpublished paper presented at the 1977 Annual Meeting of the American Political Science Association, Washington, D.C.).

42. This section is condensed from the first part of a recent article by the author, "The New Soviet Environmental Program: Do the Soviets Really Mean Business?" *Public Policy* (Summer, 1978).

43. B.N. Laskorin et alii, "Kachestvo i okhrana vody v basseine reki-Volgi," *Vodnye Resursy*, 4-1975, 23-25.

44. O.M. Voronova, "Uvelichenie stoimosti ochistki stochnykh vod i tekhniko-ekonomicheskie aspekty etoi problemy," *Vodnye Resursy*, 1-1976, 141.

45. B.N. Laskorin et alii, "Kachestvo i okhrana vody v basseine reki-Volgi," *Vodnye Resursy*, 4-1975, 23-25.

46. I.I. Borodavchenko, "Problemy ispol'zovaniia i okhrany vodnykh resursov SSSR," *Gidroteknika i Melioratsiia,* 4-1976, 9.

47. For discussions of the antecedents of the Soviet water-quality program, see Marshall Goldman, *The Spoils of Progress: Environmental Pollution in the Soviet Union* (Cambridge, MA: MIT Press, 1972). See also Donald R. Kelley, "Environmental Policy-Making in the USSR: The Role of Industrial and Environmental Interest Groups," *Soviet Studies,* Vol. XXVIII, No. 4 (October 1976), 570-589; Fred Singleton, ed., *Environmental Misuse in the Soviet Union* (New York: Praeger, 1976); David E. Powell, "The Social Costs of Modernization: Ecological Problems in the USSR," *World Politics,* Volume 23, Number 4, (July 1971); and John W. Kramer, *The Politics of Conservation and Pollution in the USSR* (Unpublished Ph.D. dissertation, University of Virginia, Charlottesville, Virginia, 1973).

48. Interview with the USSR Minister of Reclamation, E.E. Alekseevskii, "Vody nado berech'," *Trud,* 24 January 1976.

49. L.I. Brezhnev, "Report of the Central Committee of the CPSU," *XXVyi. s"ezd Kommunisticheskoi Partii Sovetskogo Soiuza* (stenograficheskii otchet), vol. I (Moscow: "Politizdat," 1976," 1976), 67.

50. A translation of the USSR Principles of Water Law can be found in Irving K. Fox, ed., *Water Resources Law and Policy in the Soviet Union* (Madison, Wisconsin: University of Wisconsin Press, 1971), 221-239.

51. Soviet Ministrov SSR-Tsentral'nyi Komitet KPSS "Ob usilenii okhrany prirody i uluchshenii ispol'zovaniia prirodnykh resursov," Decree no. 898, 29 December 1972. For background information on the reclamation program, see Thane Gustafson, "Transforming Soviet Agriculture."

52. P. Poletaev, "Plan i okhrana prirody," *Planovoe Khoziaistvo,* 4-1976.

53. Poletaev.

PART II
BENEFITS VERSUS RISKS

Many controversies develop out of fear of the risks from a new technology or industrial process. Sometimes risks are small, difficult to calculate, but potentially extremely serious. (In the case of nuclear waste disposal, it is the fear of an unlikely but potentially devastating catastrophe that fuels the dispute.) In other cases, risks are known but must be weighed against potential benefits. The dispute, then, focuses on balancing competing priorities in decisions about regulation.

In this section, three controversies illustrate the problems of evaluating and regulating risk.

Susan Fallows reviews the complex history of the dispute over nuclear waste disposal. The long failure to demonstrate the safety of radiation disposal techniques has exacerbated fear of radiation and mistrust in the ability of the nuclear industry and regulatory agencies to deal with the problem. The protracted controversy illustrates the growing power of citizen groups to obstruct a technology through diverse channels of protest: the courts, the media, the ballot box, and the manipulation of local, state, and federal authorities. Nuclear critics also exploit technical uncertainties to support their opposition to nuclear power. The case is marked by disagreement among scientists about the adequacy of different radiation disposal techniques.

Susan Hadden's case concerns the regulation of the growth-promoting drug DES, given to animals to increase efficient production of meat. Knowledge about the effect of this potentially carcinogenic drug was initially uncertain and open to diverse interpretation. Scientific advice was exploited by many interests to support their diverse policy preferences. In regulating this drug, the trade-off was between the potential risks of using DES and its obvious benefit in expanding the supply and lowering the cost of meat. As long as uncertainty about its carcinogenic effect prevailed and was reflected in disputes among scientists, the Food and Drug Administration was vulnerable to pressures from powerful industrial interests.

In the third case in this section Michael Brown uses the Vinyl Chloride controversy to illustrate the difficulty of setting standards to minimize occupational risks. In this case the issue came on the agenda not because of scientific concern, but because a number of workers suddenly died from occupationally related disease. The recently formed Occupational Safety and Health Administration (OSHA) had as a first priority the protection of worker health. When faced with the vinyl chloride decision, however, the issue of health was framed in terms of "worker protection vs. jobs." The agency soon found it necessary to balance questions of risk against economic and technical feasibility.

In all these cases, the central issue is not the degree of risk but its social acceptability when weighed against the social benefits of the technology in question. Yet the debates in each case often focus on technical questions— the adequacy of waste disposal techniques, or the extent of risk from using drugs in beef cattle.

THE NUCLEAR WASTE DISPOSAL CONTROVERSY

Susan Fallows

Public alarm over the radioactive waste disposal problem may ultimately bring an end to nuclear power development.[1] A 1976 Harris poll reported that 67% of Americans perceive this as a major problem. In 1978, the California state legislature rejected a reactor development plan until the utilities and the federal government demonstrated an acceptable scheme for safe disposal of wastes. Similarly the U.S. House Government Operations Committee recommended a moratorium on federal licensing of nuclear power plants until a feasible disposal plan is developed.

Military and commercial reactors have been producing millions of gallons of highly radioactive wastes since the mid-1940s, but scientists have not yet agreed on the best technological means for permanently isolating these wastes from the biosphere. Moreover, the government has not yet resolved the fundamental political and institutional issues surrounding the waste management problem.

This chapter examines the political and technological history of the nuclear waste disposal problem in the United States as a vehicle for exploring the process of decision-making in a public policy area plagued by risk and uncertainty, and therefore political controversy. Key questions will be: what are the impacts of technical disputes among experts on the public's perception of the waste management issue? who becomes involved in the political debate that emerges from the scientific dispute? how do these groups express their opinions and influence public decision-making? how have government institutions responded to political pressures in the face of technological uncertainty?

The technical and policy context of the radioactive waste disposal issue is developed first by explaining the significance of waste management in the nuclear fuel cycle and the technologies which have been proposed to contain and isolate high-level wastes. Next we trace the evolution of public interest in nuclear waste disposal. The public response is analyzed by comparing two cases of aborted attempts to site radioactive waste facilities.

THE NUCLEAR FUEL CYCLE

The nuclear fuel cycle includes many processes between the mining of uranium and the ultimate disposal of radioactive wastes. Once basic uranium has been mined and enriched, it is fabricated into fuel assemblies for use in nuclear reactors. In the reactor, energy is released by splitting the U-235 atoms housed in the fuel rods. The process produces several dozen radioactive byproducts (including plutonium-237). When the number of fissionable U-235 atoms in the rods diminishes below a certain level, the rods—now called "spent" and constituting nuclear waste—are removed. The spent rods then go into temporary storage in large ponds of water for a "cooling-off" period of at least 150 days—enough time for certain short-lived radioactive byproducts to decay.

From the holding ponds, spent fuel rods can follow one of two paths toward final "disposal." They can be transported directly to a permanent waste-management facility designed to isolate the spent fuel for hundreds of thousands of years. Or the spent fuel assemblies are shipped to a reprocessing plant, where the unconsumed U-235 and the fissionable plutonium can be extracted and manufactured into new fuel rods. The wastes left after reprocessing are then solidified and transported to the permanent waste storage facilities.

At present, this back end of the fuel cycle remains inoperative. Nearly all the 85 million gallons of high-level radioactive wastes produced so far by the nation's military and commercial reactors exist in temporary storage, either in the form of spent fuel rods in holding ponds at each of the commercial reactors in operation, or in steel tanks at military installations and reprocessing plants. This bottleneck in the fuel cycle results at least partly from indecision on whether to promote commercial development of the breeder reactor which would use reprocessed fuel. A more significant obstacle is the difficulty of finding a method for permanently managing the high-level radioactive wastes that is both technologically feasible and politically acceptable. Irresolution and uncertainty prevail while spent fuel rods accumulate in cooling ponds at the individual reactor sites; as these pools fill up, the decision about what to do with the wastes becomes more and more critical.

Radioactive byproducts resulting from the fissioning of uranium remain "hot" for centuries. As the radioisotopes (such as plutonium, iodine, cesium, and strontium) decay, the level of radioactivity declines. The rate of decay, measured in "half-lives," is constant and differs for each radioisotope. Generally, toxic radioisotopes must remain isolated from the biosphere for a period equal to 20 times their half-lives. This means that strontium-90 and cesium-137, each with a half-life of about 30 years, must be isolated for approximately 700 years. Plutonium, whose half-life is about 24,000 years, must be quarantined for nearly half a million years.

Radioactive byproducts are extremely threatening. Iodine-131 produces cancer of the thyroid gland when absorbed internally. Strontium-90 can enter the food chain as a substitute for calcium and cause bones and teeth to disintegrate. Plutonium is perhaps the strongest carcinogen of all. When inhaled even in particulate form, it is lethal; when it enters the body through skin wounds, plutonium can produce cancers of the liver, lymph nodes, or bones. Because of such health hazards, radioisotopes must be kept isolated for extraordinary lengths of time.

THE TECHNICAL DEBATE

As early as the mid-1950s, scientists recognized the need to develop safe methods of storing nuclear wastes. The wastes generated up to this point were under military control and were stored in carbon-steel tanks at the Hanford Atomic Reservation in Washington State. This method requires later transfer to a more permanent form of isolation. It is also extremely expensive because of the required leakproof containment for the very large volume of wastes with only a low concentration of radioactive elements.[2]

In 1957 and 1958, two major scientific appraisals of the waste disposal problem were presented to the Atomic Energy Commission (AEC), then the federal regulator and promoter of commercial nuclear development. These studies warned that the problem of atomic waste disposal would determine the future of nuclear power development in the private sector.

"Safe disposal is a major problem in the future growth of the atomic industry. . . . Radioactive wastes are a greater potential danger than the fallout from atomic bomb tests."[3] This position was reiterated in expert testimony before the Congressional Joint Committee on Atomic Energy (JCAE): "No satisfactory solution has been found for disposing of radioactive wastes from atomic industry. Rapid development of the industry is in no small measure contingent upon finding a prompt answer."[4]

Studies by the National Academy of Sciences and by a group of Berkeley scientists outlined alternative storage schemes. The most popular proposal, then as now, involved depositing the wastes in large-scale, stable, underground geological features, such as abandoned salt mines. Salt deposits appeared promising because of the absence of moving water—a requirement for isolating the wastes from the biosphere. Furthermore the salt is likely to envelop the wastes and sequester them, reducing the need for surveillance of a repository in salt mines.[5] Salt deposits are still recognized as the most promising method for storing radioactive wastes. One scientist who participated on the early NAS report repeated his support for salt mine waste repositories in testimony before the JCAE in 1976: "No better alternative to salt beds has emerged. I don't know whether we should feel dismayed that so little progress has apparently been made or proud that we saw a reasonable solution so long ago."[6]

Scientists who have criticized salt mine burial of wastes contend that not enough is known about the properties of salt when bombarded by radioisotopes. Some experts differ on the details of salt's plasticity and its strength under the pressure of tons of radioactive wastes. Scientists from the Geological Survey in Kansas, where abandoned salt mines have been identified as possible sites for waste repositories, have questioned several technical factors, including the possibility of the salt cracking, either from recrystallization or from the intense heat emitted from the wastes. Cracks would allow water to penetrate the burial ground and expose underground reservoirs to radioactivity. The Kansas geologists also argue that regional geological conditions are likely to alter significantly over the next half-million years, and that current knowledge does not allow accurate prediction of such changes.[7]

Studies during the 1950s identified an alternative method of waste disposal, deep-well injection. This technique involves converting high-level wastes to a gel or inert-solid form and burying small quantities directly into deep wells in the ground. Some experts remain cautiously optimistic about this method, which has been utilized at military installations to bury medium-level wastes. A scientist from the U.S. Water Pollution Control

Agency reported in 1969 that "If a deep-well injection program is properly planned and implemented, the wastes introduced into an underground stratum will remain there indefinitely with little or no danger to potable water or other natural resources."[8] Other experts disagree, saying that deep-well disposal is only a short-run solution to a long-run problem. Moreover they argue that the waste may eventually filter down to the underground water system and poison the environment, and that the process of pumping wastes directly into the ground could trigger earthquakes. Despite such criticisms, the Energy Research and Development Administration (ERDA) announced in late 1976 that it was initiating a search in 36 states for appropriate deep-well drilling sites.

A third technique for isolating nuclear wastes proposed during the late 1950s involved dumping casks of wastes into deep and relatively immobile bodies of water such as portions of the ocean.[9] In fact, from 1959 to 1961 the Navy experimented with dumping steel drums containing nuclear wastes into the ocean. Subsequently this practice was stopped—a fortunate move in light of recent tests which detected traces of plutonium and cesium on the sea floor near the Pacific burial sites used in the early 1960s.[10]

The next major studies were conducted in the mid-1960s. In 1965, the NAS investigated the operating procedures of AEC licensees, including their treatment of radioactive wastes. The report was highly critical of waste disposal practices both at the AEC's own installations and at commercial nuclear facilities. It faulted the AEC for storing wastes at sites with unstable geological conditions and for maintaining loose technical standards for containment. The report sharply criticized "the working philosophy of certain operators (of nuclear reactors) . . . that safety and economy are factors of equal weight in radioactive waste disposal."[11] The AEC declined to publish the report, stating that it was full of errors, and it forbade the NAS to distribute it on its own. Not until 1970, when Senator Frank Church demanded a copy, did the critical NAS study become public.

Other analyses emerged in the mid-1970s which reinforced the NAS criticism. An internal AEC memorandum, prepared in 1975 by the Office of Program Analysis, indicated that some commercial reactors currently operating in the United States might soon have to close due to the shortage of space for storing spent fuel rods on their own premises.

The next major waste storage proposal appeared in 1971-1972, for a Retrievable Surface Storage Facility (RSSF). This outlined a means to contain high-level wastes for up to 100 years. The RSSF plan consisted of "a large field of numerous, individual concrete mausolea into which thick-walled casks containing canisters of solidified wastes were to be inserted; the wastes were to be cooled by natural air flows."[12] In 1974-1975, ERDA requested $5 million from Congress as the initial installment of the estimated $55 million construction costs for an RSSF project. The Environmental Protection Agency (EPA), which had opposed this method since it first appeared, produced a highly critical preliminary Environmental Impact Statement. This forced ERDA to withdraw its funding request and to delay the project while EPA reevaluated the potential environmental impact of surface storage of nuclear wastes.

In 1972, another idea for handling wastes emerged, one that would use the Antarctic icecap to isolate the wastes from the biosphere. Sealed in glass containers, the wastes would melt their way to the bottom of the Antarctic ice sheet where they would remain isolated for 250,000 years.[13]

In the mid-1970s, the debate escalated. Various scientists began to speak out about safety problems associated with the waste management methods of commercial operators. The National Research Council, for example, recommended in May 1975 that the U.S. government postpone its decision to develop plutonium-based commercial breeder reactors for at least three years in order to study the radiological safety of reprocessing facilities and the technical methods for tightening the security of those installations to insure against sabotage and theft of plutonium. The EPA agreed with this recommendation. Other nuclear experts, led by Nobel laureate Hans Bethe, dismissed the problems raised by antinuclear critics, saying that waste disposal was just "not a major problem." Nevertheless, criticism of the government's role was encouraged by testimony of ERDA officials in 1976 before the Energy Subcommittee of the House Government Operations Committee. Government witnesses reported that some migration of radioactivity had indeed occurred at several federal nuclear installations where wastes had been deposited directly into the ground.[14]

The most recent proposal for waste management appeared in spring 1977. A study prepared for ERDA by a team of nuclear engineers and marine scientists suggested that the ocean floor might provide a stable, safe place for embedding high-level wastes. Preliminary tests on the ocean bottom indicate that the environment there has been undisturbed for hundreds of thousands of years. Scientists, however, agree that this method requires considerably more investigation. Meanwhile, in April 1977, President Carter revealed his policy of indefinitely deferring the reprocessing of spent fuel. Following this announcement, ERDA indicated its intention to construct an Interim Surface Unreprocessed Fuel Facility

(SURFF). Under this program, spent fuel would stay in cooling ponds at individual reactor sites for 5-10 years, after which it would be stored at the SURFF for another 10-20 years before being transferred to a permanent repository. This plan would make the fuel retrievable for up to 20 years, and allow more time to find a suitable permanent repository.

The evolution of theories and techniques for effective nuclear waste management expresses the low level of agreement within the scientific community and among government regulators. Technical disputes have raised many questions: does the current state of knowledge in the physical sciences allow us to predict fully geologic activity over the next half million years—the length of time required to keep some radioisotopes isolated from the biosphere? Do geologists accurately understand the properties of salt, ice, clay, or shale exposed to the long-lasting heat emitted by radioactive elements? Can materials experts and engineers design containers strong enough to resist corrosion from both their external environment (salt water, clay, acids) and their internal load of radioactive wastes? The inability of experts to agree on such issues has engendered public confusion and debate.

THE PUBLIC DEBATE

Until the late 1960s, commercial development of nuclear power remained essentially on the drawing board and no wastes were generated by the private sector. The military wastes produced by the weapons program were situated far away from populated areas and were outside the domain of public knowledge and control. An early, isolated instance of public concern was sparked by a 1959 proposal of the Navy and the AEC to dump casks containing medium-level wastes into the Gulf of Mexico. When Congress learned of this program, a contingent of Gulf-state congressmen protested and the dumping program was killed despite the AEC's contention that the matter should be determined by the Commission rather than by Congress.

In 1963, David Lilienthal, the AEC's first chairman, exposed the issue of nuclear waste management to national attention when he testified before the JCAE. Lilienthal criticized the AEC's "irresponsible" wait-and-see policy on waste disposal. A spokesman for the atomic industry responded, criticizing Lilienthal's "lack of faith in the ability of scientists and engineers."[15] But very little active public concern about high-level radioactive waste disposal surfaced until 1970.

When, during the early 1960s, the New York State Atomic Development Authority announced its plans to build an atomic service center in western New York, residents in the region supported the project as an employment boon to the depressed local economy. The plants were constructed and began operations by 1966, and it was not until years later that local groups began to question the safety of the facility's operations and the wisdom of turning their region into a nuclear dump.

By 1970, however, two proposals to develop waste management facilities ignited local protests. An attempt by the Chemical Nuclear Services to locate a dump for medium-level radioactive wastes in a sparsely inhabited portion of rural, eastern Oregon was abandoned following protest by local residents who feared the installation would jeopardize their water supply and property values. In the same year, the AEC announced plans to utilize an abandoned salt mine in a sparsely populated region near Lyons, Kansas, as the nation's first permanent, underground nuclear waste repository. The Kansas State Geological Survey criticized the technical integrity of this proposal and by 1971, the AEC shelved its plans as a result of the technical criticisms and the subsequent political pressure.

In addition to specific instances of protest, a more generalized public interest in the nuclear waste problem began to mature around 1970 when conservation groups throughout the country became increasingly concerned with the negative environmental side-effects of atomic power plants.[16] The passage of the Nationl Environmental Protection Act of 1969 (NEPA) reinforced this concern and increased public sensitivity to nuclear energy. This set the stage for intense debate about nuclear waste disposal.

By 1973, the issue of waste disposal was becoming increasingly central to policy discussions about nuclear energy in general. For example, in hearings on the Price-Anderson Act, Ralph Nader cited the unresolved questions of transporting and disposing of radioactive wastes as two major dangers of operating nuclear reactors.[17] In AEC hearings the Union of Concerned Scientists and the Consolidated National Intervenors criticized the Commission's approach to the long-term problem of waste storage. Dr. Henry Kendall of MIT reminded the AEC that some wastes represented a "legacy" that would remain radioactive for hundreds of thousands of years. "It's a new kind of risk-benefit calculation where we get the benefit now and hand the risks on to other generations, which will get no benefit at all."[18]

In September 1973, at JCAE hearings on the safety of the nuclear power industry, the AEC attempted to refute the critiques of the industry's nuclear waste management program by simply claiming that a safe, proven method for waste management did exist.[19]

In September 1974, conflicting expert testimony pervaded the hearings for the licensing of a nuclear fuel reprocessing plant near Barnswell, South Carolina. Representatives of environmental groups charged that safety standards for reprocessing facilities were unacceptable, citing the dangerously high levels of radioactivity coming from the reprocessing plant in West Valley, New York, as an example of the industry's inability to contain the wastes. Spokesmen for Allied General Nuclear Services, which owned the Barnswell facility, flatly denied this and played down the risks relative to the critical need for reprocessing facilities.[20]

Later in 1974, Ralph Nader organized a conference called "Critical Mass 74," to enhance the public's grasp of health, environmental, and security problems associated with nuclear power. The conference drew over 650 representatives, many of them noted scientists in the nuclear energy field. Again the problem of how to provide long-term secure storage facilities for nuclear wastes was perceived as central.

In the same year, Congress passed the Energy Reorganization Act of 1974 which dismantled the AEC and created two separate agencies to undertake the old Commission's conflicting purposes: the Energy Research and Development Administration (ERDA) to promote nuclear development, and the Nuclear Regulatory Commission to control it. Over the next two years, public concern with nuclear power in general, and with waste disposal in particular, increased dramatically. An environmental coalition, the California Committee for Nuclear Safeguards,"[21] gathered enough voter support throughout the state to place a proposition on a ballot. This proposition would have required utility applicants to prove to the public the safety of their radioactive waste disposal systems before they could receive an operating license from the state. After holding public hearings on the proposal in late 1975, the California State Legislature reported:

> After listening to 120 learned witnesses who could not agree on the merits of the initiative or the safety of nuclear power, it is clear that no objective conclusions can be drawn. The issues are not solely resolvable through application of scientific expertise. The debate is more the result of differing views on human fallibility and human behavior than anything else. The questions involved require value judgments, and the voter is no less equipped to make such judgments than the most brilliant Nobel laureate.[22]

In the popular referendum of June 1976, Proposition 15 was defeated. But the defeat was almost after the fact, for the California legislature had already approved bills with comparable effects on controlling nuclear development within the state.

Similar voter-initiative campaigns sprang up in 17 other western and midwestern states in 1975, and in seven states, environmental groups had been able to galvanize enough support to place their propositions on state ballots. In the end, none of these referenda passed. Proponents of these initiatives attributed their losses to a propaganda campaign funded by the nuclear industry's Atomic Industrial Forum and by corporations with direct interests in the future growth of nuclear power. Together these groups poured an estimated $2.5 million into the countercampaign in California alone; proponents had spent only $634,000.[23] The industry's drive was bolstered when a pro-nuclear scientist group called "Scientists and Engineers for Secure Energy" joined the effort to block the various voter propositions.[24]

Many national public-interest groups issued statements in 1975 and 1976 demanding a slowdown in the development of nuclear power until the health and safety questions involved in nuclear waste disposal were better understood and resolved. Under the sponsorship of the Union of Concerned Scientists, more than 2,300 scientists petitioned Congress and the President, pressing for a "drastic reduction" in the construction of new reactors, emphasizing the major unresolved problem of radioactive wastes. In early 1976, the National Research Council held public hearings in five major cities in the United States to discuss this and other questions of risk, but pressure continued. The National Council of Churches labeled the commercial reprocessing and use of plutonium as "morally indefensible and technically objectionable," and urged a moratorium.

A federal court of appeals handed down a significant decision in June 1976 that favored special consideration of the radioactive waste problem in decisions to license nuclear reactors. In *Natural Resources Defense Council v. Nuclear Regulatory Commission and Vermont Yankee Nuclear Power Corp.*, the NRDC was supported by the court in its insistence that the generic health and safety problems of reprocessing plants and the permanent disposal of wastes be considered in licensing decisions concerning atomic reactors. This seemed an important step until, in April 1978, the U.S. Supreme Court ruled that the Court of Appeals had overstepped its jurisdiction by intervening in the decision-making procedures of an agency entrusted with regulatory authority.

Protest over specific proposals to site waste disposal facilities continued in 1976. During the spring, ERDA announced that it had contracted with Union Carbide to begin exploratory drillings in northern Michigan to test salt deposits for storing nuclear wastes. This announcement kindled a local protest which eventually forced ERDA to abandon its plans. Then the NRC ordered a temporary halt to the construction of a nuclear reactor in

Seabrook, New Hampshire, after antinuclear power groups demanded that the Commission deal with unanswered questions about nuclear waste disposal. When the NRC lifted its moratorium about 2,000 demonstrators occupied the site, vowing a campaign of civil disobedience until the NRC seriously faced the problem of radioactive wastes.

That same year also witnessed several defections of scientists and engineers from the pro-nuclear camp. Three managing engineers from the nuclear division of General Electric left their jobs to protest the further development of nuclear power, which they considered to represent a "profound threat to man." Robert Pollard, one of the NRC's chief safety engineers, resigned because of his belief that government and industry were proceeding to develop nuclear power without resolving important technical problems such as managing high-level radioactive wastes. Another NRC reactor engineer, Ronald Fluegge, charged that "the NRC has covered up or brushed aside nuclear safety problems of far-reaching significance."

The most recent public attempts to control the development of nuclear power, however, have come from local and state legislative bodies which have passed resolutions superseding the federal government's jurisdiction in the siting and licensing of nuclear waste storage facilities.

For example, South Dakota's legislature passed a resolution in early 1977 asking the federal government to remove the state from its list of possible sites for waste storage facilities. In March 1977, residents of 35 communities in Vermont held town meetings where they adopted local resolutions banning the construction of nuclear reactors and the transportation and storage of radioactive wastes within their geographic borders. The Vermont General Assembly later passed a law giving the Assembly preemptive control over any construction of nuclear waste storage facilities in the state. In early 1978, the California Assembly, following the advice of the State Energy Resource Conservation and Development Commission, voted not to exempt the proposed Sun Desert nuclear power plant from 1976 legislation prohibiting licensing of new reactors until waste-management problems had been resolved. Taking a similar position in April 1978, the U.S. House Government Operations Committee proposed a moratorium on the licensing of additional reactors as long as there remained no feasible method for permanent waste disposal.

As we review this catalogue of events, it becomes obvious that public anxiety over nuclear waste management has grown into a major public policy issue. Both locally affected groups and national environmental and political organizations have joined in their opposition. The early antinuclear political discussions tended to center on the technical problems of

alternative solutions to nuclear waste disposal. Such concerns have endured, but as the dispute moved beyond the scientific community, the
continued technical uncertainty has led to questions about the legitimacy
of existing decision-making authority and the ability of federal regulatory
agencies to act in the public interest.

TWO CONFLICTS

A comparison of two attempts—one successful and the other unsuccessful—to site waste management facilities illustrates the nature of the politics
associated with decision-making on nuclear wastes. The two cases clarify
the role of technical experts in decision-making, the attitudes of public
officials and their treatment of technical uncertainty, and the local public
reaction. The first deals with the actual development of a reprocessing
plant in West Valley, New York, from 1961 to the present. The other case
involves an unsuccessful proposal to locate a permanent waste repository
near Lyons, Kansas, between 1970 and 1972.

WEST VALLEY

The West Valley story began in 1961 when Governor Nelson Rockefeller announced the establishment of the nation's first state-owned atomic
waste storage facility on a 3,500-acre site near West Valley, in Cattaraugus
County. At this time, there were no other plans underway for a commercial reprocessing plant, and the Governor saw a chance to help the state's
industries get into the business.

In 1962, New York set up an Atomic Development Authority (ADA)
to guide and regulate the orderly development of nuclear activities. ADA
joined with the Nuclear Fuel Services Corporation to apply for an AEC
license to construct the West Valley nuclear facility. The application was
for a reprocessing plant to recover the reusable portions of nuclear fuel,
and a storage facility for temporary maintenance of radioactive wastes.

Under the terms of the 1963 contract, Nuclear Fuel Services (NFS)
would manage the construction of the $20 million reprocessing plant and
the $8 million storage facilities which the State would own. The State's
ADA would receive $9.9 million from NFS to lease and operate the center
until 1980, at which time it would have an option to renew its lease. In
addition, NFS would set up a $4 million fund for the "perpetual care" of
the wastes. In its impatience to promote the development of this nuclear
service center, the State agreed to underwrite NFS's financial risk, assert-

ing that this financial backing was "to protect the health and safety of the public."

In early 1966, with construction complete, the AEC issued a license to NFS and New York State to operate the facility and the plant began to service commercial customers. Because commercial reactors were not yet generating enough wastes to keep the NFS plant busy all the time, the AEC began sending military wastes from Hanford. By the early 1970s, nearly three-quarters of the West Valley workload was generated by the AEC Hanford installation.

In 1969, NFS applied for permits to conduct tests on the technical potential for storing radioactive wastes in the shale formations on the West Valley site by means of deep-well injection. Until then, NFS had stored its wastes in underground steel tanks; now the company believed that burial in shale might be more efficient and accommodate larger quantities of wastes.

By January 1970, the first protest was heard. A group of local farmers and a few scientists from the University of Buffalo protested to the State Health Department about the NFS request to use the deep-well injection technique. The scientists argued that it was still uncertain how shale would react to the fracturing process and bombardment by radioactive materials, while the farmers feared that leaks from this permanent storage facility might contaminate the area's water system.

The NFS stopped reprocessing operations at the West Valley plant in 1972, ostensibly to retool its equipment in order to meet the stricter safety requirements established by the AEC in 1971. But NFS had many other reasons for closing the plant: workers had been exposed to increasingly high levels of radioactivity; the steel tanks holding the wastes from reprocessing were nearing capacity; several of the trenches holding low-level wastes had recently leaked; the federal government would soon require transforming stored liquid wastes into solid form; and the source of supply was threatened by increased competition in the reprocessing business.

In 1973, when NFS applied to the AEC to expand and reopen the plant, New York State Attorney General Lefkowitz filed papers with the Commission opposing approval of NFS's application. Lefkowitz's action, done at the request of the Sierra Club, claimed that West Valley had "an operational record which raises serious questions about risks to those who work there." The New York Department of Environmental Conservation also opposed the NFS request.

New York State abolished the Atomic Development Authority in the fall of 1975, and created the New York State Energy Research and Development Authority (NYSERDA) in its place to undertake a more balanced approach to developing alternative energy sources for the state.

On April 29, 1976, NFS informed NYSERDA that it intended to transfer responsibility for the radioactive wastes at West Valley back to the state sooner than 1980, when the NFS lease would officially expire. NYSERDA advised NFS that it could not legally surrender responsibility for the wastes in 1976; it would have to wait until the federal NRC issued an amendment to the NFS operating license.

Later in that same year, state energy officials and environmental observers began to worry about NFS's commitment to maintaining safe storage of the wastes it was seeking to unload. A letter to the editor of the *New York Times,* written by a local cancer specialist, warned of the precarious state of waste management at West Valley.

> The nuclear wastes are stored in a hazardous liquid form . . . originally intended as temporary storage for the reprocessing operations, not as permanent storage. However, the shutdown of the NFS plant means that the waste must be stored in this form for an indefinite period. . . . As long as the wastes are in liquid form, West Valley is a time bomb that could contaminate large areas of New York, New England, and Eastern Canada.[25]

As New York State began to realize the magnitude of the problem resulting from the idle West Valley facility, it sought to have the federal government assume responsibility for the center and its 600,000 gallons of liquid wastes. On November 30, 1976, NYSERDA asked ERDA to take over ownership of the plant and responsibility for its radioactive contents. At congressional hearings in March 1977, NYSERDA argued for a federal takeover of West Valley, reasoning that

> It was at the AEC's urging that NFS and the State undertook the venture at West Valley, that the AEC and NRC have been responsible for setting—and changing—the rules of waste management, and, finally, that only the Federal government has both the technical and financial resources and broad overview necessary to cope effectively with the problem. . . . If the Federal government cannot demonstrate that it can handle the West Valley problem, it will not demonstrate that it has adequately resolved the generalized radioactive waste disposal problem for the country.[26]

The Government Accounting Office concurred with NYSERDA's appraisal to the extent that the State of New York lacked the resources to remove the wastes from West Valley, transport them to a permanent repository, and decommission the radioactive plant. Since no nuclear facility had ever been decommissioned, costs were unknown, and estimates ranged from $600 million to $1 billion.

A stalemate exists over what to do with the wastes at West Valley. Before it can be resolved, the federal government must decide whether nuclear fuel reprocessing will take place in the United States at all; whether the NFS facility has the technological potential for safe and efficient operations; and whether the federal government is willing to subsidize the work to bring the NFS plant up to federal safety standards.

At West Valley itself there is much support for starting-up reprocessing operations again. The plant offers some employment potential and a stable tax base—two attractive features for the depressed economy of western New York. In addition, after its 1973 effort to prevent West Valley from becoming a permanent nuclear dump, the Sierra Club has not taken much interest in the plant. The state, however, appears to see no possibility of NFS resuming operations until it fully upgrades its facilities at federal expense.

The NFS plant has become an albatross; it demonstrates what can happen when a large-scale project is promoted solely on the basis of its immediate promise for stimulating the regional economy, disregarding the unresolved technical questions that are ultimately associated with it.

LYONS

The AEC has actively explored various locations throughout the country as potential sites for a permanent federal repository of the radioactive wastes generated by nuclear facilities. One such attempt centered on a salt mine near the town of Lyons, Kansas. This proposal was undermined by the combined criticism of local technical experts and environmental groups, as well as by pressure from state and local governmental officials.

The Kansas case opened in mid-1970 when the AEC announced the tentative selection of an abandoned salt mine near Lyons, in Rice County, as the nation's first permanent underground storage facility for radioactive wastes. Before it announced the plan, the federal agency had received the qualified concurrence of the Kansas Nuclear Energy Council, pending further technical and environmental impact studies.

The AEC requested $25 million from Congress for the Lyons project. This sum would cover initial costs, such as purchase of the 1,000-acre site, acquisition of the abandoned salt mine itself, and initial preparation of the ground to handle wastes. But the Kansas State Geological Survey refused to endorse the AEC's request until detailed geologic studies of the site had been conducted. In August 1970, the Sierra Club of Kansas publicly supported the cautious approach urged by the State Geological Survey.[27]

The Kansas Geological Survey had been preparing a preliminary study of the conditions at Lyons, and in December 1970, sent its report to Governor Robert Docking sharply criticizing the AEC's reluctance to delay the project on environmental grounds.

> [T]he AEC ... has exhibited remarkably little interest in studying the effects of radiation and heat on the salt. Plans for the transport of radioactive wastes across the state to the burial site are completely inadequate and plans for removing the radioactive substances, if something should go wrong, do not exist at all.[28]

Kansas Congressman Joe Skubitz, a member of the House Interior Committee, began a campaign to halt the AEC's development of the Lyons site. Skubitz wrote a letter to Governor Docking asking him to join the opposition to the AEC plan.

> [H]owever the AEC may phrase it semantically, a part of Kansas is proposed as a dump for the most dangerous garbage in the knowledge of mankind. A dump is a dump no matter how the garbage is packed. ... The federal government cannot compel a sovereign state to do itself and its citizens possible irreparable injury if its officials refuse to be stampeded and bow to federal pressure.[29]

Skubitz's opposition was reinforced by public statements by scientists and environmentalists in Kansas who questioned the knowledge of the AEC's experts about the long-term effects of high-intensity radiation on salt, and they urged that more tests be undertaken before the Lyons area became permanently contaminated.

The AEC defended itself by saying that its own scientists had already addressed the problems cited in the Geological Survey's report. According to the AEC, the "risks [of the Lyons plan] are negligible." The wastes themselves would be contained in heavily shielded containers and deposited safely in the salt beds. Furthermore, the Lyons site had not been disturbed by flood or earthquake for more than 200 million years.

A significant majority of the local inhabitants were willing to go along with the AEC's appraisal: "I trust my government." "Not only are those government scientists trustworthy, but when they come here to run tests, they turned out to be good guys and good church-going folks."[30] A poll conducted in early 1971 showed that most residents in the immediate area expressed general support for developing the Lyons project. As in West Valley, it would bring new jobs and tax dollars to the area.

In March 1971, the Joint Committee on Atomic Energy held hearings on the Lyons waste-management proposal. The director of the Kansas Geological Survey testified that more environmental and geological studies of the Lyons site must be made before the AEC committed itself to such an enormous financial investment and, moreover, before it unknowingly contaminated the state of Kansas. The U.S. Department of Interior presented testimony that strongly concurred with the Geological Survey's concern, that criticized the project for its technical uncertainties and potential environmental hazards. Congressman Chet Holifield of the JCAE responded to these criticisms by simply saying "the experts tell us that this is the safest place in the world to put these wastes."[31]

Opposition to the AEC plan escalated after the JCAE hearings. In May 1971, the Sierra Club's Board of Directors petitioned the AEC to delay decisions on specific waste disposal projects until the clear safety standards were established and in-depth environmental studies were completed. In July, the U.S. Senate adopted an amendment offered by Kansas Senator Robert Dole to prohibit purchase of the Lyons site as a waste repository for at least three years, and to set up a Presidential Advisory Commission to study the problem of transporting and storing nuclear wastes. In August, the Attorney General of Kansas sought to join the Natural Resources Defense Council as a party to hearings in Vermont, since Kansas—as the site of the proposed waste storage facility—shared a concern with the NRDC over the disposal of the radioactive wastes generated by the Vermont Yankee Atomic Power Plant.

By fall 1971, the AEC conceded that the exploratory tests it had conducted on the Lyons site revealed unexpected technical problems. In light of this, a group of officials, including two members of Congress, the Governor, and the Chairman of the Kansas Sierra Club, asked the AEC to remove the state from consideration as a possible location for future waste storage facilities. The Governor argued that "the AEC's steamroller approach and its early statement that the Lyons site was safe have given me little reason to have any confidence in its future claims."[32] Subsequently the AEC announced that it would shelve—perhaps permanently—its plans for the Lyons site.

COMPARISONS

In Lyons, Kansas, public officials and private citizens mobilized a political campaign, armed with technical support, to halt a federal attempt to site a nuclear waste storage facility in their region. The success of the Kansans in thwarting the project before it had broken ground contrasts with the earlier situation in West Valley, New York, where only limited citizen protest occurred, and then only after the reprocessing plant had been operating for several years. There are several reasons for the differences in these two cases.

First, the West Valley project was initiated in the early 1960s, several years before significant public interest in the impact of nuclear power had developed. No conservation groups emerged to assess the reprocessing facility when it obtained its construction license in 1963, or even when it began operations in 1966. Environmentalist activity at West Valley began only in 1970, after the New York State Department of Environmental Conservation detected leakages of radioactivity at the facility. The atmosphere of growing national environmental consciousness in 1970 explains in part why conservationists became involved in both the West Valley and Lyons projects during that year.

A second distinction between the two cases followed from the different justifications for the facilities. West Valley had been promoted by the State of New York, essentially as an economic-development project. The state selected the location in order to revitalize an underdeveloped area and local residents and public officials welcomed the project as a boost to their economy. In contrast, the Lyons project was sponsored by the federal government solely as a means to meet the nation's need for a permanent repository for nuclear wastes. The AEC chose the abandoned salt mine at Lyons because it offered a technically suitable geological structure at a relatively low cost. While residents of the town immediately adjacent to the old salt mine welcomed the employment and tax advantages associated with the proposed waste facility, nearly all other interested groups and public officials in Kansas resisted the project, recognizing that its short-term benefits were minimal compared to the possible long-term health and safety hazards.

A third distinction relates to the nature of the two projects themselves. The West Valley plant was primarily a reprocessing facility, with a secondary capacity for storing the radioactive byproducts which remained after fissionable elements had been extracted from the spent fuel. Waste storage was considered a temporary function, as one step in a pass-through process in which individual utilities sent their spent fuel to the plant, the fuel rods were reprocessed, and the leftover wastes were stored before being transported to a permanent repository. The facility gave the impression of being a factory—a factory that happened to be highly radioactive. In contrast, the Lyons project was a nuclear dump. The state would have to deal with the wastes forever. The Kansas officials who questioned the proposal saw their region subjected to a 250,000-year commitment to safeguarding radioactive garbage.

Finally, a fourth difference in the two cases was the role played by technical experts. The main proponents of the West Valley project were state officials who had the backing of scientists from the New York Atomic Development Authority as well as from the AEC. When the plan took shape in the early 1960s, there was little open criticism of the hazards of radioactive waste disposal techniques. There were no public-interest scientists to register their opposition to building the NFS facility. By the time the AEC proposed the Lyons installation, considerable dissent existed in the scientific community over nuclear technologies and especially over the technical feasibility of different waste-disposal methods. From the early stages of the Lyons proposal, scientists voiced their concern about developing a nuclear waste center before adequately resolving crucial technical uncertainties. In the Lyons case, geologists, physicists, and engineers played a significant role in informing public officials and citizen groups about the technical risks associated with the AEC plan. The conflict among technical experts heated up the political debate which ultimately scuttled the Lyons project.

IMPLICATIONS OF THE WASTE-DISPOSAL ISSUE

The history of the nuclear waste-disposal problem, and the particular cases of Lyons and West Valley, suggest the important role that disputes among experts can play in the political arena. Only when scientists openly debated the technical uncertainties and hazards involved in different nuclear waste containment techniques did the public become aware of the problems of the technology. The disputes among experts stimulated political debate, quickly shifting the locus of decision-making from the technical to the political arena. Value questions began to override the question of technological alternatives.

How, as a society, do we balance our short-run energy needs against the risks to future generations? Do we have a right to impose on our descendants the burden of protecting high-intensity radioactive wastes? Or, as many nuclear advocates suggest, do we have a moral responsibility to go ahead with nuclear development rather than using up irreplaceable oil, natural gas, and coal reserves? Assuming that we proceed with developing nuclear power, do we defer the problem of disposal of wastes by putting them in retrievable storage facilities? Or should we dispose of the wastes in an irretrievable fashion? Should we compute the expense of storing the wastes for years to come into the present costs of electricity generated by nuclear power? How do we balance local versus national needs—the interests and preferences of those people who live near a nuclear facility against the interests of the citizenry as a whole? And is it reckless to proceed with further development of nuclear energy when the technical problems of perpetual waste management have not yet been resolved?

In fact, significant choices have been made concerning waste disposal through a process of nondecision. During the 1950s, the nation embarked on a program to develop commercial nuclear power, and in its enthusiasm remained blind to many of the potential technical problems and negative consequences of the technology. Early promoters of nuclear power expressed faith in the power of science and technology eventually to resolve technical uncertainties and to deal with nuclear power's negative impacts as they arose. This attitude remains strong to this day.

> There is nothing else that is so strictly and securely regulated [as the nuclear industry]. So it is the faith in this system, and the faith in the development of skills and the development of our technology that some of the unresolved problems will most certainly be solved by the time we have to address them.[33]

Early research efforts did not attack the waste disposal problem with a real sense of urgency, and now, 25 years later, little progress has been made toward developing a technologically and politically feasible means of waste management. A report published by ERDA in 1975 recognized this situation.

> There are still many technical problems and uncertainties in the overall area of processing of spent fuel and properly managing its radioactive waste. . . . [The public] fears that the radioactive wastes generated . . . will either be neglected, and thus place an unacceptable hazard potential on mankind, or be managed in a way that will place an unacceptable burden on future generations to assure continued public safety. These fears are supported by a fair segment of the scientific community.[34]

As radioactive wastes stockpile at various nuclear facilities around the country, the continued failure to deal with the commercial waste disposal problem could result in a halt in the growth of nuclear power.

That the nuclear industry and its governmental promoters effectively ignored the waste disposal issue is in many ways bizarre. The health and safety risks associated with waste disposal pose unique institutional as well as technical problems, and this has long been recognized. In 1970, the AEC noted that:

> Fission technology requires that man issue guarantees on events far into the future, and it is not clear in most cases how this can be done. Institutional arrangements do not exist and never have existed to guarantee the monitoring of or attendance upon storage facilities over a millennium.[35]

Yet until recently little attention was devoted to these problems. The present political controversy suggests a public desire to defer further development of nuclear power "until an acceptable solution to the waste management problem has been demonstrated—not just a solution in principle, which the majority of knowledgeable experts are comfortable with— but a definitive plan that can be sold to the public in the face of an open technical criticism."[36]

In addition, dissenting groups are often critical of the decision-making structures that they feel have failed to respond to their health and safety interests. They have questioned the legitimacy and authority of the industry and regulatory agencies. In response, Congress abolished the Atomic Energy Commission in 1974 and dismantled its own Joint Committee on Atomic Energy in 1977.

Public groups have continued to use a variety of techniques to influence nuclear policy; they have used dissenting scientists to inform the lay public of the risks of nuclear power. They have mobilized national public-interest groups to pressure Congress and the administration for resolution of the waste-disposal issue. They have gone to the courts to oppose the administrative decision-making process. They have fought against the federal government's exclusive ability to make decisions on nuclear power by means of voter initiatives and state legislative actions. And they have resorted to political protest and civil disobedience to demonstrate the strength of their antinuclear conviction.

NOTES

1. Harvey Brooks, "Waste Management," paper presented at the International Symposium on the Management of Wastes from the LWR Fuel Cycle, Denver, Colorado, July 12, 1976, 1.

2. By 1971, several of the Hanford Tanks had leaked small quantities of radioactive liquids, and there had been a few instances of near ruptures. Dr. Chauncey Starr, founder and past president of the American Nuclear Society, was quoted in

1971 as saying: "I do not conceive of leaking tanks as acceptable storage." "Sludge, Smells, Sights, Slums, Sprays, Smog, and Seepage," *The New York Times,* September 26, 1971, X:15.

3. Quoted from a 1957 National Academy of Sciences/National Research Council report prepared for the AEC. James Reston, "A Peril of the Atom Age: An Analysis of the Radioactive Waste Problem and Moves by the U.S. to Meet It," *The New York Times,* July 16, 1957, 3:2. See also Report prepared by a panel of scientists at U.C. Berkeley in 1957. "Panel Gives Plan on Atomic Wastes," *The New York Times,* October 6, 1957, 40:1.

4. "Congress Studies Atomic Waste Issue," *The New York Times,* January 29, 1959, 24:8.

5. Alvin Weinberg, "Social Institutions and Nuclear Energy," *Science* 177 (1972), 32-33.

6. Testimony presented by John Frye, formerly chairman of the 1958 NAS Committee on Radioactive Waste Management, and now executive director of the Geological Society of America. "Geologist Optimistic on Atomic Waste," *The New York Times,* May 12, 1976, 64:4.

7. Richard Lewis, "The Radioactive Salt Mine," *Bulletin of the Atomic Scientists,* June 1971, 28-29.

8. Quote from Report prepared by Dr. Don Warner of the USWPCA, an expert on the deep-well method. David Bird, "Deep Well Industrial Waste Disposal Stirs Dispute," *The New York Times* (September 1, 1969), 25:8.

9. The lake proposal was suggested by Dr. Curtis Newcombe of the U.S. Naval Radiological Defense Lab.

10. The tests, conducted by Robert Dyer of the U.S. Environmental Protection Agency, showed that some of the steel casks showed signs of corrosion and others had been crushed, through the combined effects of ocean currents and water pressure. David Burnham, "Radioactive Materials Found in Oceans," *The New York Times* (May 21, 1976), 14:2.

11. Quoting from the 1966 NAS report. Robert Smith, "AEC Scored on Storing Waste," *The New York Times,* March 7, 1970, 12:6.

12. Luther Carter, "Radioactive Wastes: Some Urgent Unfinished Business," *Science* 195 (February 18, 1977), 664.

13. E. J. Zeller, D. F. Saunders, and E. E. Angus, "Putting Radioactive Wastes on Ice," *Bulletin of the Atomic Scientists* (January 1973), 4. The proposal's own sponsors cite such technical problems as: (1) determining ice-canister interactions; (2) obtaining detailed information on ice thicknesses, movements, and sub-ice topography; and (3) determining temperature gradients down to the ice-rock interface. The complex problems of international politics begin with the Antarctic Treaty of 1959 which prohibits disposal of radioactive wastes there.

14. Carl E. Behrens, "Nuclear Waste Management: Issue Brief Number IB75012," Library of Congress/Congressional Research Service, Washington, D.C. (January 16, 1978).

15. Theodore Jones, "Lilienthal Fears Atom Plant Here," *The New York Times* (April 5, 1963), 11:1.

16. The protest over the proposed siting of Bell Nuclear Power Station on Cayuga Lake in upstate New York in 1968-1969 exemplifies the public's demands for AEC licensing decisions more sensitive to the environment. For a detailed analysis of this case, see: Dorothy Nelkin, *Nuclear Power and Its Critics: The Cayuga Lake Controversy* (Ithaca, NY: Cornell University Press, 1971).

17. The three other dangers mentioned by Nader were: the "big accident," resulting from a meltdown of the radioactive core; sabotage of a nuclear facility; and acts of God, such as earthquakes. "Nader Asserts Nuclear Industry Forces Public to Accept Plants," *The New York Times* (August 15, 1973), 34:4.

18. Anthony Ripley, "AEC Hears Critics of Atomic Plants," *The New York Times* (February 5, 1973), 18:1.

19. This particular testimony was presented by Dr. Clarence Larson of the AEC. Victor McElheny, "AEC Aide Finds Wastes Kept Safe," *The New York Times* (September 27, 1973), 77:6.

20. By the time of the 1974 hearings, Allied-General had already invested $230 million in the plant, then about 75% complete. "Witnesses Differ on Atom Hazards," *The New York Times* (September 22, 1974), 33:1. Allied-General was particularly impatient to receive its operating license from the AEC, after construction on the General Electric reprocessing plant in Morris, Illinois, had recently been halted.

21. The coalition included: the Sierra Club; Friends of the Earth; Zero Population Growth; California Public Interest Research Group; People's Lobby; and the Los Angeles Citizen Action Group.

22. Report of 15 days of hearings held before the California State Assembly Committee on Resources, Land Use, and Energy in fall 1976. Gladwin Hill, "Nuclear Power Facing Key Coast Vote Tuesday," *The New York Times* (June 2, 1976), 1:1.

23. In announcing its campaign, the Atomic Industrial Forum mentioned its two purposes. One would be "designed to get balanced nuclear power information to decision makers, both legislative and executive, in the Federal government, and with the assistance of AIF members, to state and local policy makers. This direct approach was required because of the unwillingness of the major media to present the positive side of nuclear power." The second aspect centered on "the generation of positive news events. . . . There is an urgent need to initiate frequent and substantive news events, to counter the pseudo-press conferences held regularly by the national critics and to provide a news peg for media attention. . . . The national media, with the middlemen of the reporter and the editor, cannot be relied upon to publish a full and balanced account of nuclear power." AIF memo, quoted in David Burnham, "Atomic Industry to Promote Views," *The New York Times* (January 17, 1975), 34:1. The Atomic Industrial Forum channeled an estimated $500,000 into the California Campaign alone; its national campaign totalled nearly $1.5 million. An assortment of national corporations with ties to the nuclear industry contributed over $2 million additional funds to the countercampaign against California Proposition 15. A sampling of these corporations included: General Electric ($50,000), Westinghouse ($50,000), Exxon Nuclear Corporation ($25,000), Atlantic Richfield ($25,000), Pacific Gas and Electric ($300,000), Con Edison ($4,500), Duke Power ($9,000), Connecticut Northeast Utilities ($9,000), Public Service Electric & Gas Co., NJ ($13,500), Commonwealth Edison, Illinois ($9,000), Bethlehem Steel Corp. ($23,000), and Consumer Power, Michigan ($9,000). Reginald Stewart, "The Vote on Nuclear Power," *The New York Times* (May 23, 1976), III, 1:1; R. Stewart, "Power Industry Wooing Voters," *The New York Times* (May 15, 1976), 31:8.

24. The group attracted over 100 scientists and engineers, including five Nobel laureates: Hans Bethe, Felix Bloch, James Rainwater, Eugene Wigner, and W. F. Libby. Its initial statement in 1976 said: "There is no reasonable alternative to increased reliance on nuclear power to satisfy our energy needs. This use of nuclear power offers a temporary easing of this worldwide need for energy and time to seek

more effective and permanent solutions through other sources." "Group Backs Use of Nuclear Power," *The New York Times* (June 2, 1976), 21:3.

25. Letter to the Editor written by Dr. Irwin Bross, director of biostatistics at Roswell Park Memorial Institute, Buffalo, *The New York Times* (November 19, 1976), 26:4.

26. Testimony of Dr. Werthamer, NYSERDA Chairman. Quoted in Luther Carter, "West Valley: The Question Is Where Does the Buck Stop on Nuclear Wastes?" *Science* 195 (March 25, 1977), 1306.

27. *Sierra Club Bulletin,* Vol. 55 #8 (August 1970), 22.

28. "Kansas Geologists Oppose a Nuclear Waste Dump," *The New York Times* (February 17, 1971), 27:5.

29. Ibid.

30. B. Drummond Ayres, "Town in Kansas Is Willing to Live with Atom Dump," *The New York Times* (March 11, 1971), 41:6.

31. The Department of Interior's testimony referred to a letter written by Assistant Secretary Hollis Dole to the AEC on February 3, 1971. Letter quoted in Lewis, "Radioactive Salt Mine," 29-30.

32. *Sierra Club Bulletin,* Vol. 56 #10 (December 1971), 18.

33. Statement made by Dr. Cecily C. Selby, president of the industry-financed Americans for Energy Independence. David Burnham, "Nuclear Energy Has Moral Components, Too," *The New York Times* (May 9, 1976), IV, 16:1.

34. ERDA, Nuclear *Fuel Cycle: A Report of the Fuel Cycle Task Force,* ERDA-33 (March 1975), 40-50.

35. AEC, "Environmental Survey of the Uranium Fuel Cycle," April 1970, quoted in Bazelon opinion in *NRDC v. NRC and Vermont Yankee Nuclear Power Corp.,* #74-1385, U.S. Court of Appeals for the D.C. Circuit, decided July 21, 1976, at 35-36.

36. Harvey Brooks, "Waste Management," 6-7.

5

DES AND THE ASSESSMENT OF RISK

Susan G. Hadden

Accurate assessment of risk often requires information that is simply not available or that is ambiguous. This creates "areas of judgment," points at which experts can legitimately differ. Advances in science may eventually produce a consensus on a formerly disputed point, but many important policy decisions are based on such ambiguous knowledge. The case of DES suggests how technical uncertainties that occur in testing for carcinogens provide broad scope for political manipulation. On the other hand, as these uncertainties are reduced, policy makers have few options and are better able to resist the political pressure placed upon them.

DES

In the last 40 years, producers of meat have increasingly relied upon drugs placed in their animals' feed to promote rapid growth and inhibit disease. By 1971, the value of growth-promoting animal drugs was nearly $2 billion. Between 80% and 90% of the meat, milk, and eggs consumed in the United States come from animals fed medicated food.

One of the most common of the growth-promoting drugs, diethylstilbestrol (DES), is a synthetic compound that mimics the action of natural female hormones. When small quantities of DES are given to cattle regularly in their feed, the cattle are said to reach a weight of 1000 pounds in 35 fewer days while eating 500 pounds less grain than cattle not fed the drug.[1] Similar effects are noted in poultry. Thus growers adopted DES and related compounds enthusiastically after their commercial introduction in 1954.

DES also has other uses. For many years before 1973, it was regularly given to women suffering from estrogen deficiencies. Another widespread use involved regular small doses in early pregnancy to prevent possible miscarriage. DES is now available in one massive dose for women seeking to prevent conception—the famous "morning after" pill (actually a series of pills). DES is also used in the treatment of certain cancers that respond to the presence of estrogen. Since the early 1940s, DES has also been recognized as one of the most potent cancer-causing agents (carcinogens) known.

Policies concerning the use of DES are defined primarily by the Food and Drug Administration and by the regulatory politics that attend the technical decisions of that agency. The FDA is a regulatory agency within the Public Health Service of the Department of Health, Education and Welfare.[2] It was established in 1931 as a successor to earlier organizations charged with protecting the purity of the food supply. The basis of its authority is the Food and Drug Act of 1907. The Act, revised in 1938 and again in 1962, directs the agency to protect the health of the nation against impure and unsafe foods, drugs, and cosmetics. In addition to defining and enforcing standards of purity and efficacy for foods and drugs, the FDA undertakes basic research into questions related to its goals.

The FDA is very much a technical agency, with a large professional staff and many outside advisory groups of expert scientists. Its highly technical nature has, however, not freed the agency from accusations of being captured by its regulated industries. A number of writers have documented the FDA's reluctance to ban substances that are harmful but also highly profitable for their manufacturers.[3] Almost 20 formal reviews of agency operations conducted over the last 40 years were directed at the relationship between the FDA and industry.[4] One reason for the close relationship is that industries frequently possess the information that the agency needs to perform its regulatory function. It is left to manufacturers, for example, to perform the animal tests which show that a new drug is safe, and the FDA does not have staff to reevaluate all of these tests.

Aware of its relationship with industry, Congress keeps close watch on the FDA through its many and detailed oversight hearings, one of which concerned DES. The White House too retains an interest in FDA decisions; in the DES case, the President supported the animal drug industry and the cattle growers. Thus the actors in the case included the animal drug industry, cattle growers, the USDA, and even the White House. Later, the public and the scientists played a part.

The Food and Drug Administration kept especially close watch on DES since it was known that oral administration of the drug could cause cancer in test animals. The agency believed, however, that it posed no threat because it left no residue in the tissues of animals which either were fed the drug or had it implanted in their ears. When DES was approved for use in cattle feed in 1954, the FDA required that drug-supplemented feed should be withheld for 48 hours before slaughter to ensure that there would be no residues. The Department of Agriculture was also to include DES in its meat-inspection program.

In 1955, a team of FDA scientists discovered a new method for the detection of chemical residues in meat. Because it detected the activity of the chemical rather than the chemical itself, the test was more sensitive than any others then known. It could detect DES residues in meat in concentrations as small as two parts per billion (ppb). As soon as the new test was applied to meat animals, DES was found in the liver, skin, and kidneys of poultry. The FDA promptly banned DES implants in poultry under the requirements of the Delaney Amendment to the Food and Drug Act which restricts the sale of any product known to be carcinogenic. The agency did not ban DES in cattle feed because smaller amounts were given to much larger animals, and because no residues had been detected.

Immediately after the ban was effected, one of the manufacturers filed suit to get it lifted because it was based on a reinterpretation of old data on DES residues.[5] However, the decision of a lower court, upheld in the U.S. Court of Appeals in 1966, was that the ban was legitimate. The known carcinogenicity of DES was sufficient reason for banning it under the Delaney Clause even though scientists were unable to determine how much of the substance causes cancer in humans.

The U.S. Department of Agriculture (USDA), under pressure from growers, did not begin testing meat for residues until 1965. There is some evidence that adverse effects of DES were observed during routine inspection of cattle but were suppressed.[6] When USDA testing did begin, it was limited to less than 1000 animals out of some 30 million slaughtered annually; under congressional pressure, this figure was increased to 6000, but still no residues were reported. In 1971, a lawyer for the Natural Resources Defense Council discovered that residues were in fact being detected and as a result the USDA finally admitted to Congress that residues had been found at levels of up to 37 ppb. The agency blamed the original misinformation on administrative error, but some observers accused USDA of protecting its farmer clients who were clearly reluctant to give up the use of DES.[7]

This incident was one of several events that cumulatively called the use of DES into question. In April 1971, an article in the *New England Journal of Medicine* showed that a rare form of vaginal cancer, which had suddenly appeared in at least eight young women in Massachusetts, could be traced to their mothers' having had DES therapy while pregnant. (At that time DES was used to prevent possible miscarriage.[8]) Following usual practice, the author of the article, Dr. Arthur Herbst, had sent his case histories and his data to FDA even before publishing his article, but the agency did not respond until October 1971. Meanwhile doctors continued to prescribe DES to pregnant women.

Further cases of the rare cancer, detected in New York State, were also traced to maternal use of DES during pregnancy. The state government then officially notified its physicians of the danger of prescribing DES. The FDA labeled this action "precipitate" and unnecessarily alarmist, and continued to delay taking any action while its staff ostensibly reanalyzed Herbst's data.[9] In fact, no record has been found that the FDA conducted any reanalysis.

In October, the Natural Resources Defense Council, which had publicized the misreporting of the residues, filed suit against the FDA seeking a total ban on the use of DES.[10] During the next month, an editorial appeared in the *Washington Post* condemning DES, and this initiated a long correspondence about the pros and cons of its continued use.[11] As pressure grew, the USDA and the FDA proposed a mandatory certification system under which farmers using DES in cattle feed would have to certify formally that they had complied with the withdrawal regulations. (Formerly slaughterhouses merely assumed compliance.) Critics questioned the effect of this system since it placed all responsibility for complying with regulations on the grower and removed responsibility from inspection agencies. Furthermore, since USDA announced that it would test no more than 6000 of the nearly 50 million cattle and sheep slaughtered annually, an individual farmer could falsely state that he had followed the withdrawal procedure and have only one chance in 8000 of being caught. Ultimately the testing procedure was powerless, for by the time DES residues could be detected, the carcass from which the sample had been taken would already have been delivered to the consumer. Critics thus contended that the new "mandatory" certification program marked no effective change from the old policy.

Finally in November and December 1971, a subcommittee of the House of Representatives Committee on Government Operations heard testimony about DES. The Committee has general oversight of federal agencies; the subcommittee, under its chairman, Representative H. L. Fountain, had already conducted several investigations of the FDA. This time it was focusing on the FDA's policies regarding DES. The day before the hearings, the FDA announced in the Federal Register that the use of DES was "contra-indicated" in pregnancy. During the hearings, the agency was criticized for ignoring the contradiction between the continued existence of residues and the previous scientific evidence which purported to show elimination of all DES within 48 hours. Its response was merely to extend the withdrawal period from two to seven days before slaughter.

Thus by the end of 1971, through the efforts of the Natural Resources Defense Council, the circle of actors in the DES case had expanded to include Congress and the public. In response to the growing public and congressional pressure, the FDA made several incremental policy changes late in 1971: it recommended that physicians not prescribe DES during pregnancy, lengthened the withdrawal period, and introduced the mandatory certification program. The agency's reluctance to act in all these instances suggests its continued responsiveness to its usual clients. The provisions of the controlling legislation permitted such delay, especially where technical uncertainties remained. It is to these uncertainties that we now turn.

SCIENTIFIC AND TECHNICAL ISSUES

The FDA evaluated DES under an amendment to the Delaney Clause. Three criteria had to be met before the drug could be approved: safety for the animal, inability to detect residues in the animal's edible tissues through an accepted test, and reasonable certainty that the labeled instructions would be followed in practice. The law assumed that legal use of DES would not result in danger; the FDA exploited this assumption by explaining away all detected residues as results of illegal use of the drug. The agency could do this because there was no experimental work that definitively showed that legal use did result in residues. Several technical questions are embodied in these criteria.

IS DES A CARCINOGEN?

Considerable scientific judgment must be brought to bear to determine whether or not a substance is carcinogenic. Great uncertainty lies in establishing convincing links between agents suspected of causing cancer and subsequent illness. Many cancers are said to occur naturally in less than 1 out of every 10,000 people (or mice, the most common experimental animal in carcinogenesis testing); to prove absolutely that cancers detected during an experiment are caused by ingesting the suspect substance, it would be necessary to test tens of thousands of mice.

The use of statistical inference to circumvent the problem has led to considerable disagreement about the cancer-causing potential of many drugs. Disagreement can arise over the procedures of the experiment: whether the number of test animals was sufficient to allow the application of statistical tests, whether these tests are valid, and whether the tissues examined are actually cancerous.

The FDA initially rejected the association between DES and cancer. Dr. Charles Edwards, then Commissioner of the FDA, denied before the Fountain Committee that a causal relationship had been established between DES therapy in mothers and vaginal cancer in their daughters. Dr. Herbst, the author of the first paper on the subject, testified that "at the moment it is an established association."[12] The FDA contradicted him by citing associations between the cancer and variables other than DES. Thus the FDA Commissioner justified his delay in banning use of the drug during pregnancy.

Another area of judgment in carcinogenesis testing is whether the results in test animals are relevant to humans. One of the most common arguments against accepting the result of animal tests is that experiments involve feeding highly concentrated amounts of the substance to the animals, amounts far greater than reasonable human consumption. In the case of DES, the dose was about 56 times larger than would be ingested by a person eating one-half pound of DES-fed liver every day. Many scientists, however, argue that people are more sensitive to carcinogens than animals, so that any substance producing tumors in animals should be considered carcinogenic to humans.[13] Even the FDA recommends a safety standard of 100 to 1, meaning that a food additive may be used at no more than 1% of the maximum level shown to be harmless in test animals.[14]

Apart from resolving the problem of carcinogenicity, the FDA required a test suitable for detecting DES residues in order to regulate its use. A new test which was both quick and sensitive had been perfected in 1971. Although the USDA made use of the new method in its testing program, the FDA failed to publish it in the Federal Register. This means that the test used to obtain evidence of residues was not official, and thus farmers could not be prosecuted for illegal use of DES.

Drug manufacturers and cattle growers felt threatened by the ever-improving technology of residue testing. They asked whether it was reasonable to expect them to change drug labels, feeding practices, or even drug composition every time a new and more sensitive test was developed. The FDA concluded that manufacturers were bound by changed standards, for only repeal of the Delaney Amendment would eliminate the problem.

IS DES SAFE?

The question of safety underlies carcinogenesis testing. The Delaney Amendment, in banning carcinogens altogether, is based on a zero-tolerance limit, implying that since we do not know how much of a carcinogen causes cancer, it is best to assume that any amount is suspect. The residue tests available when the Delaney Clause was passed in 1958 were not very sensitive, and it seemed desirable to ban carcinogens entirely rather than risk having dangerous but undetectable levels left in food.

Many experts today still adhere to the principle of zero tolerance: statistical tests from experiments on animals are clearly indeterminate. Others believe that there are low levels of carcinogens which will not induce a response and that increasingly sensitive tests will allow us to determine these minimum levels. They point to the existence of natural estrogens in the body, whose chemical compositions are similar to those of known carcinogens such as DES. They also note long-term use of compounds without ill effects.

Unable to determine safe levels of carcinogens, some experts have advocated the idea of "socially acceptable" risk.[15] This concept acknowledges that there may be no way of avoiding a carcinogen: the goal is then to minimize, not eliminate, the risk. Is it "socially acceptable" to assume the risk that the projected residues will result in a probable additional incidence of cancer in one person out of 10,000 or more? While this risk seems quite small, many people question whether any drug is worth the lives of several hundred people per year. The FDA and others counter that "banning many foods . . . without due consideration for the importance of such foods in the human diet . . . would lead to chaos and inordinate wastage of vitally needed foods."[16]

To determine the social acceptability of risk requires weighing benefits. Proponents of DES argue that if there are any risks from eating a piece of meat with DES residue, these are more than balanced by the benefits of the drug's use. Much of FDA testimony to Congress consisted of pointing out the smallness of the risks and the magnitude of the benefits. The agency argued that banning DES but maintaining beef production at 1971 levels would have raised the cost of beef about 3½ cents per pound or about $3.85 per person per year. This would involve consumption of an additional 136.5 million bushels of grain. The extra feed and feeding time was also said to add to the problem of eutrophication of streams by creating an additional 17.5 billion pounds of animal waste.[17]

Opponents countered these arguments. They insisted on the risks of adding to the natural level of estrogen in the human body. The level of circulating estradiol (estrogen) in postmenopausal women is about 15 parts per *trillion*. If such a woman ate four ounces of liver containing one ppb of DES, she would be adding about 17% to her existing level. Since DES has ten times the activity of natural estradiol, the liver would in fact triple the physiological level.[18]

Critics also questioned the concept of socially acceptable risk. Benefit-risk calculations of safety were first developed for human drugs, in which advantages from treatment could be compared with the side effects or disadvantages of not using the drug. Benefit-risk calculations that compare health risks with dollar savings are much more difficult, for too many incommensurables are being balanced. Yet this is what the proponents of DES sought to do.

Furthermore, benefit-risk calculations for drugs assume that the patient knowingly takes on the risk because of the possible benefits. The consumer, however, assumes the risk of DES unknowingly and often without any choice. DES-fed meat is not labeled as such and the consumer has little alternative since 80% to 90% of U.S. cattle receive the drug.

The "areas of judgment" in carcinogenesis testing have had two effects on FDA decisions. First, the FDA used the lack of definitive knowledge to justify postponing a decision. For example, in testifying to Congress about the relationship between DES and vaginal carcinoma, the Commissioner of the FDA (Dr. Charles Edwards) noted its presence in girls whose mothers apparently did not receive DES.

> It is these puzzling things that lead us to be extremely careful. And even at the time that [the] study was published Dr. Sangmur said that there is a need for further careful study before it can be considered as a cause-and-effect relationship.[19]

Second, the policy makers used the scientific uncertainty to choose interpretations which supported their own policy preferences. Tests indicating that DES should be more strictly regulated were questioned because of the difficulty of extrapolating experimental data from mice to humans. The statistical validity of experiments and the means of determining levels and causes of residues in beef cattle tested by USDA were criticized. The difficulty of establishing causal relationships statistically created a grey area in which the FDA exploited the disagreement among scientists to justify pulling back from regulation in response to pressure from drug manufacturers and cattle growers. By late 1971, however, the growing number of interested parties combined with the development of a stronger scientific concensus on the dangers of DES to precipitate a change in agency policy.

THE FDA BANS DES

On December 3, 1971, an FDA researcher was asked to review a paper by Carl Gass et al. that had just come to notice although it had been published seven years earlier.[20] The Gass paper contained evidence that 6.25 ppb of DES in the diet caused a significant increase in cancer (mammary adenocarcinoma) in mice. The 6.25 ppb figure was especially striking to the FDA staff because it had previously appeared in a letter to the editor of the *Washington Post* with the signature of David Hawkins of the Natural Resources Defense Council (NRDC).[21] This council was filing suit to force the FDA to ban DES in cattle feed. It was assumed that the NRDC would use the evidence from the Gass paper in its litigation, so it appeared to be critical for the FDA to evaluate it immediately.

An FDA researcher devoted a weekend to the complex calculations needed to evaluate the paper, and presented his conclusions to his colleagues on Monday. By Wednesday, the evaluation of the Gass paper was in the hands of the Fountain subcommittee, and lengthy hearings were held the next week. The conclusion of this evaluation was that DES will cause cancer in concentrations so low that no available test could detect it. The FDA reaction was strong. The Fountain committee reprinted a number of internal FDA memoranda from December 1971 and early 1972 which document the detail and vehemence of the scientific debate within the agency.

The Gass paper used a method of determining carcinogenesis that differed from the usual FDA procedure. The FDA relied primarily on the statistical significance of the experimental results. Gass relied upon the Mantel-Bryan approximation. The latter approach uses experimental data on level of response, number of subjects, and magnitude of test levels to answer the question, "What can one project with high assurance to be a safe level at a given specified risk?"[22] Thus the researcher decides before-hand what level of risk he is willing to accept and then determines what dose corresponds to that risk. A one in one million risk level seems to be standard for carcinogens, but the specification of acceptable risk levels is clearly a policy, rather than a technical decision.

In addition to specification of the risk level, the Mantel-Bryan method involves extrapolating downwards from the smallest experimental dose that elicits a response to the safe level previously chosen. The researcher has some choice about the slope of the curve used in the extrapolation to the safe level: the steeper the slope, the higher the level of safety.

The Mantel-Bryan concept is widely accepted by toxicologists as a reasonable solution to several of the problems in evaluating risk. It avoids using only significance tests because the experimental data differ according to numbers of animals and dose levels; and it circumvents the questions of causality and of safety by seeking a safe dose at a *specified* level of risk. It does not resolve, however, the problem of the relative susceptibilities of animals and humans to carcinogens. Rather, in choosing the confidence level, the slope of the extrapolation line, and the acceptable risk, the researcher is making judgments about this relationship. The lower the confidence level and the steeper the slope, the more nearly is the human response assumed to be like the animal's. Using the most conservative figures for the Mantel-Bryan approximation, that is, the figures most like animal responses, the Gass data suggest that a "virtually safe" level was .3 ppb for an acceptable risk of 1 in 100 million.[23]

Although one FDA administrator endorsed the Mantel-Bryan method as a sensible solution to the "impossible" decision between carcinogeneity and noncarcinogeneity,[24] it was immediately attacked. One serious criti-cism is that the method consistently gives "safe" estimates that are so low as to be the practical equivalent of zero. Thus in effect it represents little change from the Delaney Clause, although with increasingly sensitive residue tests it could make a difference at some time in the future. Other critics said that such low tolerances contradicted "sound toxicological judgment," which suggested that much higher tolerance levels are reason-able.

By 1972, most of the important scientific issues had been carefully scrutinized by FDA staff members. Though agreement had not emerged, there was certainly a greatly increased level of awareness among the staff, especially administrators, about the importance of the Mantel-Bryan approach in determining which substances are carcinogens. Differences still existed about the implied policy, but common acceptance of the utility of the approach formed a basis for discussion. By 1973, the FDA was incorporating the Mantel-Bryan method into its provisional standards for carcinogens in food.

Those who attacked the new approach were concerned more with its policy implications than with the method itself. DES manufacturers and cattle growers all supported the most conservative DES policy. FDA officials were concerned about growing public awareness of DES and about the uses to which the Gass data might be put, especially in the suit filed by the Natural Resources Defense Council. The crucial development, however, was the growing debate among FDA's own experts, suggesting that it would be difficult to refute the Gass paper in court. At last the FDA changed its policy.

On March 11, 1972, the agency published a notice of opportunity for a hearing on a proposed ban on the use of DES in liquid premixes of cattle and sheep feed. In June, a notice appeared in the Federal Register calling for a hearing as the best way to make public the benefits and disadvantages of alternate courses of action about DES. The Commissioner of FDA emphasized that he saw no public health hazards but wished to explore information on residues and regulatory possibilities. In early July 1972, the USDA announced finding the highest residues of the year of DES in beef and lamb, and the Director of the National Cancer Institute promptly stated publicly that it would be "prudent" to ban DES.[25]

On July 28, results of a new radioactive tracer study became available. It conclusively showed detectable residues in beef liver after withdrawal periods of three, five, and even seven days, and suggested that DES might be present for at least 30 days.[26] This new study meant that an area of judgment in residue testing was no longer open to differing interpretations. Despite replies from 15 of the 25 DES manufacturers stating their objections to the proposed ban, on July 31, the FDA withdrew approval for all liquid and dry premixes containing DES. It did, however, continue to permit ear implants.

The FDA carefully avoided justifying the ban through use of the Delaney Clause, noting that 17 years' use had brought no evidence of a health hazard. The decision emphasized instead that the requirements of the animal drug amendments had not been strictly fulfilled. This same argument was used when the FDA banned all DES implants in April 1973 after another new study showed residues in livers as many as 120 days after implantation.[27]

The FDA hesitated to use the Delaney Clause for several reasons. First, the agency avoided using the legislation in any of its decisions as part of a campaign to change that law. The agency preferred to determine the relative safety of carcinogenic substances rather than simply banning all of them.[28] It was supported in this campaign by President Nixon, who proposed to Congress in 1972 that it dilute the Delaney Clause in order to avoid having to ban all foods because they contain a few molecules of naturally occurring carcinogens.[29]

Second, in couching its decision in narrow regulatory terms, the agency left itself open to attack. Critics claimed the FDA chose this route so that the ban would not stand up in court, and DES could continue to be used while public and scientific pressures on the FDA would ease.[30] Indeed the U.S. Court of Appeals in Washington, D.C. overturned both FDA orders on appeal by several manufacturers, citing a lack of compliance with fixed regulatory procedures. Commenting on the issues, the Court said that in the explicitly stated absence of a public health hazard, the FDA had no reason to act hastily, without hearings and without noting the "benefits of DES in enhancing meat production."[31] Those who were skeptical of the FDA's intentions in the original withdrawal notice were further convinced when the agency announced that it would not appeal the decision, but would instead hold a new hearing within 30 days to determine whether new information was available to warrant continued use of DES. No hearing was ever held.

The FDA has never reissued its withdrawal orders, and the USDA has continued to find residues of DES in the samples it tests. In September 1975, the Senate voted a ban on the use of DES in cattle feed effective until the Secretary of HEW decides on the basis of scientific studies that it is safe for human consumption. The House has never voted on the bill.

Finally the medical use of DES as a morning-after pill became a public issue. Under pressure from Ralph Nader and others, the FDA agreed in 1973 to require manufacturers to include a pamphlet explaining the risks and possible side-effects of the pill, and to ask doctors to tell the patient about its risks and benefits, so that she can make an informed choice.

Despite its inconclusive status, the DES case is representative of many cases in which the public and experts play a part in obtaining a change in public policy. As long as available technical data were ambiguous, political criteria for regulation prevailed. Pressure of a pending lawsuit, however, precipitated the reworking of data and led to greater technical consensus. This reduced the political latitude of the agency and imposed limits on its options. Although the FDA managed to circumvent these limits in its policy toward DES, its later actions in the broader area of animal food additives have been constrained by the consensus achieved in the DES case. Thus this study suggests the role of scientific consensus in narrowing policy options and achieving more effective public control over a wide range of policy decisions.

NOTES

1. Nicholas Wade, "DES: A Case Study of Regulatory Abdication," *Science* 177 (July 28, 1972), 335.

2. See Joseph D. Cooper, ed., *Decision-Making on the Efficacy and Safety of Drugs* (Washington, DC: Interdisciplinary Communication Associates, Inc., 1971), pp. 23, 29. See also Marver Bernstein, *Regulating Business by Independent Commission* (Princeton, NJ: Princeton University Press, 1955), 101, 114. For a more current bibliography on regulation and a useful analysis in itself, see Roger G. Noll, *Reforming Regulation* (Washington, DC: Brookings Institution, 1971).

3. Morton Mintz, *By Prescription Only* (Boston: Houghton Mifflin, 1967); James S. Turner, *The Chemical Feast: Ralph Nader's Study Group Report on the FDA* (New York: Grossman, 1970); and John Pekkanen, *The American Connection* (Chicago: Follett, 1973) are examples. These works are primarily popular exposés of the FDA's faults.

4. An account of the most recent agency review panel appears in "FDA: Review Panel Faults Commissioner's Defense of Agency," *Science* 192 (June 11, 1976), 1084-1087.

5. *Bell v. Goddard*, 366 F. 2d 177 (CA.7, 1966).

6. See John White, "The Stilbestrol Controversy," *National Health Foundation Bulletin,* January 1970, 10-14.

7. See Wade, and Committee on Government Operations, 12th Report, Regulation of Diethylstilbestrol (Washington, DC: GPO, 1972), hereafter DES Report, 18-20.

8. A. L. Herbst, H. Ulfelder, D. C. Poskanzer, "Adenocarcinoma of the Vagina: Association of Maternal Stilbestrol Therapy with Tumor Appearance in Young Women," *New England Journal of Medicine,* 284 (1971), 878-881.

9. Committee on Government Operations, Hearings, Regulation of Diethylstilbestrol (Washington, DC: GPO, 1972), hereafter DES Hearings, Part I, esp. 7-9, 13-17, 51-52, 98-100. Also DES Report, 47-50.

10. *Natural Resources Defense Council v. Elliott Richardson.* Case was never heard as plaintiff dropped the suit when DES was banned in 1972. See DES Hearings, 205-207.

11. *Washington Post,* November 12, 19, 30, December 8, 1971; February 14, 1972.

12. DES Hearings, 7.

13. Report to the Surgeon General by the Ad Hoc Committee on the Evaluation of Low Levels of Environmental Chemical Carcinogens. Report reprinted in DES Hearings, 230-246.

14. FDA regulation 121.5, quoted in DES Hearings, 213.

15. DES Hearings, 247-248; and Surgeon General's Ad Hoc Committee.

16. DES Hearings, 230.

17. Food Additive Hearings, 453; DES Hearings, 253-254.

18. On a whole body weight basis. If we assume estrogens are only in the blood, the increase would be 22 times normal. DES Hearings, 175.

19. DES Hearings, 84.

20. "Carcinogenic Dose-Response Curve to Oral Diethylstilbestrol," *Journal of the National Cancer Institute* 33 (1964), 917-977.

21. Letter to the Editor, *Washington Post,* November 30, 1978.

22. Nathan Mantel and W. K. Bryan, "Safety Testing of Carcinogenic Agents," *Journal of the National Cancer Institute* 27 (August 1961), 455-470.

23. See FDA Memo, January 26, 1975; also Gross memo reprinted in DES Hearings, 115-118.

24. DES Hearings, 62.

25. *Washington Post,* July 10, 1972.

26. Study reported in 37FR 15748.

27. 38FR 10485.

28. Peter Hutt, in *How Safe is Safe,* 118.

29. See *Science,* 179: 666-668.

30. Interviews.

31. January 25, 1974. This followed a reiteration of the FDA decision on October 22, 1973 in response to appeals by two manufacturers. Also see *New York Times,* January 26, 1974.

6

SETTING OCCUPATIONAL HEALTH STANDARDS: THE VINYL CHLORIDE CASE

Michael Brown

On January 22, 1974, the B. F. Goodrich Company announced that three workers from one of its polyvinyl chloride production plants had died from angiosarcoma of the liver. The disease, a form of cancer that attacks the liver's blood vessels, was considered to be relatively rare, killing 25-30 people each year in the United States. Soon after the announcement, other companies in the vinyl chloride industry reported deaths from the same disease. By May, 13 vinyl chloride workers had died.

These reports brought public and government attention to an industry that employs more than 7,000 people. Labor unions called for stringent government regulation of workplace exposure to vinyl chloride. The Occupational Safety and Health Administration (OSHA), the federal agency responsible for workplace safety and health, began an investigation into the relationship of vinyl chloride to occupational illness. In April 1974, the agency enacted an emergency temporary standard that reduced exposure from previously acceptable levels. Following publication of a proposed permanent standard which would severely restrict levels of vinyl chloride in the work environment, OSHA invited comment at a series of public hearings.

The hearings generated criticism and debate and underscored some of the technical difficulties involved in setting standards where there is contested scientific evidence. Debate arose over determining safe exposure levels to carcinogenic substances, the technological feasibility of controlling exposures, and the potential economic effects of regulation. Eventually OSHA established a permanent standard that reduced employee exposure to what was considered the lowest feasible level.

In the years following the creation of OSHA, attention had focused on its internal organizational development. Relatively little attention was paid to criteria for setting health and safety standards. Although OSHA had established limits for exposure to other carcinogenic substances, the vinyl chloride standard represented the first attempt to delineate guidelines for the standard setting process.

OSHA had a choice between two fundamental concepts of occupational safety and health. One assumes that the only object of a regulatory agency is to protect employees from all workplace hazards to health and safety. The central question is whether or not production adversely affects the health of workers. Exposure limits would then be set at levels that best assure employee health, regardless of its implications for production. Indeed production would cease where government regulators determine that it is technically impossible to alter production processes to assure the safety of workers through limits on exposures.

The other possible foundation for a regulatory policy assumes that occupational health and safety is only one component in a set of social benefits and costs. While health and safety may be of primary importance to the individual employee, they may be of secondary importance to the society as a whole. This concept suggests that where it is technically unfeasible or economically too costly to eliminate workplace hazards, compromises will be made between health and production. In contrast to the first concept, the absence of safety techniques does not imply stopping production, but balancing its benefits against employee health.

During its formative years, OSHA tended to rely on this second policy concept, although not in a systematic way. The vinyl chloride case legitimized the introduction of technical and economic considerations into the setting of standards; for the permanent standard that was set balanced worker health and safety against economic and technical feasibility. The establishment of exposure limits to toxic substances thus became a debate over what constituted "feasible" standards.

GOVERNMENT INVOLVEMENT IN
OCCUPATIONAL HEALTH AND SAFETY

Federal interest in occupational health and safety began with financial aid to state-run programs during World War II. In 1952, Senator Hubert

Humphrey introduced legislation that would have authorized the federal government to set and enforce safety standards, but the bill was not approved. Other bills proposed throughout the 1950s and early 1960s to aid the development of state programs also failed. The first successful fight for a strong safety and health law and compensation benefits was organized by rank and file miners around the issue of black lung disease. The campaign resulted in the Coal Mine Health and Safety Act of 1969 and the Black Lung Benefits Act of 1972.[1]

Agitation for large scale federal involvement in occupational health and safety led to the introduction of a bill in 1969, and again in 1970, supported by the Oil, Chemical, and Atomic Workers, the Steelworkers, the AFL-CIO, and public interest groups. The opposition of industry and the efforts by the Nixon administration to substitute a weaker bill did not prevent passage and the Occupational Safety and Health Act was signed into law by President Nixon at the end of 1970.[2]

This Act required the Secretary of Labor to develop and establish safety and health standards, conduct inspections and investigations of workplaces, issue citations and propose penalties for noncompliance, and promote worker education concerning occupational safety and health practices. These functions were placed under the newly formed Occupational Safety and Health Administration (OSHA).

In its initial years, OSHA promulgated interim standards based on criteria set by voluntary private organizations, such as the American National Standards Institute. These standards had been determined by a consensus in the particular industry. Most related to safety: those directed toward health were often out of date and inapplicable to present conditions.[3] OSHA was required to set permanent standards within two years.

New standards are developed with the aid of advisory committees and public hearings, and are based on recommendations from the National Institute of Occupational Safety and Health (NIOSH) in the Department of Health, Education and Welfare. Advisory committees are usually composed of less than 20 members balanced between employers and employees, technical personnel, and representatives of state and other federal agencies. Once a standard has been proposed by OSHA and published in the Federal Register, public comment is invited. The permanent standard is the responsibility of the Secretary of Labor, but enforcement is the responsibility of OSHA's field offices.

OSHA has faced a variety of problems. Inadequate budgets and limited technical staff have led to inconsistent inspections and reliance on voluntary compliance. Industry has complained that the standards are either too vague or too complex and are enormously expensive. Labor unions on the other hand accused OSHA of being lax, missing deadlines for establishment of new standards, failing to follow up employee requests for on-site inspection, and relaxing standards in the face of industry pressure. The unions argued that OSHA emphasized accident prevention while ignoring workplace exposures to toxic substances that result in the deaths of more than 100,000 people each year. They called for increased attention to the effects of toxic substances on the health of workers.[4] By 1975, OSHA had issued four emergency temporary standards related to health, all prompted by union petitions. Only three new permanent health standards—asbestos, 14 carcinogens, and vinyl chloride—have been adopted.

NIOSH in its early years was also limited by a low budget and could produce at most 30 criteria documents for proposed standards.[5] With over 1200 toxic substances on its 1973 list, not much impact on occupational health could be expected.

VINYL CHLORIDE PRODUCTION

Vinyl chloride monomer (VCM) has been in commercial production since the 1920s. The monomer, rarely used in finished products, is employed for the most part in the manufacture of polyvinyl chloride (PVC) and related copolymers. The United States consumed 3.7 billion pounds of PVC and other copolymers in 1975, enough to make it the second most widely used plastic in the country. It has many advantages; it is cheap, resistant to fire, water, and chemicals, and malleable into a variety of shapes. Consumer uses include pipes and tubing, floor tiles, phonograph records, automobile seatcovers, and wire and cable insulation.

VCM AND PVC PRODUCTION PRIOR TO 1974

The vinyl chloride industry is divided into three segments: VCM production, PVC resin production, and consumer product fabrication. VCM production employed about 1,500 workers in 1974. The production process was highly automated in open-air facilities involving minimal employee contact with the chemical. Most plants were located in warm climates near petroleum-rich areas in order to minimize the transport costs of the raw materials.

The PVC segment of the industry tended to be in colder northern climates, requiring enclosed structures. Major producers of PVC resins included B. F. Goodrich, Firestone, Conoco, and Diamond Shamrock. Employment in 1974 was about 5,600 people. The most widely used method of PVC production involved pumping water and the proper chemicals into a sealed container called a reactor and adding liquefied VCM (a process called "charging"). The batch was heated under pressure, mixed, and converted to PVC. After being pumped out of the reactor, it was drained, dried into a powdery material, bagged, and then shipped to fabricators who created the finished products.

After the polymer had been discharged from the vessel and the pressure reduced to normal, the reactor was aired out by dropping a hose to the bottom of the tank. The reactor was then ventilated into the workroom area. Loose residue was washed out with water and one or two workers entered the reactor to remove the polymer that remained on the reactor walls and mixer blades. This involved manual scraping with putty knives or the use of hammer and chisel. Residual VCM, trapped between the residue and the reactor walls, was released into the air when workers chipped off the polymer. Alternative cleaning methods, including high pressure water jets and solvents, were not widely used. The job of reactor cleaner was usually reserved for new employees; as they gained seniority they were transferred to other plant functions.[6]

RESEARCH ON TOXICITY

Studies of vinyl chloride's toxicity began as early as 1925 when experiments showed that VCM caused fatty degeneration in the liver and kidneys of test animals. Studies in 1930 described acute toxic effects in guinea pigs.[7] Large scale production began in the 1930s, and reports of serious injury appeared in the 1940s. During World War II, vinyl chloride, suggested as a surgical anesthetic, was found to cause heart irritation in animals. The first serious epidemiological evidence of vinyl chloride's toxicity was presented in a Russian medical journal in 1949. The researchers found "hepatitis-like changes" in the livers of 18 out of 73 workers in a Soviet PVC plant. They attributed the injuries to exposure to polychlorobiphenyl (PCB) plasticizer rather than vinyl chloride.[8]

Other problems identified by European researchers included skin lesions, circulatory disorders, and gastritis.[9] Exposure levels, however, were not monitored, for producers had little incentive to attend to occupational hazards.

At the end of the 1950s, Dow Chemical Company began research on the effects of repeated exposures by inhalation at different levels of vinyl chloride. Their results suggested that vinyl chloride had a "slight capacity to cause liver and kidney injury on repeated exposures," and they suggested a maximum exposure level for the substance of 100 parts per million parts air (ppm) with the time-weighted average over eight hours not to exceed 50 ppm.[10] Dow Chemical began to lower exposures in its own production facilities but did not inform its employees of the dangers from VCM exposure.

Researchers at Rutgers University, supported by Allied Chemical Corporation, challenged Dow's assertions of toxicity, claiming that long-term exposures had no toxic significance and recommending a threshold limit value of 500 ppm.[11]

In 1960, two men died following acute inhalation of vinyl chloride monomer. Autopsies showed massive changes in their liver, spleen, and kidneys, but the researcher did not attribute death solely to vinyl chloride exposure.[12]

While Dow began reducing worker exposure, the rest of the industry relied on the suggested level of 500 ppm. The American Industrial Hygienists Association reviewed the available studies and recommended retaining the 500 ppm limit. Ignoring the acute inhalation report, they argued that, at high levels, anesthesia was the only significant effect of acute exposure and, at low levels, the vapor had little or no irritating effect. They stated, however, that the evidence was "conflicting concerning cumulative toxicity."[13]

In the mid-1960s, company physicians began noting a high incidence of clubbed fingers, severe pain, bone changes, and a phenomenon known as Raynaud's syndrome—cyanosis of the extremities—among vinyl chloride workers. The disease became known as acroosteolysis. Researchers at the B. F. Goodrich Company conducted an epidemiological study investigating the relationship between vinyl chloride and the disease, and found 31 cases of acroosteolysis in the hands of polymerization workers. Researchers believed the disease to be the result of physical and chemical exposure and individual susceptibility. Noting that improvement often occurred after discontinuing exposure to vinyl chloride, they recommended medical screening to remove vulnerable individuals from reactor cleaning jobs, rather than altering work practices. A similar study sponsored by the Manufacturing Chemists Association reported in 1971 that a definite causal relationship between vinyl chloride and acroosteolysis could not be established. This study also suggested screening practices rather than control of vinyl chloride levels in the work environment.[14]

The lack of concern over VCM's low-level toxicity was reflected in OSHA's initial acceptance of the 500 ppm suggested limit. Vinyl chloride appeared on NIOSH's 1972 toxic substance priority list, but it was expected to take a number of years before they could develop criteria for a new standard.

The first public announcement of a link between VCM and cancer was made at the 10th International Cancer Congress held in 1970 in Houston. Dr. Pierluigi Viola, an Italian physician employed by the Belgian firm of Solvay & Cie, presented evidence that rats exposed over time to 30,000 ppm concentrations of VCM developed cancers in the ear canals, lungs, and bones.[15] Further research by Viola, released in 1974, revealed tumors in rats exposed to concentrations as low as 500 ppm.

Another group of Italian researchers led by Cesare Maltoni had been pursuing studies of the effects of different chemicals on the respiratory tracts of Italian workers. In 1970, the research was broadened to include workers in VCM and PVC production facilities. Reviewing Viola's work, the researchers planned experiments to clarify the carcinogenic risk from vinyl chloride. These studies, sponsored by several other large European chemical companies, duplicated occupational conditions to determine the effects of different exposures down to levels of 250 ppm. Early results showed that extended exposures to 250 ppm produced various cancers, including angiosarcoma, in the liver, kidneys, and ear canals of rats.[16]

Maltoni's contract with the industrial firms stipulated that the results of the research and the rights to public disclosure were to be controlled by the sponsors. Information on the studies was offered to the Manufacturing Chemists Association with the proviso that the U.S. companies keep the information confidential. MCA agreed and received the Maltoni study and the early results in January 1973. Neither employees, company doctors, nor government officials knew about the studies. MCA asked Industrial Bio-Test Laboratories, Inc. to replicate Maltoni's research and, in addition, asked Tabershaw-Cooper Associates, Inc. to conduct an epidemiological mortality study of current and former workers in the U.S. vinyl chloride industry. MCA received permission in July 1973 to give the information to government officials.

At a later meeting between industry representatives and the government, the nature of the information exchanged was disputed. Industry representatives contended they had given all relevant information to NIOSH. NIOSH officials maintained that the significance of preliminary studies by a little-known Italian researcher was not readily apparent in July 1973. Both sides admit that angiosarcoma of the liver was not discussed. In any case, at the time NIOSH did not consider the findings serious enough to warrant immediate attention, and the 500 ppm standard remained in effect until after B. F. Goodrich disclosed the deaths of three PVC workers in January 1974.

In December 1973, an employee at B. F. Goodrich's Louisville, Kentucky, PVC plant had died from angiosarcoma of the liver. His doctor, a medical consultant to the company, recalled similar deaths at the plant, and, following a review of death records, confirmed that three (and possibly four) deaths of plant employees had been due to the disease.[17] Company officials informed NIOSH on January 22, 1974, which then relayed the information to OSHA. Both agencies turned to establishing criteria for safe exposure to vinyl chloride. OSHA began plant inspections and, on February 15, held a public fact-finding hearing where Dr. Maltoni presented new results which showed cancers produced in test animals at levels as low at 50 ppm. The Industrial Union Department of the AFL-CIO and the United Rubber Workers Union signed a joint petition, later supported by the Oil, Chemical, and Atomic Workers International Union, for an emergency temporary standard that would severely restrict VCM exposure. Industry, however, urged that normal rule-making procedures be followed, and that a thoroughgoing investigation be undertaken before government takes action.[18]

SETTING THE STANDARD

On April 5, 1974, OSHA issued an emergency standard which required VCM and PVC producers to reduce exposure levels to 50 ppm. The temporary standard had to be replaced by a permanent standard within six months. The proposed permanent standard published on May 10 established a maximum "no-detectable level" of exposure, to be met through engineering controls on the industrial process. It permitted the use of respiratory equipment in emergencies or where even the lowest feasible exposure attainable through engineering controls failed to meet the standard. OSHA sought to involve affected groups and the public in the standard-setting process by scheduling public hearings.

Prior to the hearings, Industrial Bio-Test Laboratories, Inc. published its preliminary findings from the study sponsored by the vinyl chloride industry. They supported Maltoni's work which demonstrated the existence of tumors in mice exposed to levels as low as 50 ppm. At a workshop, scientists presented 20 papers documenting the dangers of VCM exposure.

The hearings resulted in over 200 oral and written statements totalling 4,000 pages. Employees, employers, labor unions, public health groups, independent experts, physicians, and government officials commented on the proposed standard. These participants polarized into two camps: industry opposed the standards, other groups supported them.

Controversy focused on two fundamental technical questions. The first was the question of a safe exposure level. The lowest level at which studies had been conducted on VCM's carcinogenicity was 50 ppm. Scientific evidence did not exist on the effects of exposure at levels between zero and 50 ppm. Second was the question of feasibility. OSHA's mandate was to set a standard to assure health "to the extent feasible," but interpretation of feasibility varied. Some referred to technological feasibility while others insisted on an economic interpretation. The hearings were swamped by concern over the technological feasibility of engineering controls and the economic costs involved. OSHA's implicit acceptance of an economic interpretation is suggested by its request for an independent evaluation of the economic impact of proposed regulations.

INDUSTRY'S VIEWS

Throughout the controversy industry sought to downplay the dangers of exposure to workers, minimize the environmental effects, and resist promulgation of standards which would require considerable investment.[19] They argued that health and safety in the workplace must be evaluated relative to the benefits of production. Most of the presentations stressed problems of technological feasibility and the economic costs of the proposed standard. They posed the issue in terms of jobs *versus* health.

Engineering studies conducted by Firestone suggested that a standard requiring a no-detectable exposure level was impossible to achieve through engineering controls given the state of the technology. Indeed the lowest achievable exposure level was not predictable. Moreover they estimated that a minimum expenditure of $50 million would be necessary to meet the standard. Firestone, claimed its president, would have to shut down its production plants if the proposed standard were put into effect. Similarly, a representative of Tenneco stated that the only options available would be to put all employees on respirators or shut down production.

The Society of the Plastics Industry hired a consultant to evaluate the effects on the American economy of a shutdown of the PVC industry. They argued that if enactment of a no-detectable standard resulted in closing all PVC resin plants, this could result in a loss of 1.7 to 2.2 million jobs in related industries and $65 to $90 billion annually in domestic production.

Industry also presented evidence against the use of respirators: it was difficult to get workers to wear them consistently because the face masks affected speech, body temperature, and breathing, often causing psychological stress. Moreover nonportable respirators would constitute a safety hazard in the plant due to air hose connections up to 50 feet long. Finally, industry presented epidemiological evidence indicating that the incidence of angiosarcoma of the liver occurred primarily among reactor cleaners. Those workers were regularly exposed to concentrations in excess of 200 ppm during an eight-hour day. The Dow study noted no increase in mortality for the population exposed to levels less than 200 ppm. OSHA, it was argued, was not justified in basing the proposed standard on evidence from experimental studies on rodents uncorroborated by human experience.

As an alternative to the proposed standard, several manufacturers proposed maximum-exposure limits in the 20-40 ppm range. A Firestone plant manager cited improvements in cleaning procedures that reduced the need for workers to enter the reactors and also reduced exposures to less than 50 ppm. Manufacturers argued that since conditions had improved through the initiative of the industry itself, the standard should be keyed to what was achievable by most companies.

Throughout, the chemical industry maintained that it had acted in the best interests of workers concerning known workplace hazards. The VCM and PVC producers maintained that they did not knowingly subject workers to dangerous substances, and noted that it was the industry, not government or independent scientists, that had initiated research when evidence of a potential toxic substance first appeared.

SUPPORTERS OF THE PROPOSED STANDARD

Organized labor, NIOSH officials, independent scientists and organizations interested in occupational health united to support the proposed standard. They stressed the duty of OSHA to protect the health and safety of workers, arguing that economic impact was irrelevant to the standard-setting process. In the adversary context of the hearings these groups were compelled to rebut industry's arguments, and much of their material tried to prove that the proposed standard was technologically feasible. Anthony Mazzochi of the Oil, Chemical, and Atomic Workers argued that since the PVC manufacturers had already achieved significantly reduced exposures in just a few months, greater reduction could be expected in the future.

Peter Bommarito, President of the United Rubber Workers, accused industry of cloaking the issues in terms of economic expenditures and technical feasibility when the real concern should be whether the plastic could be produced safely. If it could not, he argued, it should be phased out and replaced by substitutes.

Countering arguments against a possible shutdown of the industry, Mazzochi reminded OSHA of the asbestos standard where similar arguments had proved spurious. He felt that the Firestone engineering studies were merely a ploy to force a weaker standard.

To support the no-detectable level, government scientists testified that it was impossible to quantify a safe exposure with the present state of knowledge. The lack of data on the different exposures precluded reliable epidemiological studies on the long-term effects of varying exposures. It was important to include an adequate margin of safety in the standard since studies had not been conducted at levels less than 50 ppm.

Moreover scientists argued that the failure of the Dow study to locate a substantial number of workers who had initially been exposed at least 20 years previously, mandated that the only prudent course was a no-detectable standard.

Like the manufacturers, the union opposed the use of respirators. But they also wanted control of PVC resin dust (which may cause pulmonary fibrosis) and residual VCM levels entrapped in PVC products to be included in the final standard.

Union representatives challenged industry's claim to have acted in the best interests of workers' health, citing requests for work clothing, more showers, and yearly medical checkups that had been consistently refused. Employee health was considered by industry to be secondary to profits. A PVC production worker stated in graphic terms the need for regulation:

> It boils down to this: If vinyl chloride isn't controlled, we probably are going to die; if it is controlled we will live healthy lives like you people behind the desks.

OTHER STUDIES CONSIDERED BY OSHA

To help evaluate the proposed standard, Tabershaw-Cooper Associates presented a mortality study to OSHA in July. The study demonstrated that "cancers of the digestive system (primarily angiosarcoma), respiratory system, brain, and cancers of unknown site, as well as lymphomas, occurred more often than expected in those members of the study population with the greatest estimated exposure."[20] The inadequate representation of workers with long exposures led Tabershaw-Cooper to indicate that further investigation was needed.

An OSHA-sponsored study by Foster D. Snell, Inc. to assess the economic impact of various alternative standards was completed in September. Data were gathered through plant visits and interviews with industry-related organizations, government agencies, and equipment manufacturers and suppliers. The study's primary conclusion indicated that it was impossible to achieve a no-detectable exposure level in VCM and PVC production solely through engineering controls. The report found that while VCM concentrations could be greatly eliminated by engineering methods, respiratory protection would be constantly needed to meet a 1 ppm standard. Costs would rise rapidly with decreasing target-exposure levels. The analysts concluded that OSHA should have a phased reduction of maximum levels keyed to available technology and equipment.[21]

OSHA'S DECISION–THE PERMANENT STANDARD

OSHA issued its permanent standard on October 4, 1974. The major change from the earlier version was the quantification of a maximum limit to exposure of 1 ppm averaged over an 8-hour period with a ceiling of 5 ppm averaged over any 15-minute period. This standard applies to all segments of the vinyl chloride industry, including fabricators, with employers required to monitor employee exposures. It further requires engineering and work-practice controls to reduce exposures to the lowest level possible; where levels do not meet the exposure limits, respiratory protection is required. The standard mandates daily record-keeping of access to areas where exposure to vinyl chloride is likely, and medical examination of all employees exposed to vinyl chloride with maintenance of medical records for a minimum of 30 years. The standard was scheduled to go into effect on January 1, 1975.

OSHA concluded that VCM "must be regarded as a human carcinogen," citing animal studies in three species. In rejecting industry's arguments for a standard in the 20 to 40 ppm range, OSHA claimed that science could not yet determine a safe exposure level for carcinogenic substances, and denied that the problem was specific to reactor cleaners. The agency referred to employees who had not worked directly in PVC production yet had succumbed to vinyl chloride-related disease. OSHA argued that the lack of experimental studies conducted at levels less than 50 ppm did not obviate the need for a lower standard.

OSHA, however, rejected a no-detectable level because "it would require maintenance of an average level significantly more difficult to attain through feasible engineering controls." Eugene Regad in OSHA's Office of Standards Development suggested the minimum detection point of widely available measuring devices was used as the effective level. More sensitive devices were deemed too expensive and required operation and evaluation by a trained chemist, rather than a technician.

OSHA believed that fabricators could easily meet the requirements while the VCM and PVC production segments would probably have several job categories requiring respiratory protection. OSHA hoped that industry would continue to develop new technology and work practices to reduce dependence on respirators, but denied that respirators should be avoided on grounds of their inconvenience.

The final summary of OSHA's decision stated:

> There is little dispute that VC is carcinogenic to man. . . . However, the precise level of exposure which poses a hazard and the question of whether a "safe" exposure level exists, cannot be definitively answered on the record. Nor is it clear to what extent exposures can be feasibly reduced. We cannot wait until indisputable answers to these questions are available, because lives of employees are at stake. Therefore, we have had to exercise our best judgment on the basis of the best available evidence. These judgments have required a balancing process, in which the overriding consideration has been the protection of employees.[22]

Legal motions by manufacturers to overturn the standard were denied by the U.S. Court of Appeals which judged that the combination of engineering controls and respirators could meet the 1 ppm level. Interestingly, the judgment did not address the issue of whether or not feasibility should be a criterion for determination of a standard.[23]

The predictions by industry about the dire consequences of a stringent standard failed to materialize. Financial costs have not devastated the industry: it is estimated that OSHA regulations (exclusive of record-keeping) will result in approximately a 5% increase in the cost of PVC.[24]

WORKPLACE HEALTH AND THE
VINYL CHLORIDE STANDARD

During the standard-setting process, OSHA rejected most of the contentions of industry and set a standard closer to the view of workers. It is likely that the establishment of an average exposure limit of 1 ppm (with excursions up to 5 ppm) will reduce vinyl chloride related disease. This "victory" for workers, however, came with a price. While the standard was stringent, and workers gained protection from vinyl chloride-related disease, the decision set a precedent for possibly less protective future standards. For the vinyl chloride case signaled a significant move to make feasibility a major consideration in the determination of a health standard. To some extent, OSHA was forced to consider feasibility by its mandate that a standard be set "which most adequately assures, to the extent feasible, . . . that no employee will suffer material impairment of health.

The question of feasibility was open to broad interpretation and could have played a very minor role. Yet OSHA was pressured to consider feasibility as an important basis for its health standards.

In the standard-setting process, OSHA rapidly discovered the difficulty of distinguishing between technological and economic feasibility. The very significance of technical feasibility rested on the economic costs of its achievement. Worker protection was not simply a question of lowering exposures; OSHA had to consider the cost to industry of meeting a stringent standard and the economic impact of a shutdown where the standard could not be met. Unwilling to impose possible severe economic costs on industry, OSHA rejected a no-detectable level standard. Moreover, by allowing the use of respiratory equipment in place of engineering controls, OSHA met the technical obligation for feasibility without a large financial impact.

OSHA was predisposed to emphasize the protection of workers, but when feasibility became central to its concern, attention necessarily shifted to the impact of regulatory decisions on the industry. One effect of the industry argument that a standard requiring a large investment would cause plant shutdowns is the possible stimulation of a flow of capital away from areas with strict workplace controls.[25] Industry posed the issue as jobs *versus* health, pointing to the severe economic consequences to the worker and to the economy as a whole. Adopting this view, OSHA defined the issue less in terms of the absolute safety of production workers (as demanded by Peter Bommarito and other economists), than the feasibility of safety measures.

Accepting feasibility as a legitimate criterion of occupational health and safety, OSHA then had to deal with its determination. Here OSHA and the vinyl chloride industry disagreed. Industry defined a safe exposure level as one that could be easily met without much investment; technical and economic considerations were the guides for determining safety. OSHA, on the other hand, resolved first to determine a safe exposure level and then to moderate it by questions of feasibility. The major problem with this approach, illustrated by the vinyl chloride experience, was that OSHA depended on industry for the bulk of its scientific information.

In the absence of government regulation, industry-sponsored research in the past has had little influence on the control of workplace exposure. This is partly due to the belief that in the absence of proven effects in humans, animal studies are not to be trusted. But it also resulted from limited dissemination of information. Rarely were employees fully informed of the dangers of exposure to toxic substances by the industry that sponsored the studies; for example, Dow's failure to inform its workers of the Torkelson study and the withholding of Maltoni's work on cancer.

Following the announcement by B. F. Goodrich, OSHA found itself in a classic dilemma. On one side was pressure to set a standard restricting exposure. On the other, since few studies outside of industry had investigated vinyl chloride's toxicity, the agency had little information on which to base a standard. Lack of time precluded the possibility of conducting new tests to determine the effects of low-level exposures. Epidemiological studies were complicated by the failure of firms to maintain accurate work records and the difficulties encountered in locating workers who had been exposed several decades previously. While determining safety was complicated by inadequate information, determining feasibility was biased by the source of information—the industry itself.

The vinyl chloride case has served as a precedent for policy guidelines on carcinogen standards. To assure consistent attention to problems created by exposure to toxic substances, OSHA proposed, in October 1977, a comprehensive cancer policy. The policy would set a permissible exposure limit "on the basis of OSHA's belief as to the lowest feasible level. . . . [W]here the proposed level in the model permanent standard is shown to be infeasible to achieve, a higher figure may appear in the final standard."[26]

It is not clear what would happen in cases where the lowest feasible level is still dangerous and substitutes are unavailable. The emphasis on feasibility that began in the vinyl chloride case portends that economic and technical considerations may circumscribe OSHA's ability to protect workers from known cancer-causing substances.

NOTES

1. Daniel Berman, "Why Work Kills," *International Journal of Health Services* 7 (1977), 863-887.

2. OSHAct of 1970, PL 91-596, U.S. Congress Senate 91st Congress 2193, December 29, 1970.

3. Nicholas Ashford, *Crisis in the Workplace* (Cambridge: MIT Press, 1976).

4. Alexander J. Reiss, "Three Years of OSHA: The View from Within," *Monthly Labor Review* 98 (March 1975), 35-36; and "OSHA: Four Years of Frustration," *American Federationist* 82 (April 1975), 12-16.

5. Dr. Marcus Key, former director of NIOSH, estimated that in 1974 the development of criteria for a proposed standard cost between $200,000 and $300,000 and required 12-18 months to complete. The entire 1974 NIOSH budget was $26 million.

6. L. F. Albright, "Vinyl Chloride Processes," *Chemical Engineering* 74 (1967), 123-130; "Manufacture of Vinyl Chloride," *Chemical Engineering* 74 (1967), 219-226; and W. A. Cook et al., "Occupational Acroosteolysis. II. An Industrial Hygiene Study," *Archives of Environmental Health* 22 (1971), 74-82.

7. M. Turshen, "Disaster in Plastic," *Health/PAC Bulletin* 71 (1976), 1-16; and F. A. Patty, W. P. Yant, and C. P. Waite, "Acute Response of Guinea Pigs to Vapors of Some New Commercial Organic Compounds: V. Vinyl Chloride," *U.S. Weekly Public Health Service Reports* 45 (1930), 1963-1971.

8. S. R. Tribukh et al., "Working Conditions and Measures for Their Sanitation in the Production and Utilization of Vinyl Chloride Plastics," *Gigiena Sanit.* 10 (1949), 38.

9. G. E. Morris, "Vinyl Plastics: Their Dermatological and Chemical Aspects," *Archives of Industrial Hygiene and Occupational Medicine* 8, 535; and R. Williams et al., "Portal Hypertension in Idiopathic Topical Splenomegaly," *Lancet* I (1966), 329.

10. T. R. Torkelson, F. Oyen, and V. K. Rowe, "The Toxicity of Vinyl Chloride as Determined by Repeated Exposure of Laboratory Animals," *American Industrial Hygiene Association Journal* 22 (1961), 354-358.

11. A threshold limit value (TLV) is a concept used to describe the point at which no effect from exposure will result but above which may be harmful. D. Lester, L. A. Greenberg, and W. R. Adams, "Effects of Single and Repeated Exposures of Humans and Rats to Vinyl Chloride," *American Industrial Hygiene Association Journal* 24 (1963), 265-275.

12. H. Danziger, "Accidental Poisoning by Vinyl Chloride—Report of Two Cases," *Canadian Medical Journal* 82 (1960), 828-829.

13. "Hygienic Guide for Vinyl Chloride," *American Industrial Hygiene Association Journal* 25 (1963), 421-423.

14. R. H. Wilson et al., "Occupational Acroosteolysis," *Journal of the American Medical Association* 201 (1967), 577-581; B. D. Dinman et al., "Occupational Acroosteolysis. I. An Epidemiological Study," *Archives of Environmental Health* 22 (1971), 61-73; and V. N. Dodson et al., "Occupational Acroosteolysis. II," *Archives of Environmental Health* 22 (1971), 84-92.

15. P. L. Viola, "Canceragenic Effect of Vinyl Chloride," *Proceedings of the 10th International Cancer Congress,* Houston (1970, abstracts), 29; 20; and P. L. Viola, A. Bigoti, and A. Caputo, "Oncogenic Response of Rat Skin, Lungs, and Bones to Vinyl Chloride," *Cancer Research* 31 (1971), 516-522.

16. C. Maltoni and G. Lefemine, "Carcinogenicity—Bioassays of Vinyl Chloride: Current Results," *New York Academy of Sciences Annals* 246 (1975), 195-218; and C. Maltoni and G. Lefemine, "Carcinogenicity Bioassays of Vinyl Chloride: I. Research Plan and Early Results," *Environmental Research* 7 (1974), 387-405.

17. J. L. Creech and M. N. Johnson, "Angiosarcoma of the Liver in the Manufacture of Polyvinyl Chloride," *Journal of Occupational Medicine* 16 (1974), 150-151.

18. From testimony at "Informal Fact-Finding Hearing on Possible Hazards of Vinyl Chloride Manufacture and Use," February 15, 1974.

19. The following discussion of the positions of industry and the unions is taken from testimony at "Hearings on Proposed Standards for Occupational Exposure to Vinyl Chloride," June 25-July 10, 1974. Industry's desire for normal rule-making procedures is significant. There is a large time difference between the establishment of an emergency temporary standard followed by a permanent standard and the

regular process utilizing an advisory committee. The latter takes one to four years and is almost certain to land in court. If industry could have prevented the establishment of an emergency temporary standard, they would have effectively prevented any new standard for a long time. See Ashford, 249-251.

20. I. Tabershaw and W. Gaffey, "Mortality Study of Workers in Manufacture of Vinyl Chloride and Its Polymers," *Journal of Occupational Medicine* 16 (1974), 509.

21. Foster D. Snell, Inc., "Economic Impact Studies of the Effects of Proposed OSHA Standards for Vinyl Chloride," mimeo, September 1974.

22. "Standard for Exposure to Vinyl Chloride," 39 Federal Register 194: 35890-35898, October 4, 1974.

23. *Society of the Plastics Industry, Inc. et al., vs. Occupational Safety and Health Administration,* 509 F.2d 1301 (1975).

24. *Chemical and Engineering News,* April 7, 1975, 4.

25. Ray H. Elling, "Industrialization and Occupational Health in Underdeveloped Countries," *International Journal of Health Services* 7 (1977), 209-235.

26. "Identification, Classification and Regulation of Toxic Substances Posing a Potential Occupational Carcinogenic Risk," 42 Federal Register 192: 54148-54247, October 4, 1977.

PART III
REGULATION VERSUS FREEDOM OF CHOICE

Governmental decisions to ban a drug or to require the use of a technology for consumer protection inevitably impose constraints that infringe on individuals' freedom of choice. Sometimes the justification for such regulatory measures is that individual choices have social costs. Automobile accidents may primarily affect an individual but ultimately medical and insurance costs are borne by society. Regulations are also based on assumptions about the ability of individuals to make rational and enlightened decisions on their own behalf. Critics of regulation, however, perceive them as evidence of "authoritarian control" by the state, as "a violation of individual rights." These perceptions underpin the protests against fluoridation of water supplies, the proposed ban on saccharin, and compulsory motorcycle helmets. In such cases governmental decisions mandate universal compliance: everyone must partake of the decision and its consequences.

Judith Reppy's study of the airbag controversy raises questions about the role of government in protecting the public through imposing mandatory automobile safety devices. Pressured by consumer advocates, the government proposed a mandatory system of passive restraints to reduce injuries and deaths from automobile accidents. Despite universal recognition of the seriousness of the problem, the proposal met a reluctant industry and many skeptical drivers. The case in support of the airbag was complicated for years by technical disputes about its reliability. Then, when most of the technical problems were resolved, the issue shifted to economic questions of cost and consumer demand. A decision was reached after ten years of debate, but only when changes in the administration altered the political context.

James S. Petersen and Gerald E. Markle analyze the controversy over the freedom to use Laetrile as a cancer therapy. The medical establishment denies the therapeutic value of Laetrile, viewing its use as "irrational" and a dangerous diversion from appropriate medical care. They justify the ban on Laetrile by arguing that its users are not in a position to make knowledgeable and rational decisions and are subject to exploitation and "quackery." Laetrile proponents, however, claim the right to determine their own therapy. Their insistence on the efficacy of Laetrile therapy in the face of contrary evidence, and the persistence of the dispute, suggest its symbolic dimension. For many Laetrile proponents do not actually use the drug but carry on the cause out of resentment of government regulation and antagonism to the established medical profession.

Controversies over compulsory implementation of technology are not a recent phenomenon. Joshua Schwartz reviews two episodes in the development of smallpox immunization and provides historic examples which share many of the characteristics of recent disputes. In the first of these two episodes, scientific uncertainty about the risks involved in innoculation led to disagreement among experts and debates over the appropriate basis of decision-making authority. The professional medical establishment initially resisted innoculation, especially since the idea originated with a theologian. The central theme in the second controversy over vaccination, however, was one of individual freedom of choice. The risks were by then of less concern, but the proposal was to make vaccination universal and compulsory. Antivaccinationists opposed this practice as well as other mandatory public health programs on the grounds that they violated individual liberty. Eventually, the dispute evaporated, but less because of the manifest success of the program than of the changing attitudes toward the role of government.

7

THE AUTOMOBILE AIR BAG

Judith Reppy

On June 30, 1977, Secretary of Transportation Brock Adams issued a rule requiring "passive restraints" in all full-sized automobiles sold in the United States after September 1, 1981, and in all smaller cars over the following two years. This decision opened the latest chapter in the long debate over the automobile air bag. The controversy began in 1969 when the National Highway Safety Bureau gave its first preliminary notice of a proposed standard for passive restraints.[1] At that time, few people had even heard of the air bag, but by 1977 the automobile industry, insurance companies, public interest groups, and government agencies had spent millions of dollars promoting their conflicting views about this technology to the public. Congressional committees and the courts have also been heavily involved in this dispute which continues, even after nearly ten years.

The government's rule-making referred only to "passive restraints," but the technological efforts to meet the proposed standard have focused on the air bag. Thus Brock Adams's ruling has been widely interpreted to mean mandatory air bags.

Air bags are passive restraints in that they deploy automatically in a crash without any action by the automobile's occupants.[2] They thus represent the ultimate in a "technological fix"—a technical solution of the social problems of traffic deaths and injuries. The bag, which inflates within a few milliseconds of impact, acts as a cushion to reduce the deceleration forces on the occupants and to protect them from colliding with the interior of the automobile. When worn, seatbelts perform much the same function. Except for the new passive seat belts, however, they have required the active participation of the occupant to be effective, and the extent of seat belt use in the United States has been very low (approximately 20%).

Both seat belts and air bags are meant to reduce the injuries and deaths which have been a conspicuous and disturbing consequence of the widespread dependence on automobiles in our society. The magnitude of the automobile safety problem is beyond dispute. Although the introduction of safer automobiles, and the recent 55 mph speed limit, have lowered the alarming death rate since 1967, the total numbers of killed and injured in highway accidents are still very large: in 1977, 47,671 persons died in motor vehicle crashes. Furthermore, it is predicted that the ongoing shift to smaller, more fuel-efficient automobiles will lead to an increase in deaths and injuries unless improved protection is included in the design of new cars.

While consensus exists about the need to reduce traffic deaths, dispute rages as to how to reach this goal. The air bag controversy emerged as part of a broader argument between those who emphasize changes in motor vehicle design and those who advocate changes in driver skills and behavior through driver education, stiffer licensing procedures, and stricter penalties against drunken driving. The traditional view of automobile safety has taken "the nut behind the wheel" approach, stressing individual responsibility. This view is challenged by those who wish to focus attention on highway design and on the manufacturers' responsibility to make changes in the vehicle to reduce both the probability of a crash and the severity of injury if a crash occurs. In recent years, this latter emphasis has gained ground. The peculiar features of the air bag, however, have generated an intense and protracted debate.

The argument over the air bag has pitted the automobile industry against the automobile insurance companies, the advocates of less governmental regulation against those who believe it a duty to regulate where so many lives are at stake, and the nation's largest automobile association against the leaders of the consumer movement.[3] The tactics employed by the combatants have included court challenges, advertising campaigns in the national media, and extensive lobbying in Congress to control the National Highway Traffic Safety Administration's (NHTSA) actions.

As a consequence of the range of interest groups arrayed on each side of the issue, the arguments have ranged widely. There has been disagreement over many technical issues, from the design of anthropomorphic dummies used in simulated crashes to the proper design of studies to evaluate seatbelt use. The technical disagreement reached its most striking expression in the cost/benefit studies sponsored by the opposing sides which, based on conflicting assumptions, yielded opposite conclusions.[4] On a more philosophic level, participants in the controversy have debated the proper role of government and the morality of compelling or not compelling an individual to protect himself from the risk of injury.

Air bag proponents have argued that it is a mature technology that could save thousands of lives annually by reducing the severity of injuries in automobile crashes. They further point out that there is no feasible alternative, given the low rates of seat belt use in the United States. The automobile industry and its allies disagree. They contend that the air bag is a new, complex technology, inherently risky, overly costly, and insufficiently tested in real-life conditions. They hold that the preferable alternative is to increase seat belt use, either through education and persuasion, or through legislation. Each side claims to represent public opinion and displays contradictory opinion polls to prove it.

As the years passed with the issue unresolved, the arguments have shifted. Opponents no longer stress the novel nature of the technology so much as its costs. Proponents make fewer extravagant claims about the efficacy of air bags, but still emphasize the difficulty of implementing seat belt use as an alternative safety measure.

THE DISPUTE

Development of the air bag can be traced to a 1952 patent awarded for an inflatable cushion that would deploy in case of a sudden deceleration. Commercial interest in the technology, however, did not come until the 1960s. Carl Clark, an engineer working on the Apollo program at Martin Corporation, proposed using air bags in the landing device for astronauts. He then attempted to adapt his ideas for a restraint system to railroad cars and automobiles, but his work did not win corporate backing.[5] At the same time, however, proprietary work on air bag technology was going on in the research departments of the automobile companies; these developments became known when Eaton, Towne, and Yale (now Eaton Corporation) presented a briefing on its air bag system to the National Highway Safety Bureau in July 1968.

The system demonstrated by Eaton was essentially the same as the one now scheduled for use in 1981. In this system, sensors mounted on the automobile bumper and in the engine compartment detect sudden changes in velocity. If deceleration is greater than a threshold value (about 12 mph) the sensor activates a gas generating system which inflates the stored air bag in less than one-twentieth of a second. The air bag deflates almost immediately so that the driver's vision is not impaired.

There were problems with the early air bag design and numerous changes were made to correct them. The shape of the bag itself has been altered to provide more support in the leg area and to minimize the effect of the air bag's deployment in the case of a child who might not be in a regular seating position. The gas generating systems have been improved to allow weight reduction of the whole system, and the reliability of the electronic circuits has improved. Some problems remain. One owner of an airbag-equipped automobile reported that the bag inflated while the automobile was parked—his son had hammered the front bumper to show off the device to a friend. This kind of incident, and the opportunity for vandalism that it suggests, can be avoided by installing a switch to prevent deployment of the air bag in a nonmoving vehicle. Although the technology first demonstrated in 1968 had many bugs, these were substantially worked out by the mid-1970s.

The air bag required not only new technology, but also a shift in thinking about automobile safety—one which focused on motor vehicle design rather than on the driver. This concept reached a receptive public in the mid-1960s, following the publication of Ralph Nader's *Unsafe at Any Speed*. The subsequent congressional hearings and the publicity generated by General Motors' harassment of Nader turned motor vehicle safety into a major public policy question. With a curious sense of relief traffic safety was readily taken up by politicians as a national issue at a time when the country was increasingly divided by the Vietnam war and racial turmoil.[6]

In this atmosphere, Congress unanimously passed the National Traffic and Motor Vehicle Safety Act of 1966, as well as its companion legislation, the National Highway Safety Act. This legislation established the federal government's authority to issue safety standards for motor vehicles and highways. An agency, the National Highway Safety Bureau (later the National Highway Traffic Safety Administration), was created to administer the legislation and to promulgate the first set of motor vehicle safety standards by January 1967.

These original standards shared two notable characteristics. First, as required by the 1966 legislation, they were based on the existing technology; they did not demand any technical advances for compliance, but merely required that safety measures be extended to all vehicles. Second, the standards were couched in terms of performance rather than design criteria. It was hoped that specifying performance levels would encourage competing innovative solutions to safety problems. Given the noncompetitive structure of the U.S. automobile industry, this hope was probably naive: in safety, as in other areas of automobile technology, the most significant competition has come from foreign manufacturers.[7] Thus when, in 1969, the safety agency issued a preliminary notice of a proposed rule on passive restraints, it was breaking new ground by trying to prod new technological development, in particular the air bag.

It succeeded. Attention and resources were quickly drawn to air bag technology. In 1970 and 1972, NATO-sponsored international meetings on passive restraints attracted technical papers from foreign as well as domestic automobile manufacturers. General Motors, with its large resource base, was soon recognized as the leader in this technology.

The NHTSA action also, however, stimulated the beginnings of organized industrial opposition. Henry Ford, II spoke strongly against air bags, and Ford Motor Company, which had been cooperating with Eaton in its innovative work, publicly opposed the air bag in a series of national advertisements. The automobile companies pursued their opposition with petitions to the agency. Their lobby was powerful, gaining a series of delays in the proposed effective dates for the passive restraint standard.

In March 1971, the agency issued its ninth rule-making action on the standard, setting August 15, 1975 as the date after which all automobiles sold in the United States must provide full passive protection. The automobile companies responded with a joint lawsuit. They argued that the standard was neither objective (because of deficiencies in the testing procedures), nor practicable (because the technology did not yet exist), nor safe (because it substituted a hazardous alternative system for seat belts). They claimed that NHTSA had acted capriciously by frequently amending the standard and by not including all relevant material in the docket before taking its rule-making action.[8] Only General Motors failed to join this suit, owing no doubt to its advanced technological position and the initial support for air bags within the company.

In December 1972, the Sixth District Court ruled in the case, finding it within the agency's authority to require passive restraints. It also maintained, however, that the criteria of the standard were invalidated by the lack of standard test dummy, since this made it difficult to reproduce test results with any certainty. Before it could require passive restraints, then, the agency had to issue detailed specifications for a standard test dummy. The automobile manufacturers had gained what they most wanted—delay.

The momentum behind passive restraints dissipated during this period of delay and shifting requirements, and the pressure against the technology increased. In 1971, representatives of the automobile companies visited the White House to complain about the passive restraint standard, and, subsequently, Secretary of Transportation John Volpe, who had been an enthusiastic proponent of air bags, was told to "back off."[9] In 1972, the Office of Science and Technology released a study of "Cumulative Regulatory Effects on the Costs of Automobile Transportation." The study was hostile to air bags and concluded that seat belts were a preferred alternative.[10]

For the next four years, NHTSA took no decisive action. Although the standard for test dummies required by the court decision was issued in 1973, the agency postponed the requirement for mandatory passive restraints until 1976, and allowed the use of seatbelts with an ignition interlock as an alternative. The requirement for full passive restraints in all automobiles sold after September 1976 remained nominally in force, but became increasingly unrealistic. Economic problems and the energy crisis of 1973-1974 shifted the industry's attention to problems of fuel efficiency and the economic consequences of government regulation. The manufacturers claimed that the cost of air bags would further reduce sales of automobiles, dealing another blow to an industry that already suffered from cost inflation and faced the need to retool for smaller models with higher gasoline mileage.

In 1971, General Motors had announced ambitious plans to equip one million automobiles with air bags beginning with its 1974 models. By 1972, the company had reduced this number to 100,000 citing uncertainties about the final form and implementation date for the passive restraint standard. In the end, the company sold even fewer air bag-equipped automobiles than this—about 10,000 by 1975—for the device was available only on luxury models and the company failed to make any concerted effort to promote the air bag as a desirable option. Dealer attitudes were negative, and those buyers who wanted air bags often found them difficult to obtain. In 1975, General Motors halted production entirely, blaming low sales and the need to save weight in new car designs.[11]

The relatively few air bag-equipped automobiles that General Motors did sell, however, played an important role in the validation of the technology, since they constitute the only large-scale field testing of the device. Many have argued that such testing should have preceded mandating a new technology for the whole population. This issue has been an embarrassment for NHTSA. Field testing of air bags began in June 1972, only 14 months before the then standing date for implementation. Large-scale field tests which had been promised by NHTSA never occurred. And yet, the probability that any given automobile will be involved in a severe crash is so low that very large numbers of cars are needed in a field test in order to produce reliable data on air bag effectiveness. The 10,281 General Motors cars had, by August 1978, experienced fewer than 200 crashes in which the air bag inflated.

During this same period, NHTSA was wrestling with political problems caused by the ignition interlock, a device which prevents an automobile from starting until after the front seat occupants fasten their seat belts. Forced to delay implementation of the passive restraint standard, NHTSA, under pressure from the White House, had turned to the ignition interlock to compel increased seat belt use.[12] The interlock was mandated for all automobiles produced after January 1, 1973, and did result in increased belt use, even though a substantial number were disconnected. This system, however, raised a storm of angry criticism from both the public and Congress. Some congressmen complained about the paternalistic government regulations, forgetting, perhaps, that Congress itself had voted unanimously for the legislation which established the standard-setting authority in the first place. One congressman attacked the interlock saying that a woman fleeing a rapist would not be able to start her car without first fastening her seat belt. In August 1974, Congress voted to remove the interlock requirement and also gave itself veto power over any subsequent rule-making action on passive restraints.

This episode was painful to the NHTSA, creating a precedent of congressional interference in agency rule-making and undermining its efforts to increase seat belt use through technological devices. In a sense, however, the episode favored the air bag. The debate had publicized the continuing low rates of seat belt use. The interlock had failed because it was so annoying to the consumer, thus providing a strong argument for a more unobtrusive, passive approach.

During these years of delay, proponents of passive restraints were also gaining strength. The Insurance Institute for Highway Safety (IIHS), headed by William Haddon, Jr. (who had been the first administrator of the National Highway Safety Bureau), was actively supporting the air bag, and had succeeded in converting most of the automobile insurance industry. Allstate Insurance Company sponsored favorable advertisements in the national media, testified before congressional committees, and offered to discount insurance premiums on air bag-equipped automobiles. The IIHS sponsored studies of seat belt use rates that repeatedly showed rates far too low to be an effective alternative to air bags. Thus the insurance industry and the IIHS provided resources and, especially, the technical expertise to counter the influence of the automobile industry. Consumer organizations such as the Nader-sponsored Center for Auto Safety lobbied for the air bag, but they simply could not provide such resources by themselves. Access to expertise was indispensable.

The air bag was a new technology, and expert judgments on its effectiveness and reliability were at the core of arguments for and against its use. Contradictory technical judgments abounded. The noise of the air bag inflating has been compared to a pop gun by proponents, but to a deafening shotgun blast by opponents. Estimates of the number of lives to be saved ranged from 2,000 to 12,000 as scientists on both sides of the issue juggled their assumptions.[13] Opponents could not even agree on observed rates of seat belt usage, let alone the probability that such rates could be raised significantly by education. Every "fact" generated an opposite "fact," as each side sought to counter the impact of new evidence. Confusion and manipulation of evidence was encouraged by the limited scientific understanding of the relationship between crash forces and human injuries and by disagreement about the significance of tests using anthropomorphic dummies.

These arguments punctuated a public hearing in August 1976.[14] Air bag proponents called once again for ending the delay in implementing the standard. The industry countered with a call for mandatory seat belt use laws, a low-cost solution which would appear to offer a high payoff, but only if individual state legislatures cooperate in passing and enforcing the laws.[15] At last, in December 1976, Transportation Secretary William T. Coleman issued his own decision on the passive restraint standard.

Coleman accepted NHTSA's calculations that the available passive restraints were technologically feasible, would save about 12,000 lives annually, and could be sold for about $100 per automobile at full production. Nevertheless, Coleman delayed issuing the passive restraint standard on political grounds, saying that consumer resistance might lead to public rejection of the standard. He instead called for a large-scale demonstration of air bag technology in 500,000 automobiles in order to educate the public about the technology and to accumulate experience with the systems. Before leaving office in January 1977, Coleman negotiated details for such a demonstration with four manufacturers—two American and two foreign.

Circumstances changed rapidly with the arrival of the Carter Administration. Brock Adams, the new Secretary of Transportation, appointed Joan Claybrook, a long-time friend of Ralph Nader, to be administrator for NHTSA. Even before taking office, Adams questioned the logic of Coleman's decision, and he reopened the issue of passive restraints with another public hearing in April 1977. Following this hearing, he issued the rule setting 1981 as the date for mandatory passive restraints in full-sized automobiles, with other models to be phased in over the next two years.

Adams's decision has been attacked from both sides—by Ralph Nader who opposes the delay in implementation for small cars, and by the automobile industry. The dispute persists, but industry is preparing to meet the standard, helped by the long lead time which the ruling provides. Ironically, industry's first response has been a large-scale effort to design passive seat belts. In February 1978, General Motors demonstrated 16 different models. These passive belts are not suitable for automobiles with bench-style front seats, but smaller cars with bucket seats are a growing segment of the market. Thus, despite the favorable ruling on passive restraints, the actual future of air bags remains in doubt.

SOME ISSUES: THE ROLE OF
GOVERNMENT AND THE PUBLIC

At a fundamental level the argument over the air bag has been an argument over the proper role of government. Freedom of choice has been a powerful issue in the controversy, perhaps because of the strong associations between personal liberty and the automobile. For some, mandatory passive restraints are a symbol of the increasing encroachment of government activity into private realms. These people object that the standard forces individuals to purchase equipment for their own safety, when the equipment could be offered as an option. State laws requiring motorcyclists to wear helmets have generated similar objections.

The counterargument points out that the social costs of automobile injuries exceed the private costs by the degree of public subsidy of medical and rehabilitation services as well as the intangible losses borne by families and friends. Furthermore, most automobiles are eventually sold to second owners, and it is unlikely that the second-hand market would supply enough options in safety equipment to allow significant consumer choice.[16]

The debate can also be analyzed as a clash between the interests of the automobile manufacturers and those of an increasingly strong alliance of consumer activists, public health specialists, and the insurance industry. The automobile industry has argued that the passive restraint standard carries costs greater than its potential benefits, at least when compared to the alternative of increased seat belt usage. Such costs fall on the industry itself, and, although they will certainly be passed on to the consumer, the industry must adjust to whatever variations in demand occur. The spectre of product liability also threatens the industry, particularly at a time when lawsuits are frequent.[17] Furthermore, the industry generally considers safety considerations to conflict with its marketing strategy. Conceivably air bags could have been aggressively marketed as an option, but such an approach was not seriously considered. Even when General Motors was offering air bags, its dealers were largely unacquainted with their availability.[18]

When first proposed, passive restraints did not have substantial public support. Supplier companies were inhibited from expressing strong support for air bags since their major customers were the automobile manufacturers. The field of traffic safety itself was still largely dominated by those who emphasized improving drivers and highways, rather than automobiles, as the best means to greater safety. The first public support for passive restraints came from the consumer activists and public health specialists who had been involved in the original effort to establish a federal role in motor vehicle design. These included Ralph Nader and William Haddon, Jr., who had been head of the traffic safety agency when air bags were first demonstrated. For this group, the guiding principle was that modification of the vehicle should be a central component in a comprehensive program to reduce injuries and deaths. Opposition from most of the automobile industry turned the consumer campaign into a crusade, and as time went on important recruits flocked to the cause. The Center for Auto Safety (a Nader-related agency) and the Insurance Institute for Highway Safety provided institutional bases and expertise for the pro-air bag forces. Within NHTSA there was support (as well as opposition) for the passive restraint standard which helped to keep the standard alive during the Nixon-Ford years. And in Congress, representatives on the key commerce committees backed passive restraints.

The important role played by the insurance companies is curious. It is, of course, to the insurance industry's advantage to promote safety measures. But the effect of a measure like passive restraints is small, since the cost of personal medical expenses is only a fraction of the total automobile insurance package. The activism of the companies seems to be largely the result of personal convictions among their top executives and, perhaps, a growing sophistication about the role that their industry could play in Washington affairs.

The forum in which the controversy has been played out is almost entirely Washington, D.C.; the only other arena of any consequence has been the editorial pages of newspapers and the trade press. This in itself suggests the extent to which major decisions about the automobile have moved from Detroit to the nation's capital. The procedures adopted by NHTSA allowed much opportunity for public comment. There was a public docket maintained at the agency for all materials submitted to NHTSA, and public hearings were held in 1975, 1976, and 1977. At the last of these, NHTSA gave financial grants to interested groups to enable them to participate. In addition, congressional committees have shown considerable interest in the issue.

These public procedures were in part a means to legitimize the agency's decision. But it is doubtful that they changed anyone's mind. As positions hardened, the public hearings turned into occasions for familiar interests to reiterate familiar arguments; even "private" individuals who testified showed a predictable pattern, with. one contingent from Detroit and its environs and another composed of individuals who had been in automobile crashes.

Automobile safety is a broad issue, touching virtually every family in the United States. But like most consumer issues it is diffuse, arousing little sustained interest except among a small group who have made traffic safety their profession; there were no rallies or demonstrations for air bags. Thus the formal procedures for participation served mainly to provide additional channels for the established interest groups. Yet long delays for public comment and court challenges also allowed new interest groups to coalesce around automobile safety issues, and gave time for many of the technical uncertainties to be resolved. Arguments shifted from engineering aspects to more political questions of cost and consumer demand. At the same time, external events such as the OPEC oil price increases of 1974 affected the industry's position and altered the political context. Ultimately the political changes that occurred with the Carter Administration were decisive in bringing about the final favorable ruling.

NOTES

1. 34 FR 11148, July 2, 1969. The National Highway Safety Bureau was renamed the National Highway Traffic Safety Administration (NHTSA) in 1970.

2. Strictly speaking, the current air bag design provides passive protection only in frontal and front angle crashes. The bags are intended to be used with a lap belt to provide protection in roll-over or side-impact crashes. More than half of all fatalities, however, occur in frontal crashes.

3. The American Automobile Association for years actively opposed mandatory air bags. It has, however, supported Secretary Adams's passive restraint ruling because the standard can be met by other technologies such as passive belts.

4. A convenient summary of a number of different estimates can be found in the report, *The Department of Transportation Automobile Occupant Passive Restraint Rule,* U.S. Congress, House of Representatives, Committee on Interstate and Foreign Commerce, Subcommittee on Consumer Protection and Finance (Washington, DC: Government Printing Office, 1977), 17-20, 27.

5. Telephone interview with Carl Clark, June 1974.

6. Elizabeth Drew, "The Politics of Auto Safety," *Atlantic Monthly,* vol. 218, no. 4 (October 1966), 95-102.

7. For example, the passive belts introduced by Volkswagen. Cf. Lawrence J. White, *The Automobile Industry Since 1945* (Cambridge: Harvard University Press, 1971), 211-216.

8. *On Petition for Review of an Order of the National Highway Traffic Safety Administration* (U.S. Court of Appeals, Sixth Circuit). Brief for Petitioner Ford Motor Company (nos. 71-1350 and 71-1826), 7-9, and Brief for Petitioner Chrysler Corporation (no. 71-1339), 17-19.

9. The story is told in Ralph Nader, "Washington under the Influence: A Ten Year Review of Auto Safety Amidst Industrial Opposition" (February 23, 1976), 30-32 (mimeo).

10. The study took the manufacturers' claims for costs of the air bag even though they were twice the cost estimate used by NHTSA. It also suggested that an 80% use rate for seat belts was attainable in the United States. *Cumulative Regulatory Effects on the Cost of Automotive Transportation, Final Report of the Ad Hoc Committee* (Washington, DC: Government Printing Office, 1972), 49-57.

11. Another factor in General Motors' shifting attitude toward air bags was the retirement in 1974 of Ed Cole, who had been a champion of the air bag within the company.

12. The interlock was proposed as an alternative to the air bag by the presidents of Ford Motor Company and Chrysler Corporation in a meeting with President Nixon in 1970. In a subsequent meeting between White House aides, including Peter Flanigan and John Erlichman, and Department of Transportation officials, the decision to adopt the interlock was made. See Ralph Nader, "Washington Under the Influence," 31-32.

13. Ibid., 57-58, 64.

14. This was the second of three sets of public hearings held on the passive restraint standard in addition to numerous congressional hearings. In May 1975, there were five days of testimony before James Gregory, then head of NHTSA. Secretary Adams repeated the exercise in April 1977 before issuing his own decision.

15. The correlation between increased seat belt use following legislation and reduced human damage in crashes has been called into question by recent studies of occupant fatalities in Scandinavia. Apparently, heavy drinkers, who are disproportionately involved in crashes, are less likely to obey the law and fasten their belts. See

"Tennessee Child Restraint Law Evaluated," *Status Report,* May 31, 1978, 1, and "Danish Researchers Urge Passive Restraint Protection," *Status Report,* August 3, 1978, 7. (*Status Report* is a publication of *The Insurance Institute for Highway Safety,* Washington, DC.)

16. Susan P. Baker and William Haddon, Jr., M.D., "Ownership of Motor Vehicles in Which People Are Injured," (Washington, DC: Insurance Institute for Highway Safety, 1978).

17. A California jury recently awarded a record $125 million in punitive damages against Ford Motor Company in a product liability case. Although the award was later reduced, it serves as a warning to the entire industry.

18. Albert R. Karr, "Saga of the Air Bag, or the Slow Deflation of a Car-Safety Idea," *The Wall Street Journal* (November 11, 1976), 1.

THE LAETRILE CONTROVERSY

James C. Petersen and Gerald E. Markle

Despite attacks from the government and orthodox medicine, interest in Laetrile, a purported cancer treatment generally obtained from apricot kernels, has grown tremendously in the 1970s. Until recently, little public attention has been paid to Laetrile. Also known as amygdalin and Vitamin B-17,[1] for 25 years it has been just one of many elements in a "cancer underground."[2] Medical experts debunked Laetrile and labeled its supporters as quacks. Government officials banned its use and sale and prosecuted those who violated the law. But now, thousands of American cancer victims are seeking Laetrile treatment and an estimated 20,000 Americans are regularly using this therapy.

Today Laetrile is a household word. A Harris Poll conducted in 1977 revealed that slightly more than three-quarters of all Americans have heard of Laetrile and two-thirds favor enactment of pro-Laetrile legislation in their state. The controversy has been the subject of hundreds of news articles and coverage on TV. Johnny Carson has included Laetrile jokes in his monologues, and "Doonesbury" cartoonist Gary Trudeau depicted the

Authors' Note: *We wish to thank Yvonne Vissing, Roger Nemeth, and Ronald Troyer for their assistance in the preparation of this chapter. We also thank Paul Sage for his helpful comments.*

character Duke planning to make a fortune by buying an apricot farm and marketing the pits in Tijuana.

The political strength of the Laetrile movement is also significant. During 1977, Laetrile supporters won key legislative and judicial victories. Seventeen states have legalized Laetrile, and advocates demonstrated considerable power in other states. A federal district court judge in Oklahoma issued a permanent injunction preventing the Food and Drug Administration (FDA) from banning interstate commerce in Laetrile. The judge described the ban as arbitrary and capricious, placing a "needless hardship and expense" on cancer victims.[3]

The popularity of Laetrile therapy is difficult to interpret from a traditional scientific viewpoint. The treatment has been investigated by the FDA, the National Cancer Institute, the California Medical Association, the Memorial Sloan-Kettering Cancer Center, and other prestigious research centers. All have concluded that Laetrile does not cure cancer. After each study the Laetrile issue is pronounced dead and buried. Yet the movement grows, to the frustration and disbelief of the medical establishment.

> It is a paradoxical phenomenon deserving our earnest scrutiny that probably the single quackery promotion receiving the largest amount of public attention in all our nation's history should be one of our own day.[4]

In labeling the use of Laetrile "quackery," medical authorities have tried to explain its popularity in terms of fear, ignorance, and gullibility. But the purported irrational behavior of thousands of citizens hardly explains the Laetrile movement's wide appeal. We shall briefly examine the history of the controversy surrounding Laetrile and then consider several factors which we believe have contributed to its popularity. Who are the proponents of Laetrile, and what are the issues behind the controversy? Why did the Laetrile movement achieve such strength in the late 1970s? These questions will be probed in order to shed light on the meaning of the Laetrile phenomenon.

HISTORY OF THE CONTROVERSY

Amygdalin, the chemical name for Laetrile, was first isolated in 1830 by French chemists and was apparently used in cancer therapy as early as 1843.[5] Members of the contemporary Laetrile movement, however, generally trace the movement to Ernst T. Krebs, Jr. In 1952, Krebs claimed to have produced Laetrile by refining an apricot extract which his father had experimented with since the late 1920s. Two years earlier the two Krebs and Howard Beard published a paper, "The Unitarian or Trophoblastic Thesis of Cancer," which provided a theoretical basis for Laetrile therapy.[6] The claims made in that paper have been denounced by medical orthodoxy but are revered and currently taught by Laetrile proponents.

During the 1950s, Laetrile researchers experimented with unorthodox techniques and methods. In 1955, for example, Krebs, Sr. and Dr. Arthur Harris published a paper, "The Treatment of Breast Cancer with Laetrile by Iontophoresis," describing the use of electric current to force Laetrile through the chest wall to the tumor. After 15 to 30 minutes, the tumor purportedly was liquefied and the "cancer juice" was drawn out with an aspirating needle. The authors presented no supporting data, and use of the technique quickly disappeared.

In 1953, the Cancer Commission of the California Medical Association issued a report rejecting the claims of Laetrile proponents. Ten years later, the Cancer Advisory Council to the Director of California's Department of Public Health concluded that Laetrile was of "no value in the diagnosis, treatment, alleviation or cure of cancer." Furthermore, the council expressed concern that orthodox treatments might be delayed while cancer patients tried Laetrile therapy. It therefore recommended that the Department of Health prohibit the treatment of cancer with Laetrile. Such a regulation was issued September 20, 1963.

The first seizure of contraband Laetrile linked its proponents with advocates of other marginal cancer therapies: in December 1960, federal officials seized 57 vials of Laetrile from an osteopath who operated the former Hoxey Cancer Clinic in Dallas.

In April 1970, the FDA assigned an IND (Investigative New Drug) number to the McNaughton Foundation, a pro-Laetrile organization, to test Laetrile clinically. Within a few days, however, the IND was revoked when deficiencies were discovered in the initial application. When Laetrile proponents charged that the denial was due to prejudice,[7] the FDA sought the advice of five well-known oncologists. That committee concurred with the FDA's decision. The McNaughton Foundation submitted additional materials to meet FDA demands, but permission for clinical testing was never obtained, thus making it illegal to do Laetrile research on human subjects.

The FDA has banned interstate commerce in Laetrile—and has even attempted to ban the sale of apricot kernels. The FDA has won court cases in which it sought to ban the interstate sale of Aprikern, Bee-17, and Bitter Food Tablets, all commercial preparations containing amygdalin. In the spring and summer of 1977, the FDA and law enforcement agents seized 50 tons of apricot pits and various supplies for manufacturing Laetrile from Wisconsin and Tennessee and injectable ampules and tablets of Laetrile in several states including Maryland, Texas, Florida, and Ohio. In the largest single court action, a federal grand jury indicted one Canadian citizen, eight U.S. citizens, seven Mexican citizens, and three Mexican companies for conspiracy to smuggle Laetrile.

By 1975 Laetrile proponents also began to use the courts successfully to block the enforcement of the FDA ban on interstate sale of Laetrile. Federal judges in several states including California, Massachusetts, New York, Oklahoma, and West Virginia have permitted individual cancer patients to import supplies of Laetrile from Mexico. One of these judges, U.S. District Court Judge Luther Bohanon (W. D. Oklahoma), has permitted over 30 cancer patients to import six-month supplies of Laetrile.

The best known of these cases, *Rutherford v. United States,* was recently made a class action lawsuit. Judge Bohanon held that Rutherford and the other plaintiffs, in being "denied freedom of choice for treatment by Laetrile to alleviate or cure their cancer, were deprived of life, liberty, or property without due process of law."[8] The FDA appealed the decision, and in October 1976, the 10th U.S. Circuit Court of Appeals ruled in favor of Rutherford. According to the Court, if Laetrile was used as a cancer drug, or was generally recognized as safe and effective before 1962, then the FDA could not regulate its current use. The court stated that "the FDA's record is grossly inadequate and consists merely of a conclusory affidavit of an official of the FDA which in effect declares that it is a new drug because the FDA says it is and thus is subject to all of the statutory vagaries of such a designation." Judge Bohanon gave the FDA 120 days to compile information on whether or not Laetrile is indeed a "new drug."

The FDA received about 5,500 pages of written testimony; in addition, 47 individuals made oral presentations at the hearing which was held in Kansas City on May 2 and 3, 1977. More than 100 Laetrile supporters attended the hearing, applauding Laetrile advocates and booing its opponents.[9] Thereafter the FDA commissioner issued a 50,000 word decision that Laetrile is not generally recognized by qualified experts as a safe and effective cancer drug and that it is not exempt from FDA regulation because of the "grandfather" provisions.[10] Despite this report, Judge Bohanon issued a permanent injunction forbidding the FDA from restricting the importation and use of Laetrile. In July 1978, the U.S. Court of Appeals, 10th Circuit, upheld the injunction limiting use of Laetrile to injections given by licensed medical practitioners to terminal cancer patients. The FDA has appealed this action and further legal action is likely.

Laetrile supporters have gained considerable success in state legislatures, as well as in the courts. Alaska, in 1976, became the first state to legalize the use of Laetrile, although it prohibits its sale or manufacture. Since commercial sources are not present and the FDA prohibits interstate commerce in Laetrile, Alaska residents may use the substance but they have no legal way of obtaining it. This leaves physicians in the strange position of being able to prescribe but not to provide Laetrile.

During 1977, 12 more states passed pro-Laetrile legislation with bills generally passing by wide margins. In Illinois and Indiana, the legislatures overrode gubernatorial vetoes, but in New York, Governor Hugh Carey successfully vetoed pro-Laetrile legislation in 1977 and 1978. By the middle of 1978, seventeen states had legalized the substance. Similar legislation has failed in several states and Laetrile proponents suffered a striking loss in Massachusetts where the House voted 161-58 to defeat a pro-Laetrile bill.

The Laetrile lobby has been able to neutralize the opposition of powerful authorities and medical experts in many states. In Indiana, for example, Laetrile legislation was opposed by the governor, the Democratic and Republican leaders of the House and Senate, and the Indiana State Medical Association. Yet the bill passed the House by 85-10 and the Senate by 44-4. Even the governor's veto failed to influence the outcome: the House and Senate overrode the veto by votes of 74-15 and 47-3, respectively.

There are some interesting differences in state legislation. The Indiana legislation deregulated the manufacture, sale, and distribution of Laetrile, but required that patients sign an informed consent sheet that notes that (1) the FDA has banned Laetrile, (2) the American Cancer Society, the American Medical Association, and the Indiana State Medical Association do not recommend its use, and (3) other recognized treatments are available. An amendment to Indiana's law legalized the use of saccharin, which the FDA was threatening to ban. The Nevada legislation imposed a 10% gross receipts tax on Laetrile manufacture. The Delaware legislation simplified several issues by defining Laetrile as a natural food substance and allowing its manufacture, sale, and use without prescription or license.

Procedures designed to protect physicians are a common feature in many of the 17 state laws. The Alaska bill prohibits hospitals from interfering with the physician's right to prescribe Laetrile and protects physicians from disciplinary actions by the state medical board. Florida's law requires patients to sign a form that releases physicians from liability.

For the Laetrile movement it has been a remarkable 25 years: in the 1950s, it was an obscure and ignored phenomenon; in the 1970s, Laetrilists have mounted a serious challenge to the medical establishment, opposing and limiting the power and authority of medical experts in the treatment of our most dread disease.

PARTICIPANTS IN THE CONFLICT

Participants in the dispute over Laetrile include a wide range of public and private organizations. The federal government through the FDA, the National Institutes of Health, and the National Cancer Institute, has been the principal opponent of Laetrile in the United States. It has been joined by the American Cancer Society, the American Medical Association, and various state agencies and medical societies. In addition, physicians and medical researchers from Memorial Sloan-Kettering Cancer Center and various hospital and university laboratories have frequently testified against Laetrile at legislative hearings and court proceedings. Together, these organizations are extremely powerful; their influence is reflected in the policies of medical schools, scientific journals, and the agencies that fund cancer research.

This prestigious coalition has been challenged by a handful of largely unknown organizations that advocate Laetrile use: the Committee for Freedom of Choice in Cancer Therapy, the Cancer Control Society, and the International Association of Cancer Victims and Friends. Together these three organizations have about 20,000 members, although their mailing lists include over 80,000 names.

The oldest of these groups, the International Association of Cancer Victims and Friends, was founded in 1963 by Cecile Hoffman, who believed that Laetrile had cured her of cancer. The organization publishes *Cancer News Journal,* which promotes Laetrile along with a wide variety of nontoxic cancer therapies. The group has about 8,000 members and 50 local chapters. Conflict within this group produced schisms leading to the formation of the Cancer Control Society in 1973, the Foundation for Alternative Cancer Therapies in 1975, and the Cancer Federation in 1977.[11]

The Cancer Control Society has about 4,000 members and five local chapters. It promotes Laetrile through meetings, the *Cancer Control Jour-*

nal, and an extensive educational program. The Society shows the filmstrip "World Without Cancer" and sells pro-Laetrile literature (including a book of Laetrile-rich receipes with the ironic title *The Little Cyanide Cookbook*). The Cancer Control Society holds two types of meetings. Some are designed to educate the general public or new members about Laetrile. Others are for regular members to discuss the latest literature in metabolic therapy or ways of obtaining Laetrile and expediting Laetrile legislation. Nationally known Laetrile advocates such as Ernst Krebs, Jr. and John Richardson often speak at these meetings.

Perhaps the most influential of all the pro-Laetrile organizations is the Committee for Freedom of Choice in Cancer Therapy, founded in 1972 to aid the defense of Dr. John Richardson, who was being tried for using Laetrile in cancer therapy. Richardson was an active member of the John Birch Society, as are most of the Committee officers. The editor of *Choice,* its official publication, stated that "There are a lot of us Birchers in the Laetrile movement because the John Birch Society has the guts to fight for what it believes in."[12] Pro-Laetrile pamphlets and books are sold at John Birch Society bookstores; and *American Opinion,* published by John Birch Society founder Robert Welch, has attacked the suppression of Laetrile.[13] The Committee, which has about 500 local chapters with 8,000 members, describes itself as "the nation's major leading advocate of the decriminalization of Laetrile."

Peripheral organizations supporting the Laetrile movement include health and nutrition groups and other organizations that advocate unorthodox cancer therapy. Supporting groups have appeared from both the political right and left. A reporter in Wisconsin linked an ultra-right group called the Posse Comitatus to the manufacture of Laetrile. From the other end of the political spectrum an organization called Second Opinion has been involved in the controversy. It was founded in 1976 by members of the New York City chapter of Science for the People, a group which has written on such issues as nuclear power, recombinant DNA, and sociobiology. Second Opinion, claiming to represent the rank-and-file employees of the prestigious Memorial Sloan-Kettering Cancer Center, accuses the Center of "racism, chauvinism, and imperialism" in its policies and work. Their newspaper, "Second Opinion," chastizes the Center for not emphasizing the prevention of cancer and for not being open-minded toward unorthodox cancer therapies. In 1977 Second Opinion issued a special report, "Laetrile at Sloan-Kettering," coauthored by Sloan-Kettering's Assistant Public Affairs Director (subsequently fired for his role in its publication), which was highly critical of the Center.

Opponents of Laetrile frequently attempt to portray its users as victims driven to irrational behavior by fears of cancer. FDA Commissioner Kennedy, in his lengthy decision on the status of Laetrile, asks "[W]hy do people bet their lives, or the lives of their loved ones, on a therapy which is rejected by almost everyone trained and experienced in cancer research and treatment?" He concludes that

> the answer lies in the fear that cancer engenders—and that proven therapies for cancer engender—and the need of patients and families for hope in a situation where the hope offered by the legitimate therapies is often modest.[14]

The Commissioner summarizes testimony charging that many cancer patients reject orthodox treatment and adopt Laetrile therapy in order to gain the social support of family and friends. They are influenced by the "highly polished and thus convincing films and books" which promote Laetrile and "frustration with a medical establishment that cannot offer the certainty of a cure."[15]

Two physicians who interviewed their own cancer patients using Laetrile argued that those involved with unorthodox therapies had difficulty relating to their physicians and exhibited personality complexes that included conspiratorial views of established medical authorities.

It is difficult to assess such explanations since, in fact, our knowledge of Laetrile users is limited. However, a study of 252 participants at a Laetrile symposium sponsored by the Cancer Control Society indicated they were predominantly white, female, rural, and educated.[16] Interviews showed that those who took Laetrile were less fearful of cancer than others. They were also somewhat more likely to take vitamins, believing this would aid in disease prevention. They patronized health food stores and disapproved of the fluoridation of public water. Symposium participants were nearly ten times more likely to visit chiropractors than are Americans generally. Furthermore, those participants who were taking Laetrile held more positive views of the effectiveness of chiropractors than of M.D.s, thus demonstrating a substantial rejection of orthodox medicine.[17]

These findings point toward a consistent set of ideas behind the use of Laetrile: belief in the overriding importance of nutrition, opposition to orthodox medicine, and acceptance of officially condemned health beliefs. Though the leaders of the Laetrile movement often have right-wing connections, the followers seem to be less involved with politics than with organic food issues. While the Laetrile controversy has different historical roots than the health food movement, there is an overlap in membership. In fact, Laetrile advocates frequently claim that Laetrile is Vitamin B-17 and often combine its use with "nutritional" or "metabolic" therapy.

To explore why people became members of pro-Laetrile groups, a researcher observed a local chapter of the Cancer Control Society and interviewed 27 people in the Laetrile movement.[18] Twelve were taking Laetrile as a cancer therapy, five as a cancer preventive, and—interestingly—the rest were active in promoting Laetrile but did not take it themselves. The respondents were educated and informed about both sides of the Laetrile controversy. They did not hold totally negative views of M.D.s, but emphasized their desire to exercise control over their lives, including medical matters. In sum, many people taking Laetrile seem to be well-informed, and while they are frustrated with orthodox medicine, such feelings are also widespread in the general public. Moreover there is little evidence that these people are more afraid of cancer than those who seek conventional medical care.

SOURCES OF CONFLICT

It is helpful to analyze the sources of the Laetrile controversy and the behavior of its participants less in terms of their irrationality than in the context of a number of social factors: the coexistence of conflicting concepts of medicine, ambiguous data that are open to contrary interpretation, questions of professional prestige, economic motives, and the ideologies that were developed to reinforce the position of each side in the controversy.

CONCEPTS OF MEDICINE

The history of medicine is marked by competing concepts of health and disease. One view (variously termed technico-morphological, empirical, or allopathic) emphasizes "the local symptoms of disease and considers the affection of each organ separately. This leads to localistic treatment . . . and to mechanistic thinking generally." The second, (known as unitarian or naturopathic) emphasizes a broader approach, viewing disease as "a general fact which strikes the whole organism and has its origins in a perturbation of natural harmony."[19] The conflict between these two views influences the interpretation of symptoms, the relationship between theory and medical practice, the definition of diseases, and the role of the physician.

Laetrile proponents identify with the naturopathic philosophy of medicine, conceptualizing disease as a natural degenerative process based on dietary or metabolic deficiency. Naturopaths emphasize the maintenance of health rather than the treatment of disease and often substitute vitamins and herbs for orthodox medical care. The popularity of organic food and of such a book as Linus Pauling's *Vitamin C and the Common Cold* attest to the vigor of the movement.

In contrast, allopathy stresses the foreign nature of disease: illnesses are combated with drugs and self-treatment is discouraged. In this tradition the physician "cures by opposing and conquering something within the patient" rather than facilitating the "patient's own intrinsic healing power."[20]

Several participants at the 1977 FDA Hearings on Laetrile recognized these differences in medical philosophy. A Laetrile proponent, for example, argues for the concept of wholistic medicine which treats

the whole man as a single entity, the sum of his parts. And once again a light year removed from the specialized, fragmented, crisis medicine whereby the patient is shuttled from dermatologists to internists to gastrologists to oncologists to psychiatrists.[21]

When disputes cross philosophical lines, they are difficult to resolve, because opposing parties do not agree on the criteria of settlement. Orthodox scientists and Laetrile advocates failed to communicate with one another because they conceptualize the nature of cancer and the idea of treatment in a totally different framework.[22]

AMBIGUITIES OF DATA

For the researcher, ambiguities in data and their interpretation are a creative challenge. For the policy maker seeking definitive answers to immediate problems, the probabilistic statements of science may be frustrating. One journalist described the Laetrile controversy as an example of "science by press conference":

In recent years, science has been done as often in a fishbowl of publicity as in an ivory tower. Technical and scientific findings have become so essential to many vital and pressing matters of public policy that politicians, the press, and finally the public have come to expect—and demand—quick and definitive answers that science, by its very nature, cannot always provide.[23]

Although cancer researchers have tested amygdalin on mice and report that it has no anticancer effect,[24] Laetrile advocates reject these findings on theoretical and methodological grounds. Some deny the basic analogy between animal and human systems. According to this logic, the success or failure of an antineoplastic agent in mice is of little use in assessing its effect on humans. In addition, Laetrile supporters reject the notion that cancer is a tumor disease; rather they view it as a metabolic disease in which the tumor is merely an obvious symptom. Just as it takes Vitamin B-12 as well as iron to cure pernicious anemia and proper diet as well as insulin to control diabetes, Laetrile supporters maintain that Vitamin B-17 cannot be evaluated in the absence of megavitamin therapy and proper diet. Laetrile is described as the "crown jewel in a total diadem of treatment." One small experimental study using a "wholistic" strategy purported to show that Laetrile effectively inhibited mouse tumors.[25]

Most criticism of the experimental studies has been methodological. Is the efficacy of treatment to be determined by the growth rate of a tumor, by its size, or by whether it metastasizes? Should tumors be identified by gross examination (visually or by palpitation) or by newer techniques such as "bioassay" which are purportedly more sensitive? These techniques of measurement may be mutually exclusive since some involve sacrificing the mouse. One criterion of efficacy important for humans, the relief of pain, cannot be used in animal studies. A second methodology question focused on the kinds of tumor system to be used in experiments. The early Laetrile studies were done on so-called "transplantable" tumor systems. But some reputable researchers now believe that these systems produce a malignancy not analogous to human cancer. Later Laetrile studies have used the more costly and time-consuming "spontaneous" tumor systems. This has not, however, ended the controversy because of a third methodological question: which strain of mice should be used in a given experiment? In some strains, known anticancer agents test negatively; other strains may incorrectly indicate the efficacy of an agent. Similar problems occur in choosing the site of the cancer: choices range from tumors of various organs to nontumorous leukemias. Different sites show varying and selective sensitivities to different drugs.

These theoretical and methodological difficulties plagued the Laetrile experiments at Memorial Sloan-Kettering Cancer Center. Sloan-Kettering, one of the most prestigious cancer centers in the world, got involved in the Laetrile controversy in 1972 expecting to answer the Laetrile question quickly. But by 1977, the head of Sloan-Kettering lamented, "I sure as hell wish the Sloan-Kettering Institute had not taken on the testing. It has been such a bag of worms. It has nothing to do with science, it has to do with politics."[26]

The first mice studies, conducted by well-known cancer expert Kane-matsu Sugiura, found that Laetrile tended to inhibit the spread of new tumors (metastasis) in spontaneous breast tumors. He repeated the experiment twice, with the same findings, but the results were never published. According to Chester Stock, Vice President of the Institute and in charge of later experiments, "If we had published those early positive data, it would have caused all kinds of havoc."[27] By 1973, these data were too controversial to hide. In a pamphlet entitled "Anatomy of a Coverup" the Committee for Freedom of Choice in Cancer Therapy published Sugiura's data along with the following unsigned letter on Sloan-Kettering stationery:[28]

> Here are some of the results of Sloan-Kettering's continuing experiments with Laetrile. Due to political pressures these results are being suppressed. Please do your best to bring these important findings to the attention of people. Krebs' theory is very promising, and Laetrile should be tested clinically to see if it really holds water.

Sloan-Kettering scientists claim that they have been unable to replicate Sugiura's findings, though they admit that some early follow-up experiments—in collaboration with the Catholic Medical Center—were flawed due to clumsy injection procedures. But in 1977, Sloan-Kettering completed the most thorough and comprehensive studies ever done on Laetrile. The findings: Laetrile is inactive against spontaneous systems. The Institute acknowledges that Sugiura still finds Laetrile to be effective in controlling tumors, but maintains that

> The significance attributed to those early observations is seriously challenged by the negative findings of three independent investigators, by two out of three negative cooperative experiments in which Sugiura participated and by the blind experiment in which he and others under blind readings found no anti-cancer activity.[29]

In the normal course of science, the Sloan-Kettering findings might have squelched the opposition. But Laetrile proponents have a long record of resiliency; within months of the release of the Sloan-Kettering data, objections were raised about the research.

Now the fight was led by *Second Opinion*. In 1977, it published a special report which charged that Sloan-Kettering had suppressed findings showing Laetrile to be efficacious. They cited the example of the work of Dr. Elizabeth Stockert, a Sloan-Kettering scientist who had found evidence suggesting Laetrile's efficacy. Chester Stock, principal investigator in the recent studies, claimed he had not known of Stockert's work, but *Second*

Opinion (January 1978) printed a memo to Dr. Stock which summarized the work in question.

Second Opinion also accused Sloan-Kettering of distorting their experiments. A similar accusation appeared in a news release from the New York Academy of Sciences which claimed the Sloan-Kettering experiments were done on "the most drug resistant of experimental cancers, and that many drugs that are effective against cancer in human patients have never been tested on them."[30]

Not all observers feel that *Second Opinion* was able to substantiate its charges, but Sloan-Kettering was embarrassed by the controversy. As the Associate Editor of *Sciences* has written:

> Differences of interpretation are a legitimate and inevitable part of the scientific process. But when they seem to be offered in response to public or political pressure, science suffers and so, ultimately, does the public which depends on it.[31]

THE PROFESSIONAL PRESTIGE SYSTEM

The reception of scientific or medical discoveries is influenced at least in part by the professional prestige of the investigator. One sociologist has found that "sometimes, when discoveries are made by scientists of lower standing, they are resisted by scientists of higher standing partly because of the authority the higher position provides."[32] A study of manuscripts submitted to *The Physical Review* found that papers from highly prestigious authors were less likely to be sent to outside referees than were papers from authors of lower prestige.[33] Typically the prestige of scientists affects the reception of their contributions.

> [T]he extrinsic social and cultural values of scientists, their other roles, and their loyalties other than to science typically intrude into the evaluation and control process in science. Perhaps the most famous anecdote among the folk literature dealing with such things is that relating how a very original paper by Lord Rayleigh (then president of the Royal Society) to which he had forgotten to affix his name was rejected--until the author's identity was uncovered.[34]

Most of the pro-Laetrile research has been carried out by individuals of low prestige within the scientific community. Dr. Ernst Krebs, Sr. originally isolated the substance during a search for methods to improve the taste of prohibition whiskey. His son, Ernst Krebs, Jr. was convicted and fined for illegally promoting Vitamin B-15 to improve race-horse performance. The FDA attacked Ernst Krebs, Jr. on prestige grounds by noting that "while he is referred to as a doctor, he did not complete medical training and is a doctor only by virtue of an honorary degree."[35] Also the FDA maintains that none of the researchers active in the movement have any "special training in oncology or in the evaluation of drug safety or effectiveness," and that they publish their results in books and pamphlets, rather than in scientific journals with peer review. Money to finance the movement has been donated by the McNaughton Foundation. Its founder, Andrew McNaughton, son of a former President of the United Nations Security Council, was a former double agent working for Fidel Castro, and was recently convicted of conspiracy to misrepresent the value of Canadian mining stock.

Some of the leaders of the movement do have strong establishment credentials. For example, among the advocates of Laetrile is Dr. Dean Burk, who until retirement was head of the Cytochemistry Section at the National Cancer Institute. At the 1978 meetings of the American Association for the Advancement of Science, however, he was characterized as someone who had "spent time" at the NCI. The fact that most physicians who use Laetrile have low prestige helped to create an initial prejudice at the established research centers.

ECONOMICS

The American Cancer Society (1975) estimates that the direct costs (hospital, nursing home care, physicians' fees, nurse services, drugs and other treatments, as well as research) to combat cancer were $3 billion in 1972. The indirect costs (loss of productivity, earning power, and so forth) added another $12 billion for a total of $15 billion. Cancer therapy is big business, and each side of the Laetrile dispute has accused the other of profiteering.

Regulatory decisions, for example, may have direct financial consequences. The FDA decision to categorize Laetrile as a drug rather than a vitamin is a case in point, for as a drug it must be approved as safe and efficacious before the FDA will permit sale for human consumption. Unfortunately, the required animal studies are expensive. Lethal doses of the drug must be established; animals must be cared for while alive; when dead they must be autopsied with histological examination by professional personnel; sufficient animals must be used to make the tests statistically meaningful; and, in animals with spontaneous tumor systems, the tests are lengthy. One official of a large pharmaceutical company has estimated that all necessary studies for a given drug may run as high as $10 million. Commercial laboratories will not study amygdalin because it is not patentable, and little profit could be made from its sale.

Laetrile advocates magnify the role of economics into a conspiracy in order to account for the opposition of orthodox medicine. "It is economics. The surgeons will lose patients, the radiologists will lose patients, X-ray machine makers will be affected, drug companies will be affected."[36] Or, in more general terms:

> Scientific rationale and clinical results are not factors influencing the acceptance of a promising prophylaxis and control of cancer except in an inverse way. The more promising such a method appears, the more strenuously do the beneficiaries of the entrenched cancer industry and their agents rationalize, malign, exaggerate and otherwise obfuscate the facts about the proposed method.[37]

The physician who prescribes Laetrile may face a costly risk of malpractice suits. U.S. Congressman Lawrence P. McDonald (D-Ga.) was sued by the widow of a cancer patient whom he had treated with Laetrile while practicing medicine. McDonald, who serves on the National Council of the John Birch Society, charged that the $3.5 million suit was politically motivated and argued that Laetrile is not a drug but a food supplement.[38] Although McDonald was found innocent, he was forced to pay $15,000 for medical and other expenses. A legal fog still surrounds the whole issue of Laetrile and malpractice. For example, the Nevada Medical Liability Insurance Association, which writes about 60% of the state's malpractice policies, has decided not to extend malpractice coverage to Laetrile suits, even though the substance is legal in the state. In Oklahoma, however, where Laetrile is also legal, the law requires patients to agree to waive malpractice suits if Laetrile is prescribed at their request.

Vested interest can work both ways, and many people have charged that Laetrile advocates make tremendous profits.[39] According to one estimate, the Chairman of the Committee for Freedom of Choice in Cancer Therapy sold $1.4 million worth of Laetrile over a 2½-year period for a profit of approximately $675,000; and a leading pro-Laetrile physician deposited $2.8 million in a checking account between January 1973 and March 1976.[40] Most often accused of profiteering is Ernesto Contreras, whose Tijuana clinic treats some 600 Americans per month. It is not clear that the data support these allegations: the full costs of a one month treatment program in Tijuana is $1,500 to $2,500. Contreras's fees are $10 for the first visit, $7 for subsequent visits, and $3 per gram of Laetrile. Those fees seem modest when compared with the cost of radiation, chemotherapy, and surgery that orthodox medicine prescribes for cancer victims; "routine" care at the Johns Hopkins Comprehensive Cancer Center costs $328.40 per day and the 1973 median cost of conventional treatment for a cancer case was $19,000.

IDEOLOGY

The medical community has tried to control the Laetrile movement by invoking an ideology of expertise. They emphasize that medical decisions must be made by highly trained experts. The Acting Commissioner of the National Cancer Institute has stated this position.

> The average citizen in this country does not have the resources and technical skills necessary to select, develop, and test materials for the treatment of disease. Neither does he have the background that will enable him to make enlightened decisions concerning the selection and use of therapeutic agents. The selection, development, testing, evaluation, marketing, prescribing, and administration of materials for disease treatment is an area in which large institutions and skilled professionals are uniquely qualified to take the measures necessary to protect the interests of the public.[41]

An elitist position logically leads to government protection. At the Kansas City Laetrile hearings, a professor of medicine from the Mayo Clinic asked, "Do we want a government which permits the strong to take advantage of the weak, or do we want a society that protects the consumer?" Government attempts to protect consumers from Laetrile have been numerous. A dramatic example occurred in 1977 in Milwaukee when a judge interceded in the case of a seven-year-old girl who had leukemia. He prohibited the child's parents from removing her from the hospital and taking her to a California clinic for Laetrile therapy.

Laetrile advocates, on the other hand, invoke a populist ideology. Rather than treating cancer by the methods of experts—so-called "slashing, burning and poisoning"—they urge deprofessionalization of medical care. Individuals are encouraged to prevent and treat cancer through the use of natural substances and, in the final analysis, to be their own physicians. This populist position leads to a position that Laetrile advocates refer to as "freedom of choice" in cancer therapy. They declare that cancer patients have a right to choose their form of treatment without interference by the medical community or the government. Freedom of choice is seen as a constitutional, as well as an individual, issue. In a series of columns over a two-year period, James J. Kilpatrick has argued in the nation's daily press that such freedom is the real point of the Laetrile debate.

> We lose it by chunks, by bits, by grains. Daily we yield more authoritarian control to the state and to the experts.[42]

In responding to this demand for freedom of choice, the FDA maintains the necessity of exchanging some freedoms in order to gain others. In the Commissioner's view:

> Congress indicated its conclusions that the absolute freedom to choose an ineffective drug was properly surrendered in exchange for the freedom from the danger to each person's health and well-being from the sale and use of worthless drugs.[43]

Expert testimony before the FDA asserted that "the emotional trauma of a cancer diagnosis severely impairs the patients' and families' abilities to engage in rational decision-making."[44] A psychiatrist declared that Laetrile users are like children—not to be trusted with freedom.

> Freedom of choice ... is the same argument that my 7-year-old daughter tells me when she uses matches and says to me, "Daddy, I am grown up enough to use these matches, and don't worry. I won't burn myself."[45]

Laetrile proponents angrily responded that they were adults.

> You people in authority consider all the rest of us a bunch of dummies. ... You set yourself up as God and Jesus Christ all rolled up into one. And we don't have any rights. ... Patrick Henry said, "Give me liberty, or give me death." Glenn Rutherford says let me choose the way I want to die. It is not your prerogative to tell me how. Only God can do that.[46]

RECENT GROWTH OF THE MOVEMENT

Why did the dispute over Laetrile emerge during the late 1970s? We have considered the role played by different concepts of medicine, the character of the data, professional prestige, economics, and ideology. But these factors, while useful in understanding the dynamics of conflict, do not fully explain the appeal of Laetrile in the latter half of the 1970s. Three other factors have contributed to the movement's growth in recent years: (1) frustration over the inability of scientists to cure cancer; (2) the decline of trust in government and medicine; and (3) changing tactics of the Laetrile movement itself.

Medical science has cured many deadly diseases. From smallpox in the 1970s to polio in the 1950s, determination and dollars led to the prevention and cure of a variety of ills. In 1971, President Nixon declared war on cancer as a primary target of medical research, and Congress passed the

National Cancer Act. The combined executive and congressional commitment to cure a specific disease led to great optimism about eliminating
cancer. But the incidence of the disease has continued to increase and the
survival rates have shown little if any improvement.[47]

In 1976, approximately 385,000 people died of cancer. Some 54
million Americans are expected to contract the disease eventually, and
once contracted, the death rate from cancer is fearfully high. In light of
these gloomy data, the Commissioner of the FDA has characterized
President Nixon's war on cancer as a "medical Vietnam." The Laetrile
phenomenon is in part a response to the intractibility of the cancer
problem in a context of greatly raised expectations. Against this backdrop
of frustration Laetrile advocates promise a simple and painless treatment
without the debility and disfigurement associated with conventional therapy.

The mistrust of the FDA must also be seen in the context of declining
trust in the leaders of major institutions. In 1966, according to a Harris
Poll, some 41% of the public had "a great deal of confidence" in the
leaders of the executive branch of the government. By 1976, only 11%
expressed that level of confidence.

From 1966 to 1976, medical institutions have enjoyed a high degree of
public confidence compared to other major institutions. But here, too,
there has been a precipitous decline of trust. In 1966, some 73% of the
American public had "a great deal of confidence" in the leaders of medical
institutions, but by 1976 only 42% expressed similar confidence.

Correlated with distrust is the growth of self-help movements in medicine. The health food movement is a prominent example of this phenomenon, although the feminist movement also advocates self-help. These
groups challenge the expert role of physicians and advocate a populist
medicine. Following this trend, pro-Laetrile groups frequently have a strong
self-help component providing health information and emotional support
to their members.

Finally, the Laetrile movement itself has adapted to changing circumstances. Proponents of Laetrile maintain that their ideas are scientific,
although they have been soundly rejected by orthodox medicine. Opponents, who view Laetrile as quackery, are unable to understand the
political victories of the movement. But Laetrile proponents are skillfully
able to integrate scientific and political tactics. When Laetrile forces lost
battles within the scientific community, they changed tactics and broad-

ened the scope of the movement through popular appeals and active campaigns to legalize the treatment. By expanding the scope of the conflict they gained new resources and improved their chance of victory.

Each side in the Laetrile dispute thus developed a consistent but different strategy to obtain a favorable outcome. Opponents of Laetrile refuted the movement's scientific claims, at least from an allopathic logic. They tried to keep the dispute at the level of scientific peer review or government agency approval. When forced into the political arena, they maintained that experts should be the ones to judge Laetrile and called for government control to enforce their decision. Laetrile advocates, on the other hand, expanded the dispute into the political arena. Using a populist ideology, they developed powerful arguments for a public judgment based on a plea for freedom of choice.

It is hard to predict the future of the Laetrile movement. Its continuing appeal, however, is likely to depend as much on the social forces described above as on any scientific evidence of the effectiveness of Laetrile as a cure for cancer.

NOTES

1. While supporters of Laetrile frequently describe it as Vitamin B-17, this claim is rejected by most critics of the substance. Furthermore there is considerable doubt that amygdalin and Laetrile are identical. See J. Trux, "New Controversy Surrounds Black Market Cancer Drug," *New Scientist* 71 (1976), 132; and D. Kennedy, "Laetrile: Commissioner's Decision on Status," *Federal Register* 42 (1977), 39770-39772.

2. Other elements of the cancer underground include Gerson's diet, Koch's antitoxins, Hoxsey's therapy, grape diet, Cresson method, and Chase dietary method. (For a more complete list, see American Cancer Society, *Unproven Methods of Cancer Management* (New York: American Cancer Society, 1976).

3. New York Times, "U.S. Judge Strikes Down New Federal Ban on Use of and Importing of Laetrile," December 6, 1977, 19.

4. James Harvey Young, "Epidemic Quackery," Paper presented at the Bureau of Drugs Seminar, Food and Drug Administration, January 17, 1978.

5. T. Inosemtzeff, "Therapeutique," *Gazette Medicale de Paris* 13 (1845), 577-582.

6. Ernst T. Krebs, Jr., Ernst T. Krebs, Sr., and Howard H. Bears, "The Unitarian or Trophoblastic Thesis Cancer," *Medical Record* 163 (1950), 158.

7. G. Edward Griffin, *World Without Cancer* [Parts I and I] (Thousand Oaks, CA: American Media, 1974).

8. Luther Bohanon, "Rutherford v. United States," *Federal Supplement* 399 (1975), 1208-1215.

9. Patrick Young, "Laetrile: Hope for Cancer Patients, or Just a Hoax?" *The National Observer* 1 (May 16, 1977), 16.

10. Kennedy, 39768-39806.

11. Ronald Troyer, "Promoting a Cancer Cure: The Laetrile Movement," Unpublished Manuscript, Western Michigan University, 1978.

12. Everett Holles, "Birch Society Members Tied to Smuggling of Illegal Drug," *New York Times* (June 1, 1976), 18.

13. A. Stang, "Laetrile: Freedom of Choice in Cancer Therapy," *American Opinion* 17 (1974), 49-66.

14. Kennedy, 39797.

15. Ibid., 39799.

16. Gerald E. Markle, James C. Petersen, and Morton O. Wagenfeld, "Notes from the Cancer Underground: Participation in the Laetrile Movement," *Social Science and Medicine* 12 (1978), 31-37.

17. Morton O. Wagenfeld, Yvonne M. Vissing, Gerald E. Markle, and James C. Petersen, "Notes from the Cancer Underground: Health Attitudes and Practices of Participants in the Laetrile Movement," presented at the annual meetings of the North Central Sociological Association, 1977.

18. Yvonne Vissing, "An Exploratory Analysis of Participation in the Laetrile Movement," unpublished M.A. thesis, Western Michigan University, 1978.

19. Harris L. Coulter, *Divided Legacy: A History of Schism in Medical Thought* (Volume I) (Washington, DC: Wehawken Press, 1975), XV.

20. Ibid., 505.

21. FDA Hearings, "Laetrile Administrative Rule Making Hearing: Oral Argument," Docket No. 77N-0048, Kansas City, MO., May 2-3, 1977), 352.

22. James C. Petersen and Gerald E. Markle, "Adjudication in Science: The Laetrile Controversy," paper presented at the annual meeting of the American Sociological Association, 1977.

23. "The Laetrile Papers," *The Sciences* 18 (1978), 10-13.

24. W. R. Laster, Jr. and F. M. Schabel, Jr., "Experimental Studies of the Anti-tumor Activity of Amygdalin MF (NSC-15780) Alone and in combination with Beta-Glucosidase (NSC-128056)," *Cancer Chemotherapy Reports* 59 (1975), 951-965; Isidore Wodinsky and Joseph K. Swiniarsky, "Anti-tumor Activity of Amygdalin-MF (NSC-15780) as a Single Agent and with Beta-Glucosidase (NSC-128056) on a Spectrum of Transplantable Rodent Tumors," *Cancer Chemotherapy Reports* 59 (1975), 939-950; George J. Hill, Thomas E. Shine, Helene Z. Hill, and Cathie Miller, "Failure of Amygdalin to Arrest B-16 Melanoma and BW5147 AKR Leukemia," *Cancer Research* 36 (1976), 2102-2107.

25. Harold W. Manner, "The Remission of Tumors with Laetrile," paper presented at the annual meetings of the National Health Federation, 1977.

26. Nicholas Wade, "Laetrile at Sloan-Kettering: A Question of Ambiguity," *Science* 198 (1977), 1231.

27. Ibid.

28. Committee for the Freedom of Choice in Cancer Therapy, *Anatomy of a Cover-up: Successful Sloan-Kettering Amygdalin (Laetrile) Animal Studies* (Los Altos, CA: The Committee for Freedom of Choice in Cancer Therapy, 1975).

29. C. Chester Stock, Daniel S. Martin, Kanematsu Sugiura, Ruth A. Fugman, Isabel M. Mountain, Elizabeth Stockert, Franz A. Schmid and George S. Tarnowski, "Anti-Tumor Tests of Amygdalin in Spontaneous Animal Tumor Systems," *Journal of Surgical Oncology* (forthcoming).

30. Richard D. Smith, "Sloan-Kettering Retracts Erroneous Claim for Laetrile Tests," News Release, New York Academy of Sciences, December 12, 1977.

31. Richard D. Smith, "The Laetrile Papers," 10-13.

32. Bernard Barber, "Resistance by Scientists to Scientific Discovery," *Science* 134 (1961), 596-602.

33. Harriet Zuckerman and Robert K. Merton, "Patterns of Evaluation in Science: Institutionalization, Structures and Functions of the Referee System," *Minerva* 9 (1971), 35-100.

34. Stuart S. Blume, *Toward a Political Sociology of Science* (New York: Free Press, 1974).

35. Kennedy, 39785.

36. Michael L. Culbert, *Vitamin B-17—Forbidden Weapon Against Cancer: The Fight for Laetrile* (New Rochelle, NY: Arlington House, 1974), 103.

37. Stewart M. Jones, *Nutrition Rudiments in Cancer* (Palo Alto, CA., 1972).

38. Robert Pear and Rebecca Leet, "Cancer Drug, FDA: Malpractice Suit," *Washington Star,* May 11, 1976; and "McDonald Hits FDA Ban on Laetrile, Defends Use," *Washington Star,* May 18, 1976.

39. Jack Anderson and Les Whitten, "This Laetrile Bootlegging 'Not Humanitarian'," *Kalamazoo Gazette,* June 28, 1977, A-7.

40. Herbert B. Hoffman, testimony at Hearing Before the Subcommittee on Health and Scientific Research of the Committee on Human Resources, United States Senate, July 12, 1977 (Washington, DC: Government Printing Office).

41. Guy Newell, testimony at Hearing before the Subcommittee on Health and Scientific Research of the Committee on Human Resources, United States Senate, July 12, 1977 (Washington, DC: Government Printing Office).

42. James J. Kilpatrick, "Another Uproar over the Freedom to Choose," *Nation's Business,* May 10, 1976.

43. Kennedy, 39803.

44. Ibid., 39804.

45. FDA, Hearings, 62.

46. Ibid., 308, 315-316.

47. James E. Enstrom and Donald R. Austin, "Interpreting Cancer Survival Rates," *Science* 195 (1977), 847-851.

9

SMALLPOX IMMUNIZATION: CONTROVERSIAL EPISODES

Joshua Ira Schwartz

Smallpox immunization has been an outstanding public health success. A campaign to eradicate the disease, undertaken by the World Health Organization in the 1960s, has apparently reached its goal. Reports of the total elimination of smallpox may be premature, but there is little doubt that the goal will soon be reached. In an era when many of the techniques of modern medicine are being criticized, smallpox vaccination has not been a controversial measure. Yet at times in the past, artificial immunization against smallpox was the subject of heated controversy, both within the medical profession and for the public at large.

In recent years, Americans have become aware of the risks and social costs associated with technological innovations and scientific discoveries. Supersonic transports, nuclear power, new medical procedures, and food and drug safety are among the issues that have attracted public discussion. Yet social conflict over the implementation of new technologies is not a new phenomenon, as I shall illustrate by describing two medical controversies over smallpox immunization, one in Boston in the 1720s and the other in the United States during the last third of the nineteenth century.

Opposition to technological change has often been regarded as a product of anti-intellectualism, theological conservatism, or plain backwardness. The persecution of Galileo, the Luddites, and the Scopes "Monkey

Trial" are brought forth as reminders of resistance to change. The two episodes of public debate over the desirability of artificial immunization against smallpox, however, were remarkably similar to modern technology-related controversies. The attributes of these historical episodes were: scientific uncertainty as to the safety and efficacy of the immunization technique, disagreement among experts, and controversy over who should participate in the decision-making process and whether the government should intervene by mandating immunization.

INOCULATION AND VACCINATION

The modern form of artificial immunization against smallpox, called vaccination, consists of introducing cowpox virus into a superficial opening in the patient's skin. The discovery of vaccination is attributed to Edward Jenner who published the results of his experiments in 1798. A cruder form of artificial immunization, called inoculation by contemporaries and variolation by modern scholars, was practiced in the eighteenth century both in Europe and in the American colonies. Inoculation consisted of the application of live smallpox virus into superficial incisions made in the patient's skin. An attempt was made to secure the virus from individuals who had a mild case of the disease, thereby transmitting a mild case of smallpox to the inoculated person under somewhat controlled conditions. The mildness of the induced disease insured that most of those inoculated recovered, and thereafter had immunity to naturally occurring virulent smallpox.

The practice of inoculation for smallpox had two major drawbacks. First, modern techniques of virus attenuation were unavailable.[1] Although there were some systematic efforts to attenuate the virus, inoculated patients occasionally contracted severe cases of smallpox, and some died. Second, even if the artificially induced case were mild, the patient was capable of transmitting virulent smallpox during the interval of contagiousness. The latter problem was significant politically, for an individual's decision to be inoculated affected his neighbors. Communities therefore felt entitled to a voice in the decision as to whether individuals could be innoculated.

THE SMALLPOX CONTROVERSY IN BOSTON, 1721-1722

Smallpox was known in Europe by the tenth century, and probably much earlier.[2] Until the seventeenth century, it was regarded as an endemic but relatively mild children's disease. In the second half of the seventeenth century, the disease assumed a more virulent form and provoked increased fear and concern.[3] Smallpox spread to the American colonies in the seventeenth century, and there were epidemics in New England in 1631, 1666, 1677, 1678, and 1702.[4] In the early years of the eighteenth century, the Royal Society of London received reports about folk practices of securing immunity to smallpox by intentional exposure to mild cases of the disease. The origins of these reports were diverse: China, India, Africa, various European countries, Greece, Turkey, and Scotland. Several reports of the Turkish practice of innoculation with smallpox pustule matter were published in the Transactions of the Royal Society in 1714 and 1716. Reports of the practice of innoculation also reached North America at this time. Several copies of the issues of the *Transactions* describing innoculation were brought to Boston by travelers. African slaves also informed their masters about the practice of innoculation when asked whether they had ever had smallpox.

The Reverend Cotton Mather, better known as a conservative Calvinist theologian and clergyman, was responsible for the first experimental use of smallpox innoculation in Boston during the smallpox epidemic of 1721. There are excellent accounts of Mather's advocacy of innoculation and the reaction to it;[5] here the episode is briefly summarized to provide a basis for analyzing it in modern terms as a case of politically controversial technological innovation.

Based on his reading, Cotton Mather decided by 1716 that he would attempt to organize an innoculation program should smallpox reappear in Boston. In 1721 when the disease broke out, Mather wrote an open letter to local physicians proposing that innoculation be tried. When this letter brought no response, Mather wrote to his personal friend, Dr. Zabadiel Boylston, a leading Boston physician. Boylston began experimental innoculation on his son and two servants. After the success of these trials, Boylston published a notice in the press announcing the availability of innoculation and arguing the efficacy and safety of the practice. In the small town of Boston, word of Boylston's and Mather's experiment spread quickly. The public reaction was generally hostile and the Boston select men warned Boylston to cease innoculation.[6] Boylston ignored the warning and began to innoculate hundreds of patients.

The leader of the opposition to innoculation was Dr. William Douglass, the only physician in Boston who held the M.D. degree, who had moved to Boston from England three years earlier. Douglass argued that innoculation spread smallpox and labeled the practice criminal. Accounts of the innoculation controversy indicate that Mather had borrowed the volumes of the *Transactions* describing innoculation from Douglass, and this circumstance exacerbated Douglass's resentment of what he considered Mather's interference in the professional practice of medicine. Orthodox European and American medical practice was extremely conservative at this time, and Douglass's opposition to the use of innoculation was characteristic of the attitudes of professional leaders. He was able to unite all of Boston's physicians, who agreed that innoculation would spread smallpox, transmit other diseases by contamination of the innoculate, and cause virulent smallpox in those innoculated.

The pro-innoculation faction was dominated by the clergy. When Douglass and other physicians began to criticize Mather and Boylston, the clergy united to defend the practice of innoculation.[7] Even liberal clergymen who usually found themselves in opposition to Cotton and Increase Mather on other issues closed ranks with the conservatives on this occasion. The active support of innoculation by the clergy turned the controversy into a struggle over clerical authority in secular matters. The two factions engaged in a pamphlet war. The mouthpiece of the anticlerical faction was James Franklin's *New England Courant* newspaper. James, and his as yet uncelebrated younger brother Benjamin, maintained a constant barrage of criticism of innoculation and personal attacks on Boylston and the Mathers.

Douglass and other physicians also published a stream of pamphlets and letters in local newspapers attacking innoculation, while the clergymen published an equal number of tracts favorable to the practice. Cotton Mather was a formidable opponent, for he was a prolific writer and was quick to attribute opposition to the devil.

The opposition, however, adopted more vigorous means of expressing their opinions. A mob besieged Cotton Mather's residence and a grenade was tossed, but failed to explode. There were threats of lynching directed against Dr. Boylston. Both men were repeatedly harassed and threatened by mob violence on the streets.

The Boston selectmen held a hearing on the merits and dangers of innoculation in 1721, and leading opponents of innoculation were invited to testify. Dr. Lawrence Dal'honde, a visiting French physician, claimed that innoculation in Europe had caused horrible diseases. Although factually innaccurate, this was regarded as persuasive by the selectmen, who ordered Boylston to cease innoculation once again. Boylston continued his defiance, but Dal'honde's testimony, which was reprinted in the newspapers, helped to foster increased public opposition.

In 1722, the colonial House of Representatives voted to ban innoculation, but the Governor and the Council, which formed the upper house of the colonial legislature, rejected the measure. However, public opposition to innoculation continued unabated, and the Boston selectmen forced Boylston to agree to stop his innoculation program. By this time, the epidemic was abating, and there were fewer patients seeking innoculation. By banning innoculation when the epidemic was virtually over, the selectmen established what became known as the "rule of 20." Under this compromise, innoculation would be permitted only when there were active cases in more than 20 families. This simple form of regulation prevailed in New England through much of the eighteenth century.

Douglass himself eventually came to approve of the practice of innoculation under appropriate circumstances. And innoculation proponents eventually recognized that many of the precautions urged by Douglass, such as limiting its use to emergency situations and isolating innoculated patients, were valuable. Douglass, however, never abandoned his personal hostility toward Boylston or altered his low estimate of Boylston's credentials. Douglass conceded that Mather's intentions were good, but continued to argue that Mather had no business offering an opinion on a medical subject.

The controversy was, among other things, a clash of competing claims of expertise. For the clergy, the theocratic traditions of New England were at stake. According to Mather's conservative interpretation of this tradition, clergymen were the ultimate authority on all matters affecting the well-being of society as a whole. The concept of secular expertise, such as the physicians' claim with respect to health, was a threat. Perry Miller interprets Mather's avid interest in natural philosophy and medicine as an attempt to capture and coopt the impetus of the Enlightenment and thereby avert displacement of religious authority by science. Naturally, the assertion of religious hegemony over a controversial health practice provided a target for anticlerical and freethinking Bostonians.

For physicians the integrity of medical professionalism was at stake. This is clearly revealed in Douglass's argument that Mather was incompetent to judge the practical merits of the method of innoculation described in the *Transactions*. As a European-trained M.D., Douglass was especially sensitive to lay infringement upon medical prerogatives, and was especially anxious to achieve public support for physicians' monopoly on medical care. The rigid antiempiricism of medical thought made it highly vulnerable to competition from a venturesome, empirically minded cleric.

Just as the clergymen were intruding into the domain of medical knowledge, physicians and lay opponents of innoculation were intruding into theology. Opponents of innoculation argued that innoculation was immoral and irreligious, either because it was sinful to intentionally contract a disease, or because it was sinful to avoid a disease sent by God. Yet usually these religious and moral arguments were used not by religious leaders, but by physicians, playing to the qualms of the religious public. In this instance, the intellectual leadership of the clergy was swayed by Enlightenment ideas, while their congregants in many cases retained a more fundamentalist position. The unity of the Boston clergy in support of innoculation is explained less by their attitudes toward this particular medical practice than by their desire to defend the prerogatives of the clergy to lead in medical and other public issues, as well as to secure their right to serve as the ultimate interpreter of moral and religious doctrine.

The factions in the innoculation controversy were also arrayed along socioeconomic lines. The upper orders of Boston society were relatively receptive to innoculation, while the common people of Boston were generally opposed. Despite the virulent opposition, hundreds of individuals sought out Dr. Boylston to be innoculated, and most of these were from the elite. One practical reason for the split along class lines was that the isolation necessary to prevent spread of the disease was seldom possible in lower class communities. But the dispute also embodied the conflict between urban and rural areas. Opposition to innoculation was especially strong in rural areas surrounding Boston, where the practice of innocula-tion was regarded as a piece of cosmopolitan folly.[8]

The innoculation dispute also revolved around a matter of political principle. John Blake argues that one basis for popular opposition to innoculation was the failure of either Mather or Boylston to consult the political authorities.[9] By continuing innoculation in the face of objections they flaunted the majority will and thereby crystallized opposition.

As in modern controversies, both sides in the innoculation dispute used statistical evidence to support their contentions. Mather and Boylston published several studies to show that the incidence of mortality among those artificially exposed to the disease was much lower than among those who had contracted it naturally. No attempt was made to account for the possibility that those not innoculated might escape the disease. It was generally considered inevitable even by those opposing innoculation that everyone would be exposed to and catch smallpox during this period, although the smaller likelihood of exposure in rural areas may partly account for the anti-innoculation sentiment in these areas. Douglass and other opponents published their own statistical studies to refute Mather's claims. Each side accused the other of manipulating data, of improper statistical techniques, and of drawing improper conclusions from the available data.

One of the moral and medical issues influencing this whole affair, but rarely discussed openly, was the relationship between smallpox and venereal disease. In medieval times, smallpox and syphilis were thought to be closely related diseases, because in both cases sores erupted from the skin. The name smallpox is derived from the French "la petite verole" (the small sore), which was distinguished from "la grande verole" (the large sore), which meant syphilis. Although medical authorities had distinguished the two diseases before the eighteenth century, the idea that some connection existed between them had not disappeared, and it helped to create opposition to the novel practice of innoculation.

Like most modern technology-related political controversies, the innoculation conflict grew on a foundation of technical uncertainty. Neither faction possessed adequate evidence to prove its claims. In the heat of dispute each side exaggerated its statements and resorted to personal attacks on the other. Historians have offered varying evaluations of the merits of the two positions. Medical historians have tended to evaluate the controversy in terms that reflect medical practice and social trends prevailing at the time at which they wrote. In the eighteenth century, both sides in the dispute resorted to history as a polemical vehicle. In the nineteenth and early twentieth centuries, medical historians espoused a conservative, ahistorical view of vaccination, denying its antecedents in innoculation. This group stressed the dangers of innoculation and cast Douglass in a favorable light. In the twentieth century, with the rise of the disciplines of history and sociology of science, there has been renewed interest in innoculation. Thus many modern historians portray Mather and Boylston as courageous, farsighted, humanitarian scientists, and treat vaccination as a mere refinement of innoculation. At least one scholar argues that Jenner did not discover a new technique, but merely used a mild strain of smallpox for innoculation.[10] In recent years, there has also been a reaction to the excesses of the historicist school by scholars who caution against attributing any profound insights to Mather and Boylston. They note that the techniques of the early innoculators were crude, that their statistics were inadequate, and that their use of innoculation without advance tests is inconsistent with scientific research practices.

There is substantial agreement that the colossal egos and substantial rhetorical abilities of the major adversaries, Mather and Douglass, heightened the antagonism surrounding the dispute. Yet the controversy was more than a matter of personalities. Stripped to its essentials, we can see that Mather proposed a controversial medical practice with exotic origins. He and Boylston implemented it without adequate testing under controlled conditions, and resisted all attempts to regulate their practices. The medical profession reacted in a rigid fashion, displaying both well-founded caution and unreasoning conservatism and antiempiricism. The public reacted to fear of unknown risks. Participants disputed their opponents' expertise, credentials, and use of evidence. Contemporary research suggests that refinements of technique and the use of careful isolation procedures could reduce the risks of innoculation. Yet neither Mather nor Boylston achieved such refinements, nor did they adequately recognize the risks involved. On the other hand, if Douglass had his way, innoculation would probably never have been tried.

In the years that followed the dispute, the public succeeded in establishing controls over innoculation. Its use was regulated. Most colonial governments limited the use of innoculation to epidemics when the risk of spread of the disease already existed. Acceptance of innoculation gradually increased throughout the 1700s, although it remained an emergency measure.

TRANSITIONAL PERIOD

In 1798, Edward Jenner published his discovery of cowpox vaccination as a preventive for smallpox. His account was soon transmitted to Dr. Benjamin Waterhouse in Boston, who first used cowpox vaccine in 1800. After trying the vaccine on his own family, Waterhouse began public vaccination. He also attempted to organize a monopoly on cowpox vaccine distribution in the United States by franchising doctors and by assigning exclusive rights to particular geographic areas. The elaborate system of legal bonds and covenants created by Waterhouse in order to assure his profits soon broke down. Thereafter he assisted freely in the spread of vaccination and the distribution of vaccine, yet his brief excursion into medical enterprise earned him the emnity of nineteenth-century physicians and medical historians.

Despite Waterhouse's personal ethical deviations, the practice of vaccination caught on relatively quickly with the public and with physicians. The Boston Board of Health conducted an experiment in which a group of children were vaccinated and thereafter exposed to virulent smallpox. When none of the children contracted smallpox, vaccination received a dramatic boost. The advantages of vaccination—the mildness of the reaction produced in the patient and the impossibility of communicating the disease to others—made it more attractive to the lay public than innoculation. Nevertheless, vaccination had to overcome several obstacles to achieve acceptance.

There were some who felt that innoculation was more trustworthy, believing instinctively that the benefits of vaccination could not be achieved without some risks. This view was encouraged by established innoculators who regarded vaccination as a competitive threat. During the eighteenth century, innoculation had developed into a medical specialty, with full-time practitioners, many of whom expressed doubts about the efficacy of vaccination. Despite these obstacles vaccination became quite general. Although immigrant and lower class groups often neglected vaccination, especially as memories of devastating smallpox epidemics receded, there was little controversy about vaccination until the last third of the nineteenth century, when a major antivaccination movement emerged.

THE ANTIVACCINATION MOVEMENT

The dispute over vaccination is another case of social controversy concerning the implementation of technical innovation. Compared to the opponents of innoculation, the opponents of vaccination were far more eccentric, less respectable, and had less scientific evidence for their position. The risks involved were small, but the antivaccination movement was not entirely devoid of scientific basis, and therefore it too offers insight into the resolution of political questions involving scientific developments. The eccentricity among vaccination opponents does not render this case irrelevant to our inquiry. On the contrary, the antivaccination movement reveals how difficult it can be to differentiate scientific uncertainty about risks and efficacy from pure fantasy, as factual issues of risk converge with political issues of acceptability.

In the 1840s and 1850s, the success of vaccination in producing widespread immunity to smallpox made the threat of the disease seem remote, and vaccination fell into relative disuse. At the same time, increased immigration to the cities of the northeastern United States increased the unvaccinated population pool. By the 1870s, this situation brought renewed epidemics and new vaccination programs rekindled the antivaccination movement. This movement did not possess a uniform doctrine and its adherents espoused a wide variety of beliefs. Some antivaccinationists were opposed only to compulsory universal vaccination. This viewpoint had many respectable adherents including some physicians and public health professionals. Most self-proclaimed antivaccinationists also opposed public or charitable programs of mass vaccination, even if conducted on a voluntary basis. The most extreme faction opposed the practice of vaccination entirely.

The antivaccination movement obtained the repeal of compulsory vaccination laws in seven midwestern and western states and retarded enforcement of such laws in many others. Major riots occurred in Montreal and in Milwaukee. In New York City and the City of Brooklyn active antivaccination groups intimidated public health agencies into abandoning advocacy of compulsory universal vaccination, and lax enforcement of compulsory vaccination laws for school children. In 1882, the Antivaccination League of New York was founded.[11] The movement grew increasingly strident in the 1880s and 1890s, and extremists within it grew increasingly dominant. The Anti-Compulsory Vaccination League of Brooklyn was founded in 1894, and challenged in court the power of the Brooklyn Board of Health to compel vaccination even in cases where a risk of exposure to the disease existed. The League won this case in the trial court, but the Board obtained a reversal on appeal. Nevertheless, a number of individuals were successful in obtaining damage awards against the Board from sympathetic juries, arguing that they had been the victims of an illegal battery when compelled to submit to vaccination.

The leader of the Anti-Compulsory Vaccination League of Brooklyn was a homeopathic physician, Dr. Alice Campbell. Irregular medical practitioners, such as the homeopaths, were one well-spring of the antivaccination movement. In the nineteenth century, a host of medical sects practicing unorthodox therapies flourished. Lest these be easily dismissed as mere quackery, it is important to remember that the orthodox therapy until nearly the end of the nineteenth century was "heroic therapy" which required frequent bleeding and administration of powerful purgatives which often killed or harmed the patient. Most of the irregular therapies could at least be said to be harmless. In the last quarter of the nineteenth century, the professional societies of orthodox practitioners gained strength and began to drive the "irregulars" out of practice. Many of the irregulars seized upon the antivaccination movement in an attempt to find an issue to discredit orthodox medicine in the eyes of the public. Based on the track record of the orthodox practitioners, it was entirely reasonable to be suspicious of vaccination. Irregulars also charged vaccinators with collecting monopoly profits and portrayed their antivaccination movement as part of the prevailing muckraking opposition to monopolies.

A powerful force behind the antivaccination movement in the early 20th century was the American Medical Liberty League, founded in 1918 as a front for patent medicine manufacturers who were fighting increasing regulation under state and federal pure food and drug acts. The irregular medical practitioners and antivaccinationists formed a coalition based on opposition to all forms of public health programs including drug regulation, medical licensure, and vaccination. The antivaccination movement also won the support of the medical diploma mills whose fear of exposure created an antipathy to all forms of government regulation.

Two other sources of support for the antivaccination movement were the antivivisectionists, who frequently enlisted in this movement although their organizations took no official position on vaccination, and the burgeoning sanitary movement. The early public health program was based on opposition to contagionist etiological theories. This efficacious health program was thus built on a theoretical foundation that turned out to be in error. In the late nineteenth century, clinical experience with cholera and the discoveries of Koch, Henle, and Pasteur in the field of bacteriology had revitalized the theory that major epidemic diseases were communicable. The new bacteriological discoveries threatened to undermine the rationale for recently established public health programs, and thus Sanitarians viewed the germ theory of disease with suspicion.[12] In particular, many Sanitarians regarded specific biological preventive measures like vaccination as retrogressive and recommended programs of environmental sanitation and nutrition as an alternative to vaccination. This group developed as a protest against the unwarranted disregard of the environmental causes of disease which had been engendered by the bacteriological revolution and the domination of health care by physicians that this revolution facilitated. Indeed it was not surprising that sanitarians could show a correlation between improved sanitation and nutrition and reduced mortality.

Opponents of vaccination employed a wide range of arguments. Those who opposed compulsory vaccination argued that it was an infringement of personal liberty. Some members of the movement stressed the poor techniques in use, the inadequate training of vaccinators, and the transmission of secondary infection by use of nonsterile equipment. More extreme opponents claimed that vaccination spread cancer, leprosy, and the black plague. The old bugaboo about venereal disease surfaced again; one opponent called vaccination the "syphilization of society." Once again it is important to bear the setting in mind in evaluating this opposition. Indeed, the early uncritical enthusiasm about vaccination and other techniques of artificial immunization had led to serious consideration of a proposal to innoculate all French youth with syphilis.

In fact, there were major drawbacks to existing vaccination practices in the area of vaccine contamination, purity, dosage control, training of vaccinators, and vaccination techniques. Supporters and opponents of vaccination traded statistical proofs of their arguments, each side succeeding in finding some empirical support of its position. Moreover, the supporters of vaccination were embarassed by their inability to answer questions about the relationship between cowpox, the various forms of smallpox, and the infection induced by vaccination.

By the 1930s, the antivaccination movement began to disintegrate. The techniques, equipment, and vaccine had improved greatly, undermining the objections of many moderates. Irregular practitioners were rapidly disappearing, eliminating another focus of opposition. The role of the government in health had achieved much wider acceptance, and thus vaccination laws seemed less outrageous.

CONCLUSION

There are some obvious differences between the antivaccination movement and the earlier innoculation controversy. Far less scientific uncertainty existed about the safety and efficacy of vaccination; indeed the risks of vaccination are much smaller than those of innoculation. By the time the antivaccination movement came along, vaccination was an established practice and was therefore more difficult to obstruct. Each controversy, however, raised similar questions about the proper role of expertise and the appropriate means to shape public policy. The strongest argument presented by opponents of innoculation was the riskiness of an unknown procedure. Because this argument did not apply with equal force to vaccination in the late nineteenth century, the latter movement had more limited success. The anti-innoculators established the principle of political control over medical practice, while the antivaccinators' strongest argument was based on the individual liberty of the citizen. This argument succeeded for a time in forestalling compulsory universal vaccination, but the more extreme elements of the movement met with less success. The use of the courts by the Anti-Compulsory Vaccination League of Brooklyn suggests that they were resigned to the use of a minority strategy for political action, while the Anti-Innoculator groups of Boston were able to command the support of selectmen and a town meeting. The courts had yet to develop into the potent tools for shaping and obstructing social policy that they have become in the second half of the twentieth century, but their potential was already evident 100 years ago.

This examination of two controversial episodes in the development of artificial immunization to smallpox demonstrates that many of the elements of modern disputes about the impact and control of technology and science are not new at all. Many of the elements of modern technopolitical disputes—the problem of decision-making in the face of scientific uncertainty, the disputes among experts, the controversy over the proper participants in the dispute, the concern about credentials, the debate over technical and statistical evidence, and the participation of diverse interest groups in the controversies—were present in both episodes. The citizens review board in Cambridge, Massachusetts, which evaluated the dangers of recombinant DNA research at Harvard in 1976, has a precedent in the actions of the Boston selectmen who held a hearing in 1722 to evaluate the dangers of innoculation and to decide whether individual scientists and physicians might continue this practice.

NOTES

1. Arnold C. Klebs, "The History of Infection," *Annals of Medical History* 1 (1917), 159-173; Richard Shryock, *The Development of Modern Medicine* (New York: Alfred A. Knopf, 1936), 294, n. 40.

2. Genevieve Miller, *The Adoption of Innoculation for Smallpox in England and France* (unpublished dissertation, Cornell University, 1955), 12-13.

3. Ibid., 15-16.

4. Francis R. Packard, *History of Medicine in the United States* (New York: Hafner Publishing, 1963); C.E.A. Winslow, "The Colonial Era and the First Years of the Republic (1607-1799): The Pestilence that Walketh in Darkness," in Franklin H. Top, ed., *The History of American Epidemiology* (St. Louis: C. V. Mosby, 1952), 11-12.

5. Otho T. Beal and Richard Shryock, *Cotton Mather* (Baltimore: Johns Hopkins University Press, 1954); Reginald Fitz, "Something Curious in the Medical Line," *Bulletin of History of Medicine* 11 (1942), 239-264; and Reginald Fitz, "Zabadiel Boylston, Innoculator, and the Epidemic of Smallpox in Boston in 1721," *Bulletin of the Johns Hopkins Hospital* 22 (1911), 315-327.

6. John Ballard Blake, *Public Health in the Town of Boston* (Cambridge: Harvard University Press, 1959), 57.

7. Perry Miller, *The New England Mind: From Colony to Province* (Cambridge: Harvard University Press, 1953), 347.

8. Ibid., 350-351.

9. John Ballard Blake, *Benjamin Waterhouse and the Introduction of Vaccination* (Philadelphia: University of Pennsylvania Press, 1957).

10. P. E. Razell, "Edward Jenner: The History of a Medical Myth," *Medical History* 9, 216-223.

11. John Duffy, *Epidemics in Colonial America* (Baton Rouge: Louisiana State University Press, 1953); *A History of Public Health in New York City, 1625-1866* (New York: Russell Sage Foundation, 1968); and *A History of Public Health in New York City, 1866-1966* (New York: Russell Sage Foundation, 1974).

12. Carl Bell, "Compulsory Vaccination," *Sanitarian* 38 (1897), 19-33.

PART IV
SCIENCE VERSUS TRADITIONAL VALUES

There appears to be a renewed concern with moral and religious values in American society and a related ambivalence toward science. To the extent that science is perceived as a dominant world view, so it is seen to threaten traditional beliefs and to supress essential elements of human experience. At a time when the accomplishments of science have fostered faith in the value of rational explanations of nature, there are concerted efforts to reinvest educational systems with traditional faith. Even as biomedical research brings about dramatic improvements in medical care, efforts go forward to curtail research and to question scientific procedures that infringe on traditional moral values. The Scopes trial is often thought to have been the last vestige of the great struggle between religion and science, but the past decade has seen the revival of creationism and has brought new complaints about the teaching of evolution in public schools. The antivivisectionists are often thought to be the last of the major critics of research procedures, but recent controversies have revealed new groups who oppose research on the human fetus and question the implications of genetic research.

Concerns about the moral implications of science nurtured the dispute over fetal research described by Steven Maynard-Moody. The 1973 Supreme Court ruling on abortion enhanced sensitivity to research using the human fetus; for right-to-life groups such research was a moral affront, an offense to their beliefs. The controversy raised many value-laden questions about the definition of life and the bearing of research on human dignity. While scientists tried to focus the issue on the technical criteria that determined the initiation of life (the size and weight of the fetus), critics of fetal research talked of human dignity and the value of life. To challenge this research practice, they brought their concerns to the courts and to state legislatures. The case suggests the continued ambivalence about scientific research among many groups who perceive science as infringing on morality.

Dorothy Nelkin's review of the creation-evolution controversy illustrates similar concerns among some religious fundamentalists. A group of these fundamentalists call themselves "scientific creationists" and demand "equal time" for creation theory whenever evolution is taught in biology classrooms or included in biology texts. Creationists feel that the current practice of teaching evolutionary biology in public schools intrudes on their religious beliefs. Yet they argue their case in technical terms, providing "scientific evidence" that the Biblical version of creation is a valid scientific alternative to evolution theory. Creationists have exerted a sufficiently powerful influence on school districts and textbook commissions that many educators, biologists, and publishers view their demands as a serious threat to science education.

Finally, Şheldon Krimsky's review of the controversy over recombinant DNA research shows how cherished values influence the position of both critics of science and scientists themselves. This very complex case raises many questions about the potential risks of research and about the possible misuse of scientific findings. The intense and protracted nature of the dispute, however, is in part due to its implications for deeply held beliefs about free will and self-determination, for new techniques of recombining DNA molecules remove barriers to the creation of new life forms. A central point in Krimsky's analysis, however, is how discussion of public regulation of research threatens basic values within science. Throughout the dispute, scientists have fought to maintain their autonomy, self-regulation, and freedom of scientific inquiry. The case is presented to emphasize the importance of these values to the scientific community and how scientists influenced the dynamics of the controversy.

THE FETAL RESEARCH DISPUTE

Steven Maynard-Moody

Research on the human fetus has been a source of considerable medical progress. It has fostered new diagnostic tools to save high-risk fetuses from therapeutic abortions. It has clarified our understanding of human fetal development and refined novel techniques of life support for premature infants. And it has permitted the testing of new drugs and vaccines. Such research poses no risk to bystanders, nor are the findings likely to be used perniciously.

Yet fetal research has also been the source of a bitter conflict between ethical and scientific priorities and over the moral implications of using human fetuses as research subjects. Researchers stress the scientific merit of their work; nonscientists stress its moral implications. Although scientists tend to frame the debate in technical terms, the controversy is rooted in basic value questions: is the fetus fully human? what are its rights and its legal and social status? who should define research ethics in disputed cases? Moreover these questions are not asked in a social vacuum. Opposition has grown as legal abortions have contributed to the frequency and scope of fetal experiments. Such research, claim antiabortionists, compounds the immorality of abortion.[1]

THE NATURE OF FETAL RESEARCH

Prior to their deliberations in 1974 on fetal research, the National Commission for the Protection of Human Subjects of Biomedical and Behavioral Research funded an extensive literature review on the nature, extent, and purpose of fetal research.[2] The review organized more than 3,000 reported projects into four categories. First were those intended to expand scientific knowledge about normal fetal development, largely to provide the basis for identifying and curing birth deformities. Most of these studies involved autopsies of dead fetuses, some of which were obtained from abortions. Several of the research protocols, such as the "isolation surgically" of fetal heads, evoked disturbing images. But research on dead fetuses aroused little controversy so long as the accepted procedures for autopsies outlined in the Uniform Anatomical Gifts Act were followed.

A second type of research focused on techniques to diagnose fetal diseases or abnormalities. Amniocentesis, for example, is an important and effective tool for prenatal diagnosis of Downs' Syndrome and Rh disease. Diagnostic research also includes the extension of amniocentesis for detection of diseases such as cystic fibrosis, the isolation and examination of fetal cells from the mother's blood, and the development of a fetoscope for direct observation of the unborn. The fetoscope permits direct examination of physical deformities and better diagnosis of a wider variety of diseases than is possible with amniocentesis. Even though animal studies preceded the fetoscope's use on humans, its initial application involved unknown risks. To minimize the risk to fetuses that are expected to go full term, researchers tried out the instrument on women planning abortions.

A third area of fetal research involved pharmacology. Many doctors believe that a substantial proportion of birth defects result from unidentified chemical or environmental influences, such as the use of antibiotics. Most pharmacological studies of the effect of drugs on the fetus are retrospective, involving the examination of the fetus or infant after an accidental exposure. The effects of oral contraceptives on fetuses were studied by following the pre- and postnatal history of children whose mothers became pregnant while using the pill. Other studies are associated with therapy such as the use of penicillin to treat fetal syphilis. A small number of investigations used living fetuses, to follow the movement across the placenta of anesthetics given to the mother during labor. To increase the rigor of such experiments, several researchers reasoned that a planned abortion would permit greater scientific control. A group of pregnant women planning abortion consented to take antibiotics so that their effect on the fetus could be observed. The later dissection of the aborted fetuses without the specific permission for autopsy brought accusations, outrage, and the indictment of four researchers for "grave robbing" under an old Massachusetts law.

A final category of research involved experiments on the nonviable fetus. This was the most controversial category since the status of the nonviable fetus is far from clear. Although alive, demonstrating a heartbeat and some nervous system activity, current medical science cannot sustain its life. Thus research on the nonviable fetus raises the basic question of defining "being alive."

Nonviable fetuses are used to measure amino acid and hemoglobin levels in the blood, or to study fetal metabolism by injecting noradrenaline and tracer chemicals into the umbilical vein. These procedures do not cause significant risk to the fetus. However, other procedures such as the testing of new life support systems for premature infants are possibly harmful. One such study immersed 15 fetuses from 9 to 24 weeks gestational age in a salt solution. By forcing oxygen through the skin, this artificial placenta maintained their life signs for up to 22 hours. Development of this technique promises medical benefits, and researchers insist that fetuses are unable to feel pain; nevertheless, maintaining a fading life without the promise of survival is perceived by many people as an improper use of human subjects.

INSTITUTIONAL CONTROL

Scientists are not completely free to determine the acceptability of their investigations. The discord over fetal research must be seen as an extension of the continuing disagreement over the use of human subjects. Demands for greater external control over research procedures have generally followed incidents of abuse.[3] Early concern for the rights of research subjects grew out of the Nazi "scientific" experiments; the Nuremberg Code (1949) established the criterion of voluntary consent prior to human experimentation. Later, in 1964, the Declaration of Helsinki required that research subjects must provide informed as well as voluntary consent, and that the research must promise important contributions to science.

However, these guidelines, providing neither for the policing of research nor the punishing of offenders, were difficult to enforce. Moreover, researcher sensitivity to the safety of human subjects was not adequate to avoid abuses.[4] Several incidents increased pressure for greater public control. Inmates of coercive institutions such as prisons and mental asylums were disproportionately used as research subjects. In the early 1960s, live cancer cells were injected into nonconsenting elderly patients, and penicillin was withheld from syphilitic patients in order to maintain a control group in a longitudinal study.

To establish public control without impeding research, the government sought to increase researchers' accountability while decentralizing control within the local research institutions. Formalizing this compromise, the Public Health Service (PHS) and the Department of Health, Education and Welfare (HEW) established Institutional Review Boards (IRB) in each university and medical center to review the adequacy of safeguards protecting human subjects and the scientific merit of each study. Once questions of safety and merit were resolved locally, federal administrators would evaluate the priority of the proposals vis-à-vis national goals. Although some researchers still regard the IRB as an "unwarranted intrusion" into their autonomy, the IRB has become the principal mechanism for insuring the protection of human subjects.[5] All federally funded fetal research has been approved by such a committee. This approval, however, has not guaranteed public acceptance.

The persistence of controversy over fetal research must be understood in terms of the limits of the Institutional Review Boards. A survey found that most include community representatives as well as medical researchers.[6] These nonscientists define the purpose of the review board in terms of the protection of human subjects, whereas scientists insist that their purpose is to balance the protection of subjects with the need for developing new knowledge. The unstated corollary to the scientists' position is that higher risks can be tolerated if research needs are great. While the nonscientists' opinions are solicited, the view that balances risks and benefits has prevailed.[7]

In another study of the IRB's, Bernard Barber identifies the pressures on researchers to give greater weight to scientific rather than ethical considerations.[8] He argues that competitive pressures within science and the absence of ethical training undermine the objectives of the IRBs, many of which never require revision of research proposals nor monitor compliance with existing standards.

THE CONTROVERSY: ISSUES

What makes certain issues controversial? A partial answer can be found in the inadequacies of the existing decision-making mechanisms. Another partial answer can be found in the different values that exist within a population. The fetal research controversy cannot be reduced to the level of simple factual misunderstanding, for it reflects opposing interpretations of facts and contrasting judgments about policy. These differences are reflected in three disputes: over the definition of the fetus, over the balance of individual risks and social benefits, and over appropriate decision-making authority.

THE DEFINITION OF THE FETUS

Is the fetus, however rudimentary, fully human, or is it merely a mass of tissue? Those insisting on the former argue that, while each level of maturity brings new social and legal rights, basic respect for human dignity must extend to every stage of biological development. They insist that any distinction between prehuman and human development is arbitrary and erodes society's commitment to the rights of individuals. In contrast, others argue that a fetus which could not independently survive is a biological extension of the mother and has no separate moral or legal standing. This second definition labels the moment of independent existence as the beginning of human life. Since the difference between a premature infant and a nonviable fetus depends on current medical criteria, the status of the fetus becomes a technical not a moral judgment.

Doctors use the criteria of heartbeat, respiration, and nervous system activity to decide if life was ever present. Prior to such life signs, doctors are not required in most states to sign death certificates, and hospitals discard the fetal remains in the same manner as the tissue byproducts of surgery.

However, few researchers take the extreme view that norms of consent and scientific merit do not apply to experiments with undeveloped fetuses. Most simply argue that physical differences (such as the lack of pain and awareness) between the undeveloped fetus and the premature infant legitimize different standards of safety and consent. This position is similar to the legal position taken in the landmark abortion case, Roe versus Wade. For purposes of legal protection it is argued that the fetus may be treated as a part of the mother and that legally the state has no compelling interest in protecting the nonviable fetus.[9]

SOCIAL GAIN OR INDIVIDUAL RISK

A second controversial issue focuses on the degree of risk that is permissible given the social benefits of research. Experiments that seem unnecessary and grotesque to the nonscientist are, to the researcher, valuable contributions to knowledge and thus to society. Improvements in medical care often depend on a few individuals assuming some risks. Like their colleagues on the IRBs, proponents of fetal research argue that public policy must consider the social benefit of research when judging its costs. Critics of the research, however, reject the attempt to balance human rights against social benefits. They insist that the value of a human life outweighs any promise of social gain. Moreover, since fetuses cannot give consent, opponents argue that they should not be the subjects of any hazardous research.

WHO DECIDES?

Research practices are normally determined within the scientific community. This is consistent with the established belief in freedom of inquiry and the public acceptance of the authority of scientific expertise. There have, however, been many serious challenges to the self-regulation of science—inevitable in light of the reliance of science on federal support and the increasing effect of science on our daily lives.

In the case of fetal research, two additional factors raised the question of "Who decides?" First, the political marriage of fetal research and abortion fundamentally changed the nature of the policy questions facing local and federal governments. Suddenly people were insisting that the research should not be done at all. Second, the IRBs were quickly perceived as an inadequate forum for introducing moral judgments into the decision-making process.[10] Because of the politicization that followed the abortion issue, new constituencies such as right-to-life groups demanded the inclusion of their views in decision-making about research practices.

THE PUBLIC DISPUTE

THE PEEL REPORT

Public concern over fetal research first surfaced in Great Britain when, in a speech before Parliament, Norman St. John-Stevens exposed the transportation of fetuses from abortion clinics to research institutes.[11] In response to mounting concern over this practice, parliament appointed an advisory group to develop regulations. Under the leadership of Sir John Peel, a fellow of the Royal College of Obstetrics and Gynecology, the committee addressed questions about the status of the fetus and the requirements for consent. The British discussion was less strident than the later American controversy, but the efforts of the Peel Committee set important precedents.

The Committee's report, issued in May 1972, took a strong stand on the question of legal status, concluding that a planned abortion in no way changes the legal protection afforded a fetus. It insisted that: (1) researchers must have no part in the decision on the fetus's eligibility for experimentation; (2) the proposed research must be essential; and (3) any money exchanged for the procurement of fetuses must cover only the costs involved. Furthermore, the report described fetuses as a new class of human subjects, requiring new restrictions on acceptable research.

The Peel Report was also careful to distinguish between dead and nonviable fetuses, concluding that research must consider all fetuses over 20 weeks of age as potentially viable. Within that group, only therapeutic research was acceptable. Nontherapeutic research was permitted on fetuses of less than 20 weeks and weighing less than 300 grams. In such cases the mother's consent was necessary and sufficient. These distinctions created several important definitions, sustaining the Nuremberg and Helsinki precedents of caution in human experimentation. The Peel Committee took a conspicuously conservative stance. Not only were their criteria for viability conservative, but their arguments gave greater weight to the individual fetus's rights than to the scientific merit of the research.

THE AMERICAN RESPONSE

In the United States, HEW noted the Peel Report and decided that similar guidelines might head off controversy at home. Between 1972 and 1973, several draft guidelines were quietly debated inside HEW. But, using the access provided by the Freedom of Information Act, the *Ob-Gyn News,* a medical newsletter, ended administrative secrecy by publishing the details of the documents being considered by the National Institute of Health's (NIH) advisory council and the study section on Human Embryology and Development. These initial disclosures, read mostly by doctors, aroused no general interest. Reporters for the *Washington Post,* however, picked up the story, interviewed government officials, and on April 10, 1973, published a story on fetal research and the proposed guidelines.[12] Several NIH officials told the *Post* the guidelines were policy, while others insisted they were only recommendations. Despite the unclear status of these guidelines, the story ignited strong and immediate public concern. Now that the NIH was actually developing guidelines for fetal research, it appeared that the government was supporting such research. The *Post* disclosures brought national news coverage, both clarifications and denials by NIH officials, and a street demonstration at the NIH offices calling for a total ban on fetal research.[13]

While the public controversy was short-lived, this incident established a pattern for subsequent conflicts. First, the immediate focus of concern was the link between fetal research and abortion. The right-to-life groups adopted this issue when they had suffered a defeat in the Supreme Court and were attempting to build a strong political lobby. Well after press coverage waned, they continued to raise the issue with government officials, arguing against permissive guidelines.

Second, the polarized viewpoints that emerged at this time persisted through the debate. Dr. Kurt Hirschorn of New York's Mount Sinai Hospital told reporters:

> I don't think it's unethical. It is not possible to make this fetus into a child, therefore we can consider it as nothing more than a piece of tissue.

Similarly, Dr. Chalkey of the NIH insisted that

> [t]he determination of what research can be . . . acceptable depends on the salvageability of the fetus. . . . If you have a clearly nonviable fetus you are in a position to . . . possibly . . . treat it as a nonviable tissue.[14]

John Cardinal Krol, on the other hand, defined the moral premises of the opposition, "If there is a more unspeakable crime than abortion itself, it is using the victims of abortion as living human guinea pigs."[15]

LEGAL DECISIONS

A year after the *Washington Post* story kindled controversy in the nation's capital, another dispute erupted in Boston. On April 11, 1974, Dr. Kenneth Edelin was arrested for the murder of a fetus.[16] The trial of the Boston physician only indirectly involved fetal research since Edelin was not engaged in an experiment. Questions about the legal status of the fetus and the authority of doctors to define its proper treatment nevertheless dominated his trial. Just as the NIH guidelines attempted to define the limits on research acceptable to administrative agencies, the prosecution of Dr. Edelin articulated the limits acceptable to the general community.

In the eyes of Edelin and his colleagues, the medical procedures that led to his arrest were merely routine. That previous October he had performed an abortion by hysterotomy after several previous attempts by saline injection had failed. The mother had postponed her abortion for one day after consenting to participate in a blood study. Edelin, however, was not part of the research team. As the attending physician, he surgically removed the fetus and sent the intact remains to the pathology department. It was there that investigators, alerted by a local anti-abortion group, found the preserved remains. In tracking down its history, they interviewed a resident who insisted that the fetus was alive after it was separated from the placenta, and that Edelin had suffocated it before removing it from the mother. These allegations led to the manslaughter charge.

At the trial, witnesses disagreed on the precise gestational age of the fetus, on whether it was "born" once it was separated from the placenta, and on whether the fetus was alive prior to the hysterotomy. To several observers, the trial produced more confusion than clarity; testimony differed even on which operating room was used.

Nevertheless the jury found the doctor guilty. To them, the fetus had been a person who was born, and Edelin was guilty of "wanton and reckless" behavior. As the judge made clear in his charge to the jury, both of these criteria are required for a guilty verdict.

Even though Edelin's sentence was light (one year of probation) and his conviction overturned in 1976, the conviction of a doctor who followed standard medical procedures during a legal operation strongly affected the relationship between the medical profession and the community. In interviews after the trial, several jurors indicated that they considered Edelin competent, but they believed that medical standards were not enough to guarantee medical responsibility. Their verdict insisted that community standards should prevail. Moreover the verdict defined this fetus, with a gestational age between 20 and 24 weeks, as a person. Facing the same questions that had confronted the Peel Commission and HEW, the jury, persuaded by a picture of the fetus, also took the most conservative position, but on subjective, nontechnical grounds.

Barbara Culliton wrote in *Science*:

> The jurors reported that they were shaken by the photograph. "It looked like a baby," Liberty Ann Conlin told reporters, ". . . it definitely had an effect on me." Paul Holland commented, "The picture helped people draw their own conclusions. Everybody in the room made up their minds that the fetus was a person."[17]

To the jury, and perhaps to much of the nonscientific community, the issues were clear. No matter how experts justified different procedures in the various stages of development, the human fetus was a human being deserving respect and protection. Even though Edelin's conviction was overturned, the unstated charge of indifference to human rights leveled against Edelin and the scientific community was sustained. Jurors felt that Edelin and the experts who testified in his behalf were indifferent to the fetus's life. It was the impression of callousness and arrogance that gave wide credibility to the antiabortion movement's pressure to increase the nonscientific control over fetal research.

These incidents drew much public attention and portended a conflict that soon spread over much of the country in the early 1970s. Articles appeared in the *Oregon Journal,* the *San Francisco Chronicle,* and *Time* Magazine. Several state and local governments held hearings on fetal research. Eight states and one municipality passed restrictive laws.[18] And eventually Congress held hearings in anticipation of national legislation and imposed a temporary ban on studies which used living fetuses. In Boston, four more doctors were arrested. This time the charge was grave robbing to procure subjects for a fetal study.[19]

The public dispute, the threat of prosecution, and the federal and state bans halted much of the controversial, and also some of the acceptable, research. The lack of clear definitions for the wide range of different fetal experiments created confusion and caution. The laws passed in eight states "are so vague that they could dissuade physicians from even examining dead fetuses in order to gain medical information valuable to both the mothers and future fetuses."[20]

While these restrictions reflected concerns about human rights, the social benefits of fetal research remained attractive. Moreover, some fetal research is mandated by law. For example, the Kefauver-Harris Act requires that drugs be tested for safety, efficiency, and dosage in pregnant women before the FDA can approve their sale. Thus the proliferation of bans created concern that the legal resolution of the conflict was not entirely in the public interest.

ADMINISTRATIVE DECISIONS

HEW took the first steps toward rectifying this situation by proposing new guidelines for public comment. They were published in the *Federal Register* on November 16, 1973.[21] Despite concern that openness might prolong the controversy, Robert Stone, the director of NIH, hoped that public scrutiny of the Department's proposals might help to resolve the dispute.

Unlike the earlier drafts, the published guidelines focused directly on issues raised by the right-to-life groups. First was the problem of consent. The guidelines restated the importance of parental consent in therapeutic research. But, when there is risk without possible benefit to the fetus,

HEW concluded that consent is insufficient. Research relying on abortion falls into this category, since the fetus is not expected to survive. HEW also proposed establishing an Ethical Review Board (ERB) at the federal level. This administrative reform would separate the scientific from the ethical issues. It would limit the authority of the Institutional Review Boards to the scientific merit of each proposal, delegating questions of social benefit and ethical standards to the ERBs. Only one-third of the ERB members would be scientists. Thus, while the proposed guidelines sustained the importance of fetal research, they attempted to identify its socially acceptable forms. HEW concluded that "respect for the dignity of human life must not be compromised whatever the age, circumstance, or expectation of life of the individuals." They substantiated this principle by prohibiting hazardous research when an abortion is planned, and by limiting research on viable fetuses to efforts that could save their lives. Furthermore, the proposals insisted that a fetus must be taken off experimental life support systems if the attending physician decides that the effort would be futile.

Perhaps most important, the guidelines concluded that the ultimate criterion in choosing whether to proceed with or to ban research is the society's values, not scientific merit. Such a distinction, however, is vague and difficult to maintain; the very fact that fetal research became controversial testifies to the different values that coexist in our society. Indeed, the only practical interpretation of this vague statement would be to avoid research that offends politically active segments of our society, such as antiabortionists.[22]

Before HEW was able to revise the draft guidelines, the President signed into law the National Research Act. This law acknowledged the advance in the quality of life produced by science and reaffirmed the nation's support for research. Nevertheless, in a single sentence the act temporarily banned the controversial forms of fetal research "unless such research is done for the purpose of the survival of said fetus."[23]

The National Research Act attempted to allow external controls over science without eliminating scientific progress. It established the National Commission for the Protection of Human Subjects, which contains 11 members, with no more than five who have engaged in biomedical or behavioral research.[24] The Commission reports to the Secretary of HEW who is required to respond in the *Federal Register* if the department rejects the recommendations.

THE REVISED GUIDELINES

Before the Commission was constituted, HEW completed its guidelines. The changes from the earlier draft document HEW's continued effort to resolve the conflict. Perhaps the most important aspect of the HEW effort was the large amount of public comment considered. Over 450 responses were sent to HEW regarding the proposals.[25] By far the greatest response came from scientific organizations, underscoring an important characteristic of the dispute. Those opposing the research tended to express their dissent not through established administrative channels but through public demonstrations, the media, the courts, or elected officials. In contrast, scientists found the administrative agencies more in line with the way they saw the issues. Therefore the influence of the scientists grew with the growing importance of administrative decision-making. This influence is verified by the actual changes in the guidelines.

The revision legitimized two types of controversial experiments that were previously disallowed. Research that relied on abortions to determine the safety of therapeutic procedures, and experiments that sustained the vital signs in the fetus, were both acceptable if their ultimate goal was the refinement of health care procedures. This is tantamount to the Helsinki requirement of social benefit and could, depending on how broadly interpreted, include all the controversial studies. Scientists had argued throughout that all fetal research contributed to improved health care. HEW conceded "that consideration of risk vs. benefit with respect to fetal research does not seem to be appropriate," but concluded that the potential benefits justified continuing fetal research. They did not, however, accept all of the scientists' arguments and they insisted that ethical questions be given great procedural importance.

THE FINAL DRAFT

The creation and deliberation of the National Commission delayed the final guidelines one year. Once formed, the Commission sponsored studies on the scope of fetal research and the operation of IRBs, sampled public opinion in open hearings, and debated the difficult issues. The final report of the Commission was similar to the revised HEW guidelines and was accepted with several semantic changes and one important policy alteration. The term "abortus" was abandoned in favor of "nonviable fetus," to minimize the association with abortion. The term "viable fetus ex-utero" was changed to "viable infant" to reflect the attitude that such fetuses deserve the same care and respect our society affords young children.[26] The Commission tried to remove any implication of callousness from earlier definitions. Although not directly addressing the "personhood" question, the Commission insisted that during experiments "regardless of its life prospects [the fetus] should be treated respectfully and with dignity." Nevertheless, when faced with defining viability, they followed the technical criteria first proposed by the Peel Commission. While recognizing that revisions might follow medical improvements, the Commission concluded that fetuses younger than 20-week gestational age and weighing less than 500 grams are not viable.

Although insisting that "the integrity of the individual is preeminent," the Commission's principles underlying fetal research included consideration of social benefit. Before using the fetus for research, prior studies with animals and nonpregnant humans must have been completed; the knowledge gained must be important, and the risks and benefits to the mother and the fetus must be detailed, informed consent must be granted, and subjects must be selected so that risks and benefits are not biased along economic, racial, and ethnic lines.

While adopting a conservative attitude toward risk, the Commission considered it to be a medical judgment. It did insist, however, that the two-tiered review system including the ethical evaluation proposed by HEW should be developed to supervise these scientific decisions. These decisions discouraged doctors from clearly hazardous studies but permitted research when hazards were either small or unknown. To avoid confusion in the case of nonviable fetuses where impending death might legitimate risky procedures, the Commission created separate criteria. Defining nonviable fetuses as dying individuals, they concluded that no research may use such subjects. They based their strong ban on two criteria: first, since the subject is dying, all research including efforts to sustain life are nontherapeutic; second, they concluded that the dignity of the dying is more important than the scientific merit of the research.[27] Here they agreed with critics that an unencumbered death is a human right that overrides socially beneficial research. Nevertheless, HEW did not include these restrictions in the final policy for they contradicted the agency's own reasoning. Unable to accept that the individual rights of the dying could preclude research, Casper Weinberger, HEW secretary, concluded that research designed to enable fetuses to survive should continue, and that the success of past experiments and the public interest in better health care for premature infants provided adequate reasons for including dying fetuses in research. On July 29, 1975, this final draft was approved to become the regulations governing all fetal research funded by the federal government.

CONCLUSIONS

Critics of fetal research presented a moral challenge to science. The conflict introduced questions about the legal and social status of the fetus, the proper balance of social benefits and individual risks, and the legitimacy of scientific control over research decisions. The resolution embodied in HEW's guidelines accepted both the importance of fetal research and the scientific reasoning behind the controversial experiments. These guidelines reinforced the importance of ethical concerns by establishing an Ethical Review Board, but rejected the moral restrictions demanded by the critics. In the end, experiments that met the requirement of scientific merit and social worth were allowed, and the scientists won a substantive victory.

In a more general light, this dispute has broad implications for other controversies over science. First, interest group politics was important in sustaining conflict. Both the antiabortion lobby and the scientific community carefully targeted pressure on those institutions sensitive to their respective views and constituents. Each pressed hard for its own self-interest, a fact sometimes obscured by the moral fervor and technical nature of many of the arguments. Essentially, then, the dispute evolved through a normal political process.

Second, this conflict followed a pattern of instigation and resolution that is characteristic of other disputes over science. Prior to the conflict, the agencies charged with resolving both the scientific and ethical questions were dominated by scientists. This had precluded consideration of certain moral issues and forced opponents to seek recourse through other institutions such as the courts and legislatures. When these institutions proved insensitive to the technical distinctions between the controversial and acceptable forms of fetal research, resolution was delegated to the administrative arm of the government. This shift from legislative initiative to administrative resolution increased the influence of scientists, and gave priority to the scientific justification of research procedures in terms of their benefits to health care.

NOTES

1. U.S. Government, Senate Committee on Labor and Public Welfare, Subcommittee on Health, *Fetal Research 1974* (Washington, DC: Government Printing Office, 1974), 58-60.

2. The National Commission for the Protection of Human Subjects of Biomedical and Behavioral Research, "Report and Recommendations," *Federal Register* 40 (August 8, 1975), 33532-33534. Unless otherwise noted, all subsequent details on the types of fetal research are taken from this source.

3. Dale Cowan, "Human Experimentation: The Review Process in Practice," *Case Western Law Review* 25 (1975) 534ff.

4. Bernard Barber, "The Ethics of Experimentation with Human Subjects," *Scientific American* 234 (1976), 31.

5. Bradford Gray, "The Functions of Human Experimentation Review Committees," presented at the American Psychiatric Association Meeting May 10, 1976, 4-5.

6. Survey Research Center, "Research Involving Human Subjects," unpublished report to the National Commission, 5.

7. Cowan, 30.

8. Barber, 30.

9. Gary Reback, "Fetal Experimentation: Moral, Legal, and Medical Implications," *Stanford Law Review* 26 (May 1974), 1193ff.

10. Robert Veatch, "Human Experimentation Committees: Professional or Representative?" *Hastings Center Report* (October 1975), 31-40.

11. Paul Ramsey, *The Ethics of Fetal Research* (New Haven: Yale Univ. Press, 1975).

12. Victor Cohn, "Live Fetus Research Debated," *Washington Post* (April 10, 1973), 1.

13. Victor Cohn, "NIH Vows Not to Fund Fetus Work," *Washington Post* (April 13, 1973), 1.

14. Cohn, April 10, 9.

15. Cohn, April 13, 8.

16. Barbara Culliton, "Manslaughter: The Charge against Edelin of Boston City Hospital," *Science* 186 (October 25, 1974), 327-330; "Edelin Trial: Jury Not Persuaded by Scientists for the Defense," *Science,* 187 (March 7, 1975), 814-816.

17. Culliton, "Edelin Trial," 816.

18. Reback, 1197.

19. Barbara Culliton, "Grave Robbing," *Science* 186 (November 1, 1974), 420-423.

20. Reback, "Fetal Experimentation."

21. Department of Health, Education and Welfare, "Protection of Human Subjects," *Federal Register* 38 (November 16, 1973), 31740.

22. Charles Lowe of NIH lends support to this interpretation in a public statement. He concluded:

> But I haven't decided in my own mind whether we can go along with Great Britain in using federal dollars [to support fetal research]. First we have an articulate Catholic minority which disagrees. Second we have a substantial and articulate black minority sensitive on issues of human life [Quoted in Cohn, April 10, 1973. 9].

23. National Research Act, Public Law 93-348, section 213.

24. The commissioners were: Kenneth Ryan, M.D.; Joseph Brady, Ph.D., Professor of Behavioral Biology; Robert Cooke, M.D.; Dorothy Height, President, National Council of Negro Women; Albert Jonsen, S.J., Ph.D.; Patricia King, Professor of Law; Karen Lecaqz, Ph.D.; David Louisell, J.D.; Donald Seldin, M.D.; Eliot Stellar, Ph.D.; and Robert Turtle, LL.B.

25. Department of Health, Education and Welfare, "Protection of Human Subjects, Proposed Policy," *Federal Register* 39 (August 23, 1974), 30648.

26. Department of Health, Education and Welfare, "Protection of Human Subjects, Fetuses, Pregnant Women in vitro Fertilizations," *Federal Register* 40 (August 8, 1975), 33526-33544.

27. National Commission, "Report and Recommendations."

11

CREATION VERSUS EVOLUTION:
THE CALIFORNIA CONTROVERSY

Dorothy Nelkin

In 1963, two women from Orange County, California, decided to "seek justice for the Christian child."[1] They justified their demand on the basis of the 1963 Supreme Court decision (*Abington School District v. Schempp*) stating that it was unconstitutional to force nonbelieving children to pray in school. They argued that if it is unconstitutional "to teach God in the school," it is equally unconstitutional "to teach the absence of God."

Assisted by a geneticist and one of the founders of the Creation Research Society, they petitioned the state board of education to require that textbooks clearly specify that evolution is a theory rather than truth. Arguing that Christian children must have equal protection under the law, they obtained a legal opinion from the Department of Justice that it would be unconstitutional for a state to prescribe atheism, agnosticism, or irreligious teaching. Max Rafferty, then California Superintendent of Public Instruction, promptly ruled that all California texts dealing with evolution must clearly label evolution as a theory.

Rafferty was sympathetic to conservative and fundamentalist causes. In a California Department of Education booklet called *Guidelines for Moral Instruction in California Schools,* he unequivocally expressed his concern with "protecting the child's morality from attack by secular humanists."

I always think that America was built on the Bible. . . . The teaching
of evolution as a part of the religion of Humanism, therefore, is yet
another area of concern. . . . If the origins of man were taught from
the point of view of both evolution and creation, the purpose of
education would be satisfied.[2]

In 1966, Rafferty encouraged creationists to demand that creation
theory be given equal time in biology classes, claiming it was consistent
with the education code of the 1964 Civil Rights Act prohibiting teaching
that reflects adversely on any persons because of race, color, or creed.
Creationists interpreted this as a sanction for the teaching of creation
theory as an alternate scientific hypothesis.

In 1969, the California State Advisory Committee on Science Education prepared a set of curriculum guidelines for its public school science
programs called *The Science Framework for California Schools,* intended
to be the model for science curriculum development in California. The
Committee presented a draft of the *Science Framework* to the board of
education. It contained two paragraphs on evolution, and several of the
nine members of the board objected. Their questions were aired in the *Los
Angeles Times.*

Several weeks later, Vernon Grose, an aerospace engineer who had read
the *Times* article presented a memorandum to the board of education,
arguing that the theory of creation be included in textbooks as an
alternative explanation for the origin of life. He reduced this to a brief
statement.

All scientific evidence to date concerning the origin of life implies at
least a dualism or the necessity to use several theories to fully
explain relationships. . . . While the Bible and other philosophical
treatises also mention creation, science has independently postulated
the various theories of creation. Therefore, creation in scientific
terms is not a religious or philosophical belief. Also note that
creation and evolutionary theories are not necessarily mutual exclu-
sives. Some of the scientific data (e.g., the regular absence of
transitional forms) may be best explained by a creation theory,
while other data (e.g., transmutation of species) substantiate a process of evolution.[3]

The board of education unanimously accepted the statement and
printed it in the *Science Framework.* Thus, 45 years after the Scopes trial,
the guidelines for a state educational system that serves one million
children included a formal recommendation to teach creation theory.

THE BIBLE AS SCIENCE

During the 1960s, a group of scientifically trained fundamentalists began to reevaluate fossil evidence from the perspective of special creation as described in the Biblical record. These creationists, much like their fundamentalist predecessors in the 1920s, accept the Biblical doctrine of creation as literal. They believe that creation theory is the most basic of all Christian beliefs, and the fact that many churches fail to emphasize special creation is a "tragic oversight that has resulted in defection . . . to the evolutionary world view, and then inevitably later to liberalism."[4] They choose to reinterpret organic evolution according to Biblical authority.

Some creationists accept aspects of evolution theory but set limits to scientific explanations, rejecting, for example, natural selection as a causal explanation of evolutionary change. The more extreme creationists deny all evolutionary processes, arguing that evolution and creation are mutually exclusive theories. Still others accept the compromise that there are two levels of reality, but they are concerned that the teaching of evolution denies and obscures all religious explanation and that failure to teach alternative hypotheses implies that science provides a complete and sufficient understanding of ultimate causes.

Among those who identify themselves as creationists are disciples of traditional fundamentalist sects, some wealthy industrialists, several astronauts, and many solid, middle-class, technically trained people working in high-technology professions in centers of science-based industry. These modern-day creationists share many of the moral and religious concerns expressed in the 1920s, but their style is strikingly different from that of their flamboyant ancestors.

Creationist confrontations are like debates within professional societies. Indeed creationists try to present their views at the annual meetings of professional organizations such as the National Association of Biology Teachers. During the California public hearings on textbook selection, creationists presented brief technical papers, and the only placard to be seen was a chart of the hydrogen atom intended to demonstrate the scientific validity of creation theory. For creationists argue that Genesis is not religious dogma but an alternative scientific hypothesis capable of evaluation by scientific procedures. They present themselves not as believers but as scientists engaged in a scholarly debate about the methodological validity of two scientific theories.

The creationist world view rejects the theory that animals and plants have descended from a single line of ancestors, evolving over billions of years through random mutation. According to creation theory, biological life began during a primeval period only five to six thousand years ago when all things were created by God's design into "permanent basic forms." Like the pre-Darwinian Charles Lyell, creationists believe that all subsequent variation has occurred within the genetic limits built into each species by the Creator. Evolution is a directed and purposeful process and present variety among animals is merely part of a blueprint to accommodate a variety of environmental conditions.[5] Change would not modify the original design, for nature is static, secure, and predictable; each species contains its full potentiality.

Clearly, creationists are faced with formidable evidence supporting the theory of evolution. This poses a cruel dilemma; they must either admit exceptions to their beliefs that would raise doubts among their constituents, or they must maintain consistency at the risk of public ridicule. They have chosen the latter alternative and spend much energy trying to demonstrate that evidence supporting evolution is biased and incomplete, or that it can be reinterpreted to fit whatever conceptual system is convenient. For example, creationist theoreticians argue that the fossil record is far from conclusive and fails to provide the transitional forms or linkages between diverse living groups that would suggest evolution from a common ancestor.

Creationists also deny the evidence from techniques of radioisotope dating, for these techniques are based on assumptions that no uranium or lead has been lost through the years and that the rate at which uranium changes has remained constant over time. Rejecting the uniformitarian hypotheses that allow evolutionists to extrapolate events in the ancient past from present evidence, they contend that if a Supreme Being created the world, and a catastrophe like the Flood altered it, then the evidence for radioisotope dating is simply irrelevant.

Creationists also reject the genetic data used to support hypotheses about random mutation, arguing that the same data can be used to deny the theory of evolution. Mutations, after all, are usually detrimental and unlikely to contribute to the continuity of life. Similarly, they claim that insights into phylogenetic relationships provided by analysis of protein structure and chromosomal arrangements are based on "dubious assumptions" about the similarity between major plant and animal groups. If one assumed that such groups are unrelated and reexamined the same data according to "polyphylogenetic" assumptions, one would reach quite different conclusions.[6]

Creationists' "scientific" arguments, which they claim to develop through concurrent studies of scripture and nature, touch on floods, on heredity and genetics, on chemical and radioisotope dating techniques, on the blood circulation system, on the earth's magnetic field, and many other topics. Their "facts" are carefully selected and suggest a limited understanding of modern biology and of scientific method. Like Darwin's contemporaries, they view science as an inductive and descriptive process and they seem to comprehend poorly the function of theories and models as useful instruments for prediction. Moreover, when pressed, creationists will argue that design in nature exists simply because of the will of the Creator. They are aware of the problems with this argument, but then they claim that evolution theory is but today's creation myth, based also on faith. If one accepts a different set of assumptions, then creation theory becomes fully as workable and fruitful a hypothesis as evolution.

Scientists try in vain to refute these arguments. They note the practical and historical problems with a literal interpretation of Genesis and the many facts that contradict creationist theories. Factual arguments and criticism, however, are not likely to change creationist beliefs. Groups committed to particular assumptions tend to suppress dissonant evidence, and criticism tends only to encourage even greater activity in support of existing beliefs.[7] For those who believe in creationism, it is a distinct and coherent logical system that fully explains the world. "Studying the facts of physics and chemistry, I find that the only way I could truly understand the present world is by the word of God and the inspiration of the Holy Spirit."[8] It is evolution theory that is the "scientific fairy tale."

SCIENTIFIC CREATIONISTS

Who are these dedicated individuals who have presumed to question one of the scientific community's more strongly held concepts? Many of the activists in the creationist movement are from the applied physical sciences and engineering. They are mostly people who once made an uncomfortable accommodation between their religious beliefs and their scientific training. Creationism appealed to them as a means to resolve contradictions. The creationists claim that applied scientists are interested in creationism because "they have their feet on the ground and are heavily committed to test out theories." Most biologists, they feel, are too "brainwashed" with evolution theory to think flexibly about the evidence. They also argue that people in technical professions, working in highly structured and ordered contexts, are inclined to think in terms of order and design. Another explanation came from Wernher von Braun, the famous NASA rocket engineer, who declared his personal support for the "case for design" as a viable scientific theory: "One cannot be exposed to the law and order of the universe without concluding that there must be design and purpose behind it all. . . . I endorse the presentation of alternative theories for the origin of the universe, life, and man in the science classroom."[9]

Clearly the scientists and engineers active in creation movements are not against science and technology. Many of them earn their living in technical industries. Indeed when questioned on specific contemporary issues, creationist leaders are generally favorable to technology. Far from being against science, they spend much of their energy legitimizing their beliefs in scientific terms, firmly convinced that failure to do so would trivialize them. Their main objection to evolution theory is that it "incorporates all the attributes of a religion"; it is "a doctrine of origin" that replaces God with eternal matter and creation with random mutation. It is a doctrine of salvation not through faith but through foresight and the manipulation of nature. Thus, claim the creationists, it violates traditional religious assumptions and endorses its own system of ethics.

It was in the context of this ambivalence toward science that the new precollege curriculum in biology and the social sciences, both based on evolutionary assumptions, became targets for textbook watchers. In addition to persistent concern with patriotism and the standards of education, textbook watchers became alerted to religious and moral issues as creationists organized to fight what they perceived to be efforts to "indoctrinate" their children with the dangerous values of "secular humanism."

The creationists are organized into "research centers." For example, the Creation Research Society (CRS) in Orange County was formed in 1963. Their objective in founding the CRS was "to reach all people with the vital message of the scientific and historic truth about creation."

To attain the status of voting membership in the organization, members must meet two requirements: a postgraduate degree in science and belief in the literal truth of the Bible. As of April 1974, there were 514 voting members, plus several thousand associates. About 50 members contribute articles to the organization's journal. With the formation of other creationist organizations in California, CRS moved to Lansing, Michigan, where a branch had developed in the early 1960s. Active Michigan members include a retired chemist from Dow Chemical, several science instructors from Concordia Lutheran College, and a professor of science education at Michigan State University.

CRS promulgates its views in a quarterly journal (circulation 2,000), as well as through notices in fundamentalist tracts. In addition, CRS supports speakers ready and willing to lecture on creationism. In 1970, in a struggle over leadership, several members broke away to form the Creation Science Research Center (CSRC) in San Diego.

CSRC is a small, tax-exempt research and publishing organization formed "to take advantage of the tremendous opportunity that God has given us . . . to reach the 63 million children in the United States with the scientific teaching of Biblical creationism."[10] Its research projects, which include investigation of the physical aspects of the Flood, are intended to "clarify problems in the field of geophysics, oceanography and structural geology as well as Biblical and geological chronology." The organization also engages in legal activities to undermine what they claim is illegitimate federal funding of school curricula. It also offers publishers its services to "neutralize" textbook material.

CSRC publishes a magazine called *Science and Scripture,* a textbook series, film strips, and cassettes, all colorfully packaged and an "action kit" including the legal, organizational, and technical information necessary to implement the teaching of creation theory in public schools.[11]

Distribution of CSRC material is facilitated by the group's association with the Southern California branch of the Bible Science Association which runs a radio ministry and an active extension service. Together the two organizations have a mailing list of about 200,000 individuals and many schools, churches, and textbook committees. In 1972, the CSRC was divided in a conflict over copyright questions and some of its members formed a new organization, the Institute for Creation Research.

The Institute for Creation Research (ICR) is the research division of Christian Heritage College, founded in 1970 with the sponsorship of the Scott Memorial Baptist Church. While not an accredited institution, the college, with about 200 students, aspires to develop full undergraduate and graduate school programs in "the Study of Christian Evidence and Scientific Creationism." The college catalog describes its introductory biology course as "a survey of the life sciences; general and molecular biology; human physiology; creationism in biological origins." Its psychology course includes a section on "the unique nature of man." Its five-man science faculty is involved in an open campaign against evolution theory. All five are staff members of the ICR. ICR works to develop a reputation as the "scholarly arm of the creationist movement" debunking the CSRC as "a promotional and sales organization." It identifies its own primary activity as research devoted to developing an empirical base for creation theory and claims to leave promotional activities to other organizations. Yet the Institute runs radio programs, conferences, workshops, and summer institutes, and it publishes a monthly magazine containing both technical articles and current news of creationists' activities. During its first two years, the Institute staff published seven books, ran seven summer institutes, delivered some 2000 lectures in 38 states and five foreign countries, and visited about 90 college campuses.

THE CALIFORNIA DISPUTE

The implications of the California Guidelines requiring "equal time" for creation theory began to be evident in 1971, when the curriculum commission selected specific biology textbooks to be used in the schools. No creationist texts were among the books submitted to the board of education, and Dr. John Ford, vice-president of the board, reminded his colleagues that "No textbook should be considered for adoption . . . that has not clearly discussed at least two major contrasting theories of origin."[12] In May 1972, the board restored the omitted texts and reorganized the curriculum commission, changing its name to the Curriculum Development and Supplemental Materials Commission. Creationists, including Vernon Grose, were well represented; the new commission included only one professional scientist, Junji Kumamoto, a chemist, who for several years was to engage in a one-man defense of evolution in California.

California has about one million children of school age and buys 10% of the nation's textbooks. Many publishers were quite willing to adapt to the new *Science Framework.* One proposed replacing a section about Leakey's archaeological discoveries of primitive man with a reproduction of Michaelangelo's Sistine Chapel painting of the Creation and a drawing of Moses. Another submitted a fourth-grade science text that claimed that science had nothing to say about who made the world. One chapter had as an exercise an investigation of the Biblical account of creation.

To prepare for the final adoption of the textbooks, the board of education called a hearing on November 9, 1972, in order to assess public opinion. The hearing became a confrontation between creationists and evolutionists. It threatened to be a circus, but bureaucratic procedures (five minute limitations on speeches) and the creationists' efforts to present themselves as scientists set a tone of sober debate. Engineers appointed to curriculum development commissions somehow lack the fire of fundamentalist preachers. Yet the ironies were striking. "Witnesses from each side appeared in each other's clothing," observed a journalist amused by the spectacle of scientists speaking for creation theory and theologians supporting science.[13] The 23 witnesses for Genesis included only three

Baptist ministers, but 12 scientists and engineers. The evolutionists, on the other hand, called forth only four scientists. Other witnesses included Presbyterian, Episcopalian, and Mormon ministers, Catholic and Buddhist priests, and a rabbi; all testified for the need to separate science and religion.

Evolutionists were incredulous that creationists could have any influence. "It just does not make sense in this day and age." Incredulity led to amused disdain. It was proposed that Bible publishers insert a sentence in Genesis to indicate that "scientific method rejects the supernatural approach to explaining the universe." A biologist and member of the state advisory committee inquired whether a scientific course on reproduction should mention the stork theory.

As creationists persisted in their efforts to influence textbook selection, amusement and disdain gave way to defensiveness. If creation theory was placed on an equal footing with Darwinism, it would confuse understanding of what science was all about. Thus scientists countered creationists' demands with legal and political strategies, and they attempted to discredit the movement by refusing to acknowledge the creationists' claim to scientific status.

The National Association of Biology Teachers (NABT) organized a political and legal opposition and tried to arouse the interest of the scientific community. It set up a Fund for Freedom in Science Teaching, receiving contributions of about $12,000 to support its legal and organizational activities, and it organized a response from professional societies.

The National Academy of Sciences was moved for the first time to interfere in an issue involving a state decision, and in October 1972 it issued a strongly worded resolution urging that science textbooks be limited to the exposition of scientific matter.

The American Association for the Advancement of Science also vigorously opposed the inclusion of creation theory in science textbooks.[14]

Biologists called the arguments for design based on the intricacy and beauty of nature "spurious and irrelevant." Belief in an intelligent designer is "as blasphemous as it is far fetched."[15] Admitting that much evidence for evolution theory is circumstantial and incomplete, they defended it as a useful model with solid support from the sum of evidence accumulated in such diverse disciplines as genetics and biochemistry.

The creationists in turn asserted that Biblical authority presents an equally useful model that is also confirmed by evidence. During public hearings on the California textbooks, each group claimed the other based its beliefs on faith; each group argued with passion for its own objectivity;

and each group brought its social and political concerns to the discussion of science curriculum. Scientists and creationists alike bemoaned the moral, political, and legal implications of the alternative ideology. The influence of alternative assumptions on religious equality, as well as on educational practice, concerned both groups. And as each side defended its position and criticized the other, their arguments were strikingly similar. Indeed the debate assumed aspects of a battle between two dogmatic groups—the antidogmatic norm of science ironically tended to erode as advocates attempted to convey the validity of the theory of evolution.

After November 1972, biologists were increasingly reluctant to acknowledge the creationist movement. Many tried to discredit it by questioning the credentials and competence of its adherents who claimed to be scientists. They were, claimed the biologists, "only engineers." "They are educated at Bible colleges." "Who are these people?" "They are false authorities." "Dullards." "Rejects from the space age." "Is it legal to misuse professional titles?" "Creationists get their doctorates in a box of crackerjacks." "It is a publishers' racket." "As phony as a $3 bill." "A way to subsidize religion." Biologists attacked textbook publishers for responding to such pressure groups.[16]

While biologists groped for an appropriate response, creationists merely interpreted their opposition as a sign of recognition and their reluctance to debate as proof that few biologists were willing to defend the theory of evolution and expose its shortcomings in a public forum.

THE CALIFORNIA SOLUTION

Educational policy-making bodies are well-accustomed to responding to political pressure. Criteria for the selection of textbooks are continually being adjusted to meet the demands of the times. A state board's responsiveness often depends on the pressure that various groups can bring to bear on board members. Thus when the California State Board of Education was deluged with letters, resolutions, and petitions from educators and scientists, it began to reexamine its policies. In December 1972, the curriculum committee announced to the board that its members had agreed on guidelines that would ensure the neutrality of science textbooks. They proposed to eliminate all scientific dogmatism by changing offending statements in textbooks to indicate their conditional nature. Books should discuss *how* things occur and avoid questions of ultimate causes. The board of education accepted these recommendations, voting 7-1 to treat evolution as a speculative theory, a decision described in the *Los Angeles Times* as "A Victory for Adam & Eve." The board appointed a committee to implement the recommendations. None of the members were biologists, and all identified themselves as creationists who accepted the teaching of evolution *if* it remained neutral on the subject of ultimate causes. This committee edited the textbooks to clarify both the potentialities and the limitations of science, intending to guard against the "religion of science" as well as "other" religious positions.

The committee prepared a statement, to be printed in all textbooks dealing with evolution, that science cannot answer questions about "where the first matter and energy come from," for scientific methods can only deal with the "physical mechanisms involved." The statement declares that while the term *evolution* can be used to describe observable processes, the accuracy of the theory of evolution in reconstructing life in the past "depends largely upon the validity of the assumptions on which it is based."

The committee screened 30 textbooks, proposing many changes, and taking particular care to replace specific words that implied acceptance of evolution theory. They changed "developed" or "evolved" to "appeared," and "unfolded" to "occurred." They deleted some words ("ancestors," "descendants," "origins"), and they added qualifying phrases ("according to one particular point of view"; "It is believed, in the theory of evolution"; "The evidence is not clear, but"). Pictures were relabeled: "This is an artist's conception of what might have been," or "Some people think that plants might have looked like this: What do you think?" And they prefaced each section discussing evolution with a statement indicating that "science has no way of knowing how life began."

Most changes were in fact unobjectionable and, indeed, some did correct unnecessarily dogmatic statements. The board accepted the revision committee's recommended changes by a vote of 5-3.

Scientists accepted the changes with relief. While they felt the qualifications did injustice to the great body of scientific expertise, the changes were far less disturbing than anticipated. Later, two biologists wrote a new page 106 for the *Science Framework,* and their revision, focusing on evolution, was accepted by the board of education in March 1974.

The scientific creationists felt "sold out" by what they viewed as minimal changes that neglected their demand for equal time—but by no means did they give up. They began to gather survey material to prove the extent of public support for their views.

But despite favorable polls and a swarm of letters and petitions to the state board of education, creationists began to lose their influence in 1974 when the board initiated a new method of evaluating educational materials. From now on they would include many more civic organizations and lay-interest groups in the textbook evaluation committee. Creation science books were promptly eliminated—the broader participatory base had reduced the influence of the creationists and other special interest groups. As a concession to creationists, however, the board sent a memo to school districts to remind teachers that whenever human origins were discussed, alternative theories should be presented.

Reviewing the creationists' demands, one is struck by three recurrent themes: first, these people, living in the heartland of advanced technology, are disillusioned with the impact of technological progress on moral behavior. They associate the evils of technology with the growth of science and the subsequent decline in religious values. Second, the creationists resent the authority they feel is represented by scientific dogmatism, and the increasing professionalism of the local school system. They seek increased local and parental control over the science curriculum. Third, in their demands for equal time they defend the pluralist and egalitarian values that they see threatened by science. In the pluralist tradition, creationists claim the right to maintain cultural and religious conventions in the face of pressures for conformity.

It is not accurate to dismiss the creationist movement as merely "antiscience." Like many other social movements, creationism is a bizarre combination of religion and science. Theological beliefs are conveyed in a context of diplomas, research monographs, and professional societies. For the creationists, modern science is at once the enemy and the model. They are hardly alone in their accommodation to the expectations and images of a scientific age. Some yogis have recommended the use of electroencephalographs to assist in meditation. The popular film "The Exorcist" portrays a doctor using sophisticated medical technology to exorcize spirits from a possessed child. The Uranius brotherhood advertises "power-packed scientific proof of the continuity of life through the intergalactic confederation." Occultists, astrologers, UFO-logists, and members of other cults often seek scientific validation for their alleged facts. Creationists and many of these groups are a reaction less against science as an activity of professionals than against its image as an infallible source of truth—as a dominant myth of industrial society.

A myth is perpetuated because it satisfies a social need. If it loses credibility ("planet earth is in trouble," the creationists claim), people will grope for more fulfilling constructs. Science threatened the plausibility of nonrational beliefs, but it did not remove the uncertainties that seem to call for such beliefs. Creationism thus fills a social need for its adherents. By using representations that are well adapted to the twentieth century, by claiming that their ideas are based on scientific evidence, they offer intellectual plausibility as well as salvation, and the authority of science as well as the certainty of Scripture. Poorly understanding the process of science, they seek to resolve the old conflict between religion and science through popular decision. Democratic values such as freedom of choice, equality, and "fairness" become the criteria by which to judge the merits of science. The creationists have thus sought to bring together science, religious faith, and populist democracy—three pieties of American culture.

NOTES

1. For a complete case study and an analysis of textbook controversies, see Dorothy Nelkin, *Science Textbook Controversies and the Politics of Equal Time* (Cambridge: MIT Press, 1977).

2. Max Rafferty, Guidelines for Moral Instruction in California, A Report Accepted by the State Board of Education (Sacramento: California State Department of Education, May 1969), 7, 64.

3. California State Department of Education, *Science Framework for California Public Schools* (Sacramento, 1970), 106.

4. Richard Bube, "Science Teaching in California," *The Reformed Journal* (April 1973), 3-4.

5. John N. Moore and Harold Slusher, *Biology: A Search for Order in Complexity* (Grand Rapids: Zondervan, 1970), 422.

6. For creationists' scientific explanations, see Duane Gish, "Creation, Evolution, and the Historical Evidence," *The American Biology Teacher* 35 (March 1973), 23-27; John N. Moore, "Evolution, Creation, and the Scientific Method," *The American Biology Teacher* 35 (January 1973), 23-27.

7. See the work on cognitive dissonance by Leon Festinger, *A Theory of Cognitive Dissonance* (Evanston, Ill.: Row Peterson, 1957). The relationship between beliefs and the interpretation of scientific information is discussed by S. B. Barnes, "On the Reception of Scientific Beliefs," in *Sociology of Science,* ed. Barry Barnes (Harmondsworth: Penguin Books, 1972), 269-291.

8. Letter in *Acts and Facts,* November/December 1973.

9. Wernher von Braun, letter to John Ford, published in *Science and Scripture* (March/April 1973), 4. Von Braun later qualified his position, stating that he believed there was "divine intent" behind the processes of nature, but did not believe that all living species were created in their final form 5000 years ago. Several of the astronauts who surrounded the NASA space program with religious ritual have also endorsed the creationist view. For example, James Irwin is a creationist. After his experience on the moon ("I feel the power of God as I'd never felt it before"), he

founded an evangelical foundation called High Flight. (*New York Times,* 26 April 1974, 18C) Astronauts Frank Borman and Edgar Mitchell also indicated that they feel the Genesis account of Creation to be an appropriate explanation. Mitchell wrote to Vernon Grose that "I strongly favor the presentation of both points of view" (Letter, 16 June 1972).

10. In 1974, the CSRC employed 18 people and used 12 outside technical consultants. They claimed to have over 10,000 regular donors who could be counted on for small gifts at every fund-raising appeal. Quoted material is from Creation Science Research Center *Report,* October 1973.

11. CSRC claims that the science and creation textbook series sold about 30,000 copies to each grade level and that one of their most popular books sold 70,000 hardcover copies.

12. Board of Education, minutes of meeting, 8 July 1971.

13. Nicholas Wade, "Creationists and Evolutionists: Confrontation in California," *Science* (17 November 1972), 724-729.

14. Resolutions from several professional societies are printed in the BSCS Newsletter of 19 November 1972.

15. G. L. Steffins, "The Evolution of Design," *The American Biology Teacher* 35 (February 1973), 58.

16. These quotes are from correspondence to the National Association of Biology Teachers in late 1972.

REGULATING RECOMBINANT DNA RESEARCH

Sheldon Krimsky

The federal government's role in regulating technologies and their byprod-ucts is well established, but a clear distinction has been drawn between science and technology. Scientific inquiry is seldom justified on short-term utilitarian grounds, and freedom to pursue knowledge is a highly valued tradition. Thus, calls for regulation of science evoke extremely negative reactions both from scientists and from legislative bodies. The intervention of government into the affairs of the research scientist has been likened to a First Amendment violation—a restriction of the scientist's right of free inquiry.[1]

Yet science as well as technology may have a serious social impact. Efforts to acquire knowledge may disturb, modify, or reshape some segment of nature in a way that introduces hazards to the scientist, laboratory worker, or the broader community. How does society respond when the art of scientific investigation poses risks? The recombinant DNA controversy offers us an episode where concern about research-induced

Author's Note: *My special thanks to Dr. Susan Wright, who commented on an earlier draft of the paper, Professor Charles Weiner for his help in guiding me through the special archival collection on the Recombinant DNA debate at Massachusetts Institute of Technology, and Professor Dorothy Nelkin for her brilliant editing and encouragement.*

risks evolved from a narrow disciplinary discussion to a national public policy debate.

The events growing out of the controversy over the use of the newly developed gene transplantation techniques were precedent-setting in important ways. While similar to other environmental debates, the issue that sets this case apart is the fact that the focus of concern is a new, exciting, and powerful scientific research technique. Recombinant DNA literally means DNA molecules that have been created in a cell-free system by joining DNA fragments from different biological sources. Over the past decade, through the discovery that certain enzymes could be used to cleave DNA molecules at specific sites, and with the knowledge gained of how to splice DNA molecules together, scientists developed the capability of combining genetic material from diverse species.[2] While the discovery of the structure of the DNA molecule exhibited a formal unity for all biological life, the development of recombinant DNA techniques was the major hurdle in overcoming any barriers that might exist between biological species in terms of their fundamental substance.

Research in molecular genetics aims to exhibit how genes function in cells, and to understand the relationship between gene structure and gene function. For any particular species of cell, one objective would be attained if the genome of an organism were fully mapped, that is if for each gene one could specify its product. With the ability to cut and splice DNA molecules scientists could select out gene fragments from complex systems (the cells of higher order organisms or eukaryotes) and transplant them into simpler systems (the cells of lower order organisms or prokaryotes) offering the first practical hope of unravelling the mysteries of genetic expression for higher order species.

Objections to the use of this technique took several forms:

- fear of the potential hazards of creating new pathogens or spreading dangerous toxins or viruses into the environment;
- concern that the new tools of science would eventuate in baneful forms of genetic engineering;
- concern that scientists have ominous power to reshape evolution without understanding its consequences.
- Ethical objections to mixing genes between species and/or reprogramming cells.
- Mistrust of industry's exploitation of the technique.

Scores of recent controversies have exposed divisions among scientific experts, usually over the effects of technological innovation or on the impacts of known technologies. In the recombinant DNA case, technical expertise turned on itself, calling for special public assessment of scientific responsibility. There are few external regulations over the activities of laboratory biologists. Standards for the safe handling of biological agents in the laboratory are issued by the Center for Disease Control, but enforcement and monitoring of laboratories are largely the responsibility of the principal investigator.[3] One of the few exceptions to scientific autonomy has been in the area of human experimentation where a two-tier institutional review panel examines research protocols to insure that the subject's rights are not violated.

During the seven years of controversy over recombinant DNA, many precedents have been established in the relation between science and the public with respect to regulation.

1. Scientists concerned about the potential hazards of a research technique which they had developed request a voluntary moratorium on a class of experiments.
2. The first set of comprehensive guidelines are issued by an agency of government for regulating basic research in the biological sciences.
3. An environmental impact statement for a biological research technique is issued.
4. A local municipality issues a moratorium on genetic experiments effectively overruling a federal agency and passes a city ordinance regulating basic research.
5. A lay citizen panel convenes to evaluate the risks of scientific research.
6. Congress entertains several bills to regulate fundamental research in biology.

This chapter analyzes the recombinant DNA controversy with special focus on the development of policy for regulating a potentially hazardous research technique and on the scientists' response as they see their autonomy threatened. After outlining the questions that frame the conflict, we shall trace the debate as it evolved from a narrow technical problem to a public policy issue that has encouraged action in Congress and in local cities and states over the rights of society to determine the direction and outcome of scientific research. The response to concerns about the potential hazards of recombinant DNA research occurred in two stages. At first, scientists sought to establish a system of self-regulation with an emphasis on voluntary compliance with experimental safeguards. In this period, principal concerns were the biohazards associated with the spread of a pathogen. Later, a significant number of scientists sought uniform federal legislation.

Congress by this time had entered the debate with a serious agenda for legislation after communities like Cambridge, Massachusetts, began to establish local policy positions.[4] The actions of small communities set off a reaction in scientific circles, stimulating an intensive lobbying effort to avoid local and state restrictions. In this second stage of the controversy, participation in the debate broadened and new issues surfaced in the social and ethical arena—the relationship of recombinant DNA research to genetic engineering, the risks of infection among workers, the patenting of new life forms, and the rights of local communities to regulate the research.

HOW THE ISSUE WAS INITIALLY DEFINED

During the summer of 1971, a graduate student of biologist Paul Berg at Stanford University attended a workshop on tumor viruses at Cold Spring Harbor. The student, Janet Mertz, described an experiment planned by her mentor in which the DNA from Simian Virus 40 (SV 40) would be implanted into a bacterium *E. Coli.* The virus was first isolated from monkeys and induced tumors when injected into newborn hamsters. SV 40 was of particular interest to scientists. Because of its ability to infect animal cells it could serve as a vector for introducing DNA to those cells. Moreover any virus that caused tumors was an encouraging sign to those who sought to find a viral component of human cancer.

The ability of scientists to recombine DNA fragments in fact established a new tool of investigation for cancer research. The DNA of animal tumor viruses could be isolated and inserted into a simplified bacterial system. By allowing the bacteria to grow, the inserted DNA would be reproduced. Investigators interested in the properties of tumor-causing viruses like SV 40 could now produce large quantities of it cheaply to study its properties. The research possibilities opened up by these new techniques held special appeal in light of the growing research funds promised by the 1971 Cancer Act—from $140 million in 1971 to $800 million in 1978.

However, when Mertz described the experiment in which SV 40 DNA would be inserted into E. Coli, a researcher at the Cold Spring Harbor Conference expressed concern about the safety of such an experiment. Although SV 40 does not appear to infect humans,[5] transplanting its DNA into a bacterium that commonly resides in the human intestinal tract could pose a potential hazard by simplifying the transmission of the virus.

Because of the latency factor associated with the onset of cancer, no one could say definitively that virus SV 40, reproducing in the human system over a 30-40 year period, could cause no harm. After holding discussions with virologists and other colleagues, Paul Berg decided to postpone the SV 40 experiment until more was known about its risks.

The concept of "scientific responsibility" drew considerable attention during the turbulent 1960s. Responsibility entails openness, the courage to speak out on the misuse of science, the tolerance of fellow scientists who take stands on moral issues, and the acknowledgement that decisions affecting public welfare should reflect the public interest. The moral climate of the 1960s had a major impact in transforming the concerns of a small group of scientists about an esoteric research technique into a major public controversy. This transformation began at a Gordon Conference on nucleic acids held on June 15, 1973, at New Hampton, New Hampshire. The scientists who cochaired the conference, Maxine Singer and Dieter Soll, agreed to place the issue of the potential hazards of recombinant DNA research on the agenda, and took votes on whether the conference would support public letters expressing concern over the new genetic manipulations. In a first vote with approximately 90 participants present, 78 supported a letter to the National Academy of Sciences. A second vote found 42 out of 48 polled in favor of a second letter to be published in *Science* on September 21, 1973.

Those who supported dissemination of the Gordon Conference letters set a standard for other members of the scientific profession. It was a principled decision whereby scientists discharged what they perceived to be their collective responsibility. The message, however, was clear: scientists had located the problem and would resolve it in their own house. Conceived as an internal scientific matter, it was natural for the National Academy of Sciences (NAS) to assume responsibility. The Academy established a study committee comprised of molecular biologists headed by Paul Berg. Then, in another precedent-setting event, eight members of the Berg committee signed a letter (published in *Science,* July 26, 1974) calling upon scientists to refrain voluntarily from performing certain classes of genetic experiments (involving transfers of DNA in which tumor-causing viruses, toxins, or antibiotic resistant genes are introduced into bacteria) until risks could be assessed. The Berg letter was a pivotal point in the ensuing debate. At no time in the history of biological science had there been anything like it. The signers of the Berg letter saw themselves as acting cautiously and responsibly. They expected, through their recommendation for a moratorium, to gain public confidence.

CONTAINMENT WITHIN PROFESSIONAL CIRCLES

Once key scientists in the field of molecular biology warned that the new research program could involve risks, several policy choices were open. The National Academy of Sciences could have alerted all relevant scientific disciplines and called for papers on potential risks.[6] The issue could have been handed directly to Congress for investigation. Or alternatively, a special congressional or presidential commission might have convened, comprised of scientists from the research disciplines, the health sciences, and representatives of public interest groups. The NAS committee chose to visualize itself as a fact-finding panel. Once the relevant technical information was in place, the policy issues would be turned over to the National Institutes of Health (NIH).

In this first stage of debate, the controversy was interpreted as a technical, in contrast to a public policy, issue. Resolution was expected to remain with scientists and scientific advisers of the principal funding agencies. The Berg letter set the context for an assessment of risk which clearly focused the problem on the issue of laboratory containment.

A report in *Science* appearing in the same issue with the Berg letter called attention to the limits of this focus on technical issues.

> The motivation of the Berg group's proposals springs not from any long range misgivings about biological warfare or the social impact of genetic engineering, but rather from direct concern about the health hazard presented by the genetically altered bacteria that are created with the new technique.[7]

In another critical decision, the Berg committee moved the issue into the public policy sphere by recommending that NIH establish an advisory body to decide how the research should be administered. At the same time, however, considerations of how the research might ultimately be used was deemed outside of that committee's sphere of responsibility and interest.

Seven months after the Berg letter appeared in *Science,* the National Academy of Sciences convened an international conference at Asilomar, California. The 155 participants attended by invitation only and were selected principally through an internal network by members of the organizing group.[8] Most were biochemists and molecular biologists, but there was also representation from the fields of law, health sciences, infectious diseases, virology, and embryology. A corps of press people covered the event but there were certain stipulations about when their stories could be released. The organizers of Asilomar were concerned that the press would blow up half-baked statements or claims that would not stand up to the test of criticism.

The Asilomar conference perpetuated the assumption that analysis of risk was narrowly technical in nature. In this context, broad public and scientific input into the process was not considered. The formal agenda for the conference reflected the concerns of those who had called for the moratorium. It emphasized the extent to which the gene-splicing techniques could be used to create and/or spread pathogenic organisms. Experts were selected for their knowledge of: the ecology of Escherichia Coli (E. Coli)—the most commonly used host for DNA recombinants; potential hazards of animal viruses and how they should be handled; the ability of free DNA or plasmids (circular pieces of DNA used as a vehicle for the gene transplants) to be taken up by bacteria.[9]

The Asilomar scientists hoped to reach a consensus on the type, character, and relative magnitude of the risks in moving genes across species lines, and to establish measures for controlling the hazards agreeable to the scientific community. The pressure was building to end the moratorium and to get the research underway.

Asilomar, however, generated a wave of criticism from the scientific community and from environmental groups. They complained that this major area of risk-assessment was closed to many scientists who had important contributions to make. Only a smattering of infectious disease experts, clinical microbiologists, and public health personnel had contributed to the decisions at this historic meeting, for papers on risk-related aspects of the research were presented by invitation only and there was no general call for papers by key professional societies. Also absent from the Asilomar proceedings were scientific representatives from the ecological sciences as well as environmentalists. Yet once the results of Asilomar were delivered to NIH, important science policy decisions would follow, placing those who did participate in a very influential policy role.

For the scientists who organized Asilomar, however, it was necessary to limit representation in order to develop a rapid consensus. This was imperative, for without such consensus, the public might sense disagreement, lose confidence, and take decisions out of the scientists' hands. Concern about losing control over their research loomed heavily on the minds of those scientists who worked conscientiously to find lines of agreement.[10] The consensus that did develop out of Asilomar was a unity constructed out of considerable diversity. Later, however, disagreements among the scientists that were expressed at Asilomar were considerably tempered as the public became involved.

THE TECHNICAL RESPONSE TO THE PROBLEM

How do scientists judge the safety of an experimental procedure? Lacking any fundamental principles against which to measure safety, the Asilomar scientists tried to classify experiments according to their estimated relative degree of risk. Transferring animal virus DNA into E. Coli or transplanting genes for antibiotic resistance into bacteria were classified as high risk experiments although it was conceded that the nature of the risk was undetermined. Experiments which transplanted unspecified types of DNA (called shotgun experiments) were considered in a higher risk category than recombinations with pure DNA fragments. Since the principal concern was risk to humans, DNA transplants were considered most hazardous where the host was a mammalian cell.

The next step in the technical solution was to match this gradation of risks with a set of laboratory procedures. The scientists created two containment parameters, termed biological and physical containment. Biological containment refers to the type of host organism that serves as the recipient of the transplanted DNA fragment. The less capacity the host has to survive and to colonize humans and animals outside of highly specified laboratory conditions, the greater is its degree of biological containment. Scientists at Asilomar discussed the technical possibilities for engineering a host bacterium with restricted survival capacities.

Physical containment is a combined indicator reflecting the physical state of the laboratory and the safety protocol. The Asilomar recommendations stated that potential hazards should be matched with physical and biological containment parameters. Following these recommendations, the National Institutes of Health developed a classification mapping the level of biological containment (EK 1 to 3) and physical containment (P1 to P4) of animal and plant DNA contributors. Many hours at Asilomar were spent rationalizing the classification of particular genetic exchanges. Later, scientists would question the decision: why, for example, were genetic exchanges from birds to E. Coli considered riskier than similar exchanges from frogs to E. Coli. One observer at Asilomar termed the negotiating "an episode of technological horse-trading conducted in a vocabulary that often seemed to fit the realm of science fiction rather better than that of hard science."[11]

James Watson, a recipient of the Nobel Prize in biology for his role in the discovery of the structure of DNA, believed that there was no scientific justification for creating this relative classification of risks into a comfortable matrix.

[T]he molecular genetics establishment at Asilomar put the weight of its authority upon guidelines implying we could honestly predict that one form of recombinant DNA experimentation might carry more potential danger than another. In contrast, I, for one, saw no way to decide whether work on fruitfly DNA, or yeast DNA, or mouse DNA should be more or less restricted, if at all, and so found the Asilomar experience in the theater of the absurd.[12]

Watson's sentiments about the irrationality of the risk analysis at Asilomar was seconded by one of the principal organizers of the conference.

[I]t was a scientific matter, with political overtones, clearly because there were people who had done experiments with cold-blooded animals who wanted to continue.[13]

To the outsider, the Asilomar Conference looked like an effort to bring scientific knowledge to bear on assessing the risks of the new gene-splicing techniques. As it turned out, the technical discussion was laced with elements of value and personal vested interests.[14] Nevertheless, the conference was significant for its subsequent influence on policy makers and agency bureaucrats as they responded to the issue of public safety.

ROLE OF NIH

The National Institutes of Health (NIH), comprised of 11 institutes, is the principal federal agency which funds biomedical research. It is under the bureaucratic wing of the Department of Health, Education and Welfare. NIH entered the recombinant DNA picture soon after the Berg committee's statement appeared in July 1974. One of the recommendations in the Berg letter was that

the director of the National Institutes of Health is requested to give immediate consideration to establishing an advisory committee charged with (i) overseeing an experimental program to evaluate the potential biological and ecological hazards of the above types of recombinant DNA molecules; (ii) developing procedures which will minimize the spread of such molecules within human and other

populations; and (iii) devising guidelines to be followed by investigators working with potentially hazardous recombinant DNA molecules.[15]

Less than three months after the letter appeared, Robert S. Stone, then
Director of NIH, announced the establishment of the Recombinant DNA
Molecule Program Advisory Committee (RPAC).[16]

The stated goals of RPAC were noticeably broader than those of the
Berg committee, but as yet no consideration was given to the social and
ethical implications of the research. RPAC was defined as a technical
committee; its scope of inquiry was severely limited at the outset

> to investigate the current state of knowledge and technology regard-
> ing DNA recombinants, their survival in nature, and transferability
> to other organisms; to recommend programs of research to assess the
> possibility of spread of specific DNA recombinants and the possible
> hazards to public health and to the environment; and to recommend
> guidelines on the basis of the research results. This committee is a
> technical committee, established to look at a specific problem.[17]

The NIH also formed a recombinant DNA advisory committee which
met immediately after Asilomar to begin the process of drawing up
research guidelines. The first draft of guidelines drew criticism from
scientists for being too weak, and two additional versions were developed.
The third was adopted by RPAC and submitted to the Director of NIH,
Donald Fredrickson, in December 1975.

At this stage, only those scientists who were part of the Asilomar
network had evaluated the guidelines. The nonscientific community had
virtually no access to the process. So in anticipation that his agency could
be rebuked for not opening up the risk assessment to broader constituencies, Fredrickson convened the Director's Advisory Committee (DAC)
which, according to one NIH/HEW document, "afforded an opportunity
for the scientific community and the public to comment on the proposed
guidelines."[18] This special advisory committee was more broadly constituted than the technical group responsible for drawing up the guidelines. It
included health sciences personnel and a group of consultants including a
judge, two bioethicists, a consumer advocate, and two attorneys. Aware of
the growing political sensitivity, Fredrickson also employed his personal
advisory committee as a vehicle for promoting public participation. The
DAC held its first open meeting on February 9-10, 1976, at the NIH
headquarters in Bethesda, Maryland.[19] But spokesmen for environmental
groups and scientists criticized this as only a very meager effort to allow
public input into a major policy issue.

NIH continued to view the problems of the new gene-splicing techniques as technical, but could not avoid the political implications of their own role in developing regulations. The primary sponsor of recombinant DNA research in the United States was now playing the role of regulator and monitor. It was not a role Fredrickson welcomed, but the alternative was to relinquish the autonomy that scientists strived so hard to maintain. NIH's bureaucratic structure was a known entity, and scientists had good working relations with NIH officials. The peer-review structure for evaluating research grants enhanced confidence, and most scientists viewed NIH more as their advocate than their adversary, even when its role included regulation.

To protect itself from public criticism about conflict of interest, NIH built into the guidelines a multitiered committee structure for overseeing recombinant DNA research projects. All institutions where research is proposed must have certified containment facilities and must establish a standing biohazards committee. Besides advising the institution on its obligations, these committees review applications for support and certify to NIH that the project can be executed in conformity with NIH Recombinant DNA Molecule guidelines. The second level of responsibility lies with the NIH peer review groups or Study Sections. These groups review the scientific merit of each grant application, the potential biohazards of the proposed research, and the recommendations of the institutional biohazards committees. The Study Sections must determine whether the proposed physical and biological containment safeguards certified by the institutional biohazards committee are appropriate. Thus, beyond their scientific review, they have quasi-regulator duties.[20]

The NIH Recombinant DNA Molecule Program Advisory Committee (RPAC), responsible to the Secretary of HEW, adds another layer to the review process. The RPAC is responsible for updating guidelines, certifying host vector systems, and approving large-scale experiments. Finally the NIH staff is given the responsibility for reviewing grants and contracts for their conformity to the guidelines.

Some scientists visualized this review as an obstacle to carrying out their research. But others criticized the guidelines as inadequate and interpreted the review as inconsequential—more a form of publicity than a meaningful response to the potential hazards of the research. Since many members of the NIH Advisory Committee were affiliated with laboratories where recombinant DNA research was conducted, critics continued to worry about conflict of interest.[21]

Responding to pressure from scientists to lift the 18-month old non-legally binding moratorium, NIH Director Fredrickson issued provisional guidelines for all classes of gene transplantation experiments on June 23, 1976. Friends of the Earth promptly criticized this move as a violation of the National Environmental Protection Act which requires an environmental impact statement (EIS) and public review prior to the promulgation of regulations. Fredrickson, however, explained his position in a 27-page comment accompanying the guidelines. "The issue is how to strike a reasonable balance—in fact, a proper policy "bias"—between concerns to "go slow" and those to progress rapidly."

The Director also made it clear that he followed the line of thinking that began with the Singer-Soll letter in *Science*. It was a technical problem that required a technical solution. "These guidelines establish carefully controlled conditions for the conduct of experiments involving the insertion of such recombinant genes into organisms, such as bacteria."[22] Although by this time concerns about the relation of the research to genetic engineering were being publicly expressed by critics of the research, Fredrickson makes only oblique reference to the problem in his statement, dismissing it as irrelevant to the problem at hand.

> Recombinant DNA research with which these guidelines are concerned involves microorganisms such as bacteria or viruses or cells of higher organisms growing in tissue culture. It is extremely important for the public to be aware that this research is not directed to altering of genes in humans although some of the techniques developed in this research may have relevance if this is attempted in the future.[23]

Few would deny the direct link between recombinant DNA and future genetic intervention. But as a matter of public policy, NIH took a posture of agnosticism.

From the viewpoint of the scientists there is a vast difference between working under NIH guidelines and working under congressionally mandated regulations. The guidelines would essentially permit scientists to monitor themselves. The multitiered NIH committee structure overseeing the research is a collegial affair. Moreover, researchers anticipated that as more knowledge of genetic exchange between higher and lower organisms was attained, laboratory restrictions for containment would be weakened to permit an acceleration of the research. NIH personnel supported the idea that the guidelines should remain flexible and respond quickly to new knowledge about the risks.

NIH, however, became increasingly uncomfortable with its new role. First, there was the problem of DNA research funded by other federal agencies such as the Departments of Defense or Agriculture. Second, the NIH guidelines had no effect on private industrial research. Third, NIH was put in a compromising role, likened to the old Atomic Energy Commission, of serving as promoter and regulator of the same research.

To blunt criticism, the Secretary of HEW, prompted by a presidential request, initiated a move to secure adoption of the guidelines in other government agencies by setting up a federal interagency committee on recombinant DNA research. Also NIH Director Fredrickson hoped for voluntary compliance of the guidelines from industry[24]—a hope regarded by some critics as the height of folly at a time when competition was building for the first industrial application of the research.[25] By and large, however, pharmaceutical and chemical industries were not lobbying strongly against regulation. Some even welcomed legislation that would place their private research labs and university facilities under the same restrictions.

PUBLIC INVOLVEMENT IN THE DEBATE

The two-day open meeting of the NIH Director's Advisory Committee on Recombinant DNA Research (February 9-10, 1976) provided the first opportunity for public input at the national policy level. NIH notified 17 public interest groups of the hearings. Those who wished to comment on the draft guidelines but could not send a representative were invited to submit statements. Friends of the Earth challenged NIH for its narrow focus and raised questions about legal liability, inspection, and enforcement procedures, social and ethical problems arising from industrial applications, and the political implications of circumventing a serious effort of public participation.

The Federation of American Scientists submitted the results of a straw poll of their members. Of 322 respondents, 30% of the nonbiologists and 25% of the biologists rated the NIH guidelines as "insufficiently cautious." This was the first attempt to draw into the debate a broader sector of the scientific community—academicians and the professional lay public. A more refined poll was engineered by the *Boston Globe* and directed to professional biologists. A *Globe* science writer, Robert Cooke, supervised a survey mailed to 1256 randomly selected experienced senior experimental biologists out of a pool of 19,000. There were 490 replies from scientists employed in universities, industry, and government. Almost all the respondents believed there is some hazard in swapping genes between unrelated creatures. Thirty-nine percent of the respondents thought that the NIH guidelines should be more strict. These anonymous polls suggest far greater skepticism about the guidelines than the public statements of scientists would suggest.

The next public response to the NIH guidelines came when the draft environmental impact statement appeared on August 19, 1976. (The EIS appeared in the *Federal Register* on September 9, 1976.) Because of growing publicity, the EIS stimulated a broad range of written responses from an increasingly diverse group of individuals.[26] The 38 written statements came from elected governmental officials, public agency personnel (from ERDA, EPA, Department of Interior, HUD, Department of State, Federal Power Commission), and citizen and science advocacy groups such as the National Resources Defense Council, the Environmental Defense Fund, the Sierra Club, and the Boston Chapter of Science for the People. While laboratory containment issues still drew the most comments, concern was also expressed about genetic engineering, the EIS process, and the problems of securing compliance to the guidelines from private industry. Many of these issues raised by respondents to the EIS, however, had no place within the framework of NIH's technical definition of the problem. And those who questioned the fundamental assumptions upon which the guidelines were conceived were treated as a vocal minority, with political or philosophical biases.

Four months after NIH first invited public comment on the guidelines, the City of Cambridge (Massachusetts) declared its own moratorium on P-3 recombinant DNA research. Other communities watched attentively as actions in state and local municipalities spread. Those scientists who had once expressed reservations about the effectiveness of the biological and physical containment standards now quickly moved toward accepting the NIH guidelines. Community actions related to genetic research had two effects. First, many scientists put aside their technical disagreements to avoid what they perceived to be a greater threat—public intervention into decisions about scientific research. Second, when the passage of local and state ordinances regulating recombinant DNA started to become a reality, scientists who would have never even considered the idea of federal legislation began looking to Congress for action.

In symbolic value alone the Cambridge action proved to be a remarkable achievement for local citizenry. But it offered more than symbolic value.

Recombinant DNA research became a public issue in Cambridge when Harvard University began plans to renovate one of its old laboratories to qualify as a P-3 recombinant DNA facility. Some members of the Harvard Biology Department opposed the construction of such a facility. They argued that the research should not be carried out in a densely populated area. After the issue was brought to the Harvard faculty, local news coverage of the meeting drew the attention of the Mayor of Cambridge who called a hearing of the City Council. With two days of conflicting testimony from local scientists to draw upon, the Council voted on a moratorium for all research that NIH had classified at the moderate risk (P-3) level. The Council also called for a review board to study the issues and to make recommendations to the city.

The nature, composition, and charge of the review panel was determined by the City Manager. He chose a panel of lay citizens called the Cambridge Experimentation Review Board (CERB), and charged it with assessing the hazards to human health of a recombinant DNA P-3 research facility in the city. CERB heard testimony from scientists for five months, and then, in a unanimous decision, recommended that safeguards be added to the NIH guidelines before the research be permitted. These safeguards included a continuous program of laboratory monitoring, mandatory testing of modified organisms for their resistance to clinically used antibiotics, and a requirement that maximum biological containment be employed for gene-splicing experiments.

The Cambridge Experimentation Review Board also commented on questions of decision-making authority.

> Throughout our inquiry we recognized that the controversy over recombinant DNA research involves profound philosophical issues that extend beyond the scope of our charge. The social and ethical implications of genetic research must receive the broadest possible dialogue in our society. That dialogue should address the issue of whether all knowledge is worth pursuing. It should examine whether any particular route to knowledge threatens to transgress upon our precious human liberties. It should raise the issue of technology assessment in relation to long range hazards to our natural and social ecology. Finally, a rational dialogue is needed to determine how such policy decisions are resolved in the framework of participatory democracy.[27]

Following CERB's recommendations, the City Council passed an ordinance that regulates all recombinant DNA research carried out locally. The ordinance calls for the creation of a city biohazard committee comprised of local residents unaffiliated with the institutional biohazards committees.

The events taking place in Cambridge were reported widely in the mass media. The community, in establishing its own standards for the research, sent its message to NIH: "We want more protection than you afforded us." In addition, CERB issued a request to Congress that it regulate the research in a proper fashion, implying that NIH was not the apropriate agency for the job.

Other communities exhibited similar concerns, and hearings and study commissions burgeoned across the country.[28] Until this time, most scientists active in the debate opposed federal legislation. But as local and state actions accelerated, scientists felt more comfortable with a single set of national guidelines (even if they were enacted by Congress) than with nonuniform standards emanating out of local decision-making bodies.

Support for uniform national standards for genetic research in the form of legislation was evident during the National Academy of Sciences Forum on recombinant DNA research in March 1977. Following an address by Donald Fredrickson on the problems of control and regulation, Norton Zinder, a biologist at Rockefeller University, expressed the growing feeling of the scientific community about the need of legislation.

> I would like to support, and I am surprised that I am going to do so, the ideas of having legislation, federal legislation, with regard to recombinant DNA research. The proliferation of local option with different guidelines in different states and different cities can only lead to a situation of chaos, confusion, and ultimately to hypocrisy amongst the scientists involved. I strongly plead that the government move ahead on this as rapidly as possible.[29]

Once federal legislation became a real possibility, scientists and university officials began an organized effort to insure that the outcome of such legislation was favorable to the researcher. In an open letter to Congress, Walter Gilbert expressed the views of scientists who attended the 1977 Gordon Conference on Nucleic Acids

> We are most concerned that the benefits to society, both practical and fundamental, that we foresee will not be forthcoming because legislation and regulation will stifle free inquiry. . . . Should legislation nevertheless be deemed necessary, it ought to prescribe uniform standards throughout the country and be carefully formed so as not to impede scientific progress.[30]

Gilbert's ambivalence was widely shared. On the one hand, federal legislation meant the bureaucratization of science and with it, scientists feared, the ultimate demise of the United States' lead in biomedical research. On the other hand, without federal legislation, recombinant DNA research could be regulated like a patchwork quilt. They could only hope for weak federal legislation that would concentrate power in NIH, and preempt local authorities from making their own restrictions.

The actions of local communities drew national and international attention. The pressure was building for congressional action from scientists who could not accept local initiatives on setting research protocol, from environmental groups who wanted strong controls on industrial research, and from scientist-critics who argued that a national moratorium on all such research was essential pending a full-scale risk assessment.

CONGRESSIONAL ACTION

The first congressional hearings on recombinant DNA research were held only two months after Asilomar. The hearings of the Senate Subcommittee on Health (April 22, 1975) were entitled "Examination of the Relationship of a Free Society and Its Scientific Community." The Chairman, Senator Edward Kennedy, understood the issues to be broader than the technical biohazards. He raised questions about how nonscientists should participate in the debate especially in light of the broad social implications of the research.

The Kennedy Subcommittee also questioned the limited applicability of the NIH guidelines. The guidelines applied only to research funded by NIH and the National Science Foundation. By November 1976, Fredrickson had convened the interagency committee to review all the policies for granting patent rights for techniques and novel organisms developed with federal monies.[31]

By the time the City of Cambridge passed its ordinance regulating the research (February 7, 1977), subcommittees of the House and Senate already had background documents on the issues.[32] A resolution in the House of Representatives on January 19 had called the research "potentially devastating to the health and safety of the American people."[33] Immediately following the Cambridge decision, congressional activity began to accelerate and consideration of DNA legislation became a serious concern of congressional leaders.

By March 1977, five bills for regulating the research had been introduced into Congress. While congressional hearings on these bills were taking place, the Interagency Committee released a report to the Secretary of HEW stating that new legislation was necessary to regulate the use and production of recombinant DNA molecules.[34]

The substance of this report was on procedure, management, and administrative responsibility for DNA regulations in the event of legislation. The committee studied the existing legislative authorities that might be called upon to regulate research. Reviewing major relevant legislation (the Occupational Safety and Health Act, the Toxic Substances Control Act, the Hazardous Materials Transportation Act, and Section 361 of the Public Health Service Act), the committee concluded that "no single legal authority, or combination of authorities, currently exists which would clearly reach all recombinant DNA research in a manner deemed necessary by the Committee." Thus it recommended new legislation requiring licensing of researchers in this field and registration of projects with the Secretary of HEW. This would preempt all local laws and leave substantial discretion in the hands of the Secretary of HEW.

It was now four years after the first group of scientists publicly expressed their concern over recombinant DNA experiments, and the biomedical research community had entered a new era complicated by hard political realities. At no time in the history of American science has a basic research program been placed under such scrupulous assessment. The various bills introduced into Congress have all struggled with regulating basic research. They differ considerably in how regulation should be accomplished and in the balance between the right of free inquiry and the right of the public to protect itself from potentially hazardous research. The most prominent and controversial policy issues are: where should administrative control rest? how should enforcement be carried out? should federal legislation preempt state and local actions? should such legislation direct some action toward the social and ethical questions raised by the research?

For scientists the issue of which public body should administer the guidelines is critical; it is of paramount importance to keep the decisions as close to NIH as possible. But since NIH has responsibility for promoting and funding recombinant DNA research through its biomedical research programs, there are also strong arguments raised against its role in administering guidelines. Embodying regulation and promotion of research and technology in a single agency has been known to fail. One bill supports the establishment of a separate independent commission (like the Nuclear

Regulatory Commission) to serve as the administrative unit for implementing the regulations. But this proposal comes at a time when simplifying governmental bureaucracy is a congressional priority. Placing responsibility in the Secretary of HEW offers the advantage of broadening the powers of an existing governmental entity rather than creating a new one.

The bills filed in Congress also reflect different opinions about the adequacy of enforcement procedures. Violation of the guidelines could mean a cutoff in research funding. Is that a strong enough sanction? How should the legislation deal with privately funded research? Some bills emphasize licensure for individuals doing the research or for institutions where research is carried out. Critics argue that HEW is ill-equipped and ill-experienced as a regulatory body, so that effective monitoring, including site inspection programs, is unlikely. Some wish to promote good faith agreements between investigators and the overseeing body (HEW), but others call for aggressive regulatory procedures, conceiving the need of an agency role like that of OSHA in the work place. They feel that simply requiring investigators to publish their laboratory safety standards would not offer sufficient protection.

The most intensely debated policy issue is federal preemption. Scientists have lobbied vigorously in favor of federal preemption, and it was this issue that ultimately turned scientists full circle from initially opposing legislation to favoring it strongly. The best case for a federal preemption clause in recombinant DNA legislation is that it insures uniform standards across the nation. With differential standards, it is argued, research would drift to places that adopted the minimum guidelines. Some universities fear they will lose eminent researchers who are frustrated with additional safety conditions. They feel that those universities where research can be done with minimum standards would also have an advantage in competing for lucrative research grants. To insure that a preemption clause is included in any bill coming out of congressional committee, Harvard University has launched an intensive lobbying effort in Washington and has helped to orchestrate a nationwide counteroffensive against antipreemption forces.[35]

The arguments against a preemption clause reflect the expectation that states, cities, and towns have the right to protect the public's health and welfare. The communities and political entities which contain research facilities argue their right to choose how much protection they wish to have against the uncertain risks and to weigh these risks against the potential benefits that such research could bring to society. The 600 member Coalition for Responsible Genetic Research, which includes scientists, physicians, humanists, and environmentalists, lobbied against the preemption clause because it would place too much authority in a single individual—the Secretary of HEW.

Further congressional policy debate has focused on the establishment of a commission to oversee recombinant DNA research. A bill introduced by Senator Edward Kennedy (S.945, 95th Congress) called for the establishment of a National Commission for the Study of Recombinant DNA Research and Technology. The Kennedy bill stipulated that membership on the commission include individuals in the fields of "medicine, law, ethics, theology, the biological, physical, and environmental sciences, philosophy, humanities, health administration, government, and public affairs." The charge of the Commission would be to undertake a comprehensive study of the ethical, social, and legal implications of advances in recombinant DNA research and technology. The Commission on the Protection of Human Subjects of Biomedical Research was proposed as a model. For Congress, the proposed Commission raises the issue of whether the federal government should initiate serious discussion on the broader and more far-reaching implications of the research or simply stick with the more immediate technical concerns—the potential hazards of the spread of infectious agents or toxins.

Critics of the Commission concept believe it would be a first step in limiting, controlling, or forbidding certain types of scientific research because of its long-range potential social implications.[36] HEW Secretary Califano has opposed the concept on the ground that there are already too many outside bodies advising HEW. The addition of another commission would, in Califano's view, only add to the confusion of regulation.[37]

Despite the many hearings and bills presented during 1977, no bill made it to a floor vote. Scientists cited two new pieces of information which helped to put off legislation. Stanley Cohen, a key researcher in the field, engineered an experiment in which DNA from higher order cells (eukaryotes) was taken up by bacteria (prokaryotes) without using recombinant DNA techniques.[38] Critics had raised the possibility that if natural barriers were circumvented it could result in a dramatic alteration of evolution. Cohen's experimental results were offered as solid evidence that natural barriers did not exist between higher- and lower-order organisms. Prepublication copies of these results were passed around the halls of Congress.

A second piece of information that helped shift congressional interest away from strong DNA legislation came from Sherwood Gorbach, Chief of Infectious Disease at the Tufts University School of Medicine. Gorbach moderated a meeting at Falmouth, Massachusetts, in which workshops were held to assess the potential risks of recombinant DNA experimentation. Before the transcripts of the meetings were available and the results of the workshops published, Gorbach wrote a letter to Fredrickson reporting that

> [an] important consensus was arrived at by the assembled group which I felt was of sufficient interest to be brought directly to your attention. The participants arrived at unanimous agreement that *E. Coli* K12 cannot be converted into an epidemic pathogen by laboratory manipulations with DNA inserts. On the basis of extensive studies already completed, it appears that *E. Coli* K12 does not implant in the intestinal track of man. There is no evidence that non-transmissible plasmids can be spread from *E. Coli* K12 to other host bacteria within the gut.[39]

Gorbach's remarks were especially influential because the 50 invited participants to Falmouth represented disciplines that had not yet had an opportunity to share their knowledge about the hazards of the research. These included experts in the areas of clinical infectious diseases, enteric bacteriology, immunology, and epidemiology. It was the first time that a key risk assessment conference on recombinant DNA was not dominated by molecular biologists.

As the 95th Congress convened in 1978, lobbying continued. Except for the Coalition for Responsible Genetic Research, Science for the People, and a sprinkling of environmental groups, other scientific constituencies were either silent or accepted the NIH guidelines. Congressional support for vigorous legislation began to erode.[40] When it appeared that community actions had ceased and that strong lobbying at the local level could prevent citizen initiatives from imposing further regulations, DNA scientists began to rethink their support of legislation. The strategy of regulation shifted away from legislation in favor of expanding the powers of HEW through Section 361 of the Public Health and Safety Act.

Meanwhile NIH amended the guidelines by substantially lowering the containment requirements for most experiments. Thus, even with legislation, scientists could feel reasonably secure that they would have easy access to most classes of gene-splicing activities.

As this paper nears completion, one bill to regulate the research has received a favorable vote both from the House Subcommittee on Health and Environment and its parent committee on Interstate and Foreign Commerce. The bill is a two-year interim control measure which includes a preemption clause, and gives the HEW Secretary authority to regulate

DNA research. The bill would also establish a study commission to look at the long-term societal implications of the gene-splicing technology.

CONCLUSION

The controversy over the use of recombinant DNA molecule research highlights many problems in the relations between science and society. One of the most crucial issues, however, revolves around the belief in the necessity of scientific autonomy. The most intense debate focused on regulation: whether scientists should regulate their own research when it may be of a hazardous nature. The threat of external control that emerged in this case may mean that, rather than setting the stage for further policy debates over science, the recombinant DNA episode could promote a backlash. Scientists who raise questions about the potential hazards of certain research programs may be advised by their colleagues to remind themselves of what happened with recombinant DNA research. But nothing much did, in fact, happen. Citizen groups did not ban the research and Congress has not strangled molecular biology. Church organizations did not renounce genetic manipulation as a violation of God's will. Books were not burned. On the contrary, some citizens began reading more about science than they had before.

But let us look more closely at the meaning of the scientists' concerns. Many scientists believe that unless science remains an internal affair—from targeting research programs, to distributing grants, to evaluating risks— then scientific activity, including the content of science, will become politicized. Yet, clearly, post-World War II science has become increasingly beholden to government as its chief benefactor.[41] That the ratio of publicly funded to privately funded research in the universities has increased considerably during the last three decades inevitably raises questions about public oversight. To most scientists, support is essential, but public oversight of science means, eventually, bad science. Consider, for example, a remark by MIT biologist David Baltimore:

> biologists are spending their time in the halls of Congress trying to prevent the establishment of the first commission to be appointed to basic research. I believe that our success or failure will determine whether America continues to have a tradition of free inquiry into matters of science or falls under the fist of orthodoxy.[42]

Worries about freedom of scientific inquiry arise whenever oversight moves from within professional scientific circles to a broader arena comprised of scientists and representatives of the public. But if we examine the expression "freedom of scientific inquiry" as it is used in the DNA debate, it seems to translate into "scientific autonomy," or "freedom of self-regulation." Moreover, the scientists involved in this dispute tended to confuse the physical act of investigation of DNA with cognitive inquiry. They made a facile transition from "regulating physical investigation" to "limiting scientific inquiry," the latter being an effective metaphor to win support against public oversight over the use of gene-splitting techniques.

What can be learned from the public policy debate over recombinant DNA research? First, we must recognize that scientific research is a competitive activity. As one prominent biochemist commented: "In times of extreme scarcity of scientific funds, only a molecular angel could resist the lure of easy and plentiful support for a fashionable project."[43] Setting up controls and standards, or establishing social governors to slow down research, all evoke angry opposition from investigators. When scientists are faced with public review of their work, they close ranks and forget their internal debates to mobilize against social pressures to open up the decision-making process. The DNA debate also illustrates that scientists can be effective lobbyists when they sense a threat to their research funding.

Second, when a public body does have an opportunity to evaluate the hazards of fundamental research, the case of recombinant DNA suggests that this does not imply the demise of science. Citizens are often alarmed at the accelerating impacts of science on society, but they also understand the benefits of science.

Third, science is a big business and recombinant DNA research is no exception. Substantial sums of money were invested in new laboratories even prior to the issuance of permanent guidelines for regulating the research. Some scientists, cognizant of the industrial applications of DNA research, have sought patent rights over the new techniques or over modified strains of life. Others have begun consulting for private industry or establishing their own privately funded laboratories.

Finally, the struggle over the regulation of recombinant DNA research illustrates the strength of the traditional but dubious distinction that is made between science as the production of knowledge, and technology as the production of commodities. The distinction between science and technology becomes less credible as the gap between a scientific achievement and its technological applications is shortened, as scientific inquiry is supported to a greater degree by public and industrial funds, and as the methods of scientific inquiry involve technologies that pose risks to society. Sound policies for controlling technology, including technology assessment and public accountability, are considered inappropriate for science. Because of this distinction, the institutions of science are poorly prepared to deal with concerns that the public may have about the nature, purpose, and social impacts of the scientific investigations which it supports.

NOTES

1. The *New York Times* reported on February 23, 1977: "Fears were expressed here today [at the annual meeting of the American Association for the Advancement of Science] that the freedom of inquiry that has enabled science to flourish since the Renaissance may become subjugated as if it were the Middle Ages by pressure from both within and outside the scientific community." Also, see discussion in the Spring 1978 issue of *Daedalus* devoted to "Limits of Scientific Inquiry."

2. For an informed description of the recombinant DNA technique, see: Stanley N. Cohen, "The Manipulation of Genes," *Scientific American,* vol. 233 (July 1975), 24-33.

3. The Center for Disease Control issues a pamphlet entitled "Classification of Etiologic Agents on the Basis of Hazard," where four classes of biological agents are defined with safety conditions recommended for each class.

4. Published congressional hearings include: *Oversight Hearing on Implementation of NIH Guidelines Governing Recombinant DNA Research.* Joint hearings before the Subcommittee on Health, Committee on Labor and Public Welfare; and the Subcommittee on Administrative Practice and Procedure, Committee on the Judiciary, U.S. Senate, 94th Congress, September 22, 1976 (Washington, DC: Government Printing Office, 1976). Science Policy Implications of DNA Recombinant Molecule Research. Hearings before the Subcommittee on Science, Research, and Technology, Committee on Science and Technology, U.S. House of Representatives, 95th Congress, March 29, 30, 31; April 27, 28; May 3, 4, 5, 25, 26; September 7 and 8, 1977 (Washington, DC: Government Printing Office, 1977).

5. See Michael Rogers, *Biohazard* (New York: Alfred A. Knopf, 1977), 34-40; Nicholas Wade, *The Ultimate Experiment* (New York: Walker & Co., 1977), 33. Wade cites the summer of 1971 as the date for the Cold Spring Harbor workshop on tumor viruses, where the initial fears of recombinant DNA molecules surfaced. Rogers mistakenly placed the date at 1972. Between the years 1955 and 1961, U.S. children received polio immunization that was infected with live SV 40 virus. Subsequent epidemiological studies have not revealed a higher incidence of malignancies in the immunized population.

6. Harlyn O. Halvorson, formerly President of the American Society for Microbiology, acknowledged in a letter to *Science* that "Although recombinant DNA research has been extensively reported in the scientific and lay press, there has been suprisingly little input from individuals or organizations accustomed to dealing with hazardous microorganisms." Vol. 196, letter to the editor.

7. *Science,* vol. 185 (July 26, 1974), 332.

8. The organizing committee for the Asilomar Conference consisted of Paul Berg, David Baltimore, Richard Roblin, Maxine Singer (all from the United States) and Sydney Brenner (England). Two journalists who attended Asilomar discuss the proceedings in their respective books: Michael Rogers, *Biohazard,* Chapters 5-7, includes some remarks on the role of the press in Chapter 5, "Meeting at Asilomar;" and Nicholas Wade, *The Ultimate Experiment,* Chapter 5, "The Conference at Asilomar."

9. The five subjects which constituted the agenda at Asilomar were: the ecology of plasmids and enterric bacteria; molecular biology of prokaryote plasmids and their use for molecular cloning; synthetic recombinants involving animal virus DNAs; synthetic recombinants involving animal virus DNAs; synthetic recombinants involving eukaryote DNAs; and legal concerns of synthetic recombinant DNA. See *Genetic Engineering, Human Genetics and Cell Biology: DNA. Recombinant Molecule Research,* Report for the Subcommittee on Science, Research and Technology (Washington, DC: Government Printing Office, December 1976), 20.

10. Conflicting concerns among Asilomar participants between scientific freedom and social accountability are discussed in June Goodfield's account: "On the issues of scientific freedom, the young people divided into two groups themselves, the vast majority supporting the idea of social accountability. The few exceptions were—it was reported—the most scientifically ambitious types who argued, 'To hell with it. I know what I'm doing, and I want to do it'." June Goodfield, *Playing God* (New York: Random House, 1977), 107.

11. Rogers, *Biohazard,* 90.

12. See James Watson's essay, "In Defense of DNA," *The New Republic,* vol. 176 (June 25, 1977), 13.

13. The quotation is attributed to Maxine Singer and it appeared in "Science that Frightens Scientists," by William Bennett and Joel Gurin, *Atlantic Monthly,* vol. 239 (February 1977), 55.

14. Wallace P. Rowe, a virologist at NIH, interpreted the development of the guidelines in a similar fashion. "In a proper sense of the word 'political,' meaning the setting of policy, the guidelines are indeed political, and not scientific. . . . Thus the decision to specify containment levels for particular experiments was primarily one of policy, being based on value judgments as to how to respond to a problem for which there was an inadequate data base, and not based on a rational estimate of the probability of risk." Dr. Rowe's letter appeared in *Science,* vol. 198 (November 11, 1977), 563-564.

15. *Science,* vol. 185 (July 26, 1974), 303.

16. The Recombinant DNA Molecule Advisory Committee (RMAC) was chartered by the Secretary of HEW by the power vested in him through Section 301 of the Public Health Service Act. Under Section 301, the Secretary can initiate studies related to public health. The administrative policy is outlined in a report prepared for the Subcommittee on Science, Research, and Technology entitled, "DNA Recombinant Molecule Research" (Washington, DC: Government Printing Office, 1976), Appendix 5, 101. NIH Director Stone announced the formulation of RMAC on October 7, 1974. The announcement appeared in the *Federal Register,* vol. 39, on November 6, 1974, 39306.

17. *DNA Recombinant Molecule Research,* report prepared for the Subcommittee on Science, Research, and Technology of the Committee on Science and Technol-

ogy (Washington, DC: Government Printing Office, December 1976), Appendix 5, 101.

18. *Recombinant DNA Research*, Vol. 1, National Institutes of Health, HEW Pub. No. (NIH) 76-1138 (August 1976), iii.

19. The journal *Science* reported: "The prime significance of the hearing was probably that it created the first opportunity for people other than scientists to comment on the rationales and procedures developed within the scientific community for handling the new technique." *Science*, vol. 191 (February 27, 1976), 834.

20. *Guidelines for Research Involving Recombinant DNA Molecules*, National Institutes of Health, June 1976, 52.

21. According to Nicholas Wade's report in *Science* on the imposition of the RPAC: "Of its 15 voting members, all but the chairman are active biological researchers who may one day wish to use the technique, and at least three members . . . are personally involved in recombinant DNA experiments of the limited type permitted by the Asilomar conference" Vol. 190 (December 19, 1973), 1175-1179. See also Francine R. Simring "Folio or Folly: NIH Guidelines for Recombinant DNA Research," *Man and Medicine*, vol. 2 (1977) of the Journal of the Columbia University College of Physicians and Surgeons; and "The Double Helix of Self-Interest," *The Sciences*, vol. 17 (May/June 1977), 10-13, 27.

22. *Decision of the Director*, National Institutes of Health, June 23, 1976, 1, 6.

23. Ibid., 9.

24. Ibid., 11: "It is my hope that the guidelines will be voluntarily adopted and honored by all who support or conduct such research throughout the United States."

25. The first two breaches of the NIH guidelines on recombinant DNA research were found to have occurred in academic institutions. At the University of California (San Francisco) an investigator in the Department of Biochemistry and Biophysics used a vector in an experiment before it was certified by the NIH. See "Recombinant DNA: NIH Rules Broken in Insulin Gene Project," *Science*, vol. 197 (September 30, 1977), 1342. In a second incident reported in the *Boston Globe* (March 26, 1978), a researcher at the Harvard Medical School was carrying on recombinant DNA experiments before NIH had given official approval to his laboratory.

26. Responses to the EIS are contained in: *Environmental Impact Statements on NIH Guidelines for Research Involving Recombinant DNA Molecules*, Part 2, National Institutes of Health (October 1976), Appendix K.

27. *Guidelines for the Use of Recombinant DNA Molecule Technology in the City of Cambridge*, Cambridge Experimentation Review Board, submitted to the City Manager, January 5, 1977. For a shorter version of the Cambridge citizen's report see: "The Cambridge Experimentation Review Board," *Bulletin of the Atomic Scientists*, vol. 33 (May 1977), 23-27.

28. Reports of local activities related to recombinant DNA research appeared in the following issues of *Science*: vol. 191 (February 27, 1976); vol. 193 (July 23, 1976); vol. 194 (November 12, 1976); vol. 195 (February 11, 1977).

29. *Research with Recombinant DNA*, An Academy Forum, March 7-9, 1977 (Washington, D.C.: National Academy of Sciences, 1977), 259.

30. *Science*, vol. 197 (July 15, 1977), 208.

31. See *The Patenting of Recombinant DNA Research Inventions Developed under DHEW Support*, Director, National Institutes of Health, November 1977.

32. A report of the joint hearings before the Subcommittee on Health of the Committee of Labor and Public Welfare and the Subcommittee on Administrative

Practice and Procedure of the Committee on the Judiciary, U.S. Senate on the NIH guidelines was issued late in 1976; also appearing at that time was the report prepared for the Subcommittee on Science, Research, and Technology of the Committee on Science and Technology, U.S. House of Representatives, entitled: *DNA Recombinant Molecule Research.*

33. *Science,* vol. 199 (January 20, 1978), 274.

34. The recommendations of the Interagency Committee were reported in an HEW news release on recombinant DNA research, March 16, 1977. See: Recombinant DNA Research, vol. 2 (March 1978), DHEW Publication No. (NIH) 78-1139, 276-289.

35. According to the *Harvard Crimson* (March 2, 1978), Harvard hired a registered lobbyist "to participate in the drafting of a bill incorporating Harvard's and other institutions' support for a strong federal standard, known as a preemption clause, to regulate recombinant DNA research." The *Crimson* reported that Harvard officials along with officials of other institutions formed an organization called "Friends of DNA," for the purpose of strengthening their lobbying effort. *Science* reported that Harvard joined Stanford and Washington University in writing a draft bill with a strong preemption clause (Vol. 199 [March 24, 1978], 1320).

36. Biologist David Baltimore is quoted in *Science* referring to the Kennedy Bill: "a clear invitation to begin the process of deciding what research shall be allowed and what research prevented" (Vol. 199 [January 20, 1978], 274).

37. *Science,* vol. 196 (April 22, 1977), 405.

38. Shing Chang and Stanley Cohen, "In vitro site-specific genetic recombination promoted by the Eco. RI restriction endoclease," Proc. National Academy of Sciences vol. 74 (November 1977), 4811-4815.

39. Letter concerning the Falmouth workshop, from S. L. Gorbach to D. S. Fredrickson, July 14, 1977; in *Environmental Impact Statement on NIH Guidelines for Research Involving Recombinant DNA Molecules, October 1977, National Institutes of Health, Appendix M.*

40. See the editorial in *Science* by H. O. Halvorson, vol. 198 (October 28, 1977); also, Barbara J. Culliton, "Recombinant DNA Bills Derailed: Congress Still Trying to Pass a Law," *Science,* vol. 199 (January 20, 1978), 274-277.

41. Susan Wright, "Molecular Politics in Britain and the United States: The Development of Policy for Recombinant DNA Technology," forthcoming in the *Southern California Law Review.* Dr. Wright traces the development of biomedical research after World II showing how changes in the funding of science has changed its institutions.

42. The quotation appeared in *Science,* vol. 199 (January 20, 1978), 274.

43. Erwin Chargoff, "A Forum on Recombinant DNA," *Chemical and Engineering News* (May 30, 1977), 41.

ABOUT THE AUTHORS

MICHAEL BROWN is a graduate student in City and Regional Planning at Cornell University where he was awarded a 1977-1978 Cornell Fellowship. He has an AB degree with Honors in Politics from the University of California at Santa Cruz.

SUSAN FALLOWS is an Assistant Professor of Planning and Public Policy at the University of California at Irvine. She is finishing her doctoral thesis on energy decision-making in Congress in the Department of City and Regional Planning at Cornell.

THANE GUSTAFSON is Associate Professor of Government at Harvard University, and Research Associate in the Center for Science and International Affairs, Kennedy School of Government, Harvard University. He specializes in science policy and Soviet studies.

SUSAN G. HADDEN is an Assistant Professor at the Southern Center for Studies in Public Policy at Clark College, Atlanta. She is a political scientist with a Ph.D. from the University of Chicago.

SHELDON KRIMSKY is Associate Director of the Graduate Program in Urban and Environmental Policy. He received a Ph.D. in Philosophy at Boston University, specializing in philosophy of science. He did postdoctoral studies in economic theory and urban and environmental policy at Tufts. He has taught at the University of South Florida, Boston University, and Wesleyan University where he is Associate Professor of Philosophy in the Graduate Summer School.

GERALD E. MARKLE is Associate Professor of Sociology at Western Michigan University. He received a Master's degree in molecular biology before becoming a sociologist. He has published in the areas of population studies, deviant behavior, and the social impact of scientific controversy.

STEVEN MAYNARD-MOODY is a doctoral candidate in the Department of Community Service Education at Cornell University. He has an A.B. degree in history from Lafayette College. He has been involved in several research studies including a study of participation in technical disputes. He was formerly the program coordinator of the Ken Crest School for Exceptional Children.

JEROME MILCH is Assistant Professor in the Department of Political Science at the University of Pittsburgh. After earning his doctoral degree from MIT, he worked in the Science, Technology, and Society Program at Cornell University. His research focuses on comparative studies of airport planning policy.

DOROTHY NELKIN is a Professor at Cornell University in the Program on Science, Technology and Society, and the Department of City and Regional Planning. She is President of the Society for the Social Studies of Science and author of a number of books on controversies over science and technology. Among Professor Nelkin's previous works is *Technological Decisions and Democracy* (Sage, 1977).

JAMES C. PETERSEN is Assistant Professor of Sociology and Associate Director of the Center for Sociological Research at Western Michigan University, and is Deputy Editor of the *Journal of Voluntary Action Research.* He has published in the areas of social participation, voluntary associations, organizational behavior, and marginal medicine.

JUDITH REPPY is a Research Associate in the Peace Studies Program at Cornell University. She has a Ph.D. in economics from Cornell. Her current research interest is in military research and development and defense procurement.

JOSHUA IRA SCHWARTZ is a lawyer and city and regional planner currently serving in the Division of Lands and Natural Resources of the United States Department of Justice in Washington, D.C. Since graduation from Harvard University in 1973, he obtained his J.D. from Cornell in 1976, and Master's in Regional Planning in 1977, and served as a federal judicial law clerk in 1977-1978.

THE RED CHURCH

Also by Scott Nicholson

THE RED CHURCH

Scott Nicholson

Haunted Computer Books

HAUNTED COMPUTER BOOKS
188AA Bernard Bledsoe Lane
Todd, NC 28684

The Red Church was originally published by
Kensington Books in 2002.
This edition was published by arrangement with Scott Nicholson.

Haunted Computer Books Edition: 2010

Publisher's Note:

This book is a work of fiction. The characters, incidents, and dialogue are drawn from the author's imagination and used fictitiously. Any resemblance to actual events or persons, living or dead, is entirely coincidental.

ISBN: 978-1-45150702-7

For God, for second chances.

✞ Chapter 1

The world never ends the way you believe it will, Ronnie Day thought.

There were the tried-and-true favorites, like nuclear holocaust and doomsday asteroid collisions and killer viruses and Preacher Staymore's all-time classic, the Second Coming of Jesus Christ. But the end really wasn't such a huge, organized affair after all. The end was right up close and personal, different for each person, a kick in the rear and a joy-buzzer handshake from the Reaper himself.

But that was the Big End. First you had to twist your way though a thousand turning points and die a little each time. One of life's lessons, learned as the by-product of thirteen years as the son of Linda and David Day and one semester sitting in class with Melanie Ward. Tough noogies, wasn't it?

Ronnie walked quickly, staring straight ahead. Another day in the idiot factory at good old Barkersville Elementary was over. Had all evening to look forward to, and a good long walk between him and home. Nothing but his feet and the smell of damp leaves, fresh grass, and the wet mud of the riverbanks. A nice plate of spring sunshine high overhead.

And he could start slowing down in a minute, delaying his arrival into the hell that home had been lately, because soon he would be around the curve and past the thing on the hill to his right, the thing he didn't want to think about, the thing he couldn't help thinking about, because he had to walk past it twice a day.

Why couldn't he be like the other kids? Their parents picked them up in shiny new Mazdas and Nissans and took them to the mall in Barkersville and dropped them off at soccer practice and then drove them right to the front door of their houses. So all they had to do was step in and stuff their faces with microwave dinners and go to their rooms and waste their brains on TV or Nintendo all night. They didn't have to be scared.

Well, it could be worse. He had a brain, but it wasn't something worth bragging about. His "overactive imagination" got him in trouble at school, but it was also kind of nice when other kids, especially Melanie, asked him for help in English.

So he'd take having a brain any day, even if he did suffer what the school counselor called "negative thoughts." At least he <u>had</u> thoughts. Unlike his little dorkwad of a brother back there, who didn't have sense enough to know that this stretch of road was no place to be messing around.

"Hey, Ronnie." His brother was calling him, it sounded like from the top of the hill. The dorkwad hadn't *stopped,* had he?

"Come on." Ronnie didn't turn around.

"Looky here."

"Come on, or I'll bust you upside the head."

"No, really, Ronnie. I see something."

Ronnie sighed and stopped walking, then slung his

book bag farther up on his shoulder. He was at least eighty feet ahead of his little brother. Tim had been doing his typical nine-year-old's dawdling, stopping occasionally to tie his sneaker strings or look in the ditch water for tadpoles or throw rocks at the river that ran below the road.

Ronnie turned—*to your left*, he told himself, *so you don't see it*—and looked back along the sweep of gravel at the hill that was almost lost among the green bulk of mountains. He could think of a hundred reasons not to walk all the way back to see what Tim wanted him to see. For one thing, Tim was at the top of the hill, which meant Ronnie would have to hike up the steep grade again. The walk home from the bus stop was nearly a mile and a half already. Why make it longer?

Plus there were at least ninety-nine other reasons—
like the red church
—not to give a flying fig what Tim was sticking his nose into now. Dad was supposed to stop by today to pick up some more stuff, and Ronnie didn't want to miss him. Maybe they'd get to talk for a minute, man-to-man. If Tim didn't hurry, Dad and Mom might have another argument first and Dad would leave like he had last week, stomping the gas pedal of his rusty Ford so the wheels threw chunks of gravel and broke a window. So that was another reason not to go back to see whatever had gotten Tim so worked up.

Tim jumped up and down, the rolled cuffs of his blue jeans sagging around his sneakers. He motioned with his thin arm, his glasses flashing in the mid-afternoon sun. "C'mon, Ronnie," he shouted.

"Dingle-dork," Ronnie muttered to himself, then started backtracking up the grade. He kept his eyes on the gravel the way he always did when he was near the church. The sun made little sparkles in the rocks, and with a little imagination, the roadbed could turn into a big galaxy with lots of stars and planets, and if he didn't look to his left he wouldn't have to see the red church.

Why should he be afraid of some dumb old church? A church was a church. It was like your heart. Once Jesus came in, He was supposed to stay there. But sometimes you did bad things that drove Him away.

Ronnie peeked at the church just to prove that he didn't care about it one way or another. *There. Nothing but wood and nails.*

But he'd hardly glanced at it. He'd really seen only a little piece of the church's mossy gray roof, because of all the trees that lined the road- big old oaks and a gnarled apple tree and a crooked dogwood that would have been great for climbing except if you got to the top, you'd be right at eye level with the steeple and the belfry.

Stupid trees, he thought. *All happy because it's May and their leaves are waving in the wind and, if they were people, I bet they'd be wearing idiotic smiles just like the one that's probably splitting up Tim's face right now. Because, just like little bro, the trees are too doggoned dumb to be scared.*

Ronnie slowed down a little. Tim had walked into the shade of the maple. Into the jungle of weeds that formed a natural fence along the road. And maybe to the edge of the graveyard.

Ronnie swallowed hard. He'd just started developing an Adam's apple, and he could feel the knot pogo in his throat. He stopped walking. He'd thought of reason number hundred and one not to go over to the churchyard. Because—and this was the best reason of all, one that made Ronnie almost giddy with relief—he was the *older* brother.

Tim had to listen to *him*. If he gave in to the little mucous midget even once, he would be asking for a lifetime of "Ronnie, do this" and "Ronnie, do that." He got enough of that kind of treatment from Mom.

"Hurry up," Tim called from the weeds. Ronnie couldn't see Tim's face. That wasn't all bad. Tim had buck teeth and his blond hair stuck out like straw and his eyes were a little buggy. Good thing he was in the fourth grade instead of the eighth grade. Because in the eighth grade, you had to impress girls like Melanie Ward, who would laugh in your face one day and sit in the desk behind you the next, until you were so torn up that you didn't even care about things like whatever mess your dorkwad brother was getting into at the moment. "Get out of there, you idiot. You know you're not supposed to go into the churchyard."

The leaves rustled where Tim had disappeared into the underbrush. He'd left his book bag lying in the grass at the base of a tree. His squeaky voice came from beyond the tangle of saplings and laurel. "I found something."

"Get out of there right this minute."

"Why?"

"Because I <u>said</u> so."

"But look what I found."

Ronnie came closer. He had to admit, he was a little bit curious, even though he was starting to get mad. Not to mention scared. Because through the gaps in the trees, he could see the graveyard.

A slope of thick, evenly cut grass broken up by white and gray slabs. Tombstones. At least forty dead people, just waiting to rise up and-

Those are just stories. *You don't actually believe that stuff, do you? Who cares what Whizzer Buchanan says? If*

he were so smart, he wouldn't be flunking three classes.

"We're going to miss Dad," Ronnie called. His voice trembled slightly. He hoped Tim hadn't noticed.

"Just a minute."

"I ain't got a minute."

"You chicken or something?"

That did it. Ronnie balled up his fists and hurried to the spot where Tim had entered the churchyard. He set his book bag beside Tim's and stepped among the crushed weeds. Furry ropes of poison sumac veined across the ground. Red-stemmed briars bent under the snowy weight of blackberry blossoms. And Ronnie would bet a Spiderman comic that snakes slithered in that high grass along the ditch.

"Where are you?" Ronnie called into the bushes.

"Over here."

He was in *the graveyard, the stupid little jerk. How many times had Dad told them to stay out of the graveyard?*

Not that Ronnie needed reminding. But that was Tim for you. Tell him to not to touch a hot stove eye and you could smell the sizzling flesh of his fingers before you even finished your sentence.

Ronnie stooped to about Tim's height—*twerp's-eye view*—and saw the graveyard through the path that Tim had stomped. Tim was kneeling beside an old marble tombstone, looking down. He picked something up and it flashed in the sun. A bottle.

Ronnie looked past his little brother to the uneven rows of markers. Some were cracked and chipped, all of them worn around the edges. Old graves. Old dead people. So long dead that they were probably too rotten to lift themselves out of the soil and walk into the red church.

No, it wasn't a church anymore, just an old building that Lester Matheson used for storing hay. Hadn't been a church for about twenty years. Like Lester had said, pausing to let a stream of brown juice arc to the ground, then wiping his lips with the scarred stump of his thumb, "It's *people* what makes a church. Without people, and what-and-all they believe, it ain't nothing but a fancy mouse motel."

Yeah. Fancy mouse motel. Nothing scary about that, is there?

It was just like the First Baptist Church, if you really thought about it. Except the Baptist church was bigger. And the only time the Baptist church was scary was when Preacher Staymore said Ronnie needed saving or else Jesus Christ would send him to burn in hell forever.

Ronnie scrambled through the bushes. A briar snagged his X-Files T-shirt, the one that Melanie thought was so cool. He backed up and pulled himself free, cursing as a thorn pierced his finger. A drop of crimson welled up and he started to wipe it on his shirt, then licked it away instead.

Tim put the bottle down and picked up something else. A magazine. Its pages fluttered in the breeze. Ronnie stepped clear of the brush and stood up.

So he was in the graveyard. No big deal. And if he kept his eyes straight ahead, he wouldn't even have to see the fancy mouse motel. But then he forgot all about trying not to be scared, because of what Tim had in his hands.

As Ronnie came beside him, Tim snapped the magazine closed. But not before Ronnie had gotten a good look at the pale flesh spread along the pages. Timmy's cheeks turned pink. He had found a *Playboy*.

"Give me that," Ronnie said.

Tim faced his brother and put the magazine behind his back. "I—I'm the one who found it."

"Yeah, and you don't even know what it is, do you?"

Tim stared at the ground. "A naked-woman book."

Ronnie started to laugh, but it choked off as he looked around the graveyard. "Where did you learn about girlie magazines?"

"Whizzer. He showed one to us behind the gym during recess."

"Probably charged you a dollar a peek."

"No, just a quarter."

"Give it here, or I'll tell Mom."

"No, you won't."

"Will, too."

"What are you going to tell her? That I found a naked-woman book and wouldn't let you see it?"

Ronnie grimaced. *Score one for dingle-dork.* He thought about jumping Tim and taking the magazine by force, but there was no need to hurry. Tricking him out of it would be a lot more fun. But he didn't want to stand around in the creepy graveyard and negotiate.

He looked at the other stuff scattered on the grass around the tombstone. The bottle had a square base and a black screw top. A few inches of golden-brown liquid were lying in the bottom. He knew it was liquor because of the turkey on the label. It was the kind that Aunt Donna drank. But Ronnie didn't want to think about Aunt Donna almost as much as he didn't want to think about being scared.

A green baseball cap lay upside down beside the tombstone. The sweatband was stained a dark gray, and the bill was so severely cupped that it came to a frayed point. Only one person rolled up their cap bill that way. Ronnie nudged the cap over with his foot. A John Deere cap. That cinched it.

"It's Boonie Houck's," Ronnie said. But Boonie never went anywhere without his cap. Kept it pulled down to the bushy line of his single eyebrow, his eyes gleaming under the shade of the bill like wet ball bearings. He probably even showered and slept with the cap plastered to the top of his wide head.

A crumpled potato chip bag quivered beside the cap, fluttering in the breeze. It was held in place by an un-opened can of Coca-Cola. The blind eye of a flashlight peeked out from under the edge of the chip bag.

Ronnie bent down and saw a flash of silver. Money. He picked up two dimes and a dull nickel. A couple of pennies were in the grass, but he left them. He straightened up.

"I'll give you twenty-five cents for the magazine," he said.

Tim backed away with his hands still behind him. He moved into the shadow of a crude stone monument, made of two pillars holding up a crosspiece. On the crosspiece was a weathered planter. A brittle sheaf of brown tulips stabbed up from the potting soil.

Tulips. So somebody had minded the graveyard at least once since winter. Probably Lester. Lester owned the property and kept the grass trimmed, but did that mean the tobacco-chewing farmer had to pay respects to those buried here? Did the dead folks come with the property deed?

But Ronnie forgot all that, because he accidentally looked over Tim's shoulder. The red church was framed up perfectly by the stone pillars.

No, NOT accidentally. You WANTED to see it. Your eyes have been crawling right toward it the whole time you've been in the graveyard.

The church sat on a broad stack of creek stones that were bleached yellow and white by eons of running water. A few of the stones had tumbled away, revealing gaps of darkness beneath the structure. The church looked a little wobbly, as if a strong wind might send it roof-over-joist down the hill.

The creepy tree stood tall and gangly by the door. Ronnie didn't believe Whizzer's story about the tree. But if even half of it were true-

"A quarter? I can take it to school and make five bucks," Tim said.

The magazine. Ronnie didn't care about the magazine anymore. "Come on. Let's get out of here."

"You're going to take it from me, ain't you?"

"No. Dad's supposed to be coming over, that's all. I don't want to miss him."

Tim suddenly took another step backward, his eyes wide.

Ronnie pointed, trying to warn him about the monument. Tim spun and bumped into one of the pillars, shaking the crosspiece. The concrete planter tipped over, sending a shower of dry black dirt onto Tim's head. The planter rolled toward the edge of the crosspiece.

"Look out," Ronnie yelled.

Tim pushed himself away from the pillar, but the entire monument toppled as if in slow motion. The heavy crosspiece was going to squash Tim's head like a rotten watermelon.

Ronnie's limbs unlocked and he leaped for Tim. Something caught his foot and he tripped, falling on his stomach. The air rushed from his lungs with a whoosh, and the smell of cut grass crowded his nostrils. He tasted

blood, and his tongue found the gash on the inside of his lip just as he rediscovered how to breathe.

A dull cracking noise echoed across the graveyard. Ronnie tilted his neck up just in time to see the planter bust open on the monument's base. Tim gave a squeak of surprise as dingy chunks of concrete rained across his chest. The pillars fell in opposite directions, the one on Tim's side catching on the ledge just above his head. The crosspiece twirled like a slow helicopter blade and came to rest on the pillar above Tim's legs.

Ronnie tried to crawl to Tim, but his shoe was still snagged. "You okay?"

Tim was crying. At least that meant he was still alive.

Ronnie kicked his foot. He looked back to his shoe—

NO NO NO

—red raw burger hand.

An arm had reached around the tombstone, a bloody arm, the knotty fingers forming a talon around his sneaker. The wet, gleaming bone of one knuckle hooked the laces.

DEADGHOSTDEADGHOST

He forgot that he'd learned how to breathe. He kicked at the hand, spun over on his rear, and tried to crab-crawl away. The hand wouldn't let go. Tears stung his eyes as he stomped his other foot against the ragged grasping thing.

"Help me," Ronnie yelled, at the same time that Tim moaned his own plea for help.

Whizzer's words careened across Ronnie's mind, joining the jumble of broken thoughts: *They trap ya, then they get ya.*

"Ronnie," came Tim's weak whine.

Ronnie wriggled like a speared eel, forcing his eyes along the slick wrist to the arm that was swathedin ragged flannel.

Flannel?

His skewed carousel of thoughts ground to a halt.

Why would a deadghost thing be wearing flannel?

The arm was attached to a bulk of something behind the tombstone.

The hand clutched tightly at nothing but air, then quivered and relaxed. Ronnie scrambled away as the fingers uncurled. Blood pooled in the shallow cup of the palm.

Ronnie reached Tim and began removing the chunks of concrete from his little brother's stomach. "You okay?"

Tim nodded, charcoal streaks of mud on his face where his tears had rolled through the sprinkling of potting soil. One cheek had a red scrape across it, but otherwise he looked unharmed. Ronnie kept looking back to the mangled arm and whatever was behind the tombstone. The hand was still, the sun drying the blood on the clotted palm. A shiny fly landed and drank.

Ronnie dragged Tim free of the toppled concrete. They both stood, Tim wiping the powdery grit from the front of his shirt. "Mom's going to kill me. . . ." he began, then saw the arm. "What in heck . . .?"

Ronnie stepped toward the tombstone, his heart hammering in his ears.

Over his pulse, he could hear Whizzer: *They got livers for eyes.*

Ronnie veered toward the edge of the graveyard, Tim close behind.

"When I say run. . ." Ronnie whispered, his throat thick.

"L-looky there," Tim said.

Dorkwad didn't have enough brains to be scared. But Ronnie looked. He couldn't help it.

The body was crowded against the tombstone, the flannel shirt shredded, showing scoured flesh. The head was pressed against the white marble, the neck arched at a crazy angle. A thread of blood trailed from the matted beard to the ground.

"Boonie," Ronnie said, his voice barely as loud as the wind in the oak leaves.

There was a path trampled in the grass, coming from the underbrush that girded the graveyard. Boonie must have crawled out of the weeds. And whatever had done that to him might still be in the stand of trees. Ronnie flicked his eyes from Boonie to the church. Had something fluttered in the belfry?

A bird, a BIRD, you idiot.

Not the thing that Whizzer said lived in the red church.

Not the thing that trapped you and then got you, not the thing that had wings and claws and livers for eyes, not the thing that had made a mess of Boonie Houck's face.

And then Ronnie was running, tearing through the undergrowth, barely aware of the briars grabbing at his face and arms, of the scrub locust that pierced his skin, of the tree branches that raked at his eyes. He heard Tim behind him- at least he <u>hoped</u> it was Tim, but he wasn't about to turn around and check, because now he was on the gravel road, his legs were pumping in the rhythm of fear—*NOT-the-thing, NOT-the-thing, NOT-the-thing*—and he didn't pause to breathe, even as he passed Lester Matheson, who was on his tractor in the middle of a hayfield, even as he passed the Potter farm, even when geezery Zeb Potter hollered out Ronnie's name from his shaded front porch, even as Zeb's hound cut loose with an uneven bray, even as Ronnie jumped the barbed wire that marked off the boundary of the Day property, even as the rusty tin roof of home came into view, even as he saw Dad's Ranger in the driveway, even as he tripped over the footbridge and saw the sharp, glistening rocks of the creek bed below, and as he fell he realized he'd hit another turning point, found yet another way for the world to end, but at least *this* end wasn't as bad as whatever had shown Boonie Houck the exit door from everywhere.

✟ Chapter 2

"Why didn't you tell me?"

"Like you'd understand? You didn't understand the first time." Linda Day balled her hands into fists. She could smell beer on David's breath.

Drunk at three o'clock, she thought. *Doesn't he know that the body is sacred? If only he were more like Archer.*

David closed in on her. She backed against the kitchen table. He'd never hit her in their fifteen years of marriage. But his face had never set in such a mix of hurt and anger before, either.

He waved the papers in the air, his thin lips crawling into a sneer. "A lie. All those years . . ."

God, he wasn't going to CRY, was he? Mr. Ain't-Nothing-It'll-Heal that time he flipped the tractor and had his forearm bone poking through his denim jacket?

She looked into his wet brown eyes. Who was he? What did she *really* know about him? Sure, they'd gone to high school together, were both in the Future Farmers of America, lost it together one fumbling Friday night in the pines above the Pickett High football field, never really dated anybody else, got married like everybody expected and—after that little California interlude—settled down on the Gregg family farm after cancer had chewed her father's lungs away.

More than half of their lives. Not nearly enough time to figure David out.

"Don't start that," she said.

"I ain't the one who started it. You said when we got married that all that foolishness was over and done with."

"I thought it was."

"Thought it was?" he mocked. His face twisted.

"I was going to tell you."

"When? After you'd sneaked another hundred lies past me?"

Linda looked away, anywhere but at his burning, red-rimmed eyes. The stick margarine on the counter was losing its sharp edges in the heat. Two black flies were playing hopscotch on the kitchen window screen. The roses that made a pattern on the yellowed wallpaper looked as if they needed watering. "It's not like that."

"Sure, it ain't." A mist of Pabst Blue Ribbon came out with his words. "When a man's wife gets love letters from another man, why, that's nothing to worry about, is it?"

"So you read them."

"Course I read them." He stepped closer, looming over her, six-three and shoulders broadened by lifting ten thousand bales of hay.

"Then maybe you noticed that the word 'love' isn't in a single one of them."

He stopped in his tracks. Linda thought about retreating to the hall entrance, but she was trying hard not to show fear. Archer said fear was for the meek, them that huddled at the feet of Christ.

David's brow lowered. "There's lots of different kinds of love."

She studied his face. Twice-broken nose. A white scar

in one corner of his mouth. A strong chin, the kind you could forge steel with. Skin browned by years of working in the sun. Had she ever really loved the man who wore that face?

"There's only one kind of love," she said. "The kind we had."

"The kind you and Archer had."

"David, please listen."

He reached out. She held her breath and leaned away. But he didn't touch her, only swept the can of Maxwell House from the table behind her. It bounced off the cabinet under the sink and the lid flew off, sending a shower of brown granules onto the vinyl floor. The rich smell of the coffee drowned out David's sweet-sour breath.

His teeth were showing. Broad and blunt. Pressed together so tightly that his jaw trembled.

Linda scooted along the edge of the table to her right. There was a knife on the counter, a skin of dried cheese dulling the flash of the blade. If she had to-

But David turned away, slumped, his shoulders quivering.

David never cried, at least not in front of her. But since he'd found the letters, he was doing a lot of things he'd never done before. Like drinking heavily. Like leaving her.

"Hon—" She caught herself. "David?"

His work boots drummed the floor as he strode away. He paused at the back door and turned, looking down at the letters in his hand. Tears had shimmied down one side of his face, but his voice was quiet, resigned. "Archer McFall. Pretty funny. Who'd you put up to doing it?"

"Doing what?"

"We both know it ain't Archer, so quit lying. Is it one of your buddies from California?"

Linda shook her head. *He doesn't understand. And I had hopes that he would join us.* "No, it's nobody."

"Nobody? *Nobody* who's been writing you letters while dumb-and-happy David Day runs a hammer and eats saw-dust for ten hours a day, only *he* don't mind because he's got a wonderful family waiting at home each night waiting to shower him with love and bullshit?"

His bulk filled the door frame, blocking her view of the barn and the pasture beyond. The room darkened as a cloud passed over the sun. "I told you, it's not the way you think," she said.

"Sure. Archer McFall just happened to walk back into your life at the exact same time that you started to get the letters. That's a mighty big coincidence."

"This isn't about Archer or the Temple. It's about *us*."

He flapped the letters again. "If it's about us, how come you didn't tell me about these?"

"I was going to."

"When? After hell finished freezing over?"

"When I thought you were ready to listen."

"You mean when I was ready to swallow it hook, line, and sinker. And get reeled into that mess the same as you. I thought you learned your lesson the last time."

The cloud passed, and the sun lit up the mottled spots on the window. She looked past them to the reddish square of the garden, at the little rows of green that were starting their seasonal push to the sky, then looked beyond to the wedge of mountains that kept North Carolina from slopping over into Tennessee. Two hundred acres of Gregg land, every inch of it stony and stained, every ash and birch and poplar stitched to her skin, every gallon of creek water running through her veins like blood. She was as old-family as anybody, and the old families belonged to the McFalls.

"It's only letters," she said. "That doesn't mean I'm going back in."

"Why did you ever have to fall for it in the first place?"

"That was nearly twenty years ago. I was a different person then. *We* were different people."

"No, *you* were different. I'm still the same. Just a mountain hick who thinks that if you say your prayers and live right, then nobody can break you down. But I reckon I was wrong."

"You can't still blame me for that, can you?" But his eyes answered her question by becoming hard and narrow. "Don't you know how terrible I thought it was to be trapped here in Whispering Pines forever? Stay around and squirt out seven kids with nothing to look forward to but the next growing season? To be like my mother with her fingers as knobby as pea pods from all the canning she did? What kind of life is *that*?"

"It's good enough for me. I didn't need to run off to California."

"I must have asked you a dozen times to come with me."

"And I asked you a dozen-and-one times to stay."

"You were just afraid you'd lose me."

He hung his head and shook it slowly. "I reckon I did," he said, barely above a whisper. "Only it took me this long to find out."

"The kids will be home soon," she said. "Ronnie's been looking forward to seeing you."

He held up the letters again. "You're not going to drag them into this mess, are you? Because, so help me, if you do—"

The threat hung in the air like an ax.

"Archer's not like that." Linda said it as if she only half-believed her own words.

"You said the group broke up."

"I . . . most of us left. I don't know. When they said he was dead, I—"

"He's dead. Now, the question is, who's trying to bring back *this*?" David held up one of the letters, more for effect than anything. Because Linda knew perfectly well what was on the letter.

She could see the symbol from across the room, even though it was bunched into the top right corner. It looked like one of those Egyptian symbols, only the cross was topped with two loops. Two suns. The Temple of the Two Suns.

Not that she needed to see it, because she was sure now that it had been seared into her brain, that its power had reached over years and across three thousand miles and through the thick white walls of her renewed faith in Jesus. Because, after all, there was only one true savior. And his name was Archer McFall.

If only David would open his heart. Sure, he'd been born with Baptist blood, he'd been dipped in the river below the red church so that his sins would be washed away, he'd given his ten percent, but there was so much more to faith than the rituals and scriptures and prayers. Her own heart was swelling again, budding, unfolding like a flower under a bright sun. No, under two suns. Twice the love. If only she could share that with David. But he wouldn't understand. He was as blinded by Jesus as everybody else was.

David watched her carefully, waiting for her reaction. She swallowed her smile and let her face slacken.

"The Temple," he said in a sneer. "You promised you

were over it. But I guess I'm the fool."

"He's not asking for money."

David laughed, a bitter sound. He rubbed his forehead with his right hand. "Probably the only thing he's not asking for, whoever it is."

"Since you read the letters, you know exactly what he wants."

"Yeah." He held up one of the letters. "'We've missed you, sister,'" he read.

"And that's all."

"'There will come great trials, but we bathe in the light of faith.'" He shuffled to the next letter. "'The stone is rolled away.'"

"Where's the love in that?" Linda was straining to show disinterest. David wasn't from one of the old families. She had been a fool to think Archer would accept him, anyway.

"Where's the love? Where's the *love*? Why, right there on the bottom, where it says 'Forever Yours, Archer McFall.' On every single one of them."

"Maybe he didn't die. Or maybe somebody started up the group again and is using his name. That's all it is. I don't care one way or another."

But I DO care. I've always cared, even when you thought you and your Christian friends had "cured" me. There was always a little room in my heart tucked away for nobody but Archer.

David's eyes had cleared a little as he sobered, but kept their bright ferocity. "You don't care so much that you didn't even bother to throw the letters away, huh?"

"Don't matter none to me."

"That so?" David started to crumple the letters into a ball.

Linda's mouth opened, and her arm reached out of its own accord.

David smiled, but it was a sick smile, the kind worn by a reluctant martyr. He crushed the paper into a hard wad of pulp and tossed it on the floor at her feet. "I seen him come around. Last week. Laid out of work just so I could hide up in the hills and watch the house. Just me and a six-pack. Mostly I was curious if you were sending out any letters yourself."

"You bastard."

David licked his lips. "Is ten o'clock the regular meeting time?"

Linda felt the blood drain from her face. How much did he know?

"Got himself a Mercedes. I guess this 'cult' business pays pretty good."

"It wasn't—" Linda started.

David nodded. "I know. It wasn't Archer McFall. Then why don't you tell me who it really was?"

Linda wondered how many times David had watched the house from the woods. Or if she could trust anything he said.

Trust. That was a good one.

David slowly approached her. She was like a deer frozen in the headlights of his hate. She looked down just as his boot flattened the wad of letters.

"How long?" he said, and his eyes were welling with tears again. As if the reservoir had been filling all his life and, finally full, now had to leak a little or bust.

"*It's not like that.*" She looked again at the butcher knife on the counter, close to tears herself.

He took another menacing step. "I wondered why you been acting strange lately. And why you ain't been up to going to church."

Linda grabbed a gulp of air and scooted from the table to the kitchen counter. David was close behind her and caught her when she spun. His hands were like steel hooks in her upper arms, holding her firmly but not squeezing hard enough to bruise.

She stared at his stranger's face with its wide eyes. She'd never noticed how deep the two creases on his forehead were. The hard planes of his cheeks were patched with stubble. He looked old, as if all his thirty-seven years had dog-piled him these last few weeks.

"Tell me who it is," he said.

She shuddered with the force of his grip. Those hands had touched her so tenderly in the night, had softly stroked her belly when she was pregnant with the boys, had tucked daisies behind her ears when they fooled around in the hayfield. But now they were cruel, the caresses forgotten, the passion in them of a different kind.

She turned her face away, afraid that he'd see the fear in her eyes. The knife was beside a bowl of melted ice cream, within reach. But David grabbed her chin and twisted her eyes back to his.

Archer had warned her what the price of belief would be. Persecution. Pain. The loss of everything human. She could hear Archer's voice now, pouring from the geysers of her heart. *There will come great trials. And great sacrifices. Because sacrifice is the currency of God.*

But the reward was greater than the sacrifice. Belief paid back a hundredfold. Devotion now brought Archer's steadfast love unto the fourth generation. Surrendering to him meant that her offspring would reap the harvest. She had been telling herself that ever since Archer and the Temple of the Two Suns reclaimed her heart. And she reminded herself now, locked in David's grip.

He'd never hurt her before. But Archer said those who didn't understand always fell back on violence, because violence was the way of their God. That was why the world had to end. From the ashes of their heavenfire would come—

"Who *is* it?" he asked.

She grunted through her clenched teeth. David relaxed his grip until her mouth could move. "Ahh—Archer."

"Archer. Don't lie to me, damn it." He clamped his fingers tight again.

She fumbled with her left hand, running it along the edge of the counter. She felt the cool rim of the bowl. If only she could keep him talking. "It is. And he doesn't want me . . . that way."

"It can't be Archer."

"He's come back."

David choked on a laugh. "The second coming. They really *do* have you again, don't they?"

"No, I meant he's come back to Whispering Pines." Her hand went around the bowl and touched wood. Her fingers crawled along the knife's handle. Archer said sometimes you had to fight fire with fire, even if it meant descending down to their level. Even if it was a sin.

"You said he was *dead*."

"They said . . . I thought . . . I never saw his body."

"It's not Archer."

"It is. You know I'd never cheat on you."

He released her arm with his left hand and drew his arm back. He was going to hit her. She snatched at the butcher knife, then had it in her palm, her fingers around it, and all the old memories flooded back, all the energy and power and purity that Archer promised and delivered. She raised the knife.

David saw it and stepped away easily. The blade sliced the air a foot from his face. He lurched forward and caught her wrist on the down-stroke. The knife clattered to the floor.

They both looked at it. Silence crowded the room like death crowded a coffin.

A chicken clucked out in the barnyard. Somewhere over the hill, in the direction of the Potter farm, a hound dog let out one brassy howl. A tractor engine murmured in the far distance. The clock in the living room ticked six times, seven, eight. David reached out with the toe of his boot and kicked the knife into he corner.

He exhaled, deflating his rage. "So it's come to this."

"I didn't mean to—"

"Is that what they preach? Stabbing your own husband?"

"I . . . you scared me." The tears erupted from hr eyes even as David's tears dried up, probably for good. "I thought you were going to hit me."

"Yeah." He was calm again, walking dead, man who wouldn't harm a fly. "I guess you never could trust me, could you? Not the way you could trust them."

"I didn't lie to you."

"Which time?"

Archer was right. Pain was a steep price. Faith required sacrifice. "When we got married, and I said I was through. I believed it then."

"And I believed it, too. Guess you're not the onlyfool in the family."

"Please, David. Don't make this any worse thn it has to be."

"Fine." He spread his arms in surrender. "I guess it

don't matter none who it is. I just don't see why you had to make up this stuff about the cult."

"It's not a cult."

"And Archer McFall just happens to walk back into your life twenty years after he died. You really must be crazy, or else you think I am."

Archer always said he would return. How could she ever have doubted him?

Easy. You had your world taken away from you, and you came back to this safe, normal, God-fearing life and slipped into it like a second skin. You hid away your heart like it was separate from loving and mothering and living. But this normal life was all a lie, wasn't it? Maybe David was right, even if he was right about the wrong thing.

"I reckon I'll get the kids, then," he said, and a chill sank into her, deep-freezing her bones.

"No." She went to him.

"Any judge in the land would give me custody. Don't worry. I won't make no claim on the farm. That's rightly yours as a Gregg, if for no other reason."

"Not the kids," she wailed. She pounded her fists on his chest. He didn't try to stop her.

The blows softened and she collapsed, grabbing his shirt for support. He kept her from falling. She felt nothing in his embrace.

"How are we going to tell the boys about us?" She sniffled.

"They already know. They ain't dumb."

"I thought . . . I don't know what I thought." But Linda knew exactly what she thought. She thought the children were hers, to love and protect and introduce to the joys of worship in the Temple of the Two Suns. To deliver unto Archer, so the generations would be spared.

"Now quit your crying. They'll be here any minute."

Damn him for trying to be strong. Acting like she didn't matter. Her eyes went to the knife in the corner.

"Don't do it, Linda. I'd hate for that to come up at the custody hearing."

Jesus-loving bastard. But she wouldn't lose hope. Archer would know what to do. Archer would—

"Did you hear that?" David asked, releasing her.

"Hear what?" She rubbed her arms, trying to wipe away the memory of his rough touch.

David went to the door. Linda thought about the knife. No, if she used the knife, they'd take the kids away for sure. She heard something that sounded like a calf caught in a crabapple thicket and bawling its heart out.

"It's Ronnie," David said, then leaped off the porch and ran toward the creek that divided a stretch of pasture from the front yard.

Ronnie raced across the pasture, moaning and wailing, waving his arms. Tim was farther back, running down the road, and even from that distance Linda saw that her youngest boy had lost his glasses.

Ronnie reached the little wooden footbridge that spanned the creek, a bridge that was nothing more than some pallet planks laid across two locust poles. His foot caught in a gap in the planks and his scream went an octave higher as he plummeted into the rocky creek bed. Her own shout caught in her throat.

David reached the creek and jumped down to where Ronnie lay. Linda scrambled down the bank after him. Ronnie was facedown, his legs in the shallow water. His head rested on a large flat stone. A trail of blood ran down the surface of the rock and dribbled into the creek, where it was quickly swept away.

"Don't move him," Linda shouted.

David gave her a look, then knelt beside Ronnie. The boy moaned and lifted his head. Blood oozed from his nose. His lip was swollen.

He moaned again.

"What?" David said.

This time Linda was close enough to hear what he was saying.

Ronnie's lips parted again. "Uhr—red church."

His eyes were looking past both of them, seeing nothing, seeing too much.

✝ Chapter 3

Sheriff Frank Littlefield looked up the hill at the church and the monstrous dogwood that hovered beside it like a guardian. He'd always hated that tree, ever since he was a boy. It hadn't changed much since the last time he'd set foot in the graveyard. But *he* had, the world had, and Boonie most definitely had.

The young get old and the dead get deader, he thought as he studied the shadowed belfry for movement.

"What do you figure done it?" asked Dr. Perry Hoyle, the Pickett County medical examiner.

Littlefield didn't turn to face the man immediately. Instead, he squinted past the church steeple to the sun setting behind the crippled cross. The cross threw a long jagged shadow over the cemetery green. Somebody was cutting hay. Littlefield could smell the crush of grass in the wind. He scratched at his buzz cut. "You're the ME."

"Wild animal, that's my guess. Mountain lion, maybe. Or a black bear."

"Sure it wasn't somebody with a knife or an ax?"

"Not real likely. Wounds are too jagged, for one thing."

Littlefield exhaled in relief. "So I guess we can't call it a murder."

"Probably not."

One of the deputies was vomiting in the weeds at the edge of the cemetery.

"Don't get that mixed in with the evidence," Littlefield hollered at him. He turned back to Hoyle. "Black bear wouldn't attack a man unless her cubs were threatened. And it'd have to be a mighty big mountain lion."

"They get up to two hundred pounds."

"But they're extinct up here."

"One of them college professors down at Westridge believes mountain lions are making their way back to these parts."

Littlefield resumed rubbing his scalp. He'd just had it trimmed at Ray's, a good clipper job that let the wind and sun get right to the scalp. The department thought he wore the short style to give himself a ramrod appearance, but the truth was, he kind of liked the shape of his skull. And his hat fit better when he went to the Borderline Tavern to kick up his heels to some Friday-night country music. Boonie used to dance at the Borderline, too. Back when he still had feet.

The two men stood quietly and looked at the church for a moment. "Never been many happy times here," Hoyle said.

Littlefield didn't rise to the bait. He was annoyed that Hoyle would fish those waters. Some things were for nothing but forgetting. He hardened his face against the past as easily as if he'd slipped on a plastic superhero mask.

"Who found the body?" Hoyle hurriedly asked.

"Couple of kids who live down the road. They were walking home from school this afternoon."

"Must have bothered them something awful."

"Hell, it's bothering *me*, and you know I've seen a few

ripe ones."

"What did they tell you?"

"The older one, he's about thirteen, fell running home and busted his face up. He'll be all right, but for some reason it got to him worse than it did the little one. Kept mumbling 'the red church' over and over again."

"How old's the little one?"

"Nine. Said he saw some stuff laying in the graveyard and went through the bushes to have a look. He said he saw a cap and a flashlight and a bottle of liquor, but he didn't touch any of it. Ronnie, the thirteen-year-old, came back to see what was taking so long, and that's when the victim must have dragged himself out from the bushes and grabbed ahold of Ronnie."

Littlefield didn't like calling Boonie Houck a victim. Boonie was a good fellow. A little bit creepy and plenty lazy, but he was in church of a Sunday morning and was known to vote Republican. Nobody deserved to die this way.

Hoyle looked like he could use a cup of coffee, maybe with a few drops of brandy in it. "He lived a lot longer than he should have with those kinds of wounds. My guess is he was attacked sometime in the early morning, between midnight and sunup."

Littlefield's stomach rolled a little. How did Boonie feel lying in the weeds, wondering about the wound between his legs, knowing that whatever had ripped him up was somewhere out there in the dark? "You going to send him to the state ME's office?"

"Reckon I ought to. They can do a better job of guessing than I can." Hoyle pulled a handkerchief from his jacket pocket and wiped the sweat from his bald head. "The press is going to want to know something."

"Wonderful."

"Plus, if it is a wild animal, might be some rabies going around. That could make an animal go nuts and do something like this."

"We haven't had that up here in a long time, either."

"Times change."

The sheriff nodded. *You used to have hair, and I used to be worth a damn. Boonie used to be alive, and the red church used to be white.*

"Let me know when you're ready to drive him down," Littlefield said. "We'll get the pieces together."

He didn't envy Hoyle. The drive to Chapel Hill took about four hours. Boonie would be kicking up a mean stench by the time the trip was over. But Littlefield decided he ought to save his pity. Unlike Boonie, at least Hoyle would be coming back.

Littlefield patted the medical examiner on the shoulder and went to examine the articles lying on the grass in clear plastic bags. He bent over the bag that held a porn magazine. He fought an odd urge to flip through the pages.

A camera flash went off. "Could you please move to one side, Sheriff?"

He looked up. Detective Sgt. Sheila Storie waved her arm. She was taking photos of the crime scene.

No, not a CRIME scene, Littlefield had to remind himself. *An accident. A tragic, violent, unexplained ACCIDENT.*

The kind of thing that happened too often in Whispering Pines. But Littlefield was relieved that a psycho with a set of Ginsu knives wasn't on the loose in his jurisdiction. They'd had one of those down the mountain in Shady Valley a few years back, and the case was never solved. *Damned inept city cops.*

He already knew he was going to put Storie in charge of the investigation. When they arrived and found the mess, she hadn't even blinked, just got out her clipboard and tape measure and went to work. She was too young to be so unmoved by death, in Littlefield's opinion. But maybe she was a little bit like him. Maybe it was the kind of thing that made them cops.

Got to keep yourself outside of it all. Don't let them get to you. No matter what they do, no matter what the world takes from you.

"What do you make of it?" he asked Storie.

Her eyes were blue enough to hide everything, as unrevealing as her camera lens. "Extensive trauma. Death probably due to exsanguination."

Storie's educated flatland accent always surprised him, even though he should have been used to it by now. Most people took her for a local until they heard her speak. "That's what Hoyle says. Only he calls it 'bled to death.'"

"Unless shock got him first. Same to the subject either way. I haven't seen this much blood since those driver's ed films they show in high school." She took two steps to her right and snapped another picture, then let the camera hang by its strap over her chest.

"Must have taken a while. You looked over in the bushes where he crawled after the attack?"

"Yes, sir. He left a few scraps."

Littlefield swallowed a knot of nausea.

"Footprints go from this grave marker here, where the boys said they found the stuff. They're deep, see?" She pointed to the pressed grass. The smaller prints of the boys were visible as well. But Boonie's were clearly marked by the thick treads of his boots.

"That means he was running, right?"

"He must have seen or heard whatever it was and gotten scared. He was probably attacked just before he started running."

"Why do you say that?"

"Blood here is coagulated almost to powder. The blood over there- "-she waved to the slick trail of slime where Boonie had crawled out of the bushes- "-isn't as oxidized."

Littlefield nodded and passed his hand over his scalp. The breeze shifted and he could smell Boonie now. A person never got used to the odor of death. The detective didn't even wrinkle her nose.

"Hoyle thinks it's a mountain lion," Littlefield said.

She shook her head. Her brown hair was a couple of inches past regulation and swished over her shoulders. "Wild animals typically go for the throat if they're treating something as prey. There are a few wounds around the eyes, but those are no more devastating than the other injuries. And it doesn't look like the subject had an animal cornered so that it would be forced to defend itself."

Littlefield was constantly amazed by the level of instruction that new officers received. A college degree in Criminal Justice, for starters. Then state training, not to mention extra seminars along the way. Littlefield had long since quit going to those things, at least the ones that didn't help him politically.

Or maybe Storie was a little too educated for her own good. Frank knew that as a female in a rural department, she had to be twice as smart and icy and sarcastic as everybody else. She couldn't go out for after-shift beers.

Pay attention, damn it. In case you're going senile and need a reminder, one of your constituents is gathering flies long before his natural time.

"So you don't necessarily hold to the wild animal attack

theory?" he asked.

"I'm not saying that. I'm just saying that if it *was* an animal, its behavior was unnatural." She looked across the stretch of tombstones to where the cemetery ended near the forest. Her brow furrowed.

"What is it?" Littlefield asked.

"The thing that bothers me the most."

If STORIE'S bothered . . . A small chill wended its way up Littlefield's spinal column and settled in the base of his neck.

"No animal tracks," she said.

The sheriff's jaw tightened. So *that* was what had been bothering him ever since he'd first walked the scene. An animal's claws would have ripped chunks out of the ground, especially if it were attacking.

"Damn," he whispered.

"No tracks means no easy answers." She almost sounded pleased. "There are no other human footprints, either."

Storie had cracked a big case last year, when an ex-cop had hauled a body up to the mountains for disposal. Perp was a big goofy guy who went around bragging about how he'd never get caught. Well, Storie set her nose on his trail and nailed him so hard that his lawyers had to recite scripture in the courtroom to save him from a lethal injection. The conviction got statewide coverage, and Storie's picture was in both the local papers.

This looked like it might be another of those high-profile mysteries that, if she solved it, would make her a legitimate candidate for sheriff. If she ever ran against him, she'd have him beat all to hell on looks. Her accent would hurt her some, though.

"Tell me, Sergeant. What do you think did it?" he

asked.

"I can honestly say I have no idea, sir." She folded her arms over the camera.

"Any chance that somebody did it with a sharp weapon, without leaving footprints that we could see?"

"The pattern of the wounds seems random at first glance. But what bugs me is the ritualistic nature of the injured areas."

Areas? Littlefield wanted to remind Storie that those body parts were once near and dear to Boonie Houck. But he only nodded at her to continue.

"Look at the major wounds. First, there's the eyes."

"We haven't found them yet."

"Exactly. That's an inconvenient spot for a rampaging animal to reach. In any event, it's unlikely that a claw would take both eyes."

"Unless they were shining, and somehow attracted the animal's attention. The moon was over half full last night."

"Okay. Let's go on to the hand. Seems like an animal would have started gnawing at a softer spot."

"Maybe it did."

"That brings us to the fatal wound."

"Now, that's not been determined yet." Littlefield felt the tingle of blood rushing to his cheeks.

"I saw the rip in the front of his pants." She lifted the camera. "I took pictures, remember?"

"Guess so." His tongue felt thick.

"With the loss of that much blood, I'm amazed he survived as long as he did."

"You said the wounds were ritualistic. What's that got to do with his . . . er . . ."

"Penis, Sheriff. You can say it in the company of a woman these days."

"Of course." His face grew warmer with embarrassment. He looked across the mountains. He would love to be walking a stream right now, flicking a hand-tied fly across the silver currents, the smell of wet stone and rotted loam in his nostrils. Alone. Anywhere but here with blood and the red church and Sheila Storie. "So what does it mean?"

"It may mean nothing. Or it may mean we have a deviant personality on the loose." The flash of her eyes gave away her belief in the latter. Or maybe she was only hopeful.

"Is it because we haven't found the . . . other part, either?"

"I don't know yet."

"Think we ought to call in the state boys?" Littlefield knew Storie would bristle at turning the case over to the State Bureau of Investigation. She would want a shot first.

"That's your decision, Sheriff."

"I suppose we'll have to wait for the state medical examiner's report. Hoyle's sending him down to Chapel Hill."

"Good."

Littlefield tried to read her expression. But the sun was in her face, so her half-closed eyes didn't give away anything. He knew she thought Perry Hoyle had about as much forensic sophistication as a hog butcher. The whole department was probably a joke to her. Well, she was a flatlander, anyway. "Hoyle doesn't think the wounds were made by a weapon."

"You asked for my opinion, sir."

Littlefield looked up the hill at the church. Suddenly he felt as if someone had reached an icy hand down his throat and squeezed his heart. His brother Samuel was on the roof of the church, waving and smiling.

His dead brother Samuel.

Littlefield blinked, then saw that the illusion was only a mossy patch on the shingles.

He sighed. "I'm putting you in charge of the investigation."

Storie almost smiled. "I'll do my best, sir."

Littlefield nodded and stepped over the strings that marked off grids at the scene. He knelt by the toppled monument. "What do you make of this?"

"The boys' footprints lead over here. I'd guess vandalism. Tipping tombstones is an old favorite. Maybe they were messing around when the subject heard them and tried to crawl out of the weeds."

"Seems like they would have heard Boonie yelling." He stopped himself. Boonie wouldn't have called out, at least in nothing more articulate than a groan. Boonie's tongue had been taken, too.

Hoyle rescued him from his embarrassment. "We're ready over here, Sheriff," the ME called. Littlefield winced and started to turn.

"I'll handle it, sir," Storie said. "It's my case, remember? I might see something I missed the first two times."

She was right. Littlefield's shoulders slumped a little in relief. He hoped Storie hadn't noticed, but she didn't miss much. She had detective's eyes, even if they were easier to look at than look through. "Go ahead."

Littlefield headed across the cemetery and up the hill toward the red church. He glanced at the markers as he passed, some so worn he could barely make out the names. Some were nothing more than stumps of broken granite. Other graves were probably forgotten altogether, just the silent powder of bones under a skin of grass.

The ground was soft under his feet- good mountain

soil, as black as coal dust. Almost a shame to waste it on a graveyard. But people had to be buried somewhere, and to the dead, maybe the most fertile soil in the world wasn't comfort enough. Maybe his kid brother Samuel had yet to settle into eternal rest.

The names on the markers read like a who's who history of this end of the county. Potter. Matheson. Absher. Buchanan. McFall. Gregg. More Picketts than you could shake a stick at.

And three Littlefields off by themselves.

He knelt by two familiar graves. His mother and father shared a single wide monument. He looked from the gray marble to a smaller marker, which had a bas-relief of a lamb chiseled in its center. Its letters were scarcely worn, and the fingerlike shadows of tree branches chilled the stone. Littlefield read the damning words without moving his lips.

Here Lies Samuel Riley Littlefield. 1968-1979. May God Protect and Keep Him.

His heart burned in his chest and he hurried away, his eyes frantic for a distraction. He stopped by the dogwood. The thing looked like it was dying. But it had looked that way for the last forty years, and every spring it managed to poke a few more blossoms out of the top branches. A memory stirred and crawled from the shadows before he could beat it back.

The red church. Halloween. The night he'd seen the Hung Preacher.

The night Samuel had died.

He shuddered and the memory fell away again, safely buried. The sun was warm on his face. Down the slope, Hoyle and Storie were hauling Boonie's body to the back of the overgrown station wagon that served as the county's non-emergency ambulance.

Littlefield moved away from the tree and put a foot on the bottom of four steps that led into the church foyer. The door was large and made of solid wooden planks. The cracks between the planks were barely distinguishable due to the buildup of paint layers. Over the door was a small strip of colored glass, two deep blue rectangular planes separated by an amber pane. Those had survived the onslaught of juvenile delinquents' rocks.

The sheriff climbed the rest of the steps. The top one was a wider landing, scarred from the tailgate of Lester Matheson's truck. Littlefield examined the thick hinges and the door lock. There was a lift latch in addition to the dull brass handle. Littlefield put his hand on the cool metal.

Wonder if I need a warrant to open it? Naw. Lester won't mind if I have a peek.

There was a small chance that if Boonie had been murdered, some evidence might be hidden inside. Or the door might be locked, but he didn't think Lester would bother keeping up with a key just to protect a hundred bales of hay. People didn't steal out in these parts. The thieves and B&E addicts kept to Barkersville, where the rich folks had their summer homes.

Littlefield turned the knob and the catch clicked back into the cylinder. He nudged the latch up with his other hand, and as the door creaked open and the rich dust of hay hit his nostrils, he realized he hadn't set foot inside since shortly after Samuel's funeral.

Please, God, just let it be a plain old ordinary murderer. Some drunk who got mad because Boonie took two swigs before passing the bottle instead of one. A Mexican Christmas tree worker with a grudge. I'll even take a crazy if you got one.

His palms were sweating, the way they had when he was seventeen and he'd first heard the laughter in the belfry.

The door opened onto a short, windowless foyer. A shaft of light pierced the ceiling from the belfry above. *Where the bell rope used to hang.*

The bell rang in his memory, a thunderclap of angry bronze, an echo of the night Samuel died.

The plank floor creaked as Littlefield crossed the foyer. Golden motes of dust spiraled in the draft. What must it have been like a century ago? The worn wood had endured a hundred thousand crossings. Trembling and red-faced virgin brides with their best dresses dragging on the pine, solemn cousins come to pay their respects to a dear departed, women in bonnets and long swirling skirts gathering for Jubilee. Littlefield could almost see the preacher at the steps, shaking the hands of the menfolk, bowing to the women, patting the heads of the children.

The sheriff peered up through the tiny rope hole, an opening barely large enough for a child to scramble through. The hollow interior of the bell was full of black shadow. But that would tell him nothing. He returned to scanning the floor for signs of blood.

The foyer opened onto the main sanctuary. The chill crawled up his spine again. He didn't know whether it was caused by childhood legends, or the chance of finding a killer hiding among the bales of hay. For a frantic moment, he almost wished he wore a firearm.

The bales were stacked to each side, forming a crooked aisle down the center of the church sanctuary. Lester had left the altar undisturbed, probably because lifting hay over the railing was too much work. The altar itself was small, the pulpit hardly more than a rectangular crate with a slanted top. A set of six wormy chestnut beams, hand-hewn, crossed the open A-frame overhead. The interior walls were unpainted chestnut as well. In the dim light, the woodwork had a rich, deep brown cast.

The bales were packed too tightly against the walls to afford hiding places.

Unless somebody had removed a few bales and made a hollow space inside the stacks.

He'd done that in his family's barn, when he wanted to hide out on an autumn day, or when he and his brother played hide-and-seek or army. But few hours could be stolen back then. Crops, livestock, firewood, fence mending-a long list of chores was waiting at six every morning that never got finished before dark. But back then, Littlefield had slept in dreams and not bad memories.

Nothing stirred amid the hay. The church was silent, as if waiting for a congregation to again fill it with life. Littlefield walked to the dais. The chill deepened even though the air was stuffy. A small wooden cross was attached to the top of the pulpit. Like the cross on the church steeple, it was missing a section of the crosspiece.

Littlefield leaned over the waist-high railing and looked into the corners of the altar. The small vestry off to the side held nothing but bare shelves and cobwebs. He didn't know what he expected to see. Maybe he was just trying to ease his own mind, to reassure himself that old rumors and long-ago strangeness were put to rest. Boonie was dead, and that had nothing to do with the red church or Samuel or the Hung Preacher.

As he was turning to leave, he noticed a dark stain on the dais floor. It was the kind made by a spill. Maybe Lester had stored building materials in here once. At any rate, the rust-brown stain was far too old to have been made by whatever had killed Boonie.

But something about it held his attention. The shape seemed familiar. He tilted his head, as if stumped by an inkblot in a Rorschach test. When he realized where he had seen the form before, he drew in a dusty gasp of air.

The dark shape in the belfry, that long-ago Halloween.

Littlefield strode back through the church, suddenly anxious to be in the sunshine. He was going to go with the animal theory for now. If Storie wanted to play her forensic games, that was fine. But he wouldn't allow himself to believe that something masquerading as human had ripped apart good old Boonie Houck. Not in Pickett County. Not on God's ground. Not on his watch.

As he closed the door and looked across the graveyard where Storie searched the weeds for clues, the chill evaporated. Something fluttered in the belfry.

Bird or raccoon, he told himself without looking up. *NOT the thing that had laughed as Samuel died.*

He hurried down the slope to see if Storie had found any of Boonie's missing parts.

✝ Chapter 4

Bummer.

That was Ronnie's first thought when the gray blindfold of unconsciousness dissolved into light. And that was the last thought he'd had when the anesthesiologist had pressed the mask to his face. Or maybe not. He'd been so stone-black-buzzed from the injection that he couldn't be sure if he'd had any prior thoughts at all.

His face, at least what he could feel of it, was like a molasses balloon. Pain tingled and teased him through a curtain of gauze. It was a sneaky, funny pain, a bully that skulked around the edge of the playground, waiting for you to chase a stray kickball. Once you were alone, it would jump on you and beat you and kick you and rip you--

More of the druggy haze fell away. Ronnie opened his eyes and the light sliced at his pupils. His eyes were over-flowing, but he couldn't feel the tears on his cheeks. His stomach turned crooked flips. Mom and Dad were blurry images beside the bed. A man with a mustache whose eyes looked like licorice drops leaned over him.

"I think we've got somebody waking up." The man's mustache twitched like a caterpillar on a hot griddle. He wore a white coat.

Doctor. Ronnie's thoughts spun, then collected. *Pain plus doctor equals hospital.*

He opened his mouth to speak, but his tongue was too thick to find his teeth.

"Easy now, little partner," the doctor said. "Take it slow."

Slow was the only way Ronnie *could* take it. His arms and legs felt like lead pipes. He turned his head to look at his parents. Despite the numbness, he felt a warmth growing in his chest. Mom and Dad were *together.*

Well, they weren't holding hands, but at least they weren't yelling at each other. And all it took to make that happen was for Ronnie to . . . what *had* he done?

He slogged through the tunnels of his memory. He remembered the ride to the hospital, Dad holding him in the back seat, Dad's shirt against his face. The shirt should have smelled of sawdust and sweat and maybe a little gasoline, but Ronnie had smelled nothing but blood.

Then, farther back, before that, the little footbridge, falling, the rocks . . .

Ouch.

Ronnie was old enough to know that the memory of pain could never quite match up to the real thing. Which was a good thing; otherwise, everybody would be running around as crazy as old Mama Bet McFall, or Grandma Gregg down at the Haywood Assisted Care Center back before she slipped into the grave. But even Ronnie's memory of the pain was strong enough to wipe out some of the numbing effects of the drugs.

Dad stepped forward, his lower lip curled, his face made sickly green by the fluorescent strip lights. Dad never looked quite right indoors, sort of like the tiger Ronnie had seen in a pen down at the Asheboro zoo. Both of them nervous and impatient, pacing, too large for walls or bars.

"Hey, Ronnie," Dad said, unsuccessfully trying to funnel his deep voice into a whisper. "How are you feeling?"

"Muuuuhr." Even Ronnie couldn't translate the sound his vocal chords made.

Mom leaned over him, a tight smile wrinkling her face. The skin under her eyes was dark blue. She reached out and brushed hair away from his forehead with a clammy hand. "It's okay, baby."

The doctor checked Ronnie's pulse. "Coming around fine. You'll be able to take him home in an hour or so. Buzz one of the nurses if you need anything."

The doctor left the room, and the draft from the closing door swept over Ronnie like a tide of water. Being a molasses-head wasn't all bad. His thoughts weren't dropping as fast as usual, but he was thinking *wider* than he ever had before. If not for the pain bully waiting behind the numbness, Ronnie wouldn't mind hanging out in this half-speed dreamscape for a while.

This was almost peaceful. If he closed his eyes, the white walls fell away and the sky got big and he could float on a cloud and no one could bother him, not even dingle-dork-

Tim. What had happened to Tim?

The molasses of his face rippled as his eyes opened wide. Mom and Dad and . . . where was Tim? Because suddenly it was all coming back, the molasses creek turning a bend and flowing into sunlight and, now hot and golden, churning over a precipice in a sugary waterfall. The run home, the hand on his foot, the bleeding thing—*they got livers for eyes*—the toppled monument, the red church, the graveyard.

Had the bleeding thing trapped Tim?

Dad must have sensed his agitation, because a hand on his shoulder prevented him from sitting up. "Now, you heard the doctor, son. Just rest up."

Mom chewed on the skin at the end of her thumb. "You got busted up pretty good when you fell. Broke your nose. The doctor said you were lucky you didn't crack your skull."

Good old Mom. Found the bright side to everything. So he had a broken nose. He thought of some of the players on his football cards, how their noses had great big humps across the bridge or were twisted off to one side. Just what a guy like him needed. Now Melanie would never talk to him.

The molasses mask slipped a little more, and the pain bully chuckled from the shadows, knowing an opportunity was drawing near. Ronnie became aware of a lower portion of his body, where the knot of snakes nested in his stomach. He was going to throw up.

Total bummer. He groaned and his tongue worked.

"What is it, honey?" Mom said, her face now paler and her eyes wider.

"Poooook," he said. His right arm flailed like a water hose under pressure.

"Puke?" She looked at Dad. "Oh, Lord, David, he's going to throw up."

Dad looked helpless. The situation called for quick action and compassion. As a caregiver, Dad made a good pallbearer.

Mom spun and began searching under a counter beside the bed. A mirror ran along the length of the counter, and Ronnie was startled by his own reflection. His nose was purple and swollen, little clots of bloody gauze hanging out of his nostrils. His eyes were like green-brown marbles pressed into ten pounds of dough.

The image accelerated his nausea. He turned his body with effort, and now Dad helped, putting a hand in his armpit to lean him over the steel railing of the bed. The scene in the mirror was doubly disorienting from being reversed. The greasy snakes crawled up Ronnie's throat.

Mom found a plastic pan made of a yucky aqua color, but that was okay because yucky was just what the situation required. She held it under his face, and the snakes exploded from his mouth. His eyes squeezed shut in the effort of vomiting, and drops of something besides molasses beaded his forehead. His abdomen spasmed twice, three times, four, a pause, then a fifth eruption.

"Oh, my Lord," Mom exclaimed to Dad. "Call the nurse."

"He said this might happen. And look, it's stopped now."

"But it's blood."

"What did you think it would be, grits and sausage gravy? They just operated on his nose."

Ronnie looked into the pan and his guts almost lurched again. A thick gruel of blood and mucus pooled in front of his face. And what were those things floating in-

Fingers. They cut off my fingers and made me eat them.

Dad's words came as if through cotton. "What the hell are *those?*"

"Get a nurse." Mom waved her hands helplessly.

The draft of the door opening wafted over Ronnie again, but this time it provided no comfort. He lay back on the raised pillows.

A tired-looking nurse looked in the pan. "Oh, those are the fingers of surgical gloves. The doctor stuffs them with gauze and uses them as packing."

"How did they get in his stomach?" Mom's voice was a thin screech.

"The packing must have worked its way down the pharyngeal openings of his Eustachian tubes. I'm sure it's nothing to worry about."

"Nothing to worry about?" Dad's voice was loud enough to make Ronnie's head hurt. "It's not your kid in the bed, is it?"

The nurse gave a forced smile that Ronnie figured she wore while giving medicine to somebody who wasn't likely to last the week. A smile that plainly said, *If there were another job in Pickett County that paid this well, he could puke rubber fingers until he choked, for all I care.*

But all she said was, "I'll see if I can find the doctor."

After she was gone, Mom said, "You didn't have to raise your voice."

"Shut up."

"David, please. For Ronnie's sake?"

Ronnie wasn't bothered by the argument. The relief of passing nausea was so great that he would have slow-danced with the pain bully, he felt so wonderful. So what if more sweat had popped out along his neck and in his armpits and down the slope of his spine? The stomach snakes were gone.

The act of vomiting also cleared his head a little. That was a mixed blessing. Or mixed curse. Because not only were the good wide thoughts gone, they were being replaced by memories.

Before he'd been wheeled into surgery, the sheriff had talked to him about the things that happened at the red church. It was scary enough just to talk to a policeman, especially one with a crew cut and a face that looked like it was chiseled out of stone. But the sheriff wanted him to remember what had happened, when Ronnie really, really, really wanted to be in the business of forgetting.

Forgetting the wet, slooshing sound his shoe had made as he jerked his foot from the graveyard grip.

Forgetting the raw, bloody arm reaching around the tombstone.

Forgetting the laughter that had fluttered from the belfry of the red church.

The sheriff finally went away, and they had rolled Ronnie to the operating room. Then came the needle and the mask and the wide thoughts and the darkness.

"How are you feeling, honey?"

He looked at his mom. Her hair was wilted and stringy, a dull chestnut color. She looked about a hundred and twelve, older even than Mama Bet McFall, the crazy woman who lived up the road from the Day farm.

"Better," he whispered, and the air of his voice scraped his throat as it passed.

The door opened again and Ronnie craned his neck. The doctor was whistling an uneven tune through the scrub brush of his mustache. Ronnie would bet money that it was a Michael Bolton song. Or maybe something even lamer. Ronnie was almost glad that his nose was clogged. He would have bet double-or-nothing that the man was wearing some sissy cologne. He flopped his heavy head back on the pillows.

"I heard you had a little episode," the doctor said.

Episode? Was that the medical term for vomiting up fingers?

"I'm okay now," Ronnie said in a wheeze, mainly because the doctor was leaning over and reaching for his nose. And even though the painkiller was still dumbing him down, he was smart enough to know that being touched there would hurt like heck. Even through the molasses that encased his brain.

The doctor backed away at the last moment. "The packing looks like it's still in place where the break occurred. I don't think any harm was done."

Nope. No harm at all to YOU, was there, Mr. Mustache?

"We could always roll him back into the OR and pack some more gauze up there," the doctor said to his parents, as if Ronnie weren't even in the room.

"What do you think?" Mom turned another shade closer to invisibility.

"I believe he's okay," the doctor said, fingering his mustache. "In fact, I'd say you could go ahead and take him home. Call me next week and we'll schedule a time to take the stitches out."

Dad nodded dumbly. Mom worked at the gnawed skin of her fingers.

Ronnie was eager to go home. By the time the nurse showed up with a fake smile and a wheelchair, he was sitting up in bed, feeling dizzy but no longer nauseated. As the nurse wheeled him to the elevators, he was floating away again. The outside air tasted strange and thick.

Ronnie was surprised to see that the sun was setting. He felt as if years had passed, not hours, since he'd fallen. Pinkish gray clouds wreathed the horizon above the dark mountains.

Mom had pulled her big black Coupe De Ville by the hospital doors. Dad eased him into the backseat and they were on their way home. They had gone about two miles when Ronnie remembered Tim.

"Where's Tim?" he managed to ask. He was sleepy

again, a molasses-head.

"At Donna's. They went back to the graveyard to find his glasses."

So Tim had survived the encounter at the red church. *The Encounter.* Sounded like a title for a cheesy monster movie. *Whatever.* His thoughts were getting wide again.

He wanted to be asleep by the time they drove past the red church.

He was.

"Didn't see nothing," Lester Matheson said. His face was crooked from decades of chewing his tobacco in the same cheek. He ground his teeth sideways, showing the dark mass inside his mouth, occasionally flicking it more firmly into place with his tongue.

"Last night, either?" Sheriff Littlefield turned from the man's smacking habit and looked out over the rolling meadows. A herd of cows dotted the ridge, all pointed in the same direction. Like their owner, they also chewed mindlessly, not caring what dribbled out of their mouths.

"No, ain't seen nothing up at the red church in a long time. Course, kids go up there to mess around from time to time. Always have."

Littlefield nodded. "Yeah. Ever think of posting a 'No Trespassing' sign?"

"That would only draw twice as many. I'd never keep nothing out there that I couldn't afford to get stolen."

Littlefield shifted his weight from one foot to another and a porch board groaned. The Mathesons lived in a board-and-batten house on the edge of two hundred acres of land. Even Lester's barns seemed better built than the house. It was roofed with cheap linoleum sheeting that had visible patches in the material. The windows were large single panes fixed with gray strips of wood. The air coming from the open front door was stale and cool, like that of a tomb.

The sun was disappearing into the angle where Buckhorn Mountain slid down to the base of Piney Top. The air was moist with the waiting dew. Pigs snorted from their wooden stalls beside the larger of Lester's two barns. Crickets had taken up their night noises, and the aroma of cow manure made Littlefield almost nostalgic for his own childhood farm days. "Have you ever seen Boonie hanging around the graveyard?"

Lester scratched his bulbous head that gleamed even in the fading light. His hand was knotted from a life of work, thick with blue veins and constellations of age spots. "Well, I found him in the red church one time, passed out in the straw. I just let him sleep it off. As long as he didn't smoke in there, he couldn't really hurt nothing."

"Have you noticed anything unusual around here?"

"Depends on what you mean by 'unusual.' The church has always been mighty unusual. But I don't have to tell *you* that, do I?"

"I'm not interested in ghost stories," Littlefield lied.

Lester emitted a gurgling laugh and leaned back in his rocker. "Fine, Sheriff. Whatever you say. And I guess Boonie just happened to get killed in one of them gang wars or something."

"Perry Hoyle thinks it was a mountain lion."

Lester laughed again, then shot a stream of black juice into the yard. "Or maybe it was Bigfoot. Used to be a lot of mountain lions in these parts, all right. Back in the thirties and forties, they were thick as flies. They'd come down out of the hills of a night and take a calf or a chicken, once in a while a dog. But they're deader than four o'clock in the morning now."

Lester was a hunter. Littlefield wasn't, these days. "When's the last time you saw one?" the sheriff asked.

"Nineteen sixty-three. I remember because everybody was just getting over the Kennedy mess. I took up yonder to Buckhorn"—he waved a gnarled hand at the darkening mountain— "because somebody said they'd seen a six-point buck. I set up a little stand at a crossing trail and waited. My stand was twenty feet up a tree, covered with canvas and cut branches. Moon come out, so I decided to stay some after dark, even though it was colder than a witch's heart.

"I heard a twig snap and got my rifle shouldered as smooth as you please. We didn't mess with scopes and such back in them days. Just pointed and shot. So I was looking down the barrel when something big stepped in the sights. Even in the bad light, I could see its gold fur. And two shiny green eyes was looking right back up the barrel at me."

Lester drained his excess juice off the side of the porch. The old man paused for dramatic effect. People still passed down stories in these parts. The front porch was Lester's stage, and they both knew his audience was duty-bound to stay.

The sheriff obliged. "You shot him," he said, even though he knew that wouldn't have made a satisfactory ending to the tale.

Lester waited another ten seconds, five seconds longer than the ritual called for. "About did. I knew what he was right off, even though his fur was about the same color as a deer's. It was the eyes, see? Deer eyes don't glow. They just sop up light like a scratch biscuit draws gravy."

"What happened next?"

"He just kind of stared back at me. Damnedest thing I ever saw. Looking at me like I was an equal, or maybe not even that. Like I was a mosquito buzzing around his head. He drew his mouth open like he was going to snarl, and his whiskers flashed in the moonlight. And I couldn't pull the trigger."

"Scared?" Littlefield asked, hoping Lester wasn't insulted. But Lester seemed to have forgotten the sheriff as he stared off at the mountain.

"In a way I was, but that's not the reason I didn't pull the trigger. There was something about him, something in the eyes, that was more than animal. You might think I'm crazy, and you probably wouldn't be too far wrong, but that cat <u>knew</u> what I was thinking. It *knew* I wouldn't pull the trigger. After maybe half a minute of us staring each other down, he slipped into the woods, his long tail twitching like he was laughing to hisself. Like I was a big ball of yarn he'd played with and gotten tired of."

The sun had slipped behind the horizon now, and Littlefield couldn't read Lester's expression in the darkness. All he could see was the crooked shape of the farmer's face.

"I was frozen, and not just from the chill, either," Lester continued. "When I finally let out a breath, it made a mist in front of my face. I was sweating like I was baling hay and racing a rainstorm. I strained my ears for any little sound, even though I knew the cat was gone."

Littlefield had been standing more or less at parade rest, a habit he had when he was on official business, even around people he knew. Now he let his shoulders droop slightly and leaned against the porch rail. As a youngster, he'd hunted at night himself. He could easily imagine Lester in the tree, muscles taut, ears picking up the slight scurry of a chipmunk or the whispering wings of a night-hawk. Like any good storyteller, Lester had put the sheriff in another place and time.

"You're probably wondering why I'm going on so about this mountain lion," Lester said. "You're asking yourself what that's got to do with Boonie Houck's death."

"That mountain lion would have died a natural death long ago."

Lester said nothing. There was a clattering inside the house, then the rusty skree of the storm door opening. Lester's wife Vivian came out on the porch. Her hair was in a bun, tied up with a scarf. She had a slight hump in her back, a counterpart to her husband's twisted face. The interior light cast her odd shadow across the yard.

"You done yapping the Sheriff's ear off?" she asked, her voice trembling and thin. She must have been a little hard of hearing, because she talked louder than necessary.

"Ain't hardly started yet," Lester said, not rising from his rocker. "Now get on back in the house before I throw a shoe at you."

"You do and I'll put vinegar in your denture glass."

Lester chuckled. "I love you, too, honey."

"You going to invite the sheriff in for pie?"

"No, thank you, ma'am," Littlefield said, bowing a little in graciousness. "I've got a few other people to talk to tonight."

"Well, don't listen too much to this old fool. He lies like a cheap rug."

"I'll take that under advisement."

The door sprang closed. The darkness sprang just as abruptly. "So you haven't seen a mountain lion since then?" the sheriff asked Lester.

"Nope."

"And you're sure you haven't seen anything strange around the red church?"

"Haven't *seen* nothing. Heard something, though."

"Heard something?"

"Last night, would've been about three o'clock. You don't sleep too well when you get to be my age. Always up and down for some reason. So when I heard them, I figured it was one of those in-between dreams. You know, right before you fall asleep and your real thoughts are mixing in with the nonsense?"

Littlefield nodded, then realized the old man couldn't see his face. "Yeah. What did you hear, or think you heard?"

Littlefield glanced at his watch, about to chalk up his time spent talking to Lester as a waste. The luminous dial showed that it was nearly nine o'clock.

"Bells," the old man said in a near-whisper.

"Bells?" Littlefield repeated, though he'd plainly heard the man.

"Real soft and faint, but a bell's a bell. Ain't no mistaking that sound."

"I hate to tell you this, Lester, but we both know that the red church has the only bell around here. And even if some kids were messing around there last night, there's no bell rope."

"And we both know *why* there ain't no bell rope. But I'm just telling you what I heard, that's all. I don't expect you to put much stock in an old man's words."

The ghost stories. Some families had passed them down until they'd acquired a mythic truth that had even more power than fact. Littlefield wasn't ready to write *Death by supernatural* causes on Boonie's incident report. Since Samuel had died, the sheriff had spent most of his life trying to convince himself that supernatural occurrences didn't occur.

Just the facts, ma'am, Littlefield told himself, hearing the words in Jack Webb's voice from the old *Dragnet* television show.

"There were no recent footprints around the church. No sign of disturbances inside the church, either," Littlefield said, piling up the evidence as if to convince himself along with Lester.

"I bet there wasn't no mountain lion paw-prints, either, was there?"

This time, Littlefield initiated the ten-second silence. "Not that we've found yet."

Lester gave his liquid laugh.

Littlefield's head filled with warm anger. "If you believe so much in the stories, why did you buy the red church in the first place?"

"Because I got it for a song. But it won't be my problem no more."

"Why not?"

"Selling it. One of the McFall boys came by the other day. You know, the one that everybody said didn't act like regular folks? The one that got beat near to a pulp behind the football bleachers one night?"

"Yeah. Archer McFall." Littlefield had been a young deputy then, on foot patrol at the football game. Archer ended up in the hospital for a week. No arrests were made, even though Littlefield had seen two or three punks rubbing their hands as if their knuckles were sore. Of course, nobody pressed the case too much. Archer was a McFall, after all, and the oddest of the bunch.

"Well, he says he went off to California and made good, working in religion and such. And now he's moving back to the area and wants to settle here."

"I'll be damned."

"Me, too. And when he offered me two hundred thousand dollars for the red church and a dozen acres of mostly scrub pine and graveyard, I had to bite my lip to keep from grinning like a possum. Supposed to go in tomorrow and sign the papers at the lawyer's office."

"Why the red church, if he's got that kind of money?" Littlefield asked, even though he was pretty sure he already knew.

"That property started off in the McFall family. They're the ones who donated the land for the church in the first place. Remember Wendell McFall?"

Coincidences. Littlefield didn't like coincidences. He liked cause-and-effect. That's what solved cases. "That's a lot of money."

"Couldn't say no to it. But I had a funny feeling that he would have offered more if I had asked. But he knew I wouldn't. It was like that time with the mountain lion, like he was staring me down, like he knew what I was thinking."

"I guess if he's a successful businessman, then he's had a lot of practice at negotiating."

"Reckon so," Lester said, unconvinced. He stood with a creaking that might have been either his joints or the rocker's wooden slats. "It's time to be putting up the cows."

"And I'd best finish my rounds. I appreciate your time, Lester."

"Sure. Come on back anytime. And next time, plan on staying for a piece of pie."

"I'll do that."

As Littlefield started the Trooper, he couldn't help

thinking about the part of Lester's story that had gone un-
told. The part about why a bell rope no longer hung in the
red church, and why Archer McFall would want to buy
back the old family birthright.

He shook his head and went down the driveway, gravel
crackling under his wheels.

✞ Chapter 5

The dawn was crisp and pink, the air moistened by dew. The scent of pine and wild cherry blossoms spread across the valley along with the thin, smoky threads of the night's hearths. Water swept its way south underneath the soft fog that veiled the river. A rooster's crow cracked the stillness of the hills.

Archer McFall nestled against the damp soil, the earth cool against his nakedness. He kept his eyes closed, looking back into the dark avenues of his dreams, chasing shadows to nowhere. The dreams were splashed with red, the color of retribution. They were human dreams, strange and new and chaotic.

The rooster crowed three times before Archer remembered where he was.

Home.

The word, even though it was only thought and not spoken, left a bitter taste in his mouth. The bitterness came from the memory of old humiliations. And an older suffering, one that ran deeper than the expansive surface of sleep.

Archer coughed. Pine needles and brittle leaves pressed against his cheek. He shivered and rolled into a sitting position, opening his eyes. After so long in darkness, he was almost surprised at the brightness of the coming day. The light slashed through the gaps in the forest canopy, sharp and merciless and full of grace.

He gazed down at his bare human flesh. His skin seemed to fit well enough. These human bags of water and bone had always seemed awkwardly constructed to him. But he'd come among these people to take up their ways. Deliverance was more joyful when the victims thought it came from one of their own kind.

More thoughts came back to him, more memories flooded the gray mass of brain that filled his skull. He spat. A reddish clot of half-digested pulp clung to a stump.

As the sun warmed him and his shifting night shapes slithered the rest of the way out of existence, he planned his route back to the Mercedes. He knew the river well. It flowed below the old home grounds, below the church. He'd left his car in the woods a mile away. A Brooks Brothers suit, pinstriped and charcoal gray, was spread out in the trunk, along with leather shoes, knit socks, cologne, a Rolex wristwatch and a sky-blue tie.

The uniform of the walking dead, the Christian soldiers, the false idol-worshippers. The pretenders. And he would pretend to be one of them.

Archer stood and brushed the clinging loam from his body. A kingfisher swooped and lit on a branch nearby, then either smelled or sensed him and disappeared with a frantic snap of wings. Archer smiled and studied the gray mountain slopes.

Home.

The Promised Land.

Creeks as old as lies, dirt as dark as hopelessness. Stones as cold as the heart of a father who had only enough love for one son. Mountains thrust like angry fists up to the sky, defying the heaven that so many people believed in, including his dear deranged mother.

The worst part of this incarnation was the emotional turmoil. No wonder these creatures sinned. No wonder they sought refuge in lust and depravity and excess. They were God's mistakes. But God's biggest mistake was jealousy, the craving to build things in His image, the demand for sacrifice.

God demanded love, but had no love of His own to spare. At least not for the second-born. Not for the one destined for dust, while the first earned a high place above. The second son was fit only to rule what he could see, left to find corrupted pleasure here on Earth.

Archer began walking down the rugged incline toward the river. Brambles and branches pricked at his skin, but he soaked up the pain and buried it inside the hollowness of his rage. Sharp outcrops of granite tore at the soles of his feet, and he relished the flow of blood from his wounds.

Jesus had walked in wilderness. So would Archer.

The blood would leave tracks. Others could find his trail, if they were clever. Let them follow. He was born to lead, after all.

And even if they found him, what were they going to do? Kill him?

His laughter echoed through the trees, as deep as the glacier-cut and time-eroded valleys, the human vocal cords vibrating strangely as he threw back his head and chilled the spine of the forest.

Sheriff Littlefield leaned back in his oak swivel chair. Not a whisper of a squeak came from the well-oiled springs.

Detective Sergeant Storie shifted uneasily in the chair across the desk from him, her suit jacket rumpled. The morning light on her face showed that she had slept little and poorly. Her eyes were puffy and narrowed from the headache caused by disrupted dreams. Her hair was still wet from a morning shower, and the smell of her conditioner filled the room.

Steam billowed from Littlefield's cup of black coffee. He looked through it, and the steam parted and swirled as he spoke. "I talked to the folks out in Whispering Pines."

"Any eyewitnesses?"

"Nobody saw anything." He put a little too much emphasis on the word saw.

"What about knowing? This isn't the big city, where people don't want to get involved. The old woman in the apartment next to mine knows it when my cat breaks wind. And the rest of the neighbors are clued in before the fumes disperse."

Littlefield winced. But he let the wince slip into what he hoped looked like a frown of concern. Storie was always calling him "old school" as it was.

"Well, two people said they heard the bells ringing at the church," he said.

"So the killer celebrated by letting everybody know what he'd done?" Storie asked incredulously.

"Must have been their imaginations. There's no bell rope."

Storie leaned forward, tapping the report that lay on Littlefield's desk. The pages were wrinkled, probably from where she had worried over them in bed while trying to fall asleep. "Nobody heard the screams, either, I suppose."

"All we have is what we had yesterday. I've got Charlie and Wade searching the hills up around the church. Wade brought his dogs. If there's anything to be found, they'll turn it up."

Storie stood. "I guess I'd better get to work. Any word from Chapel Hill yet?"

"Hoyle says they should get around to the autopsy Monday. Ought to have preliminary results by Wednesday or so."

"What if it *is* a psycho?"

Littlefield looked past her to the glass case that lined one wall of his office. He had a collection of confiscated drug paraphernalia that would make a doper weep with envy. Colorful bongs and ornately carved pipes adorned the shelves, along with photographs of a younger Littlefield posing next to marijuana plants. In the center of the case stood a brass cup emblazoned with a badge: the 1998 Law Enforcement Officer of the Year Award, bestowed by the North Carolina Sheriff's Association.

There wasn't much crime in Pickett County. In Littlefield's seven years as sheriff, there had been a total of two murders. In one, the killer himself called the department, and blubberingly narrated how he had just blown his wife's head open with a .38 revolver. He was waiting on the porch when officers arrived, draining the last of his liquor, the gun cleaned and returned to its cabinet. His wife's body was in the garage, gingerly covered with a hand-woven shawl.

The other was Storie's case, the one that had established her as a legitimate detective. In Littlefield's mind, all the technical training in the world was useless until you actually snapped the cuffs on a perpetrator. And Storie had done that with style, making headlines across the region by helping prosecute the cop-turned-killer. After the trial, she gave the press a highly quotable statement: "If I had written the book, the final chapter would have been different. He would have gotten the death penalty."

So Littlefield was left with domestic disputes and civil disturbances. Some kids with a stereo blasting too loud, a drunk breaking windows, somebody rearranging the letters on Barkersville's Main Street Theater marquee to spell out crude words. Or some longhair in an army jacket would sell oregano joints behind the high school. The crime stats looked great on paper, which was part of the reason Littlefield had won his Sheriff's Association award.

But sometimes he was afraid that Pickett County was just a little too sleepy, that underneath the shimmering overlay of tight community and good-natured harmony was a layer of moral rot. After all, people were people. Maybe having a mad killer on the loose wasn't really so hard to imagine, not with what played out in other small towns across the country on the nightly news.

"Dogs should be able to track it, whether it's a mountain lion or a human."

Storie put her hands on her hips. "And?"

"And what?"

"The rest of the sentence. I get the feeling that you aren't telling me everything."

Littlefield sighed and rubbed his eyes. Storie was now wide-awake, as if she had magically cast her weariness over to him. He didn't know how to begin, but it would be unfair to withhold the information.

Information, hell. It was flat-out rubber-room stuff. But she would find out sooner or later, if she talked to any of the oldtimers in Whispering Pines.

"Well," he started, "it's about the church."

"The church?" Her eyebrows lifted into her wet bangs. "What about the church? Did you find something yesterday?"

"Nothing that you could call a clue," he lied. "Maybe you'd better sit back down."

Storie sat on the arm of the chair, clasping her hands together. Like Wade's hounds, she was excited by the fresh scent of prey. Littlefield pretended to look through a stack of papers on his desk, then cleared his throat.

"The church is haunted."

Littlefield could have sworn he heard his wristwatch ticking in the sudden silence, but that was impossible. His wristwatch was electronic. Even the police scanner, which sat on a stack of manuals in the corner, quit its squelching in response to his statement. He searched Storie's face.

Her eyes were wide, disbelieving, as if she had misheard him. But they quickly hardened back into a cool, professional gaze.

"Okay, Sheriff," she said with an irritated laugh. "That explains everything. A ghost sneaks out at night, maybe it's pissed off because its sheets got mildewed in the wash, whatever. So it finds a drunk in the graveyard with a dirty magazine and a bottle of bourbon and decides to vent its wrath. That explains why we didn't find any footprints at the scene. Case closed."

Littlefield folded his arms over his chest and let the wave of sarcasm sweep over him and die in the corners of the room.

His tight lips must have aroused Detective Storie's curiosity, because she looked as if she expected him to admit he was joking. "What?" Her mouth dropped open. "Sheesh, you're *serious*, aren't you?"

He said nothing. The coffeemaker on a side table gurgled. He walked slowly over to the machine and refilled his cup. "Want some?" he said, lifting the pot in Storie's direction.

She shook her head. Littlefield had been dreading this moment ever since they'd gotten the call yesterday. The thing at the church had never left. All these years of hoping, wishing, and his best attempts at praying hadn't made it go away.

"In the 1860s, the church was the only one in these parts," he began, walking to the closed door of his office. He looked at the hardware store calendar hanging there. The almanac said the moon was favorable for planting root crops.

He continued, keeping his back to the detective. "Back then it was called Potter's Mill Baptist Church, after the old grist mill that operated down by the river. Wendell McFall was the pastor. He was an 'old school' preacher"— he turned to judge her reaction and saw she was carefully controlling her expression, which didn't surprise him— "all fire and brimstone and hell to pay. But during the Civil War, they say he started stretching his interpretation of the Gospel.

"I don't know how much you know about the history of these parts, but the war pretty much made a hard life harder for the people who lived here," he said. "Pickett County men were part of the Fifty-eighth North Carolina Troops, and almost two-thirds of them were killed in action. Women were keeping up the fields and home chores at the same time. It was a bad stretch, as you can imagine. And Reverend McFall started preaching that the end of the world was nigh."

"Now, *there's* an original idea," Storie said. "They've been peddling that line for at least four thousand years."

Littlefield gulped his coffee, welcoming the hot sting in his throat. At least Storie hadn't walked out of the office yet. Maybe rank had its privileges after all.

"Some of the soldiers' bodies were shipped back here to be buried," Littlefield said. "Reverend McFall insisted on holding midnight vigils over the graves, because he said they would rise up and walk again otherwise. At the same time, he was preaching some nonsense about how God had two sons, and while the first one was merciful and good and holy, this second son was just the opposite."

"Too bad this guy wasn't around in the 1980s," Storie said. "He could have made a fortune selling cheesy paperbacks."

Littlefield ignored her. "So McFall starts warning the congregation that this second son would return to the earth, come to undo the good done by Jesus. Said the second son demanded love and sacrifice, like God's spoiled little brat. In those times, the preacher was pretty much the leader of the community. While those ideas might seem a little flaky now, people were more imaginative back then, carrying with them all the legends and beliefs of their Scottish and English ancestors. So when a man of the cloth told you he had a vision, then you were bound to believe it. And with their fathers and brothers and sons dying and hunger spreading, the congregation must have felt that they hadn't given enough tribute to God. Or His sons."

Littlefield had never discussed religion with Storie, or with much of anyone else, for that matter. He'd invited her to attend the First Baptist Church in Barkersville, but that was more of a rote politeness than a serious recruiting pitch. Littlefield himself usually went to services about once a month. He'd stopped reading the Bible after he finished his run through Sunday school and there was no longer anyone to force to him memorize verse. But he'd been raised Baptist, and he was going to die Baptist, even if he'd never devoted a minute to finding out what that really meant. Jesus was Lord, and that was that.

His grandmother on his mother's side used to tell the story of the red church while she snapped peas or shucked corn. He would sit at her feet, helping with the chore at his own awkward pace, listening too closely to the story to do much work. Sometimes Littlefield's mother would come in and say, "Don't fill Frankie's head with that foolishness," but Grandma would start right in again the minute Littlefield's mother left the kitchen.

Littlefield closed his eyes and tried to hear her voice in his mind. But it was no use. He fumbled for eloquent words, found none. "McFall was the one who painted the church red. Said that would bring the first son around to save them, to defeat the second son. Plus the congregation had to start meeting at midnight on Sunday instead of in the morning. By this time, according to the way the oldtimers tell it, McFall was feverish and white as a sheet. He'd stand in the pulpit, a dozen candles lighting up the old wooden interior of the church, and he'd describe his visions. He'd go into convulsions and rant about sin and violent ways and the punishment of the wicked and false idols and a blight carried unto umpteen generations. And the strange thing was, McFall never did prescribe a remedy for this punishment. No prayers, nothing. He wasn't even passing the plate."

Storie was rapt now, staring at the sheriff. He didn't know if it was because she found the legend fascinating or whether she was transfixed by her boss's making a fool of himself. "So this second son...was he supposed to be the devil or something?"

Littlefield shook his head. "McFall believed this second

son had a power equal to Jesus'. And according to my grandmother, McFall had most of the congregation believing it. So the preacher was riding high, dishing out his revelations while the congregation cowered speechless in the pews. And I guess he started getting a little delusional after that."

"After *that*? Like he wasn't before?"

"He started taking advantage," Littlefield continued. "Said he was the instrument of the Lord, and only he could protect them from the second son. Well, he got a woman pregnant, the wife of a soldier who was off fighting at Gainesville. People started whispering then, though they were too afraid to confront the preacher. Then, one morning following a midnight service, one of the parishioners found her young child mutilated at the altar of the red church.

"Well, as crazy as the preacher had been acting, they figured he had played Abraham or something. Only God didn't tell him to stop as he raised the knife, so he chopped up the child as a sacrifice. That Sunday night in 1864, the parishioners showed up for service and hauled the preacher from the pulpit. Somebody climbed up the bell rope and cut it loose, threw it out on the ground where the others stood holding torches."

"They didn't," Storie cut in. Littlefield couldn't tell if she was still mocking him. He decided to bust on through the tale and get it over with. He could feel his neck blushing.

"You know that dogwood by the church door? They hanged him from it."

"So that was that. Except his ghost still haunts the church, right?"

"I guess the Potters and the Mathesons and the Buchanans started feeling a little guilty and decided that maybe 'an eye for an eye' was all fine and dandy, but once a sin was paid for, all was forgiven. They buried him out in the woods, covered him with rocks in a place long forgotten. But they said prayers over his grave even if he didn't deserve them. They even took care of the woman he got pregnant."

The police scanner squawked, and a female dispatcher's voice came over. "Ten-sixty-eight. Ten-sixty-eight on Old Turnpike Road."

The tension in Littlefield's office eased slightly. "Denny Eggers's cows got out again," Littlefield said.

A deputy on patrol responded to the call. "Ten-four, base. Unit Four, en route."

"Ten-four," said the dispatcher. The scanner returned to broadcasting its ambient hiss.

The sheriff looked at Storie. She stood and stretched. "Well, I'd better get out to the church and see if I missed anything yesterday," she said.

She was at the door, with her hand on the knob, when Littlefield spoke. "The woman he got pregnant brought flowers to his grave. They say that three days after the hanging, she came running out of the woods with tears in her eyes, her clothes torn by the tree branches. She said, 'Praise God, the stone's been rolled away.'"

Detective Storie didn't turn around. The sheriff continued, his words spilling over each other, as if he were experiencing an attack of nausea and wanted it to pass. "When she said that, the church bell started ringing. Only the bell had no rope. And nobody was in the church at the time."

Storie turned. "So *that's* why you told me all this. That'll really stand up in court." She dropped her voice into a low, professional delivery. "'Your Honor, I would like to submit as state's evidence thirty-two a tape recording of church bells ringing, made on the night of Mr. Houck's death.'"

Littlefield stared into the black pool of his cup of coffee. "Maybe all that has nothing to do with Boonie's death. I sure as hell hope not. A psycho might be able to hide out in the woods for a few weeks, but the bloodhounds would get him sooner or later. Same with a mountain lion. But I hear that one of McFall's descendants is back in town."

"So you expect me to believe in coincidence?" she said. "They didn't teach paranormal investigation at the academy. As for Reverend McFall's ghost, I'll believe it when you can prove it in court."

"I've got an eyewitness for you," he said, his voice tired now, an old man's defeated voice.

"Who?"

He glanced at the Officer of the Year award, glinting dully in the morning sun that sliced through the parted blinds. Storie approached his desk. She leaned over it in a position of superiority, like a teacher berating a daydreaming student.

"Who?" she repeated. "Who's going to testify that a ghost committed murder?"

"Me."

✞ Chapter 6

"You?" Storie shook her head.

Littlefield sat back, feeling twice his forty years. The good thing about the past was that you left it farther and farther behind each day. The bad thing was that you also got closer to the day when you could no longer hide from the past. A day of reckoning and judgment.

"I was seventeen," he said, his flesh cold. "It was Halloween night. Back then, and probably still to this day, getting drunk and driving over to the red church was the thing to do on Halloween. Me and a few of my high school buddies loaded into a pickup I borrowed from my dad. Well, my kid brother Samuel, he was eleven at the time, saw the beer in the bed of the pickup and said he was going to tell on me."

Littlefield rubbed his eyes. He wasn't going to let himself cry in front of a woman or another cop. He cleared his throat. "So I told him he could come along if he'd keep his stupid little mouth shut. We went out to the church- we only lived about two miles away, up near the McFalls at the foot of Buckhorn- and parked in the trees off to one side of the graveyard. We drank the beer and dared each other to go inside the church, you know how teenagers will do."

"Sure I do," Storie said. "I just never expected you to

have been such a scofflaw."

Littlefield wasn't sure if her sarcasm was designed to provoke him or encourage him to continue. But he'd kept the story bottled up for too long. He'd never had anyone to confide in.

"Naturally, we were all too scared to do it. Like I said, the ghost stories were pretty well known in these parts. Which was funny as hell, because that's where most of us went to church on Sundays. During the day, with all the people there and the sun in the windows, it wasn't scary at all. But at night, with the dark shadows of the woods, your imagination had a lot of room to play.

"So then we got to picking on Samuel, calling him a chicken, as if we were any braver. And, damn me, I was as bad as any of the others. Samuel sat in the bed of that pick-up truck, his eyes wide and shiny in the moonlight and his lip quivering. What else could he do but go up to the church?"

Storie leaned against the wall. The sheriff glanced at her, but she was staring at the floor, looking uncomfortable. She was a cop. Maybe she was as emotionally inhibited as he was and hated this type of intimacy. Well, she could walk out if she wanted. Now that he had started, he was going to finish the story, even if the walls and God were his only audience.

"He went across the graveyard, wearing a cape that was part of his trick-or-treating getup. He was Batman that year, and the cape was a beach towel tied in a knot around his neck. Maybe as he walked, he tried to convince himself that he was a brave superhero."

Littlefield closed his eyes, and it was as if an October wind had carried him back to that night. He could almost smell the freshly fallen leaves, the sweetness of the late-autumn grass, the beer that had spilled in the truck bed, the smoke from the cigarettes one of the boys smoked. He continued in a monotone.

"By the time he passed those lonely tombstones, I started feeling a little guilty. I jumped out of the truck and ran across the graveyard to get him and drag him away. I hollered, and I guess he thought I was going to do something to him. He ran up the steps and lifted the latch to the church door, then went inside. The rest of the guys were hooting and moaning, making ghost noises while trying not to snicker.

"I followed Samuel inside the church and closed the door behind me. That's when I got the idea. 'Let's scare the bejesus out of them,' I said, mad at the other guys mostly because I was so much like them. The entryway was dark, but the moonlight spilled through the belfry and lit up that little square where the bell rope used to hang. The hole was about two feet by two feet, too small for most people to squeeze through. But Samuel was slender and wiggly, so I knew he could slip through there if I boosted him up."

Unit Four's voice came through on the police radio and interrupted Littlefield's story. "Come in, base. Found the cows, all right. Denny's getting them rounded up. I'll be ten-ten for a few—"

Storie crossed the room and cut off the radio, then turned back to Littlefield. Her eyes flicked to the sheriff's face, then away, as if she were as ashamed of his vulnerability as he was.

He continued. "I told him, 'Get up there and hide, and I'll run out screaming and say that the Bell Monster got you.' He must have been scared, but I'd always been his hero, and I guess he trusted me that everything would be okay, that nothing bad could happen while I was there. So

I boosted him up, and he scrambled through, then I saw his pale face framed in the rope hole. 'When I wave my arms, you kick the bell,' I said. He nodded, and I ran outside, waving my arms and screaming like a crazy man.

"'It *got* him, it *got* him,' I yelled. 'The Bell Monster got him.' And all those drunken guys jumped out of the pickup and took off running down the road. I turned and pointed to the belfry, signaling Samuel to ring the bell. I saw his eyes, his white forehead, and the dark mess of his curly hair. And behind him, behind him . . .'"

Littlefield took three swallows of cold black coffee. He looked at the sunlight sneaking around the window shade. He'd never told anybody this part. Except for himself. He'd relived it during a thousand sweaty, sleepless nights.

"The Bell Monster was there," he said, his whisper filling the room.

"It was really just a shadow, but it was there. It had sharp edges, and it moved toward Samuel. I screamed for real then, and I guess Samuel thought it was part of the act. Then he turned around and saw the thing, God only knows what it looked like from that close up. He scrambled over the edge of the belfry and started to slide down the roof. It was a short drop, he should have been fine. But that stupid cape got caught on a nail or something, and I heard the pop from clear across the graveyard." Littlefield's whisper dropped a notch quieter. "His neck broke."

Littlefield could still see Samuel's startled expression, his eyes and tongue bulging as his body spun beneath the eave of the church. The image had been burned into his retinas, coming to him in dreams and while awake, crisper than a high-definition television signal, more vivid than any movie.

Storie came to him and put a hand on his forearm. "I'm sorry."

The tears came now, hot and wet and stinging, but not enough to flush away the image of his dead brother's face. "We buried him there at the church. Sometimes I think that's the worst part, that we left him buried there forever. The place got what it wanted. The place got *him*."

Littlefield wiped his nose on his sleeve. "And here I am, blubbering like an idiot."

Storie came closer. "It's okay, Frank," she said, and for a moment he thought she was going to hug him. That would be the final humiliation. He spun so that the back of his chair was facing her.

"I saw him," he said.

"I know. It must have been awful."

"No, not Samuel. I saw *him*. Right when Samuel's neck broke, I saw the Hung Preacher. Just for a second. He shimmered there at the end of a rope, hanging from that goddamned dogwood tree that I've never had the nerve to chop down. He was looking at me like he knew what he'd done. And he was mighty damned pleased with himself."

Littlefield was deflated, tired. He was sorry he'd said anything. How could he expect anyone to believe what he barely believed himself? He knew what had happened that night. He'd *seen* it with his own eyes. But that night existed as if in a separate reality, a private hell, apart from the safe and sane world of Pickett County.

"Did any of your drinking buddies witness anything?" Storie asked.

Damn her. Of course SHE'D want hard evidence. A broken soul wasn't enough to convince her. His anger dried his eyes.

"No," he said, staring at a drug prevention poster on

the wall. "Officially, it was a prank that turned into a tragedy. Freak accident. Of course, the oldtimers muttered and added Samuel's death to the legend of the red church. The rest of the world went on with the business of living."

"Except you," Storie said.

Except me. Storie *did* have a detective's eyes. Littlefield ran his hand over his scalp and stood. "Well, now you know your sheriff is apeshit crazy."

"The eyes can play tricks. In my psychology classes, they taught us that bad memories can trigger—"

Littlefield sliced his palm across the air to silence her. "I don't give a damn about theories. I know what I saw."

She clenched her fists and looked at him, the hurt clear on her face. She hurried out of the office, and he did nothing to stop her. She slammed the door, and Littlefield's Officer of the Year award rattled in its case.

Elizabeth McFall, known to the old families as Mama Bet, knelt in the damp forest soil.

The dead belong to the dirt. And the dirt belongs to Him that shaped it all.

The dirt would have her soon enough. She was nearly eighty, suffering from diabetes, cataracts, and high blood pressure. But at least God allowed her legs to work still, and her mind was a lot clearer than her eyesight. She looked through the treetops, at the blue sky and the invisible kingdom waiting behind it.

A hand touched her shoulder.

"You done yet, Mama Bet?"

It was Sonny Absher, the biggest small-time thief this side of Tennessee. She hoped his sins didn't jump onto her, like lice or fleas jumping to greener pastures.

The worst part of this whole business was that the Abshers were in on it. The Buchanans were bad enough, what with their moonshining and wife-beating and chicken-stealing ways. But at least the Buchanans knew how to get down on their knees and say they were sorry. The Abshers would just as soon spit at God, even if the saliva fell right back onto their oily faces.

But the Abshers couldn't be culled from the congregation. All the families had a hand in the original persecution, and they all carried a common debt in their hearts. After all these years, they were practically of the same blood anyway. And that blood would have to spill, and spill, and spill.

"I'll be done shortly," Mama Bet answered. "Gotta suffer a little, get right down here on my knees and feel a little pain."

"So this is where they buried him?"

Mama Bet bowed over the small pile of stones. "Yeah. But without a body, a grave's just a hole in the ground."

Sonny Absher snorted. She could smell the white lightning on his breath, in his clothes, strong enough to drown out his rancid sweat. "You mean you believe all that bullshit about Wendell McFall coming back from the dead?"

"You better hush yourself," Mama Bet said, shrugging his hand away from her shoulder. "God might strike you down. Look what He done to Boonie."

"God's done and struck me," Sonny said. "He got me born here. Why in hell else would I be part of this bunch?"

Sonny drew a cigarette from his stained shirt pocket, lit it, and blew a gray cloud of smoke to the sky. He retreated to a stand of laurels, where his brother Haywood and Haywood's wife and teenage daughter waited. Stepford

Matheson sat on a stump, whittling on a little chunk of white ash.

Haywood had tried to aspire to a little dignity, taking up with the Baptists and selling insurance in Barkersville. His hands were folded in reverence, but he didn't fool Mama Bet. A person of true faith didn't believe in insurance. But Haywood was all show anyway. His retail-rack suit swamped his skinny frame.

You put a weasel in a forty-dollar suit, and you get a forty-dollar weasel. And Nell ain't quite got all the ingredients to be a trophy wife. I mean, a quart of makeup and a weekly trip to the hair salon ought to give better results than THAT. Why, I've seen better eyeliner jobs down at Mooney's Funeral Home.

Mama Bet turned back to the loose pile of stones that marked her great-grandfather's former resting place.

Forgive me, God, for thinking ill of others. I guess I suffer the sin of pride. I'm just a little shaky, is all. Scared. You can understand, can't You?

Sure, God could understand. God was really the blame for this whole mess, when you got right down to it. God was the one who put those fool notions in Wendell McFall's head. God was the one who put temptation in Wendell's path. God was the one who sat right up there in the clouds and didn't lift a finger while Wendell sliced up that pretty little girl.

God sat right there and laughed. And God laughed the night He slipped His seed into Mama Bet's belly. Oh, yes, God was a sneaky little devil, all right. Came to her in the dark and made her forget all about it after.

Until she missed a few of her monthlies. Her belly had started to swell and her breasts grew heavy with milk. Everyone thought she had suffered a sin of the flesh, had fallen in with one of those door-to-door Bible salesmen who had a reputation for rutting like stallions going after a pent-up mare. And so the little hens clucked, Alma Potter and Vivian Matheson and all the other no-good gossips of Whispering Pines.

She didn't tell anybody she was still a virgin. Then, now, and forever, as far as she could tell. Virgins couldn't get pregnant, could they? Only one had in the whole history of the world, the way the Bible told it.

Mama Bet delivered the baby without help, had strained and groaned and screamed for twenty hours, as her water burst and her uterine walls spasmed. God forgive her, she had even cussed that baby's Father. Borrowed every bad word in the Absher repertoire, then added a few of her own. Finally that slimy head popped through, followed by little shoulders and arms and belly and legs.

Can a body love something so much that her heart aches with the loving?

She had often wondered. Because she fell in love with that child, she pulled him onto her belly and then hugged him against her face, her tears running like whatever was leaking from her broken place down there. Her whole world, her whole reason for living, was realized in that moment after birth.

"How long you going to pray over that damned old pile of rocks?" Sonny called.

"Shut up," Haywood said.

Mama Bet slowly rose to her feet, pushing on the mossy stones for support. Haywood started forward to help her, but she waved him away.

"I get my strength from God and Archer," she said.

Oh, yes, it was strength, all right. The strength born of stubbornness and determination. God was the worst absentee father of all time. Because He never really just showed up and did his business, never made this or that happen directly, though He had his hand in every little breath that human beings took. He kept himself invisible, because He wanted nary bit of the blame when things went wrong. That was why He'd planted the seed and sneaked away in the night without even leaving an instruction manual on how to raise a messiah.

Mama Bet peeled her scarf back and let it rest around her neck. The sun was high enough to break through the canopy of forest. The leaves weren't at full size yet. Otherwise, the grave would be in the shadows all day. Mama Bet took a deep swallow of the fresh mountain air. She could taste the past winter's ice and the coming summer's oak blooms in the same breath.

Round and round these dadgummed seasons go. Seems like they get faster and faster, mixing together and not stopping to rest, like the world's in a great big hurry to get to the reckoning.

She hobbled across the damp leaves of the forest clearing until she reached the others. The congregation. Only they didn't know it yet. They knew only that they had to come, had to join in, had to open their hearts. Mama Bet was the only one who knew that the Second Son was back, and now there would be hell to pay. But she had never whispered a word of the truth, except to Archer. Darned if she couldn't keep a secret as good as God could.

"I reckon we ought to pray," she said. She held out her wrinkled hand to Stepford, who folded his pocketknife and put away his carving. He wiped the wood chips from his hand and clasped it to Mama Bet's. Noreen took her other hand, smiling. She was a pretty girl, not as moon-faced as the rest of the Abshers. Maybe she had Potter blood in her. Zeb Potter had been known to cat around a little, back before his health started failing. Maybe Nell had succumbed to old Zebulon's sinful charms.

There I go again, God. Thinking ill of others, as if I got no sins of my own to worry about. Strike me down if it be Thy will. Just please don't plant another seed in me. I don't think I could take another go-round as bad as the last one.

Well, that, plus she had no more love to spare for another child. Archer Dell McFall took up every square inch of her heart. Archer had given her more joy than she ever thought heaven could hold. Archer was the most beautiful creature under Creation. Darned if God couldn't produce a fine offspring when He set His mind to it.

The others gathered in a circle and held hands, though Sonny gave another of his little grunts of annoyance. Mama Bet shot him a wicked look. He blinked and went coweyed. The gathered bowed their heads.

"Dear God, give us the strength to do Your will, and to accept our part in Your work," she said, her voice taking on a tremulous quality. "We know we have sinned and come short of the glory, but we know You love us anyway. Lead our eyes from evil visions and lead our ears from the call of false prophets. Allow us to make whatever sacrifices You require, that we may not stray from the one true path. Keep us and protect us unto the fourth generation. Amen."

And may Archer do this thing right, she silently added, as the others echoed "Amen."

"Are we done now?" Sonny said, pulling out another cigarette.

"We might not ever be done," Mama Bet said.

"When the Lord Jesus gives you a mission, you follow

it to the end," Haywood said.

Poor Haywood. Swallowing that New Testament tom-foolery hook, line, and sinker. Well, Archer will shine the light on him soon enough.

Stepford spat onto the trunk of a poplar. "Come on, Sonny. I'm thirsty," he said. He turned and started down the path that led to the rutted dirt road. They had parked their cars at the foot of the trail.

"Wait a second," Sonny yelled. He turned to Mama Bet. "Do we got to go to the red church tomorrow night?"

"I said so, didn't I?"

He frowned at the forest floor. "It's getting so a body ain't got time to pitch a good drunk, what with all this bowing and scraping and worshiping."

"Well, Mr. Absher, you're welcome to go straight on down to hell if you want, but this ain't about you, is it?"

He looked at the small overgrown grave.

"The stone's been rolled away," Mama Bet said. "We all got sacrifices to make."

Sonny's thin lips curled. "Well, we may have to follow the call, but we sure don't have to like it none."

He turned and hurried after Stepford, his boots kicking up a wash of leaves. Haywood came to Mama Bet's side and took her arm. "Come on, Mama Bet," he said. "Let's get you home so you can rest up."

She smiled at him, at Noreen, even at Nell. The congregation. Well, part of it, anyway. That Noreen was so pretty, there in her Easter dress the color of robin's eggs. Almost a shame that beauty such as that would have to fall by the wayside.

Because all a pretty face does is hide the ugly underneath, don't it?

"Yeah, I guess we all better rest up," she said. "There

will come great trials."

The sky seemed to darken a little at her words, or maybe God took up into the trees and reached His fingers out to throw a shadow in her eyes. He liked to keep things confusing, all right. She sometimes wondered if He loved her, if He really loved any of them. Or was He just pretending so He could get the things He wanted, like love?

Haywood led her down the mountain path to her home, to the birthplace of the Second Son.

✟ Chapter 7

Linda watched the sun crawl down toward the ridge of Buckhorn Mountain. Just a few more hours. She was wondering how she could slip away without the boys noticing. She almost wished David had stayed. He swallowed lies more easily than the boys did.

She turned from the door and went back to the kitchen. Timmy would be hungry when he got in from his chores. She could see him through the window above the sink, chopping at the brown garden soil with his hoe. The cabbage and peas and potatoes were in the ground, and soon it would be time to plant corn and cucumbers. She didn't know how she was going to manage the farm alone. Even though the fields were leased out for growing hay, the garden took a lot of backbreaking time and sacrifice.

Sacrifice.

Archer always said that sacrifice was the currency of God.

Linda bit her lip. Tears stung her eyes, and she didn't know whether they were brought by regret or joy. The fold would prosper in the next life and unto the fourth generation, but letting go of the things in this life was hard. There were joys to be had here: her children and sometimes even David, a walk in the wet grass of a morning, standing in the barn during a rainstorm with the music of the drops on the tin roof.

No, that was mortal thinking, covetous and vain and destructive. But she was a mortal. Still. A mother of two wonderful boys. Until Archer demanded it, she wouldn't forsake them.

Linda stopped at the refrigerator. One of Ronnie's poems from school was hanging from a banana magnet. His teacher had circled a large red A on the corner of the page. "The Tree," it was called.

> The tree has arms
> that hug,
> not as warm as Mother's.
> Sometimes when I walk by,
> the tree waves
> and I run away.
> The tree barks at me.

Ronnie was doing okay. He had slept most of the time since coming back from the hospital. His face was pale and his nose was lost in gauze and padding. Once he had vomited blood and stained the carpet in the boys' room. The place smelled like carpet-cleaning spray, but luckily it was warm enough that she could leave the windows open.

Linda pulled some hamburger from the refrigerator. They had killed their final cow the previous fall. Linda wondered if the dead cow counted as a sacrifice. Maybe for the God of cows. Let Archer worry about that kind of stuff.

Tim came in the back door.

"Go wash your hands, honey," she said over the rush of water as she rinsed some potatoes.

"They're sore." Not too much whine in his voice.

"I know. You'll get used to it."

Tim came to the sink and saw the hamburger. "It looks like that guy's face."

"Hush, honey."

"I dreamed about him last night."

"Was it scary?" She searched his face, looking for weakness. All she saw were David's eyes, the stubborn gift of genetics. She moved over and let Timmy wash his hands.

The sink turned brown-red from the dirt. "No. In my dream, the graveyard was sort of dark, but not a bad dark. A fun dark, like a carnival or something. And the dead man was all ripped up and stuff, but he was walking around the tombstones."

"You're a brave boy. That sure would have scared me." Was Archer coming to the boys? Or had it just been the usual trick of dreams?

Tim turned off the taps and wiped his hands on the dishcloth that hung from a cabinet knob. "There was another person, a boy, up at the church. Except the church wasn't a church, it was lit up like a spookhouse. This boy was up in the place with the bell, just laughing and laughing and laughing and ringing the bell. And the dead man danced around the tombstones, pieces of him falling off the whole time."

Archer. It had to be Archer. *The truth has many faces*, he always said. "Well, you've been through a lot. It's no wonder you had such a weird dream," Linda said, pressing out two patties and placing them in a black iron skillet on the stove. The heat made the meat sizzle, the white noise of energy transformation.

"That dream was nowhere near as scary as talking to the sheriff. Or seeing Ronnie in the hospital."

The sheriff. No wonder Tim had thought the man was

going to arrest him. The sheriff had stood like an army man in the hospital lobby, asking Tim questions in his deep, patient voice. He was a threat. But he was of the old blood, and had his own debt to pay. Archer could handle him.

The burgers popped as she flipped them, sending tiny sparks of pain up her bare arms as hot grease spattered on her skin. The bell rang on the microwave. "Dinner's ready," she said.

While Tim ate at the kitchen table, Linda took some apple juice to Ronnie. She turned on the light, and he moaned. "It's okay, honey," she said. "I brought you some- thing to drink."

He was feverish and pale against the pillow. His nose was still plumped by packing, and a stray bloody thread of gauze dangled from one nostril.

"N—not thirsty," Ronnie said.

She sat beside him on the lower bunk. As the oldest, he usually slept in the upper bunk, but she didn't want to risk his falling during the night. Archer would want him mended, healed, whole. Not like this.

Why did you have to go and break your nose? He looked so small, with his hair brushed back and the *Star Wars* sheets pulled up to his chin. Theo, his stuffed bear, had fallen to the side, the stiff arms providing no comfort.

For a split second, she blamed Archer for the injury. Of course, she knew that Archer had taken Boonie Houck, had made the drunkard pay for his sins at the same time Archer rejuvenated himself for holy work. Boonie's worth- less life had culminated with a great act of giving. Serving as a sacrifice was Boonie's highest possible purpose in this world. He should have been whimpering in gratitude as Archer took his wicked eyes and tongue and other sinful parts.

Ronnie's accident was only a down payment, she knew. Many innocents would fall so that none of the guilty escaped. That was the Word, that was the Way. She had accepted the testament long ago.

Archer warned that some choices would be difficult. But he reminded the fold that earthly love was only another vanity, another sin. All love must be directed to the Temple of the Two Suns. And none of that love could be wasted on the First Son, Jesus.

Jesus, the plague maker. The damning one. The liar. A mask of light and peace covering a devil's scarred and pocked face. Linda shivered, recalling how deeply the Baptists had brainwashed her. And to think that she'd been making the boys go to their church.

A Jesus trick, Archer had explained. Using David to trap her. To "save" her.

She shuddered and put the apple juice to Ronnie's lips. He strained his head forward and took a swallow, then collapsed back against the pillow. "How are you feeling, sugar?"

"Hurts," he whispered.

"I know, baby. It'll be okay soon."

"I just want to sleep."

"Sure." She kissed him on the forehead, careful to avoid the purpled flesh around his eyes. "Sweet dreams."

Timmy was finished eating by the time she got back to the kitchen. She sent him to wash his face and brush his teeth, and then to bed. She turned on the radio, the local station. A Beatles song was playing, "Strawberry Fields Forever." Sinful. But she was strong. She could withstand this test of faith.

Yes, Archer, I am strong. I am worthy. The music can't

touch me, because I know it for what it is.

She listened as the song segued into its second fadeout, the backward tape effects filled with secret messages. The taunts and seductive whispers of Jesus. Something about burying Paul, the cursed apostle. Dozens of people across the county, maybe hundreds, were being exposed to this depraved Christ-worship. She said a quick prayer to Archer for their souls.

Another song came on. The Culture Club, a band she used to like. Back before she met Archer. "Karma chameleon," Boy George sang. Karma chameleon. More sacrilege, more perverted celebrations of the spirit, another false Way.

The boys would be asleep now. She turned off the radio and silently crept out the door. The sky was charcoal gray in the west, where the waxing moon hung bloated and obscene. But the ground, the earth, the mountains were black as absolution. As near Archer's promised peace as one could hope, at least in this mortal world.

Crickets. The chuckle of the creek. The wind soughing through the trees, hiding the noises of nocturnal creatures.

She didn't need light in order to see.

She needed only faith.

And darkness.

Archer's darkness summoned her, a beacon so righteously black that it was blinding.

She crossed the damp meadow and slipped into the forest.

Zeb Potter cradled the shotgun across one flannel-wrapped arm. He shined the flashlight into the belly of the barn. The cows were banging against the walls of their stall, uneasy lowing coming from their throats. The air was thick with the smell of fresh manure.

Something's scared 'em bad.

Zeb had been getting ready for bed, had taken out his chewing tobacco and his teeth and was deciding whether or not he could go one more night in the same pair of long johns when the bawling of a calf filled the night. A calf could wail its lungs out if it wanted, but hardly ever cut loose without a good reason.

Most people thought cows were dumb as dirt, but they had peculiarities that none of those genius "agronomists" from NC State would ever be able to explain. A healthy cow, you hit it in that place just between and a little above the eyes with a sledgehammer, and it dropped dead on the spot, ready to turn to steak and hamburger. But a sick cow, you had to hit it five or six times before it went down. And why was that? The sick cow was living to get healthy, but the healthy cow was about as well off as it could hope to be. So the healthy cow didn't have as much to look forward to. Cows knew a thing or two about life.

So they always kicked up a fuss when they smelled something bad. Though all the big predators had died out, once in a while a pack of wild dogs came over the hills from Tennessee-ways, where people let such things go on. But on this side of the state line, people took care of their problems. They didn't wait for problems to do their damage and move on.

After the first commotion, Zeb had cussed once and slipped into his boots without bothering to find his socks. He'd stopped by the door and put on his hat and collected his twenty-gauge and his spotlight. If Betty were still alive, she would be waiting by the door in her nightgown, telling him to be careful. And he would have patted the shotgun and said, "This is all the care I need." But Betty had gone to be with the Lord, and the farm was big and lonely and the house made noises at night. And the damned hound had probably skulked away into the woods at the slightest scent of trouble.

The shotgun was heavy, and Zeb's muscles ached from tension. He flicked the light over the barn, its yellow beam bouncing around among locust posts and old wire and rotted feed sacks. Hay dust choked the air, and the crumbs from last fall's tobacco snowed between the cracks in the loft floor above. Something was moving around up there.

That ain't no damned wild Tennessee dogs.

Zeb clenched his bare gums together and moved as smoothly as his old bones would let him over to the loft stairs. A chicken was disturbed from its nest under the steps and almost got its knobby head blown off when it erupted into Zeb's face. Zeb picked up the flashlight he had dropped. The cows were noisier now, their milling more frantic.

Zeb put a trembling foot on the stairs. "Who's up yonder?" he hollered, hoping he sounded angry instead of scared. Nothing but moos answered him.

He'd heard what had happened to Boonie, and there was no way in hell that it was going to happen to him. The sheriff had even been out, asking if Zeb had seen or heard anything unusual. But the only thing Zeb had heard was those damned bells in the middle of the night, what was probably some of them high school kids finding a way to bug as many people as possible.

He thought now about going up to the house and ringing the sheriff's department. Littlefield told him to call if anything "unusual" happened. Littlefield sure liked that word. But Zeb had known Littlefield when the boy was knee-high to a scarecrow, and he didn't want the sheriff to think that he couldn't take care of his own problems. That was why Tennessee and the rest of the damned country was in such a mess. Everybody closed their eyes when the bad stuff came along.

John Wayne never even blinked.

Zeb played the spotlight into the darkness at the top of the stairs. He put a boot on the second tread, and before he could decide whether he was really going to or not, he had taken another step, then another, and he was halfway up before he even started thinking again. He laid the barrel of the shotgun over his left wrist so he could shine the light while still keeping his right hand at the trigger. If he fired the gun in that position, with it held beside his hip, the recoil would probably break his trigger finger. That was one worry that John Wayne never had.

"Might have been somebody with a knife or an ax," the sheriff had said. "Either that, or a wild animal."

Sure, it could be somebody with a blade. City folks had moved into Whispering Pines, up from Florida or down from New York, come to escape those streets that were full of maniacs with drugged-out eyes and hands that would rather slap you than lift in greeting. But guess what? The city folks had brought the bad things with them. A killer's instinct was as easily packed away in a U-Haul as a fitness machine or a golf cart was.

He'd told the sheriff in no uncertain terms that there wasn't an animal around here big enough to mutilate a man like that. Maybe off in Africa or something, but things were tamed over here. So when Littlefield said Perry Hoyle had mentioned a mountain lion, Zeb laughed out loud. The idea of a touched-in-the-head killer running around was way easier to swallow than believing a mountain lion was on the loose.

But right now, Zeb was in no mood to laugh at anything. His stomach was a wet sack of cornmeal, tied closed by the knot in his throat. He had ascended enough to poke his head into the loft, and the spotlight jittered from corner to corner, too fast for him to really see much.

Hay, stacked crooked like a child's wooden blocks.

The bright metal glint of his tools hanging on the wall by his workbench.

Night, cool beyond the chicken wire that covered the open windows.

Posts, the dull underside of the tin roofing, the hewed stakes where the tobacco hung to dry, the-

The dark thing, swooping, a sudden papery rattle breaking the strained quiet.

Zeb jerked the spotlight and his trigger hand tensed.

Bat.

Goddamned no-good mouse with wings.

Zeb exhaled, his heart pounding in his eardrums. A small warm ache filled his chest.

Easy now, Zebulon. Don't be putting yourself in no hospital.

He'd been in the hospital last year, and that was as close to prison as he ever wanted to be. Doctors sticking things inside every hole in his body, nurses seeing him naked, people in white coats telling him when to eat what pills. Couldn't have a chaw, no, sir. *Have you ever had this, this, or this?*

Finally, they'd cut him open and taken out his gall bladder. He suspected it was just for the hell of it, that they really couldn't find anything wrong but didn't want to admit it. But he figured the surgery would make them happy, and he'd never needed the damned gallbladder anyway. At least they didn't take anything important, and he got to go home again, even if he still felt like warmed-over liver mush about half the time.

Zeb was mad at himself for shaking. And to prove to himself that he didn't close his eyes to problems, and that, by God, *he* didn't have no sorry Tennessee blood in him, he walked across the loft, careful to avoid the black squares cut in the floor where he threw down hay to the cattle in the winter months.

If anybody was up here, they were trespassing, plain and simple.

And if it was a touched-in-the-head druggie escaped from the city, Zeb could handle him.

No matter the ax or knife.

A shadow of movement caught his eye, and he brought up the light to see that it was only a piece of hemp rope, swaying in the breeze that leaked in from the windows.

A metallic squeak came from behind him. Zeb spun, the flashlight beam crawling over the workbench. A short piece of stovepipe rocked back and forth. *Wasn't no wind blowed that.*

He crept toward the bench, the pump-action shotgun leading the way. It occurred to him that the flashlight was giving away his position. The druggie or whatnot knew exactly where Zeb was.

Nothing to do but walk brave and proud. He stood John Wayne straight and said, "Come on out where I can see you."

Only silence and the muted ruckus of the cows.

"Got a gun here."

A cricket chirped somewhere amid the hay.

Zeb played the light along the wall above the workbench. Something wasn't right.

There was the pitchfork, hanging by two rusty nails. A pulley, used for raising cows so they could be properly gutted. A cross-saw. An ax. A crop sprayer with a shoulder strap. A loop of harness. A shovel. Two hoes. An old mowing bar for the tractor. Three different thicknesses of chain.

And what else? What was missing?

The wall went dark and it took Zeb a second to realize that the light had been blocked.

Druggie.

A face filled the circle of light, a face that looked familiar but unreal. Zeb's chest was boiling, as hot as a chicken-scalding cauldron.

Not a druggie. A . . .

Zeb's finger tightened on the trigger, and the roar of exploding gunpowder slapped against the tin roofing, then echoed to give Zeb's ears an extra deafening blow. Pellets ripped scars in the wormy chestnut walls. And the thing that had been standing before him was blown back to hell where it belonged.

Except . . .

Sweet merciful Jesus.

The thing was still there, the face split into a sharp grin as the features around it rippled between skin and scale and fur and a shapeless, slick gray. But the eyes were the worst, those green stabbing rays that loved and hated worse than any dream or nightmare, eyes that owned, eyes that blessed and cursed, eyes that—

Zeb could hear himself whimpering as he tried to pull back the pumping stock. He'd been right: firing the gun *had* broken his shooting finger, but no time to worry about the pain in his heart and hand. He might have missed the first time, but the thing was closer now, only he was too weak to reload—this would never happen to John Wayne.

The spotlight had fallen in the hay, but its beam was angled upward. The bright-eyed thing filled the circle of light like the star of a demented puppet show. It raised the sledge, Zeb's cow-killing hammer, and as the eight-pound metal head began its downward stroke, aimed for that place just between and a little above the eyes, he realized that maybe those Tennessee-born bastards were right.

There *was* a time to close your eyes until the bad stuff went away.

✝ Chapter 8

Frank Littlefield topped the hill in his Trooper, blinking against the dawn as he threaded his way into the valley of Whispering Pines. He had the window rolled down because the smell of green spring was so much sweeter this far from town. The few houses were set away from the road, with stretches of pasture and tobacco fields broken by stands of hardwood forest. Below, the silver and brown of barn roofs made tiny rectangles along the plain of the river. Cows ambled near the fence lines, moving as sleepily and lazily as the river, their heads all pointed in the same direction.

A few vehicles passed, their occupants in dark suits and starched dresses, with hair respectfully combed or brushed. They were headed toward Barkersville, toward church. Sunday was supposed to be a holy day, a day of rest and fellowship, of fried chicken and televised sports. Not a day of death.

He reached the valley floor and turned onto the gravel road that he knew too well. A boy was fishing off the one-lane bridge, and Littlefield slowed to minimize the dust raised by the Trooper's passing. The sheriff checked the boy's stringer line to see if the trout were biting. The stringer was slack. Even the fish were lazy today.

He rounded a bend and the red church came into view. From this distance, the structure seemed to have a face. The windows were like flat eyes, the eaves a brooding brow, the uneven stone foundation a cruel grin of broken teeth. The church glowered, smug and hateful on its cemetery hill. Littlefield looked away to rid himself of the image of Samuel hanging from the eaves.

A strip of yellow plastic at the lower edge of the cemetery marked off the scene where Boonie Houck had died. *Do Not Cross*, the police line commanded. Funny how those words always came a little too late. If only the barrier had been in place a week ago. Then Boonie might be waking up with a hangover instead of sleeping on a metal gurney in the state medical examiner's meat locker.

All we have to do is mark off the whole world. Little yellow strips for everybody.

A truck was backed up to the church's door. It was Lester's farm truck, a big black Dodge two-ton. Bales of hay were stacked in the cattle bed. Lester had never worked on Sundays. The only time he missed a morning worship service was when he had to make a November run to the tobacco market in Durham.

Littlefield decided to have another talk with Lester. Storie would be waiting for him at Zeb Potter's place, but from what the detective had told him over the phone that morning, there wasn't much Littlefield could do for the old farmer. And the sheriff had a feeling that whatever was going on at the red church might have some connection to last night's murder. Because Zeb Potter most definitely had not been attacked by a mountain lion. Unless mountain lions had learned how to swing sledgehammers.

He pulled into the twin ruts that served as the church's driveway and parked by the Dodge. Lester was standing at the church door, a bale of brown-yellow hay in his gloved hands. "Howdy, Sheriff. You're getting to be a regular around these parts."

"A mite *too* regular," Littlefield said, getting out of the Trooper. He looked up at the dogwood, at the thin black branches that never died. He started to glance at the belfry, but caught himself and turned his attention back to Lester. "I guess the sale went through okay."

"Sure did. I ain't seen that many zeroes since my last report card, way back in the fourth grade." Lester drained the excess tobacco juice from his mouth.

Someone came out of the sanctuary. It was the Day woman, the mother of the boys who had found Boonie's body. A red kerchief held her hair out of her face, and her shirtsleeves were rolled halfway up. Bits of straw clung to the flannel.

"Hi, Sheriff," she said, tossing a bale of hay into the truck and starting back inside the church.

"Good morning, ma'am. How's your boy this morning?"

She looked confused at first, as if she didn't know who he was talking about. "Ronnie? Oh, he's fine. Just fine. They bounce back fast when they're that age."

Fast enough so that you can go out and leave them unattended? "Glad to hear it, ma'am. What about the little one?"

"Timmy's okay, too. He's at the house, keeping watch for me."

"Did he remember anything else about finding the body? Anything that might help us?"

She looked at Lester, then into the dark belly of the church. "I think it's best that he forget all about it, don't you?"

"Maybe so." Who or what was inside the church that

was making her so nervous? And what was she doing here in the first place? To Littlefield, the chore seemed like something more than just a case of neighbor helping neighbor.

Lester squinted up at the sun. "Excuse us, Sheriff. We got work to do."

"Sure. One thing, though. You hear anything last night?"

Lester's eyes flicked almost imperceptibly to the belfry. Almost. "No. I slept like a hibernating log. Why?"

"I thought you might have heard something. What about you, Mrs. Day?"

The woman was leaning against the door frame, biting her lip. "Heard something? What do you mean?"

"Like maybe something from over your neighbor's way? On the Potter farm?"

She shook her head. "Why, no, Sheriff."

He eased closer to the steps that led into the red church, veering clear of the dogwood. The air coming from the church was cool, even though light slanted through the windows. Lester and Linda stepped side by side as if to block his way.

"Somebody killed Zeb Potter last night." The sheriff watched for any reaction. Lester quickened the pace of his tobacco chewing. Linda Day looked in the direction of the Potter farm.

"I guess it for sure wasn't no mountain lion this time, was it?" Lester said.

"That's what my deputies say. Zeb was killed with a sledgehammer."

"Huh. They know who done it?"

"Not yet. We're trying to lift some fingerprints." But Littlefield suspected they would find no clues. No fingerprints, no footprints, no clothing fibers. And no eyewitnesses. "I was wondering if you heard the bells ring last night?"

Littlefield had learned from long experience how to tell if a person was about to lie. And Lester fit the profile. The old farmer's nostrils flared slightly with indignation, he drew in a sharp breath, his eyes shifted left and right, and he stood a little straighter. "Like I told you, I was sleeping like the dead."

The sheriff nodded. "What about you, ma'am? Or your husband?"

She was a better liar than Lester. Maybe she had done it too often. "Well, I had the radio on most of the night, at least till I fell asleep. I wouldn't have heard nothing. David was . . . asleep."

"I see. Well, I guess I better get over to Zeb's."

He started to turn, then quickly looked up at the pair, trying to catch them off guard. "You mind if I have a quick look inside the church? You know, in case the killer stopped by. I'm kind of figuring that the same person that killed Zeb killed Boonie."

Sweat glistened underneath Lester's eyes. He pulled at the straps of his coveralls. "Well, Sheriff, I don't mind a bit, but it ain't my property no more. I don't know if I can give permission like that unless you got a search warrant."

A smooth voice boomed from inside the church. "Now, now, Lester. Our church is always open."

Lester and Linda parted, standing one on each side of the door like concrete lions at a library entrance.

A man stepped into the light. He was tall, with dark curly hair and healthy, tanned skin. He had a slight touch of gray hair at the temples. His cheeks crinkled when he smiled, but his deep brown eyes were unreadable. He wore a white cotton shirt and a gray tie, slacks, and a pair of leather shoes that cost about two weeks' worth of Littlefield's salary.

"A church should turn away no one, especially a man who seeks the truth," the man said. An aroma of cologne wafted from him, but underneath the spicy musk was a disturbing smell that Littlefield couldn't place. The man stooped and extended a hand. "Sheriff Littlefield. I'm glad we have a capable man on the job in these uncertain and dangerous times."

The sheriff climbed to the landing. The preacher's hand was as cool as a fish. "Pleased to meet you, uh . . ."

"It's been a long time. Nearly a lifetime ago."

Now his face was familiar. McFall. Except he didn't have that typical McFall slump, that devious way of moving, the almost cowering attitude that ran in the McFall family as a result of being snubbed and kicked around. "I'm Archer McFall," he said, in that used-car-salesman voice of his.

"Archer. Lester told me you were moving back here." Littlefield glanced at Lester, who had suddenly become highly interested in the flaking paint of the truck's cattle bed.

"Well, Sheriff, everybody loves these mountains," Archer said. "It gets in your blood."

"And you bought this here church?"

"Yes, sir. I'm going to open it up again. God's work has been sorely neglected in these parts. People are in desperate need of the Word and the Way. That we have a murderer in our midst is only one more sign of how far we've fallen."

Littlefield nodded. He never knew how to conduct himself in the presence of a preacher. He always felt a flash of guilt for his sins and his irregular church visitations, but usually an aura of forgiving calm emanated from someone of the cloth. With Archer, though, he felt nothing but the guilt.

"Come on inside, Sheriff. Make sure there's no killer here. We can't have a devil hiding out in the house of God."

Suddenly the sheriff didn't want to step inside. In his mind, he could hear the fluttery Halloween laugh from his childhood. The boards were clapping, clawing, the church door was a mouth, he was going to be swallowed, like Jonah into the belly of the whale. Like his brother Samuel.

He swayed dizzily and felt the preacher's strong grip on his forearm. "Are you okay, Sheriff?"

"Uh . . ." Littlefield rubbed his temples. "Not getting much sleep lately. These damned—excuse me, Reverend—these doggoned murder cases must be getting to me."

"There's peace in prayer, Sheriff. You will find your killer. All things in God's good time."

Littlefield felt his feet shuffle forward, almost against his will, and then he was inside the church. Most of the hay was gone. The handmade pews that had been stacked against one wall the day before were now lined unevenly across the floor. Brooms, pitchforks, mops, and buckets were scattered across the sanctuary. The room smelled of candle wax. They had accomplished a lot this morning.

Or had they been working all night?

Behind him, Lester and Linda resumed their work. A woman emerged from the small wing at one side of the dais. Littlefield recognized her face but didn't know her name. She gave a short nod and began dusting the lectern. Littlefield thought he might sneeze, but he rubbed his nose until the urge passed.

"Looks like you'll soon be ready for a service," Littlefield said.

"There are different kinds of service, Sheriff. I work for God, you work for the people. But we're a lot alike, in a way."

"What way?"

"We both know there's more to this church than just nails and chestnut and rippled glass."

Littlefield tried again to read the man's eyes. The irises glittered like muddy diamonds with many facets, each facet hiding a different secret. Archer surely was well versed about the legends, handed down in his family for generations. Those were the sources of his childhood beatings. That he could maintain faith in God after such suffering was a miracle in itself.

"My father used to say, 'It's people what makes a church,'" Littlefield said.

Archer smiled, showing perfect white teeth. "He was a wise man."

"Aren't you afraid of what people are going to say when you open the church again?"

"God delivered Daniel from the lion's den. He delivered Isaac from Abraham's sacrificial altar. Why should I expect any less?"

"Well, for one thing, push never came to shove for Abraham, because he never had to deliver the knife blow. And Daniel didn't have a great-great-grandfather named Wendell McFall."

The preacher let out a laugh that rolled from deep inside his diaphragm. The sound echoed in the wooden hollow of the church, the acoustics amplifying the power of Archer's voice. "Ah, the scandals and the ghost stories," he said. "There's only one ghost here and that's the Holy Ghost. As for the rest of it, I hope that the legends might draw a few curiosity seekers to our services. There are many paths to the one true Way."

"Amen to that." Littlefield walked to the dais, the fall of his boots resounding in the hollow of the church. He leaned over the railing that fronted the pulpit. The stain was still there. Littlefield's dizziness returned as he tried to attach an image to the random shape.

And he saw that it was the shape of an angel, or a Bell Monster, winged and fierce, with jagged claws and . . .

Yeah, sure. Sounds like something a murderer's lawyer would make up. It's nothing but a stain, old paint or something.

It was larger than it had been the day before, yet still retained its weathered quality, as if the stain had been embedded in the floor ages ago. And Littlefield wondered if it had been even smaller before Boonie's death. As if ...

He didn't want to give legitimacy to his superstitious turn of mind. Telling Detective Sergeant Storie about the ghosts had been foolish enough. But now that the thought was trying to form, he held it outside himself, examined it rationally.

. . . as if the stain is made from the blood of its victims.

There. Now that he admitted it, it seemed safe and perfectly silly. A psychotic killer wasn't on the loose. Something worse was on the loose, somehow finding legs and hands and a pair of eyes and a soul.

A soul.

"See anything unusual, Sheriff?"

Archer's voice pulled him from a pool of dizziness. He met those brown eyes again, eyes that were now as dull and faded as the ancient woodwork of the church. Some famous person had said that eyes were the windows to the soul. Well, Archer's windows needed a good washing. Except then, you might be able to see inside.

"I don't believe you have anything to worry about," Littlefield said. "Now that you've cleaned up, there's no place for a killer to hide."

Except right out in the open.

Archer smiled, standing with his arms crossed. He was taller than the sheriff. "I never worry. I have God on my side, remember?"

"Yeah, but isn't that what the other side always says, too?"

Archer laughed again. "So they do, Sheriff. So they do."

Littlefield walked back through the church, Archer following. "I used to come to services here when I was young," the sheriff said. "Back when it was Potter's Mill Baptist Church."

"Oh, is that so? Being inside it must bring back a lot of memories."

Littlefield didn't respond. He paused in the foyer to look up at the square hole in the ceiling. "You going to get a new rope?"

"Sooner or later. And I hope none of the congregation gets a crazy notion to hang their preacher."

"God stopped Abraham's knife." Lester and the Day woman were standing in the doorway. They drew back as he went back into the sunshine. "Thanks for your time. Guess I'd better get on over to Zeb's."

As Littlefield was getting in the Trooper, Archer called to him from the steps: "Say, Sheriff. Why don't you come back sometime for a service?"

"When?"

"First one's tonight at midnight."

Midnight. It figured. Nothing could be ordinary about this church.

Maybe he *would* come to a service, Littlefield thought as he drove away. Crazy as it was, maybe he would.

The thing with wings and claws and livers for eyes clicked sharp bone against Ronnie's window. *Can you hear him aknocking?*

Ronnie was trapped by the weight of blankets, frozen in sweat, clenched around the tight fire in his belly. *Close your eyes and it will go away. Close your eyes—*

His eyes were already closed. He opened them.

The sunlight coming through the window made his head hurt. He'd been asleep for so long that he couldn't remember where he was for about a minute. Plus he'd been having really weird dreams about the red church and a walking bloody thing and something to do with Mom.

"Mom?" he called, his throat dry.

His nose wasn't as sore today, but he felt as if somebody had taken a hand pump and blown his face full of air. He licked his thick lips. "Mom?"

Tim came into the room, still wearing his pajamas. And he was eating chocolate-chip cookies. Mom was going to kill the little dork if she caught him eating cookies so early in the day. But, after the scary dreams, Ronnie was actually kind of glad to see his brother, though he'd never admit it in a million years.

"Where's Mom?" Ronnie asked.

Tim shrugged. His belly button showed below the fabric of his top. "Ain't seen her this morning."

"What time is it?" Ronnie groaned as he tried to sit up,

then fell back onto the pillows.

"Almost eleven."

"*Eleven*?" That meant that Mom was skipping church again. It was the first time she'd missed church two weeks in a row since Tim was a baby. Not that Ronnie minded, because his Sunday school teacher, Preacher Staymore, usually told him he needed to be saved, then made him wait after class while everybody else went to the main sanctuary for worship service.

Preacher Staymore would sit beside Ronnie and ask the spirit of Jesus to move into Ronnie's heart so that the child might be spared, and though Jesus loved the little children, there was only one path to salvation and that was through the blood of the Lord. And Preacher Staymore would tremble and put his palm on Ronnie's head and invoke the mercy and the power and the goodness, then ask Ronnie if he could hear the Lord aknocking. And the whole time Ronnie would be thinking about how Preacher Staymore's breath smelled like a basket of rotten fruit.

"Can you hear Him aknocking?" the preacher would say, his eyes shining and glassy. "He's awanting in. And all you got to do is say, 'Come on in, Jesus. Come right on into this sorry sinful heart of mine and clean house.' If you won't do that one little thing, then don't go crying to the Lord when the devil comes to drag you into the pits of hell."

And Ronnie would always be afraid. That message, along with the preacher's pungent breath, made him hastily agree to be saved, to let the Lord shine His everlasting light into the darkness of Ronnie's heart, to throw the door wide open and say, "Come in, come in, come in."

Getting saved always filled him with a kind of warmth, as if something really *had* come into his heart. But the feeling always faded, and he'd slip back into his sinning ways. Preacher Staymore said there were two kinds of sin: the kind of the flesh, and the kind of the spirit. Ronnie suspected that sins of the flesh had something to do with the naked women like those in Boonie's magazine, but his own sins were mostly those of the spirit. Still, any kind of sin made his heart beat faster, and maybe that drove the Lord away, what with all the noise and commotion in his chest.

So every few weeks, Preacher Staymore would sense that Ronnie needed another saving. Ronnie was scared enough of the hellfire not to take any chances, even though sometimes he wondered, if the Lord was merciful, why would He make people go to such a bad hot place? And if sinners went to hell, what was the point of Jesus dying for them in the first place? And if the Lord was all-powerful, why didn't He just make people so they didn't sin? And if He already knew what happened in people's hearts, why did there have to be a Judgment Day when all the sins were revealed?

But those kinds of thoughts were sins of the spirit, and led to a fresh need to be saved. Ronnie didn't want to think about that right now. He had enough troubles, like a broken nose and his parents separated and a scary red church and bad dreams.

"Have you seen Mom?" he asked Tim.

Tim bit a crescent of cookie and shook his head. "Not since last night," he said, spraying cookie crumbs onto the floor as he spoke.

"Dang."

"The police are out again."

Ronnie sat up. "*Here*?"

"No. They're over at Mr. Potter's."

"Mr. Potter? I guess maybe the sheriff wanted to ask him some questions."

Tim shook his head. His bowl haircut made him look like a turtle. "I don't think so. Their blue lights were flashing when they drove up. And I saw the ambulance over by the barn."

"You're fooling."

Tim's eyes widened behind his spectacles. "No, I ain't. You can go look."

Ronnie rolled himself out of bed with a groan. He leaned against the railing of the top bunk, dizzy from spending nearly two days in bed. Through the window, he could see two police cars on the Potter farm. The sheriff's vehicle was parked by the house. One of the deputies walked toward the barn, the sun glinting off his handcuffs and black shoes.

"You don't suppose . . . ?" Ronnie said.

"That whatever got Boonie Houck got Mr. Potter?" Tim sounded almost pleased at the prospect. "That would be cool. Like one of those movies Mom won't let us watch."

Ronnie remembered his dream. Maybe it was just his overactive imagination again. "Did you hear anything last night?" he asked, trying to sound like he didn't care one way or another.

"Not really. I heard some bells ringing. I don't know what time, except for it was dark."

"I hope Mom is okay." Sure, Mom would be okay. Nothing would get her.

Not even the thing with wings and claws and livers for eyes.

Ronnie thought of Preacher Staymore's words: *Can you hear Him aknocking? He's awanting in.*

No way in hell would Ronnie let *that* thing come in. He shivered in the sunlight.

✝ Chapter 9

Sunday. A holy day, at least to the Protestants and Catholics and Mormons. Fools all. But Mama Bet comforted herself with the knowledge that they'd be burned by the light in due time.

It was almost as if God had roped off a little section of the Blue Ridge and saved it for the Potters, Abshers, McFalls, and the rest. The original families came from Scotland and England, as white as the driven snow, though their hearts were as dark and Jesus-laden as any of their ancestors' hearts. And somehow those families had managed to protect this piece of valley at the foot of Buckhorn from invaders and outsiders. Kept it pure, except for the original taint that they brought with them when they settled in the 1780s.

You can't ever shake the blood.

She sat in her front porch rocker, looking out over the mountains she loved so much. Heaven ought to be this nice. A fresh spring breeze cut through a gap, working up from the foothills to stir the jack pines and locusts and poplars. The sky was clear enough for her to see the gray face of Grandfather Mountain forty miles in the distance. Even with her cataracts, she could make out the features that looked like a brow, a nose, and a long granite beard.

Her goat bleated below the porch. She kept a few chickens, too, but they were free-ranging up in the woods. She was getting too old to track down their eggs, and plucking their feathers was too rough on her fingers. Come to think of it, she didn't know why she bothered with a goat, either. She hated the taste of goat's milk, and she didn't know how to cook the animal up even if she could bear to kill it.

"What are you thinking about, Mother?" asked Archer. He sat on the porch swing, uncomfortable, his face rigid, as if holding his earthly flesh together took all his concentration. He was a fine boy, handsome and respectably clean-shaven, with the whole world laid out before him. All a mother could want for her son.

She felt a tug in her heart, or maybe it was a spell of the murmurs. The murmurs were coming on a lot more often lately. God was priming her for a trip up to the kingdom, striking her with all the little ailments that added up to the miseries of old age. God could be downright cruel when He set his mind to it. But He allowed good stuff to happen, too. Like Archer.

"I was just remembering," she said. "When you was little, you used to go up yonder on that knoll and pick gooseberries. You'd eat them things till you turned green and got sick to your stomach. And I'd lay you down in bed, tuck you in, and give you a nice cup of peppermint tea."

"And you'd tell me stories," Archer said. His voice was different from the one he'd used on television. It was softer, more down-home, a little of his Carolina mountain accent creeping in between those California words.

"Sure did. You probably don't remember any of them silly stories."

Archer leaned forward, sniffed the air. "I remember them all."

"All of them?"

"Yeah. The Old Testament. Jack tales. Ghost stories. And the real story of Jesus. Except that one always gave me nightmares."

"I hope I done right. It wasn't easy, raising you by myself. I reckon I made some mistakes along the way, but I always acted out of love."

Archer left his porch swing and knelt before her rocker. He took her hands and looked up, his brown eyes shining with that same radiant depth they'd had when he was a baby. As he grew older, those eyes got him in trouble. They made the other kids suspicious and made adults uncomfortable. Those eyes, plus the fact that he was a McFall, pretty much brought the persecution on him. Many was the time he came home from school with a black eye or a skinned knee or his little shoulders shaking with sobs.

All she could tell him was that the lamb must walk among wolves. He seemed to accept that he would be persecuted, that the human hatred was all part of God's plan. He came up with that bit about "There will come great trials" all by himself. What willpower it must have taken to keep from lashing out, what patience and understanding Archer had possessed even from an early age. Of course, he always knew that he was the Second Son. She was upfront about that right from the moment he could speak.

"You did everything perfectly," Archer said. "God should be proud."

"Well, I ain't so sure about that. If I was so all-fired perfect, maybe I'd be out of this place by now."

"Why don't you let me buy you one of those chalets at Ski Village?"

Mama Bet looked at the scar that ran up Wellborn Mountain. The steel threads of the lift cables arced along the barren slope. The snow had melted weeks ago, leaving nothing but a mud patch. She despised those ski people. "No. People best stick to their own kind. Besides, I reckon God put us here for a reason."

And that reason just MIGHT have something to do with that little hell-hole in back of the root cellar, the one I got to keep plugged with prayers. But I ain't going to worry YOU with that.

Something beeped in Archer's pocket. Mama Bet looked at him suspiciously.

He smiled. "Cellular phone. You ought to let me get you one, Mother."

"That's the devil's tool," she said, frowning. "I don't even trust words that come over wires. When it's invisible, there's no telling where the messages are coming from."

Archer pulled his phone from his jacket pocket and flipped it open. He put it to his head. "Archer McFall."

He listened for a moment, then put his hand over the mouthpiece. "Excuse me, Mother. It's the foundation offices in California."

She nodded. She'd been against his exodus to California from the start. Nothing out there but heathens and hippies and all manner of strange cults. Archer had no business among that sort.

But children had to learn on their own, didn't they? All you could do was fill them up with love, and let them wander the path. You couldn't hammer faith into the. You couldn't drive goodliness and grace into them like nails. You couldn't *make* them believe the things God wanted them to believe. They just had to search in their own hearts, and, God willing, come up with the truth.

She watched him as he carried on a conversation, something about stock splits, portfolios, and divestitures. She didn't understand why God kept Archer meddling in such affairs. But then, there was a lot she didn't understand about God. And she had to admit, that black Mercedes looked awfully shiny and clean down there in the driveway.

She rose from her rocker and headed for the door. Archer glanced at her questioningly, but she waved him back to his phone conversation. She entered the house, walking over the same boards that the McFalls had trodden for more than two hundred years. The main room was the original cabin, thick hand-hewed logs chinked with yellowed cement. Not much had changed in the room since her great-great-great-grandparents Robert and Hepzibah McFall had first blessed these walls with love and devotion.

The old stone fireplace was black from ten thousand fires. The room was dark, the small wooden windows nailed shut. Three sides of the cabin were partially underground, built that way to cut down on the wind leaking through the cracks, though the room always stayed as cold as a Christian's heart. Water was piped from a spring up the hill, and a leak dripped steadily into the freestanding ceramic sink in the corner.

A few rooms had been added onto the south side of the cabin, and these had glass windows. The sun poured through, God's pure light, but it barely touched what had once served as kitchen, bedroom, and living room combined. When electricity first reached these parts in the 1950s, Mama Bet wouldn't allow them to hook up the original part of the house. Some things were to be kept sacred, untouched by the progress that marked the spread of the devil's influence.

Mama Bet went past the rough hemlock table where Wendell McFall had once taken his meals. She parted the gingham that curtained off the pantry. She took a candle from a counter and lit it, and looked to make sure Archer was still outside. She stepped inside among the shelves and rows of canning jars, dried beans, and sacks of cornmeal. The chill from the back of the pantry crept over her like a live thing, a giant shadow, an ice-cold invisible lover.

She pushed aside the rotted boards that lined the back of the pantry. A fungal, earthy smell filled her nostrils. She extended the candle into the root cellar, peering over the rows of potatoes and red apples into the darkness. The candle shrank from the stale, still air, its light swallowed by the dirt walls of the cellar.

"I'm getting too old for this, God," she whispered in silent prayer. God said nothing, but she knew He was up there, watching, biting His tongue to keep from laughing. She wiggled the base of the candle into the red clay until it stood without her holding it. She could see the stone that blocked the narrow tunnel, a tunnel that wound down and down and deep into the earth.

This was the one secret she had spared Archer, the one that had been passed down through eight generations of McFalls. The Appalachians were the oldest mountains in the world, had risen from the hot magma when God crushed the world together. And she knew exactly why God made the earth. He had trapped the devil inside it, wrapped billions of tons of rock and dirt and molten lava around the beast. And, oh, how the devil must have kicked and struggled to get free, shoving up mountains and causing the rifts that became the oceans.

She knew this as surely as she knew that Archer was a

savior. You didn't question universal truths. You accepted them on faith. You tucked them in your heart and made the best of them. You fought for them. You made the sacrifices that kept those truths alive.

Who knew when the devil had first wormed its way finally to the surface of the world? It could have been tens of thousands of years ago, or a few hundred. All that mattered now was that the devil was loose upon the face of the earth, and Archer had to defeat it.

That had to be why Archer had returned to Whispering Pines, why God had called His son back home. The devil was still here, tied to this mouth of hell, living in those original families. The devil had hidden behind the faces of the Littlefields, worn the masks of the Houcks, slipped into the blood and meat of the Mathesons.

Archer would have to perform the cleansing. And she had to help. Even though she was as worn as these mountains, eroded by time and tides, by the forces of God's tireless punishment. Even though she was only mortal.

She crawled to the rear of the root cellar and rolled away the flat stone. In the weak light, she could see the small crippled cross that had been carved into its surface. She stuck her face near the black opening. She never understood why the path to hell was so bone-chillingly cold. It should have been blazing hot, and smelling of sulfur and brimstone and smoke instead of dirt. But God worked in mysterious ways, and the devil worked just as strangely.

She cast her prayers into the pit. She could hold back the hordes. With her faith, she could win the battle below. Let God and Archer take care of the devil up here.

Mama Bet finished her prayers, the same ones the McFalls had been saying for over two centuries. She replaced the stone, sweating with effort even though her fingers were stiff from the cold. On aching knees she backed her way to the pantry, retrieved the candle, and replaced the boards along the back wall. She wiped the dirt from her hands and cussed God for burdening her with this holy work. As if filling her up with a messiah weren't bad enough. No, He made her crawl on her belly like a serpent.

She blew out the candle and peeked through the gingham curtains. Archer was still outside. She could hear him carrying on with his business deals over the telephone, acting for all the world like an ordinary person. Well, Jesus had taken on work as a carpenter before starting up his career as a liar. Archer might as well be a rich preacher as a poor one.

She turned on the kitchen tap and stuck her hands under the frigid springwater. The dirt ran red down the drain. She put the candle away and wiped her hands on a towel. Her dress was stained at the knees, but she didn't like to change clothes in midday. That was wasteful, the kind of thing a Christian might do.

She heard voices outside. *They ain't supposed to gather here, not with Archer around. The church will be ready soon enough.*

She hurried onto the porch. Archer folded his phone and put it away. At the edge of the yard, in the shade of the trees, stood some members of the congregation: Stepford Matheson, Sonny Absher, Donna Gregg, and Rudy Buchanan. Rudy carried a shotgun and a Bible.

They started forward, Rudy's broad face split with a grin, Sonny and Stepford red-faced from drink. Donna Gregg hung back, tugging Sonny's sleeve. He brushed her away and scowled.

"What do y'all want?" Mama Bet called, shading her eyes so she could see them better. Archer stood beside her, looking down on them.

"We been thinking," said Rudy, apparently the leader of this shoddy crew.

"Well, there's a first time for everything."

Rudy's thick lips curled. Mama Bet could almost hear the gears churning rustily inside his head as he tried to think of a comeback. He soon gave up, and settled for raising the shotgun barrel until it pointed at the sky.

"We've been hearing a lot about the red church, and the day of reckoning, and all this foolishness about 'great trials,'" Rudy said. "Now all of a sudden you're telling us that Archer's the Second Son of God. And that somehow we're all part of it, because of what our kin did way back when." He looked at Stepford and Sonny.

Stepford swayed a little, and Rudy pressed the Bible against him until he regained his balance.

"Yeah," Stepford said. "You're telling us that *this*"—he pointed to Archer— "is the earthly face of God? Then God must be one hell of a practical joker, I say."

Mama Bet started to speak, but Archer raised his hand. "I don't blame you for your doubts," he said to them. "I know some of you were raised as Christians. But people use God for their own purposes, they twist His ways to benefit themselves. People build up the idols that are easy to accept. And they always destroy what they can't understand."

Sonny spat. His eyes were bloodshot and bright. "We didn't hang Wendell McFall."

"You don't think it's fair that you have to suffer for the sins of your ancestors. But blood sins require payment in blood. And sacrifice now will protect your blood unto the fourth generation."

Rudy elbowed Stepford. "Tell him."

Stepford moved reluctantly closer, until he was at the foot of the porch steps. Mama Bet's goat, which was tied to the porch rail, came over and sniffed his dirty jeans. Stepford shooed the goat away and looked up at Archer. "We decided we ain't so sure you're a messiah after all."

Rudy nodded, his courage bolstered by the shotgun. "Yeah. All we hear is fancy talk. Sure, Boonie Houck and Zeb Potter got killed. But how do we know that has anything to do with these 'great trials' we keep hearing about?"

"Getting killed sure don't take no sacrifice," Stepford said. "It ain't like they were asking to die, or anything."

Donna Gregg pressed close behind Sonny, her chest against his back.

Dirty sinners, Mama Bet thought. *It's a wonder that God and Archer don't strike them down on the spot. And Sonny married, at that. Of course, his wife took down to Raleigh after she got tired of getting beat up every time he got drunk. I can hardly wait to see them adulterers get cleansed.*

"This *is* about sacrifice," Archer said, his voice lifting now, resounding with the power of his faith. Mama Bet's heart swelled with pride.

"More big talk," Sonny said. "But we ain't seen no signs."

"Yeah," taunted Rudy. "Why don't you whip us up a miracle? Maybe break us up some loaves and fishes?"

"To hell with that," slurred Sonny. "Do something worthwhile, like changing some water into wine."

The drunken trio laughed, Donna smiling uncertainly behind them.

"True faith doesn't require proof," Archer said.

"Exactly what I'm saying," Rudy said. "I can't rightly

call my faith 'true.' It's more like it's been shoved down my throat. And I don't much like the taste of it."

Mama Bet saw that Sonny and Stepford wore similar expressions of rebellion.

The devil's in them so deep they can't even separate it out from their own selves. Can't they just accept that the time for the cleansing is here, that God's back and ready to do the job right this time?

"Archer?" Mama Bet said. Her son was holding his head in his hands, his knuckles white from the pressure of squeezing. He bowed forward, wobbling unsteadily, and nearly fell against the porch rail. Mama Bet hurried to catch him.

My poor baby.

Muffled moans of anguish came from behind his hands. His legs and shoulders quivered. She touched him, and her fingers felt electrified. Suddenly the moans turned into roars and Archer threw his arms wide.

The sky darkened as if a large cloud had passed over the sun.

Donna screamed, and Sonny joined in. Rudy dropped the shotgun and clasped the Bible to his chest. Stepford fainted dead away, his legs folding up like a wet stretch of rope and his eyes rolling up to stare at the top of his skull.

Mama Bet looked on her son with love. Archer smiled, all wings and claws and livers for eyes.

Detective Storie knelt in the hayloft of the Potter barn. The sledgehammer lay on the warped boards of the floor, its handle slick with blood, the eight-pound head clotted with grue. A few strands of gray hair clung to the shredded matter that had once been encased in the delicate shell of Zebulon Potter's skull.

The sheriff's face turned ashen as he looked at the body. "Zeb was a friend of my parents," he said, looking out the window as though the mountain slopes were a movie screen and the past were being projected onto them. "I used to help him bale hay during the summer. He even gave me a hound puppy a long time ago. So long ago that Samuel was still alive."

Storie didn't like the vacant look in the sheriff's eyes. She'd seen that look once. During a criminal transport, in her first week on the Charlotte Metro force, she had met evil, if such a thing could possibly be embodied. She'd been green then, a rookie who thought that police officers could actually make a difference simply by caring.

The middle-aged suspect in the back of the car had allegedly raped an eight-year-old girl. He bragged about it as they drove to the Mecklenburg County jail, his unshaven face broken into a satisfied grin, his eyes afire with some secret madness. Storie was riding shotgun, fuming and helpless. *Innocent until proven guilty, even if they're guilty*. That was what they taught in cop school.

"The puppy was named Roscoe," Littlefield said quietly, rubbing his scalp. "Got run over before it was barely big enough to bark."

Perry Hoyle knelt and examined the open cavity of the victim's skull. Storie took another photograph and the camera's flash glinted off Hoyle's bald head. She pulled a metal tape measure from her jacket pocket. "You mind holding that end?" she asked the sheriff.

He started as if jerked from a dream and took the end of the tape. Storie pointed to the hammer. The sheriff held the tape near the handle and Storie let the tape unwind until it stretched near the body.

"Seventeen feet," she said, though she doubted the sheriff was listening. He was so damned hard to figure out, at times friendly, at times cold and distant. But she didn't need friends, and she didn't need to waste thoughts on Frank Littlefield. She wrote the measurement in her notebook.

Long ago, the child rapist had put his face near the wire screen that separated the front seat from the rear. His breath smelled like sardines and gasoline. "Hey, good-looking, what you doing after work?" he'd said.

Storie had clenched her fists, fighting the urge to pull her nightstick from her belt and drive it into the rapist's face. But, no, he was a suspect and he had rights. No matter that he'd already pulled three years for two separate indecent liberties raps. No matter that he'd be out on the street in two years. No matter anything but that the world was absolutely, hopelessly insane. God had made a pretty good stew, then He'd screwed it up by mixing in humans and giving them free will and brains.

Brains. Zeb Potter's brains were as gray as the old oak boards that covered the barn walls.

"I can finish up here, Sheriff," she said. He nodded absently and moved to the workbench. Deputy Wade Wellborn helped Hoyle put the body on a stretcher. The body made a sticky sloughing noise as it was lifted from the pool of blood.

"Guess I'm not helping much," Littlefield said quietly. Storie didn't want to show him up in front of the others. She understood that vacant look. Because she knew it well.

She'd seen it herself, in her own eyes, in the mirror of a Charlotte Metro police car. As she was transporting a rape suspect with a familiar face and secret mad eyes. It was the same suspect she'd arrested a few months earlier. Purest evil wearing meat. This time, he'd gone for a six-year-old. The girl had died on the way to the hospital.

The rapist recognized Storie. "Hey, honey, you can lock me up, but I'll be back. One of these days, I might even get around to *your* part of town."

Storie had nearly pulled the car over and shot the creep in the head. But she did her job and took him in, handed him over to a judicial system that was fair but over-matched.

That was when Storie made two decisions: she would leave the Metro force and get a job with a rural depart-ment. And she would try her damnedest to make a small difference, even though the world was absolutely, hope-lessly insane. Even though God was insane.

Or was God, like the serial rapist, also innocent until proven guilty?

She watched Littlefield follow Hoyle, Wellborn, and the cold body of Zeb Potter down the loft stairs. Outside, a small breeze played through the trees, the sound she im-agined gave Whispering Pines its name. Somewhere out there, a killer was harboring a secret madness in his eyes. Storie didn't like secrets.

✞ Chapter 10

David Day watched from the hills as the sunset threw bands of orange over the dark lines of the horizon. The air was moist and smelled of damp leaves. Normally, being alone in the woods gave him a sense of peace. But under these trees where he had spent some of the happiest hours of his life, he felt like an intruder. Because now the forest belonged to something else.

Below him, the old Gregg farm was spread out like a wrinkled green carpet. He still thought of it as home, even though he hadn't slept there in weeks. But all the things that made the place home were still behind those white walls of the house: the boys, the bed, the maple gun cabinet, the trophy heads on the wall. Everything but her.

He hated that the boys were alone. But they were safer at the house than with Linda at the church. She would give them to Archer sooner or later, unless David could find a way to stop Archer again. But this time would be more difficult.

The red church was crouched on a little rise to his left, above the road and the curve of the river. Six or eight cars were parked by the old building. People milled around the cemetery grounds, going into and out of the church. They moved like ants on a sugar hill, heads meeting, seeming to communicate silently from that distance. One of those ants was Linda.

The police were finally finished at the Potter farm. David had seen them carrying a stretcher from the barn. From the way the deputies' backs stooped, the load must have been heavy. The sheet-draped load was marred by a dark stain. They'd slid their burden into Perry Hoyle's station wagon. Then the vehicles had driven away one by one, including the sheriff's Trooper. The cruiser driven by that woman deputy was the last to leave, about an hour ago.

Poor old Zeb. And Boonie before him. In California, the killing hadn't seemed as brutal, as casual. But David hadn't known any of those victims. Boonie and Zeb were mountain folks. These were <u>his</u> people who were dying this time, not nameless longhairs and drifters.

Archer was gathering a flock, just as he had done in California. And David had learned that there were only two kinds of people who followed Archer McFall: the dead and the about to be.

David lifted his Marlin rifle and peered into the scope, the odor of gun oil comfortingly strong. Through the magnifying lenses, he saw Lester at the church door. The crosshairs were centered on the man's beet-red face. David shifted the scope and saw Becca Faye Greene, her smile a rapture of lipstick. Another shift, and Linda's face filled the small circle of the scope.

Linda.

They'd met in the ninth grade, a Buckhorn Mountain boy and a valley farm girl. Most of the families, including the Days, who lived on the back side of Buckhorn were the descendants of Union sympathizers. Some people in these parts still held a grudge, the ones who had Rebel-flag license plates and considered summer tourists to be invaders. In seedy bars at each corner of the county, the Civil War was renewed every Friday night.

But, Day or not, Linda had let him pick her books up that time she'd dropped them in the mud getting off the school bus. She had thick books, math and social studies. All David had was an auto-repair manual and a set of plans for a wooden desk.

She had pushed her hair back with one hand and actually looked into his face. Her eyes were deep and blue and seemed to penetrate his skin so that she could see everything he kept hidden. He looked back and grinned like a sick mule. His hands felt as if they were made of wood as he wiped the books clean against his pants.

"Thanks," she said, smiling. Her teeth were only a little crooked, just enough so that David didn't feel self-conscious. He gave her the books. She walked away, her figure shifting attractively inside her knee-length dress.

He had solved the mystery of those curves, though it had taken years. But the waiting was far from a waste. David knew that she liked yellow squash better than butternut, and she hadn't laughed at his big dream of owning a saw mill. She liked Bob Seger, and David liked him a little. She cried every time they slaughtered a beef steer. He cried when each of the boys was born.

Through the scope, her blue eyes were damp and bright. But the depth had been replaced by a flat glaze, her pupils large. She was scared or excited or aroused. Or maybe all three. Just the way she had looked in California.

David swiveled the rifle barrel slightly to the right. Archer smiled into the crosshairs of the scope. The preacher was looking through the lenses at David, the magnifying process somehow reversed, David the prey and Archer the hunter. David shuddered and blinked and the illusion passed.

He couldn't hold the rifle steady. From this range, the
.30-06 round would drop only a few inches in trajectory.
The hot bullet would pierce Archer's chest, chew up his
heart, and shatter his ribs. And then what?

He pictured Linda, screaming, spattered by the gore of
her messiah. She would kneel by Archer, the other disciples crowding around as his death tremors passed and his
blood cooled. Then their wailing would lift and fill the
darkening sky, the moon would moan, the red church
would howl in anguish. Just as legend said happened the
last time one of the McFall preachers was killed. And
those buried in the cemetery would . . .

David closed his eyes and let the barrel of the gun tilt
slowly to the ground. Sweat stung his eyes, and the metallic stench of his fear overwhelmed the green smells of the
forest.

Forgive me, Lord, for I am weak.

He leaned against a cold hickory and waited for midnight.

"It'll be dark soon," Sheriff Littlefield said, turning from
the window in Storie's cramped office. Papers were piled
high on the sofa, crime reports and DARE brochures and
gun magazines. He had nowhere to sit. He couldn't be
comfortable in front of Sheila anyway, even if he were lying in a feather bed. "You coming?"

"Afraid not." She didn't look up from her cluttered
desk. "I'd better go over these reports one more time."

Littlefield sagged against the wall, the years heavy on
him, the last two days heavier still. "I guess you never
thought you'd get a serial killer here."

She looked up. "I guess you didn't, either."

She hadn't mentioned Littlefield's confession, the way he'd broken down in front of her about Samuel. Whether it was kindness or embarrassment that kept her off the subject, he hoped it would continue. "We'll be calling in the SBI."

Storie's lips tightened. "I want this bastard."

Littlefield contemplated the black sludge in the coffeepot. "No witnesses. No prints. No suspects. No motives. Probably no DNA evidence."

"Let's wait for the state lab to have a look. Or did I forget that ghosts don't have DNA?"

Littlefield slammed his fist against the wall. Storie's framed copy of a newspaper article trembled from the blow.

"Look, forget what I said about the ghosts. I wouldn't expect you to understand, anyway. You're not from around here."

Storie stood, the wheels of her chair squealing in the rush. She parodied a hillbilly accent. "'Cause I ain't mountain, I don't know nothin'. Well, Sheriff, I wouldn't believe in ghosts or boogiemen or haunted churches even if I lived in Transylvania County. I'm sorry about your brother, and I know his death must have . . . *upset* you. But this is the twenty-first century, even in the Appalachians."

They stared each other down. Littlefield finally looked away, out the small window to the lights of town below. "You do it your way. I'll solve it mine."

Storie held up some papers. "The answer's here somewhere. And we'll get the coroner's report back in a few days."

"A few days might be too late."

"You think there's going to be another one?" She sat

down, her anger deflated.

"Maybe more."

"You really *do* think the church has something to do with all this, don't you?"

"There's no such thing as coincidence."

"What's the background on this Archer McFall character? You think we should bring him in?"

Storie was interrupted by the receptionist's voice paging from the speakerphone. "Sheriff, you have a call on line two."

"Who is it?"

"The radio station. Wants to know about reports of murders in the county."

"That's all we need, getting everybody worked up," he said to Storie, then louder, to the dispatcher, "Tell them we'll have a press release going out next week. In the meantime, they can make do with the obituaries."

"Yes, Sheriff." The static was silenced.

"I'd better get to the church. It's going on midnight," he said.

Storie called to him as he reached the doorway. "Sheriff . . ."

Her face was hard, but her eyes were soft. "Sorry I lost my temper," she said.

"We all want to solve this case. And I hope I'm wrong about the church. Lord only knows how wrong I want to be."

"What kind of crazy has a church service at midnight?"

"The kind named Archer McFall."

"Well, be careful."

"I'm going to church. What's the worst that could happen?"

Littlefield was relieved that she didn't prod him for an

answer.

"I got to go," Ronnie said.

"You're crazy." Tim was still in his pajamas, watching television with the living room lights off. A half-empty bag of cookies and a bottle of Pepsi were beside him on the couch. The flickering from the screen strobed over him and made his movements jerky. Twin reflections of the on-screen action played themselves out in his glasses as well as in the false eyes of the deer heads mounted on the walls.

"You can either stay here by yourself or come with me." Ronnie's dizziness had passed, and he'd taken one of the pills that made his nose stop hurting. But the pill also made him feel as if he had pillows under his feet.

"What if Mom comes back?"

"Mom won't be back. Not until morning."

"How do you know?"

"I just know, dingle-dork."

"I'm scared."

"The moon's out and we can take a flashlight." Ronnie didn't know why he wanted to go to the red church. Especially at night. But maybe he didn't want to. Maybe something was making him go.

Like the thing with wings and claws and livers for eyes.

He swallowed invisible dry needles. Tim was looking at him, waiting. Maybe it would be better if Tim stayed here. But then the thing might get him. No, better to stick together.

Ronnie went to the closet by the front door. Tim reluctantly followed. "Better take a jacket," Ronnie said.

He rummaged in the closet for a flashlight. His heart stopped for a moment when he saw Dad's fishing pole,

leaning all thin and lonely in the corner. A pair of hip wad-
ers flopped bonelessly against the wall.

If only Dad were here . . .

But Dad wasn't here, for whatever mysterious reason
people got mad at each other. Mad enough to hate. Maybe
Jesus was paying Ronnie back for all those sins of the spirit, all those questions he asked himself that Preacher
Staymore said would lead to eternal damnation.

"The answer is Jesus," Preacher Staymore said, every
time Ronnie was getting saved and asked one of those
questions. But Jesus was the question. How could He be
the answer to His own question? But Dad said the Baptists
were the true religion, and Dad was smart enough to catch
a trout in four inches of water.

Ronnie found the flashlight and put on a jacket and they
went out the door. The driveway and the gravel road were
pale under the big moon, like white rivers in the night. But
the wooded hills rose black around them, filled with the
chatter of a million restless insects. Across the meadows,
the Potter farm was dark and still. The stars above were
far and cold with great spaces between them. Ronnie
wanted so much for there to be a Jesus behind the stars.

"I'm scared," whispered Tim.

"Shh. It's okay. I'm here."

"I want Dad."

"Me, too. But Dad's not here."

"Even Mom."

"We'll get to Mom."

"Are you scared?"

"No," Ronnie lied.

"Then why are you whispering?"

Ronnie looked off the porch into the thick shadow of
the barn, then down along the creek bank. The thing with

wings and claws and livers for eyes was nowhere around, or else was really good at hiding.

"I'm not whispering," he said aloud. He hoped Tim didn't hear the tremble in his voice. "Now come on," he said, stepping off the squeaky porch.

"Where are we going?"

"You know."

"Do we *have* to?"

"Yeah."

"How come?"

"We just have to, that's all. Remember what Dad says: 'Some things, a man's just gotta do.'" Ronnie didn't want to point out that Dad could do anything, wasn't scared of anything, and was a man, and they were only boys.

They started down the driveway, Tim huddling close and Ronnie not minding a bit. When they reached the road, Ronnie looked back at the house and its squares of yellow light. For a moment the light beckoned, promising safety and warmth and the possibility of love. But love wasn't found behind walls. It was found in Mom and Dad and Jesus.

He switched on the flashlight when they reached the road. It made an orange circle in the gray gravel. Ronnie shifted his head back and forth, studying the dark roadside weeds for any movement. The sounds of the forest were smothered by their footsteps crunching on the gravel.

"I thought you didn't like the church," Tim said.

"I don't. But we have to go anyway."

"Do you think whatever got Boonie Houck and Mr. Potter- ?"

"No," Ronnie said too quickly. "There's nothing out here now. It's . . ."

It's WHAT? Eaten its fill and flown home to the belfry?

"We'll be okay," Ronnie said.

"Do you think it was the thing that lives in the church steeple?"

"What thing?"

"You know. What Whizzer says. The thing with wings and claws and livers for eyes."

"Whizzer's a dork."

They went around a bend and were out of sight of the house. Ronnie couldn't smell the river, but he could feel its fishy dampness on his face. They passed the last of Zeb Potter's pasture. The barbed-wire fence ran into the forest, and the trees pressed close on both sides of the road. The moon sliced through a narrow gap between the treetops.

"How come Mom's at the church so late at night?" Tim asked. There was a note of complaint in his voice.

"What am I, Einstein or something? And do you have to ask so many stupid questions?"

"Talking makes me not as scared."

They walked faster now, the exertion driving away the moist chill of the spring night. They hit an incline and slowed. One side of the road sloped away into blackness. The river rushed over rocks below, the water gurgling liked a choking victim trying to breathe.

They rounded another turn, and the red church stood on a hill, black under the moonlight. The moon glinted off the windshields of cars that were huddled around the church. Behind the cars, the pale slabs of tombstones stood like soldiers. The dogwood was all black bones and sharp fingers and reaching hands of wood.

The church's front door was open, a gray rectangle against the darkness of the church structure. Yellow light flickered from the church windows, tiny pinpricks that would flash and then disappear. *Candles*, Ronnie thought.

The church had never been wired for electricity.

Singing drifted from the church, a choir of several dozen voices. The music was nothing like the songs they sang at First Baptist. This singing was hollow and creepy, as if half the people were singing off-key on purpose. But if they were singing about Jesus and God's love and mercy and salvation, that would make the music not so creepy. Ronnie listened but couldn't make out the words.

"That song is creepy," Tim said.

"Shh." Ronnie grabbed the sleeve of Tim's jacket and led him toward the edge of the woods where the nearest cars were parked. He wanted to be as far away from the dark wall of forest as possible, but he also was reluctant to approach the graveyard. He pulled Tim down to the ground and they crawled between the cars until they could see into the church. The singing stopped.

"Do you see Mom?" Tim whispered. Ronnie elbowed him in the ribs.

A man's voice resonated inside the church and spilled into the night.

"My fellow worshipers," the voice rang out. During the pause, someone coughed. The voice continued. "We are gathered here tonight to honor the one true God. For He is a jealous God, and many are the lies that fall on our ears. Many are the promises made to us by those who wear faces of evil. Many are the paths that lead from the true Way."

Ronnie peeked over the hood of the vehicle they had hidden behind. The engine was still warm. He saw the rounded light on the dashboard. It was the sheriff's Trooper.

Ronnie felt a little better. Nothing bad could happen if the sheriff was here. Ronnie knew that the cops on the TV shows were all fake, but the sheriff had seemed like a nice guy when he'd asked Ronnie about finding Boonie. So if both the sheriff and Mom were here . . .

". . . and the First Son was a carpenter," came the voice. "The First Son went among the people, among the sick and the outcast and the poor. The First Son taught of love and peace and salvation."

Salvation. So the man was a regular preacher after all. Though he spoke more like an actor than any of the preachers Ronnie had ever heard, the man's voice made Ronnie less afraid.

"And God called the First Son back to heaven, letting Him die on the cross so that we might find grace," the preacher said, his voice rising. "But God always promised that the Son would return. And the Son has returned. The Son walks among us. But it's not the First Son that God has sent. God gave Jesus a chance to save the world, and Jesus failed. Jesus with his false miracles and lies. So now the job goes to the Second Son."

"Second Son," murmured a few in the audience.

Second Son. That didn't sound like something a Baptist preacher would say. But now that he thought about it, it kind of made sense. Why should Jesus be an only child, when God could make as many offspring as He wanted? Jesus certainly hadn't made the world a perfect and sinless place.

And the red church wasn't as scary anymore. In fact, Ronnie felt a kind of warmth radiating from the structure. How silly and dumb and third-grade he had been, thinking the church was a bad place. The church was a *good* place.

The preacher increased his cadence. "The Second Son spares no one from His love. This one needs no money, asks for no servitude, demands no tribute. The Son has found the path, and it leads through people's hearts. The Son wants to take us all home. But every journey begins with a single step. Tonight, in this house of the Lord, let us begin."

"Let us begin," echoed twenty voices.

"Let us begin," Ronnie whispered.

"Why are you saying that?" Tim said, still crouched behind the Trooper.

"Didn't you hear?"

"Hear *what?*"

"The Second Son."

"What about it?"

Tim wouldn't understand. All he cared about was cartoons and comic books and miniature action figures and sweets. Preacher Staymore hadn't made Tim get saved yet. Tim didn't know the warm feeling of something moving into your heart. And this warmth- spreading from this preacher's voice straight into Ronnie's blood- was better than anything Ronnie had ever known. This time he was saved for real.

Ronnie felt light, as if made of cotton candy. Even his broken nose, which had been throbbing with every beat of his heart, was forgotten in the rush of purest love. And love was what was between the preacher's words, love was what filled the wooden cavity of the church, love was what emanated like a welcoming fog from the red church and crept out across the hills of Whispering Pines. Love was more numbing than the pain pills.

"Let's go in," Ronnie said.

"Are you crazy?"

"It needs us." Ronnie started around the front of the Trooper. Tim grabbed his shirt from behind and pulled him backward. They fell on the ground, and Tim's flailing hand struck Ronnie's nose. Pain flashed behind Ronnie's eyes in streaks of bright purple and electric lime green. He yelped in agony.

"You dork." He grunted at Tim between clenched teeth. He pushed Tim away and rolled to his knees. He put a hand to his nose and felt something warm and wet.

The people inside the church had started singing again, but Ronnie scarcely heard it. He shivered and realized the night was chilly. The warmth of love had left him, as if he'd been asleep and someone had yanked the winter quilts off his body. An empty ache filled his chest. Something had been taken, and he couldn't remember what it was.

"You ain't going in there," Tim said, his eyes wide behind his glasses. The moon gave Tim's eyes a feral, eager quality.

"Now why in the heck would I want to go in there?"

"You just had a funny look in your eye."

"Shh. Listen—"

The singing stopped. A silence settled over the mountains. The wind waited in the tops of the trees. Not an insect stirred. Even the river seemed to pause in its twisting bed.

Then, a soft sound.

A scratching, fluttering sound.

Not inside the church.

Above.

In the steeple.

A shadow moved, a lesser gray against the church bell.

"Holy crud." Tim gasped.

Ronnie swallowed hard, and some of the blood from his nosebleed snaked down his throat.

It smells the blood. The thing with wings and claws and livers for eyes . . .

"Run!" he shouted at Tim, but his little brother was already a step ahead of him. They dashed between the cars and hit the gravel road, rocks flying as they scampered away from the red church. They were exposed, vulnerable in the open, but Ronnie didn't dare head into the forest. The pounding in Ronnie's ears almost sounded like laughter, but he didn't stop to listen.

Instead he ran into the night, hunching his shoulders against the monster that swept down from the blackness.

✞ Chapter 11

Ronnie ducked low, sensing the cold shadow sweeping down over him and blocking out the moon. Ahead, Tim stumbled in the gravel and veered toward the ditch that ran along the edge of the road. Tim looked back at his older brother, his mouth a round well of fear. Ronnie saw a fluttering shape reflected in Tim's glasses.

Then Tim hurdled the ditch and headed into the trees.

No, no, no, NOT the forest, Ronnie silently screamed.

But Tim was already out of sight, lost amid thrashing branches. Ronnie followed, sizing up the dark gaps between the trees, each like a door to nowhere. Something brushed his shoulder, and he bit back a shout. His body was electrified, sweat thick around his ankles and armpits and trickling down the ladder of his spine.

The monster is going to get me.

Ronnie thought of Boonie Houck, eyeless and mutilated and groping for a handhold to drag himself back to the ordinary, sane world.

Going to get me get me get me.

He held his breath and jumped the black ditch. A pine branch whacked him across the face, and he yelped in pain, then fell to his knees. Blood was flowing steadily from his nose. It made a warm rope down his chin.

Tree limbs snapped above and behind him in the dark.
The trees had arms, would hug him and hold him. The
trees were part of the nightmare.

He scrambled to his feet, throwing damp leaves and dirt
as he regained his balance. He ran ten steps, twenty steps,
blind, his arm raised over his face to fend off the branches.
His heart spasmed like a trapped animal in his chest.

Ronnie didn't know where the road was, and couldn't
hear Tim above the noise of his own passing. He dodged
between the trees, unaware of his feet.

Run, dingle-dork.

*Maybe if the Bell Monster follows me, you can get
away. If the thing's not too hungry, maybe one boy will be
enough for it.*

Shards of moonlight cut into the forest canopy in places, creating a mad strobe as he ran from darkness to light,
darkness to light. Then all was dark as he moved under the
thicker canopy of old oak and hickory, and the branches
were higher, no longer beating at his sides.

He was going downhill now, skidding in the mud. He
stepped on a flat rock and fell on his rear, sliding and then
rolling back to his feet.

A damp chill overlaid his sweat, and he knew he was
near the river. Though his nose was blocked, he carried
the river's fishy and muddy smell in his memory. The rushing water roared faintly in his ears.

Follow me, but not TOO close, Ronnie silently willed
the Bell Monster.

The trees opened and he reached the river. Moonlight
glinted off the black water. The froth of waterfalls spar-
kled like ten million eyes. The air was colder here, fresh
and heavy in Ronnie's gasping lungs. The earth vibrated
under his feet as he dodged among the gray rocks along

the riverbank.

He huddled in a gap between two boulders, peering back up the slope. The tops of the trees moved, all big black creatures, live things, hostile and bristling and in league with the Bell Monster.

Ronnie didn't know how long he had been running, but it felt like years. He breathed with his mouth open, his throat sore. His nose had stopped bleeding. He wiped his chin with his hand.

If the thing smells blood . . .

Ronnie crawled along the rocks until he reached the water. He stuck his hand in the current and a frigid shock ran up his arm. But he cupped his palm and brought the water to his face, wiping, then repeating the process until he thought his face was clean.

The front of his jacket was wet. He drew himself into a ball and waited for the Bell Monster to find him.

Waited.

Waited.

The river roared on, sweeping down below him past the red church and under the bridge into the valley.

A few thin clouds drifted across the sky, made silver-gray by the moonlight.

Did Tim make it? Or did the Bell Monster lose track of me and go after him?

Ronnie suddenly felt ashamed, remembering how he ran away when they'd found Boonie Houck. He'd left Tim behind to face the red, raw horror alone. And now he was abandoning him again.

Big brothers were supposed to take care of little brothers. Even if little brothers were dorks.

Dad was gone, and Mom was at that weird meeting in the red church. Tim had nobody to help him. Except Ronnie.

"Danged rocks are getting cold anyway," he whispered to himself. He stood on trembling legs, his bones aching and stiff. The trees around him were still, their leaves wet and heavy.

He eased his way from behind the boulders, his back to the river. If he went upstream he would eventually come to Buckhorn Mountain, where a series of creeks ran together. If he went downstream he'd reach the bridge near the red church. If he went back into the woods, he would have to climb a hill to see where he was.

The river wasn't too deep to cross, only waist-high in most places, but he was already nearly frozen. Besides, Tim wouldn't dare cross the river. Tim had fallen into it once, and had been scared of deep water ever since.

Ronnie hunched low and headed back the way he thought he had come. His nose was not hurting much but, like the river, pulsed steadily under the bandages. He moved quietly through the trees, the way he did when he was playing Indian scout. He kept his palms up to push the branches from his face.

Once away from the river, he found an old hunting trail. A little moonlight splashed along the clearing, and he paused to listen for Tim. The Bell Monster probably hadn't found Tim yet, or screams would be shattering the night silence.

Ronnie gulped at that thought. What if the thing had gotten Tim while Ronnie was cowering by the water? What if the Bell Monster had come aknocking on Tim's rib cage? What if the thing with wings and claws and livers for eyes was even now scooping out Tim's guts and having a late-night snack?

No. Think happy thoughts.

When you have one of those waking nightmares, when you think bad things in the dark and can't go to sleep, you think happy thoughts. Cartoon dogs, fat clowns, things like that. Except sometimes the cartoon dogs bite and the fat clowns grow sharp smiles.

Happy thoughts.

Ronnie kept walking, using those words as a mantra, falling into their rhythm.

Think happy thoughts, think happy thoughts, think happy thoughts . . .

He tried to picture those stupid yellow smiley faces, but the faces kept turning into Preacher Staymore from Sunday School, lips pursed and asking, *Can you hear Him aknocking?*

Ronnie staggered on, tripping over roots and stones, mentally clinging to his happy-thoughts mantra.

He was nearly on his hundredth repetition when he first heard the twigs snapping.

He froze.

Whatever had been following him rustled some low bushes to his left.

A whisper of wings.

A soft clicking, like that of claws meeting in anticipation.

A wet flutter, like that made by liverish eyes opening and closing.

Ronnie's limbs turned wooden, his feet grew roots, he was part of the dark soil he would die on. As the bushes exploded with movement, Ronnie's last thought was that maybe Tim got away.

And then the monster had him, in a fury of tooth and wing and razor hatred.

The monster had smelled his blood in the dark.

The monster embraced him, eager and sharp-fingered.
The monster—
Ronnie kicked and screamed, flailing his elbows. He pressed his eyes closed, not wanting to watch the thing open his insides and pull out his dripping wet heart.

Ronnie balled his fists.

The creature growled in his ear.

"Ronnie, it's *me*."

Dad?

Yes, it was. Ronnie imagined Dad's smell, all aftershave and sawdust and boot leather.

He relaxed in his dad's strong arms, finally opening his eyes. Dad's face was pale in the weak wash of moonlight.

"The . . . the thing," Ronnie said, fighting back tears.

"Shh," Dad said. "It's okay now. Nothing's going to get you."

Ronnie shivered against his Dad, burrowing close for warmth. Ronnie was relieved to note that Dad had a gun with him. He suddenly pushed away. "Tim. Where's Tim?"

"Right here." Tim came out from the shadow of the trees.

"Did you see it?"

Tim's glasses flashed as he nodded.

"What *is* it, Dad?" Ronnie asked.

"I'll tell you later. Right now, let's get to the house." Dad put an arm around each boy and led them up the hill.

"Is Mom going to be okay?"

"I hope so, son. I hope so."

They walked past midnight and into safety.

Midnight.

Linda was lifted by invisible loving arms. The singing,

the sermon, the pure love of her fellow worshippers, all flowed through her like the charged juice of her blood. Every cell of her body glowed in the warmth of Archer's glory. Her mouth was flooded with the sweetness of the communion they had taken.

She felt as if she had returned from a long sleep. But it had been a long sleep, years and years and years of religious tyranny, licking at the pierced feet of David's foolish Jesus. But now Archer was back, and everything would be the way it was before.

She would belong again.

She looked to her right, to the owner of the hand she was holding. Sheriff Littlefield. Of course. The Littlefields were one of the old families. They, like the Greggs, Mathesons, Potters, and others, had attended the church back in Wendell McFall's day. Now the families were reuniting, answering a call that was deeper than flesh and blood.

Archer McFall leaned over the lectern, spent from his rampaging sermon. His eyelids fluttered and the muscles in his shoulders twitched. He lifted his head and smiled. The sweat on his face glistened in the candlelight. He reached out with a trembling hand and caressed the broken wooden cross that jutted from the top of the lectern.

"He has found us worthy," Archer said, in a drained voice that had none of its earlier thunder.

"Amen," echoed the parishioners.

Linda turned from her front-row pew and looked at the others. Lester Matheson smiled at her, his teeth yellow. His wife Vivian swayed as if in rhythm to an inaudible hymn, her eyes closed. Old Mamie Pickett was beside Vivian, her wrinkled and spotted hands folded carefully across the waist of her blouse.

Nell and Haywood Absher sat erect in the back row,

Nell in her blue hat with the diaphanous netting. Their daughter Noreen wore a blissful, vacant expression. Others filled the church, their eyes bright with joy. Mama Bet sat in the last row, her wrinkled mouth pressed in solemn joy.

Abshers. Mathesons. Greggs. Picketts. McFalls. Only one family was missing. No, two. The Potters and the Houcks.

The sheriff had said that old man Potter had died. And Boonie Houck had lost his sinful eyes and tongue and penis. Linda couldn't mourn their loss. They had found their own path to the everlasting glory that Archer spoke of. They had paid in blood so that the other families might live unto the fourth generation.

Nobody gets anything without a little sacrifice. Archer needed them. He just sent them home ahead of the rest of us, that's all.

Archer lifted his head, his brown eyes as intense as truck headlights. Linda quit thinking. He was about to speak.

"We have done God's work," Archer said, swiveling his head to indicate the refurbished interior of the church.

"We done Him proud," Lester shouted.

"Amen," Vivian said, not opening her eyes. A clamor of approval spread across the room. Linda glanced at the black world outside the windows, momentarily sorry for all the blind, misguided fools who had been led astray by that devil, Jesus. Even her very own sons had fallen for the devil's tricks.

Her eyes welled and spilled over.

I'll bring them. They should know of the true path before it's too late.

She looked back at Archer, so grateful for his rescuing

her from the flames of Christianity. She slid from her hard
pew and knelt on the floorboards, bowing to Archer. Her
heart was a tortured mix of love and regret. She had found
Archer, then had lost him, and now she had found him
again.

*Archer says that the truth will always win out. Faith
will beat Satan and Jesus both.*

She bent lower, her head near the floor she had spent
hours cleaning.

Faith is sacrifice. And sacrifice is the currency of God.

She kissed the floor, tasted the red church. And she
knew—*knew*—that Archer would need her children.

Ronnie and Tim.

But what were their sins?

A voice came to her, unbidden: *They don't pay for their
own sins. They pay for YOURS, Linda.*

She looked up from where she was kneeling on the
floor. Archer smiled at her, eyes moist and arms spread in
supplication.

*Remember Abraham from the Old Testament? When
God asked him to kill his beloved son Isaac? Do you think
Isaac was the one who had sins to pay for? Of course not.
Abraham was the one who needed to suffer a little, who
needed to prove his faith.*

Around her, the parishioners stood and began to file
out, talking quietly among themselves. Their words were
joyless now, muted, as if the gathered had given all their
emotions to the walls of the church. Outside they went,
shuffling sacks of skin and fluid and organs, while within,
the wood seemed vibrant, soaked with light and energy
and the ghosts of prayers.

Archer stepped off the dais and came to Linda. He offered her his hands. For a moment she thought she saw

stigmata, tiny red pocks in the white palms. *The mark of Jesus.* She recoiled in horror even as the image faded.

"What's wrong, my child?" Archer said. He was the Archer of old, aged and ageless, wise and innocent, his eyes sparkling with love and hate.

"I—I'm . . ." she stammered, looking back down to the floor. She couldn't meet his eyes, couldn't stare into the hot hells inside them, couldn't bear his gracious cruelty. Because she knew she would see the threat in them, the hunger, the need for her children.

But then, Archer was a divine incarnation, the flesh of God, sent among the mortals with a mission to perform. What were her needs next to the needs of Archer?

She felt Archer's strong arms pulling her to her feet.

"Do you doubt?" he asked simply. There was no anger in his voice, no accusation.

Linda shook her head. She could hear the others talking outside, seemingly revived by the fresh spring night. A few cars started and drove away with a crunch of gravel.

Archer cupped her chin and tilted her head up until their eyes met. "You're as lovely as you were in California."

Linda thought for a moment that he was going to kiss her. *If only . . .*

But she was mortal and he was the Second Son. He didn't need love the way that others did, the way that David did. For Archer, love was a fuel, a human juice that would propel the world to heaven. Love wasn't for the soul, not a contract between two people in defiance of death; no, to Archer, love was for the *Soul*, the collective, the glory. Not an ounce of it could be spared on carnal yearnings.

Oh, she had loved him. Archer with his long hair and

his Volkswagen bus with peace signs painted on the rear and sides. Archer who could never fit into the small-town mountain life. Archer who had dreams, who saw visions, who accepted the taunts and jeers with equanimity.

It was just after her high school graduation, when she and David had been busy planning their marriage and their careers and their future together. And that was when Linda first recognized the glass walls that surrounded her, that would forever keep her caged in the mountains. Oh, she could leave, she could go to Charlotte or the Outer Banks, but only for days at a time. Her life was here, as bound to the mountains as the granite foundations of the earth were. That long-ago summer, she had carried the certainty of it like a lump in her throat.

She was waiting tables at the Mountaineer Diner when Archer came in. She'd noticed Archer in high school, but he kept to himself, carrying at times a Bible or thick books that weren't required reading. That in itself was enough to mark him as an outcast. But coupled with the fact that he was the great-great-grandson of the Hung Preacher, he might as well have had a sign that read *Kick Me* stuck to the back of his shirt.

He sat in a corner booth that day, under the fake antique Pepsi-Cola sign. Linda looked around, hoping Sue Ann, the other waitress on duty, would take the "weird one." But Sue Ann was leaning over the counter, showing her cleavage to some red-eyed trucker. So Linda pulled out her order pad and walked over to the booth.

"What do you want?" she said, sizing him up as a lousy tipper in addition to being a long-haired creep. He fumbled with the menu and scraped a bit of gravy away with his thumb.

"Coffee," he said.

"That all?" She was irritated by the way he watched her, as if she were a piece of chocolate cake.

He nodded. She turned to hurry back to the kitchen.

"Your name's Linda, isn't it?" he said.

Maybe he would tip after all. "Yeah," she said, giving him her two-dollar smile.

"My name's Archer."

"I know. You go to Pickett High, don't you?"

"Did. I graduated."

Linda didn't remember him from the ceremony. Of course, she and David had hit a little Jim Beam before crossing the stage. Suddenly she felt guilty, as if his stare saw through her, into her. Then she was angry at herself for feeling guilty. Who cared what some longhaired bum thought?

His eyes were brown, vibrant yet distant. She felt dizzy looking into them.

"Uh . . . coffee, coming right up."

She brought the coffee but he didn't drink it. "The body is a temple," he said. "And sacrifice is the currency of God. For He is a jealous God, and He punishes children for the iniquity of the parents."

What a weirdo, she thought, but within fifteen minutes she was taking a break and sitting across from him in the booth, on the edge of the cheap vinyl seat. He talked matter-of-factly, and damned if he didn't know just what he was talking about.

"You're tired of this place," Archer said. "You're tired of these people and all this arguing over whether Chevy is better than Ford and what caliber bullet takes down a deer the fastest. You're about to be married, your union blessed by God, and you think that this is your dream come true, that it's happily-ever-after from now on. But scratch the surface" —he leaned forward as he said this, their faces only a foot apart— "and you find that you're scared to death that this is *it*, this is all there is to life."

She tried to protest, tried not to show that he had completely peeled back the layers of her soul like an onion. But she was already enthralled, already hooked, already mesmerized by the cadences of his speech. And by the time Sue Ann was calling Linda to get back to work, she had agreed to meet Archer for dinner.

She had to lie to David, but sinning was much easier back then. She and Archer ate at the Chick'n Shack over the line in Tennessee. She didn't resist when Archer took her out behind the old red church after dinner. They rode back through town in his van, her with her head down, hoping no one would see her. At the same time, she was thinking that this was it, she was going to do it, she was going to cheat on David and damn the consequences. It was time to finally get around to the business of taking chances.

But Archer only wanted to talk. She thought at first it was just another come-on line. He wasn't really her type. She was no longer sure just what *was* her type, even though she had always thought it was David. So they sat in the dark and Archer talked, and even though she was aching with lust and the fire of her flesh would lead her to the fires of hell, she somehow couldn't get up the courage to touch him.

Archer talked of strange things. He made her look at the stars. He pointed to the church bell and the dogwood and told the story of the Hung Preacher. Linda thought at first he was trying to spook her so that she would slide close and he could put his arm around her. But he told the story wrong.

In Archer's version, the Hung Preacher was a victim of persecution. "It was all a conspiracy of Jesus," he said. His eyes seemed to gather the scraps of stray light and glistened like oil. "Jesus got in the heads of all those people and made them kill my great-great-grandfather. And Jesus had to pay nothing for his own sins. Because God loved Jesus more than He loves the entire world."

Linda knew she should be getting the hell out of the van, that he was insane, but he spoke so reasonably and kept his voice level. So she listened to the rest of it, how Jesus hated the McFalls because they would bring forth the holy child. And that child would rise up and reveal Jesus for the fallen angel that he was. By morning, when the first timid rays of the sun peeked over the hills, she was more than in love; she was devoted.

She went through that summer with a bounce in her step, seeing David throughout the week but saving every Sunday night for Archer and his private sermons. When she found out that Archer had others, like Mandy Potter and Esther Matheson, she got jealous. But Archer explained how each had a part in the Divine Plan and that Linda would always hold a special place in his heart.

They moved to California at the end of the summer. Linda wrote a good-bye letter to David, three pages. At the end, she'd written, *I hope you understand, but there's a larger mission that I must attend to. I love you.* Archer helped her write that last bit, and she cried until Archer made her stop.

They headed west in the van, Archer driving, the seven girls taking turns sleeping, singing silly songs by the Eagles and the Beach Boys, at least until Archer pointed out the sinful subtexts in the lyrics. Then they passed the time wondering aloud what California would be like.

"What are we going to do out there?" Linda asked from the front passenger seat. They were halfway across Tennessee, and the hills were rounded and green. Archer was hunched over the steering wheel, wearing a faint peaceful smile.

"Get delivered," he had said.

Now, with his face only inches from hers, Linda wanted so very much for Archer to deliver her once and for all.

✝ Chapter 12

Sheriff Littlefield looked around the churchyard at the trees. The moon bathed the open hill with light, and the tombstones were like silver sentinels, mute and mocking. Littlefield took a deep breath of the chilly air, trying to clear his head. His tongue was fouled with a sweetly putrid aftertaste. He felt as if he had just walked out of the long tunnel of a dream.

He had come to the church to see if he could learn more about Archer McFall. His plan had been to keep a polite smile on his face and sit quietly through the service. He would shake hands if necessary and bow in prayer at the right time. But his eyes would always be slightly open.

His plan had failed. The green digital display on his watch read 1:57. Somehow he had lost nearly two hours. He leaned against the front of the Trooper and tried to remember what had brought him to the red church.

The others had gone already, shaking hands with each other and saying "God bless," and driving back to their dark farmhouses. Linda Day and the preacher were inside the church. He could hear them talking.

The sheriff was hit by a sudden wave of nausea that almost drove him to his knees. The candlelight dancing from the open church door blurred in his vision. The huge, twisted dogwood swayed, as if moving to invisible music. His head roared with the first soul-ripping toll of the church bell.

He covered his ears and looked up at the bell tower, his mind scattered by the noise.

No rope. It CAN'T be ringing.

The dull cast iron of the bell glinted under the moon. As the note pealed through Littlefield, vibrating every nerve ending in his body, he fought to keep his eyelids from snapping shut in agony. The bell hadn't moved an inch.

Archer was at the mouth of the church now, arms spread to the sky. The preacher was a dark shape shimmering in Littlefield's tears. Behind Archer, Linda was bowed in reverence or else hunched in an agony that echoed Littlefield's own.

With the second toll of the bell, Littlefield knew the deep resonance had driven him insane. Because the night *walked.*

A shape fluttered from the forest and settled in the belfry, a ragged black thing, an insult to the swimming beauty of the stars. The red church took on a glow, as if consumed with bright fire. A rope dangled from a strong, high limb of the dogwood. Pulling the rope taut was a body, full and heavy and limp.

It's HIM.

The thought came to Littlefield along with a flood of other broken thoughts and images. The cemetery ground buckled and swelled, and the turf beneath the headstones rippled like boiling water. Archer grew in Littlefield's vision—*grew*—until he filled the church door, and the edges of Archer's body sharpened. The nearby trees leaned forward as if to ogle the unreal spectacle before them.

Littlefield surrendered to gravity and fell to his hands and knees. With effort, he lifted his head, transfixed by the still form of the Hung Preacher shimmering twenty feet away. The man's face was waxen, and the skin reminded Littlefield of the way Freeman Harper had looked after floating dead in the river for two weeks. The tongue protruded like a blacksnake's head. The eyes bulged, maniacally gleaming as if lit by strange suns.

The Hung Preacher wore a vested suit of ill-cut cotton that draped about the body like burlap, the ivory buttons resembling teeth. The dull leather square-toed shoes dangled inches above the ground. A leaf stirred between the feet, and Littlefield watched the leaf's shadow skip across the grass on the breeze. He visually traced the shadow of the tree, thrown long across the hill by the candlelit church. But the Hung Preacher cast no shadow.

Littlefield stared the illusion full in the face. But he knew the Hung Preacher was no illusion. He had almost been able to convince himself that the first time had been a trick of the mind, the night that Samuel died. Now here was the ghost again, dangling like a slip of lost light, back to prove that the long-ago Halloween was as horrible as Littlefield remembered.

But in some small part of himself, he knew that such things were impossible, irrational. *Dead people don't come back.* Samuel had died, and was as dead or deader now than he had ever been. This hideous vision hanging before him had no right to be here. Dead people belonged in the dirt.

He focused on the Hung Preacher's bloated, wan face.

See? It can't be real. You've let it build up in your mind, giving shape to your guilt over Samuel. You've just heard too many stories, that's all.

And the stories are wrong. Because in the stories, right after the Hung Preacher comes back, the congregation gathers around him—

The bell rang a third time, louder and more jarring than before, and the Hung Preacher blinked and smiled.

The black tongue flitted back inside the swollen head. The dead arms trembled and raised as if testing the gravity of a new reality. The Hung Preacher parted his blood-engorged lips and laughed. It was the Halloween laugh, the terrible and unforgettable sound from Littlefield's childhood. All the fear came flooding back, all the memories, only this time he couldn't run away.

Around and behind Littlefield, the cemetery came alive.

His screams sheared the damp silence of the night.

"Do you smell that?" Tim said.

David Day *did* smell it. He knew the smell intimately. He was a hunter. Death had its own essence, a thick, heady quality that went beyond the olfactory sense. Death seeped inside of you like a mist.

"Smell what?" Ronnie said, his voice nasally because of his bandages. David looked down at the wide eyes of his oldest son. Ronnie was lucky that he couldn't smell. The coppery odor of blood and a sickly-sweet aroma of decay mixed in the night air, tinged with an underlying pungency.

David looked down the gravel road, then back to the woods. He didn't know what was safer, being out in the open stretch of moonlit road or sneaking through the dark forest. Their house was still half a mile away, and the only nearby houses, those of the Potters and the Mathesons, were dark. He gripped the gun more tightly. The weapon probably wouldn't do any good, but it made him feel better.

Tim kept trying to run ahead of their little group. He didn't seem scared anymore, just excited, as if he had sneaked out past bedtime to play some silly chasing game. David tried to keep his fear to himself, but Ronnie was smart. Ronnie knew that something bad had come to Whispering Pines.

"Hey, looky," Tim said, pulling his hand from David's. He pointed into the tall grass along the side of the road ahead. "There's somebody."

It could just as easily have been a sack of grain or a pile of rags, except for the pale hand that extended from the weeds onto the roadbed. Even in the dimness, there was no mistaking the fact that it was a human hand, its fingers curled upward in motionless begging. The hand was slender, feminine.

"Stay here," David whispered, taking a quick look around. The breeze that had steadily risen and fallen was now in a lull. The stillness was almost more unbearable than the flapping of leaves and the groaning of trees bending in the wind. He crept toward the body, his rifle tilted in front of him.

David fought back the vomit that tried to leap from his stomach. He recognized the woman's blouse. He thought at first that her blouse was unbuttoned and that she was wearing a dark, rumpled shirt underneath. But now he realized that her chest was open, not her blouse, and that someone or something had parted her rib cage. Blood pooled in the cavity, a slight steam rising toward the moon.

Her heart was gone.

David glanced at the woman's face. Her eyes were open, her mouth gaping in an endless, voiceless scream. It was Donna. Linda's cousin.

Linda had given Donna the blouse for Christmas two years ago. David hadn't liked Donna because he always got the sense that she didn't approve of Linda's marrying a redneck. But nobody deserved to die like this, to be ripped open like a cow at the slaughterhouse. Horror and sorrow and fear welled up in David's chest, fought each other for space, and then settled into a miserable mixture.

"What is it, Daddy?" Ronnie called.

"Somebody . . ." He fought to keep his voice calm. "Somebody had an accident."

"Are they dead?" Tim asked.

David knelt in the grass and looked at the boys waiting thirty feet behind him. They would have to walk past the body, and he didn't want them to know that it was Donna. He settled his fingers on her eyelids and pulled them closed, the way he had seen soldier buddies do in war movies. He tried to nudge her mouth closed, but her jaw muscles had locked in an everlasting scream.

He pulled the blouse closed across her wound, careful not to get blood on his hands. He took off his deerskin jacket, even though the night was chilly. Then he whispered a quick prayer.

"Dear Lord, I know she took You into her heart. And I know she was messing around at that awful church. But please don't hold that against her. The devil spins a mighty good yarn, and I don't think it's fair if she got tricked off the path of salvation. Judge her by the way she was *before* Archer got ahold of her. So if it be Thy will, please take her away from him and bring her up into the heavenly fold where she rightly belongs. Amen."

David looked into the woman's face. Death was supposed to be peaceful. But there was no peace in those rigid features. Worst of all, the thin nose and the sharp cheekbones and the rounded eyebrows were Gregg family characteristics. Exactly the same as Linda's. He laid the jacket across Donna's face.

"Are they dead?" Tim repeated, coming forward despite David's order to stay put. Ronnie followed, hesitantly.

"Looks like it, son," David said, standing. "We'd best get home and call the sheriff."

"The sheriff?" Ronnie said. "We saw his truck back at the church."

Tim tried to peer at the body. David put his arm around Tim and led him to the far side of the road. "Come on. Let's get home."

They walked in silence past the forest and into the open stretch of pasture and fields. The Potter farm sprawled dark and empty at the foot of the mountains. The farmhouse and barns were like tiny boats in a rough sea. Nobody let their lights burn all night in Whispering Pines. That was wasteful and expensive. But somehow the darkness in Zeb's windows was more desolate and final than if the occupant had been merely sleeping.

Boonie, Zeb, and now Donna. It's starting again, getting faster. Just like Archer done in California. Except this time I don't know if I can even slow him down, much less stop him.

"How come people are dying, Daddy?" Tim asked.

David thought about how to answer.

The devil's setting up revival camp in Whispering Pines? A preacher got hung over a hundred years ago and he's been pissed off ever since? We've all collected on the wages of sin and now it's payback time?

"I don't rightly know, son," he finally said. "I just know

it's going to be all right."

Lying, like marksmanship and tomato growing, got easier with practice.

He could see their house ahead, the mailbox shining in the moonlight. It somehow made him feel safer, even though he knew that mere walls wouldn't keep the Bell Monster away. The lights were off in their house, too.

"Is Mama home?" Tim asked.

"Don't believe so," David said, hoping he could keep his worry hidden.

"How come she was at the church?" Ronnie asked. "We always go on Sunday morning, not late at night."

"Well, she was just being neighborly, helping out," David lied for the third time. Well, it wasn't a complete lie. She was helping out, all right, just not the kind of help a person usually gave to their church. Her service went way beyond bake sales and sending get-well cards and arranging flowers.

She would be out with Archer, taking part in whatever crazy ritual the freak thought up next. She was helping him bring death and fear and hell's madness into their little valley. His chest tightened, this time hot with failure.

He'd rescued Linda once, led her back into the Baptist fold, into the love and light of the Lord. But maybe that wasn't good enough for her, because she'd taken a second taste of the devil's temptation and found it to be sweeter than Christ's redeeming blood.

He clenched his hands tight around his rifle. He tried to offer a prayer, to ask for God's strength, but he'd run out of words. He glanced at the sky, ink-dark and star-filled and stretching from mountaintop to mountaintop.

Just exactly who owns this damned world?

David shivered at the slight weakening of his faith.

He led the boys up the driveway and into the house. He was momentarily afraid that, even if he managed a prayer, it would fall on deaf ears. Or worse, ears that heard but just didn't plain care.

When the bell rang, Linda didn't cover her ears, though the church shook with the vibrations.

That was part of the ritual, Archer had said. The bell had to ring to drive away that crazy Jesus and all the other demons that clouded people's minds. The bell must toll as a reminder of the iniquities of murderous ancestors.

So she welcomed the sound, and each rich resonance washed over her body like a cleansing wave of holy water. Archer folded his hands together and bowed his head.

"Stronger," he whispered after the third toll. "It's getting stronger."

What's getting stronger? Linda wondered. But she dared not break his reverie to ask. She craned her neck to peer outside the church. That was when the sheriff screamed.

Archer ran down the church steps and stood over Littlefield's prostrate form. Linda followed slowly, waiting for a sign from Archer. The sheriff had been looking at the tree. Linda wondered what he had seen that was so frightening. The churchyard was a place of peace and beauty, not a place of fear. Perhaps the sheriff was faithless, weak, unworthy.

Archer knelt on the ground beside the sheriff and lifted his face to the sky.

"O Father," he intoned in that preacher voice that sent shivers of rapture up Linda's spine, "See me take this sinner into my church. He has joined us in communion and has eaten of the host. O Father, watch him join us in the battle against the unrighteousness and evil that masquerades as salvation, so that he may walk into light forever, amen."

"Amen," Linda echoed automatically. She felt a piece of the communion between her teeth. She worked it free with her tongue, then swallowed the soft flesh that Archer had consecrated and administered. The sense of well-being expanded in her chest, swelled her head, made her light with love.

And then she *saw*.

The Hung Preacher rolled his eyes in her direction, looking at her appreciatively. Then the thick apparition turned his face back to Archer.

The Hung Preacher's black lips parted, and insubstantial things wiggled inside his mouth. "More," he said, moving his lips again, but the second time he made no sound.

A vision, Linda told herself. *An honest-to-God VISION. Just like Archer always promised.*

The Baptists had raved on and on about Elijah and the burning bush, about how such-and-such was revealed to God's chosen, but nobody at First Baptist had ever had a vision of his or her own. Well, Boonie Houck had laid claim to a few, but his revelations never seemed religious in nature, especially since they usually came after a week of the trembles. But this . . . *this* . . .

The Hung Preacher dangled in full glory before her. But even now he was shimmering, fading back into his holy realm beyond this earth. Linda felt her heart leap with uncertain loss.

Archer clutched his hands together and edged toward the dogwood tree on his knees. "Don't go, oh sweet prophet," he pleaded, his voice almost childlike.

The Hung Preacher mouthed the word *more* a final time, the dead face contorted in rage. His arms fell limp at his sides, and he drifted into invisibility.

Archer stood and ran to the spot beneath the tree. He reached his arms out and hugged the empty air to his chest. "Come back," he said softly. He had a lost look on his face.

Linda had never seen Archer appear in any way vulnerable. It made her heart soar with joy. She could be of use to him. He *did* have needs. He needed *her*.

Archer had given her so much, opened her eyes to the follies of Christianity, saved her soul. The least she could do was comfort him now in his time of trouble. At last she had something to offer. She touched his shoulder. His coat was so hot that it almost burned her fingers.

He spun. Linda drew back, her hand covering her mouth in shock.

Archer's face contorted as if the bones of his skull had broken and the fragments were trying to push through his skin. His forehead flattened and elongated, the lower part of his face funneled together, the nose broadened over the mouth. His eyes widened, and a fierce golden color ringed the black, marble-sized pupils. Archer's eyes glittered, capturing the moonlight and turning it into green and yellow diamonds.

A low, animal growl came from his throat, and triangular ears pricked up at the top of his head. Whiskers like silver wire sprouted from the sides of the black-gummed mouth. The eyes narrowed, cat-like, and Archer fell onto his hands.

No, not his hands. PAWS.

Archer's suit ripped, and reddish-brown fur sprouted over the preacher's flesh. The creature stepped forward,

out of Archer's shoes, its thick claws curling into the
ground through the socks.

A mountain lion.

David had told her stories about them, her father had
hunted them, and the Appalachian settlers used to fear
them so much that they became the stuff of fireplace scare
stories. But all the mountain lions were dead.

She had never doubted that Archer could work miracles. Now, with this undeniable proof, she gave the last
of herself to him. She fell before the great cat and bowed
her head, trembling, awaiting the mighty gnash of its teeth
or the swift stroke of its talons, whatever method Archer
deemed most fitting. Salvation was all about sacrifice, Archer had told her, and she was willing to make the ultimate
one.

Jesus divided loaves and fishes and walked on water.
Big deal. Jesus had never been anything but Jesus. This
proved that Archer was better, the true savior, the real
Son of God. This proved that Archer was master of the
atoms and cells and all that other invisible stuff that made
things what they were.

The animal growled again, a low rumbling noise in its
chest. It moved forward and sniffed at Linda. Despite herself, she shivered as warm, moist breath passed across the
back of her neck.

Please make it not hurt, Archer.

The mountain lion waited. The sky was a shade lighter
now, a deeper blue from the east pushing away the black.
The forest was still, hushed in that moment just before
dawn when the diurnal and nocturnal animals changed
shifts. The great cat's soft breathing was the only sound
besides the pounding of Linda's heart.

The cat moved away, toward the still-unconscious sheriff. Linda felt a small surge of disappointment, but also a rush of relief.

So I'm to be spared. I promise to have a purpose if you only let me live, God. You need me here to serve Archer, to help him do whatever he needs done to save the world. To beat Jesus and Satan forever.

She watched as the cat lowered its head toward the sheriff's neck.

✝ Chapter 13

The house was dark when Linda drove up. That meant the boys were asleep. She hated to neglect them the way she had been, but Archer needed her more than the boys did. A servant should have only one master, Archer always said. And God was a jealous God.

She had passed the body that had been lying on the side of the road. Some of the other parishioners had probably passed it as well, though all would murmur to themselves, "There must be great sacrifices." Linda recognized David's jacket draped across the body. So her husband had been out nosing around.

She hoped he would stay out of the way. If David left her alone, maybe Archer would spare him. David had married into the Gregg family, not earned the birthright with blood. The Days weren't one of the old families, so they owed no tribute to the red church and had no iniquities to pay for.

She got out of the car and took a breath of fresh air. The smells of the farm, freshly tilled soil, hay, and chicken manure always comforted her. That was one of the ironies of her life: she'd always been afraid that she'd wind up trapped in Whispering Pines, yet she had never really felt comfortable anywhere else, especially in California. Not even Archer's wonderful presence there could totally erase her homesickness.

The moon was low in the sky, three-quarters full over the uneven mountain ridges. The deep indigo of the night and the scattered pinpricks of stars were beautiful. She would miss this world. It was hard to believe that a better one existed, but Archer said he had a place for her waiting in heaven. The *real* heaven, not that mock-up illusion that the Christians peddled.

Harps and white robes. What a laugh.

She went into the house, careful not to make any noise. She would go in and kiss the boys good night and make sure the blankets were tucked under their chins. Her hand fumbled along the wall until she found the light switch, and she flipped it up.

"Well, well, well . . ." David said. She jumped back against the door.

". . . if it ain't the whore of Babylon," David finished. He sat on the couch, still in his work clothes, eyes alert. His rifle was across his lap.

"What in the world do you think you're doing here?" she whispered, as loudly as she could without waking the boys.

"Taking care of my own." His eyes narrowed as he patted the gun barrel. "Somebody's got to do it."

"Get out."

"Not while that . . . that McFall bastard is on the prowl."

"Leave Archer out of this."

"I wish I could."

"You think this is all about you? This doesn't have anything to do with you, so just mind your own business."

David watched her as she stepped away from the open

door and eased toward the kitchen. Only his eyes moved. The rest of him remained rigid. "What's going on up at the church, Linda?"

"Nothing. Just getting services going again." Linda looked away to escape his gaze. "How are the boys?"

"Oh, they're just fine. Ain't nothing like being scared to death and having their mother taking up with a touched-in-the-head bunch of midnight worshipers."

"Those are good folks. You know most of them. They're our neighbors."

"Yeah, at least the ones who are still alive."

"You saw her?"

"Yeah."

Linda's eyes grew moist. She had not allowed herself to mourn for Donna. But now that David had reminded her, she couldn't fight the mortal weakness of tears.

"Boys saw her, too." David's voice was sharper now that he saw he could cut her with his words. "Lucky for them, they didn't find out who it was."

Linda leaned against the jamb of the entryway that led into the hall. The guilty had to die. But why did it have to be Donna? Her cousin had never really done anything wrong, except maybe committing a little adultery. Was Donna's heart really that tainted, just because she liked to love other women's husbands?

"That makes three," David said. "One every night. Just like in California."

Linda slammed her fist against the cheap paneling, and the trophy heads on the wall shook. "Why didn't you just let me stay in California?" she said, louder than she wanted to.

"You're going to wake the boys."

She crossed the room and stood over him. "Why didn't

you leave me out there? I was happy. Maybe for the first time ever."

David took his hands from the rifle and cupped them over his knees. "Because you turned your back on the Lord. And on me. I couldn't let Archer McFall and that bunch rot your soul."

She snorted, her nose red from crying. "Soul? What do you know about having a soul?"

"I know what's right. And Archer ain't right. He's the devil. He's worse than the devil. At least the devil plays by God's rules, and knows good from evil. Your precious preacher seems to get them a little mixed up."

"You're crazy, David."

"I ain't the one praying to a murdering monster."

"Archer has nothing to do with the killings."

"Sure he don't. Mighty big damned coincidence, wouldn't you say? Archer goes to California, people die hard. Archer comes back to Whispering Pines, people die hard."

"Sometimes the innocent must die-"

"I got news for you. None of us are innocent."

Linda shook her head. "You don't get it, do you? I've been praying and praying, asking God to throw some light on you so you'd see that Archer is the real savior. But I guess that ten-dollar-a-week Jesus is all you've got the brains for. Serves you right to follow him to hell."

David stood suddenly, the rifle thumping to the floor. He glared down into her eyes, but Linda wasn't afraid. *There will come great trials*, Archer said. She would be strong. Her faith would not waver.

"You can follow that fool," David said between clenched teeth. "But I'll be damned if you're going to take the boys with you."

"That's right. You'll be damned," she said, angry now that David was taking her greatest possessions, the greatest tithe she could make to Archer. The boys were her ticket into Archer's heart, into the kingdom of God.

David bent and picked up the rifle, holding it across his chest between them. "Then let the son of a bitch come and get them. But he'll have to come through <u>me</u> first."

David's eyes were hard. She knew how stubborn he could be. He had worn that same expression in California, when he came into the temple after Archer had disappeared. He'd carried her out to his pickup, then drove back to the mountains, stopping only for gas and food or when exhaustion forced him to nap for a few hours. Now, as then, Linda realized just how much she loved him. But love was a trick, a scare tactic that led to desperation. Archer said that earthly love was just another vanity, didn't he?

Love in its way was a false idol. Love was as hollow as a golden calf- all shiny and bright on the outside, and nothing but bad dark air on the inside. Love gave you nothing, but took every little thing that you had.

Human love was an altar that you crawled on and then asked to be slaughtered.

Love was Jesus' greatest lie.

She would be strong.

"I hate you," she said, her chest cold, her heart coated with the iron will that Archer had instilled.

David held up a hand, glanced at the front door and then the window. "Did you hear that?"

"Hear what?"

David thumbed the rifle's safety off and tilted his head to listen. "Shh."

"It won't come here," Linda whispered, trying to reassure herself. Archer would send his heavenly agent for the boys. But he'd promised to wait until they'd become part of the fold. That would ensure their place in Archer's eternal glory, and secure her place by Archer's side.

Something rattled at the front door.

It can't be. Tonight's sacrifice has already been made.

In the silence, the ticking of the clock was like raindrops on a coffin.

David put his cheek to the gunstock and waited for whatever was outside to enter.

Can you hear Him aknocking?

Ronnie pulled the covers over his head, but the suffocating darkness made his fear grow instead of disappear. Mom and Dad had stopped arguing, so maybe they had heard the noise, too. Tim was snoring, but Ronnie hadn't been able to close his eyes since they'd arrived home. He was afraid that if he slept, he'd dream about the black shape that flapped across the sky like a jaggedy kite.

And now it was here, the Bell Monster, the scary thing from the church that had wings and claws and livers for eyes. It had followed them home, and Ronnie knew— *knew*—that it had come just for him. Because he had sinned in his heart, and the devil had sent a demon from the pits of hell, just the way Preacher Staymore had threatened in Sunday school.

The claws clicked on the glass. Ronnie chewed nervously on the blankets and a stray fiber got in his throat and made him cough. The clicking stopped. The monster had heard him. In the stillness, Ronnie listened to the wet mist of its waiting breath.

Ronnie tried to pray. The preacher said that the Lord

forgave all sins and protected the children. If God had control over the heavens and the earth, then surely He controlled the demons as well.

Dear Jesus, please forgive me for my sins of the heart. I know I've suffered bad thoughts, and I haven't been saved in three weeks. But I want YOU in my heart and not the thing with livers for eyes. Please, please, get me out of this and I promise I'll get saved every week from now on, even if Preacher Staymore's breath smells like rotten fruit. Amen.

Ronnie opened his eyes under the blankets. It was working. The wet noises went away. The prayer had sent the demon back to hell, or maybe back to the red church.

Thankyou thankyou thankyou, O Jesus—

The clicking started again, and Ronnie felt as if the door to his heart had slammed shut. Across the room, Tim rolled over in his sleep. If the Bell Monster came in through the window, it might get Tim.

And maybe if it gets Tim, it will leave me alone.

As soon as he had the thought, his face warmed with shame. Didn't Jesus say to love thy brother? Or was that one of the Ten Commandments? Either way, he had suffered another sin of the heart, and Jesus would punish him even more.

The brave thing to do would be to go out and face the monster. To let the thing rip him open and gnaw on his sinning heart, the way it had ripped up Boonie Houck and probably Zeb Potter and that person on the side of the road.

Mom said that Archer McFall said that sacrifice was the way to heaven. If Ronnie sacrificed himself, maybe Jesus would take him instead of letting the demon drag him down to the hot place. But Archer McFall was weirder than any preacher Ronnie had ever heard of. Who else would hold services in a haunted church? And the memory of those strange hymns that Mom and the others had been singing made him shiver with strange, sick pleasure.

The claws were on the windowsill now, exploring the crack at the base of the window. Ronnie couldn't remember if the window was locked. Mom had raised it yesterday to let in some fresh air, and Ronnie went right after she left and latched it again. But maybe she had unlatched it again while he was asleep.

Footsteps came down the hall, heavy footsteps. Dad's boots. Ronnie pulled the covers off his head and sat up, braver now that Dad was coming to the rescue. He couldn't help himself. He had to glance at the window.

Through the curtains, Ronnie saw the Bell Monster pressed against the glass. It was moist, changing shape as he watched, the lesser gray of its mouth parting in some kind of anger or longing.

And he saw the eyes.

Livers.

Wet, drippy, slick, and red.

Eyes that looked right into Ronnie's, that seemed to crawl down his eyeball sockets and into his brain, to reach from his brain to his heart, as if to say, *You're mine now, you've always been mine, can you hear me aknocking?*

Then the door to the bedroom crashed open and light from the hall spilled across the room and Dad's long shadow filled the doorway.

"Get down," Dad yelled, and Ronnie fell back against the pillows as the first shot exploded from Dad's rifle.

Glass shattered as the percussion echoed off the walls.

Dad yanked the bolt back, reloaded, and fired again.

Gun smoke filled Ronnie's lungs, and though he

couldn't smell it, he could taste it, as acrid as car exhaust on his tongue.

Tim woke up screaming. Mom ran into the room and hugged him, pausing for a moment to look at the window.

Dad hurried across the room and looked through the broken panes. Jagged glass framed him, sparkling in the moonlight like sharp teeth.

"Is it gone?" Mom asked. Tim cried into her chest, his shudders shaking them both.

"I don't see it," Dad said, the rifle at his shoulder.

"Did you kill it?" she asked.

"Who the hell knows?"

"Will it come back?"

Dad turned from the window and glared at her. "You tell me. You're the damned prophet."

Prophet? thought Ronnie. *Like Ezekiel and Abraham and all those? Was Dad committing a sin of the heart?*

Dad bent over Ronnie's bed. "You okay?"

Ronnie nodded.

Yeah, I'm as okay as I'm ever going to be, considering that the thing with livers for eyes is after me because I've sinned in my heart, and now it's after YOU, too. And my nose hurts and you and Mom are fighting again and I'm not going to cry, I'm not going to—

Dad sat on the bed and wiped Ronnie's tears away. "It's gone now. You're safe. I won't let that thing get you."

"P—promise?"

"Yeah."

"Will you stay here?"

Dad tensed, then looked at Mom. Ronnie felt their hatred in the air, a black electricity, as mean as the Bell Monster and almost as scary.

Tim had stopped crying, and now whimpered a little into the folds of Mom's shirt. Ronnie knew his little brother was waiting for what would happen next. They both knew what was at stake. If Dad left again, they would be helpless against the Bell Monster. And despite the promises, Dad might just be angry enough to leave them all, to go somewhere in his truck and drink beer and do other things that he'd never done before.

This was one of those turning points, like when the Lord came aknocking, and you either opened the door or you didn't. Where everything changed, either for better or worse. No going back to last week, when life was nearly normal and all Ronnie had to worry about was homework and Melanie Ward. This was for all the marbles.

Dad looked at Mom again, then at Tim, then at the shattered window. The sky had settled into that deep blue of early morning and even the crickets had quit their chirping. Somewhere in the hills, a hound dog bayed, a lost, lonely sound in the predawn stillness.

"I'll stay," Dad said, staring out the window at the black slopes of the mountains.

Ronnie admired the muscles in his dad's jaws, the way Dad held his head up proudly, without a bit of back-down in him. Dad said that a man ought to draw his strength from the Lord, that nobody who trusted the Man Upstairs needed to be afraid of anything. And Dad made a pretty good case for it, too: why should you be afraid of dying if dying only brought you into the presence of everlasting glory?

When Ronnie thought of heaven, he always imagined that color illustration in Dad's Bible, right before the New Testament. The picture showed Jesus at the top of a set of golden stairs that rose up into the clouds. Jesus had long hair and a brown beard and the saddest eyes Ronnie had ever seen. He had his arms out and his palms lifted in welcome, but there was nobody on the stairs. Heaven looked like a lonely place.

And besides, no matter how wonderful heaven was, new things were always scary. Like the first day of school, the time he'd given that poem to Melanie, the first time he'd been inside the red church, this business about Mom and Dad being mad at each other. So he'd rather stay right here in bed, with Dad sitting beside him and Mom and Tim under the same roof. He'd rather just go on living, thank you very much.

Even with a broken nose and a monster after him and schoolwork and Mom hanging out with that creepy preacher.

Even with all that.

He closed his eyes and waited for the sun to come up.

Archer crouched in the forest near the church. He had dragged the sheriff under the trees after sending Linda away. She wouldn't understand why the sheriff should be suffered to live. She was a good disciple, and she would willingly sacrifice herself, but she wasn't prepared for the truth. None of them were.

Archer surveyed the landscape, his great cat's eyes piercing the darkness. God ruled the kingdom of heaven, but He had given Archer the kingdom of the Earth, along with dominion over all of its creatures. Archer's brother Jesus had misused that power, had wandered among the humans and confused them with messages of love and hope. Before the rise of Christianity, heaven was attained only through pain, trials, and sacrifice. After Jesus's blasphemy was erased from the earth, people would again turn to those true tests of faith.

Of all the ludicrous Christian beliefs, the most laughable was that being forgiven would earn the sinner a ticket to heaven. Yet it was so utterly human. Why bother living right and enduring the rigors of true faith when all you had to do was say, "Come into my heart" and Jesus would be right there tricking you with lies?

Archer would also grant forgiveness. But his would be delivered after the sinner got on bended knee and begged, begged, even as the dark claws of justice performed the cleansing. Deliverance must be paid in blood. Redemption must be earned the hard way.

And Father above would burn with jealousy as Archer succeeded where Jesus had failed.

Archer felt a brief twinge. Bullets passed through the manifested spirit that lurked at the Days' house three miles away. Archer threw back his head and growled a laugh at the moon, then sent the manifestation back to its home in the belfry. Let it eat the shadows there until the next night's work.

Dawn would be breaking soon. The forest was in the held breath between the changing of the guards, the nocturnal animals returning to their nests and burrows and the morning songbirds shaking sleep from their heads. What a beautiful world God had made. Except for the blight of human hearts, a blight born of God's insecurity, the earth nearly approached heaven in its glory.

But Archer was here to erase that blight. All that sinned must be destroyed, so that a new, pure world could emerge. And all on Earth had sinned, even Jesus. Especially Jesus. All except the Second Son.

Archer licked his fur, patient in the knowledge that he had forever. In the meantime, he would continue the cleansing right here in the place of his mortal birth. Here where Wendell McFall's soul had been trapped, where Archer himself had suffered the taunts and abuses of the unrighteous. Here where the sinless ones could come forth in an exodus of blasphemy and mockery.

Archer brought his teeth to the sheriff's collar and gently closed his mouth around the cloth. The sheriff's eyelids twitched as Archer's warm breath tickled his neck, but he didn't awaken. The smell of the man's sin, and those of all the generations of Littlefields, crowded Archer's sensitive nose.

Before Littlefield paid for his own sins, the sheriff first had to suffer for the sins of his ancestors. Archer dragged Littlefield across the churchyard, to a special place of punishment. Littlefield thought that the death of his younger brother had been enough to atone for Wendell McFall's hanging. But he would soon learn that sacrifice was the currency of a jealous God, and of jealous sons as well.

There was joy in being a messiah.

✝ Chapter 14

Det. Sgt. Sheila Storie looked at the clock above her office door. It was one of those old round clocks of the kind that hung in elementary schools, with a black casing and plain, oversize numerals. The second hand didn't sweep smoothly. It locked into place on each tiny mark, then twitched over to the next. She watched twenty-three of the spastic seconds pass before she took her eyes away.

She had spent the night in the office, napping a few hours in her chair. Now her back was stiff. She stood and stretched and made another pot of coffee, even though her stomach ached from the abusive night of caffeine and snack food from the machine in the hall. Just before the midnight shift change, Deputy Wellborn had called in to report that the hounds had found nothing.

Somehow, she wasn't surprised by the negative report. Hounds might be okay for chasing down runaway convicts, but this was the twenty-first century. Sifting forensic evidence and poring through criminal databases were the ways to solve crimes, not sniffing around the woods. But she had to admit that a night spent at the desk with her reports had brought her no closer to solving the two murders.

Where was the motive?

That was one of the first lessons of homicide investigation: find the motive, and you find the murderer. But she had a near-penniless drunk mutilated in a churchyard and a farmer with his head caved in by a sledgehammer. As far as anyone could determine, robbery was not a motive in either crime. In fact, the only connection between the two victims was that both lived in the Whispering Pines area.

No, that wasn't the only connection. There were more of what she called the BDC's—big damned coincidences. And most of the coincidences seemed to center on the old church.

McFall's buying of it. Frank's spilling his guts about the childhood tragedy he'd endured there. Even the ghost stories seemed to be a red flag of some kind, though she would never in a million years admit that she gave them any credence at all.

Storie looked out the window. The sky was just turning pink behind Barkersville. The two blocks of Main Street were shadowed, the brick buildings cold and empty in the gasp of dawn. A few vehicles were on the road, most of them pickup trucks with tools in the back. People were heading to work, another week to get through before another payday, and then another two days to forget that they had to do it all over again on the following Monday.

The Chamber of Commerce mailed out glossy brochures that said, *Up here, life moves at a different speed.* The idea was to lure rich tourists with the promise of front-porch rockers and lazy river breezes. Of course, once they got here, they were bored out of their minds after two days and then dumped a few thousand dollars in the area craft shops and restaurants. Some different speed.

Then why are you here?

She chewed her pencil. Why the hell *was* she here?

Running from the Metro force and big-city crime, she had wanted as rural a life as she could find. Maybe she thought this would be an easy place to cut her teeth, move up a little in rank, and then make a run for sheriff.

She'd always wanted a department of her own. Storie wanted it the way other people craved sex or fame or a family. Solving high-profile cases was just the means to that end. But she also had developed this very scary need to understand Frank Littlefield, to get beneath his professional veneer and his good-ol'-boy act and figure out just what in the hell he was about.

She didn't know much about him. She didn't know enough about the red church or Archer McFall, either. It was time to change that. She pulled her keys from her desk and poured herself a last cup of coffee.

She pressed a button on her two-way. "Unit Two will be in service."

"Ten-four," came the third-shift dispatcher's voice.

She strapped on her shoulder holster before putting on her blazer. The .38 revolver was comforting against her rib cage. As she went outside, she was struck by the moist scent of life: lilies crawling out of their night pajamas, the wild cherry in front of the library snow white with blossoms, birds chattering from branches and utility poles. She took a deep breath and gazed over the mountains.

On those hills were houses, filled with people who were as deeply rooted as the old-growth hardwoods. Smoke curled from a couple of the chimneys, despite the warmth of the morning. These people were no different from the urbanites she had grown up with. They slept with dreams, and the dreams dissolved when they awoke. Time passed for them as rapidly as it passed for everyone.

Yep, some different speed, all right.

She got in her cruiser and headed for Whispering Pines, staying just under the limit all the way.

Frank.
  Get up.
Frank didn't want to get up. He was lying under some hay, and the sun was coming through the open loft door and warming his bones until they were like cooked noodles.

"Get up, Frankie."

Frank opened his eyes. The world was yellow, all sunlight and straw dust. The straps of his overalls dug into his neck, making him itch. But that was only a minor problem. He could endure the itch, and he could ignore Samuel. Samuel was about as minor a problem as a little brother could be.

"Come on, let's go fishing."

"Go away," Frank murmured. If Grandpa or Dad found him lazing off, they'd wear out his rear end with a hickory switch. He could hear Grandpa's crotchety voice now: *Corn to be hoed and hogs to be slopped and the gol-durned dinner chicken's still wearing its feathers.* The chainsaw buzzed like a drunken bee where the two men were cutting firewood on one of the hillsides.

Something poked Frank in the side. He reluctantly rolled over and saw Samuel with a cane pole in his hands, feet bare and an Atlanta Braves cap perched on his head. A grin filled with crooked teeth threatened to split Samuel's freckled face in half. "Come down to the river, Frankie."

Frank sat up, dazzled by the sun. Outside, the fields were a brilliant shade of green. The mountains were sharply in focus, as if each individual tree and rock had been carefully etched onto a fine cotton paper. The sky was so vividly blue that he rubbed his eyes, because the air was like water, thick with currents and eddies and languorous coolness. He stood on wobbly scarecrow legs.

"Got your pole, too," said Samuel. He held out another bamboo cane. A round red-and-white float and a small silver hook dangled from the monofilament line. Frank took the pole without a word, then followed Samuel across the hayloft. His feet felt as if they were wrapped in fat clouds and scarcely seemed to touch the ground. Then they were down the ladder and out of the barn and crossing a long meadow. The grass was alive, like the crisp hair of the earth.

The chainsaw stopped and its echo fell like smoke across the valley and dissolved. In the sudden silence, a bird cried from the trees near the river. Samuel led the way across the meadow, below the garden with its tomato vines and leafy cabbage heads and cornstalks tipped with golden buds. He felt as if he were attached to an invisible line, being reeled toward an unknown shore.

Samuel hummed a church hymn that was a little too somber for such a bright summer day. And Samuel should be skipping, laughing, beating at the thistles with his cane pole. He should be running ahead of Frank to find a hiding place under the cottonwoods. Instead his little brother walked solemnly, watching his toes.

The sky pressed down and Frank swam against it. They were at the river now, and its sparkling silvery eyes watched them.

"We're going to catch the big one," Samuel said, standing on a sandbar and freeing his line. He sneaked a look at Frank and put his hand to his mouth. Then he held out his palm to Frank, showing a writhing mass of thick, glistening nightcrawlers. Frank took one and speared it on his hook. Samuel took one for himself and returned the rest of the worms to his mouth. Frank's stomach tightened in nausea.

The boys launched their baited hooks almost in unison. Dragonflies scooted along the riverbank, their green wings beating against the air. Water splashed over stones, snickering.

"It's almost like Sunday," Samuel said.

"Yeah. Here we are being lazy when there's chores to be done. Dad will get ill as a hornet if he finds out we're fishing." Frank moved down the sandbar a little so the sun didn't flash off the water into his eyes.

"Lazy Sunday. Makes you want to go to church, don't it?"

"Church?"

Samuel smiled and his head lolled limply to one side. "Fun place to hang around, know what I mean?"

"We don't have time for that," Frank said, his hands sweating and his heart pounding.

"I got all the time in the world," Samuel said, as a thick worm crawled from his mouth. The brown tip of it squirmed as if sniffing the air, then the worm inched down Samuel's chin.

"I don't go the church anymore," Frank said. "Not since . . ."

"Since *what*, brother?"

Samuel's float bobbed once, twice. Then he jerked his pole and it bowed nearly double. "Got one, got one." He squealed in delight.

Frank dropped his own pole and lay on his belly so he could reach into the water and land the fish. In the calm water near the shore, he saw the reflection of the sky and the high white clouds. His own face was dark on the water, unwrinkled, unworried. Young.

"Pull him in," Samuel said. Frank reached out and grabbed the taut line. As he tugged, the river erupted in a silver avalanche.

The Hung Preacher rose from the water.

The fishing line was a rope, the hook a noose that encircled the preacher's neck. The pale figure clawed at the strands, and the skin was purple where the rope dug into flesh.

The Hung Preacher's mouth parted in a suffocated scream, except—no, that wasn't the river, that was the *preacher*—he was laughing, gurgling, a font of morbid merriment.

Frank's own scream was a dull fist in his throat, a mossy stone, a cold fish. He tried to scramble up the bank, but a hand on his arm held him down.

"Time for a baptism, Frankie," came Samuel's voice, only it wasn't the voice of a child. It was a low voice from beyond the grave, a putrid exhalation of hate, the words rustling and slithering like snakes through a catacomb.

Frank looked up at his dead brother, into the eyes that had once been mercifully sewn closed by the funeral director, eyes that now stared accusingly, filled with the hot hunger of vengeance delayed. Samuel's crooked teeth were sharp, moldy, the spaces between them filled with quick darkness.

Samuel was knee-deep in the water now, his gaunt hand tight on Frank's arm, drawing him across the mud and soggy roots into the lapping, laughing tongue of the river. The Hung Preacher tented his hands in a prayer, and his bowed head was smiling, smiling.

Samuel tugged, and Frank was in the river, his dead little brother pushing down on the top of his head, submerging him, and the water tasted like death, the water was crypt air and flooded his lungs even while he struggled toward the surface that was so far away. He fought, even though he knew he deserved to die for what he had done to Samuel.

The hands tugged, pulled. He felt himself going under, deeper—

"Sheriff, wake up."

Littlefield kicked and flailed, moaning.

"Get up, you're having a bad dream."

Littlefield tensed, his muscles spasming from the struggle. "Sh—Sheila?"

"Yeah, Sheriff. Are you okay?"

He opened his eyes. The morning sun was painful. He blinked up into Detective Storie's face. She was so close that he could smell the coffee on her breath. Her hair fell softly about her cheekbones, but her mouth was lined with worry.

What a pleasant sight to wake up to.

Littlefield's head felt as if Zeb Potter's murderer had done another sledgehammer job. A sweetly foul aftertaste coated the inside of his mouth. He could smell his own body odor.

Storie helped him sit up. His uniform was moist with sweat and dew. Or maybe baptismal water . . .

"What happened?" Storie asked.

"I don't know," said the sheriff, shaking his head. "Last thing I remember . . ."

He looked across the churchyard. The Trooper was where he had parked it the night before, but that was his last memory. Had he been inside the church?

Gravestones surrounded him, the marble and granite bright in the sun. He knew this area of the cemetery. He had brought flowers here many times. He turned and glanced at the marker where his head had been resting.

A small lamb was engraved on the top of the tombstone. The etched symbols beneath the image pierced his heart, just as they had always done:

HERE LIES
SAMUEL RILEY LITTLEFIELD
1968-1979
May God Protect and Keep Him

May God protect him. Because Frank Littlefield sure hadn't. Frank had practically sealed Samuel's coffin shut through stupidity and indifference. A big brother was supposed to be his brother's keeper.

The dream.

"Look," said Storie, pulling Littlefield from his reverie. She pointed to a flattened path in the grass that led from the forest.

"Something dragged me here."

"Something?"

Sure. The Hung Preacher, the Bell Monster, the Tooth Fairy. Maybe even the Bride of Frankenstein. Take your pick. She'll believe any of them, won't she?

"The back of your shirt is dirty," she said. "And your collar's torn. You look like you pulled an all-night drunk."

"Gee, thanks. I feel like it."

"Must have been a hell of a church service. What did they do, make you go back for second helpings of the wine until you blacked out?"

Communion. Vague images floated through his head,

images of taking something into his mouth from Archer McFall's fingers. He swallowed and probed his mouth with a thick tongue. He wanted to spit but couldn't muster enough saliva.

The red church stood silent at the top of the rise. The belfry was black with shadows. He watched for a moment, but the shadows didn't move. His fingers explored the shredded fabric of his collar. Whatever had made the wounds had stopped inches from his neck. He had been spared, but why?

He wasn't sure he wanted to know.

"Looky," said Tim. "There's the sheriff and that lady cop. Out in the churchyard."

Ronnie looked past his dad to the two police officers. The sheriff was sitting in front of a tombstone, his hair all messed up. The woman waved at them. He started to wave back, then remembered what Dad had said.

Dad glanced over into the cemetery, then back to the gravel road. He kept his hands clenched around the steering wheel. Ronnie knew that when Dad set his jaw so that it creased, he didn't want to be bothered.

"Shouldn't we tell them about the dead person we saw last night? And the monster?"

David glanced into the rearview mirror and froze Tim with a hard look. "Those things are best not talked about."

"Is it because the sheriff was at the church with Mom? Is he one of the bad people?" Tim didn't know when to shut up.

"Let the Lord sort that out," Dad said. "Our job is to keep our eyes on our own paths."

They rounded the bend and the church was out of sight.

Below the road, the river raced them, losing by a wide margin. The water was low because no rain had fallen in weeks. Ronnie looked for places that might make good swimming holes. Anything to avoid thinking about you-know-what.

"Why do we have to go to school, Daddy?" The motor of Tim's mouth couldn't idle for long.

"The best thing to do is to keep everything as normal as possible."

"Is that why we can't tell anybody what happened?"

"Yep. So you two are going to school and I'm going to work."

"What about Mom?"

Oops, Ronnie thought. *What a dingle-dork.*

"Your mom will be okay," Dad said. "Just took a fool notion. We all do that once in a while. Now let's talk about something else."

Ronnie looked out the window. He didn't mind going to school, even if his nose was still a little sore. The swelling had gone down, and the only problem was that the packing in his nose muffled his speech. Kids would be making fun of him. But at least at school, the Bell Monster had plenty of victims to choose from if it came aknocking. Ronnie wouldn't mind seeing two or three of his class-mates come face-to-face with whatever the thing was. But that wish sounded like a sin of the heart, and Ronnie couldn't risk any more of those.

"Got your medicine?" Dad asked. Ronnie nodded.

Yep. A good old pain pill. He would go through the day with a dorked-up brain, that was for sure. He wondered if that was why Whizzer Buchanan smoked those stinky pot cigarettes he brought to school. If so, maybe Whizzer wasn't as loony as Ronnie thought.

Because there was something to be said for going through life in a fog. In the fog, you couldn't see the monsters coming. In the fog, they got you before you knew what hit you.

They reached Barkersville Elementary about a half hour late. Dad said he would pick them up in the afternoon. Ronnie was relieved he didn't have to spend all day worrying about having to walk past the red church. He and Tim got excuse notes from the principal's office and went into the hall.

"See you, Tim," said Ronnie.

"Are you going to tell anybody?"

"Tell anybody what?"

Tim just didn't get it. If Dad said do something, you did it. Dad had his reasons.

"You know. The monster."

"Lock it and throw away the key," said Ronnie, imitating turning a key against his tight lips and tossing the invisible key over his shoulder.

"Even about finding Boonie Houck?"

"If anybody asks, just say the police told you not to talk about it."

"Cool," said Tim, his eyes widening behind his glasses. "We're sort of like heroes."

"Yeah, sure." Heroes. Brave as hell, that was Ronnie, all right. Ran from Boonie Houck and busted his nose. Left Tim to fend for himself when the monster had chased them both. Chickened out when something came scratching around the bedroom window.

At least here at school, the biggest horror was Mrs. Rathbone's pre-algebra class.

"Meet me out front after school," Ronnie said. He turned toward the upper-grade wing. He'd taken about six steps before Tim called.

"Ronnie?" The word echoed off the cinder block walls. Ronnie looked around, hoping none of the teachers came out in the hall to shush them.

"Yeah?"

"Is everything going to be okay?"

"Of course it is."

"With Mom and Dad? And everything?"

Ronnie walked back, made sure no one was in the hall, and gave Tim a quick hug. "Sure. Your big brother's here. I'll make sure nothing happens to us."

Tim almost looked convinced.

"Now get to class, squirt," Ronnie said. Tim hustled down the hall. Ronnie got his books from his locker, then went to Mrs. Rathbone's room. He hung his head as he walked to his assigned desk near the back of the class.

"Why, Mr. Day, we're fortunate that you have graced us with your presence today," Mrs. Rathbone said, folding her arms, stretching her ever-present acrylic sweater over her sharp shoulders.

Ronnie stifled a groan and glanced at Melanie in the next row. He slid into his desk and said, "Sorry, Mrs. Rathbone. We . . . had an accident at home."

"I see," she said, touching her nose in derision. She imitated his stuffy tone as the class giggled. "I trust you have your homework, nevertheless?"

"Uh, yeah, sure." He shuffled through his papers. He hadn't done his homework. Who else but crazy Mrs. Rathbone assigned homework over the weekend?

"Then would you share with us the answer to problem number seventeen?"

Ronnie gulped and pretended to scan down a piece of paper. Mrs. Rathbone was almost as scary as the Bell

Monster. Sweat collected along his hairline. He was about to blurt a random answer when, out of the corner of his eye, he saw Melanie wiggling her fingers. He rolled his eyes toward her while holding up his paper to hide his face. Melanie had scrawled something and angled her paper toward him so that Mrs. Rathbone couldn't see it.

$X = 7$.

He looked over his paper at Mrs. Rathbone. "X equals seven?"

The teacher frowned. "Very good," she said, unable to hide the sour disappointment in her voice. She turned her attention to the next victim.

After class, Ronnie caught up with Melanie at her locker. With his heart pounding, he said, "Thanks."

"It was nothing." She smiled. Ronnie grew about two feet and felt as if he'd already taken the pain pill. "Besides, you've helped me a couple of times."

He nodded, unable to think of what to say next.

"What happened to your nose?" she asked.

"Broke it."

"Ouch. Does it hurt?"

"Yeah."

Around them, kids slammed lockers and the intercom ordered somebody to the office. Ronnie checked the clock on the wall. He'd better hurry to his next class before he'd have to think of something else to say.

"How did you break it?" she asked, her eyes blue and bright and her pretty lips parted in waiting.

He swallowed. Better to stare down Mrs. Rathbone than to talk face-to-face with Melanie. But she was looking at him as if what he had to say actually mattered.

It was now or never, one of those stupid turning points again. Did everything require bravery?

We're sort of like heroes.

Well, maybe.

He lowered his voice conspiratorially, his heart fluttering as she leaned closer to listen. He wished his nose worked so he could smell her hair. "You ever heard of Boonie Houck?"

She shook her head. The warning bell rang.

"I got to go," he said.

She put her hand on his arm. "Sit with me at lunch and tell me about it," she said, then disappeared into the bustle of students.

Ronnie floated to his next class. He'd just learned that fogs came in different flavors.

✟ Chapter 15

Sheila stood on the steps of the red church and stared it down.

Just a building. Wood and nails and stone and glass. A little shabby, the roof bowed in the middle from age. Walls that creak a little when the wind blows, and mice probably skittering around under the foundation. Nothing but a building.

Then why all the ghost stories? Sure, the Scottish and English and Irish settlers brought their folk legends to the mountains, something to spook the children when gathered around a winter's fire. Maybe preachers were always a favorite target of gossipers, and gossip turned to whispered legend. If Frank could fall for that "Hung Preacher" nonsense, then that was a testament to the power of a whisper.

Even in the flatlands, every town had a haunted house or two. There was one in Charlotte, an old brick house a few blocks from where she had grown up. She had pedaled her bike past it several times, searching the darkness of the broken windows for movement.

One bright autumn morning, Sheila saw something move in the dead space behind a shutter. She stopped her bike and looked up from the edge of the overgrown yard.

Something or someone was watching her. She had shivered and pedaled madly away. She hadn't believed the place was haunted, yet she had never accepted her friends' Halloween dares to enter it.

Now, after all her derision of Frank's stories, she hesitated at the church door. Of course this place held horrors for Frank. His brother had died here while Frank watched. A memory like that would haunt anybody. But did that explain why the hair on her forearms tingled erect when she touched the doorknob?

Sheila looked around the churchyard. Frank was at the edge of the forest, searching the ground. Other than the noise of his moving through the brush, the hill was quiet. Though the sun glared down, she was chilled by the shadow of the huge old dogwood. Its branches hovered over her, long bony fingers, reaching, reaching . . . .

Nonsense. You're just catching whatever craziness is infecting everybody else in Whispering Pines. You deal in facts, and don't you forget it.

She went inside. The foyer was dark, since it had no windows. She blinked and headed into the sanctuary. The handmade pews were lined neatly on both sides, even though the heights of them varied slightly. Storie admired the woodwork of the beams and the carved railing that marked off the dais. Once upon a time, somebody had put a lot of love into this church.

The church smelled of hay and her nose itched from dust. The church had been used as a barn, Frank had said. The church had undergone a haphazard cleaning job since the Houck murder. She wondered if the intent had been to hide evidence, and regretted not ordering the church sealed off with yellow crime scene tape. But Frank said he'd checked the church thoroughly.

She approached the pulpit, aware of her footsteps and heartbeat intruding on the stillness of the church. She wasn't religious, but she was respectful of houses of God. Still, the Christian God was all about getting to the truth, right? So maybe Jesus wouldn't mind her snooping around a bit.

Nothing seemed amiss in the sanctuary and a quick look in the vestry revealed only cobwebs and dark corners. She crossed the dais and stood at the lectern, looking out over pews and imagining what it would be like to have a congregation to address. If she were going to understand Archer McFall's motives, she had to put herself in his place. All murderers had a motive, however senseless in the eyes of sane people.

A preacher as prime suspect? That's about as loopy as a murderous ghost.

She put her hands on the lectern and realized her palms were sweating. Was this the power that lured McFall from California, to leave a life of sun and cash to preach in these cold mountains? Did McFall have a messiah complex or something? No, that was giving him too much credit. The only reason he was a suspect at all was that she couldn't come up with anything better.

She checked over the dais one more time, and on the second pass she saw the stain. It was old and brown, faded into the oak floorboards. It looked like a bloodstain, though too ancient to be from Boonie Houck's murder. She knelt and traced her finger around the edges of it.

The stain made a pattern. She stood and studied it. If you looked hard enough, you could imagine it was an angel, all wings and...

She smiled to herself. Yep, she'd failed her own Rorschach test. So much for those criminal psychology classes. It was time to see if Frank had found anything.

She touched the railing as she stepped off the dais, and something clung to her hand. At first she thought it was dust, but she held her hand to the light coming through the windows. Rust-colored flakes glistened against her skin. Dried blood.

Sheila stooped and looked at the rail, wishing that she'd brought a flashlight. A few flakes of dried blood were scattered across the wood. How had Frank missed seeing them? She thought maybe she'd better be more discriminating about the things Frank said. After all, he believed in ghosts.

She had a solid clue at last, something the labs could work with. They could at least determine whether the blood was Houck's or, if she were lucky, the killer's. She wondered how many fingerprints were lying about the church. Even if they were from fifty different hands, at least she would have a suspect pool.

Sheila backtracked down the aisle, scanning the floor for more bloodstains. No luck.

She went through the foyer, better able to see this time because her eyes had adjusted to the dimness. A coat rack was nailed to one wall, wooden pegs angled out like deer antlers. Sheila bumped into the bell rope and it swayed against her blazer with a whispering sound. The rope led up into the belfry.

Wait a second. Frank said there wasn't a bell rope. Why would he lie about something like that? And what ELSE has he lied about?

Well, at least this explains why those witnesses had reported hearing bells on the nights of the murders. Probably some kids messing around in here.

She hurried from the church to share her news with

Frank. She wanted to see his face when he was confronted with his lies. "Hey, Sheriff," she called.

He stepped out from a laurel thicket. He looked a little better now, though his eyes were bloodshot and his hair unkempt. "I didn't find anything," he said with a shrug.

Big surprise.

"Well, I did. Bloodstains."

"Bloodstains?"

"In the church."

Frank's eyebrows rose. "I'll be damned."

"I thought you would be. And another thing. You know the ringing bells that you kept talking about?"

"Yeah?"

"Well, I have a simple explanation for that."

"How simple?"

"Follow me."

She jogged to the church steps and waited for Frank. "In here. I thought you said there wasn't a bell rope because of-"

"Right. There hasn't been a bell rope for over a hundred and thirty years. Because people wanted to forget that mess about the Hung Preacher."

Sure. That's why the legend is alive and kicking today, isn't it? Because they did such a damned good job of forgetting?

She smiled to herself as she followed Frank up the steps. *THIS will show him.*

She blinked. The rope was gone.

She gazed up into the small hole that led to the belfry. Nothing. Had someone pulled it up? If so, whoever it was would still be up there. They would have seen anybody running from the church.

Frank had his hands on his hips, looking at her.

"I swear. There was a rope here."

"Ha, ha. Very funny."

"I'm serious. Give me a boost up to that hole."

The sheriff shook his head. "No way in hell, Sheila. The last time I did that, I lost a brother. I'm not about to lose you."

She balled her fists. "Damn it, I saw a rope. Are you going to tell me one of your ghosts tied it to the bell?"

"There's no rope."

"Do you think I imagined it? That I'm catching whatever craziness seems to be spreading around these parts?"

The sheriff sighed. "Look, maybe I've been a fool. Forget all that crap about the ghosts. If I really believed in ghosts, why would I bother to investigate the case?"

"Because you're the sheriff. You *have* to act like you know what you're doing."

"You're not going up in the belfry."

"There's no way *you're* going to fit. One of us has to look. We can't just sit back and cower while people keep getting murdered."

Sheila grabbed two of the coat-rack pegs and pulled herself up, then positioned one foot against the doorknob. If the murderer was dumb enough to play stupid tricks, he was just begging to be caught. She wondered if she should draw her revolver, but her hands were occupied. If the murderer was waiting with a weapon . . .

She poked her head through the belfry, her anger giving her strength despite the poor grip she had on the wood.

Nothing.

Nothing in the belfry but a cold, tarnished cast-iron bell. A few leaves skittered in the breeze, caught in the corners since last autumn. Nothing else.

After a moment she jumped down, the impact jarring

her knees. Frank caught her and helped her regain her balance. Their eyes met at the contact and they both looked away.

"Satisfied?" asked the sheriff.

"I swear I saw a rope," she said, failing to convince even herself. *Had* she seen it?

Well, at least there was the blood. That was real enough. She vividly recalled the texture of the coagulated flakes. Good, hard forensic evidence, with none of the problems caused by haunted eyewitnesses.

She brushed past Frank and hurried to the rail. The blood was gone.

"So where's this blood?" Frank asked when he caught up with her.

She stared at her hand, thinking of that Shakespeare play. Out, out, damned spot. Had she imagined it, just as Lady Macbeth had?

"It was right here," she whispered.

"Maybe it was ghost's blood."

From the windows, shafts of sunlight sliced across the church. Golden dust spun slowly in the air. Wood and nails and stone and glass. The building, the walls, waited.

"Are you ready to call in the SBI?" Frank asked after an awkward stretch of silence.

"Why? So they can certify me as insane as everybody else in these mountains?"

She went outside and sat on the church steps, alone with her confusion.

Linda drove up the narrow dirt road that led to Mama Bet's house. The driveway became so rutted that she had to park along the fence beside the other cars. She walked the last hundred yards, up the hill to a little glen in the forest. She heard the music before she saw the house. Sounded like a fiddle and a guitar playing "Fox on the Run."

Mama Bet's house was one of the oldest structures in Whispering Pines, and generations of McFalls had been born, grew old, and died behind those warped gray walls. It was a perfect place for a good old-fashioned revival, away from the snooping eyes of the cops and those brownnosers from Barkersville. It was only fitting that the church members congregate here. After all, besides Archer, Mama Bet was the last of her line. Though Linda had always thought the old woman was strange, a little bit haughty and holier-than-thou.

Lester Matheson had brought his four-wheel-drive truck all the way up to the house. The truck was parked under a half-dead apple tree. Two of the Buchanan sisters sat on the sidewalls, moonfaced and dull-eyed. The oldest wore a red plastic clip in her greasy hair.

A goat was tied to the apple tree, browsing along the banks of the creek. The goat stared at Linda, its dark eyes knowing and cold. It sniffed the air. The goat's jaws worked sideways, then it shook the flies from its ears and dipped its head back to the brush.

Jim Potter and Stepford Matheson continued their counterpoint melody on guitar and fiddle. Vivian, Lester's wife, sat in a rocker beside them, tapping her toe in time to the music. Rudy Buchanan stood at one end of the porch, nodding his head, though he was about a half beat off the rhythm.

Sonny Absher leaned against a corner post, smoking a cigarette. His eyes moved to the woods behind the house, then fixed on Linda. "You're late," he said, smoke drifting through his ragged mustache as he spoke.

"I got here as soon as I could."

"The reverend don't like people to be late."

"Archer says, 'Everything in God's good time,' brother," she answered.

The Abshers were a bunch of inbred ignorants, and Sonny was the worst of the lot. That was one of the things that burned her up about some of her neighbors: they were on the doorstep to heaven here in Archer's mountains, but instead of reveling in the glory, they lived off food stamps and bootlegging and selling the occasional beef steer. Archer would cleanse them, though. She could hardly wait.

She entered the house without knocking. Mama Bet sat in an overstuffed armchair, a shawl over her lap. Her lower legs were thick-veined below the hem of her dress. The woman smelled of smoke and salt, like a cured ham.

"Hi, Mama Bet." Linda bent and kissed the woman's cheek.

"Hey, honey. How's that man of yours coming along?"

"Not real good. I was hoping he would see the light and be spared, but-"

The old woman cut her off with a hard look, her eyes misted by cataracts. "Ain't for us to decide such as that."

Linda lowered her head.

"Only Archer knows the proper time and place for each man's death," Mama Bet continued. "*You* ain't the one turned David into a sinner, are you? You ain't the one packed him off to the Baptist church when he was a boy and too young to know any better. So Jesus is to blame for leading David astray, not you."

"Amen to that," said Nell Absher. Her husband Haywood nodded in solemn agreement. Their daughter Noreen went to the window and looked out over the clouded mountains.

"Here come Hank and Beulah," Noreen said.

"Good," said Mama Bet. "Is that everybody?"

Becca Faye Greene came in from the kitchen, a cup of coffee in her hand. She gave it to Mama Bet and stood beside the old woman's chair. She flashed a smug smile at Linda.

Becca Faye was a Potter by blood, but had married and kept the Greene name after her husband ran off to Minnesota. She was part of Archer's circle back in high school, but had chickened out when Archer asked her to help found the Temple in California. Since Archer had returned, Becca Faye was doing everything in her power to stay in the reverend's good graces, perhaps to make up for her earlier betrayal.

Or perhaps for something more. Becca Faye's blouse was low-cut, and she was flashing enough cleavage to earn her a severe spiritual cleansing. Linda had seen the way Becca Faye had sidled up to Archer at last night's service. She wondered if the woman had had better luck than Linda in Archer's parked van.

Jealousy. One of the greatest sins of all. Forgive me, Archer.

"Call them on in," said Mama Bet. She put the coffee cup to her wrinkled lips and took a sip.

One of the Mathesons went outside, and the music stopped. The others filed in, silent Potters, Abshers, Mathesons, Buchanans, and two Greggs, both Linda's cousins. One of them met her eyes, then turned away in shame.

Linda wanted to shout, *There will come great trials, cousin. Archer says sacrifice is the true test of faith. Donna needed cleansing as much as anybody.*

But she kept her tongue. No words would bring Donna back from the dead. Except perhaps Archer's words.

About thirty people packed the living room, lined along the stone hearth and against the corner cupboard, filling the kitchen entrance. Some of the Mathesons skulked in the hall, looking into the room over Lester's shoulders. Mama Bet scanned the waiting faces. She worked her mouth in approval.

"You all know why we're here," she began. "The time's almost upon us. We prayed for the return, and now He's returned. We have all sinned and come short of the glory of heaven. Our ancestors came unto these mountains to worship in peace, but then their hearts turned hard and cold and went to Jesus. We thought saying 'I'm sorry' would make all the old sins go away."

The assembled crowd grew silent at the mention of that foul name "Jesus." Linda's stomach clenched in anger. Mama Bet nodded in appreciation of their revulsion, then continued.

"We got away from all the good things we worshiped," she said. "We strayed from the one true path. We needed the savior to return and deliver us from evil. So God sent Archer into the world of us mortals. And God punished us by making our seed go barren and letting our families die out, punishing the sinners unto the fourth generation."

"Amen," said Lester, and a smattering of others echoed the sentiment.

"We are wicked," said Mama Bet.

"Amen," said Haywood and Nell in unison. Haywood adjusted the knot of his red silk tie.

"We deserve God's wrath," the old woman said, her voice trembling as it increased in volume.

Becca Faye raised her hands and threw back her head.

"There will come great trials."

The woman's breasts swelled against the fabric of her blouse as she arched her back. Linda sneered, wondering who the hussy was showing off for. Archer wasn't here, and God could care less.

The air in the room was electric, thick with the odor of sweat and tension. "Some of us have suffered loss," Mama Bet said.

Linda looked at her cousins. They lowered their heads. The Potters also looked at each other. Old Alma Potter, Zeb's sister, choked on a sob.

"But don't mourn those who have gone before," Mama Bet said, finding her rhythm. "Sacrifice is the currency of God. It's part of Archer's work. We'll all have to make sacrifices before it's done."

Mama Bet's eyes brimmed with tears. Archer was her son, the last of the McFalls. Linda knew that all the families had suffered losses. But the losses were justified, because all of them, the Greggs, Abshers, Potters, Buchanans, and Mathesons, were touched with sin. All of them had a hand in the murder of Wendell McFall.

"What do we do about the sheriff?" Lester asked. The room grew quiet.

Mama Bet clutched the worn arms of her chair. Her fingers crooked as if she were suffering a spasm of pain. "Archer can deal with the sheriff."

"There's others that are against the church," said Becca Faye, staring at Linda.

Linda's face flushed with anger and shame. "He's my husband. The Old Testament says to honor your husband."

Not that you would know about honoring a husband. The only thing YOU honor is whatever big-spending cowboy picks you up at Gulpin' Gulch on Friday night.

"What about your boys?" Becca Faye said, her eyes half-lidded with pleasure at Linda's discomfort. The other members of the congregation looked on with interest. Ronnie and Tim were the youngest descendants of the families that had committed deicide more than a century ago.

Linda looked out the window, at the trees green in the sun, at the dark ridges, at the creek winding between the slopes toward the river. She wished she had stayed in California. Then Ronnie and Tim would have never been born. But she couldn't imagine a life without them, even a life spent in Archer's divine arms.

"I pray for Archer's mercy," Linda finally said. Becca Faye had no response to that simple plea.

Sonny Absher broke the silence. "They got to pay like everybody else."

"But they're innocent," Linda said, angry now.

"Ain't nobody innocent."

Especially you, Linda thought, but she shouldn't pass judgment on a fellow sinner. All were equal in the eyes of Archer. All were equally guilty, and all would pay the same price.

No, not exactly the same price. Sonny would lose only his own miserable life. Linda was more than ready to give Archer her life if that was required to complete his sacred work. She even understood that David would have to die if he insisted on interfering. But the boys . . .

The boys shouldn't have to pay for sins that only barely touched them. Their blood was nearly pure. But so had Isaac's blood been pure, and Abraham still had to lay him on the altar.

Mama Bet tried to stand and fell back into the armchair. Two of the Potter brothers moved forward to help her rise. She wobbled slightly in their grip.

"Archer be praised," she said. "Y'all go on now. I'll see you at church tonight."

"Archer be praised," said Haywood Absher. He had been one of the last to leave the Baptist fold, but he had embraced Archer's gospel as wholeheartedly as anyone. At least, he put on a good act of believing.

Linda joined the others in a closing "Amen."

The families began filing out, their heads down. Linda thought they should be joyful, but instead they were worried about their own mortal flesh. Death wasn't the end: death was the beginning of a new life in the kingdom. The coming deliverance was a time of celebration and exaltation, not punishment. God had blessed them by sending Archer to serve as His mighty sword.

Then why did she so dread giving her boys away?

Linda waited on the porch for the crowd to thin. Becca Faye brushed past, leaving a trail of dimestore perfume. Sonny Absher flashed his four-toothed grin and nodded good-bye, then took Becca Faye's arm. He escorted her to his rusty Chevelle, where they would probably spend the afternoon sinning in the backseat.

"You coming to the church early tonight?" asked Lester.

Linda chewed at her thumb. "If it's Archer's will."

"Don't worry none about your boys. Mine went to God years ago, and I've come to accept it." Lester nervously chewed his tobacco.

"What if Vivian is the next sacrifice? How would you feel then?"

"Sins got to be paid for."

"Why can't we just pay for our own sins?"

Mama Bet was listening from the screen door. "It don't

work that way, child. Sacrifice is the true test of faith. Remember the lesson of Abraham? It ain't a sacrifice unless you lose something dear."

"And what are you losing, Mama Bet?"

The old woman looked out across the mountains, squinting her milky eyes. A small breeze was blowing from Tennessee, carrying with it the smell of sourwood blooms and pine.

"Flesh and blood," Mama Bet finally said. "Just like everybody else."

✟ Chapter 16

The last bell rang, and Ronnie ran to his locker, holding his books in front of his face so that no stray elbows would bump him in the nose. The injury throbbed a little, but he'd decided not to take the pain pill. After he'd spent lunchtime with Melanie, pain barely touched him. He felt bulletproof, especially because she said maybe they should eat lunch together every day.

He was mentally going over the poem that he'd given her last month. He had tried to be funny and sweet at the same time, so that maybe if she read between the lines, she'd see that he thought she was the most beautiful flower in the whole garden. Dripping in the rain. Soaking color from the sun. Flashing beauty in the breeze.

Plucking petals. *She loves me. She loves me not.* Well, he'd left out that last part. No way was he going to say *love* in a poem. Plus, she might think that, since she was the flower, that would mean he wanted to pull her arms and legs off.

The best thing about the poem was that she didn't giggle and show it to all her girlfriends. Ronnie didn't think he could stand that. A lot of the other kids already thought he was weird because he carried around books that weren't even assigned. He also wore bargain-brand blue jeans and sometimes his T-shirts didn't even have messages on them. He wasn't cool: he didn't play sports, hang around the Barkersville mall, or watch MTV.

But right now, he didn't care what people thought or how far out of it he was. All he cared about was that Melanie would sit with him at lunch. He recalled the breathless way she had said, "I promise," when he told her not to tell anyone else about Boonie Houck and the Bell Monster. His heart was made of helium.

A commotion in the hall pulled him from his pleasant thoughts. Shouts erupted, and a gawking ring of students had gathered in the math wing. Something was happening, possibly a fight. Most likely a fight. That was about the only thing that drew people's attention these days.

"Leave me alone," came a scared voice.

Tim! Ronnie fought through the circle. He heard Whizzer Buchanan's smoky, snickering voice.

"Tell us about it, goober-head," taunted Whizzer. "Tell us about the thing with wings and claws and livers for eyes."

"No," whimpered Tim. "Let me go."

Ronnie shouldered past the eighth graders in the front row. Whizzer had Tim by the shoulders, shaking him. Tears trailed down Tim's cheeks. His glasses were on the floor, and books were scattered around his feet.

"Tell us, Tim," said Whizzer. "Inquiring minds want to know."

This drew a laugh from the crowd. Ronnie threw down his books and shoved Whizzer in the back. The crowd gasped and grew silent. Whizzer turned, all five feet ten of him, jaw muscles twitching. Ronnie imagined the bully's muscles tensing under his camouflage jacket.

"Well, well, well," said Whizzer. "If it ain't Mr. Hero

himself."

Whizzer's eyes half closed, as if Ronnie were a bug that he wanted to squash with one big lace-up boot. Ronnie looked around the looming hulk at Tim, who was pressed back against the lockers that lined the hall. "You okay, Tim?"

Tim sniffed and nodded.

"Get your books, then. Dad's waiting."

"And what if I say it ain't time for you to go yet?" said Whizzer.

Ronnie looked at the faces in the crowd. Their expressions were eager, expectant, relieved that they weren't Whizzer's victims of choice this time. If only a teacher would come. He'd even be happy to see Mrs. Rathbone.

"We didn't do anything to you," Ronnie said.

"Yeah, you did. You got born, didn't you?" This drew another laugh, but Whizzer wasn't smiling.

Tim stooped to pick up his books. Whizzer kicked them away.

"Heard you been to church," said Whizzer. "And you got a little friend there. Something with wings and claws and livers for eyes. Everybody likes a good ghost story, Mr. Hero-Man. Tell us about how you saved Tim from the Bell Monster."

Ronnie's heart lodged in his throat. "Did you tell anybody, Timmy?"

Tim shook his head, then knelt and found his glasses and put them back on.

If *Tim* hadn't told, then . . .

Ronnie spun and searched the crowd. Melanie was on the edge of it. To her credit, she was a little pale. She looked away in shame.

He would not cry. Oh, no, Ronnie would not cry, at

least not here and not now. He balled his fists, and a sigh of satisfaction rose from the crowd.

"Tell us about the rest of it," said Whizzer, looking down at Ronnie, his smile like a possum's. "Tell us about your Mama and the temple in California."

Temple? California? His mom had never been to California. "You're crazy, you . . . you—"

Ronnie was aware that he could never take back what he would say next. "—*you gap-toothed redneck.*"

A murmur rippled through the hall. Some of the kids had buses to catch, but the crowd had grown larger. Sweat trickled down the back of Ronnie's neck.

Where were those teachers?

Whizzer shoved Ronnie in the chest. Ronnie stumbled but kept his feet.

"Now you done it, you sissy," said Whizzer. "The reverend says everybody got to pay for their sins in blood. So maybe I'll just let you make an advance payment."

The reverend? Ronnie's head spun in confusion. His ears rang because of the pulse throbbing in his head. He was scarcely aware of the crowd now. It was just him and Whizzer and hate and pain.

Whizzer drew back a fist that looked the size of a football. Ronnie heard the whisper of air just before the fist crashed into the side of his head. His vision went black for a moment, and when it returned, he was looking at Whizzer's boots only inches away.

One of the boots nudged him on the shoulder. "Get up, weasel. Or you want me to step on you a little?"

Ronnie struggled to his knees, then stood on wobbly legs. He realized that the crowd was roaring, shouts and laughter and jeers. Tim had slipped to safety. The blood hunters had bigger game now.

Ronnie pretended to be hurt. It wasn't a far stretch of his imagination. His ears rang and the side of his face throbbed.

"Come on. Archer says there will come great trials," taunted Whizzer. "Archer says it's high time for a cleansing."

Did none of the other kids realize Whizzer was a raving lunatic? No. They didn't care. Reasons didn't matter. Only entertainment at someone else's expense.

Ronnie stooped and bulled his way into Whizzer's belly. He heard the wind rush from Whizzer's gut, and they both slammed into the lockers. Whizzer pounded on his back, but he could hardly feel it. He held on and squeezed, his nose pulsing now. He tasted blood on his lips.

An authoritative voice boomed through the hall. "What's going on here?"

It was Mr. Gladstone, the principal. The one everybody called either Glad-Stoned or Fred Flintstone. The students backed away, and Ronnie relaxed his grip on Whizzer, though he didn't let go. The principal grabbed Ronnie by the collar and finally dragged him to his feet. Whizzer stood and smoothed his jacket, his face red.

"Ah, Mr. Buchanan," Mr. Gladstone said. "Why am I not surprised?"

He turned to Ronnie. "And you are . . . ?"

Lying was useless. Everything was useless. "Ronnie. Ronnie Day."

"Okay, gentlemen. Let's take a trip to my office."

Ronnie and Whizzer marched down the hall like prisoners at gunpoint. The crowd had broken into lines on each side of the hall, whispering among themselves, already expanding the fight into a bloody schoolyard legend. Ronnie realized he was the first person stupid enough to stand up to Whizzer Buchanan. He wiped his nose with his hand. At least Whizzer hadn't punched him there.

Sins paid for in blood. Well, how much freaking blood does it TAKE?

He looked behind him. The kids were juiced on adrenaline, dispersing now, a few shadow-boxing to re-create the fight. Tim's tears had dried and he followed Mr. Gladstone as if in shock, carrying an armful of books. Melanie was behind Tim, and Ronnie looked back into her blue eyes.

So this is what it feels like when the Bell Monster rips open your chest and takes your heart. Except this way, you don't die. This way, your heart keeps working, and you get a dose of nails and barbed wire and broken glass with every beat.

Melanie opened her mouth as if to explain, then looked down at the floor and shook her head. Her lip quivered and her eyes were moist.

She loves me. She loves me not.

At least that was one less thing to worry about. The principal nudged Whizzer and Ronnie into his office and closed the door.

"Another one dead." Sheriff Littlefield let the deerskin jacket fall back over the face of the mutilated woman. "One of the Gregg girls."

"You know her?" Detective Storie asked.

"Used to date her sister back in high school." Littlefield looked up the road, where it wound into the hills. He knew this area well. A half dozen houses were tucked away in the shadowed folds. Behind them, Buckhorn Mountain rose so steep and rocky that no one could settle there. The mountain was the end of the world, a great wall

that imprisoned as much as it protected.

Littlefield had grown up in one of those old houses. He still owned a couple of acres of sloping timberland at the foot of the mountain. He had visited the land only twice since his mom had died some ten years ago. She had gone to her grave still heartbroken over the deaths of her husband and youngest son.

Frank was the last of the Littlefields. Maybe that wasn't a bad thing. Seemed all the old families were dying out. The world had changed under them, time had left them in the dust, and all that remained was the demolishing of homesteads and the erecting of monuments. Stone markers that read, *May God Protect and—*

"Sheriff?" Storie called from the ditch.

He rubbed his eyes and looked up from where he was kneeling over the body. Whatever haze he'd been in last night still affected him. He felt as if he were moving underwater. "Did you find something?"

She held up a yellow receipt, gripping it carefully by the edge so that she wouldn't smudge any fingerprints. "This must have fallen out of the jacket."

"What does it say?"

"It's from Barkersville Hardware. Made out to Day Construction."

"David Day. He lives about a mile up the road."

"We couldn't be that lucky, could we?"

"David ain't a murderer. I've known him since we were kids."

David sometimes wore a jacket like the one over Donna Gregg's body.

"How well do you know him?"

Littlefield stood, his knees sore. "Well enough."

"As well as you know Archer McFall?"

The sheriff looked up the road, then at Sheila. "I'd better go question him."

"I'll call for Perry Hoyle," Sheila said.

The county's station wagon was putting on a lot of miles these days. Sheila headed back to her cruiser, which was pulled off the side of the road behind the sheriff's Trooper.

Littlefield checked around the body. Chest ripped open. Heart gone. No mountain lion had performed that particular atrocity.

How about the Bell Monster, Frankie?

Samuel's voice. Littlefield glanced into the forest on both sides of the road. His ears rang, a high-pitched buzz that ripped like a jigsaw blade through his brain.

He tried to blink away the darkness that seeped from the corners of his vision.

Not another blackout. Not in front of Sheila.

He wouldn't allow himself to go insane. Too many people were counting on him. Samuel was dead. So were Donna Gregg and two others. More, unless he did something.

A car came down the road and slowed as it approached the scene. Littlefield forced himself to stand erect and wave the car past. One of the Absher boys was driving. Becca Faye smiled at him from the passenger's side. Neither of the pair looked at the body lying in the weeds, though it was visible from the road.

The sheriff waited until his hands stopped trembling, then walked to Sheila's cruiser. She was just hanging up her radio handset when he reached her open door.

"Another unit's on the way, and Hoyle will be out in a half hour." Her eyes narrowed. "Are you okay, Sheriff?"

He nodded, hoping she didn't notice the sweat on his

face. "I'm going to ride up to the Day place."

"Good. I'll wait here for backup, then I'm going to pay a little visit of my own."

"Who to?"

"The Reverend Archer McFall."

He came around the door and leaned over her. "Listen, Shei—" He started to say her first name, then caught himself. "Sergeant. We got nothing on him."

"In that case, he won't mind answering a few questions."

"Maybe we should go together."

She shook her head. "We don't have time. Who knows when the killer's going to strike again? We need to jump on every lead we've got."

"Then let me take Archer."

Her eyes shone with defiance. "This is my case, remember? You assigned it to me. What are you so worried about, anyway?"

Ghosts don't exist. Archer McFall is just another preacher, another ordinary person who took up the Bible and found something in its pages that meant something. That doesn't make him dangerous. That doesn't even make him that unusual.

He didn't want to admit that he was scared. The detective would perform a better interrogation without him around to muddy the waters. After all, Littlefield had taken his chances with Archer the evening before, and had nothing but a gaping hole in his memory to show for it. Littlefield was losing faith in his own abilities, and that was even scarier than the Hung Preacher's ghost.

"Do you know where he's staying?" he asked.

She nodded. "I checked around. He's rented a room down at the Holiday Inn."

"That's funny. His mother has a place up the road. Wonder why he's not staying with her?"

"With his money, you'd think he'd rent one of those chalets by the ski slopes. You're the one who's supposed to know him, remember?"

He looked at Donna Gregg's cold body. "No," he said quietly. "I *don't* remember."

"Maybe after you talk to David Day, you should get some sleep." Sheila went past him and continued her search of the scene. Littlefield got in his Trooper and started the engine. He rolled down the window as he pulled away. "Be careful," he called over the motor's roar.

She nodded absently, her mind already consumed with analyzing the victim's ragged flesh. Littlefield swallowed hard and headed toward Buckhorn Mountain.

It was past four o'clock. David and the boys should have been home by now.

I hope Archer didn't take them early, Linda thought. The angel of God would be coming for them all sooner or later. She couldn't help but hope it was later. She was going to miss the boys when they were gone. But at least the reunion would be sweet and everlasting.

For the tenth time, she peered anxiously through the curtains. The sheriff's Trooper turned off the river road onto their packed dirt driveway. Linda dropped the curtain, heart pounding. Even though he'd attended last night's service, she didn't trust him.

She waited by the front door until she heard his feet on the porch. She swung the door open and forced a smile. "Hey, Sheriff. What brings you out to these parts?"

The sheriff bobbed his head in greeting. "Bad news, I'm

afraid."

Was there any other kind?

She cleared her throat. "It's not the boys, is it?" Hoping, hoping.

Please, God, don't take them yet.

"No." The sheriff looked at her closely, as if they had once shared some secret that he'd forgotten. Then he pointed to the side of the house, where David had nailed a piece of plywood over the window. "Looks like you got a broken window."

"Yeah. Those darned blue jays, they see their reflection and just got to pick a fight. One of them hit it just a little too hard."

"Is David home?"

"He went to pick up the boys at school. Should be back any minute."

"Mind if I wait for him?"

Linda opened the door all the way and stepped aside. "Please come in."

The sheriff sat on the edge of the easy chair and leaned forward. Linda sat across from him, not knowing what to do with her hands. She straightened the magazines on the coffee table, wrinkled copies of David's *Field & Stream* and her *Woman's World Weekly*.

She sat back and cupped her hands over her knees, then pushed her hair away from her forehead. "Wasn't that a wonderful service last night?"

"Reverend McFall sure knows how to preach up a storm. I'll say that for him."

The sheriff's eyes focused behind her. She turned to see what he was looking at. It was a knitted sampler, one Grandma Gregg had made for her, which read, *May God Protect And Keep This House.* A little farm scene was stitched below the words.

"We're mighty blessed that he came back," she said.

"Came back?"

"To the mountains."

The sheriff nodded. The room was cramped with silence. The air smelled of the trout she had cooked for lunch.

"So what do you think of this weather?" she asked.

"Pretty nice."

"Yeah, we've got to get our pole beans planted. Been in such a commotion lately, we got behind on our chores."

"How's Ronnie?"

"Ronnie? Oh, he's fine. Good enough to go back to school today. I got to take him to the doctor next week to get his stitches out, but he won't have a permanent hump on his nose or anything."

"That's good."

Another long silence. The sheriff looked at the wall again. "What's that?" he asked.

Linda's heart warmed as she looked at the small metal ankh on the wall. She had put the symbol of the temple in place of the old wooden cross David had nailed there. "It's a joyous time, isn't it?"

"Linda, what's going on at the church?"

She swallowed some air and nearly choked on it. "You heard Archer last night. It's time for a cleansing, time to pay for iniquities."

"People are getting killed."

"Archer says sins have to be paid for in blood."

"Jesus did that for all of us by dying on the cross."

Linda held her breath. *Blasphemy.* Archer had allowed this nonbeliever into the church?

Archer must have his reasons. Who was she to doubt

his holy ways?

Outside, a vehicle pulled up. She jumped up from the sofa and ran to the door. The sheriff followed her out onto the porch. David and a glum-looking Ronnie and Tim got out of the Ranger.

David cast a hostile look at the sheriff. "What do you want?"

The sheriff looked at the two boys, then back to David. "It's about Donna Gregg."

Linda put her hand over her mouth. David turned to the boys. "Why don't y'all go play in the barn for a while?" he said to them.

"What's wrong?" Tim asked. His glasses sat askew on his nose. He pushed them up with a thin forefinger.

"Come on," Ronnie said to Tim. "Let's get out of here."

As Ronnie turned, Linda saw the large bruise on his temple. "What happened?" she asked David.

"He got in a fight."

Ronnie? In a fight? He wouldn't hurt an earthworm.

"Something bad happened, didn't it?" Tim said to Linda. "You always send us away when you want to talk about bad stuff."

Ronnie took his brother's arm and led him across the uneven stretch of green lawn. The sheriff waited until the boys had disappeared inside the barn, then said, "Donna's dead."

David looked at Buckhorn Mountain as if he wished he were walking its ridgeline. He always wanted to be away, alone, in troubled times. Linda tried to fake a sob, but failed.

"I found your jacket at the scene," the sheriff said to David. "And a receipt made out to Day Construction. That kind of evidence is enough for me to take you in for questioning, but I'd just as soon do it here."

"She was still warm when I found her," David said, his voice as hollow as a potato barrel in spring. "Must have been about two in the morning."

"Why didn't you report it?"

"You were around. I figured you knew about it before I did."

"Did you see anybody?"

"Depends on your definition of 'anybody.'"

Linda tried to signal David with her eyes. Then she realized she didn't know whose side to be on. The sheriff was one of the flock, but somehow *wrong*, Jesus-tainted and closed-hearted. And David was . . . well, she didn't know what David was.

"Tell me what you saw," the sheriff said.

"Probably the same thing you saw." David folded his arms. "After all, you're one of them, ain't you?"

"One of what?"

He nodded at Linda. "Them. Archer's little angels. I saw you at the church last night."

Linda looked from the sheriff to David, as if she were watching a badminton match being played with a live grenade. She chewed at her fingernail. Blood rushed from the ragged quick and filled her mouth with a brassy sweetness.

"Three people are dead," the sheriff said. "All of them were somehow connected to the church."

"It's not Archer," Linda said too quickly and forcefully.

"The old families," Littlefield said. "Houck. Potter. Gregg."

"They needed cleansing," Linda said. "Archer says we all need cleansing."

"Shut up," David said. "I'm sick to death of 'Archer this' and 'Archer that.' I had enough of that the first time."

"The first time?" the sheriff asked.

"Yeah," David said. "In California."

"What's California got to do with what's happening now?" Linda asked.

David slowly shook his head. "You don't get it, do you? He was a lot smarter out in California. Or maybe he just didn't know his own power."

"Don't bring your blamed old jealousy into this."

"You didn't see him," David said, his voice rising in pitch. "You didn't see him carry the bodies into the so-called temple."

"What are you talking about?" Linda said.

"The Temple of the Two Suns," he spat. "You didn't hear about the murders out there. Who misses another lost drifter on the Santa Monica freeway? Even a half dozen. Plenty more where they came from. Now I just got to figure out why Archer came back."

Linda shook her head. What was he saying? Archer didn't kill anybody. It was *God* who performed the cleansings. Archer was merely the savior, the earthly vessel.

"You're saying that he committed murders in California?" she heard the sheriff ask David.

"Saw it with my own eyes. How do they taste, Linda?"

Linda looked in horror at the gnawed flesh of her fingertips.

"How do they taste, Sheriff?" David asked.

"What the hell?" the sheriff asked.

"Communion. The body. The bread of life." David walked to the Ranger.

The sheriff looked questioningly at Linda, then called to David, "I'm not through talking yet."

"Well, I am." David pulled his rifle out from under the Ranger's seat.

"Don't do it," the sheriff warned. He fell into a crouch, like one of those television cowboys in a showdown. Except Linda saw that the sheriff wore no firearm.

David laughed. "Don't worry. I won't waste good bullets on the likes of you and her. These are for Archer. I'm going to kill him as many damned times as it takes. This time, I'm going to blow him back to hell for good."

✝ Chapter 17

"What's going on?"

"Shh." Ronnie pressed his cheek against the board so that he could see through the knothole. The air was thick with dust. He wondered what would happen to the packing in his broken nose if he sneezed. Could he even sneeze if he couldn't smell?

Dad strode back to the Ranger, leaving Mom and the sheriff standing on the porch. When Ronnie saw the rifle, his heart stuttered in his chest. "No," he whispered.

"What?" Tim said.

Dad went into the house. Mom said something to the sheriff that Ronnie couldn't hear. The sheriff got in his Trooper and drove away. Mom looked around, then also went into the house.

Ronnie moved away so that Tim could look through the knothole. Tim stood on an overturned bucket to get eye-level with the hole.

"I don't see nothing," Tim said.

"They're in the house."

"Is it bad?"

Tim's not dumb. He knows what's going on. I guess this is the part where I have to play brave big brother.

Ronnie tried to sound nonchalant. "Dad's home, isn't he? How bad can it be?"

"I'm scared."

"It's daytime," Ronnie said, though the shadows and dusty cobwebs and the creaking planks of the barn made him nervous. "Monsters don't get you in the daytime."

"No, I mean scared about Mom and Dad." Tim stepped off the bucket and sat on a bale of hay.

Ronnie stared into the row of wooden stalls that lined the far side of the barn. They didn't keep cows anymore. Dad said with beef prices being so low, it was cheaper to buy meat at the supermarket than to raise it. Ronnie almost missed taking care of the animals, putting them up at night and making sure they had hay in the winter. Dad and Ronnie had slaughtered cows, too, hung them up by a chain and cut them open, the steam rising from the animals' insides. Ronnie didn't miss that part of it.

"Mom and Dad will work it out," Ronnie said. "They have to."

"What if they don't? What if she makes him mad again and he leaves? Who will protect us then?" Tim's lower lip trembled.

"Look, I saved you from Whizzer, didn't I? You have to trust me."

"Yeah, right. Like you're going to be able to beat up the Bell Monster?"

Ronnie coughed from the dust. "I'll think of something."

"Anyway, how do you kill a ghost? Dad shot it, but I know it's coming back."

Ronnie had been wondering that himself. Why would a ghost want to kill people? It didn't make sense. If a ghost were crazy, maybe, but just a plain old ordinary ghost?

Whatever it was, the red church was to blame. He'd read books about hauntings. Supposedly, "psychic imprints" could be projected into the walls if a person suffered great emotional turmoil. That seemed kind of stupid to Ronnie, but the Bell Monster was real. What if the Bell Monster was the spirit of the preacher who had been hanged there? Surely having a rope around your throat would cause some emotional turmoil.

But then, everything that had ever died would leave a ghost. What living thing hadn't suffered a little emotional turmoil in its life? A lot of cows had been killed right there in the middle of the barn, shot in the brains with a rifle and cut into pieces and their guts hauled away in a wheelbarrow. But you didn't see ghost cows lurking around everywhere.

Maybe God was trying to take the preacher's soul to heaven, but decided halfway up that the preacher was too evil to enter the kingdom. Maybe the devil didn't want the preacher, either, because the preacher knew too many Bible verses and would tell them to the other people in hell. Maybe the preacher would try to save people who had already been condemned to the everlasting fire. No way the devil would want something like that going on. So the preacher got stuck in the middle, and killed people because he was lonely and wanted some ghosts for company.

That was dorky. He was thinking like a third grader.

"You don't have to kill a ghost," Ronnie finally said. "It's already dead. The trick is to make it *stay* dead."

"How do you do that?"

"By giving it what it wants."

They looked at each other. "What it wants is to kill us," said Tim.

"Yeah." Ronnie sighed. "A real kick in the rear."

"I don't want to die."

Ronnie didn't, either- no matter how many times

Preacher Staymore tried to tell him that God had a special place for children. The preacher had also introduced him to the idea of committing sins of the heart. It was bad enough back when doing something bad would get you scratched out of the Big Golden Book. Now he'd learned that just *thinking* about bad stuff would damn him to hell.

He'd asked Jesus into his heart every few weeks, just like Preacher Staymore wanted. How long did your heart stay clean after Jesus washed away the sins? What if you died while you were thinking a bad thought, and didn't have time to ask forgiveness? The whole business sounded pretty risky to Ronnie.

And he was in no hurry to find out for sure.

"You're not going to die, Tim," Ronnie promised, hoping he sounded more reassuring than he felt. He was about to say something else when the shot rang out.

The Holiday Inn was off the only four-lane highway through Pickett County, just outside the Barkersville exit. Sheila Storie pulled into the parking lot. The lot was nearly empty. Tourists were rare between the ski season and summer, when Floridians came to escape the heat and New Yorkers came to escape New York.

Archer McFall's room was on the first floor, just beside the motel's drained pool. McFall's black Mercedes was parked in front of 107. Storie parked beside it and got out, checking her watch and wondering how the sheriff was coming along. She glanced through the driver's-side window of the Mercedes. The interior was spotless. She knocked on the door of 107.

A tall man answered the knock. He was handsome, but a little slick-looking, like a lawyer on a television show.

He had strong cheekbones and a wide face that was freshly shaven. He smiled at her.

"Archer McFall?" she asked.

"Yes, my child. How may I help you?"

The way he called her "child" irritated Storie. He couldn't have been more than ten years older than she was, about Frank's age. He smelled faintly of cologne and a more pungent odor that she couldn't identify. The room behind him was dark, the shades drawn.

"I'm Det. Sgt. Sheila Storie, Pickett County Sheriff's Department," she said, not bothering to dig her badge out of her jacket.

McFall blinked, but his smile didn't waver. "It's a pleasure to meet you, ma'am. Your sheriff and I go way back."

How far back?

Storie looked into his eyes, trying to read them. He gave nothing away. "I was wondering if I could ask you a few questions."

"Oh, about Mr. Houck." His eyes went colder, darker. "That poor, unfortunate man. I hope you've caught his killer."

"No, sir, but we have a few leads."

"I'm glad. What kind of perverse notion leads someone to commit such an act on holy ground?"

"Well, sir, at the time, the red church was being used as a barn."

McFall laughed, a low sound that started in his abdomen and shook his entire body. "That's true. Without a congregation, a church isn't much of a church, is it? Without people, and what they believe-"

"Did they believe in you in California?" Storie said. She gave him her "sunglasses stare," the kind of cool look that some of her fellow cops gave only when hidden behind the safety of tinted shields.

"The people of Whispering Pines need ministering as much as anyone else."

"Badly enough to make you give up an easy life in California?"

"Why, Sergeant," he said, tugging at his tie. "I do believe you are interrogating me."

"Not really. Just dropped by for a chat."

"In that case, please come in." He showed his capped teeth and pushed the door wide.

Storie went inside. The bed was neatly made, with no clothes or suitcases in sight. A Bible lay open on the bedside table. McFall shut the door and flipped the shades. Afternoon sunlight striped the room.

She sat in the stiff-backed chair by the desk. McFall sat on the edge of the bed, looking uncomfortable. "So why did you come back?" she asked.

"I'm of the mountains. My heart has always belonged here. My mother still lives in Whispering Pines, in a little farmhouse at the base of Buckhorn Mountain."

Storie nodded at him, encouraging him to continue.

"I felt the calling as a child," he said. "As you may know, my family has a long history of serving God and spreading the Holy Word. Even as a child, I always knew I was going to be a preacher."

"Like your great-great-grandfather?"

McFall looked out the window, his jaw twitching. "Wendell McFall was an unpleasant twig on the family tree. Still, I don't think he deserved hanging, do you?"

"I don't know anything about him but the legend."

"Oh, the so-called 'ghost' story. Let me assure you that the only spirit that walks the church is the Holy Spirit. I should know. I spent a lot of time there as a teenager, praying to God for direction."

Storie shifted in her chair. "Tell me about California."

"I thought I would start a church out there. A few local girls went with me. We were a fine bunch, not a sinful thought among us, our hearts as pure as the sun. We were going to start a commune and live a simple, ascetic life."

"Seven girls went out there, I hear." Storie had traced the seven. Of them, only Linda Gregg, now Linda Day, had ever been heard from again.

"When we got there, most of the girls wandered off to Los Angeles and San Francisco. I guess the big-city life was more enticing than a life spent in the service of God."

"How come your church out there failed?"

McFall smiled at her. "It didn't fail. The Temple of the Two Suns prospered, thanks be to God. I had a television show that ministered to thousands. I opened a music store, a religious bookstore, and some other businesses. Even with the success, even though I was reaching the people, my heart held an emptiness. I prayed for guidance, and God told me to go home. So here I am."

Storie watched his face carefully. "If you don't mind my saying so, the Temple of the Two Suns sounds like an unusual name for a church founded by someone from the Bible Belt."

"There are many paths to God. The true path is to follow your own heart. My heart says that what I do is right."

"What denomination is your religion?"

"Christian, in a manner of speaking. Of course, every sect or order has its unique qualities. 'Two Suns' comes from the idea of God sending a second light into the world. That's one of God's promises, you know."

"It certainly didn't take you long to get a church up and running here," she said.

"I was fortunate that Lester Matheson let me buy the property and return it to the family. And the people of Whispering Pines opened their hearts and welcomed me into their community."

"You have to admit, it's something of a coincidence that murders started occurring as soon as you came back to the area."

"I came because God called." He leaned forward. "He calls all of us. He asked to be invited into our hearts. Is He inside you?"

Storie shifted in her chair. "That's not important."

His mouth twisted. "It's the *only* thing that's important. What's in your heart?"

"Look, Mr. McFall--"

His eyes were bright, feverish. "*What's in your heart?*"

Storie stood and headed for the door. A hand fell on her shoulder. She spun, instinctively crouching into the defensive judo stance she had learned in cop school. For a long second, her muscles froze.

His FACE.

McFall's chin lengthened, and his teeth sharpened between his wide black lips. His eyes were feral, so glitteringly yellow that they seemed to float in front of his face. His nose lifted in a snarl.

Just as suddenly, the illusion passed. McFall stood before her, his hands up in apology. "I didn't mean to startle you, my child," he said in a calm voice.

Great. As if seeing bloodstains and ropes that don't exist wasn't bad enough, now I'm starting to think . . .

She put her hand to her forehead. Stress, that was what it was. Three murders to solve before more people died. Her people, the ones she had sworn to uphold and protect.

"What's troubling you, Sergeant?"

His voice soothed her. She had a sudden urge to break down in front of this man who was unruffled by life's traumas and worries. He was like the sun on the smooth surface of a lake. His serenity radiated in almost palpable waves.

"It's nothing, Reverend. Nothing at all."

"You don't have to keep it inside," he said, taking a step nearer. She backed against the door.

"Just turn your troubles over to a higher power," he continued in his soft, firm voice. "Open your heart and trust in God."

That sounded like a good idea. And as soon as she realized it sounded like a good idea, a warning flare rocketed across her mind.

Wait a second. I don't trust ANYBODY, much less a man who's on a suspect list for three counts of murder.

But there was something about his tone, the gentleness and concern in his dark eyes. He was close enough so that she could smell mint mouthwash on his breath. For a moment, she thought he was going to lean forward and kiss her, and the worst part was that she didn't think she would stop him.

Instead he said, "Don't be afraid. Open your heart. Have faith."

She looked into his eyes, and her skin tingled with mild electricity. Such warmth, such promise, such *peace* emanated from his eyes. Such humanity.

Oh, yes. She had faith. She believed. Her heart felt swollen and warm in her chest, like a balloon on a summer day.

I believe. Just tell me WHAT to believe.

This was insane. She should have called for backup, told Communications what her 10-20 was. The only person who knew what she was doing was Frank. She tried to picture his face, but all she could see was the golden light that emanated from Archer.

He touched her face. His fingers were hot. She couldn't look away from his eyes, though part of her wanted to vomit, to punch him, to claw at the corners of his smile.

"Faith comes with a price," he said. "All you have to do is give me everything. But the rewards are great, too. The kingdom of heaven can be yours, which contains all the world and more."

She would give and give and give. No, she wouldn't. She served only the taxpayers and law-abiding citizens. She—

"The congregation must have communion," he said. "One bread, one body. And sacrifice is the currency of God. All I ask of you is that you serve."

She nodded. She could do that. Faith required a little sacrifice, but the rewards were everlasting, weren't they?

"Please," she said, lowering herself to her knees. She gazed up into that beatific face. "Let me serve."

He gave a benevolent nod. "You're not one of the old families. But you are working against the purpose of God."

I have fallen short. I am unworthy. I deserve punishment.

What could she offer that would compensate for her sins? What did she have? She could offer her soul, but that was nearly worthless. She did have flesh. She could sacrifice that, and perhaps appease the God she had so callously ignored all the days of her life.

"Take me," she said, her voice hoarse and her eyes moist. So great was the glory of God. And equally great was the glory of Archer McFall. "Use me any way you need."

McFall cocked his head, as if he were consulting God, listening to a divine command that would determine her fate. He knelt quickly and lifted her by the shoulders of her jacket, then wiped the tears from the corners of her eyes.

"Don't cry, my child," he said.

She smiled at him. How could she bury the happiness that filled her and brimmed over, the joy and rapture that he had delivered unto her?

He pulled her away from the door. "Say nothing of this. Tonight you will serve, and thus gain a place in the bosom of God."

Oh, glory! Oh, how merciful is God in his wisdom! She would make the sacrifice to earn her place, to please Archer, to pay for the sin of pride that had shadowed her life.

"Come to the church tonight," he said, then turned and crossed the room, again sitting on the bed.

He adjusted his tie, then clasped his hands lightly in his lap just as someone knocked on the door. "Would you get that, please?" Archer said.

Storie spun, fumbling with the doorknob in her haste to serve. She opened the door and Frank Littlefield stood before her, his fist held sideways, preparing to knock again.

"Hi, Sergeant," Frank said, no surprise in his voice.

She blinked against the sudden rush of sun, annoyed by this trespass into her spiritual communion with Archer. "What are you doing here?" she said.

He looked past her to the reverend. "I came to get some answers, same as you."

"Come in, Sheriff. We've been expecting you," McFall said.

***

David lowered the rifle and smiled.

The front door burst open, and David thought the sheriff might have returned to sneak up on him and jump him. He swiveled the rifle toward the door, his finger tight on the trigger. Ronnie stood in the doorway, Tim small behind him.

David sniffed the comforting aroma of gun smoke. Linda was facedown on the living room floor. Tim ran to her and got on his knees, touching her hair, murmuring "Mommy" over and over again. Ronnie stared at David, his eyes wide with shock, his face pale.

"Did you . . . did you shoot her?" Ronnie asked.

David leaned the rifle against the coffee table. "I ain't that crazy yet."

Linda groaned and Tim helped her sit up.

Ronnie clenched his hands, a tear running down his cheek. "What in the hell's going on, Dad?" he said, shuddering with sobs. "Why are you trying to kill her?"

"I'm not the one trying to kill her," he said, looking down at his wife. "It's that damned Archer McFall."

"Archer McFall's the *preacher*. The preacher's supposed to be the good guy."

"Don't believe everything you hear in Sunday school, son."

"You're *scaring* me, Dad. You told us a family's supposed to stick together when times get bad." Ronnie helped Tim lean Linda against the easy chair. She had a welt above her eye. Ronnie looked at it and then glared at David.

He looks so damned much like his mother.

"I didn't touch her," he said. "She fell when I shot that damned thing."

He pointed to the little symbol that hung on the wall, the lopsided cross that Linda had kept from her days in California. She'd told David she'd thrown it away, that all the old nonsense was over. Well, the devil's hooks sank deep. All it took was a little whiff of sulfur and brimstone to fan the embers in a sinner's heart.

The bullet had penetrated the center of the mock cross. The metal arms had twisted outward, curled by the impact. Gypsum powder trickled from a hole in the sheet rock. David nodded in satisfaction at a good shot.

"Hell followed her from California," he said.

"California?" Ronnie said. "She's never been to California."

David wiped sweat from his forehead. Maybe some secrets were best left buried.

"Are you okay, Mommy?" Tim sounded like a four-year-old.

"Yeah, honey," she said, pushing her hair away from her face and looking at David with mean eyes. "There will come great trials, but we keep on walking."

David was filled with renewed rage. So this was what Archer had driven his family to. Linda, ready to give up everything she owned, including her own flesh and blood. Tim, not knowing which of his parents to trust. Ronnie, learning too young that the world was a screwed-up and hard-assed place. And he himself wondering if faith was enough, if he could single-handedly take on the devil who wore lamb's clothing.

No, I won't be single-handed. I've got God and Jesus and a rifle and everything that's right on my side. Surely that will be enough. I pray to the Lord that will be enough.

"What are we going to do, Dad?" Ronnie looked pathetic, his eyes red and moist, his swollen nose a bruised shade of purple.

"It's high time for a cleansing," Linda said, her voice distant. She rocked back and forth as if tuned into an invisible gospel radio station.

David looked out the open door. Dark mountains huddled on the horizon, cowering before the sinking sun. Even the trees seemed to dread the coming night. The shadows held their breath, waiting to send out an army of monsters under cover of darkness.

Linda's eyes focused on a high spot behind the wall. Tim and Ronnie looked at David, expectant and fearful.

Maybe it *was* high time for a cleansing.

"We're going to beat that thing," he said, more to himself than to the boys.

"How do you kill a ghost?" Tim asked.

David rubbed the stubble on his chin. "Hell if I know, Tim."

"Ronnie says the trick is to make it stay dead. By giving it what it wants."

"Maybe so. We're just going to have to trust in the Lord."

"The *Lord*," Linda said with a sneer. She stiffened and contorted her features. She resembled the wrinkle-faced bat that David had found dead in the barn one morning. The old Linda, the pretty wife and loving mother and good sin-despising Christian, was as dead as Donna Gregg.

David knew Linda had been saved. He had knelt with her at the foot of the pulpit and held her hand while she tearfully asked Jesus into her heart. Once Jesus was in there, He belonged forever. Or was being saved a privilege that He could take away, like the court took away your driver's license if you drove drunk?

David was getting a headache thinking about it. That was God's business, and not for him to worry about. His mission was to protect the innocent, and let the guilty be damned.

"Get out," he said to Linda, trying not to raise his voice.

She lifted her face to him, her eyes wild. The boys wore twin masks of terror.

"Get out," David said more firmly. He gripped the rifle. "Go to the red church or Archer McFall's bed or straight to hell if you want. Just as long as you stay away from the boys."

Linda trembled as she stood.

"Don't hurt her, Daddy," Tim yelled.

David felt a smile crawl across his face, and a chill wended up his spine. He was sickened by the realization that he was enjoying this. A Christian was supposed to hate the sin but love the sinner. A man was supposed to honor his wife. The Lord's number one lesson was that people ought to forgive trespasses.

But the Lord also knew that the human heart was weak.

David pointed the rifle at her.

Tim jumped at Linda and hugged her, his face tight against her chest. "Don't go, Mommy," he pleaded.

David motioned with the rifle barrel toward the door. Linda glared at him, then leaned down and kissed Tim on top of the head. "Shh, baby. It will be okay."

She gently pushed Tim's arms from her waist. Her blue blouse was dark with Tim's tears. She rubbed Ronnie's hair and smiled at him. "Take care of your brother, okay?"

Ronnie nodded. Linda pulled the mangled cross from the wall and clenched her hand around it. She paused at the door. "It's tonight, you know," she said to David.

He swallowed hard. He started to tell her that he still loved her, despite it all. But he could only stare numbly, his fingers like wood on the rifle.

"Lord help us all," he whispered as she headed into the shroud of twilight. His prayer tasted of dried blood and ash.

✟ Chapter 18

The sunset threw an orange wash over the ribbed clouds in the west. The strong green smell of the day's growing died away on the evening breeze. The river's muddy aroma rose like a fog, seeping across the churchyard so thick that Mama Bet could almost taste it. She eyed the shadows in the belfry, clutching her shawl tightly across her chest.

This was bad ground, here at the church. She didn't know why Archer insisted on holding services in this marred house of worship. Wendell McFall had died right there at the end of a rope, one end of it tied high in that bedeviled dogwood. The tree's branches stretched both high and low, toward the sky and the ground, like fingers reaching to grab everything and everybody.

"What's wrong, Mama Bet?"

She turned and looked into the dirty face of Whizzer Buchanan. Fourteen and already in need of a shave. He was all Buchanan, wall-eyed and his hands as plump and clumsy as rubber gloves filled with water. And to think his family used to be fine whittlers, back in the days when people made what they needed instead of buying it down at the Wal-Mart.

"Why, nothing's wrong, child." She smiled at him.

Whizzer smelled of sweet smoke, probably that wacky

weed she heard some of the hippies were growing up in the mountains. Archer would cleanse them, sure as day. Archer held no truck with such trash. Hippies were as bad as the hard-drinking Mathesons and Abshers. Sins of the flesh, sins of the heart. All sins led down one road, down one tunnel, into the dark heart of hell.

"How come we ain't seen the Bell Monster yet?" Whizzer asked. Like the Bell Monster was some kind of video game that you could switch on and off at your convenience. The boy had a lot to learn about the workings of God.

"We got to be patient," she said.

Whizzer nodded and ran into the church, his boots thumping across the wooden floor. She looked across the cemetery. Stepford was relieving himself against a tall granite statue. The faded angel accepted the insult with nary a peep.

In the woods, shadows moved and separated. Becca Faye and Sonny came out from the trees, holding hands and giggling like kids at an Easter egg hunt. Crumpled leaves stuck to Becca Faye's blouse, and the top button was undone. Mama Bet hoped the hussy enjoyed her sweaty little frolic. Because soon she would be sweating the long sweat, the devil riding her back, until forever ate its own sorry tail.

Mama Bet walked across the gravel to the church steps. Diabetes was making her feet hurt something awful. She slowly went up the steps, keeping a grip on the worn handrail. She figured she might as well get used to taking them one step at a time, because she just knew that God had a mighty high set of golden stairs for her to climb to get to heaven.

She rested in the windowless foyer, in the cool darkness. Voices came from the main sanctuary, scattered and echoing in the hushed hollow of the church. She overheard Haywood telling Nell about the benefits of a high deductible with a low co-pay.

"You see, honey," he said, as Mama Bet entered the main body of the church, "odds are that if you do get sick enough to meet your deductible, it's going to run into the tens of thousands of dollars anyway. And the way hospitals charge these days, a body pretty much meets their deductible just walking in the door. So you might as well save that money up front with the cheaper plan."

Nell nodded and put the back of her hand to her mouth to hide her yawn. A couple of pews in front of them, Jim and Alma whispered about Zeb's funeral arrangements. Rudy Buchanan knelt near the lectern, on both knees, practicing his Archer-worship. Almost as phony as a bootlicking Christian.

Mama Bet chewed her lower lip between the nubs of her gums. She didn't want to have one of her spells, not on Archer's night. She took slow deep breaths until her rage subsided.

Some congregation this was. As addle-brained as fishhead stew. But it wasn't Archer's fault. Her boy worked with what material God gave him. If anybody was to blame for this shoddy bunch of backwoods nonbelievers, then you had to turn your eyes upwards- to Him that would plant the seed and then laugh until the skies busted open. And all you could do was let your belly swell until you busted open yourself, until the child crawled out from between your legs and took its rightful throne.

"It's going to be tonight, ain't it?" said Jim, pulling her from her reverie.

"That's for God and Archer to know," she answered.

"It ain't for the likes of us to worry about."

"Can't help but worry," he said, sweat under his eyes.

"It might be any of us up on the chopping block."

"Pray that you're worthy." She couldn't abide such selfishness in the face of a great moment, the moment the whole world was born to see, the reason God clabbered the mud together and shaped the mountains and spit the seas and breathed life into dust. This one shining moment of glory. This end to everything, and the start of the business beyond everything.

She gazed upon the dark stain on the dais. The thing was taking shape, drawing on the sacrificial blood spilled onto its wooden skin. It had slept for 140 years, fighting free once in a while to drift across the night hills or to spook up some teenagers. But now it was awakening for real, busting loose of whatever kind of invisible chains bound the past.

Archer said the red church had to feed, so let it be fed. Let the juice of these sorry souls soak into the floorboards. Let this church absorb all their human blood and sweat and sin. Let them be cleansed for the final journey. Because Archer so ordained.

A tear collected in the corner of her eye. Jim stood and gently clasped her hand, thinking she was afraid or mournful. No, she was *joyful*, grateful to be allowed to hobble into the church, though it was tainted with the sins of their ancestors. Even aching and stiff, her bones as brittle as chalk sticks and her blood vessels as narrow as flaxen threads, even with eyes that could barely tell day from night and fire from ice, even with all the crush of eighty-odd years weighing down and crooking her spine, she could stand proud before the altar.

Here, she could surrender. In this sick house of God,

she could give up her flesh and blood.

Frank Littlefield looked around the motel room. Sheila appeared dazed, her eyes wide and her pupils unnaturally large. Archer McFall sat on the bed like a patient king who was deigning to accept tribute from a minor subject.

"Did you learn anything from David Day?" Sheila asked, though judging from the tone of her voice, she could care less.

"He pulled a gun on me, mostly just for show," Frank said. "He's crazy, but not the kind of crazy that kills three people."

"David Day?" Archer said. "I believe his wife is a member of the congregation."

"Linda," said Frank. "And if I remember right, she was one of the ones who took off to California with you."

Archer looked from Frank to Sheila, and back again. "California has nothing to do with what's happening here. Please put your minds at rest about that. We're all home now, and that's what's important. We're all fulfilling God's plan."

"God's plan," said Frank. "God's plan has left three innocent people dead, assuming that God is the one who pulls the strings."

"Nobody's innocent," said Archer. "And God doesn't pull the strings."

"Sure," Frank said. "I forgot. *You* do."

"Have you been talking to my mother?" Archer smiled. Shadows flitted in the corner of his mouth, or maybe it was worms crawling from between his lips. . . .

***

Frank blinked away the illusion. "Oh, no, Mr. McFall. I don't have to talk to your mother. Because on the way over here, I was thinking back on a night a long time ago. One night when you and me were both younger and, I reckon, more innocent."

"Nobody's innocent," Archer repeated.

"Samuel was," Frank said.

"What's your brother got to do with this?" Sheila asked, her voice hesitant. She put a hand to her head, then rubbed her face as if wiping away sleep.

"That Halloween night at the red church," Frank said hurriedly. His blood raced, his face grew warm, his stomach clenched around a bag of hot nails.

Archer's eyes widened in interest, his face passive and unconcerned, his hands in his lap. As if he were watching a bug in jar, curious to see what it would do next. "Halloween? There've been so many Halloweens."

"When Samuel climbed up into the belfry, something came up behind him. A shadow. Except the shadow laughed." Frank balled his hands into fists.

"Please, Sheriff, not the ghost story again," Sheila said. She seemed to have recovered from her daze, and was probably worried that Frank would make a fool of himself in front of the public. Probably thought that Frank would blow his law enforcement career, maybe his whole future in Pickett County. But right now, Frank wasn't thinking about the future. He was thinking about the past. About the dead and buried. And about a familiar laugh.

"I recognized that laugh," Frank said. "Sent a chill through me, the first time I heard it again- at the red church, the day after Zeb Potter was killed."

The Halloween laugh. Frank had heard it hundreds of

times, keeping him awake at 4 A.M. or jerking him from nightmares. He heard it in the squeal of car tires, in the wail of a police siren, in the rush of the cold river. He heard it in the howl of the wind, and he even heard it in silence. The laugh was loudest in silence.

"You were there." Frank raised his fist toward Archer's face. Archer ignored the threatening gesture.

"Sheriff," Sheila said, in her stern cop voice.

"You were in the belfry that night," Frank said to Archer.

He'd heard assault suspects talk about being so mad they "saw red," and now Frank knew what they meant. It was a real thing, the red brighter than the blood of the sun. It poured down over his vision, blocking out Sheila, blocking out the Bible on the nightstand, blocking out the consequences.

"You scared Samuel." Frank was trembling now. "You made him jump. You killed him."

"Sheriff, Sheriff, Sheriff," Archer said, shaking his head slowly as if having to explain an obvious truth to a child. "I didn't kill Samuel. *You* did."

Frank leaped at Archer, the red in his vision now completely obscuring everything but the smile on Archer's face. Frank wanted to tear that smile from the man's face, to hear the satisfying rip of flesh and crack of bone. Frank wanted to feed the man his own smile, shove it down his throat until he choked.

His hands snaked around Archer's neck, squeezing. Frank looked at his own fingers, white from the pressure. He felt removed from the attack, as if it were someone else's hands shutting the air from Archer's lungs. As if he were watching a movie. The thought angered him. He didn't want to be distanced, removed, cheated of his satisfaction.

Hands pounded on his back, pulled at his shirt. He barely felt the blows. Sheila's voice came to him as if through a thick curtain of dreams.

"Stop it, Frank," she shouted. "Damn you, you're killing him."

Killing him.

A wave of pleasure surged through Frank, almost sexual in its intensity. At the same moment, he was repelled by his joyful vengeance. He was no better than Archer, no better than whoever had killed Boonie Houck, Zeb Potter, Donna Gregg.

Sheila had one arm hooked under his right bicep, the other pressing on his neck, her weight full on his back. Frank kept his grip on Archer's neck, watching the carotid artery swell from the stifled circulation. Throughout the attack, Archer had made no move to defend himself. As if he were submitting, a willing victim. A sacrifice.

Frank stared into Archer's eyes. He saw nothing human, no fear, no anger, no pity.

"If he did it, we can take him to trial." Sheila grunted, levering her body against his, trying to break his chokehold. "Let the justice system make him pay."

Justice system.

God supposedly ran a justice system, one where the meek and the just earned a place in the kingdom of heaven. One where the guilty paid for their sins eternally. But eternity was a long way away, and revenge was like chocolate on his tongue, the taste sweet and rich and consuming.

Frank pictured Samuel in his mind as he pressed his fingers tighter. The gristle of Archer's throat popped and clicked, his breath coming in shallow, whistling gasps. Still

Archer endured his own murder without raising a finger to protect himself.

Sheila's knee pressed against Frank's lower spine and he shouted in pain. Sheila seized the opening, bending him backward and jerking one of his hands from Archer's throat. She twisted her hip against Frank, and the sheriff slammed against the nightstand as Archer fell back onto the rumpled bed.

Sheila drew her .38 and stood in cop stance, both arms extended, legs spread, jaw tense. Frank looked up at her. His shoulder throbbed. He ignored it, and rubbed his scalp instead.

"Are you okay, Reverend?" Sheila asked, her hard gaze never leaving Frank's face. Archer didn't answer.

"Reverend McFall?" she said, her voice rising in both pitch and volume. Still she didn't look away from Frank.

The sheriff tried to stand.

"Don't do it, sir," she ordered.

Archer rose slowly from the bed behind her. Floated up without bending his legs. As if God were pulling invisible strings.

"Look out, Sheila," Frank yelled. "Behind you."

She gave him a disbelieving look, as if use of this oldest trick in the book was proof of his utter madness.

Behind her, Archer came to full life, the skin of his neck unblemished, his face contorted.

Changing.

Archer's smile returned, a curved gash of bright, sharp teeth that dripped hate. His wings filled the room behind Sheila, stretching themselves and stirring a wind to life.

Something broke inside Frank's head, some thin threshold was breached, and his thoughts spilled out into dark places where thoughts should never go. He sprang at Sheila, trying for her knees in a perfect flying tackle.

Her gun went off, and the blood spilled along with his thoughts.

It all happened at once, distorted in jerky slow motion, as if the filmstrip of reality had jumped its sprockets and was jamming the projector.

Frank had cracked. Sheila had no doubt at all about that. Attacking a suspect like that, trying to choke Archer, trying to . . .

She still felt groggy, and barely trusted her own thoughts, but now she was acting on instinct. She heard a whisper of movement behind her at the same time that Frank jumped at her knees.

Aiming to wound instead of kill was also instinctive, the product of countless hours of training. Still, she was surprised when the revolver roared in her ears and twitched in her hands. Frank shouted in pain as a red rip erupted in his left shoulder. Frank slammed against the nightstand, the bedside lamp and Bible knocked to the floor, his head bouncing off the edge of the mattress as he crumpled to the floor.

The sulfurous tang of gunpowder reached Sheila's nose at the same moment she realized what she had just done. She had shot Frank. Her sheriff and the man she cared about most in the world was bleeding at her feet. And Archer was laughing.

The source of the laughter was so close that she could feel its wind stirring her hair. The preacher's breath was cold on her neck, sending icy rivers down her spine. Or maybe it was the quality of the laugh itself that chilled her. The voice was scarcely human, a cross between an animal's growl and an asylum inmate's demented cackle. Or maybe Archer's windpipe was so damaged that he could scarcely breathe. It was a miracle he could stand at all.

She stepped backward and pivoted to face Archer, expecting to see red fingerprints around the preacher's throat. She nearly dropped her revolver.

The thing hovering before her was not real. *Not real, not real, not real.* She had cracked, same as Frank. Too many murders to solve, not enough sleep, too much processed food, she shouldn't have watched *Rosemary's Baby* as a child, yeah, that was it, that was why she was crazy, and she began laughing herself.

Because this just ain't HAPPENING, this thing's got wings and nothing that big has wings and oh my what big TEETH you have, the better to eat you with, my dear and Oh God your EYES, what have they done to your EYES they look like split meat in a butcher's counter and where's Archer and hee hee since I'm absolute apeshit crazy it's OKAY if I shoot you, especially if you don't exist.

Sheila pulled the trigger, the firm metal beneath her finger her only link with reality. The .38 flashed a second time, and the window exploded. Still the impossible vision hovered before her, the hideous face gleaming with a wet, sharp smile. She fired again, and Frank groaned from the floor. The sheriff's hand gripped her pant leg as if he were trying to pull himself to his feet.

"Nice try," said the thing, only now it was using Archer's voice, and the flesh rippled and changed and became the preacher again. His suit had three holes in the breast. He fingered them and smiled. "This is a three-thousand-dollar suit," he said.

Yeah Judge, I swear to tell the truth the whole truth

and nothing but the truth, if only I could figure out what it IS, but I testify that one Archer McFall turned into a . . . a THING . . . yeah, right in front of my eyes, it had big teeth and gray wings and you could smell the rot in the wrinkles of its meat and . . . no, of COURSE I didn't sneak into the evidence room and sample the contraband drugs, hee hee, I'm just apeshit crazy, that's all—

"And I would be a good boy and lie down and die, but that isn't the way this works," Archer said. "Is it, Frank?"

Archer's face changed again, the body quivered and shrank, and a young boy of about eleven stood before her, his hair mussed and his eyes sparkling blue above his freckled cheeks. Beneath the freckles, his skin was as pale as milk. A beach towel was tied around his neck and hung down his back like a cape.

"Tell her, Frankie," said the boy in a rural mountain accent. "Tell her how it's got to be done."

Frank leaned against the bed, his right hand pressed against the gunshot wound, his left arm dangling limply. "Suh . . . Samuel?" he whispered, his voice cracking.

Sheila looked in disbelief from Frank to the pale boy, then to the revolver in her hand. A small trail of smoke wended from its barrel.

I killed him, Judge. I swear, as God is my witness. I shot Archer dead, but you know the rules. Innocent until proven guilty.

"Tell her how it is, Frankie," said the boy, his eyes darkening. "What the legend says. The gospel according to the Hung Preacher."

"Sacrifice is the currency of God," Frank said in a hiss between clenched teeth.

"And everybody pays," said the smiling boy. The gap between his top front teeth did nothing to dampen the corruption of his smile.

"Not you, Samuel," Frank said, struggling to his knees. Tears pooled in his eyes. "You're innocent."

The boy's face changed yet again, became that of a balding middle-aged man with sweat beading his upper lip. "Innocent until proven guilty," he said. "Just ask your lady-cop friend."

Storie recognized that voice, the one that sometimes slithered into her own nightmares. *Hey, honey, you can lock me up, but I'll be BACK.*

Years ago in Charlotte, she couldn't ram the nightstick into the kiddie-rapist's face or pull the car over and shoot him in the head. But she was already a murderer now, so one more victim wouldn't matter. She pulled the trigger, then again, then again, only the last time the hammer clicked on a spent shell. And still the pudgy man licked his lips and leered at her.

"Except nobody's innocent," the man said, his shape shifting again, growing taller and becoming Archer McFall.

"What have you done to Samuel?" Frank shouted.

"I told you, it's not what *I've* done to Samuel," Archer said. "It's what *you've* done."

Archer touched the spot on his forehead where Sheila had aimed the revolver. "Not bad," he said to her, in his calm televangelist voice. "But you have some deep sins in your heart, Sheila Storie. If only you would open up and let God come inside, give over all your troubles, then you'd find the one true Way."

Sheila stumbled slowly backward, away from this insane vision, away from the black pit of madness that threatened to swallow her whole.

If I close my eyes, it will all go away. Criminal Psych

101: "psychotic episodes can be triggered by extreme emotional stress, leaving the subject temporarily displaced from reality," yeah, that's a good one, I'll have to remember to tell that to my defense lawyer, because when I open my eyes, Archer McFall is going to be lying dead on the floor of a Holiday Inn motel room, unarmed, with five bullet holes in his body.

And with luck, I'll only get six to ten for manslaughter, only I've got the funny feeling that this is a life sentence. Innocent until proven guilty? Hell, we're ALL guilty, just like the man says.

She sat on the bed, eyes still closed, the .38 in her limp fingers. She could smell Frank's blood and her own sweat. A breeze seeped through the broken window, raising goosebumps on her neck. A hand touched her just above the knee, and she tensed. Frank's voice broke through the knotted fabric of her thoughts. "Sheila? Are you okay?"

"She'll live," Archer said. "At least for a while."

Sheila's eyelids fluttered open despite her best efforts to keep them clamped tight. Archer smiled at her with his most benevolent and beatific expression.

"I'm sorry to have misled you earlier, Detective," the preacher said. "You will not serve me, nor God, nor the church. That's only for the old families, right, Sheriff?"

Frank's lips pressed tightly together, as if his anger would crawl up his throat and erupt in sharp claws and needles of fire and silver blades.

"Now if you two will excuse me, I have a congregration in need of tending." Archer turned and walked to the door. Three holes formed a triangle in the back of his jacket. Archer opened the door, and the darkening hills were behind him, the security lights in the parking lot blinking on. A car whisked by on the highway beyond the lot. A siren, probably from a patrol car responding to re-ported gunshots, bounced off the high, hard mountains.

"See you at church, Frank? It's the Third Day, you know." Archer stepped into the twilight and closed the door.

✞ Chapter 19

Night.

It pressed down on the whole world, stretching out and smothering the trees, crushing the mountains, swallowing the weak light of the stars. The night pressed against the remaining bedroom window, and Ronnie knew it was equally thick outside the walls. The scariest thing about the night was that it always came back. You could shine the universe's brightest light into it, make it run away, but the second you switched that light off—*whoosh*—the night came swooping back in blacker than ever.

"We're going to be okay, ain't we?" Tim said. He was in the bottom bunk, bundled in blankets.

Ronnie nodded in the bunk above him, not trusting his voice. Then he realized that Tim couldn't see him, though Dad had left the light on. He took a quick breath and spoke. "How many times do I have to tell you it's going to be all right?"

His anger had no force, like a bad actor's in those stupid daytime soaps that Mom used to watch, back before she joined the red church.

"What about Mom?"

Ronnie rolled over and stuck his head over the edge of the bunk. "She'll be fine. Things will work out. You'll see."

"I don't like it when they fight." Tim squinted, his glasses put away for bedtime.

"They don't like it, either."

"Then why do they do it?"

Why? That was the big question, wasn't it? Why did the Bell Monster want to eat Ronnie's heart? Why did Mom have to join the red church? Why did Melanie turn out to be the queen of mean girls?

And there was always the big question: why did God let bad things happen? God let Boonie Houck and Mr. Potter and that woman by the side of the road get killed. He even let people kill His only begotten son. What sort of all-merciful God was that? Maybe Ronnie would ask Preacher Staymore that one, if Ronnie was lucky enough to live until the next Sunday school meeting.

"Ronnie?"

Ronnie realized that Tim had been talking for at least half a minute, but Ronnie had just zoned out. Better to keep the kid occupied, so he didn't completely lose it. "I'm listening."

"We have to give it what it wants."

"Give what to who?" Ronnie said, though he knew exactly what Tim was talking about.

"To . . . you know."

"Yeah, yeah. The thing with wings and claws and livers for eyes."

Tim pulled the blankets up to his chin. His eyes were wide now, his lip quivering from fear. Ronnie swung down off the bunk and got in bed with him.

"I won't let it get you," Ronnie said. "No matter what. Dad will beat it somehow."

Tim didn't look like he believed Ronnie, but he didn't say anything. He closed his eyes and Ronnie told him the story of Sleeping Beauty, and he was halfway through "Hansel and Gretel" when Tim fell asleep. Ronnie lay beside him in the cramped bunk, trying to figure a way out of this mess.

Then it struck him, the revelation like an icicle in the chest: God was sending all these trials down on Ronnie as some kind of test. If there was one thing that stood out clearly in the Bible, it was that God liked to test the faith of His people. Job, Daniel, Abraham, why, heck, even Jesus got tempted by the devil, and if God was all-powerful, surely He pulled the devil's strings, too.

Imagine that. Jesus was God's own son, His flesh and blood, His earthly incarnation, yet even Jesus had to measure up. And with Ronnie committing all these sins of the heart lately, it was no wonder that God wanted to visit some great trials on him. And that was the scariest thing of all.

Because Dad said that when the night was dark and the pain was great and you were all alone, then you turned your eyes up to God and you opened up your heart and let Jesus come on inside. You let God take away the fear. You let Him work out your problems, you let Him push back your enemies. But what if *God* was the enemy? What if God was the source of your fear?

Even as he thought it, he knew it was wrong. The idea of God as the bad guy was just too awful. You had to have faith. If you didn't, you might as well curl up in a ball and let the Bell Monsters of the world eat your insides. You might as well roll away the stone and head down into hell. So Ronnie tried to picture the face of Jesus from those color plates in the Bible, that man with the beard, long brown hair, and sad, loving blue eyes.

Something clicked against the window.

A rap on the glass at the good window, the one that hadn't been boarded up.

Can you hear him aknocking?

Oh, yes, Ronnie could hear the knock. Only this wasn't Jesus. This was the Bell Monster, come back to finish the job.

This was what God wanted—for Ronnie to get up out of bed and open the window and give himself away. Then the dead would stay dead, ghosts would stay in the ground, and Tim would be saved. And Ronnie would have passed the test.

Ronnie almost yelled for Dad, so Dad could come in with the rifle and kill the thing again. But what good would that do? You could kill it a million times, but still it would come back, night after night forever. Until it had what it wanted.

Until it had Ronnie.

He slid out from under the covers, looked at Tim's face relaxed by sleep, and crossed the room. Even though he was wearing pajamas, he shivered. The thing rapped on the glass again, and Ronnie heard slithery whispers. He hoped the claws were fast, so that he could die without pain.

He was carrying plenty of pain already. His broken nose, the welt on his face where Whizzer had punched him, the stone lump in his chest. At least all those would pass away. Soon Jesus would come and take his hand and float with him up to heaven, where there was a cure for every pain. Because Ronnie believed.

Don't you, Ronnie?

He took another trembling step to the window. He couldn't see through the blackness beyond the glass. All he saw was his own reflection and the lighted bedroom. It was better this way. If he saw the Bell Monster, he would scream, Tim would wake up, Dad would come in, and the Bell Monster would get all of them. Or Dad would kill the Bell Monster and they'd have to do it all again, every night forever, until the test was taken.

So he pulled back the sash-lock and held his breath and slowly slid the window up. It squeaked in its frame, and the cold night air poured through the crack and chilled his belly. He tensed for the claws to his gut, his eyes closed. Nothing happened, so he lifted the window another few inches.

"Ronnie," came the whisper.

Mom.

Relief surged through his body, a warmth similar to the one made by Jesus coming into his heart. But what was Mom doing out there with the Bell Monster?

Confused, Ronnie opened his eyes. The light from the room spilled on Mom's face. She didn't look scared at all. She smiled and put her finger to her lips. "Shh. Where's your dad?"

Ronnie stooped until his head was near hers. "In the living room. He thinks the Bell Monster will come through the front door this time."

"Let's go," she said, waving at him to come outside.

"Where are we going?"

"The church."

The red church. At night. Maybe Dad was right. Maybe Mom really was crazy.

"Get Tim," she said.

"Tim?" Ronnie glanced back at his brother. Tim moaned in his sleep from a bad dream. "Why does Tim have to come?"

"He's of the blood." Her eyes were strangely bright.

"We all are."

"What about Dad?"

Mom's eyes narrowed. "He's not a member of the church."

Ronnie started to add that he and Tim weren't, either. Mom smiled again, and it was the old Mom smile, the one that said *Everything's going to be all right* and *Mom will kiss it and make it better* and *I love you more than anything in the world.*

"I'm scared of the red church," Ronnie said.

She took down the screen, reached through the window, and gently squeezed his shoulder. "Honey, it's so wonderful. You know how good it feels to be in the First Baptist Church?"

Ronnie nodded.

"Well, this is a hundred times better. This is like having God right in the same room with you. No more pain, no more anger, no more earthly worries. Nothing but everlasting peace."

Being in the red church was starting to sound a whole lot like being dead. But Ronnie thought that if he went with Mom just this once, he could figure out why she loved the place so much. Besides, she wouldn't let anything happen to her sons. She would protect Tim from the Bell Monster and other bad things, and she'd help Ronnie pass the test.

He woke Tim, putting a hand over Tim's mouth before he could yell out. "Mom's here," he whispered. "We have to go to the church."

Tim's lips moved beneath his palm, so Ronnie moved his hand away. "Why do we have to go to the church?" he said drowsily.

"Why do we ever go to church? Because we *have* to,

that's why. Mom's here to take us."

At the mention of Mom, Tim came fully awake and sat up. "Is she here?"

"At the window."

"Hi, sugar," she said. "Now hurry, before Dad hears. Don't worry about changing clothes. We won't be there long. Just put your shoes on."

"Don't we need to tell Dad?" Tim asked.

"He'll only get mad, honey. He'll yell at me. You don't want him to yell at me, do you?"

Tim rushed to the window and hugged her. Ronnie locked the door and the boys put on their sneakers. Then Ronnie helped Tim slip through the window. Ronnie followed, taking a last look into the lighted room before heading into the night.

The siren was louder now, closer. Frank shut his eyes and leaned against the bed. His shoulder throbbed, but he could still flex the fingers of his left hand. No major nerve damage, at least from the bullet wound. But Archer McFall had damaged his nerves plenty.

Sheila's fingers explored the area around the wound. "Does it hurt?" she asked, her voice as spaced-out as it had been when he'd first entered the motel room. He thought about trying to make a wisecrack, like Bruce Willis in "Die Hard," but he gave up. Bruce Willis had a writer to feed him lines. All Frank had was a jangled-up nest of thoughts and red wires of hurt in his brain.

He grunted and opened his eyes. Sheila's face was corpse white, as white as Samuel's had been.

Samuel.

Anger and hate pushed Frank's pain away. That bastard

Archer had killed Samuel. Whoever or whatever Archer was, ghost or demon or the best damned magician this side of Houdini, the "preacher" was to blame for Samuel's death. And for Frank's long years of guilt.

"You know what's funny?" Frank said.

"Nothing's funny," Sheila said. "I just shot you."

"No, really, it *is* funny," he said. "Once you throw away all the old rules, all the things you thought you knew and that you counted on, then you can believe just about anything."

"What in the hell are you talking about?"

"Ghosts. Archer McFall. Whatever he is, he's real. Not some trick of the mind, or a vision to fit in with your criminal psychology theories."

"He's real, all right," she said, though she sounded unsure. She folded back the bedspread and yanked the sheet free. She tore a long strip from the sheet and wrapped it around Frank's shoulder and upper arm. He winced at the fresh pain.

"Damn, it's only a flesh wound," she said.

"That's good."

"No, it's not. I was aiming for your heart."

"I'll take that under advisement, for the next time you threaten to shoot me."

She tied off the bandage as the wailing patrol car pulled up to the door. It skidded to a stop, tires squealing, and Wade Wellborn shouted from the parking lot.

"Sheriff? Detective Storie?" He had seen their vehicles.

"It's all clear, Wade," Frank yelled back.

Wade rushed through the open door, gun pointed to the ceiling. "What in the holy heck happened?" he said, eyes wide.

"We had us what you call an 'incident,'" Frank said. His

blood stained the makeshift bandage, but the spreading seemed to have slowed. He stood, Sheila taking his good arm and helping him up.

As he struggled to keep his balance, he said, "Maybe it was more of an 'encounter' than an incident."

"Sir?" Wade said.

"Call in backup. Then stay and secure the scene."

"Who done it?" Wade gaped at the bandage, then at the broken window and the holes in the motel's sheetrock wall.

"You'll have to wait for the incident report like every-body else," said Frank. "I won't even know what happened until I make it up."

Wade hesitated, a confused expression on his face. Then he obeyed Frank's command. When Wade left the room, Frank said to Sheila, "You up for a church service?"

"I don't know. I always thought I'd believe in ghosts when I saw them. Only now I've seen one, and I still don't believe it."

"You ought to have a little faith, Sergeant."

"Faith?"

"Yeah. I *told* you the church was haunted. I just didn't know what was doing the haunting."

"Like I was supposed to believe you when you babbled on about the Hung Preacher?" Sheila seemed to be coming around, emerging from her daze and regaining her sarcas-tic edge. Frank was glad she was her old self again. He kind of liked her old self. Maybe the old Sheila wouldn't shoot him next time.

They went out the door, Frank taking a last look at the bloodstain on the carpet, the mussed bed, the Bible on the floor. "You drive," he said to Sheila.

"Yes, sir."

"Stop calling me 'sir.' If we're going to try to kill a ghost together, we might as well be on a first-name basis."

The few motel tenants had left their rooms and stood in clumps of two or three, whispering to one another in the parking lot. Blue lights strobed off the windows, adding to the disorienting power of the experience. The Holiday Inn's night manager stood at the far end of the parking lot, half-hidden behind a concrete planter.

"Everything's under control," Frank shouted to him.

"Don't look so damned under control to me," said the manager in a squeaky voice. "Where's Mr. McFall?"

"Checked out early," Sheila replied. She got in the driver's side of her patrol car and opened the passenger door for Frank. As he settled onto the seat, Wade ran over to their car.

"Where are you going?" he asked, his face red from exertion.

"Following up on a lead," Frank said. "We'll radio in the details."

Sheila gunned the engine to life, backed up, then fishtailed out of the parking lot. When they were on the highway and accelerating smoothly, Sheila pulled her revolver from her shoulder holster.

"You're not going to finish the job, are you? Shoot me for real?" he asked.

She handed the gun to him. "Need to reload."

"Why? We already know that bullets can't stop him. Or *it*. Whatever the hell it is."

"There's still such a thing called 'proper procedure.' It might be the last thing I can do by the book." She hit eighty and held steady, running without siren or blue lights. He watched her face as she drove.

He liked her.

Crazy as it was, he liked her. Hell, the world was touched-in-the-head crazy anyway, with its haunted churches, shape-shifters, Hung Preachers, and Looney Toons sheriffs. Why couldn't he like a woman he had worked with for years? So what if she'd shot him? He knew men who'd been treated worse.

Sheila glanced at him for a moment, and must have seen his strange expression. She glanced again. "What are you looking at?"

"You."

She gave a tired smile. "Just reload the gun."

"Yes, sir," he said, struggling to open the box of shells she'd flipped onto the seat. She turned off the highway onto a narrow road that was paved but unmarked. Frank looked up at the dim stars. A high haze belted the sky, and the three-quarters wedge of moon was wreathed with electric-blue clouds just above the mountains.

"Sheila?" he said, the first time he'd said her name aloud. At least to her. He'd tried it on his tongue a few times, back in his small apartment in the wee hours between nightmares.

"What?" she said.

"What are we going to do when we get to the red church?"

"You're the sheriff," she said.

"I mean, how do you kill a ghost?"

"Good question," she said.

They rode in silence as Frank clumsily dumped the spent shell casings and reloaded the revolver using his one good hand. He passed it back to Sheila.

"Feel better?" he asked after she'd returned it to its holster.

"No," she said. "What about you?"

His shoulder still throbbed with every beat of his heart, but the pain was just a background distraction now, mental white noise. "I'll live. More or less."

The dispatcher's voice fuzzed from the radio. "Base to Unit Two, come in, Unit Two."

Frank turned the radio off.

Sheila glanced at him, her hands still tight on the steering wheel. "Guess we do this without backup?"

"Seems like those are the rules."

Her next question made his breath catch. "Do you believe in God?"

"Sure," he said without thinking. "Jesus is our Lord and Savior."

"No," she said. "I mean *really* believe."

"Look, if you think Archer is the devil and this is the ultimate battle of good and evil—"

"Don't be a jerk, Frank."

"I don't think it's ever that simple," he said. "I mean, God is good and the devil is evil. One's right and one's wrong. You ever known anything that clear-cut?"

"Well, we're only human," she said with some sarcasm. "What the hell do we know?"

"Archer says it's the flesh itself that leads to sin," Frank said, wondering where he'd picked up that little nugget of wisdom. "The heart is pure, but the flesh gets us in trouble."

"Archer says a lot of things." Sheila slowed the cruiser and turned onto the gravel road leading to Whispering Pines. The river glinted below them, the silver of the moon dappled across its surface. They rounded a bend and the dark shape of the church stood out on the hill above them.

"Here goes nothing," Frank said, his voice barely audible over the gravel crackling beneath the wheels.

"What's the plan?"

Frank looked at the long dark fingers of the dogwood, at the black belfry, at the white bones of the tombstones. Figures moved around the church, and cars were clustered in the driveway. Archer's fold was gathering.

"If I come up with one, you'll be the first to know," he said.

It happened so fast that it seemed like slow motion.

He yelled, Sheila braked, and the cruiser slid sideways. Her elbows flailed as she fought the steering wheel, trying to avoid the boy standing in the road. The momentum slammed Frank against Sheila's side and she lost control. The car skated across the loose gravel onto the soft dirt shoulder, then slipped down the embankment to the black river below.

Frank's head bounced off the dashboard, then rammed into the roof, and he reached for Sheila as metal twisted and glass shattered and the world turned cartwheels. As his thoughts turned black and blue, he held on to the image of Samuel in the road, arms spread in welcome, worms dripping from his smile.

Then, wet darkness.

✝ Chapter 20

"Where's your car?" Mama Bet asked in the dimness of the vestry. Not that a car mattered much to her, but few around these parts had raised a son who made good in the world. Maybe she suffered from sinful pride, but a flashy luxury car just flat-out said, *I done proud.* Soon cars and pride and such wouldn't matter, but you clung to life's little joys while you had them.

"I won't need a car where I'm going," Archer said. "Where *we're* going."

Archer lit a candle. Waxy smoke mingled with the smell of the communion. The reverent murmurs of the congregation filled the wooden shell of the church, anticipation in the air as thick as flies on roadkill.

Archer's suit was a little rumpled. Mama Bet frowned and straightened his tie. A messiah had to look the part. People didn't fall in for just any old body.

"You going to make me walk into the kingdom on these tired old feet?" she said, trying to get Archer to smile. He was so blamed serious all the time.

"We each must make the sacrifice," he said.

Mama Bet worked her shoulders so that the lace of her dress collar stopped tickling her neck. "Guess we'd best get on with it."

"Yes . . . you go ahead. Give me a moment to commune with God the Father," Archer said without a hint of irony.

That was one part of this deal that worried Mama Bet. She was finally going to come face-to-face with that lowdown, sneaky thing. The one who'd planted the seed and left her with all the pain and trials of raising a messiah. Well, He couldn't properly claim any of the benefits. *She* was the one who had made the hard decisions, the sacrifices, endured the whispers. Even though the reward of heaven was great, she felt she deserved a little something more.

Like maybe God ought to get down on His knees and beg her forgiveness.

She smiled at the image, though she had no clear picture of what God should look like. She remembered that night of sweaty pleasure, but His flesh had been moist and cool as clay. She hadn't glimpsed His face, but had felt his mouth slick on her neck, her shoulders, her chest. She shuddered in a mixture of remembered pleasure and revulsion.

Everybody knew that saying, "An eye for an eye," from the Old Testament. But not many knew the part right after, Mama Bet's favorite verse: "A stripe for a stripe, a burning for a burning."

You got what was coming to you, what was due, the very thing you deserved. That was the best thing about God. He was fair. What you dished out to the world, He fed back to you, over and over, for an eternity.

And her heart swelled at the thought of her part in it, of Archer's part. They were doing holy work. Nothing so dirt-common as fulfilling a prophecy, but rather they were guiding people onto the True Path. Every nutcase who ever took a knife to little girls and boys claimed they had a hotline to God. But Archer was the real thing, the Second Son, God in the flesh.

She paused at the threshold of the vestry. Archer stood with his head bowed, eyes closed, the candles throwing golden light on his peaceful face, the deep brown of the wooden walls busy with shadows. Tears came to her eyes at the beauty of the scene. She could give him up.

See, God, how strong I am? I know You need to take him, that's the Way and the Word. But I hope You got some idea just how much it pains me. If I didn't know the stone would soon be rolled away forever, I'd throw myself down at Archer's feet and not let him go through with it.

Then Mama Bet realized she hadn't been totally truthful to God. She was actually looking forward to the cleansing. Sure, most of the old biddies who had whispered about her unexpected pregnancy were long dead, were under the cold dirt and damp grass of the cemetery. But she had a feeling that those long-dead weren't out of the woods yet. They still had a part in Archer's plan. Archer would sink his claws into them, one way or another.

Thy will be done, amen, she silently added as a catch-all apology to God. Just in case He was one to hold a grudge. He had a long memory, that much was plain. The whole history of the human race was one everlasting bout of suffering.

She opened the door and slipped into the sanctuary of the church. The murmurs quieted, then picked back up again as the parishioners realized Archer wasn't coming out. She glanced at the dark shape on the floorboards of the altar, saw that it had grown larger and sharper, that the Death's Angel was nearly formed. Just a little more blood and it would be whole. Mama Bet lifted her skirt so that the hem didn't brush the floor, then raised her chin proudly and walked across the dais to take her place in the front row.

Nearly thirty of the faithful had gathered. The candles mounted on the wall bathed their faces in unsteady shadows. Mama Bet was pleased to note that the Abshers lined the pew in the second row, Sonny looking uncomfortable in a button-down shirt and bow tie. Becca Faye sat beside him, the vee of her dress offering up the pillars of her flesh. At least the slatternly hussy had worn a bra, even if it was one of those push-up kinds that made a woman look more womanly than was proper.

Becca Faye was wasting her time. Archer had no need for such offerings, and Mama Bet wouldn't let him sample the vile fruits even if he was of a mind to. Sonny could drool over that harlot all day, but Sonny would pay and pay and pay for the privilege, maybe with his tongue, maybe with his eyes, maybe with other things, according to God's will.

"Don't see why we have to put up with this foolishness," Sonny muttered just loudly enough for Mama Bet to hear. "I got better things to do than hobnob with you God-fearing folk."

"Shush," Becca Faye said, though she giggled. Haywood cleared his throat uncomfortably.

Mama Bet turned around and looked Sonny in his oily eyes. "You'd best open them big ears, mister," she said. "You don't get many chances at salvation in this life. So you best be ready when the light shines on your stupid greasy head."

Becca Faye looked around nervously, like a cat caught in a hedgerow, a whiff of her fear carried on the scent of department-store perfume that probably went by the name of Passion Flower or Wild Meadows or such. Sonny's eyes grew bright and fierce.

"I ain't the one that hung Wendell McFall," he said. "None of us are. So why do we got to pay for it?"

Mama Bet shook her head, her mouth wrinkled in weary amusement. "You ain't heard a single word Archer's said. Sacrifice is the currency of God. It ain't a sacrifice if all you're doing is paying what you owe. No, you got to pay *more* than you owe."

Haywood tried to change the subject. "Did y'all hear about the car that run off the road? Jim Potter says it just went over the side for no good reason. Probably a drunk or something."

"Nobody went to help them?" his wife Noreen said.

Haywood glared at her. "They ain't of the old families, so what's it to us?" He added, as if to himself, "Wonder if they had insurance?"

Mama Bet glanced past them to the other rows, at Alma Potter, Lester and Vivian and Stepford Matheson, the Buchanans in the back row, where their barnyard smell barely reached her, Whizzer sullenly chewing on the stump of a half-smoked cigarette. And across the aisle, oh, yes, there they were.

The Day family, minus that meddling David, the boys wide-eyed and fidgeting, the mother glowing with an expectant pride.

There *he* was, the one Archer needed.

A warmth expanded from Mama Bet's chest to the rest of her body. Let the cleansing begin.

Icy coffin black.

Drifting, on beyond black. So easy.

So cold.

At Samuel's viewing, Frank had touched his little brother's hand. Samuel had looked lost in the splendid folds of the casket, a little too pink-skinned and hollow-cheeked. His lips were unnaturally red, a shade they had never been in life. But worse than the interrupted smile was the coldness of Samuel's skin, colder than November air, colder than shaded marble.

That same coldness gripped Frank now. It flowed through his veins, clasped him in its shocking dullness, enveloped him in its numbing shroud. He was dimly aware of the currents around him, the water softly swirling around his skin. The river murmured in his ears, telling him to drift, to surrender, to submit to the embrace of long sleep.

Years passed in that near-perfect state, years in which Frank remembered the roughness of his father's hands, callused and cracked from farmwork, hands that could break a locust rail if they had to. Those same hands had met, tucked under chin in desolate prayer, during Samuel's funeral. A week after, those same hands had threaded and looped one end of a thick rope. Then the hands' owner joined his youngest boy in whatever afterlife they each deserved.

And Frank's mother followed six months later. She also killed herself, though she wasn't cowardly or brave enough to take a direct route like her husband. No, she was subtle. She went into the darkness by fading a little at a time, losing appetite and health and soul to the great erosion of apathy. And only Frank had carried on, the weight of all their deaths on his shoulders, pressing down on him as heavy as a cross, the guilt a constant, cold lump in his heart.

And now he followed them into darkness. He could almost hear their whispers drawing him forward, pulling him more deeply into the numbing cold. They were waiting.

He almost smiled in his sleep. So many years of waiting, so many more years of journey ahead.

But what would be waiting?

The bright light of heaven, as promised by his parents and the Baptist preacher and practically everybody in Pickett County.

But if heaven was bright and warm and welcoming, then the change should start occurring any moment now. Because if God and Jesus wanted the eternity of worship they deserved and demanded, then they were being robbed of Frank's servitude by this extended dark purgatory. This cold and peaceful drifting. This slow suffocation.

He was aware of hands reaching, hands darker than the darkness, gentle hands. He relaxed, glad for the end to this interim end. Anxious for heaven. Anxious for the love and light and heat.

Then the hands clamped onto his wounded shoulder, and he screamed into the darkness.

His eyes snapped open against wetness, and he realized he was underwater. Then he remembered the crash. He struggled against the current as the years of drifting became seconds of chaotic tumbling and thrashing and pain. His body was trapped in the submerged car.

The hands on his shoulder . . .

Sheila.

The hands worked down his arm, and Frank stopped flailing, realizing she was trying to help him. The seat belt loosened across his chest. He reached for her, and his fingers brushed her softly flowing hair, and then she was gone.

He blinked into the blackness, his limbs stiffening from

the intense chill. His right hand found the door, then the opening of the shattered window.

The water he'd inhaled burned in his lungs as he kicked through the window. A small pocket of air in his chest told him in which direction the surface lay, and he fought toward it.

The car had tumbled into a deeper part of the river, so the current was sluggish, but the weight of his wet uniform limited his progress. Bright streaks of lime and fluorescent orange rocketed across the backs of his eyelids as he paddled upward. Then he broke through the skin of the river, his lungs greedy as he gulped at the night air.

The air tasted of muck and mud and fish, and he spat to clear his mouth, then drew in another gargling gasp. The current tumbled him lazily against a boulder, then another, the rush of the river like white noise.

In the glimmer of the moon, he saw the scarred ground and broken saplings where the car had rolled down the bank. He spun around in the water, looking for Sheila. Nothing but black stones and the white phosphor of the current.

He spat once more, took a deep breath, and dove toward the twin streams of yellow light that rippled ghostlike in the riverbed.

The current pulled him away from the underwater lights. He frantically paddled toward the bank until his feet hit bottom, then waded back upstream, his teeth chattering. He'd been up for nearly a minute. Could Sheila hold her breath that long?

When he reached the spot where the car had gone under, he dove in headfirst. His hand hit smooth metal and he opened his eyes. Judging from the position of the swirling headlight beams, he was on the roof of the car. He let the current drag him to the driver's side. Luckily, the car had settled nearly flat on the riverbed, so he didn't have to worry about the door's being jammed.

Frank forced himself deeper, his lungs already longing for a taste of oxygen and nitrogen. He found the door handle, opened his eyes again, and thought he made out a shadow in the front seat. But the water was dark, as dark as his drifting dream of death.

He yanked the handle up, and the dented door opened with a burp of released air. Reaching inside, he felt the vinyl of the seat, the warped steering wheel, the freely drifting seat belt.

He probed deeper, holding himself suspended in the cold water with his left hand on the chassis. He found her draped halfway across the seat, her legs dangling limply.

How long had she been under? Had she reached the surface, then come back to rescue him? Or had she been submerged all along? Frank was losing track of time, his thoughts gone fuzzy from lack of air, and he knew they were in trouble.

He squirmed his body into the cab and reached for her torso. Wrapping his arm around her, he tugged her toward the door. His knee caught on the steering wheel and the horn emitted a pathetic, drowning bleat. He pulled again, and the current nudged them out of the vehicle. Vomit and fear forced Frank's mouth open, and rank, muddy water rushed between his teeth.

He spun lazily and acrobatically with Sheila in his arms. He thought of Friday night hoe downs at the Gulp 'n' Gulch, how he'd never had a partner this graceful. He nearly laughed. Choking on Potter's Mill River, with the ghost of his dead brother waiting for them up on the road, with the red church owned by whatever nightmare inhabited Archer McFall's transient flesh, with everything he'd ever held as sane and right and normal now as distant as the sweet night air above, he'd finally found a dance partner.

At least I'll die in somebody's arms, and not all alone, like I always figured would happen.

And he almost surrendered again, almost opened his mouth and let the river sing its song, almost let the cold black in-between sweep them both away to the endless sea. But just as he thought of it, just as he realized that your life doesn't flash before your dying eyes, only the very end of it does, he pictured Sheila. He pictured her behind her desk, and him standing before it, explaining to her why he'd given up.

A little bit of pain? she would say. *You were cold and tired and just wanted to rest? It was easier to give up than face a world where things were topsy-turvy gone-to-hell, where spirits walked and shape-shifters drove luxury cars and you had to stare your embodied guilt in the eyes? You gave up on me, you gave up on yourself, you gave up on us, just because you didn't have faith?*

And her imagined anger flooded his wet and scalding chest, lit a fire in his rib cage, made *him* angry. Frank kicked until his feet found solid purchase. He shoved upward, his arms tightly clutching Sheila around the waist.

He silently prayed as they rose through the water, though he could not decide to whom to send his prayers or what he should ask for. His limbs were so numb he wasn't even entirely sure it was Sheila in his grasp. It could easily have been an old sodden stump.

And then they broke the surface, the air as sweet as a ripe plum, the moon as welcome as a smile, the million bubbles of froth on the river joyously whispering in Frank's ears.

He tilted Sheila's head back so that her mouth and nostrils were clear of the water, then half swam, half drifted to a sandy shallow. He carried Sheila to a flat outcropping of rock and laid her gently on her back.

He had learned CPR as part of his officer certification, and leaned over her face, ready to pinch her nose and force breath into her lungs and reach inside her shirt to massage her heart back to action.

But suddenly she coughed, spat, and blew a clear viscid fluid from her nose. She coughed again, and Frank called her name, then rolled her onto her side so that she wouldn't choke. Her skin was white in the moonlight, almost glowing in its bloodless pallor.

"Sheila?" he called again, louder this time, so that his voice carried over the rushing waters. Her eyelids fluttered weakly, and she coughed again. Then her eyes snapped open and she raised herself on one elbow, her hair trailing water onto the gray stone.

"C—cold," she said, teeth chattering. That reminded Frank of his own chill, settling as bone-deep as a toothache. But he brushed aside his discomfort in the face of this miracle. How long had she been under? Two minutes? Three? Five?

"Are you okay?" he asked, knowing how stupid his words sounded even as he said them.

"Next time . . . you take me for a swim . . ." she said, panting, her throat rattling with trapped liquid, "can you make it . . . a heated pool?"

She sat up, tucking her knees against her chest and hugging them. Her body trembled, and Frank pressed against her, even though he had little body heat to offer.

"You saved my life," he told her. She felt good in his

arms, even with cold flesh.

"No . . . *you* saved *my* life," she said. Her shoulders rose and fell with her deep, even breathing. She was recovering quickly.

Too quickly.

There must have been a pocket of air trapped in the car, perhaps near the back windshield where her head had been. That was the only explanation. That, or else maybe there really was a God, prayers sometimes *did* get answered, sometimes miracles happened.

Frank glanced at the deep black sea of sky overhead, at the winking blue-white stars that stretched out and out forever. Then he cleared the brackish aftertaste of the river from his mouth and spat into the dark water. Sure, God just happened to break from His constant job of keeping the stars burning to actually save a human being. That was a laugh.

God hadn't bothered with saving Samuel, or Frank's father and mother. He hadn't saved Boonie Houck or Zeb Potter or Donna Gregg. Hell, if you got right down to it, He hadn't even saved His only son, Jesus. God was cold and uncaring, as distant as the blue behind stars. God didn't even deserve Frank's hate, only the apathy He showered upon those who would love Him, so Frank spat once more and turned his attention to Sheila.

"Are we dead yet?" Sheila said, her eyes bright with her old sarcasm and verve and maybe that little glint that comes only from seeing the light of life's end.

"No, but you're going to have so much paperwork, you might wish you were," he said. "You wrecked a Pickett County patrol car, and the taxpayers are going to want an explanation."

"And the worst part is, you're only half joking," she

said, followed by a laugh that turned into a cough.

"That Frankie, he's a laugh a minute," came a voice from the shadows along the riverbank.

Frank's blood temperature plummeted the rest of the way to zero. Sheila tensed beneath his embrace.

A milky shape came out from the dark trees.

"Samuel?" Frank said.

"Thought you were going to get baptized for sure that time," the dead boy said. "Somebody up there must like you."

Frank had often dreamed of the apologies he wished he could make to Samuel, all the ways he could try to put things right, a hundred ways to say he was sorry. But now that he had the chance, all he could do was respond dumbly to his brother's ghost. "You mean God?"

Samuel's laughter drifted across the river like a mournful fog.

"No," came the hollow voice. The ghost turned its head up the embankment toward the hill, where the orange lights of the church windows flickered between the trees. "I mean Archer McFall. Him what owns God."

"Samuel?" Frank held up a quivering hand as if to touch the thing that couldn't be there, that couldn't possibly exist. "Is that really you?"

"What's left of me."

Sheila squeezed Frank's forearm. Frank wanted to ask Samuel so many things. But his dead brother spoke before he could think of anything to say.

"Why did you let me die, Frankie?" The hollow eyes became part of the greater night. The wispy threads of the ghosts rippled as if fighting a breeze. Then the ghost turned away.

Samuel drifted up the steep bank and disappeared between the mossy boulders. Frank stood, his wet clothes hugging him like a second skin. He was to follow. He knew it as surely as he knew that all the roads of his life led to the red church, led back to that night of his greatest failure, led forward to Archer and the Hung Preacher and the Bell Monster with its Halloween laugh. As surely as he knew that even the dead weren't allowed to rest in peace. Until Archer said so.

And the thing behind Archer?

Did it have a name, or did it have its own Archer, its own God to obey?

No matter. All that counted now was the arrival of midnight. He took Sheila's hand and helped her to her feet. Wordlessly they began the climb to the red church.

✟ Chapter 21

Ronnie's nose hurt.

Not so badly that the pain drove away the throbbing in the side of his head where Whizzer had punched him, but plenty bad enough. Whizzer had glared at him when the Day family entered the church, had even tried to stand, but one of Whizzer's moronic brothers held him back. Whizzer grinned around his cigarette butt in an *I'll see you after church* expression.

Ronnie flipped him a secretive finger and followed Mom to the second row. Tim sat between Ronnie and Mom, looking around the church with an awe struck expression. Tim wasn't that hard to impress. Ronnie had trembled a little coming up the church steps, but now that he was inside and could see this was just a church like any other, only a little bit older, he was able to bite back his fear.

He recognized most of the people in the church, though he didn't know everybody's name. There sat creepy Mama Bet McFall, who had stopped by last week to sell Mom a few jars of pickled okra. Anybody who ate okra at all, much less pickled it, must be batty. Plus she was Archer McFall's mother, and Ronnie knew that Archer had something to do with the trouble between his parents.

"Sit still," Mom whispered to Tim, who had been kicking his legs back and forth in his excitement. He sat back in the pew and held himself stiff for about twenty seconds, then started swinging his legs again.

Ronnie looked at Mom. She seemed happy, her eyes shiny in the candlelight, a little smile wrinkling the corners of her mouth. She hadn't smiled this much in years, not ever in the Baptist Church, hardly ever at home, not even at the Heritage Festival at the school when Dad made her get out on the floor and do a little flatfoot dancing. But she was happy now, her hands held over her heart as if she were going to reach in and grab it, then give it away.

The other parishioners whispered to each other, as agitated as Tim. Something was up. You could feel it in the air like a mild dose of electricity, sort of like the shock you got when you touched a wire between the posts of a car battery. Not bad enough to hurt, but enough to make you uneasy.

This felt like one of those turning points. Ronnie didn't like so many turning points popping up in such a short period of time. If you turned in too many different directions, you got twisted up in knots and couldn't tell which way you were headed.

Mama Bet turned around in her seat and smiled back at the Days. She was missing three of her teeth, and the grin looked like that of a sick jack-o'-lantern. "Glad you could make it tonight, Linda," she said, her words liquid and snuffy.

"Wouldn't miss it for the world," Mom said, smiling in that empty and satisfied way.

"See you brought the boys." Mama Bet nodded at Ronnie, then reached out to pat Tim on the head. "Little Timothy Day. What do you think of the church?"

Tim shrank back from her gnarled fingers, then shook

his head from side to side as if to shed himself of her lingering touch. "It ain't so scary," he said in that defiant nine-year-old way. "They said it was scary."

Mama Bet's eyes narrowed, and some of the Mathesons at the other end of the pew stopped whispering and stared.

Tim went on. "I mean, it's supposed to be haunted, but it's just like the Baptist church, only it smells funny. Like wax and old meat and-"

Ronnie elbowed Tim in the side.

"Your mom did a lot of work on it," Mama Bet said. "Cleaned it up right good, along with some of the other folks. Made it worthy of Archer's glory."

Ronnie frowned. Archer's glory? In the Baptist church, they always talked about the glory of Jesus and God. *People* weren't supposed to be glorious, at least not until they were dead. But here was Mama Bet saying bad stuff right in the middle of the church. And God didn't come out of the woodwork and strike her dead.

Mom's smile faded. "What's wrong, honey?" she asked Ronnie.

"Preacher Staymore says that everything is for the glory of Jesus."

Mom and Mama Bet laughed in unison.

"This church is a little different," Mom said.

"You mean like the Methodists and Catholics and all those other people that Dad says don't know any better?" Tim said.

"Sort of like that, yeah," Mom said. "Only here, when the plate is passed, you get to take instead of having to give."

"Cool," Tim said.

Ronnie had a bad feeling in his stomach, as if he had swallowed a boot. "Mom?"

"What?"

"You ever been to California?"

Mom and Mama Bet exchanged glances. The Mathesons had gone back to whispering among themselves, but suddenly fell silent again as the little door off to the side of the pulpit opened. Mama Bet turned and faced forward. Even the candles stopped flickering, as if not daring to absorb any of the preacher's precious oxygen. The night beyond the windows turned a shade blacker. A stillness crowded the church like water filling a bottle, and thirty pairs of eyes fixed on the man in the doorway.

Archer crossed the stage like an actor. Mom's mouth parted slightly, as if she were witnessing a miracle. Ronnie studied the preacher's face, trying to see what the others must see, the special quality that held the congregation rapt. Archer met his gaze, though surely that was Ronnie's imagination, because the preacher was looking everywhere at once, meeting every eye in the church.

Ronnie had seen eyes that intense only once before. Painted eyes. In the color plate of his Bible, on the portrait of Jesus. Sad, loving eyes. Eyes that said, *I'm sad that you must kill me, but I forgive you.*

Ronnie shivered. He wished Preacher Staymore were here. The preacher would tell Ronnie in a calm yet strong voice that Jesus was the light and the truth and the way, that the Lord was aknocking and all you had to do was open up. But Preacher Staymore was miles away, and this wasn't even Sunday. Ronnie didn't even know if you could be saved on any day besides Sunday.

If only Preacher Staymore had told him all the rules. Then this new preacher with his peaceful face and wise eyes and graceful hands gripping the lectern wouldn't scare him so much. If Ronnie knew the rules, if he didn't need the preacher to help show Jesus the way into his sinning black heart, then maybe Ronnie wouldn't dread the words about to come from the preacher's mouth. If Ronnie could be positive that Jesus was still inside him, then nothing else would matter. Except Mom and Tim and Dad.

But he wasn't sure.

Archer smiled from the lectern, his teeth gleaming in the candlelight. And twenty-nine people smiled back, Mama Bet and Whizzer and Lester Matheson and Mom and even Tim. Only Ronnie doubted. It seemed in all the world, only Ronnie failed to understand and believe.

And Ronnie wondered if he was the only one who heard the stirrings and scratchings in the church belfry.

"Sacrifice is the currency of God," Archer said to the flock, gathering the prepared communion from a shelf beneath the lectern. The plate was covered with a dark cloth, but stains were still visible on the fabric. Archer inhaled its sweet aroma.

Conducting the ritual was Archer's favorite part of playing messiah.

Rituals were important to the congregation. It was as true for the Catholics and the Baptists and the Jews and the Muslims as it had been for the unfortunate members of the Temple of the Two Suns, and now, the fold of the red church. This was the act that bound them together and bound them to Archer, that made them willing to pay the currency of sacrifice. And the preacher's job was to make the show worth the price of admission.

"And God sent the Son, who led the world astray," Archer said, lifting the communion. "And that Son, the terrible, blasphemous Jesus, who was called the Christ, gave his flesh to the people, that they might be tainted. And God looked down, and saw that evil had been set loose upon the world."

Archer looked out at the congregation. The "old families." The living flesh of the those who had murdered Wendell McFall so many decades ago. They deserved their cleansing. Anger burned his chest, but he kept the beatific smile on his face. One corner of his mouth twitched, but he doubted that anyone noticed. The lambs were too intent on the offering.

"And because we have been tainted, we must be cleansed," he continued, raising his voice, working toward the payoff.

He sensed the stirrings in the belfry, and knew that his shadow had chosen a new victim. Tonight it would be the boy.

But first, the families must taste the bitterness of their treason. They must know the depth of their iniquities. They must prove themselves worthy of cleansing. He would feed them. Matheson, Buchanan, Potter, Day, all.

He looked down at his mother in the first row. Even dear Mother must be cleansed. Perhaps she was more deserving than anyone. The ritual was his sacred duty, the reason he had been fashioned into flesh. He would not disappoint her.

Archer held the plate before him and gazed upward.

For you are a jealous God.

He bowed his head to hide his smile, then stepped off the altar and gave the plate to his mother. He removed the cloth and watched her face as she took some of the communion in her fingers. She opened her mouth and slid the host between her rotten teeth.

Outside, the world slithered toward midnight.

***

Frank and Sheila were on the roadbed below the church when the congregation fell silent. Then a sermon began, filling the wooden shell of the church, and though the words echoed together into an indecipherable wall of sound, Frank recognized Archer's voice.

Through the trees twenty feet ahead, the washed-out flesh of Frank's brother floated among the bright tombstones. In the still night, Frank could almost hear the whisper of the clouds that brushed the face of the moon. The sheriff gripped Sheila's hand tightly, as much to reassure himself that she was real as to ease his fear. She squeezed back.

Samuel turned, Frank's dear, departed brother, Frank's greatest failure. "You gotta kill me again, Frankie," Samuel rasped. Though the ghost smiled, the blue eyes revealed nothing.

"Kill you?" Frank stumbled into the border of weeds and saplings that surrounded the cemetery. He knew where Samuel was now. He recognized the curve of the granite marker, the two tombstones beside it. Home. Samuel's home.

"Samuel?" Frank said, keeping his voice low. He had talked to his dead brother many times, kneeling in that lush grass whose roots were fed by his brother's decay. But he never dreamed that Samuel would one day talk back.

"Kill me, Frankie," pleaded the ghost, and suddenly Samuel was a small boy again, not a thing to be feared, just a scared and lost and lonely little boy. A brother. "You got to set me free."

"Why me?" Frank said.

"Because it will hurt you," Sheila said. Samuel's mouth parted in a wicked grin as he nodded agreement.

"What the hell does that mean?" Frank said, angry at his own helplessness and confusion. Guilt and fear were in a battle that rivaled the great bloodfests of the Old Testament.

"Because it's the hardest thing you can ever do," Sheila said. "Killing Samuel again would be your greatest sacrifice."

"And sacrifice is the currency of God," Samuel said.

"You got your gun?" Frank asked Sheila.

"No. Lost it in the river."

Frank crashed through the brush, not caring if the congregation heard him. Sheila was right behind him. Frank felt foolish, thinking of killing a ghost. But what else could he do? He finally had a chance to fix a past mistake, but all he could do was repeat it. He had to kill Samuel for real this time, up close and personal. He had to take Samuel away from whatever or whoever owned the boy's spirit.

Samuel spread his arms in supplication, awaiting whatever would happen after the afterlife. His mouth writhed and bulged with the worms that crawled among his teeth. One slipped out and poked its sightless head around, and Frank fought back the revulsion that curdled his stomach. He crossed the grass, weaving between grave markers and monuments. As he came nearer he could smell Samuel, the odor of maggots and loam hot in the air.

He reached Samuel's grave, saw the shadow of the bas-relief lamb engraved on the marker, read the words "May God Keep and Protect Him," felt the coldness radiating from his dead brother's flesh as he reached his hands up to grip Samuel's neck. And his hands met empty air as the apparition flickered and faded before his eyes.

Frank fell to his hands and knees and ripped at the grass, heedless of his shoulder wound.

"Samuel," he yelled, his voice breaking. He clawed at the soil, ignoring the pain as his fingers raked over small stones. He dug like a starved dog after a buried bone, throwing dirt high in the air. Finally he collapsed on the marred grave, the deep reservoir of his tears overflowing, the water of pity and self-pity backed up for too many years.

Archer's sermon was building in intensity inside the church. Frank listened to the mad rhythm of the words as his sobs subsided. After a long, slow thunder of heartbeats, Frank felt a hand on his head.

"It's okay, Frank." Sheila's voice was as soothing as an evening summer breeze, silk on a sunburn.

He lifted his face from the mud he had made. "I failed him again."

"What could you do? Just then, or twenty years ago? It's not your fault."

He met her eyes. They were understanding, forgiving, sympathetic. All things that he had never seen in a woman's eyes. All the things he had never looked for, until now.

"I don't know why, but Samuel still needs me," Frank said.

A shadow fell over Sheila as a dark hulk blocked out the moon. Frank stiffened. What madness was the night sending next?

"You have to kill these things more than once," said the looming figure.

David Day.

The barrel of David's rifle caught the moonlight and sent a menacing glint into Frank's eyes. Sheila tensed beside Frank, ready to attack. The sheriff clutched her arm to restrain her.

"Only, I can't be the one who does the killing," David said.

Frank suspected the carpenter had a screw loose. David had already pulled the gun on him once today, had already proven himself dangerous. But there was something conspiratorial in David's tone, and his eyes were focused on the church instead of on Frank and Sheila.

"What are you talking about?" Frank asked him.

Sheila interrupted. "He's crazy, Frank."

"And what ain't, around here?" David replied, crouching behind a concrete angel whose wings were so rainworn that the feathers had lost detail. David aimed the rifle toward one of the windows of the church and squinted through the rifle's scope. He seemed to have forgotten all about Frank and Sheila.

Inside the church, Archer's voice rose to a fevered pitch, though the words were unintelligible. It reminded Frank of those old film clips of Adolf Hitler's speeches he'd seen, the same thundering and maniacal tirade. He'd always wondered how people could be so stupid as to fall in with anybody so obviously insane. Now he knew the kind of odd power and charisma that could totally pull the wool over people's eyes, power that could make them forget their own hopes and hearts and even humanity.

It was the kind of power that Archer possessed. Or that possessed *him*.

Power that no human should have, because no human knew how to wield it. But then, Archer wasn't human. Frank looked at David's form huddled around the rifle and wondered if *anybody* was human. Then he felt Sheila's hand in his.

Yes. Somebody was human.

Somebody lived and breathed and loved.

"What did you mean by 'You have to kill these things more than once'?" Frank asked David.

The man turned from his aiming, the shadows eerie on his eyes. "Remember what I said to you out at the house today? About killing Archer as many times as it takes?"

"Yeah?"

"When he took all those local girls out to California, he set up the Temple of the Two Suns. Don't know if you knew that part of it, but I expect it was just more of the devil's work. I went out there to bring Linda back. She was eighteen. Hell, she didn't know what she was doing. I guess I didn't, neither. All I knew was that I loved her, and I wasn't going to give her up without a fight."

"Some people don't need to be saved," said Sheila.

"No offense, Detective, but them twenty-dollar opinions won't buy you a dirty cup of water in these parts," David said. "I went out to California for Linda's good, not my good. That's when I saw what happened to one of them girls that went out there with Archer."

Frank's stomach tightened. Archer's voice ranted, roared, reached heights of frenzy that even a Baptist evangelist at a tent revival couldn't match.

"He killed her," David said. "Cut her up. Took her heart, and maybe some other things. I shut my eyes after that first part. But not before I seen them pass around the plate of meat."

"Just like he did the ones here," Frank whispered. Then he remembered the odd taste that had filled his mouth after attending Archer's service. What had happened during those lost hours?

"No," Sheila said, shaking her head in disbelief.

But nothing was beyond belief anymore. They had both seen Archer McFall change shape before their eyes. They both had watched as Sheila shot him five times at point-blank range. Yet here the preacher was, tending to his flock, culling the stray lambs, feeding them the Word.

"That's why I shot him," David said. "Killed him, or so I thought."

A thick cloud passed over the face of the moon, momentarily darkening the hill. The candles burning in the church cast the only visible light. There were no streetlights in Whispering Pines, and the scattered houses were hidden by the hills. Frank felt as though they were the only people in the world, that everything outside the cemetery and the surrounding mountains had fallen away into a dark emptiness. And all that remained of civilization, of humanity, hope, and sanity, resided right here. Frank and Sheila and David. Archer and the congregation.

And the church.

The red church, with its golden eyes.

The church that had swallowed Samuel.

The church that also claimed Frank's father and mother.

The church that held secrets in its stained and stubborn boards.

The church that had hoarded the iniquities of the old families, that had leered at their weddings and eavesdropped on their funerals and absorbed the soft, spirited seepage of their prayers.

The church that housed the ghosts of memories.

The cloud drifted on and the moon again gave its baleful glare. The steeple thrust toward the sky, the awkward broken cross barely visible against the night sky. The dogwood's branches dangled in the gentle breeze, brushing the steeple like a mother caressing a babe. The shadows shifted in the belfry, the darkness dividing itself.

"You see it, too, don't you?" David said.

Frank nodded.

"What?" Sheila said.

"The Bell Monster," David said.

"The thing that killed Samuel," Frank said.

Yes, the *church* was to blame, not Frank. If the church hadn't stood all those years, gathering legends like a stone gathered moss, then Frank, Samuel, and the others wouldn't have been there that fateful Halloween night. If not for Wendell McFall's sins, none of the tragedies would have occurred. If, if, if.

If Samuel were still alive, he wouldn't be dead. If Samuel were still dead, he wouldn't be a ghost.

David's next words interrupted Frank's thoughts and brought back the river chill that he'd been trying to ignore.

"You're the one that's got to do the killing, Sheriff."

"What are you talking about?" Sheila said.

"You're of the blood," David said, ignoring her. "You're of the old families. That's why my bullets don't do nothing. It's got to be done by one of Archer's own."

Maybe. Sheila didn't say anything, but Frank knew what she was thinking. Her bullets hadn't killed Archer, either. Maybe that was the way this thing worked.

Wendell McFall had been killed by his own people. And if Wendell was behind this, if Wendell was a restless spirit that was tied forever to the church, then maybe the scene had to play itself out again. . . .

Frank balled his hand and ground his fist into his temple. The pain drove away the foolish thoughts. What was the use of trying to figure out why Whispering Pines was go-to-hell inside out? The important thing was to make it all go away.

"He's right, Frank," Sheila said. "I know it sounds silly-hell, you know I don't believe any of this- but if there are rules to this game, that one makes as much sense as any. That's what Samuel was trying to tell you."

"My boys are in there," David said, nodding toward the church. "You've got to save them. And Linda, too. I reckon if the Lord can forgive her, I can, too. I guess when you save somebody once, you owe them."

David handed the rifle to Frank. He glanced at the belfry, at the quivering fabric of darkness. Frank took the rifle.

It was heavy and awkward in his hands. He'd never liked guns much. He'd hunted as a boy, had shown enough targeting skill to earn his police certification, but had rarely fired a gun since. He'd stopped wearing a holster piece when he'd been elected sheriff eight years ago.

"What if you're wrong?" Frank said to David.

"He's not wrong," Sheila said. "Archer says sacrifice is the currency of God."

Frank's jaw tightened. "What did you say?"

Sheila fell silent, her face pale in the moonlight. Frank was about to ask her again, to slap her, to do something to drive her words from his memory, to make her take them back and swallow them, but the day died as he stood before her.

Midnight.

The air screamed with the first toll of the bell.

✝ Chapter 22

This is just like the Baptist church, Ronnie thought. *Nothing to be scared of here. They're just passing the plate, taking up money for God. So what if Reverend McFall's sermons are a little wacky? When you think about it, Preacher Staymore's gone off the deep end a time or two.*

In the pew in front of him, Mama Bet took the plate, her hands trembling. The reverend pulled the cloth from the heaping plate. Tim wrinkled his nose, then pinched it closed. Other members of the congregation craned their necks, trying to see the offering.

"Shoo," Tim said. "Something smells like donkey crap."

Ronnie elbowed Tim at the same time that Mom squeezed Tim's forearm. "Ow," he yelped.

"Shh," Mom whispered. "Show some respect in church."

That was just what Dad always said. This place was getting more and more like the Baptist church with every second. If you could forget that it was the middle of the night and that the red church was haunted, why, you might as well be in any of them. You still had to be quiet whenever somebody performed some ritual or other. You had to pretend like you were paying attention, and you couldn't talk or laugh. You had to sit up straight and stay awake.

And sitting up straight was getting harder and harder to do. The pain pill Ronnie had taken before bedtime was kicking in. His thoughts spread fat and happy, the joy juice was sloshing around in his brain, the hard wooden pew felt like cotton candy under his bottom. He was almost having fun in church. If old Preacher Staymore could see him now, then Ronnie would be in for a serious session of heart-opening, head-bowing penance.

Mama Bet held the plate, then bent and mumbled what sounded like prayers. Becca Faye's and Sonny's faces both curdled in disgust. Stepford held his nose closed as if he were diving into a swimming hole. If something stank that bad, Ronnie was glad his nose was packed with gauze. He almost giggled. That pain pill was sure doing a number on his head.

Mama Bet reached into the plate, and Ronnie leaned forward for a closer look. Mama Bet was putting whatever was in the plate to her mouth. Dad said that the Catholics ate bread and pretended it was Jesus' body, and drank wine pretending it was the blood of the Lamb. But this looked even weirder than that.

A string of thick fluid escaped from Mama Bet's fingers. It glistened in the candlelight, looking for all the world like . . .

The happy pill was definitely messing with him. Because it looked like <u>blood</u> dripping from her hand, but before he could get another look, she had put the stuff in her mouth and started chewing.

"Gross," Tim said.

Mom didn't even pinch him this time, because she was gripping the back of Mama Bet's pew so hard that her fingers were white. She had a strange smile on her face. Mama Bet smacked her lips as she worked the offering.

"The body of God," the reverend said.

"Amen," Mama Bet responded, the word sloppy because of her chewing.

Archer McFall took the plate from her and stepped to the end of the next pew. Mom eagerly looked up at him, and he held out the plate to her. Tim edged away from her until he was pressing against Ronnie. Mom reached out, her eyes bright as ice, and Ronnie saw what was in the offering plate.

Clumps of tattered meat.

Moist, raw, and stringy.

Barf-out. She's not EATING that stuff, is she?

Mom took a morsel between her fingers and brought it to her lips. She bit down and turned and smiled at Tim and Ronnie. Bits of the pink meat dangled between her teeth. Ronnie's stomach tumbled and knotted.

"The body of God," Archer McFall said. He reached out and patted Tim's head. Then he looked at Ronnie. McFall's eyes were as deep as quarry holes, black and hiding secrets. Ronnie shivered and tried to look away, but the man's gaze held him hypnotized.

It's the PAIN PILL, dummy. You've fallen asleep and you're just having a stupid dream. Little snakes are NOT squiggling in his eyes.

"Amen," Mom said in response to the reverend's blessing. She passed the plate to Tim, who slid back in his seat away from it. Ronnie moved away, too, but Sonny Absher pressed against him from the other side.

"Where you going, runt?" Sonny said, his lips curled in menace.

Ronnie looked wildly about the church. Whizzer made a chewing motion with his mouth and leered at him. Mama

Bet nodded encouragement, her rheumy eyes like pails of rainwater. McFall leaned forward, his mouth hanging open.

Worms. Worms between his teeth.

"Come on, Timmy," Mom said, her voice creepy and soothing. "It's good for you."

She nudged the plate against his arm. Some of the grue slopped over onto Tim's flesh, and he stared it. He looked at Mom, eyebrows raised.

"Do it, honey," she said. "Let the reverend bless you."

Tim reached toward the offering plate.

No. NO. NOOOO.

Ronnie reached out and slapped Tim's hand away. The plate flipped out of Mom's hand, hitting the back of the pew and splashing into Mama Bet's face. The viscid blood clung to her wrinkles, small tatters of pulpy flesh on her checks.

McFall roared, his voice thundering, the wooden shell of the church vibrating with his rage.

And the bell struck.

The coppery, heavy taste of the communion filled Linda's mouth, her heart, her soul. She felt strong, reborn, just as she had in California in the Temple of the Two Suns. Just like always.

She lovingly held the offering out to Tim, and he was almost convinced, almost saved, almost *there*, when Ronnie knocked the plate away.

Archer's anger was radiating in waves of heat beside her. He wasn't angry over the spilled offering; no, there was plenty more where that came from, and a little dirt never hurt the sacramental flesh. But Archer couldn't abide betrayal in any form.

Neither could Linda.

God knew she loved her boys, but Ronnie was getting to be a real pain in the rump. Ronnie was displeasing Archer. Ronnie was sitting there with that defiant look in his eyes, looking so much like his dad did when he set his mind to something. It was that same stupid Christian stubbornness, the look that said, *Don't tell ME there's another path to God.*

Well, she wasn't going to let Ronnie get into the clutches of that devil-worm Jesus without a fight.

But she wouldn't have to fight alone.

She smiled as the bell's long arcing note rattled her eardrums.

Now would come the cleansing, the true reason Archer had been sent to this earth.

Perhaps it didn't matter that the vessel had not been fully prepared, that the sacred meat had not passed his lips. He still needed to be given to God.

Ronnie needed to die for the glory of Archer, of Wendell McFall, of the old families. He needed to pay for the iniquities of the Days. Most of all, he needed to die for the greater glory of herself. God would surely smile upon this great sacrifice she was making.

Around her, members of the congregation were rising, some heading for the door, some shouting in anger at Ronnie's betrayal. Sonny Absher grabbed Ronnie's sleeve, but Ronnie pulled free and scrambled to the floor.

"Come on, Timmy," Ronnie screeched, tugging on Tim's right arm.

No. He can't get away.

She grabbed Tim's left arm and held on with all the strength borne of desperate love. A mother's love.

For a brief moment, Tim was caught in the middle of the tug-of-war, and Archer reached over, talons extended, to take the boy. But then Tim was gone, stolen by the meddling Ronnie.

The boys scurried underneath the pew as Linda's anger rose to match Archer's. She wouldn't let Ronnie rob her of this chance to win Archer's favor. She'd wanted the reverend for so long. Not just in the lustful flesh, though that would be fine with her, but she wanted to join in spirit.

And now Ronnie was depriving her of the gift that would buy Archer's undying love.

Her oldest son had always been a troublemaker, now that she thought about it. Always reading books and getting ideas and asking dumb questions when there was really only one question. And the answer to that question was Archer.

She added her voice to the clamor and vaulted over the front pew, where the boys had gone. She lost her balance and slammed against Mama Bet, and the old woman fell heavily to the floor. Mama Bet moaned in pain, but Linda ignored her. Mama Bet may have given birth to Archer, but she was just another vessel, just another piece of meat used by God to bring Archer to Linda. Mama Bet mattered no more than rain mattered to a river.

Ronnie pulled Tim to the dais and helped him over the railing. Linda followed. Where was Archer? Didn't he see that Tim, the youngest descendant of all the old families, was getting away? Didn't he care? Didn't he want to accept the sacrifice as badly as she wanted to offer it?

Wasn't sacrifice the currency of God?

She crossed the railing and looked down at the shape on the old boards. Wings, claws outstretched, a terrible angel of dark blood.

Back again.

The work that Wendell McFall had begun was now nearly complete. Only one more sinner's blood needed to be spilled to flesh it out and bring the Bell Monster's spirit from shadow to fully formed life.

Only one more cleansing.

She yelled at the boys to stop, but they didn't even look back. They ran into the vestry and the door slammed shut. Linda clenched her fists until her knuckles ached, then turned to look back at the congregation.

The Buchanans had spilled out the front door, their spell broken. Sonny and Becca Faye were edging toward the side of the church, away from Mama Bet, who had risen to her knees and lifted her arms.

"Look what you done to me now," Mama Bet yelled to the ceiling. She paused to lick at the offal in the corners of her mouth, then said, "You ain't made me suffer enough, now you got to go and mess up my Sunday-go-to-meeting dress. I can't wait to get my hands on you."

Linda glanced across the rapidly thinning crowd. Where was Archer?

"Let's get the hell out of here," Sonny yelled to Becca Faye. "This bunch is crazier than a bug in a bottle."

Mama Bet chanted again, a toothless prayer: "I can't wait to get face-to-face with you, mister. Then, by God, there'll be hell to pay. Cause you owe me big."

Oh, them of little faith, Linda thought, but Archer would deal with them later. After tonight's sacrifice, Archer would have all the time and power and anger in the world.

She shivered with rapture and went to the vestry to fetch her boys.

"Holy hell and D-double-damned," David muttered.

The bell's clangor rolled across the hilltops, slapping the mountain slopes and reverberating back in a trapped tide. The vibrations wriggled against David's skin, a thousand live things.

"There's no rope," Sheila said to herself.

She was starting to get on David's nerves. Damned woman ought not be a cop, anyway. Women were too sensitive, too caring. Too easily fooled. And that thing she'd said about sacrifice being the currency of God, why, she'd said it exactly the way Linda did.

Kind of worshipy and dreamy, in-love, like.

But she was the sheriff's problem, not his.

Because his problem was *What in hell do I do about that shadow-shape thing coming out of the steeple?*

But maybe that was everybody's problem, because the thing swooping down was full of sharp edges.

The shadow swerved and skimmed across the roof of the church, then tangled in the branches of the old dogwood. David glanced away to look inside the church. The congregation was scattering and shouting, and for a brief instant David saw Ronnie and Tim scrambling toward the front of the church.

And behind them, Linda.

He saw Ronnie lead Tim into the vestry.

"Get Archer," David shouted at the sheriff, who stood as stiffly as any of the stone angels around them, the rifle like a weight in his hands.

Sheila said, "It's not Archer's fault. He's just doing God's work."

"What in hell?" David shouted at her, and now the church door had slammed open and people were spilling out onto the cool dewy grass.

Sheila had turned. Archer had gotten to her somehow. Softened her up. Fed her the big lie and shut the door to her heart away from the saving grace of Jesus.

But the sheriff . . . well, the sheriff would take care of business.

Except he was from one of the old families.

Same as Linda, same as Mama Bet, same as Donna and Zeb and Boonie.

Same as them that was running away from the church like rabbits from a brushfire.

And David had seen Sheriff Littlefield at last night's service.

Chowing down with the rest of them.

Eating what Archer offered.

Damn.

Was *everybody* on the side of Satan?

And David had given him a rifle.

About the smartest thing you ever done, Mr. David Day. Now you'd best forget about him, forget about all of them. Save the only things that matter.

Save the boys.

And to hell with the rest.

He raced across the graveyard to the rear of the church, keeping one eye on the dark branches of the dogwood and the other on the sheriff.

Frank watched David disappear into the shadows behind the church.

The congregation, Frank's constituents, the people who had once been his neighbors, scattered across the graveyard, some getting into their cars. Others disappeared into the trees. Haywood and Nell Absher crouched behind a large marker near the sheriff and Sheila.

"You've got to kill him," Sheila said.

"Haywood?"

"No, *Archer*."

"I . . . I don't know if I can."

"That's the way it has to be done. For God so loved the world, He gave His only other begotten son. Kill Archer, and set Samuel free. Set all the sinners free."

Frank shook his head. His clenched his jaw to keep his teeth from chattering. His wet clothes gave off a mist in the moonlight.

"You got to, Frankie," came a muffled, hollow voice from the ground, the sky, nowhere. Samuel's voice.

Frank gripped the rifle, stood and strode toward the church. Stepford Matheson ran toward him, saw the rifle and froze, then fled in the opposite direction. The night was filled with the gargle of car ignitions and excited shouts. Twin beams swept over Frank as the Buchanans' pickup turned around. Frank didn't even blink as the headlights pierced his eyes and the truck growled its way to the main road.

He came to the foot of the old dogwood and stared up into its black branches, to the scattered white blossoms at its top.

Where is that damned brother-killing shadow?

But he knew that the shadow wasn't the real monster. The real monster was the one who cast the shadow.

The Reverend Archer McFall.

Frank climbed the steps and entered the church foyer. He heard Sheila behind him. She would want to see. She was part of it now. Though she wasn't of the old families, she had been touched and changed by Archer.

In Archer, they were all one big happy family.

Frank entered the dimly lit sanctuary. Some of the candles had blown out because of the open door, and it took Frank's eyes a moment to adjust. Someone moaned near the front of the church. Another person—it looked like Linda Day—stood to one side of the altar, her back to him.

"You got to do it, Frankie," said Samuel.

He spun, and Sheila smiled at him. "Sacrifice is the currency of God," she said in Samuel's voice.

"What the hell *are* you?" Frank said, the muscles in his neck rigid.

Sheila batted her eyelashes. She spoke in her own voice this time. "Just a woman, Frank. Just somebody else for you to love and lose. Just another piece of God's great puzzle."

Her face twisted, dissolved, shifted into Archer's.

"Just somebody else for me to take away from you," Archer said.

Frank swung the butt of the rifle at Archer's smirk, wanting to drive the bright, secretive glee from the monster's eyes. Just before the wood struck flesh, the face shifted back into Sheila's.

Her eyes widened in surprise and anticipated pain.

Dark.

So black that Ronnie couldn't see his hand in front of his face.

He was in a box, a coffin, with nothing but the hard thud of his heart to mark the passing of time.

"I'm scared," Tim whispered.

"Shh," Ronnie said. "They'll hear us."

Though *they* already knew the two of them were locked in the vestry. It wasn't as though there were a whole lot of places to hide inside the red church.

Ronnie finally opened his eyes. The weak gleam of moon fought through a small window set high in the back wall. He could barely make out Tim's pale face, though his eyes and mouth were steeped in shadows. He pressed his ear to the door again.

She was out there.

Waiting.

Wanting.

Ronnie shivered, remembering the deep and creepy look in his mother's eyes as she ate the raw meat, as she passed the plate to Tim, as she screamed at them for running away from Archer McFall.

Mom knocked again. "Let me in, boys."

Ronnie put his hand over Tim's mouth before his younger brother could cry out. Tim's hot, rapid breath passed between his fingers.

"Mommy won't hurt you," she said.

Ronnie put one finger to his lips to shush Tim, then slid quietly around until his back was against the door. To get inside, she'd have to bust the old metal lock. But they couldn't stay here forever. Some of the other church people might help her. Like Mama Bet. Like Whizzer.

They'd have to find a way out.

The window was too high to reach. Ronnie wasn't sure if he could even fit through it. But maybe Tim could.

The door rattled. "Come out, my honeys. I'll protect you."

Said the spider to the fly.

But that was Ronnie's *mom* out there, the one who had raised him and burped him and kissed the scrapes on his

knee and stood up for him when the school counselor said
Ronnie wasn't playing well with others.

This was the only mom he had.

He fought back the tears that burned his eyes and wet
the bandages on his nose.

*Think, think, think. You're supposed to be smart, re-
member? At least, that's what all those tests say.*

What would Dad do?

Something shuffled in the corner, a light, whispery
sound.

A leaf?

A mouse?

This was supposed to be a fancy mouse motel, after all.

That was what Lester Matheson had called the church.
But Lester also said, *It's people what makes a church, and
what and all they believe.*

The people here believed some pretty weird stuff.

People like his mom. And he was so scared of his Mom
that he wouldn't open the door.

The soft, dry rattling came again, so quietly that he
barely heard it over his pounding pulse.

He'd have to do something fast.

"Ronnie," Mom said from the other side of the door.

He tensed.

"Listen," she said. "It's Tim that Archer needs. Open
the door and let me have Tim, and you can go. Mommy
promises."

Tim gasped.

Mom usually kept her promises.

Ronnie looked into his brother's face, saw the glint of
tears on his cheeks, the weak reflection of the moon in his
glasses.

This was the dingle-dork who pestered him and tore the

covers off his Spiderman comics and said that Melanie Ward wanted to give him a big, sloppy kiss.

Tim was the biggest pain-in-the-rear of all time.

And this moment, this choice, was another of those turning points that were popping up so often lately. This was some kind of test.

Everything was a test.

And to win, to make an A-plus, all he had to do was stand up, turn the brass catch, and let the door swing open, let Mom give Tim a big, bloody hug and carry him off to Archer. And Ronnie could walk right down the road to the rest of his life.

Yeah, RIGHT.

Mom knocked again, more firmly. "Ronnie? Be my big boy."

"Mommy," Tim whimpered, a bubble of mucus popping in his nose.

"Tim?" Mom said. "Open the door. Come to Mommy."

Tim's hand snaked toward the door handle, trembled, and stopped halfway. Ronnie reached out and caught it, then pulled Tim to his feet.

The thing in the dark corners shuffled again.

Mice.

He led Tim underneath the window, then put his mouth to his brother's ear. "When I boost you up, break the window and crawl out."

Tim's glasses flashed in the moonlight as he nodded.

Ronnie stooped and cupped his hands, and Tim put a foot in them. Ronnie grunted as he lifted, and Tim grabbed the small splintered ledge and pulled himself up to the glass.

"Close your eyes and hit it with your elbow," Ronnie commanded. "Hurry."

Ronnie didn't worry about remaining quiet, because whatever was in the corner was growing louder and larger and darker than the shadows. Tim hit the window once, and nothing happened.

"Harder," Ronnie yelled, his voice cracking.

Tim smacked the window again and the brittle explosion was followed by the tinkle of showering glass.

"What are you boys up to in there?" Mom shouted, banging on the door.

Ronnie pushed Tim higher. "Watch out for the glass," he said, as Tim scurried through the small frame. When Tim had tumbled through, probably landing shoulder-first on the grass outside, Ronnie jumped as high as he could. His fingers scratched inches short of the window ledge.

At least Tim made it.

He leaned against the wall. Alone. He would have to face the darkness alone.

The darkness moved away from the lesser darkness, and the moon fell on its face.

His face.

Preacher Staymore.

Ronnie exhaled a lungful of held fear as the preacher's voice reached and soothed him. "With the Son of God in your heart, you're never alone."

The preacher stepped forward, calm and smiling.

✞ Chapter 23

Wait a second.

What's the preacher doing here? During the First Baptist services, he said time and again that all the other churches led people straight to hell.

Ronnie stepped back from the man's broad, grinning face and fervent eyes.

"You're wondering what I'm doing here, aren't you, my child?" Preacher Staymore spread his arms and held his palms upward, like Jesus in those Bible color plates.

"Let me in, Ronnie," Mom yelled, rattling the door again.

"I hid back here so I could help save you, Ronnie," the preacher said, ignoring her. "God sent me special just to watch you. We knew you'd be tempted."

"Tempted?" Ronnie glanced at the window.

"Yes. You know there's only one true way."

Mom pounded on the door.

"Can you hear Him aknockin', Ronnie?"

I can try for the window one more time. Maybe if I get a running start—

Mom flailed at the door. "You boys had better get out here right this second," she said, her voice a mixture of anger and hysteria.

"Escaping won't save you, Ronnie." Preacher Staymore took another step closer. "You can run to the ends of the earth, but you can't get away from your own sorry heart. Only one person can cleanse you."

Ronnie pressed against the wall, clawing at the wood behind him.

The moon bathed the preacher's face, almost like a dramatic spotlight on some crazy stage.

"Can you hear Him aknockin'?" the preacher repeated.

Mom pounded on the door. "*Ron-NEEEEE.*"

The preacher reached out to touch Ronnie's forehead, just as he had done the dozen or so other times he'd helped Ronnie get saved. Ronnie closed his eyes and bowed his head slightly, the way he was supposed to do.

At least I'll get saved one last time before Mom and Archer and the Bell Monster get me. And dear Jesus, when you come in this time, please stay awhile. Please don't let me have more of those sins of the heart that make you so mad. And please, please, please, let Tim get away.

"You got to throw open the door, Ronnie," the preacher whispered, his hand moist and cool on Ronnie's forehead. "You got to let Him in."

The feeling came, that mixture of warmth and airiness expanding in his chest.

The good feeling.

The kind of feeling he got when Mom hugged him or Dad mussed his hair.

A feeling of being wanted, of being loved.

Of belonging.

He smiled, because he was going to tell Preacher Staymore that the door was open, that the Lord had come right on in and then slammed it shut so that no sins could sneak in behind Him.

Ronnie opened his eyes to thank the preacher, but the preacher wasn't there.

A slick stack of something that looked like gray mud stood before him. Touching him.

Some of the mud slid down his forehead and clung to his bandaged nose.

The mudstack made wet noises, a bubbling like snotty breath.

Ronnie choked back a scream. The darkness took shape, the shadow behind the mud gaining sharp edges.

The Bell Monster.

Ronnie slapped away the branch of mud that stretched to his head. It was like punching a giant slug.

Mom screamed his name again from behind the door.

The mudstack jiggled forward, the shadow looming behind it.

It's moving, oh, sweet Jesus Christ, it's MOVING.

Ronnie tried to tell himself it was the pain pill, this was a stupid dream and he'd wake up with a pillowcase tangled around his head. That he'd wake up and the only problems he would have were Mom and Dad's arguing, Tim's pestering, Melanie Ward's hot-and-cold flirting, and all the hundreds of ordinary problems that boys across the world faced every day.

Oh, yeah, and the big one: whether Jesus Christ was going to stay with him and help him get through it all, or whether He was going to cut and run at the first tiny sin of the heart.

But the mud monster moved again, pressing against Ronnie, and he could no longer lie to himself. This was real.

And the worst got worser, as Tim would say.

Because the thing *spoke.*

"Come into me, Ronnie," came the slobbery, mumbling voice. "Give it up. It's the only way to get cleansed forever."

Ronnie didn't ask how getting smothered in a nasty, creepy mound of walking, talking mud would make him clean.

"I need you," the mud monster said. The shadow grew larger behind it, filling the room, blocking the window. "Give yourself to me."

Yeah, RIGHT.

It's all about sacrifice, ain't it? I give myself up, and you let Tim go. That's the deal, huh?

Ronnie struggled against the crush of mud.

But then you'll be back, and it will be TIM'S turn to sacrifice. And then Dad's, and then everybody else's. And everybody loses but you.

Because YOU don't have to sacrifice anything.

All you do is take and take and take.

The weight of the mud pressed Ronnie to his knees. The slimy fluid soaked through his clothes. Mom called again and pounded on the door, the sound a million miles away.

All he wanted to do was sleep. He was so tired. It was so much easier to just give yourself up than actually try to fight.

So much easier.

Frank tried to pull back on the rifle, but his swing had too much momentum.

Sheila's eyes widened as the rifle butt struck her cheek.

Oh, my God. No, no, NOOOO.

The wooden stock glanced off her jaw, and for a split second, Frank had the illusion that the butt had passed *through* her skull. But he'd been suffering a lot of illusions lately, and the slapping sound echoed off the church and tombstones.

Sheila dropped like a sack of wet seed corn, and Frank dropped to her side almost as rapidly, calling her name.

A red splotch spread across her cheek. Frank put his fingers gently against the bruise. "You okay?" he whispered.

Her eyes fluttered open and she groaned.

"I didn't . . . you were *Archer* . . ."

She gripped his shoulder, the one she had shot hours earlier. Frank winced but swallowed his grunt of pain.

She worked her jaw sideways twice, then said, "It still works."

So maybe he'd held back enough.

"You were Archer," Frank repeated stupidly.

"Gee, thanks for the compliment," she said. "Have I told you lately that you're ape shit crazy?"

"Not in the last five minutes or so." Frank glanced into the branches of the dogwood above, making sure nothing sharp and black was moving around up there.

Where *was* Archer? And how was Frank going to kill something that couldn't be killed when he couldn't even trust his own eyes?

Sheila sat up, rubbing her jaw. "Guess that was payback," she said, pointing at the blood seeping through his bandage.

"Yeah," he said, gripping the rifle. "Now we're even, but somebody else has a debt to settle."

He rose and headed for the church. Most of the congregation had scattered, and the church was silent except for Linda Day's shouting. Frank stood before the door and stared at the belfry, then into the dim interior of the church.

Twenty-three years ago, at Samuel's funeral, Frank had entered this structure with only one comfort: that God would take care of Samuel in the afterlife.

And that comfort had kept Frank going all these years, even though a tiny niggling voice in the back of his mind never let him forget what the Bell Monster had done. God had been with Frank then, had helped him deal with the sorrow of losing his family, had laid by him and with him and inside him during a thousand sleepless nights.

But now, as Frank entered the church, he knew the kind of tricks that God liked to play. And that God's closeness was only another illusion.

This time Frank walked alone.

Mama Bet crawled on her hands and knees across the floor to the altar. The muck that had been Donna Gregg's internal organs soaked into Mama Bet's Sunday dress and coated her skin. She didn't mind the sticky blood on her face or the rank, coppery taste that clung to the inside of her mouth. This was an offering, after all. A sacrifice.

There's nothing as glorious as the flesh of one of the old families.

The others had fled, those of little faith who shied from the brilliance of Archer's power. But not her. No, she would follow to the end. And the others were only delaying what was meant to be, what was ordained by God. The only thing that heavenly son of a snake ever did right was to give Archer to the world.

To her.

She licked her lips and raised up in worship of the
crooked cross. The wood caught the dying light from the
candles, standing as defiantly as a true believer on a devil's
playground. The Jesus-demon had been nailed to such a
cross, and people had fallen all over themselves to get on
the bandwagon. But when the real thing, the true messiah,
came unto their midst, they scattered like a bunch of hens
running from a fox.

Except Linda Day.

The woman banged on the vestry door like there was
no tomorrow, screaming Ronnie's name over and over
again. Mama Bet chuckled to herself.

*I reckon faith is either all or nothing. Linda's gone
whole hog for Archer, giving up her boys without a
second thought just so Archer will pat her on the head
and flash that television smile. And people think I'M
crazy.*

She wiped a fleck of flesh from her chin and stood on
trembling legs.

*I'm getting too old for such foolishness. About time I
took Archer up on that eternal peace he keeps promising.
As long as God stays way over to the other end of heaven,
I don't think I'll mind one bit. I believe I've earned a little
rest.*

But first they had to nail down one little piece of unfinished business. Business by the name of Ronnie Day.
Mama Bet looked at the dark shadow on the dais, at its
flickering edges, at the blackness that seemed to burn
through to the belly of the earth.

She started laughing.

Linda turned from the door, her face wet with hysteri-
cal tears. "He won't let me in."

Mama Bet was enjoying the woman's misery. After all,

the blood of the old families ran through Linda's veins. Linda was one of *them*—them that had hung Wendell McFall, because they were just as blind to glory back then as they were today. Them that deserved all the suffering that Archer could dish out.

You showed them the way, you lit the path, you spoon-fed them the truth, and they spat in your face.

People didn't change.

"You didn't say the magic words."

"Magic words?" Linda blubbered, her eyes roaming wildly over the church as if a message might be written on the walls. "What magic words? Archer didn't say anything about magic words."

"I believe the words are 'let me die,'" boomed a voice from the back of the church.

Mama Bet turned.

Sheriff Frank Littlefield strode up the aisle, carrying a rifle, his eyes narrowed and his face clenched in a strange smile. Blood soaked the left half of his uniform shirt. In the foyer behind him, the detective woman leaned against the wall.

Mama Bet laughed again. "You think Archer will fall down for a bullet? You're crazier than a liquored-up Absher."

"Archer *wants* to be killed. And it's got to be done by one of us. One of us who belong to Archer."

Maybe so. Maybe Littlefield's been chosen. Though he didn't seem all that gung-ho at the service the other night. Just nibbled on a bit of old Zeb's stringy flesh like it was a piece of black licorice. Didn't put a whole lot of gumption in it.

But Archer had his own ways, and who was she to question his workings? One Judas was as good as any other. Let the sheriff come.

"He's in there," Mama Bet said, pointing past Linda to the door. "Doing a little holy work."

Linda gasped and put her hand to her mouth.

As the sheriff stepped before the vestry door, Mama Bet said, "You ain't got it quite right, Sheriff. The magic words ain't 'let me die.' They're 'let me die for *you*.'"

The sheriff pounded on the door. "Open up, McFall. I got a message for you. From a boy named Samuel."

Mama Bet rubbed her hands together, smearing the coagulated blood. This was going to be good.

The old brass handle turned and the door swung open.

David crept from the woods behind the church, keeping his eyes on the dark canopy overhead. But one of those hell holes might be under his feet, one of those gateways that allowed the devil to crawl up out of his hot pit in the center of the Earth and stir up a ruckus. God had kicked the devil's hind end a thousand times over, but still the red-faced son of a skunk kept on trying. You had to hand it to the devil: long odds never dampened his enthusiasm one bit.

David almost felt guilty about sending the sheriff into battle. You couldn't fight a holy war unless you were serious about the "holy" part. The sheriff hadn't been to church of late, and never had been a regular. David had seen the man baptized when they were both children, but sometimes the water didn't soak completely through.

Branches snapped about a hundred feet to his right, and he tensed and crouched behind a thick oak. The sound faded. Probably one of Archer's folks. One of the stray lambs, bolting the pen now that the gate was unlatched.

David reached the clearing behind the church just as glass shattered. The moon flashed on the jagged pieces that flew from the high window. Then he heard Ronnie's frantic voice.

David ran from the trees, not caring that he was out in the open where the devil could strike him down. All he cared about was that his two children, the dearest things a father could have, were inside that church with the devil's incarnation. And, almost as bad, they were with Linda, who was so cross-eyed over Archer that she couldn't tell right from wrong.

He almost shouted, but the devil's keepers were all around. Some of those stray lambs might have a few teeth. They might just want to get a good bite of God-fearing flesh, so they could chew it up in mockery of dear sweet Jesus. Just like they had in California, and just like they had in the red church.

And then David put it all together.

The boys.

Linda was going to give them to Archer as an offering. As soul food.

He ran, sweat bleeding through his pores faster than the night could chill his skin. Tim's head appeared in the broken window, then his shoulders and arms, and he was falling head first ten feet to the ground.

Tim gasped in expected pain.

But David was there to catch him. He'd always be there to protect his boys. Him and Jesus.

"Shhh," David said, putting his hand over Tim's mouth before the boy could scream. Tim's glasses bounced away, settling softly in the graveyard grass.

"It's me," David said, then moved his hand away.

"Ronnie," Tim whispered, his throat tight. "It's got

Ronnie."

"Who?" David said, though his heart sank like a stone down to his belly.

"The preacher."

Littlefield had better have enough faith. Littlefield had better do what the Lord required. Littlefield had better make the sacrifice.

Because even though God always won the battle of good and evil, sometimes innocent blood was shed. That much was plain through all the books of the Bible.

"Ronnie will be saved," David said, as convincingly as he could manage.

Slurping noises from inside the vestry spilled through the window. Talking. Ronnie and someone whose voice was familiar.

Naw, couldn't be.

"You said the *preacher* got Ronnie?" David asked.

"Yeah. Preacher Staymore."

Staymore. David smiled and looked to the sky. God always sent a champion when times were tough, when the good guys had their backs against the wall.

A *real* preacher, a bathed-in-the-blood Baptist preacher.

Ronnie would be all right.

"Mom's in there, and she's acting really weird," Tim said. David set him down and the boy knelt to retrieve his glasses.

"She don't know what she's doing, son. The Lord will set her straight."

Just like He had twice before. Once when Linda was young and pure, and once after she had returned from California. *Third time's a charm*, they said.

David led Tim past the gray tombstones to the edge of

the woods. They could wait there, in the safety of shadows, for the battle to end and the Lord to come out on top.

Just like always.

Frank nearly dropped the rifle as Ronnie came from the dark vestry. The boy's face was pale, his eyes feverish on either side of the soiled bandage that covered his nose. His lips moved as if to speak, or maybe he was whispering something to himself.

It was the same look Samuel had worn the moment he realized that the Bell Monster was behind him and was going to get him, get him, get him. Frank's heart twisted in rage, but he instantly forgot Samuel.

Because behind Ronnie shambled a creature that was the crowning glory of a day full of impossibilities. The mud and clay of the thing's flesh glistened in the candlelight, its limbs an awkward and perverted imitation of a human's. Worst of all were the black slits that hinted at eyes and a mouth.

The mouth flapped, the edges like cold gray syrup.

Mama Bet and Linda gasped in unison, and Linda grabbed Ronnie to pull him away.

"Welcome," said the thing, and even though the word was drawn-out and slushy, Frank knew it was Archer's voice.

"Archer?" Mama Bet said, her withered face taut.

"Mother," the thing said. The clay rippled, shifted, and for a split second, the preacher's face appeared, the powerful eyes sweeping over them like a lighthouse beacon over a troubled sea.

Linda drew back from the preacher, Ronnie tucked be-

hind her. The preacher turned his smile to her and then the
flesh fell back into corrupted mud.

"Linda, give me the child," the thing commanded.

She shook her head, speechless and numbed.

"Give me the child," it repeated.

Frank lifted the rifle.

"You got to kill it, Frank," Sheila said from behind him.

How could you kill . . . *this*?

But he pointed the rifle anyway, lodged the stock
against his shoulder and looked down the barrel. The rifle
weighed a thousand pounds, and he felt as if he were still
underwater.

"Give me the child," the thing said a third time.

Mama Bet fell on her knees before the mudstack.

"You . . . you're not Archer," Linda said.

"Does it matter what face God wears?" the thing said in
Archer's smooth and seductive voice. "You promised. And
I ask so little, after all."

Linda backed away another couple of steps. "Not like
this," she said. "You're not Archer. You can't have my baby."

The mudstack trembled, dropping bits of itself on the
dais. The tiny clods writhed like worms on the blotched
dark angel that stained the boards.

"Sacrifice is the currency of God," it said. "And Ronnie
is the sacrifice."

"I won't let you kill him," Linda said.

The thing gurgled a laugh. "Oh, *I'm* not going to kill
him. *You* are. That's what sacrifice is all about. Blessings
are better given than received."

Linda looked at her son, whose eyes were wet with
tears.

"Mom?" Ronnie whispered. He gulped.

Frank fought the strange gravity that wrapped him like a thick skin. He could kill it. Sure, he was of the old families. He had a right. It was his job.

"Do it," Sheila whispered in his ear, a little too gleefully.

Frank remembered how the rifle butt had seemingly passed through her cheek, how she had been underwater for far too long. How she recited Archer's words in a chilling and worshipful way.

He glanced back at her. For just a moment, so briefly that before this recent madness he would have chalked it up to illusion, she wore Archer's eyes, deep and brown and brimming with secrets. She blinked them back to blue.

"You heard what Samuel said," she whispered, her eyes never leaving the quivering pile of clay. Her doting eyes, her eyes hot with a faraway and deep and inhuman love. A fervor that went beyond the flesh.

She was Archer's now.

Frank's throat tightened.

They were all Archer's. They always had been. Frank had tasted, and found it sweet. He had swallowed his way into the red church and he had let the monster into his heart. And he hated his own weakness almost as much as he hated Archer.

Yes, he could kill it.

But as his finger tightened on the trigger, the mud rippled again and shrank. Samuel stood before him with pleading eyes.

"You can do it, Frankie," his dead brother said. The boy pulled a worm from his mouth and held it up. It squirmed between white fingers.

Samuel put the worm back in his mouth and chewed noisily. "Archer ate me, you know. He eats all of us."

Then Samuel blossomed hideously into the mass of putrid clay.

Archer *wanted* to be killed.

As if somehow being killed by one of his own would give him great power. Just as Judas had given up Jesus. The sons of God always needed a betrayer. Even though Frank no longer believed in God, it was just the sort of logic that ruled in an insane universe.

And he wouldn't obey. He wouldn't give Archer what he—or *it*, whatever it was—wanted most of all. Frank wouldn't make the sacrifice.

He dropped the rifle and it clattered across the hard floor.

The thing let out a damp moan, its thick arms reaching for Ronnie.

✝ Chapter 24

Mama Bet gazed up at the thing she had made, birthed, delivered unto the world.

A flawless monstrosity.

Her perfect, sinless child.

She reached out and touched the moist clay. This was the flesh of her flesh. Had she ever dreamed she would be part of something so glorious, so big?

And I done it all by myself. I brung it out myself, taught my Archer all about the wicked ways of the world, about the evil of the old families. I passed down the story of Wendell McFall, about how preaching was in the blood, how it was Archer's job to bring salvation to these heathen Jesus followers.

She slid her hand down the slope of the mud shape. Dimly, she heard Archer's golden-throated voice demanding the Day child.

Let them be cleansed, young and old. Then, when we're done with the Days and the Mathesons and the Potters, we can go on to bigger work. Because Jesus is legion. A whole lot of hearts got to be plucked out of tainted chests. A whole heap of iniquities got to be paid for.

The Archer-mud shook and became the boy, the one whose corpse she had dug up and pickled and then canned in glass jars so that young Archer could have offerings throughout the year. There had been other corpses along the way, a Day here, another Littlefield there, the whole graveyard like a fresh, sacred garden. Even the embalmed ones were worthy.

But getting them fresh was so much better.

The cold mockery of flesh rippled again and changed back into the mud shape.

The rifle that the sheriff had been carrying landed on the floor beside her. The sheriff was weak. That was just like a Littlefield, to fold like an accordion when there was work to be done. Well, he'd get his in due time.

Mama Bet sank her fingers into the mud and pulled a clump free. She put it to her face and rubbed it over the blood that had coagulated on her cheeks. Her boy. Her son and savior.

She pressed it against her lips, savoring the humus, this flesh of the earth.

It was between her lips, her tongue probing the holy matter, when she recognized the texture. She froze.

That night.

Nearly forty years ago.

When she gave away her virginity and took the seed.

And she remembered how, the next day, she'd found the stone rolled away, the stone that sealed off the hole in the back of the pantry. The hole that led down into the dark, moist tunnels of hell.

The clay squirmed between her gums. She tried to spit it out, but it thrust toward the opening of her throat, wriggling toward her belly.

As its rank flavor flooded her mouth, she tasted the bitter truth.

It wasn't God that had impregnated her.

It was . . . *this.*

No.

Archer was her flesh, her body, her blood. He was born of the heavens, not the earth.

Not like this thing.

But this *was* Archer. Her only son.

The word made flesh.

The flesh made mud, from that which crawled up through deep holes in the ground.

How could she ever have loved this thing?

This *thing* that walked among humans like some gift from above, throwing off lies and laying out tricks that made Jesus look like a two-bit street magician.

This thing that stood at the pulpit, slick and foul and throwing off a fungal rotten smell. The odor of the grave.

A deceiver.

Just another in a long line of false prophets and God-pretenders.

May God forgive me, I HELPED it. I gave it LIFE.

She clamped her legs together, as if she could change the past and keep the thing's head from appearing, to prevent its birth. But it was too late. It had always been too late.

The McFall secret was even more secret than she had known.

The thing, the hideous coalition of accumulated sin and pain and sorrow, moved toward Linda and Ronnie.

It wanted a last supper.

Mama Bet looked at the thing that was its own father, the thing that had fooled her more deeply than it had fooled anyone, and anger burned her from the inside out. It began in her chest, where the small clump of mud had lodged, and expanded out to her skin. Her head felt as if it were glowing, as if some power from beyond had lit her hair like a torch.

Strength flooded her aged limbs, a strength born of self-loathing.

Sacrifice was the currency of God.

And damned if she didn't know what sacrifice was all about.

Ronnie stepped in front of his mother, protecting her, though the creepy mountain of mud was the worst nightmare ever made.

Mom tried to pull him back, but he shrugged her hands away. "I got to do this, Mom," he said, trying to keep his voice from cracking, but failing.

"No, Ronnie," she said.

"If I give myself to it, maybe that will be enough. That's all it wants."

So I hope and pray. Because if it takes me in, and I'm full of Jesus, then it will be filled with Jesus, too.

Though Ronnie's vision blurred with tears, he knew he was doing the right thing. After all those sins of the heart, all those selfish things, this was something he could do for the whole world. He would give himself so that the world could live. And if Mom loved him enough, she would give him up, too.

His heart, which had been shriveled with fear, now felt light and warm in his chest. A strange calmness came over him. This thing could eat him, smother him, rip him apart, whatever it wanted to do, but it could never touch the *real* him.

The part of him that floated in his heart.

With Jesus.

Because Jesus was there, all right, big and happy and brave. Jesus had always been there, only Ronnie realized sometimes you couldn't see Him because you got caught up in your own little sorrows and worries and dreams. All your little selfish things.

But Jesus stuck right there with you, no matter what.

And Ronnie knew that Jesus wouldn't step in and save him from the monster.

Because Jesus had already saved him.

He twisted away from Mom and stepped forward to meet the monster's embrace, a smile on his face, the pain in his nose and heart now as far away as heaven was near.

Mama Bet picked up the rifle.

She had no doubt that Archer could die, *would* die. And only she, who had given it life, could free it. Hers was the greatest sacrifice, after all. She was giving up her only begotten son.

Her cataracted eyes fixed upon the mass of mud that was only inches from taking the boy.

Sure, that boy deserved cleansing- he had that awful and tainted Day blood in him- but the sins of the old families were nothing next to the blaspheming joke of an angel that slopped before her.

Angels didn't fall from heaven. They rose up from the meat of the earth.

Her guts ached at the thought that this *thing* had been harbored in her belly, had grown by sapping her strength, had come forth under the lie of a miracle.

"Archer," she called with all the strength she could muster. Her diabetic limbs trembled as she aimed the rifle. The mud shape turned, its slab of face rippling. The mud changed, slid into Archer's human features.

"Mother?" he said, eyes wide and pleading and oh so damned innocent. Like he'd never had a nasty thought in his life. Like God was the one lighting up his eyes, a holy filament burning inside that glorious, handsome head.

Mama Bet wavered. She'd suckled this thing. She'd told it bedtime stories. She'd fed it from a hundred worthless sinners. Why, surely there was *one* good thing about it, one thing worth a mother's love.

"Archer," she whispered. The rifle tilted down toward the floor, and she saw the dark stain moving, rising up like a fat and sinuous snake, draping Archer like an oversize shadow. Something else moved out of the corner of Mama Bet's eye—the sheriff jumping over the railing.

"The Bell Monster," Ronnie screamed.

The Bell Monster.

The *real* evil.

Because evil didn't wear flesh. Evil didn't need substance.

As the black shape settled over Archer and sank into him, soaked through his smooth suit and styled hair, Mama Bet's son smiled at her.

"I love you, Mother," the preacher said, though his teeth said exactly the opposite.

His teeth said, *You're about due for a turn in the offering plate, you stupid blind bitch. And let me tell you something: you're worse than all the others put together. Because you served me, and you LOVED it. You loved having your face pushed into the corrupted flesh of the old families. You swallowed the body of God like a pig snorting at the trough.*

And the horrible truth of it slammed into her like a twenty-pound Bible dropped from the heights of heaven.

She lifted the rifle and pulled the trigger, and the stock kicked against her shoulder as the report bounced off the wooden walls of the red church.

Frank eased over to the railing. The others had forgotten him, all except Archer, who knew everything and seemed to always have a gleaming eye on the sheriff. Even in his mud incarnation, the preacher owned the red church.

But when the shadow of the Bell Monster had risen, Frank knew that Archer had always been here, in many forms, troubling the people of Whispering Pines since the first family had settled in these hard hills. Maybe it had been here since the first sun rose. Maybe it was an evil older than hope, older than religion, older than everything that people thought they understood. And since Frank no longer believed in God, he no longer believed in the devil, either.

Those things didn't matter. Who cared about some nameless, faceless eternity? What counted was that he could save Ronnie, right here and right now. Frank had failed Samuel, but maybe this was a chance at redemption.

The sheriff jumped over the rail and grabbed the boy, lifted him and carried him away from the preacher. Archer didn't even glance at them, his hands spread wide in acceptance as he spoke to his mother. Linda stood in shock at the edge of the altar, slowly shaking her head as if someone had told her that the emperor had no clothes, and she had just noticed the nakedness.

Shoot it.

Frank couldn't kill it, because that would only bring the thing back, more powerful than ever. But Mama Bet was its creator, in a way. At least in the human way. If the Archer-shadow-thing was an ancient evil, it must have started somewhere. And everything that had a beginning also had an end.

Ronnie was light in the sheriff's arms as they fled from the altar and down the aisle. Sheila, or whatever Sheila had been, was gone. Frank thought of her touch, but only briefly. He was getting better at forgetting.

The shot exploded when he was in the middle of the church, and he couldn't help himself. He had to turn and look.

Archer, arms wide, palms up, eyebrows raised, mouth stunned open, a messiah on an invisible cross.

A small red spot appeared on his white shirt, just to the left of his tie.

Shot in the heart.

Archer's lips moved, but no words came. The face shifted rapidly, to mud and mountain lion to Samuel and then to a dozen, no, a *hundred* faces that Frank didn't recognize. Then it settled back into Archer's face.

"Jeez," whispered Ronnie.

Archer's eyes rolled heavenward, as if looking for some large, compassionate hand to come down and collect him. But above them was only the dark ceiling of the red church.

Then the bell rang, a belch of hellwind ripping the night.

"Mom," Ronnie called, struggling in Frank's grasp.

Linda looked from Ronnie to Archer, then back again, as if making a hard choice.

The wound on Archer's chest blossomed wider, leaking a gray gelatinous substance along with the blood. Frank thought he saw bits of stone and root in the seepage. Archer lurched toward Mama Bet as the bell rang a second time.

"Why hast thou forsaken me?" the preacher-thing said to its cowering mother. The words were as thunderous as the tolling bell, but Archer was *smiling*. As if getting killed was all part of some perverted sacrament.

"Come *on*, Linda," Frank shouted.

"Ronnie," she called, holding her arms up and running from the altar. This time they were a mother's loving arms, not the snatching arms of a conspirator.

Frank set Ronnie down, and the boy hugged his weeping mother.

"Let's get the hell out of here," Frank said, leading them down the aisle.

He turned one last time, just before they went out the door. Mama Bet had stood and was meeting her son's embrace. Except her son, her savior, her hope for the world, was a glistening mass of clay. The mudslide swept over her and suffocated her screams. Frank's feet were in the graveyard grass when the bell rang for the third and final time.

This is it, Ronnie thought. *The all-time, Whopper-with-extra-cheese turning point, the up-close-and-personal end of the world.*

And the weirdest thing was, he was no longer afraid. No matter what happened from here on in, he knew he wasn't alone. Because when Jesus came into your heart, He signed a lifetime contract with a no-trade clause. Ronnie wished someone had told him how simple it was, that you didn't need Preacher Staymore or an angel or even Dad to tell you that God was right there all the time.

He gripped Mom's hand as they ran across the graveyard. A smattering of starlight and the half-faced moon threw the shadow of the dogwood tree over them. The black branches swayed in an unfelt breeze like fingers reaching to grab them.

"Are you okay?" Mom asked.

"Yeah," he said.

"I- I'm sorry," she said, but Ronnie barely heard her, because the bell rang for a third time and the ground trembled beneath his feet.

"Over here," someone shouted.

Dad!

Ronnie dashed for the trees at the edge of the woods. Dad stepped from the darkness and grabbed him, hugged him, and pulled him into the underbrush.

Tim squinted from behind a laurel.

"Timmy," Ronnie said, his heart lighter than it had ever been. Prayers *worked*. Prayers kicked ass.

"What happened?" Tim asked.

"Did the sheriff kill him?" Dad asked, before Ronnie could answer Tim.

"*She* did."

"She? The deptective?"

"No, Mama Bet."

"Did they hurt you, son?"

"No," he said, wanting to tell Dad about his new discovery, that Jesus was a pal and an ally, and who cared about an old stupid Bell Monster when you had the top gun on your side?

But he forgot about Jesus.

Because Mom was standing in the graveyard, and so was the sheriff, and the grass stretched open and the ground cracked and tombstones shivered.

Archer appeared in the doorway of the red church, the

hole in his chest miraculously healed, the shirt unstained. He was bathed in a strange light, a sick yellowish orange the color of a dying fire. His face was sad and peaceful, and once again Ronnie was reminded of Jesus' face in the Bible pictures.

Ronnie swallowed hard. Because what if this *was* the Second Coming, only this time God did it in a roundabout way, the ultimate big-time test of faith?

"What's happening?" Tim said, nearly blind without his glasses.

"God only knows," David said.

Archer walked—no, *floated*—down the steps. Mama Bet was behind him, looking nearly the same as she had, the dried blood and dirt streaking her face. But her eyes were somehow *wrong*, looking past the seen and known world.

Then the ground quivered again. The dirt at the base of the grave markers roiled, and pale, wispy shapes slithered up into the night air.

Arms topped with clawing, grasping hands.

Arms followed by heads, whitish lumps that were half skull, half milkish vapor.

Then more, rising up from the ground like heavy fog. A sound like a hurt breeze wended through the forest.

The shapes solidified, became translucent people. Some wore old clothes, long dresses and bonnets, some of the men in Confederate Civil War uniforms, their blanched faces stretched and sagging, mouths yawning mournfully as they moaned. Others wore clothes of more recent vintage, suits and cravats or ties, with or without shoes. Ronnie recognized some of the more freshly dead.

There, Willie Absher, who had been crushed to death while working on a truck last year. Jeannie Matheson, an old schoolteacher who had finally given in to cancer. And Grandma Gregg.

The same Grandma who used to perch Ronnie on her knee and tell about the old ways and the old stories. Now she shook the dark dirt from her burial gown and moved forward, feet hovering above the ground, vacant eyes shadowed.

A dozen, a hundred dead, all rising up from the grave, answering the call of the bell.

Summoned by Archer.

The preacher was beneath the dogwood now, reaching out with his luminous hands to rip the air in front of him. A separate entity shimmered into being.

"The Hung Preacher," whispered Ronnie.

"May the good Lord protect us and keep us," Dad prayed aloud.

"What about Mom?" Tim whimpered.

"She bargained with the devil. Now she's got to pay the price."

"No," Ronnie said. "She changed. When Archer got shot, she became one of us again. We can't give up on her now."

Ronnie couldn't explain. Mom was Mom. Mom belonged to *them*, not Archer. And Archer wasn't the devil, anyway. For the first time ever, Dad was wrong.

Ronnie looked for her in the herd of haunted figures. At first he saw only the aching dead collecting around Archer. Then he saw Mom, hiding behind Grandma Gregg's tombstone. The sheriff was with her.

"There she is," Ronnie said. "You got to save her."

"Only Jesus saves, son."

"But you *love* her. You can't let Archer have her."

"She was more than ready to give *you* up. She thought

she was making *that* sacrifice for love."

"What's happening to Mommy?" Tim said.

"Please, Dad," Ronnie said. He was nearly ready to run out there himself, out in the middle of those dead creepy things, to help Mom. "Jesus will run with you. Archer can't touch you if you're carrying Jesus in your blood."

Dad said nothing. As they watched, the Hung Preacher materialized, his plump bloated face beaming with joy. Archer embraced his ancestor, lifted him as three of the new congregation removed the noose. The sinuous threads that comprised the Hung Preacher's revenance collapsed onto Archer, and the two coalesced into one body.

Then the crowd of corpses parted, and Archer headed across the corrupted cemetery. The others fell in line, a ghostly caravan.

The sheriff shouted and ran from his hiding place. He caught up to one of the figures, a young boy.

"Samuel," the sheriff screamed. "Don't go."

The sheriff grabbed at the apparition, tried to embrace it, but he might as well have been harvesting the air. The boy didn't even turn, just kept marching in that solemn regiment. The sheriff fell to his knees, weeping.

When the last of the dead disappeared into the brush, Dad said to Ronnie, "Stay here with your brother. I'll get your mom."

Ronnie looked at the dark gaps in the bushes where the dead had gone, wondering where Archer was leading them. Then he looked at the belfry, at the unmoving shadows that filled its hollowness. The candles burned low in the red church, the eerie flickering making the building seem alive.

"I can't see nothing," Timmy said. "My glasses broke. Tell me what's happening."

"Exactly what you see," Ronnie answered. "*Nothing* is happening."

The sheriff crawled into the shrubs. Below him, the road and the valley lay spread beneath the grim moon. The congregation drifted down the embankment, and there, near the end of the speechless column, was Samuel.

His dead brother, now and forever Archer's.

Frank watched as Archer reached the great stones bordering the river. The monstrosity stepped into the water. No, not into—*onto*. Because the preacher walked on water.

Archer turned and waited as his congregation followed, first Mama Bet, then others old and new, including Frank's grim parents, all entering the black river. The water swallowed them, took them under its frothy tongue and carried them back to the ancient belly of the Earth.

Frank hoped Samuel would look back and wave, do anything to show that he remembered, that part of Samuel's human life would remain even in this bleak new eternity. But Samuel slipped beneath the currents as silently as the others had, and when the last ghost faded, Archer himself dissipated and sank into the water.

Only the river mist remained, like the shroud of a final burial. The water laughed as it carried Archer's people to the deadest sea.

✝ Chapter 25

Frank returned to the red church three weeks later.

The cemetery was quiet, the grass thick from gentle rains, the earth undisturbed. Birds chirped in the nearby forest. Wildflowers erupted along the road, black-eyed Susans and Queen Anne's lace and winding morning glories. At the feet of the giant slumbering mountains, the river rolled on.

They'd found Sheila's body two miles downstream. Hoyle said that sometimes fish or turtles nibbled on the flesh when it became softened by prolonged exposure. Frank tried to believe that. At the hard edge of midnight, as he convinced himself that haunted congregations didn't exist, Hoyle's little forensic tidbit gave a tiny comfort.

But right now, he didn't need comfort.

He pulled the cord, and the chainsaw leaped to life, its racket drowning out nature's blissful stirrings. As he dug the spinning blade into the base of the dogwood, his teeth were clamped so tightly together that his jaw ached. The sawdust was bitter on his lips and in his nostrils as he sliced into the wood. Finally the deformed tree fell, and the sun bathed the red church with its cleansing rays.

He'd filled out a missing persons report on Mama Bet and Archer McFall, writing that he suspected they'd moved to California. He also postulated that Archer had murdered Boonie Houck, Zeb Potter, and Donna Gregg. Never mind that no solid evidence had ever been recovered, and that the state medical examiners were left as baffled as everybody else. Who cared if the FBI spent ten years tracking down a person who no longer existed, who may never have lived?

Frank sawed the dogwood into smaller lengths, then carried the brush to the edge of the forest. The work raised a good, honest sweat. Lester rode by on his tractor, gave a neighborly wave, and keep driving. The people of Whispering Pines were good at keeping things to themselves. Sonny Absher had tried to blabber, but everybody chalked it up to liquor-induced delusions.

When Frank was finished, he took off his gloves and went into the church. A pile of dry, gray dirt lay in the spot where Archer had been shot. Frank kicked at it, and dust spun in the air. The stain on the altar was gone.

He had thought about burning the church. Arson was a difficult crime to trace. But a church couldn't be good or evil—only people could. Or things that walked as people. Without people, and what they believed, a church was just a bunch of wood and nails and stone and glass.

Maybe someday God would return to this church. Maybe pure-hearted people would take up psalms and hymns and prayers here. Maybe a preacher would come here as God's servant, not as a jealous rival.

Maybe.

Frank went outside and gathered some wildflowers. He put some on the grave of his parents, then knelt before the stone that contained the engraving of a lamb.

If only God truly did keep and protect people.

If only.

***

Forgiveness.

That was something Jesus taught.

So Ronnie figured it was only right that he forgive Mom for trying to sacrifice him to Archer. Besides, Dad said that Jesus had already forgiven her. If Jesus, with all His problems and worries and duties, had room in His heart for Mom, then surely Ronnie had room, too. It helped that Mom and Dad had made up, and that Mom had joined the choir at Barkersville Baptist, and life was almost back to normal.

His nose was healing nicely, though he suspected he'd have a small hump on the bridge. Gave it character, Mom said. He looked forward to being able to smell flowers again.

Because he'd also forgiven Melanie. They sat together every day at lunch, and maybe in a week or two, he'd be able to smell that sweet little smell that her hair gave off. Melanie had asked him several times about what had happened at the church, but he'd never told her. At least, not yet. Every time she batted those long eyelashes and made his heart float, he weakened. Maybe someday he'd tell her, as soon as he figured it out for himself.

Summer was coming, the days long and full of sunshine. And the sun had a way of killing darkness and dark thoughts. He still walked past the red church, and he still shivered when he was near it. The Days didn't talk about what had happened at the church. Forgetting was part of forgiving.

But sometimes, when the sun was burying itself in the cut of Buckhorn Mountain, Ronnie couldn't help glancing at the belfry. And he couldn't help remembering how, that night of the ghosts when the Hung Preacher moved into Archer, the black shadow had slipped away and seeped into the old dogwood tree.

But surely that was only his overactive imagination trying to get him in trouble again. The sheriff had cut the tree down. Besides, Ronnie had Jesus, didn't he? Jesus would protect him. Doubting would be a sin of the heart, and Ronnie had suffered enough of those to last a lifetime.

So he kept his eyes away from the shadows and looked ahead to a life where dead things stayed dead, except for good things like Jesus.

These humans were the source of endless joy, endless fascination.

The thing had played many games throughout the billion passages of the sun, but this new one, the one of godhood, was the best.

With their belief in miracles, with their faith, with their frailties and failures, humans were a rich and abundant playground. From the beginning, when it had first burrowed up from the core of the Earth, it had inspired awe among those who wore flesh. The thing had taken many forms, many faces, and they had given it many names, but most of all, they had fed it fear and worship, and it craved those things that had been reserved for the gods.

And though it had been many things, trees and rocks and wind and meat, all those things were of the Earth. As it settled into the sandy riverbed and seeped back toward the hot magma of the earth's core, it considered the human thoughts it had stolen.

The time as Archer McFall had been pleasurable, as had its venture as Wendell McFall. But so had a thousand other forays into the flesh. So had many other possessions. Perhaps it would return one day, to shape clay into human form, to breathe life into hollow vessels and again bring a McFall among the people who lived in those old mountains. Or perhaps it would rise somewhere else, to play havoc in a new place, or revisit the site of other former miracles.

Because miracles never ceased.

Sometimes, when it owned thoughts, it wondered if its own existence was a miracle.

No. That would mean that greater things, greater forces, existed.

And the thing did not believe in anything greater than itself.

In the riverbed, it surrendered thought.

The master of the world returned to the dirt from which it had arisen.

Scott Nicholson is the author of seven novels, including THEY HUNGER and THE SKULL RING. He's also written the story collections ASHES, FLOWERS, and THE FIRST, as well as the comic series DIRT and five screenplays. He lives in the Blue Ridge Mountains of North Carolina and at **www.hauntedcomputer.com**.

E-books are available through:
> **hauntedcomputerbooks.blogspot.com.**

You can email Nicholson at:
> **hauntedcomputer@yahoo.com.**